T0180261

Communications in Computer and Information Science 1249

More information about this series at http://www.springer.com/series/7899

R. Venkatesh Babu · Mahadeva Prasanna ·
Vinay P. Namboodiri (Eds.)

Computer Vision, Pattern Recognition, Image Processing, and Graphics

7th National Conference, NCVPRIPG 2019
Hubballi, India, December 22–24, 2019
Revised Selected Papers

Springer

Editors
R. Venkatesh Babu ⓘ
Department of Computational
and Data Sciences
Indian Institute of Science Bangalore
Bangalore, India

Mahadeva Prasanna ⓘ
Department of Electrical Engineering
Indian Institute of Technology Dharwad
Dharwad, India

Vinay P. Namboodiri ⓘ
Computer Science & Engineering
Indian Institute of Technology Kanpur
Kanpur, India

ISSN 1865-0929   ISSN 1865-0937 (electronic)
Communications in Computer and Information Science
ISBN 978-981-15-8696-5   ISBN 978-981-15-8697-2 (eBook)
https://doi.org/10.1007/978-981-15-8697-2

This Springer imprint is published by the registered company Springer Nature Singapore Pte Ltd.
The registered company address is: 152 Beach Road, #21-01/04 Gateway East, Singapore 189721, Singapore

Preface

The seventh National Conference on Computer Vision, Pattern Recognition, Image Processing and Graphics (NCVPRIPG) was held at Hubli, Karnataka is organized by the KLE Technological University in association with the Indian Unit for Pattern Recognition and Artificial Intelligence (IUPRAI), an affiliate of the International Association for Pattern Recognition (IAPR). The primary goal of NCVPRIPG is to bring together researchers working in the broad areas of Computer Vision, Graphics, Image Processing, Pattern Recognition and related fields to promote community-wide discussion of ideas that will influence and foster continued research in these fields. The NCVPRIPG family of conferences has evolved from national-level workshops and is held every alternate year since 2004 while the much-acclaimed Indian Conference on Vision, Graphics and Image Processing (ICVGIP) is being organized since 1998.

This conference received 210 papers from all over India and we must thank the contributors who have considered NCVPRIPG 2019 to be an important event in which they could showcase their research works. This was obtained from a wide variety of institutes, both academia and industry. After a thorough review process, 58 papers were presented and these are included in the proceedings. The program of the conference included oral and poster presentation sessions. We had six plenary keynotes that were presented by Andrew Zisserman, Amit Roy Chowdhury, Namrata Vaswani, Dima Damen, Siddhartha Chaudhuri and Ardhendu Behera. We are grateful to them for having agreed to present the keynote talks. We also had two Vision India sessions where prominent papers by Indian students presented in top conferences and journals abroad were presented. Besides this, we had a Panel Discussion related to Start-Ups and Industry talks at the conference. Additionally, the conference featured 4 tutorial sessions and a special "India Driving Dataset" based workshop. The proceedings of the conference are being published by Springer as part of their CCIS Conference Proceedings. We would like to thank Sanja Evenson from Springer and Ujwala P, Deepak K.T. and Kaushik M who have helped in arranging for the NCVPRIPG 2019 proceedings.

Excellence of a conference program depends much on the selection of papers. The support from the program committee and the additional reviewers is very crucial in the selection process.

We are fortunate to have a group of diligent program committee members and reviewers without whose active support we could not have designed such an enriching program. We must also acknowledge the support of dynamic advisory committee members and sub-steering committee in having lent their valuable suggestions and guidance. We thank the session chairs for readily agreeing to our proposal to chair the sessions. We express our gratitude to Uma Mudenagudi and A.N. Rajagopalan, general chairs and Prabhakar Kore and Ashok Shettar, patrons of the conference for their support and guidance. We would like to thank the tutorial chairs Vineeth Balasubramanian and Soma Biswas for their wonderful work. We also thank the sponsors of the conference for their support. We would like to thank the Start-Up Chairs Nitin Kulkarni and Lokesh Boregouda for their help in organizing the sessionand the Demo Chairs and Doctoral Symposium Chairs as well for their help in the contribution to the program. We acknowledge Meena S.M, Nalini C., Shankar Gangisetty, Ujwala P. and Sujata C., organizing committee members and the Outreach Chairs B.S. Anami, Mansoor Roomi, and Arnav Bhavsar for putting in their best effort in creating a powerful knowledge network.

NCVPRIPG 2019 is yet another step forward in making a stronger research community in the areas of computer vision, pattern recognition, image processing and graphics. We shall consider our efforts to be satisfying if you all can take back enriched experiences from the conference.

December 2019   R. Venkatesh Babu
                                                             Mahadeva Prasanna
                                                             Vinay P. Namboodiri

Organization

Chief Patron

Prabhakar Kore   KLE Society, India

Patron

Ashok Shettar   KLE Technological University, India

General Chairs

Uma Mudenagudi   KLE Technological University, India
A. N. Rajagopalan   IIT Madras, India

Organizing Chairs

Meena S. M.   KLE Technological University, India
Nalini Iyer   KLE Technological University, India
Ujwala Patil   KLE Technological University, India
Narayan D. G.   KLE Technological University, India
Shankar G.   KLE Technological University, India
Suneetha B.   KLE Technological University, India
Sujatha C.   KLE Technological University, India
Uday K.   KLE Technological University, India
Ramesh T.   KLE Technological University, India
Sunil V. G.   KLE Technological University, India
Chaitra D.   KLE Technological University, India

Program Chairs

R. Venkatesh Babu   IISc Bangalore, India
Mahadeva Prasanna   IIT Dharwad, India
Vinay P. Namboodiri   IIT Kanpur, India

Vision and Geometry (VG) Track Chairs

Gaurav Harit   IIT Jodhpur, India
Venkat Ramana P.   Samsung Research Institute (SRIB), India

Learning and Vision (L&V) Track Chairs

Dinesh Babu J.	IIIT Bangalore, India
Lokesh B.	Samsung Research Institute (SRIB), India
C. V. Jiji	College of Engineering, Trivandrum, India

Image Processing and Document Analysis (IP&DA) Track Chairs

Suneel T. S.	TataInnoverse, India
Biplab Banerjee	IIT Bombay, India

Detection and Recognition (D&R) Track Chairs

Md. Mansoor Roomi	TEC Madurai, India
K. Palaniappan	University of Missouri, USA
B. Sathya Bama	TEC Madurai, India

Advisory Committee Members

Subhashis Banerjee	IIT Delhi, India
Subhasis Chauduri	IIT Bombay, India
P. J. Narayanan	IIIT Hyderabad, India
C. V. Jawahar	IIIT Hyderabad, India
Santanu Chaudhary	IIT Jodhpur, India
P. K. Biswas	IIT Kharagpur, India

Contents

Vision and Geometry

Fast Stereo Depth Estimation in Smartphone Devices with Narrow Baseline

Saikat Kumar Das[✉], Pankaj Kumar Bajpai, and Rituparna Sarkar

Samsung Research Institute India - Bangalore, Bengaluru, India
{saikat.das1,pankaj.b}@samsung.com

Abstract. With an expanding market of mobile devices consisting of dual camera configuration, depth estimation has become a core technology for various camera applications. However, due to the constraints imposed by camera configurations and relatively lower computational capabilities of mobile devices, state of the art methods, do not fare well on embedded devices. In this work, we address the challenges in designing a fast depth estimation method for asymmetric dual camera, with narrow baseline and limited computing power on a smartphone device. We propose a novel approach to efficiently compute accurate matching cost volume using sub-pixel steps. Additionally, a modified Semi Global Matching cost optimization and confidence measure based on binary edge maps are used for dense depth map estimation. To validate the proposed method, we use a dataset consisting of 600 stereo image pairs captured using two smart phones with dual cameras. The proposed method demonstrates significant visual improvements in areas involving repeating patterns, smooth regions and complex object boundaries compared to prior methods.

Keywords: Stereo vision · 3D Geometry · Disparity.

1 Introduction

Many consumer features in mobile devices such as synthetic background blur and 3D object placement as well as various image analysis tasks such as semantic segmentation, optical flow estimation rely heavily on accurate and efficient estimation of depth information of scenes. Depth inferred from stereo cameras using computer vision based algorithm is preferred for many of these applications as it can provide dense depth maps in varied conditions unlike some of the active depth sensors.

The realization of stereo vision setup in mobile devices have introduced new challenges in the domain. The main challenge in the embedded environment is limited memory and computational capabilities, specially for a volumetric search algorithm like stereo correspondence. For the past few decades, various traditional patch-matching based methods [12,13,30,33], as well as deep learning approaches [4,9,19,21,23,31] have been developed which achieved considerably high accuracies on stereo benchmark datasets [5,14,17].

© Springer Nature Singapore Pte Ltd. 2020
R. V. Babu et al. (Eds.): NCVPRIPG 2019, CCIS 1249, pp. 3–13, 2020.
https://doi.org/10.1007/978-981-15-8697-2_1

Fig. 1. Target view I_t, Reference View I_r and Estimated disparity Map (L-to-R). Accurate disparity estimation inspite of significant change in intensity level. Integrity of fine structures and repetitive patterns are maintained throughout the disparity map.

The traditional methods generally use hand crafted features for correspondence search and various edge aware filtering techniques to obtain dense disparity map. In recent years, significant progress has been made in stereo depth estimation using deep learning [21,31] approaches. However, deep learning methods for stereo disparity are computationally demanding for embedded system implementation and require large training data with depth ground truth of scenes. The mobile device stereo camera setup has a very narrow baseline (small baseline-to-height ratio) unlike the stereo data in any stereo benchmarking dataset [5,14,17]. The traditional as well as deep learning based stereo disparity estimation algorithms, designed with an assumption of 0.6 to 1 B-H ratio [15], do not scale well to the challenges of a narrow baseline.

In this paper, we propose a efficient stereo disparity estimation system with following salient contributions:

1. A novel approach to reduce the search space by reducing the cost volume dimensions for computational efficiency and using sub-pixel disparity step to estimate disparity with high accuracy in embedded devices.
2. Modified semi-global matching (SGM) [7] optimization by employing a novel edge based penalty function in smooth regions and repetitive structures.
3. Edge aware cost volume smoothing and cross consistency check is used to prevent errors in regions involving thin structures.

The proposed method does not discuss image rectification and works on rectified images.

2 Related Works

Stereo depth estimation is a classic and well-studied problem in computer vision and has been an active research area for decades. The existing works in literature can be broadly classified as (a) traditional patch match based methods and (b) deep learning based approaches.

(a) **Traditional approaches** rely on hand crafted features for computing stereo correspondence. Scharstein *et al.* [18] provide an encompassing taxonomy of stereo matching methods till 2002 and created the Middlebury Stereo Benchmark [17]. The traditional approach in stereo depth estimation is discussed in terms of steps involved below.

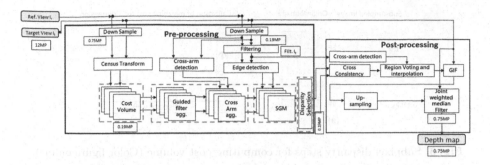

Fig. 2. Block Diagram of Proposed Stereo Depth Estimation method

Cost Volume Computation: Sum of squared differences, absolute intensity difference (AD) and mean square error were the cost functions used in the earliest works. However, these are susceptible to illumination difference in the two views and do not embed any neighbourhood information. Klaus *et al.* [10] proposed using gradient based cost. Zabih *et al.* [30] introduced a non-parametric local transform, *census transform*, a robust matching cost for its invariance to intensity changes. [8] has a detailed evaluation of cost functions.

Cost volume aggregation: Cost aggregation methods can be classified into three distinct categories: local window based, filter based and global methods. Tombari *et al.* prepared a taxonomy of cost aggregation methods for stereo correspondence in [22]. Local window based methods assume implicit smoothness constraint during the cost aggregation step. These methods range from simple box filter based aggregation to adaptive window based cross arm aggregation [33]. Lei *et al.* [2] used a cost aggregation based on color and intensity similarity. Filter based local cost aggregation includes using edge aware filters like bilateral filter [29], guided image filter [6] for depth edge preservation.

Cost optimization: These methods range from dynamic programming [24], belief propagation [28], Semi Global Matching (SGM) [7] to minimum spanning tree (MST) [27] and segment tree [13]. This step uses an explicit smoothness term and works on the principle of minimizing a global energy function.

(b) **Deep learning approaches** use deep features, which produce better matching cost as they do not suffer from the known pitfalls of the traditional matching costs. LeCun *et al.* [31] proposed using deep features for cost volume computation. Subsequent works like [4,23] achieved good accuracy in terms of Middlebury Stereo Benchmark [17]. Multiscale deep features have also been used [9] to incorporate context at different scales. In [19], authors use SGM with adaptive smoothness and discontinuity penalty terms estimated by deep learning alleviating reliance on heuristic penalties. Mayer *et al.* [11] proposed a fully convolutional network that determines stereo correspondence between two views in an end-to-end fashion. Many researchers modelled stereo depth estimation as a joint estimation problem with others problems in computer vision such as object segmentation [1], optical flow estimation [26], edge map estimation [20] etc.

Subsampled Image Original Image   Visualization of matching cost for 1 dimension

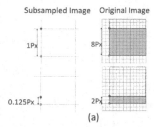 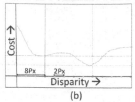

(a)   (b)

Fig. 3. Subpixel dispairty steps for computing cost volume (Color figure online)

However, despite all the advantages of deep-learning methods, using them is not the best choice for us because the main focus of our work is to build a stereo disparity estimation system for embedded devices with limited memory and processing power. With deep learning components it becomes challenging to build a fast method with small memory footprint. Additionally, for the system to generalize well we would have required a large training dataset of images with annotated ground-truth depth. Therefore, we design the proposed method by adopting a combination of different parametric feature extraction for matching cost computation and edge aware filtering for cost aggregation.

3 Method

As shown in Fig. 2, the proposed stereo depth estimation method involves four major steps (blue dotted boxes), discussed in the following subsections.

3.1 Cost Volume Computation

In our method, we use a combination of AD and census transform [30] to compute matching cost. The major challenge in achieving efficiency in stereo correspondence computation is processing the cost volume, which takes up a size of image resolution times the disparity levels. To alleviate this, we compute the cost volume at a lower resolution, which also reduces the search range. However, reducing spatial resolution has adverse effects on accuracy due to coarse disparity steps and amounts to data loss for fine structures. Selecting optimal disparity step to compute matching cost volume is crucial for converging to a global minimum in disparity selection. The disparity computation for a pixel $x_t \in I_t$ (target image) and $x_r \in I_r$ (reference image) is given by Eq. 1

$$D(x_t) = \min_{\forall i \in [0,n]} [T(x_t) - T(x_r + i \times d_s)] \quad (1)$$

$$d_s' = d_s \times I'/I \quad (2)$$

D(.) denotes disparity of a pixel and T(.) is parametric feature transformation (e.g. census) of a pixel. d_s is the disparity step used for calculating cost volume

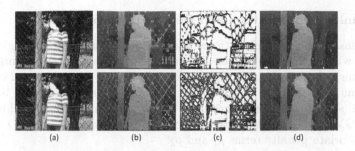

Fig. 4. Refinement improvements, top: existing methods, bottom: proposed, a) Input image, disparity map after b) SGM, c) Confidence Map, d) Depth filling based on (c)

at n disparity levels. The relation between disparity step and image resolution is given by Eq. 2. Here I'/I is the sub-sampling ratio and d'_s is the equivalent disparity step in the original higher resolution image I'. For increased efficiency, we compute the cost volume at 1/64th (H/8 and W/8) of the original resolution. Thus, 1-pixel shift along baseline direction in the sub-sampled image (I) will be equivalent to 8 pixels shift for original image (I'). In Fig. 3a the blue dot represents the current pixel location and the purple dot shows the next pixel location where matching cost is computed. The shaded part denotes the search space where matching cost is not computed. It can be seen clearly that using a integer step at I will have incomplete matching information. In terms of 1D visualization of matching cost (Fig. 3b), we can see that the cost curve, when sampled finely (yellow points) with the sub-pixel step is less likely to converge at local minima (red lines) than when sampled at integer disparity (red points). Thus, using sub-pixel disparity shifts we can search the solution space better for the global minima(green dotted lines) for every pixel.

Symmetric Bidirectional Cost Volume: In proposed method, we compute bidirectional cost volumes [16] i.e. one cost volume taking each image from the stereo pair as the target view (I_t) and other as the reference view (I_r).

3.2 Cost Volume Aggregation

The cost volumes (CV) computed in the previous step can contain noises and errors due to mismatch occurring from occlusions, texture-less regions, repetitive patterns, noises etc. The cost planes are aggregated using a Guided Image Filter (GIF) [6] with the RGB images as guide image to reduce the errors due to wrong matches and compensate data loss at regions with fine details. In addition to GIF, we use a cross-arm based aggregator [33], which aggregates cost of each pixel based on color and intensity similarity. Other methods like MST [27] based aggregation consider a more global scope for cost aggregation but can be expensive for embedded devices.

3.3   Scanline Optimization and Depth Discontinuities

To compensate the local operational window of the aggregation, a global cost optimizer with explicit smoothness constraint is required. These optimizers work on the principal of minimizing a global energy. For its computational efficiency, we use Semi Global Matching (SGM) by Hirschmuller *et al.* [7]. SGM is a multi-directional scanline cost optimizer used for further eliminating matching ambiguities. SGM aggregates the cost of a pixel at disparity d along 1D scanlines with appropriate penalty terms ρ_1 and ρ_2.

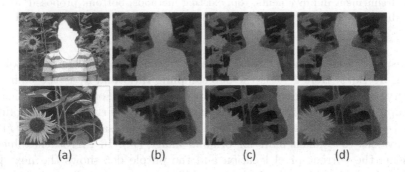

(a)   (b)   (c)   (d)

Fig. 5. Disparity refinement: a) Input image, b) GIF refinement, c) JWMF refinement [34] d) GIF and JWMF

We use edge maps to decide the penalty terms in the SGM process. We apply a high penalty (ρ_1) for pixels, which are not separated by an edge and low penalty (ρ_2) for pixels, which are separated by an edge. This ensures that all the pixels on a surface have similar disparity and distinct boundaries near depth discontinuities (Fig. 5).

$$P = \begin{cases} \rho_1, & \begin{aligned} EM_t(x) = 1 \text{ or} \\ EM_r(x) = 1 \end{aligned} \\ \rho_2, & \begin{aligned} EM_t(x) = 0 \text{ and} \\ EM_r(x) = 0 \end{aligned} \end{cases} \tag{3}$$

The edge map used for deciding smoothness penalties in SGM is crucial for producing a disparity map with piecewise smooth depth and sharp steps near depth discontinuities. The edge map should only contain object boundaries and not include any edges indicating surface textures or illumination difference in same object. In our experiments it was observed that learning based methods like HED [25] or Structured edge (SE) [3] performed much better than statistical edge detectors. SE was chosen for our final method as it is more efficient.

Preserving Fine Structures: Although, SGM smooths out most local variations in the disparity map but it can have adverse effects on fine structures (see Fig. 4). To mitigate this instead of deciding the penalty terms based on edge map of target view, edge maps of both views should be checked jointly for each pixel. If any of the view has a edge between two points then those points should be processed with a low penalty (see Eq. 3). P is the penalty term which uses ρ_1 and ρ_2 based on the edge map, where ($\rho_1 < \rho_2$). EM_t and EM_r denote the binary edge map of target and reference image, respectively. The effect of proposed modification can be seen in Fig. 4, which shows forward and backward disparities (dF, dB) processed with regular SGM in the 1st column and dF, dB processed with proposed modified SGM in the 2nd column.

3.4 Disparity Selection and Refinement

Disparity maps (dF, dB) from the bidirectional cost volumes (CV_F, CV_B) are computed by Winner Take All (WTA) method. WTA selects the disparity for a pixel that has minimum cost across the volume. The pixels for which the Winner Margin is not higher than a pre-decided threshold are marked as unsure [18].

Cross Consistency Check: In addition to the unsure pixels, pixels with mismatching disparity values in dF and dB are also marked as error areas. These areas which fail consistency check can include occlusions also along with genuine mismatches [12]. Only these and unsure regions mentioned previously are further processed in depth refinement step.

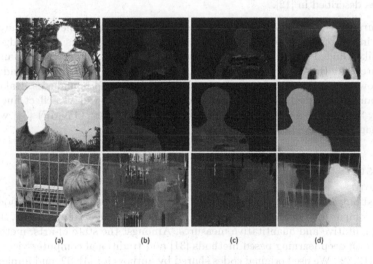

Fig. 6. Results: a) Input image, b) MC-CNN [31], c) Mei *et al.*[12] d) Proposed

Preserving fine structures in Consistency Check: Areas with fine structures and details are susceptible to errors as they can be wrongly identified as failed pixels in the consistency check due to parallax in two views. Fine structures like net, fences, fingers etc. (see Fig. 8) can have very minimal overlap between their relative positions in two views which can ambiguously mark them as error areas.

Fig. 7. Quantitative result images: (left to right) left image, GT, [21,32], proposed

We tackle this issue by jointly inspecting disparity map and edge maps. Areas which are enclosed by edges in the edge map are considered as areas having fine structures and are not subjected to consistency check like other pixels.

$$CC(x) = \begin{cases} 1, & \begin{array}{l} dF(x) = n - dB(x) \\ \text{or } EM_t(x) = 1, \\ \text{or } EM_r(x) = 1, \end{array} \\ 0, & otherwise \end{cases} \tag{4}$$

Here CC(x) is the cross consistency map where 1 means sure pixel and 0 means unsure/error pixels, n is the total disparity The occlusions, mismatches and unsure pixels are corrected by a neighbourhood region voting method and region interpolation method as described in [12].

Edge Aware Filtering For Disparity Enhancement: In order to refine the disparity map obtained in the previous steps and smooth out small irregularities we use edge aware filtering like Guided Image Filter [6] and Weighted Median Filter. This enhancement makes sure that the depth boundaries are consistent with the object boundaries in image. However, GIF suffers from a known halo effect around boundaries. Halo effects by GIF can be smoothed out by median filter. However, this will also effect fine details adversely. So, instead we use a Joint Weighted Median Filter (JWMF) [34] with the target image as the guide.

4 Results

We carried out an extensive analysis of the results of each of the proposed module, as well as a comparative study of our method against the state-of-art methods, in terms of both qualitative and quantitative measures. Amongst the state-of-arts, methods we consider both deep learning based methods [31] and traditional computer vision based methods [12,32]. We used original codes shared by authors for [31,32] and implemented the method in [12] independently according to the description in the literature. *The faces in the images are masked out to protect anonymity of the subjects.*

4.1 Qualitative Comparison

Figure 6 shows the qualitative comparison of our method with two state of the art methods [12,31]. From Fig. 6 it can be observed that MC-CNN [31] and the method by Mei *et al.* [12] have problems handling complex scenes with repeating structures.

Moreover, as MC-CNN is trained on images captured with significantly different setup, hence the results suffers much more than traditional computer vision methods. In order to obtain more decent results from a deep learning based method like MC-CNN, it should have been fine-tuned on the specific dataset, which was not possible in our case due to absence of ground truths. The proposed method excels in estimating smooth and crisp disparity map even in areas with repetitive patterns, fine structures and smooth regions. It is also able to achieve decent stereo matching results despite intensity differences between the two views (see Fig. 1).

4.2 Quantitative Comparison

Table 1 shows the quantitative comparison with state of the art methods [21] and [32] in terms of RMSE on Middlebury datasets for half (H) resolution images (RMSE of [21,32] recomputed from Middlebury leader board results). We chose a non-deep learning based method [32], apart from deep learning base method [21], for quantitative comparison because deep learning based methods are fine tuned for performance on a specific dataset and may show appreciably higher numbers on them which can be difficult to surpass by using hand crafted computer vision techniques designed for efficiency. The qualitative comparison for a sample image from Middlebury dataset is shown in Fig. 7. Proposed method performs at par with the non-deep-learning state-of-art method and even surpassing the same on few datasets. However, despite being computationally expensive the deep learning method [21] has better number than the proposed method.

4.3 Computational Efficiency

Table 2 shows the comparison of performance. The performance of the proposed method is recorded on an Samsung Galaxy S9+ using two threads on CPU. It can be observed that the proposed method is more than 500 times faster than [21].

Table 1. Quantitative result

	Shelves	Piano	Playroom
Proposed	**5.64**	5.3	7.54
[21]	6.81	**2.275**	**4.41**
[32]	5.67	2.435	4.54

Table 2. Computational efficiency

Method	Proposed	[21]	[32]
secs/MP	**1.1**	706	55.5

5 Conclusion

For a stereo disparity estimation method to be widely used in an embedded device as a core service for other features, along with being highly accurate in natural scenes it is equally important that it shows near real time performance. The disparity map estimated by the proposed method surpasses most state-of-art real-time methods on a custom challenging dataset, captured with a narrow baseline stereo setup. The proposed modifications in sub-pixel disparity search, cost volume optimization and depth refinement provides significantly improved results in areas involving repetitive pattern, smooth regions and fine structures and provides a very sharp and accurate disparity map. In terms of Middlebury stereo datasets it performs decently to achieves competitive scores on the train dataset (2014). We theoretically validated the potential for achieving real-time performance on embedded devices by using hardware accelerators. With ARM-NEON SIMD optimization, custom DSP and latest mobile GPUs the proposed method can possibly run at over 10 fps for VGA depth output.

References

1. Bleyer, M., Rother, C., Kohli, P., Scharstein, D., Sinha, S.: Object stereo – joint stereo matching and object segmentation. In: 2011 IEEE CVPR, pp. 3081–3088, June 2011
2. Lei, C., Selzer, J., Yang, Y.-H.: Region-tree based stereo using dynamic programming optimization. In: 2006 IEEE CVPR, vol. 2, pp. 2378–2385, June 2006
3. Dollar, P., Zitnick, C.L.: Structured forests for fast edge detection. In: IEEE ICCV, December 2013
4. Drouyer, S., Beucher, S., Bilodeau, M., Moreaud, M., Sorbier, L.: Sparse stereo disparity map densification using hierarchical image segmentation. In: Angulo, J., Velasco-Forero, S., Meyer, F. (eds.) ISMM 2017. LNCS, vol. 10225, pp. 172–184. Springer, Cham (2017). https://doi.org/10.1007/978-3-319-57240-6_14
5. Geiger, A., Lenz, P., Urtasun, R.: Are we ready for autonomous driving? The kitti vision benchmark suite. In: 2012 IEEE CVPR, pp. 3354–3361, June 2012
6. He, K., Sun, J., Tang, X.: Guided image filtering. IEEE TPAMI **35**(6), 1397–1409 (2013)
7. Hirschmuller, H.: Stereo processing by semiglobal matching and mutual information. IEEE TPAMI **30**(2), 328–341 (2008)
8. Hirschmuller, H., Scharstein, D.: Evaluation of cost functions for stereo matching. In: 2007 IEEE CVPR, pp. 1–8, June 2007
9. Kim, K., Koh, Y.J., Kim, C.: Multiscale feature extractors for stereo matching cost computation. IEEE Access **6**, 27971–27983 (2018)
10. Klaus, A., Sormann, M., Karner, K.: Segment-based stereo matching using belief propagation and a self-adapting dissimilarity measure. In: 18th ICPR 2006, vol. 3, pp. 15–18, August 2006
11. Mayer, N., et al. A large dataset to train convolutional networks for disparity, optical flow, and scene flow estimation. In: The IEEE CVPR, June 2016
12. Mei, X., Sun, X., Zhou, M., Jiao, S., Wang, H., Zhang, X.: On building an accurate stereo matching system on graphics hardware. In: 2011 IEEE ICCV Workshops, pp. 467–474, November 2011
13. Mei, X., Sun, X., Dong, W., Wang, H., Zhang, X.: Segment-tree based cost aggregation for stereo matching. In: The IEEE CVPR, June 2013
14. Menze, M., Geiger, A.: Object scene flow for autonomous vehicles. In: The IEEE CVPR, June 2015
15. Morgan, G.L.K., Liu, J.G., Yan, H.: Precise subpixel disparity measurement from very narrow baseline stereo. IEEE TGRS **48**(9), 3424–3433 (2010)
16. An, P., Lu, Zhang, Z.: Object segmentation using stereo images. In: 2004 IEEE ICCCS, vol. 1, pp. 534–538, June 2004
17. Scharstein, D., et al.: High-resolution stereo datasets with subpixel-accurate ground truth. In: Jiang, X., Hornegger, J., Koch, R. (eds.) GCPR 2014. LNCS, vol. 8753, pp. 31–42. Springer, Cham (2014). https://doi.org/10.1007/978-3-319-11752-2_3

18. Scharstein, D., Szeliski, R.: A taxonomy and evaluation of dense two-frame stereo correspondence algorithms. IJCV **47**(1), 7–42 (2002)
19. Seki, A., Pollefeys, M.: SGM-nets: semi-global matching with neural networks. In: The IEEE CVPR, July 2017
20. Song, X., Zhao, X., Hu, H., Fang, L.: EdgeStereo: a context integrated residual pyramid network for stereo matching (2019)
21. Taniai, T., Matsushita, Y., Sato, Y., Naemura, T.: Continuous 3D label stereo matching using local expansion moves. IEEE TPAMI **40**(11), 2725–2739 (2018)
22. Tombari, F., Mattoccia, S., Di Stefano, L., Addimanda, E.: Classification and evaluation of cost aggregation methods for stereo correspondence. In: 2008 IEEE CVPR, pp. 1–8, June 2008
23. Tulyakov, S., Ivanov, A., Fleuret, F.: Weakly supervised learning of deep metrics for stereo reconstruction. In: The IEEE ICCV, October 2017
24. Veksler, O.: Stereo correspondence by dynamic programming on a tree. In: 2005 IEEE CVPR, vol. 2, pp. 384–390, June 2005
25. Xie, S., Tu, Z.: Holistically-nested edge detection. In: IEEE ICCV, December 2015
26. Yamaguchi, K., McAllester, D., Urtasun, R.: Efficient joint segmentation, occlusion labeling, stereo and flow estimation. In: Fleet, D., Pajdla, T., Schiele, B., Tuytelaars, T. (eds.) ECCV 2014. LNCS, vol. 8693, pp. 756–771. Springer, Cham (2014). https://doi.org/10.1007/978-3-319-10602-1_49
27. Yang, Q.: A non-local cost aggregation method for stereo matching. In: 2012 IEEE CVPR, pp. 1402–1409, June 2012
28. Yang, Q., Wang, L., Yang, R., Stewénius, H., Nistér, D.: Stereo matching with color-weighted correlation, hierarchical belief propagation, and occlusion handling. IEEE TPAMI **31**(3), 492–504 (2009)
29. Yoon, K.J., Kweon, I.S.: Adaptive support-weight approach for correspondence search. IEEE TPAMI **4**, 650–656 (2006)
30. Zabih, R., Woodfill, J.: Non-parametric local transforms for computing visual correspondence. In: Eklundh, J.-O. (ed.) ECCV 1994. LNCS, vol. 801, pp. 151–158. Springer, Heidelberg (1994). https://doi.org/10.1007/BFb0028345
31. Zbontar, J., LeCun, Y., et al.: Stereo matching by training a convolutional neural network to compare image patches. JMLR **17**(1–32), 2 (2016)
32. Zhang, C., Li, Z., Cheng, Y., Cai, R., Chao, H., Rui, Y.: MeshStereo: a global stereo model with mesh alignment regularization for view interpolation. In: IEEE ICCV, December 2015
33. Zhang, K., Lu, J., Lafruit, G.: Cross-based local stereo matching using orthogonal integral images. IEEE TCSVT **19**(7), 1073–1079 (2009)
34. Zhang, Q., Xu, L., Jia, J.: 100+ times faster weighted median filter (WMF). In: IEEE CVPR, June 2014

Single Storage Semi-Global Matching
for Real Time Depth Processing

Prathmesh Sawant[1](✉), Yashwant Temburu[1](✉), Mandar Datar[1](✉),
Imran Ahmed[2](✉), Vinayak Shriniwas[2](✉), and Sachin Patkar[1](✉)

[1] Department of Electrical Engineering, Indian Institute of Technology Bombay,
Mumbai, India
prathmesh.vsawant@gmail.com, temburuyk@gmail.com,
mandardatar@ee.iitb.ac.in, patkar@bhairav.ee.iitb.ac.in
[2] Defence Research and Development Organization, New Delhi, India
imran.livt@gmail.com, nvshriniwas@cair.drdo.in

Abstract. Depth-map is the key computation in computer vision and
robotics. One of the most popular approach is via computation of
disparity-map of images obtained from Stereo Camera. Semi Global
Matching (SGM) method is a popular choice for good accuracy with
reasonable computation time. To use such compute-intensive algorithms
for real-time applications such as for autonomous aerial vehicles, blind
Aid, etc. acceleration using GPU, FPGA is necessary. In this paper, we
show the design and implementation of a stereo-vision system, which is
based on FPGA-implementation of More Global Matching (MGM) [7].
MGM is a variant of SGM. We use 4 paths but store a single cumulative cost value for a corresponding pixel. Our stereo-vision prototype
uses Zedboard containing an ARM-based Zynq-SoC [10], ZED-stereo-
camera/ELP stereo-camera/Intel RealSense D435i, and VGA for visualization. The power consumption attributed to the custom FPGA-based
acceleration of disparity map computation required for depth-map is just
0.72 watt. The update rate of the disparity map is realistic 10.5 fps.

Keywords: Semi Global Matching (SGM) · More Global Matching
(MGM) · Field programmable gate array (FGPA) · System on chip
(SOC) · Zedboard · Census transform · High Level Synthesis (HLS)

1 Introduction

Although 2D and 3D LIDARs (Light Detection and Ranging Sensors) provided
accuracy, they did not succeed with the economics of power and bill of materials
for portable goods. Stereo cameras cost less, but need a lot of computational
processing, and this aspect is getting good attention of research community,
spurring the development of FPGA and GPU based acceleration of stereo-vision
related computation. The low power consumption of fpga-based solutions are
attractive and crucial for high performance embedded computing too.

This paper describes our design and implementation of a real-time stereo
depth estimation system with Zedboard [10] (housing ARM-SoC based FPGA)

© Springer Nature Singapore Pte Ltd. 2020
R. V. Babu et al. (Eds.): NCVPRIPG 2019, CCIS 1249, pp. 14–31, 2020.
https://doi.org/10.1007/978-981-15-8697-2_2

at its center. This system uses Zed stereo camera [16], Intel RealSense D435i [15] or ELP stereo-camera for capturing images. Real-time Raster-Respecting Semi-Global Matching [6] (R3SGM) along with Census Transform are used for disparity estimation. The system takes in real-time data from the cameras and generates a depth image from it. Rectification of the images, as well as stereo matching, is implemented in the FPGA whereas capturing data from USB cameras and controlling the FPGA peripherals is done via application programs which run on the hard ARM processor on Zedboard. Development of the FPGA IP's is done using High-Level Synthesis (HLS) tools. A VGA monitor is interfaced to Zedboard to display the computed depth image in real-time.

Our approach is inspired by R3SGM [6] a hardware implementation of SGM. Table 3 (at the later portion of the paper) shows the comparison of hardware utilization between our approach and [6] which shows ours uses much lesser Hardware Resources and thus having less power consumption. It may be emphasized that we have focused on very low power consumption as well as small form factor that is necessary for drones vision, blind aid etc.

2   Literature Review

There has been a lot of research on the topic of disparity map generation dating back to 1980s. [8] reviews most of the works including both software and hardware implementations. A binocular Stereo Camera estimates disparity or the difference in the position of the pixel of a corresponding location in the camera view by finding similarities in the left and right image. There have been various costs governing the extent of the similarity. Some of them are Sum of Absolute Differences(SAD), Sum of Squared Differences (SSD), Normalized Cross-Correlation and the recent Rank Transform and Census Transforms. They are window-based local approaches where the cost value of a particular window in the left image is compared to the right image window by spanning it along a horizontal axis for multiple disparity ranges. The window coordinate for which the metric cost is the least is selected which gives us the disparity for that corresponding center pixel. From the disparity, the depth value is computed by Eq. 1 where the baseline is the distance between the optical centers of two cameras.

$$Depth = Baseline * (FocalLength)/disparity \tag{1}$$

Local window-based approaches suffer when the matching is not reliable which mostly happens when there are very few features in the surrounding. This results in the rapid variations of the disparities. This problem is solved by global approaches which use a smoothing cost to penalize wide variations in the disparity and trying to propagate the cost across various pixels. The following are some of the global approaches.

2.1   Semi Global Matching (SGM)

SGM is a stereo disparity estimation method based on global cost function minimization. Various versions of this method (SGM, SGBM, SGBM forest) are still among the top-performing stereo algorithm on Middlebury datasets. This method minimizes the global cost function between the base image and match image and a smoothness constraint that penalizes sudden changes in neighboring disparities. Mutual information between images, which is defined as the negative of joint entropy of the two images, is used in the paper [3] as a distance metric. Other distance metrics can also be used with a similar effect as has been demonstrated with census distance metric in our implementation. Since we already had a Census Implementation, we used it for our SGM implementation. The Hamming Distance returned by Census stereo matching is used as the matching cost function for SGM. The parameters for Census are window size 7×7, disparity search range 92. The image resolution is 640×480. Sum of Absolute Differences (SAD) was also considered as a matching cost function. But it was observed that SAD implementation consumes more FPGA resources than the Census implementation with same parameters. This may be due to the fact that SAD computation is an arithmetic operation whereas Census computation is a logical operation.

Simple census stereo matching has a cost computation step in which for a particular pixel we generate an array of costs (Hamming distances). The length of this array is equal to the disparity search range. The next step is cost minimization in which the minimum of this array (minimum cost) is computed and the index of the minimum cost is assigned as disparity. In SGM, an additional step of cost aggregation is performed between cost computation and cost minimization. The aggregated cost for a particular pixel p for a disparity index d is given by Eq. 2.

$$L_r(p, d) = C(p.d) + min(L_r(p - r, d),$$
$$L_r(p - r, d - 1) + P_1,$$
$$L_r(p - r, d + 1) + P_1, \tag{2}$$
$$min_i(L_r(p - r, i) + P_2))$$
$$-min_k(L_r(p - r, k))$$

For each pixel at direction 'r', the aggregated cost is computed by adding the current cost and minimum of the previous pixel cost by taking care of penalties as shown in Eq. 2. First-term $C(p, d)$ is the pixel matching cost for disparity d. In our case, it is the Hamming distance returned by Census window matching. It is apparent that the algorithm is recursive in the sense that to find the aggregated cost of a pixel $L'_r(p,)$, one requires the aggregated cost of its neighbors $L'_r(p - r,)$. P_1 and P_2 are empirically determined constants. For detailed discussion refer to [3].

2.2   More Global Matching (MGM)

As SGM tries to minimize the cost along a line it suffers from streaking effect. When there is texture less surface or plane surface the matching function of census vector may return different values in two adjacent rows but due to SGM, the wrong disparity may get propagated along one of the paths and can result in streaking lines.

MGM [7] solves this problem by taking the average of the path cost along 2 or more paths incorporating information from multiple paths into a single cost. It uses this result for the next pixel in the recursion of Eq. 2. The resultant aggregated cost at a pixel is then given by the Eq. 3

$$
\begin{aligned}
L_r(p,d) = C(p.d) + 1/n \sum_{x\varepsilon\{r_n\}} (min(&L_r(p-x,d), \\
&L_r(p-x,d-1)+P_1, \\
&L_r(p-x,d+1)+P_1, \\
&min_i(L_r(p-x,i)+P_2)) \\
&-min_k(L_r(p-x,k)))
\end{aligned}
\tag{3}
$$

where n has the value depending on the number of paths that we want to integrate into the information of single cost. For example, in Fig. 1a two paths are grouped into 1 so n has value 2 and there are a total of 4 groups. Thus we need to store 4 cost vectors in this case and while updating 1 cost value in the center pixel have to read cost vector of the same group from 2 pixels. Lets say $r = 1$ for blue boxes group in Fig. 1a, while updating the L_r for this group of the centre pixel in Eq. 3 we have x as left and top pixels. From here on SGM refers to MGM variant of it.

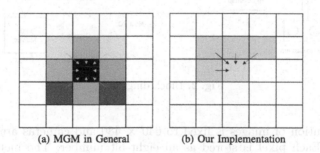

(a) MGM in General   (b) Our Implementation

Fig. 1. Grouping of paths in MGM

3   Hardware Architecture and Implementation

3.1   System Design

Figure 2 shows an overview of the implemented system. Left and right images captured from the Zed camera [16] are stored into DDR RAM (off-chip RAM). Maps required for the stereo rectification of the images are statically generated offline using OpenCV [17]. These maps are also stored into DDR RAM.

We need two Remap peripherals which perform stereo rectification for the left and right images respectively. The Remap peripheral reads the raw image frame and the corresponding map and generates a rectified image frame. The rectified images are again stored into DDR. The Intel RealSense camera requires USB3.0 or higher to stream left and right images. However, Zedboard does not have USB3.0. Hence the camera cannot be directly interfaced to the board. So images were continuously captured and streamed from a computer using ethernet. The left and right image streams were received by a socket client running on the ARM processor on Zedboard. The camera outputs rectified images, hence remap peripheral is not required in this case. The images received from the socket client are stored into DDR RAM. We have also implemented it for Zed Camera [16]. For both camera modules in Binocular cameras, the stereo matching peripheral (SGM block in the Fig. 2) then reads the left and right rectified frame and generates disparity image which is again stored into DDR. The VGA peripheral is configured to read and display the disparity image onto a VGA monitor. FPGA peripherals perform memory access using the AXI4 protocol.

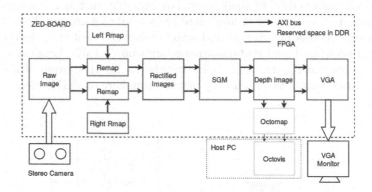

Fig. 2. Block diagram

The resolution of images is fixed to 640 × 480 and cameras are configured accordingly. Each pixel is stored as an eight-bit number. The metric used to profile the computation times of different peripherals and also the cameras is fps (frames per second). From here on a frame means 640 × 480 pixels. We could have skipped storing the rectified images and passed the output of the Remap peripheral directly to the stereo matching peripheral. We chose not to do this because our performance is not limited by memory read-write but by the FPGA peripherals themselves. We use the AXI4 protocol to perform memory read-write. The read-write rates are 3 orders of magnitude greater than the compute times of FPGA peripherals.

The images are captured using application programs running on the ARM processor on Zedboard. The programs make use of v4l2 library for image capture. The ARM processor is also used to control the FPGA peripherals.

3.2   Undistortion and Rectification

Stereo camera calibration and rectification (one time step) is done using the OpenCV library. Calibration and rectification process produces distortion coefficients and camera matrix. From these parameters, using the OpenCV library, two maps are generated, one for each camera. Size of a map is the same as image size. Rectified images are built by picking up pixel values from raw images as dictated by the maps. The map entry (i,j) contains a coordinate pair (x, y); and the (i, j) pixel in the rectified image gets the value of the pixel at (x, y) from the raw image. x and y values need not be integers. In such a case, linear interpolation is used to produce final pixel value. Figure 3 shows the remap operation with 4 neighbour bilinear interpolation.

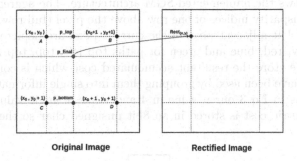

Original Image   Rectified Image

Fig. 3. Remap operation

On-chip memory is limited in size, and it is required by the stereo-depth hardware module. So, we store the maps generated during calibration and rectification in system DDR. The map entries are in fixed-point format with five fractional bits. Captured images are stored in DDR too. The hardware module iterates over the maps, and builds up the result (left and right) images by picking pixels from raw images. Note that, while the maps can be read in a streaming manner, the random-access is required for reading the raw images. For fractional map values, bilinear interpolation (fixed point) is performed. Resulting images are stored back in DDR. As this hardware module has to only - "read maps and raw images pixels from DDR, perform bilinear interpolation, and store the pixels back", it needs less than 5% resources of the Zynq chip.

3.3   SGM Block Architecture

In Census implementation we scan using row-major order through every pixel in the image and perform stereo matching. Thus for the SGM implementation built upon this, we consider only four neighbors for a pixel under processing as shown in red in Fig. 4. This is done because we have the required data from neighbors along these paths. The quality degradation by using 4 paths instead of 8 paths is 2–4%[4].

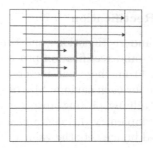

Fig. 4. Four neighbour paths considered for SGM

Figure 5 shows the implemented SGM architecture. The aggregated cost for all paths and disparity indices of one row above the pixel (full row not shown in figure) and the left adjacent pixel of the current pixel are depicted as columns of colour yellow, red, blue and green for paths top left, top, top right and left respectively. We store the resultant accumulated cost which is computed using Eq. 3. 4 Paths have been used by grouping them into single information as shown in Fig. 1b. Thus in Eq. 3 our n value in 4 and r has a single value for a pixel. The Census metric cost is stored in an 8bit unsigned char so the total size of

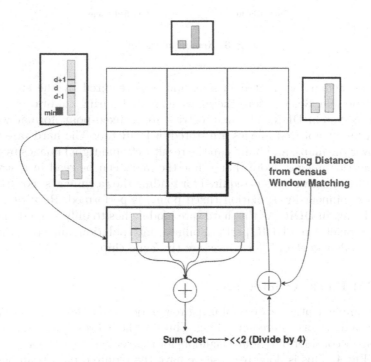

Fig. 5. SGM cost computation. Steps involved in calculating the disparity for the current pixel.

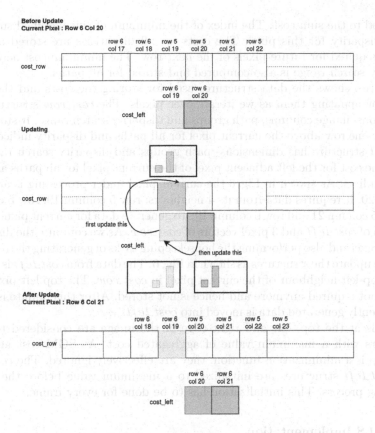

Fig. 6. SGM array updation.

memory occupied by the cost is given as $SizeofRowCostArray = (ImageWidth) * (DisparityRange) * (NoofPathGroups) = 640 * 92 * 1 = 57.5KB$.

Minimum cost across disparity search range is computed once and stored for the above row and left adjacent pixel. These scalar quantities are shown as small boxes of the same color. Since the minimum cost values are accessed multiple times, storing the minimum values instead of recomputing them every time they are required saves a lot of computations. The pixels in the row above the current pixel can be either top-left, top or top-right neighbors of the current pixels. Hence costs along the left path (green columns) are not stored for the row above the pixel.

Figure 5 also shows the data required and the steps for computing the aggregated cost for a certain pixel considering all the 4 paths. Smoothing term(2nd part in the RHS of Eq. 3) along all paths are summed up to obtain a sum cost which has to be divided by n(4). Since division is resource-intensive hardware we use left a shift by 2 to divide by 4. Then the resulting value is added with the current hamming distance (1st part in the RHS of Eq. 3). An upper bound is applied to the sum cost. The index of the minimum of this modified sum cost is the disparity for this pixel. The costs for all disparities are stored as they will be required for future pixels of the next row. The minimum cost across the disparity search range is also computed and stored for all paths.

Figure 6 shows the data structures used for storing the costs and the algorithm for updating them as we iterate over pixels. The *cost_row* structure has dimensions- image columns, path groups and disparity search range. It stores the costs for one row above the current pixel for all paths and disparity indices. The *cost_left* structure has dimensions- path groups and disparity search range. It stores the cost for the left adjacent pixel of the current pixel for all paths and disparity indices. As shown in Fig. 6 the current pixel under processing is at row 6 column 20. It requires data from its 4 neighbors: row 5 column 19, row 5 column 20, row 5 column 21 and row 6 column 19. To generate data for current pixel we use the data of *cost_left* and 3 pixel vectors of *cost_row*. As we compute the disparity for this pixel and also performing the housekeeping tasks of generating the required data, we update the structures as shown in Fig. 6. The data from *cost_left* is moved to the top-left neighbour of the current pixel in *cost_row*. The top left pixel cost data is not required anymore and hence is not stored. After this update is done, the currently generated data is moved into *cost_left*.

Pixels at the top, left and right edge of the image are considered to have neighbors with a maximum value of aggregated cost. As SGM cost aggregation step is a minimization function, they are effectively ignored. The *cost_row* and *cost_left* structures are initialized to a maximum value before the stereo matching process. This initialization has to be done for every frame.

3.4 HLS Implementation

High-level Synthesis(HLS) platform such as Vivado HLS (from Xilinx) facilitates a suitably annotated description of compute-architecture in high level language like C or C++, which it converts to a low-level HDL based description of the same computing architecture. The generated VHDL or Verilog code is then synthesized to target fpgas. We have used Vivado HLS tools provided by Xilinx to convert our C implementation to HDL and package it to an IP for further use. The structure of HLS stereo matching code is as follows.

```
void stereo_matching_function(){
for(int row=0; row<IMG_HEIGHT; row++) {
 for(int col=0; col<IMG_WIDTH; col++) {
  //Reading pixel from DDR through AXI4
  protocol in row-major order
  //Shifting the Census Match window in
  the left and right blocks
  for(int d=0; d<SEARCH_RANGE; d++) {
   //Match l_window with r_window[d]
   //Update the min cost index
   //Add the necessary output to the cost
```

```
    row and cost left vectors
  }
 //write disparity image pixel to DDR
  }
}
}
```

There are no operations between the row and col loop, hence they can be effectively flattened into a single loop. The plan was to pipeline the merged row-column loop. Thus resulting in increase of frame rate by disparity range times if the pipeline throughput had been 1. However the resources in fpga device on Zedboard are not enough to permit the pipelining the row column loop. Hence, only the search range loop was pipelined. The arrays used in the implementation have been partitioned effectively to reduce the latency. Based on the availability of Hardware resources we have divided the whole image into sections and disparity of each section is computed in parallel. It was observed that a frame rate of 2.1 fps is obtained with the most used resource being Block RAM (BRAM) 17%. The time required for processing one frame for such an implementation can be given as

$$T \propto no.\ of\ rows\ \times no.\ of\ columns \times \\ (search\ range\ + pipeline\ depth\ ) \qquad (4)$$

The characteristic of this implementation is that the logic synthesized roughly corresponds to the matching of two Census windows, the cost aggregation arithmetic and on-chip memory to store data for the next iterations. As we sequentially iterate over rows, columns and disparity search range we reuse the same hardware. Thus, the FPGA resources required are independent of the number of rows, columns and search range but computation time required is proportional to these parameters as shown by Eq. 4. This gives us the idea to divide the images into a number of sections along the rows and process the sections independently by multiple such SGM blocks. As the most used resource is BRAM at 17%, we can fit 5 such SGM blocks with each block having to process 5 sections of the image i.e., 128 rows in parallel. Thus we increase resource usage 5 times and reduced the time required for computation by the same resulting in 10.5 fps.

One flaw to this approach is that if we divide the input image into exactly 5 parts, there will be a strip of width window size at the center of the disparity image where the pixels will be invalid. The solution to this is that the height of each section is $image\_height/5 + window\_size/2$. This is shown in Fig. 7 for an example of 2 sections.

3.5 Hardware Setup

Figure 8 shows the hardware setup. The Zed camera is connected to a USB 2.0 port of the Zedboard. The Zedboard is booted with petalinux through SD card. In the case where Intel RealSense camera is used, we require ethernet to receive the images. The only other connections to Zedboard are the connection to VGA display and power.

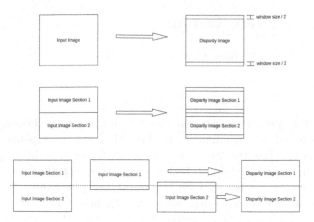

Fig. 7. Dividing the input image into two sections to be processed by two blocks simultaneously

4   Experimental Results and Evaluation

The obtained frame rate for the implemented system is 10.5 fps with Zedboard running at 100 MHz. The Power consumption of the computation which is performed in FPGA is 0.72 W whereas the on-chip arm processor which is being used to capture the images and start the FPGA peripherals along with the ELP stereo-camera consumes 1.68 watt, thereby raising consumption to 2.4W. A $10m\Omega$, 1W current sense resistor is in series with the 12 V input power supply on the Zedboard. Header J21 straddles this resistor to measure the voltage across this resistor for calculating Zedboard power [10]. The resource usage is summarized in Table 1. It is observed that the BRAM utilization is the most. This is due to storing large cost arrays.

Fig. 8. Hardware setup

Table 1. Resource utilization for the entire design in Zedboard

	BRAM	DSP	FF	LUT	LUTRAM
Utilization	132	65	39159	37070	981
Available	140	220	106400	53200	17400
% Utilization	94.3	29.5	36.8	69.6	5.64

(a) Left image

(b) Ground truth

(c) SGM 4 paths software

(d) SGM 8 paths software

(e) SGM 4 paths hardware

(f) SGM with arrays initialized to zeros

Fig. 9. SGM results on Middlebury images

The algorithmic accuracy is measured using Root mean square of difference in the disparity values obtained by our implementation with the ground truth on Middlebury test images given in Table 2 column 2. It can also be measured by percentages of erroneous disparities in Table 2 column 3. A 5 pixel tolerance is considered due to intensity variation caused by changing resolution of raw image. It is notable that no post processing has been done on the SGM output.

Table 2. Accuracy metric of ours disparity image pixels as compared to ground truth for Middlebury images

Image	RMSE	% Erroneous disparities
Teddy	5.43	11
Dolls	6.79	17
Books	6.82	20
Moebius	7.54	20
Laundry	9.22	27
Reindeer	9.17	27
Art	9.24	30

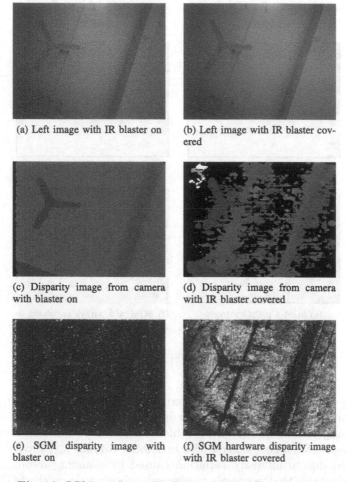

(a) Left image with IR blaster on

(b) Left image with IR blaster covered

(c) Disparity image from camera with blaster on

(d) Disparity image from camera with IR blaster covered

(e) SGM disparity image with blaster on

(f) SGM hardware disparity image with IR blaster covered

Fig. 10. SGM results on Realsense image: effect of texture

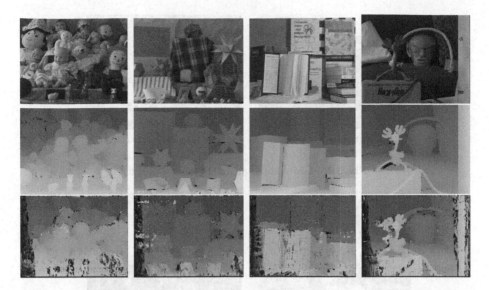

Fig. 11. Qualitative Comparison of our results with some of the Middlebury data set. 1st Row contains the Left Raw Images, 2nd Row contains the ground truth of the corresponding Images and 3rd Row contains the Output of our Implementation.

Figure 9 shows the software and hardware implementation results on Teddy image from Middlebury 2003 dataset [5]. Figure 9c-d show the results of an inhouse software implementation of SGM and Figure 9e shows the result of the hardware implementation. It can be observed that SGM with 8 paths gives the best results. SGM with 4 paths in software gives slightly better results than the hardware implementation. The difference in results is due to the fact that the way the algorithm is implemented in software and hardware is different. Figure 9f shows the SGM disparity image with $cost\_row$ and $cost\_left$ initialized to zero. Since the cost aggregation function is minimization function, the zeros from the arrays propagate to further pixels. The trickle down effect causes the degradation of the disparity image. Similar results with frame rate around 8.3 fps were also achieved by an inhouse GPU implementation of SGM on Jetson TK1 board which is of MAXWELL architecture with 256 cores and power consumption < 10 watts. This implementation is analyzed and optimized by using OpenMP for multi-threading and AVX (Advanced Vector Extension) registers for vectorization. GPU shared memory is used to reduce the global memory access. CUDA shuffle instructions are used to speed-up the algorithm and vector processing is also applied.

Figure 12 and 13 shows the captured image and the corresponding disparity image obtained using the SGM implementation. The Intel RealSense camera also provides a disparity image. This is shown in Fig. 13b. The convention followed here is opposite i.e., closer objects appear darker.

(a) Left image classroom   (b) SGM disparity image classroom

Fig. 12. SGM results on ZED camera image

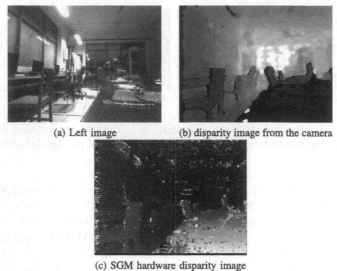

(a) Left image   (b) disparity image from the camera

(c) SGM hardware disparity image

Fig. 13. SGM results on Realsense image: lab

The Intel RealSense camera has an infrared (IR) light projector which projects structured light onto the scene. This pattern can be seen in Fig. 13a. Figure 10 shows the effect of the infrared projector on disparity estimation. Figure 10ace show the captured left image from the camera, disparity image obtained from the camera and the computed disparity image when IR blaster was on. Figure 10bdf show the same images when the IR blaster was covered. Incase of 10e although the image contains salt noise, it can be easily filtered out. The fan blades can be easily seen in the disparity image. In Fig. 10f there are more number of white pixels which imply that the object is very near to the camera which is a false result. As can be seen, the structured light projector helps in stereo matching by adding texture to non-textured surfaces.

Figure 14 shows the scene and the corresponding disparity image obtained on the VGA monitor. The camera can be seen on the left side of the image.

Fig. 14. Scene and disparity image on VGA monitor

Table 3. Comparison of FPGA Hardware Resources(Approx) and power consumption between our approach and [6]

	BRAM18K	DSP	FF	LUT	Frame Rate	Power (Approx)
Ours	132	65	39159	37070	10.5	0.72W
[6]	163	-	153000	109300	72	3W

Figure 11 shows the qualitative comparison or our results with Middlebury data set. We can see that the objects placed near are not accurate this is because we have used the disparity range of 92 pixels and so it is not able to find a match in the corresponding left and right images. Thus for a better accuracy, disparity range can be increased with the trade-off being update rate as the pipeline latency will increase.

Finally we inform the reader about our comparison with R3SGM [6] work. Table 3 shows the comparison of hardware utilization between our approach and [6] which shows ours uses much lesser Hardware Resources and thus having less power consumption. Furthermore, if we were to use fpga used in [6], we would have far more liberty with resources that can be leveraged to further pipeline the design and obtain another order of speedup. However we have focused on very low power consumption as well as small form factor that is necessary for drones vision, blind aid etc. We can extrapolate the frame rate likely to be achieved by our design on ZC706 board as below. We can replicate the hardware four times (assuming other resources are under limit) to utilize all of the BRAM, and get 40 fps performance. However, it would increase the power consumed by zynq chip, as well as by camera and DDR subsystems for this higher frame capture and processing rate.

5   Conclusion

In this paper we presented the hardware implementation of the MGM [7] which is a variant of SGM [3] on Zedboard [10] an FPGA-ARM based SOC inspired by R3SGM [6]. In order to reduce the memory consumption, we have grouped 4 paths- left, top left, top, and top right, whose pixel data are available while processing as a result of row-major order streaming process. The efficient utilization of hardware resources resulted in a low power consumption of 0.72 W for data processing on FPGA that computes the Rectification and disparity Map generation and with 1.68 W for data acquisition from Cameras along with starting the peripherals using the on board ARM processor achieving an update rate of 10.5 Hz with a good accuracy as was shown in Table 2 and Fig. 11. This system is highly suitable to be used in micro UAVs, blind Aids or any portable types of equipment with a small form factor and high power constraints.

References

1. Zabih, R., Woodfill, J.: Non-parametric local transforms for computing visual correspondence. In: Eklundh, J.-O. (ed.) ECCV 1994. LNCS, vol. 801, pp. 151–158. Springer, Heidelberg (1994). https://doi.org/10.1007/BFb0028345
2. Kanade, T.: Development of a video-rate stereo machine. In: Proceedings of International Robotics and Systems Conference (IROS'1995), Pittsburgh, Pennsylvania, August 5–9, pp. 95–100 (1995)
3. Hirschmuller, H.: Stereo processing by semi global matching and mutual information. IEEE Trans. Pattern Anal. Mach. Intell. **30**(2), 328–341 (2008)
4. Roszkowski, M., Pastuszak, G.: FPGA design of the computation unit for the semi-global stereo matching algorithm. https://doi.org/10.1109/DDECS.2014.6868796
5. Scharstein, D., Szeliski, R.: High-accuracy stereo depth maps using structured light. In: IEEE Computer Society Conference on Computer Vision and Pattern Recognition (CVPR 2003), Madison, WI, vol. 1, pp. 195–202 June 2003
6. Rahnama, O., Cavallari, T., Golodetz, S., Walker, S., Torr, P.H.S.: R3SGM: real-time raster-respecting semi-global matching for power-constrained systems. In: International Conference on Field-Programmable Technology (FPT), Vietnam (2018)
7. Facciolo, G., de Franchis, C., Meinhardt, E.: MGM: a significantly more global matching for stereovision. In: BMVC (2015)
8. Hamzah, R.A., Ibrahim, H.: Literature survey on stereo vision disparity map algorithms, vol. 2016, Article ID 8742920, p. 23 (2016)
9. Daolei, W., Lim, K.B.: Obtaining depth maps from segment-based stereo matching using graph cuts. J. Vis. Commun. Image Representation **22**, 325–331 (2011)
10. Zedboard datasheet. http://zedboard.org/sites/default/files/documentations/ZedBoard_HW_UG_v2_2.pdf, Accessed 25 Aug 2019
11. Zynq 7000 datasheet. https://www.xilinx.com/support/documentation/data_sheets/ds190-Zynq-7000-Overview.pdf, Accessed 25 Aug 2019
12. Vivado HLS user guide. https://www.xilinx.com/support/documentation/sw_manuals/xilinx2014_1/ug902-vivado-high-level-synthesis.pdf, Accessed 25 Aug 2019

13. Vivado Synthesis user guide. https://www.xilinx.com/support/documentation/ sw_manuals/xilinx2017_3/ug901-vivado-synthesis.pdf, Accessed 25 Aug 2019
14. XSCT reference guide. https://www.xilinx.com/support/documentation/sw_manuals/xilinx2016_2/ug1208-xsct-reference-guide.pdf, Accessed 25 Aug 2019
15. Intel Realsense D435i Depth Camera. https://www.intelrealsense.com/depth-camera-d435i/, Accessed 25 Aug 2019
16. Zed Camera. https://www.stereolabs.com, Accessed 25 Aug 2019
17. OpenCV. https://www.opencv.org/, Accessed 25 Aug 2019

SynCGAN: Using Learnable Class Specific Priors to Generate Synthetic Data for Improving Classifier Performance on Cytological Images

Soumyajyoti Dey[1], Soham Das[1], Swarnendu Ghosh[1], Shyamali Mitra[1], Sukanta Chakrabarty[2], and Nibaran Das[1(✉)]

[1] Jadavpur University, Kolkata 700032, WB, India
{soumyajyoti.cse.rs,shyamalimitra.iee,nibaran.das}@jadavpuruniversity.in,
soham.das0000@gmail.com, swarbir@gmail.com
[2] Theism Medical Diagnostics Centre, Kolkata 700030, India
drsukantachakraborty@gmail.com

Abstract. One of the most challenging aspects of medical image analysis is the lack of a high quantity of annotated data. This makes it difficult for deep learning algorithms to perform well due to a lack of variations in the input space. While generative adversarial networks have shown promise in the field of synthetic data generation, but without a carefully designed prior the generation procedure can not be performed well. In the proposed approach we have demonstrated the use of automatically generated segmentation masks as learnable class-specific priors to guide a conditional GAN for the generation of patho-realistic samples for cytology image. We have observed that augmentation of data using the proposed pipeline called "SynCGAN" improves the performance of state of the art classifiers such as ResNet-152, DenseNet-161, Inception-V3 significantly.

Keywords: Conditional generative adversarial networks (CGAN) · Synthetic data generation · Cytology image classification · Deep learning

1 Introduction

The modern machine learning algorithms such as deep learning, have been greatly dependent on the availability of a large amount of high-quality data. But for various niche domains such as medical imaging large quantities of data are generally unavailable due to various constraints, such as lack of patients, infrastructural inadequacy, noisy environments, lack of experts for annotations and so on. However, with the advent of *generative adversarial networks* (GANs) [6], an avenue for high quality data generation has opened. In its base form, GANs

© Springer Nature Singapore Pte Ltd. 2020
R. V. Babu et al. (Eds.): NCVPRIPG 2019, CCIS 1249, pp. 32–42, 2020.
https://doi.org/10.1007/978-981-15-8697-2_3

are capable of generating samples from a randomly sampled prior which demonstrates likeliness to a predefined data distribution. However, without proper guidance, the generation process can result in eccentric outputs. However, conditional GANs (CGANs) [12], on the other hand, use a semantically sensible prior for guiding the data generation process to generate more accurate and meaningful samples. In the proposed work, we explore the ability of CGANs to work with learnable priors for efficient data generation to improve classifier performance on cytology images. In most practical cases the number of available data samples is too limited for deep learning approaches to thrive. Thus data augmentation serves as a primary tool for improving learning ability. Though annotating pixel specific masks for cytology images is a difficult and expensive job, however, with adequate expertise and a decent amount of labor it is possible to annotate at least a small batch of samples for a better semantic representation. The proposed approach makes use of such semantic masks to serve as a prior for CGANs. While generating fully detailed cytology images without priors is much difficult, the generation of segmentation masks from scratch is a much simpler task given that the output distribution is binomial. Our proposed approach makes use of this factor to create learnable segmentation masks that can guide CGANs for synthetic data generation. Some relevant studies are discussed in the next section. The proposed methodology is provided in the subsequent section followed by experimental setups, results, and discussions in Sect. 4 and future scopes are discussed in the conclusion thereafter.

2   Related Works

Most common methods for data augmentation involved affine transformations [5] such as translation, rotation, scaling, shear, flipping and so on. Also, it has been noticed that training with added noise results in a much more robust classifier. The introduction of *generative adversarial networks* (GANs) has brought a shift in the paradigm of generative processes in computer vision. Several approaches have made use of GANs for data augmentation. Adar et al. [3] proposed a GAN based liver lesion data augmentation technique where after the extraction of ROI for classification was done using CNN. Dataset was augmented in two ways: i) the ROIs were augmented by affine transformations ii) the synthetic data was generated from ROIs using DCGAN (Deep Convolution Generative adversarial Network) and ACGAN(Auxiliary Classifier GAN). DCGAN showed greater performance compared to ACGAN. Shin, et al. [13] proposed a GAN based model to segment tumor of brain MRI images of two traditional datasets: ADNI and BRATs. Normal brain MRI images were segmented using an image to image translation model using CGAN [9]. Synthetic abnormal brain MRI scans were obtained from labels (tumors) by incorporating some changes in the label (e.g. increasing the size, changing the position of the label, or placing the tumor in a healthy brain MRI segmentation map). The synthetic images were used in data augmentation for training the model. Improved performance of tumor segmentation was observed by adding the synthetic data to the real data but without using normal data augmentation methods. Tom et al. [15] simulated patho-realistic ultrasound images of the IVUS dataset using deep generative models. Tissue echogenicity maps were generated from the ground truth of the dataset. From these maps simulation of ultrasound images was produced using a physics-based simulator. Two-staged GAN was used to generate patho-realistic ultrasound images and stability of training state. In the first stage, images from the simulator were taken as input to GAN from which low-resolution images were generated. In the second stage, these low-resolution images from the first stage of GAN were transformed into high-resolution images. Bissoto et al. [2] suggested a GAN based model to generate high-resolution images of skin lesion of the ISIC challenge dataset. Classifiers were trained on real data as well as on synthetic data.

3   Proposed Methodology

The goal of the current work is to generate realistic cytology images similar to images collected during FNAC (Fine Needle Aspiration Cytology) test. The cytology images were collected from Theism Medical Diagnostics Centre, Dumdum, Kolkata. These cytological data were mainly collected by FNAC test, and were captured using an Olympus microscope at 40X magnification in the presence of the professional practitioners. Around 156 cytology images were collected among which 77 were benign samples and 79 were malignant samples (Fig. 1).

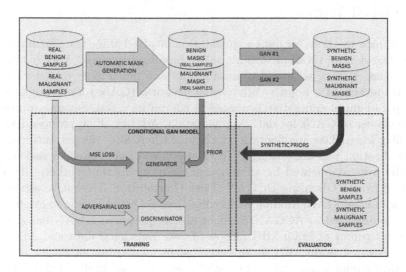

Fig. 1. SynCGAN: the proposed data augmentation pipeline

3.1   The Data Augmentation Pipeline

The proposed method of synthetic data generation consists of 3 phases. Firstly, segmentation masks are collected from real images using an unsupervised method. Secondly, a CGAN is trained on these pairs of images and auto-generated segmentation masks. Two sets of synthetic segmentation masks are generated using a GAN for each of the two classes. Finally, these synthetic segmentation masks are used to guide the previously trained CGANs to generate patho-realistic samples for data augmentation.

3.2   Mask Generation

The proposed methodology requires a set of pixel-level annotations to guide a CGAN for data generation. Due to the lack of hand-annotated samples, an unsupervised approach was used for nuclei segmentation. There have been many developments in the field of image segmentation lately [4]. For our work, first, the contrast of the RGB cytology image is increased by the histogram stretching method. The image is then converted to a grayscale image. To eliminate the irrelevant portions, adaptive thresholding [10] based segmentation algorithm is adopted and the RGB image is converted to a binary segmented mask. But the red blood cell, cytoplasm which had similar high local contrast is distinguished using the Gaussian Mixture clustering algorithm. Finally, the refined binary segmented mask is extracted. The presence of an unsupervised mask generation technique alleviates the necessity of large amount of training data (Fig. 2).

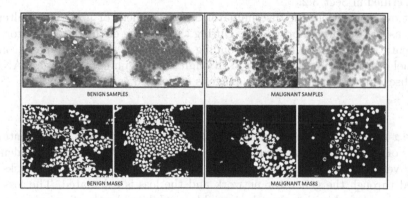

Fig. 2. Auto generated segmentation masks using [10] from real samples

3.3   Training the CGAN to Generate Patho-Realistic RGB Images from Segmentation Masks

Generating RGB images from scratch using a traditional GAN is difficult as the generation procedure can be represented as a prediction of 256-dimensional multinomial distribution across three channels for each pixel. However, the segmentation mask is simply a pixel specific binomial distribution which is much easier to predict when starting without a predefined prior. Thus a CGAN [12] must be trained which takes the segmentation masks generated in the previous step as a prior and a generator loss is reduced against the corresponding RGB image. We derive inspiration from the pix2pix network [9]. For the generator, we use a modified UNet like architecture. Normally the UNet architecture used transposed convolution for upscaling the feature maps. However, that results in checkerboard artifacts due to overlap of kernels during the fractional stride. Instead, bilinear interpolation opted for upscaling the feature map followed by a 3×3 convolution layer for refinement. The discriminator network has been directly implemented using the PatchGAN discriminator as demonstrated in [9]. The discriminator attempts to detect real and fake samples from the dataset and the generator respectively. The objective function V can be written as:

$$\min_{G} \max_{D} V(D, G) = \mathbb{E}_{(x,y)\sim p_{data}(x,y)}[\log(D(x|y))]$$
$$+ \mathbb{E}_{y\sim p_{data}(y)}[\log(1 - D(G(y)))]. \tag{1}$$

Here G and D refers to the generator and discriminator. x represents the RGB sample, y represents the corresponding auxiliary representation which serves as a prior for the generator. The x and y samples are drawn from the input data distribution $p_{data}(x, y)$ that consists of RGB images and their auxiliary representations or segmentation masks in the current scenario. In our case, the auxiliary representations are the automatically generated segmentation masks as described in Sect. 3.2.

At every iteration, the discriminator and the generator are trained alternatively as was performed previously. During the training of the discriminator, the segmentation mask and its corresponding RGB image are concatenated on its channel dimension. It is then passed through the discriminator (Patch GAN) [9] and discriminator loss of the real image is calculated as below

$$D_{loss} = -\log(D(x)) + \log(1 - D(G(y))), \tag{2}$$

where x represent samples from the input database and y refers to segmentation masks of those samples. A binary cross-entropy loss function is used to calculate the adversarial loss. While training the generator, the segmentation masks are passed through the generator network and the loss is calculated. The loss has two components denoting the adversarial loss exhibited by the discriminator and the mean square error between the generated sample and the actual RGB image from the dataset that corresponds to the mask y.

$$G_{loss} = -\log(D(G(y))) + \lambda \, \text{MSE}(G(y), x|y) \tag{3}$$

where λ is the weight of Mean Squared Error (MSE) loss. The weight of the mean squared error loss is set to 100 based on empirical analysis on a small validation set. x and y represent samples from the RGB image and the segmentation mask dataset.

3.4   Training the GAN to Generate Segmentation Masks

A conditional GAN(CGAN) usually generates synthetic samples conditioned by some predefined priors. In the current scenario, the CGAN has been trained to generate samples from segmentation masks highlighting the spatial distribution of nuclei across the cytoplasm. To generate patho-realistic synthetic samples during the evaluation phase a class-specific prior distribution is necessary. For that purpose, we train a GAN model [6] to generate binary segmentation masks based on a randomly drawn seed from a gaussian distribution. While models like CycleGAN [16] can be used for image translation, it is not suitable for synthetic data generation. The most straight forward method to generate synthetic samples would have been to train an end-to-end GAN. However, it has been noticed in ablation studies that without a prior the quality of outputs is very poor. The primary reason being the complexity of predicting the intensity value of a pixel. Given the output image has three channels, each pixel exists within a search space with 256^3. However, a binary segmentation mask is a much easier output to predict given that each pixel belongs to a binomial distribution. On the other hand, the shape information encoded within these segmentation masks is quite informative about the class of the samples, namely, benign or malignant. We train two separate GANs trained on segmentation masks belonging to each of the predefined classes.

The objective of the GAN network is simply defined as

$$\min_G \max_D V(D,G) = \mathbb{E}_{x \sim p_{data}(x)}[\log(D(x))]$$
$$+ \mathbb{E}_{z \sim p(z)}[\log(1 - D(G(z)))] \tag{4}$$

Here x refers to samples drawn from the input data distribution $p_{data}(x)$. z refers to randomly sampled priors from a Gaussian distribution $p(z)$. G and D refers to the generator and discriminator network. The architecture of the GAN used in the current work is very similar to the one described in the previous section. It consists of a generator inspired from UNet whos transposed convolutions have been replaced with bilinear interpolation for upscaling and a convolution layer for refinement. The discriminator is derived from the PatchGAN discriminator as demonstrated in [9]. During the training phase, the discriminator loss is given by,

$$D_{Loss} = -(\log(D(x)) + \log(1 - D(G(z)))) \tag{5}$$

and the generator loss is given by:

$$G_{Loss} = -\log(D(G(z))) \tag{6}$$

However, due to very low number of samples, the discriminator was too overpowering and saturates at a very early stage. To deal with this issue some additional measures were taken as described below [11].

– **Label smoothing:** The labels for real and fake samples are set as 1 and 0 by default. To enforce some fuzziness in the system, a random number between

0.9 and 1 was taken for real samples and a random number between 0.1 and 0 was taken for fake samples while training. However, this is unnecessary while training the generator as we want to bottleneck the learning curve of the discriminator and not the generator.

- **Randomly flipping labels:** To even further confuse the discriminator at some random iterations real samples are labeled as fake and vice versa. This confusion results provide some breathing space for the generator so that it can learn the requisite features.

Other models such as Wasserstein GAN [1] can further improve results.

3.5   Evaluating on the Trained Model to Generate Synthetic Images

The final phase generates class specific patho-realistic synthetic samples. According to the pipeline discussed in Sect. 3.1, at first the class-specific GANs are used to generated segmentation masks (refer Sect. 3.4). Then the generated segmentation masks are fed into the trained CGAN model (refer Sect. 3.3) to obtain the RGB synthetic images. The synthetic data distribution is modeled as,

$$p_{data(z)} = \mathbb{E}_{z \sim p(z)}[G_{CGAN}(G_{GAN}(z))] \tag{7}$$

where, G_{CGAN} and G_{GAN} refers to the generators of the CGAN and GAN model described in Sect. 3.3 and 3.4 respectively.

While a simple CGAN trained on a prior denoting the class of samples could also be viable, having a richer representation like a mask provides more flexibility in terms of variations in the synthetic dataset.

4   Experiments and Results

The main objective of the work is to generate class-specific synthetic data similar to microscopic cytology images that can boost the performance of standard image classification algorithms. For our experiments we have used three classifiers namely, ResNet-152 [7], Inception-V3 [14] and DenseNet-161 [8]. Each of these networks has a proven track record in tough image classifications tasks such as the ILSVRC. In the original dataset, there were 156 images in total. Out of which 77 were benign samples and 79 were malignant samples. For the benefit of a cleaner calculation, a total of 150 images were selected with 75 images from each class. The dataset was randomly divided in the ratio of 3:1:1 into training, validation, and testing set with an equal number of samples in each class. The ratio of synthetic data to original training data was maintained at 2:1. Thus 90 synthetic training images were generated per class (Table 1).

4.1   Experimental Setup

The performance metric defining the goodness of the synthetic data generation pipeline, referred to as SynCGAN in the current work, is given by its impact

Table 1. Number of samples in the original and synthetic dataset

Dataset	Training	Validation	Testing
Original images	90	30	30
Synthetic images	180	–	–

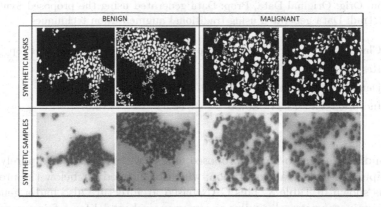

Fig. 3. Synthetic masks generated by class specific GANs (top) are fed as priors to the conditional GAN during evaluation phase to generate patho-realistic samples (bottom) for benign (left) and malignant (right) classes separately

on the test accuracy obtained using the three previously mentioned network, namely, ResNet-152, Inception-V3, and DenseNet-161. The experiment was conducted to analyze the impact of synthetic data augmentation on several grounds (Fig. 3).

1. Impact of augmentation using data generated by SynCGAN,
2. Performance of SynCGAN generated data augmentation against traditional data augmentation,
3. Performance of SynCGAN generated data augmentation against GAN generated data augmentation.

The CGAN model trained for a maximum of 200 epochs and the best model was saved based on minimum generator loss on the validation dataset. While the GAN model was trained for almost until the generator loss saturated(1600 epochs). For both the cases adam optimizer was used. All the experiments were conducted on Nvidia GTX 1060 GPU.

4.2   Observations and Analysis

The first observation as shown in Table 2, shows that augmentation of data generated with the proposed SynCGAN improves the performance of classifiers. When compared with traditional augmentation techniques like random horizontal and vertical flipping, random rotation and addition of Gaussian noise, the proposed method of augmentation has a higher impact. When traditional data augmentation was combined with SynCGAN based augmentation, the performance was either at par or lower than exclusive SynCGAN based augmentation.

Table 2. Performance of classifiers while using the dataset with and without augmentation. Orig: Original Data, Prop: Data generated using the proposed SynCGAN pipeline, Trad: Data generated using traditional augmentation techniques

Classifier	Orig	Orig+Prop	Orig+Trad	Orig+Trad+Prop
ResNet-152	73.33	**76.67**	70.00	**76.67**
DenseNet-161	80.00	**86.67**	83.33	84.67
Inception-V3	73.33	**80.00**	63.33	76.67

Secondly, as a control to our proposed model, we implemented a purely GAN based pipeline for data augmentation, which performed far below the proposed model as shown in Table 3. This GAN based architecture also had a generator and discriminator network similar to our proposed model for a fair comparison.

Table 3. Performance of classifiers while using the dataset with and without augmentation. Orig: Original Data, Prop: Data generated using proposed SynCGAN pipeline, GAN: Data generated using vanilla GAN.

Classifier	Orig	Prop	Orig+Prop	GAN	Orig+GAN
ResNet-152	73.33	73.33	**76.67**	50.00	63.33
DenseNet-161	80.00	63.33	**86.67**	50.00	60.00
Inception-V3	73.33	66.67	**80.00**	56.67	66.67

5   Conclusion

In the present work, a CGAN based data augmentation technique has been proposed using class specific priors that improves the performance of various state of the art CNNs such as ResNet-152, DenseNet-161, and Inception-V3 on cytology images corresponding to FNAC tests. Unlike a normal GAN, we have used learnable segmentation masks as class-specific priors to guide a conditional GAN for more robust synthetic data generation. It is to be noted that the method is quite dependent on the mask generation algorithm and hence extensive studies may be performed using other available nuclei segmentation techniques for further analysis. Furthermore, the method may be further generalized to adapt to other types of cytological data.

Acknowledgement. This work is funded by SERB (DST), Govt. of India (Ref no. EEQ/2018/000963). The authors are thankful to Theism Medical Diagnostics Centre, Kolkata, West Bengal, India for providing cytology samples and also thanks to Centre for Microprocessor Application for Training, Education, and Research, Jadavpur University for providing additional infrastructure for the research.

References

1. Arjovsky, M., Chintala, S., Bottou, L.: Wasserstein GAN. arXiv preprint arXiv:1701.07875 (2017)
2. Bissoto, A., Perez, F., Valle, E., Avila, S.: Skin lesion synthesis with generative adversarial networks. In: Stoyanov, D., et al. (eds.) CARE/CLIP/OR 2.0/ISIC - 2018. LNCS, vol. 11041, pp. 294–302. Springer, Cham (2018). https://doi.org/10.1007/978-3-030-01201-4_32
3. Frid-Adar, M., Diamant, I., Klang, E., Amitai, M., Goldberger, J., Greenspan, H.: Gan-based synthetic medical image augmentation for increased CNN performance in liver lesion classification. Neurocomputing **321**, 321–331 (2018)
4. Ghosh, S., Das, N., Das, I.S., Maulik, U.: Understanding deep learning techniques for image segmentation. ArXiv abs/1907.06119 (2019)
5. Ghosh, S., Das, N., Nasipuri, M.: Reshaping inputs for convolutional neural network: some common and uncommon methods. Pattern Recogn. **93**, 79–94 (2019)
6. Goodfellow, I., et al.: Generative adversarial nets. In: Advances in Neural Information Processing Systems, pp. 2672–2680 (2014)
7. He, K., Zhang, X., Ren, S., Sun, J.: Deep residual learning for image recognition. In: Proceedings of the IEEE Conference on Computer Vision and Pattern Recognition, pp. 770–778 (2016)
8. Huang, G., Liu, Z., Van Der Maaten, L., Weinberger, K.Q.: Densely connected convolutional networks. In: Proceedings of the IEEE Conference on Computer Vision and Pattern Recognition, pp. 4700–4708 (2017)
9. Isola, P., Zhu, J.Y., Zhou, T., Efros, A.A.: Image-to-image translation with conditional adversarial networks. In: Proceedings of the IEEE Conference on Computer Vision and Pattern Recognition, pp. 1125–1134 (2017)
10. Kowal, M., Filipczuk, P., Obuchowicz, A., Korbicz, J.: Computer-aided diagnosis of breast cancer using gaussian mixture cytological image segmentation. J. Med. Inf. Technol. **17** (2011)
11. Kumar, S., Gupta, M.D.: C+GAN: complementary fashion item recommendation. arXiv preprint arXiv:1906.05596 (2019)
12. Mirza, M., Osindero, S.: Conditional generative adversarial nets. arXiv preprint arXiv:1411.1784 (2014)
13. Shin, H.-C., et al.: Medical image synthesis for data augmentation and anonymization using generative adversarial networks. In: Gooya, A., Goksel, O., Oguz, I., Burgos, N. (eds.) SASHIMI 2018. LNCS, vol. 11037, pp. 1–11. Springer, Cham (2018). https://doi.org/10.1007/978-3-030-00536-8_1
14. Szegedy, C., Vanhoucke, V., Ioffe, S., Shlens, J., Wojna, Z.: Rethinking the inception architecture for computer vision. In: Proceedings of the IEEE Conference on Computer Vision and Pattern Recognition, pp. 2818–2826 (2016)

15. Tom, F., Sheet, D.: Simulating patho-realistic ultrasound images using deep generative networks with adversarial learning. In: 2018 IEEE 15th International Symposium on Biomedical Imaging (ISBI 2018), pp. 1174–1177. IEEE (2018)
16. Zhu, J.Y., Park, T., Isola, P., Efros, A.A.: Unpaired image-to-image translation using cycle-consistent adversarial networks. In: Proceedings of the IEEE International Conference on Computer Vision, pp. 2223–2232 (2017)

Fish-Eye Image Based Cross Traffic Alert System

Madhurima Bandyopadhyay[✉], Ankit Kumar, and Anoop Pathayapurakkal

Continental Automotive Components (India) Pvt. Ltd., Bengaluru, India
Madhurima.Bandyopadhyay@continental-corporation.com

Abstract. In the automotive industry, the use of advanced driver assisted systems (ADAS) is gaining a lot of traction. ADAS systems are designed to assist the driver by providing information regarding road users, lane information, traffic infrastructures etc., and improve the road safety aspects of an automobile. In this paper, we propose a real-time cross traffic alert (CTA) system based on fisheye camera images having ~180° field of view (FOV). The main purpose of CTA is to avoid unwanted collision with any approaching target by issuing an alert to the driver at a T-junction. The main components of the proposed CTA algorithm are, sparse optical flow vector tracking, object cluster formation and estimation of time to collision (TTC) for each object cluster. The TTC calculation can be performed without explicit depth reconstruction. We compute TTC based on homography estimation between similar features of consecutive image frames. Under good weather condition, the performance of the proposed CTA algorithm in detecting approaching target is reasonably good with a true positive rate of nearly 88%, but with significant false positive rate to the tune of 19%. A major contributing factor to this high false positive is identified to be the inability to distinguish a real crossing object and objects moving parallel to the host vehicle just using TTC estimates. To suppress the unintended false positive cases, we propose a novel solution based on statistics of the flow vector cluster and showcase its efficacy. The classification result for the proposed approach indicates that we have achieved to reduce the false positive rate to nearly 10% while maintaining the true positive rate.

Keywords: Cross traffic alert · Homography · Time to collision

1 Introduction

ADAS has great potential to enhance the driving comfort and more over the road safety aspects. Road accidents are one of the leading causes of death and health hazards in India. According to the Ministry of road transport and highways of India, during 2016, there were cases of 55 road accidents and 17 deaths in every hour. This emphasizes the necessity of ADAS, which can promote a safe driving by monitoring, warning, and reducing the controlling efforts of a driver. The research on ADAS has become the current trend in the automobile industry, which has been fueled by the consumer interest and guidelines of regulatory bodies to strengthen the road safety measures.

© Springer Nature Singapore Pte Ltd. 2020
R. V. Babu et al. (Eds.): NCVPRIPG 2019, CCIS 1249, pp. 43–52, 2020.
https://doi.org/10.1007/978-981-15-8697-2_4

Now-a-days different ADAS functionalities are available, such as, adaptive cruise control, blind spot detection, collision avoidance system, traffic sign recognition, lane change assistance, pedestrian detection, parking assist among few of them. ADAS uses different environmental sensors like RADAR, LiDAR, ultrasound, visible/infrared imagers to assist the driver in recognizing and reacting to potentially dangerous traffic situations. Each sensor has its own benefits and limitations. Data fusion techniques provide best solution by utilizing the complimentary nature of data [1, 2]. However, such systems are expensive to enter the mass automobile market.

Designing any real-time system requires efficient algorithm with fast processing time. Different techniques have been proposed by various authors. Cui et al. (2010), used Haar and Adaboost classifier to detect moving objects [3]. In other research, Dagan et al. (2004), estimated collision time directly from the size and position of the vehicle in the image without computing a 3D representation of the scene [4]. To detect forward vehicle detection and warning system, Jheng et al. (2015), designed Bayes classifier along with vehicular symmetry detection and shadow detection technique [5]. Yet in another research, Deng et al. (2014), used Haar-like feature and Adaboost classifier together with SVM-based classifier with HOG feature to build forward collision warning system based on monocular vision [6].

In this paper, we are proposing a real-time solution for front CTA system based on fish-eye image for static host vehicle. The main steps in CTA are, feature detection, spare optical flow tracking, object cluster formation and finally estimation of the collision time, i.e., TTC. To calculate TTC, algorithm does not rely on the depth reconstruction between the host and the target object, rather TTC is estimated by determining the homography between cluster features obtained in the consecutive image frames. The proposed CTA module demonstrated good performance statistics, however, it had a serious limitation, where it was failing to differentiate between an object approaching the host and an object moving parallel to the host. This contributed in a high false positive number. To overcome this problem, we have come up with a solution which utilizes the statistical characteristic of the flow vectors of an object cluster. Using this approach, we are able to suppress the false positive cases to a greater extend. The rest of the paper is organized in four major sections. We will start with the method, followed by the results, discussion, and conclusion.

2 Method

The block diagram of the CTA system is shown in Fig. 1. To capture images, a video camera with fish-eye lens is placed at the front bumper of the car. The fish-eye lens has ~180° FOV to capture image of a wide region. The video camera captures 30 image frames per second, with image resolution of 1 megapixel. A pre-processing step is performed, such as noise removal, brightness adjustment etc. before sending the image to the CTA module. Next, CTA module detects any object approaching the host vehicle, it generates alert. The alert can be either in visual or acoustic form. To save further processing time CTA application runs only for two selected portions of the image. These are called region of interest (ROI). There are two ROIs, left and right ROI. The choice of ROI regions is to ensure that the movement of approaching objects (either from left to right for left ROI, or right to left for right ROI) can be captured unhindered.

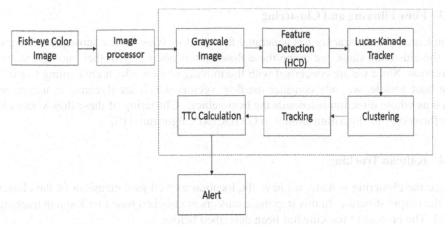

Fig. 1. The block diagram of CTA module, the main components are camera, image processor, CTA module.

Different components of the CTA module are discussed below.

2.1 Feature Detection

Harries corner Detector (HCD): Initial feature points were selected using HCD [7], followed by feature densification method to further enhance the number of feature points.

Feature Densification. Apart from the HCD points for each frame, we try to populate some more feature points, so that we do not miss any features which is not picked up by HCD. Feature densification works like this, it picks up a random point of the image. Over a 3x3 window region around that pixel it computes the luminance difference between the central and surrounding pixels. If majority number of pixels inside that window have luminance difference more than a predefined threshold, then we consider that pixel as a feature point.

Once the features points are identified our next task is feature tracking. We have used Lukas Kanade (LK) optical flow tracker for this purpose.

2.2 Lukas Kanade (LK) Optical Flow

Estimating the location of any image feature point between time frame t and t + 1 is called tracking. There are many tracking techniques available. Lucas kanade (LK) optical flow tracker [8] is most popularly used sparse tracking technique. However, with the conventional LK tracker the problem is to track larger movement or object with high speed of motion. We have implemented four pyramidal layer LK tracker [9] to overcome this issue.

Our next step is to group or cluster the flow vectors, which is performed in the next step.

2.3 Flow Filtering and Clustering

The Lucas-Kanade tracker has generated flow vectors between the subsequent frames. In the clustering stage, we group these flow vectors according to their movement and direction. Since we are concerned with the moving objects which are coming towards the host vehicle, we only consider the flow vectors which are dynamic in nature, as well as whose direction is towards the host vehicle. Clustering of these flow vectors is performed by an algorithm similar to GRIDCLUS algorithm [10].

2.4 Kalman Tracking

Once the clustering is done, we have the location as well as dimensions of the cluster as the output structure. In this step these clusters are tracked based on Kalman tracking [11]. The process of tracking has been described below:

1. For all the available tracks, we set the Kalman state transition matrix and predict the next state of the tracks. The state matrix of the track is given as:

$$X = \begin{bmatrix} xPos & xVel & yPos & yVel & wBox & 0 & hBox & 0 \end{bmatrix}^T \tag{1}$$

The state transition matrix is based on the basic kinematics formula
We can write the above kinematics equation in the matrix form as

$$X(t) = A * X(t-1) \tag{2}$$

The Kalman prediction of the next state [12] of the tracks is done using below equations:

-   $X(t) = A * X(t-1)$

    Here we are predicting the mean of the next state. We assume that the target vehicles are travelling at a constant speed, so the acceleration of the vehicles is zero. Therefore, in the above equation, we are neglecting the control matrix since there is no known external force.

-   $P(t) = A * P(t-1) * A^T + Q$

    Here we are predicting the next state covariance [12]. Q is the Process noise covariance matrix.

2. The track status is updated with respect to the objects in the frame. The types of operation done on the tracks are track association, track deletion, and track merge.

Once object tracking is done next the TTC is computed for the object cluster.

2.5 Time of Collision (TTC) Calculation

In this section we estimate the collision time between the host vehicle and target. TTC is purely computed based on homography estimation using the feature points of a cluster between two consecutive image frames. Hartley and Zisserman, 2000 have shown that the homography induced by a 3D plane between two views is given by,

$$H = K'\left(R - t\tilde{n}^T/D\right)K^{-1} \tag{3}$$

where R and t are the rotation and translation between two camera centres. K and K' are the intrinsic calibration matrix of the two cameras. D is the distance between the first camera centre and the 3D plane, and $\tilde{n}$ is the normal vector of the 3D plane.

Now, according to our setup, the host vehicle and the camera attached to it are static. Images of any 3D object which is approaching towards the host is captured by the camera at different time are being used to calculate homography H. These images are having similar normal vector $\tilde{n}$. Figure 2 depicts the situation.

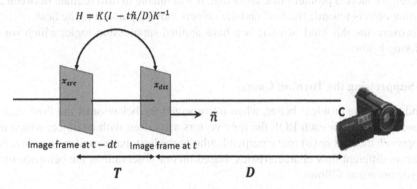

$$H = K(I - t\tilde{n}/D)K^{-1}$$

Fig. 2. Homography introduced by 3D plane

Based on the above condition, Eq. (5) becomes,

$$H = K\left(I - T\tilde{n}^T/D\right)K^{-1} \tag{4}$$

where, D is the distance between object and camera at time t. T is the translation/relative displacement between the object at $t - dt$ and t. The intrinsic calibration matrix K is same as only single camera is involded here. Also there is no rotation between two image frames thus rotation matrix R is an identity matix I. According to the above figure, the TTC can be expressed as,

$$\text{Time to collision } (TTC) = D/\|T\| * dt = D/V \tag{5}$$

where $V = T/dt$ is the relative speed between the object and the camera.

Now, suppose, x_{src}, and x_{dst} are the source and destination point of a flow vector. These two points are connected by the homography matrix H, given by Eq. (6).

$$x_{src} = H * x_{dst}$$

$$x_{src} = K\left(I - T\tilde{n}^T/D\right)K^{-1} * x_{dst} \tag{6}$$

In the above equation, the only unknown is T/D, which we have termed as inverse TTC (iTTC). We can approximate the normal vector $\tilde{n}$, without introducing much error in the system, since we are only concern about the moving objects which are crossing the host vehicle. To solve the unknown quantity, we have built a system of linear equation using all the flow vectors inside the cluster obtained from the tracking module. The system of linear equation takes a form given by,

$$A * iTTC = B \tag{7}$$

By solving the above equation, we get iTTC, inverse of this gives us as the collision time TTC. The TTC is computed for each cluster which are having more than three flow vectors.

The algorithm design of the CTA module is discussed above. It can run real time with, with a processing speed of 33 ms and gives a reasonably good detection accuracy. However, we faced a problem in CTA is that, it was unable to differentiate between any incoming objects towards the host and the objects moving parallel to the host.

To overcome this kind of issue, we have applied suppression logic, which we are discussing below.

2.6 Suppressing the Turning Cases

To understand the problem better, when introspected the behavior of the flow vectors, we found out that, for each ROI, the flow vectors associated with an object which may (a) approach the host or (b) move perpendicular to the host, have similar flow direction, but shows different flow characteristics. Based on our observations the behavior of the flow vectors are as follows,

- Approaching object: The object cluster which is approaching the host vehicle gets bigger size due to the fact that flow vectors inside that cluster show divergence.
- Perpendicular moving/turning objects: The object cluster which is moving perpendicular to the host vehicle gets smaller in size due to the fact that flow vectors inside that cluster show convergence.

The above observations are attributed to the fish-eye distortion of the image. Figure 3 illustrates the flow characteristics. To suppress the detection of perpendicular moving vehicle, for each cluster the standard deviation of the source points and destination points was compared. If $\sigma_{src} > \sigma_{dst}$ – cluster is converging, perpendicular movement. If $\sigma_{src} < \sigma_{dst}$ - cluster is diverging, approaching towards host. The suppression logic removes the object cluster which shows $\sigma_{src} > \sigma_{dst}$.

3 Result and Discussion

The major challenge we have faced while designing this driving solutions is that we have to consider various weather conditions, different lighting condition throughout to the day

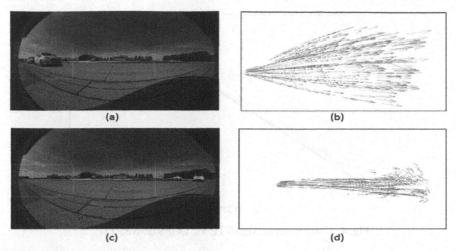

Fig. 3. The flow characteristics is shown in the figure. In figure (a) and (c) the images from three different time frames has been superimposed to show the object trajectory. Figure (b) shows the flow vectors associated with the (a) approaching vehicle (from left to right towards the host). Here the flow vectors are diverging in nature. Figure (d) shows the flow vectors associated with the (c) moving away vehicle. Here the flow vectors are converging in nature.

time, type of target objects and various road conditions (different road junctions, parking bay etc.). Therefore, we have tested our algorithm based on different 1) weather condition (rainy, fog, dry, wet), 2) time of the day (Early morning, Mid-day, Late afternoon), 3) target objects (bus, truck, car, two-wheeler etc.).

To validate the performance of the proposed CTA algorithm, we compared its result with ground truth videos. These videos were captured by placing the differential global positioning systems (DGPS) in the host and the target object. The DGPS is accurate up to 10 cm. Videos of various length were captured ranging from 1 min up to 15 min. Ground truth data were prepared by manually labelling the approaching objects towards the host from either left or right ROI. The DGPS measured distance between the host and target was used to calculated collision time per frame, which was treated as ground truth TTC to compare the accuracy of the TTC alert of CTA.

3.1 Assessment of CTA Measured TTC

As mentioned earlier CTA estimated TTC was compared based on the DGPS derived TTC. Figure 4 shows the plot of CTA TTC vs. DGPS measured TTC, for a target vehicle of speed 35 kph.

As shown in the above graph, the CTA estimated TTC and the DGPS TTC almost follow a 1:1 relation. We can see some deviation, which is more prominent when the target vehicle is far from the host. This was expected, as we are calculating TTC based on homography between two clusters of an image frame. This method of TTC calculation is adopted to reduce the run time. So, it can be said, to improve the run time, we have compromised in the accuracy of collision time. However, as the target comes nearer to

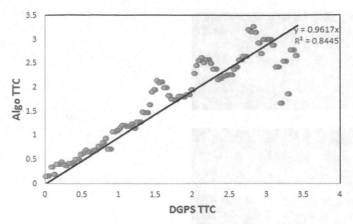

Fig. 4. Comparison of Algo TTC vs. DGPS derived TTC

the host, say between 1.5 s to 0 s, (in this particular case target is ~15 m away from the host) the CTA derived TTC is accurate, which is crucial, as chances of accident is more in this zone.

3.2 Classification Assessment of CTA

We have tested the CTA application under varying environmental conditions. Data catalogue was created to cover all weather conditions, road scenarios, target objects. Table 1 shows the classification accuracy of the proposed CTA module, along with the number of video clips used to test CTA under different weather and lighting conditions. Table 1 shows that except high luminance and foggy condition, the performance of CTA is reasonably good with true positive rate of ~86%. The reason behind the poor performance of CTA for above mentioned cases is that there is a drop in overall scene contrast, which affects the algorithm performance. As mentioned earlier, before the implementation of flow suppression logic, CTA was wrongly detecting parallel (w.r.t host vehicle) moving target objects, which was degrading the false positive rate. For example, the 1st row of Table 1 has total 1049 videos, among them nearly 400 videos have turning case scenario. Due to this reason, the false positive rate was ~19% before the flow vector suppression. Our proposed solution, based on the statistical characteristics of the flow vectors shows a good suppression of the turning cases, and thus the false positive rate has improved to 15%. If we compare the overall performance of the CTA module we can see the overall false positive detection has been improved from 11% to 9% without affecting the true positive detection rate.

Table 1. Classification matrix of CTA module

	Test conditions		Total video clips	Before turning case suppression logic		After turning case suppression logic	
	Weather	Luminance		TP (%)	FP (%)	TP (%)	FP (%)
1	Dry	Low	1059	88.88	19.19	88.07	15.66
2	Dry	Medium	952	94.24	3.35	93.88	2.86
3	Dry	High	813	68.21	10.69	67.39	9.36
4	Wet	Low	909	91.71	7.92	91.25	5.86
5	Wet	Medium	576	90.07	8.06	89.66	6.63
6	Wet	High	365	81.79	18.85	81.07	15.07
7	Snow/Rain	Low	910	86.21	12.36	85.75	11.05
8	Snow/Rain	Medium	339	73.56	18.69	73.32	16.59
9	Fog	Low	328	55.66	9.98	54.65	10.22
10	Fog	Medium	418	54.24	1.2	53.45	1.33
		Average (%)		78.45	11.03	77.84	9.46

4 Conclusion

In this paper, we have presented real-time CTA application with run time of 33 ms. The main functionality of CTA is to alert the driver for approaching target, at T-junction or parking bay. Proposed system purely works based on feature detection and tracking. The TTC calculation is based on homography estimation between two planes. Estimated TTC is accurate when the target vehicle is in the vicinity of the host (Fig. 6). Overall the detection accuracy of the CTA is 80%, with a false positive rate of 9%. Earlier, CTA was suffering from inability of detecting crossing traffic targets with the targets moving parallel to the host. We have addressed this by exploiting the converging/diverging nature of the optical flow to improve the overall performance. This is evident from Table 1, which shows a drop in false positive rate from 11% to 9%, without affecting the true positive detection (~80%). Our proposed CTA module can deal with the cases of static as well as moving host vehicle with small velocity between 0–10 KMPH. In the case of dynamic host, we use ego-motion compensation. The ego motion compensation part is not mentioned in this paper as our main purpose here was to present the main CTA algorithm. Since there is no real-time benchmarking data available, so there is no baselining for CTA. But we have extensively studied the performance of the proposed system with collected ground truth data (Table 1), and able to achieve intended performance. In future, we will try to improve the classification accuracy, without compromising the processing time. Currently, CTA works under day light condition, so in future, we are planning to increase its applicability by running it under dark, where the possibility of accident is more. Also, our plan is to not to constraint the application inside ROI, rather build a semantic segmentation-based detection system.

Acknowledgement. This paper is the result of the collective work of all teams involved in the project. Particularly we want to thank to Boris Lugez (Continental Automotive, France) and Behshad Memari (Continentla Automotive, UK) for their technical support and guidance.

References

1. Tokoro, S., Moriizumi, K., Kawasaki, T., Nagao, T., Abe, K., Fujita, K.: Sensor fusion system for pre-crash safety system. In: 2004 IEEE Intelligent Vehicles Symposium, pp. 945–950. IEEE (2004)
2. Hsieh, Y.-C., Lian, F.-L., Hsu, C.-M.: Optimal multi-sensor selection for driver assistance systems under dynamical driving environment. In: 2007 IEEE Intelligent Transportation Systems Conference, ITSC 2007, pp. 696–701. IEEE (2007)
3. Cui, J., Liu, F., Li, Z., Jia, Z.: Vehicle localisation using a single camera. In: 2010 IEEE Intelligent Vehicles Symposium (IV), pp. 871–876. IEEE (2010)
4. Mano, O.S., Stein, G.P., Dagan, E., Shashua, A.: Forward collision warning with a single camera. In: 2004 IEEE Intelligent Vehicles Symposium, pp. 37–42. IEEE (2004)
5. Jheng, Y.-J., Yen, Y.-H., Sun, T.-Y.: A symmetry-based forward vehicle detection and collision warning system on android smartphone. In: 2015 IEEE International Conference on Consumer Electronics-Taiwan (ICCE-TW), pp. 212–213. IEEE (2015)
6. Deng, Y., Liang, H., Wang, Z., Huang, J.: An integrated forward collision warning system based on monocular vision. In: 2014 IEEE International Conference on Robotics and Biomimetics (ROBIO), pp. 1219–1223. IEEE (2014)
7. Harris, C., Stephens, M.: A combined corner and edge detector. In: Alvey Vision Conference, vol. 15. Citeseer (1988). https://doi.org/10.5244/C.2.23
8. Lucas, B.D., Kanade, T.: An iterative image registration technique with an application to stereo vision (1981)
9. Bouguet, J.-Y.: Pyramidal implementation of the affine lucas kanade feature tracker description of the algorithm. Intel Corp. **5**(1–10), 4 (2001)
10. Schikuta, E.: Grid-clustering: an efficient hierarchical clustering method for very large data sets. In: 1996 Proceedings of the 13th International Conference on Pattern Recognition, vol. 2, pp. 101–105. IEEE (1996)
11. Kalman, Rudolf E.: A new approach to linear filtering and prediction problems. J. Basic Eng. **82**(1), 35–45 (1960)
12. Faragher, Ramsey: Understanding the basis of the kalman filter via a simple and intuitive derivation. IEEE Signal Process. Mag. **29**(5), 128–132 (2012)
13. Hartley, R., Zisserman, A.: Multiple View Geometry in Computer Vision. Cambridge University Press, Cambridge (2003)

Evidence Based Image Selection for 3D Reconstruction

Smita C. Yadavannavar$^{(\boxtimes)}$, Varad Vinod Prabhu, Ramesh Ashok Tabib,
Ujwala Patil, and Uma Mudengudi

KLE Technological University, Hubli, India
scy15398@gmail.com

Abstract. In this paper, we propose a framework for image selection
using evidence theory, towards 3D reconstruction. The process of 3D
reconstruction involves image acquisition, image selection, feature extraction, calculating camera parameters, and generation of the point cloud.
Of these all, image selection plays a significant role, as it has a significant
impact on the final 3D model. However, in large scale 3D reconstruction,
image selection based on a single parameter is not sufficient. We measure the similarity between the images using multiple parameters and
generate a combined confidence score towards discarding similar images.
Experimental results show that the quality of 3D reconstruction is better
using images selected by the proposed method.

Keywords: 3D reconstruction · Image selection · Dempster Shafer
Combination Rule (DSCR) · SSIM · FLANN based parameter.

1 Introduction

In this paper, we propose a framework for image selection towards 3D reconstruction using evidence theory. 3D reconstruction is the process of the generation of
three-dimensional models from multiple images of the object. 3D reconstruction
finds its applications in the field of Computer Aided Geometric Design (CAGD),
computer graphics, computer vision, computer animation, medical imaging, computational science, virtual reality, digital media, reconstruction of heritage sites,
etc.

Typically image acquisition, image selection, evaluation of camera parameters
and point cloud generation are the modules in 3D reconstruction. The challenges
involved in 3D reconstruction are: less variation in data, variation in lighting
conditions, pairwise matching between images is computationally expensive.

To address these challenges, there is a need for efficient image selection algorithm which selects the valid images, improves the reconstruction quality and
optimizes the time required for reconstruction. In large scale 3D reconstruction
we perform reconstruction of large sites, cities, heritage sites.

Several methods, pipelines have been proposed towards 3D reconstruction
using large scale data. Authors in [6] propose a technique for image selection

© Springer Nature Singapore Pte Ltd. 2020
R. V. Babu et al. (Eds.): NCVPRIPG 2019, CCIS 1249, pp. 53–63, 2020.
https://doi.org/10.1007/978-981-15-8697-2_5

using Structure From Motion (SFM) to compute the position and orientation of each camera and the contribution of each image towards 3D reconstruction is computed. Based on the contribution of each image and effect of its contribution to 3D reconstruction a decision is made to select the image. The limitation in this approach is that time taken is more than a traditional approach since each image is checked for its contribution to the final 3D reconstruction. Authors in [3] propose an image-pair selection by creating a bag of visual words based on vector similarity and set similarity. The term frequency-inverse document frequency (tf-idf) weighting based similarity is used as vector similarity and modified Simpson's similarity is used as a set similarity. The image pairs are selected based on the intersection of the results obtained by vector similarity and set similarity. Due to the creation of a bag of visual words for large scale 3D reconstruction, there may be memory issues. The tool used in the paper [2] named Imaging Network Designer (IND) to cluster and select vantage images in a dense imaging network. They require a suitable hardware arrangement.

Researchers have also proposed the images selection based on key-frame selection. The authors in [4] discuss the keyframe selection algorithm. Keyframes are defined as the set of a frame that satisfies the epipolar geometry between the views. The keyframe selection algorithm is based on the "Geometric Robust Information Criterion (GRIC)". In this case, the number of feature points may decrease significantly as the baseline between the current frame and the last key-frame increases. Authors in [5] use a keyframe selection algorithm based on those images which have a large number of feature points and a sufficient baseline between each keyframe. Here the keyframe pairing is done to improve the probability of convergence of bundle adjustment.

Authors in [1] propose an image selection by the removal of redundant images. Images are first sorted in the increasing order of the image size, so that smaller size images are removed first. Then each image is removed to check if the coverage constraint holds well after removal of the image. If the coverage constraint is satisfied, then the image is permanently removed. This process is continued over all the sorted images.

Presently people use single parameter or hardware adjustments for 3D reconstruction, but large scale, 3D reconstruction one parameter cannot give the desired results and there cannot be hardware setup for this case. [3] uses two parameters but as a bag of visual words is used it may not work on large scale reconstruction. To overcome this, we propose an approach where we use two parameters and based on an evidence-based technique [9] to perform image selection for 3D reconstruction. Towards this,

- We propose to model a similarity score for the selection of images towards 3D reconstruction.
    - We choose two parametric scores namely Structural Similarity Index (SSIM) and Fast Library for Approximate Nearest Neighbor (FLANN) based parameter to generate a combined score.
    - We propose to combine similarity parametric scores using Dempster Shafer Combination Rule (DSCR) [7] to generate a confidence score.

– We propose to use the confidence score to eliminate redundant images.
- We demonstrate the results using a heritage dataset and compare the results using state-of-art methods.

2   Evidence Based Image Selection

We demonstrate the proposed framework in Fig. 1 to find the contribution of the images by detecting the similarity between images and find the parametric score of images being similar by using two parameters. Further, combine the two parametric scores using DSCR to obtain the confidence score. We decide if the given image is suitable for 3D reconstruction based on the decision threshold set upon the confidence score.

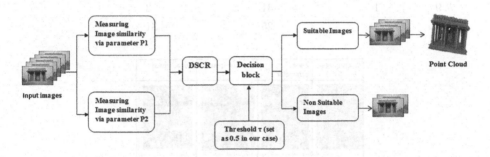

Fig. 1. Evidence based image selection

2.1   Parameters for Image Similarity

In large scale 3D reconstruction, measuring the similarity via a single parameter is not sufficient. This is demonstrated as shown in Table 1. Considering the row 1 of Table 1 column 1 signifies that image 1 was chosen for the image similarity. Flann based method estimated image 1 is similar to image 2 whereas SSIM based similarity estimated image 1 is similar to image 27. The DSCR rule is used to obtain the confidence score based on the two parametric scores and said image 1 was similar to image 27.

We use FLANN (Fast Library for Approximate Nearest Neighbors) based matcher as the first parameter (P_1). FLANN is a library for performing fast approximate nearest neighbor searches in high dimensional spaces. Classical feature descriptors (SIFT [12], SURF [13]) are typically compared and matched using the Euclidean distance (or L2-norm).

$$Euclidean\ distance = \sqrt{(x_1 - x_2)^2 + (y_1 - y_2)^2} \qquad (1)$$

Table 1. Results on the dataset

Image number	Flann Based similar image number	SSIM based similar image number	Our approach based similar image number
1	2	27	27
2	1	15	16
3	1	10	15
4	2	5	35
5	20	33	34
6	5	8	18
7	9	30	3
8	7	14	16
9	1	31	3
10	1	25	31

Fig. 2. Images corresponding to Table 1

Here (x_1, y_1) represents the location of feature 1 in $image_1$ and (x_2, y_2) represents the location of feature 2 in $image_2$. Whereas, binary descriptors (ORB [14], BRISK [15]) are also used for matching using Hamming distance.

$$d_{hamming}(a, b) = \sum_{i=0}^{n-1}(a_i \oplus b_i) \tag{2}$$

Here a and b are binary strings of length n. This distance is equivalent to count the number of different elements for binary strings (population count after applying an XOR operation).

We use the Structural Similarity Index (SSIM) as the second parameter (P_2). SSIM measures the perceptual difference between two similar images. SSIM is based on visible structures of the images. The SSIM index is calculated on various pairs of a window taken from both the images. Then the measure of SSIM between two windows x of $image_1$ and y of $image_2$ of common size N × N is:

$$SSIM(x,y) = \frac{(2\mu_x\mu_y + c_1)(2\sigma_{xy} + c_2)}{(\mu_x^2 + \mu_y^2 + c_1)(\sigma_x^2 + \sigma_y^2 + c_2)} \tag{3}$$

where:

μ_x is average of x;
μ_y is average of y;
σ_x^2 is variance of x;
σ_y^2 is variance of y;
$c_1 - (k_1L)^2, c_2 - (k_2L)^2$ two variables to stabilize the division with weak denominator;
L the dynamic range of the pixel-values (typically this is $2^{\# \text{ bits per pixel}} - 1$);
$k_1 = 0.01$ and $k_2 = 0.03$ by default and kept constant throughout our experimentation.

Let N be the total number of images in the dataset for 3D reconstruction. We perform one versus all similarity check. Let $image_i$ be the current query image. It is compared with all the other $(N-1)$ images in the dataset, based on this parametric score P_1 and P_2 are calculated. The Flann based parametric score P_1 is obtained by the number of valid matches between the image pair divided by the total number of features detected for one image (in our case the total number of features to be detected for one image is fixed to 500). The SSIM based parametric score P_2 is obtained by the SSIM score between the image pairs. The obtained parametric scores are combined using DSCR.

2.2   Confidence Score Using DSCR

We combine the two parametric scores using the Dempster Shafer Combination Rule (DSCR) to obtain the confidence score. Confidence score is obtained using DSCR based on the two parametric scores. We decide if the given query image is suitable for 3D reconstruction based on the decision threshold set upon the confidence score to maximize the probability of images being similar. Let P_1 and P_2 be the parametric score to be combined. DSCR combines two hypotheses consisting of three parameters, mass of belief, the mass of disbelief and mass of uncertainty rather than two parametric scores. We construct a hypothesis, hyp_1, and hyp_2 as a set of the mass of belief $(m(b))$, disbelief $(m(d))$ and uncertainty. $(m(u))$ respectively. We set the mass of belief $(m_1(b))$ for hyp_1 as P_1 and mass of belief $(m_2(b))$ for hyp_2 be P_2. We assume the mass of disbelief $(m_1(d))$ for hyp_1 and hyp_2 to be 0 and mass of uncertainty $(m_1(u)$ and $m_2(u))$ for hyp_1 and hyp_2 as $1 - P_1$ and $1 - P_2$ respectively. We combine hyp_1 and hyp_2 using a combination table as shown in Table 2.

In the above combination table, the product of the mass of belief of one hypothesis and mass of disbelief of other hypothesis gives rise to conflict and is represented by ϕ. The product of the mass of belief and mass of belief or the

Table 2. Combinational table

$\cap$	m_1^{belief}	$m_1^{disbelief}$	$m_1^{ambiguity}$
m_2^{belief}	ψ_1	ϕ	ψ_1
$m_2^{disbelief}$	ϕ	ψ_2	ψ_2
$m_2^{ambiguity}$	ψ_1	ψ_2	Ω

product of the mass of belief and mass of uncertainty represents joint belief and is represented by ψ_1. Similarly, ψ_2 represents the joint disbelief. The combined belief of two pieces of evidence is considered as confidence score and is given by:

$$Confidence\ score = \frac{\sum \psi_1}{1 - \sum \phi} \tag{4}$$

We decide if the given frame is suitable for 3D reconstruction based on the decision threshold τ set upon the confidence score [8]. The advantage of using DSCR for combining the two parametric scores is that it emphasizes the fact that if P_1 is the probability of the image being suitable for 3D reconstruction, then $1 - P_1$ need not be the probability of image not being suitable for 3D reconstruction. It can be uncertainty as well. Heuristically the value of decision threshold τ is set to 0.5 based on various heritage sites.

2.3 Algorithm

Algorithm 1. Evidence-based image selection

Input: *Images* $(i_1 \dots i_N)$
Output: *Selected Images*
 1: **for** $i \leftarrow 1$ to N **do**
 2:    **for** $j \leftarrow 1$ to N **do**
 3:        **if** i is not j **then**
 4:            $P_1 \leftarrow FLANN\_Based\_parameter(image_i, image_j)$
 5:            $P_2 \leftarrow SSIM(image_i, image_j)$
 6:            $Confidence factor \leftarrow DSCR(P_1, P_2)$
 7:            **if** $Confidence factor$ greater than 0.5 **then**
 8:                *Image is rejected*
 9:            **else**
10:                *Image is selected*
11:            **end if**
12:        **end if**
13:    **end for**
14: **end for**

By using Algorithm 1 we perform evidence-based image selection on heritage sites.

3   Results and Discussions

In this section, we demonstrate our results using real-time heritage datasets. We compare our results with the state-of-art [10,11] methods using the number of images retained after the image selection process. We have experimented with two heritage sites of Karnataka 1) Sasivekalu Ganapati of Hampi, 2) Mahadeva Temple of Koppal and one dataset generated by us bell dataset with no redundant images and which consists of 48 non-redundant images taken around a bell. We analyze our results quantitatively and qualitatively.

3.1   Quantitative Analysis

Table 3. Results on the dataset

Dataset	Number of images in dataset	Number of redundant images	Number of images retained using our approach	Time taken for 3D reconstruction (using all images) using MVG-MVS pipeline	Time taken for 3D reconstruction (our approach)
Sasivekalu Ganapati of Hampi	129	49	80	4 h 57 min	2 h 51 min
Bell	48	0	48	1 h 25 min	1 h 40 min
Mahadeva Temple of Koppal	301	75	226	2 days 43 min (for texture memory insufficient)	1 day 1 h 21 min

The proposed framework is implemented on the HP workstation with 64 GB of RAM.

Table 3 shows the results with and without using our framework. The Sasivekalu Ganapati of Hampi dataset consists of 129 images, 49 images were redundant according to our framework. The point cloud obtained by our framework is comparable with the state of art. The point cloud of the Sasivekalu Ganapati of Hampi is shown in Fig. 3.

We also experimented with the framework on bell dataset results of which are shown in Table 3. The bell dataset contains no redundant images. Our framework took 25 minutes extra when compared to that of the state of art (MVG-MVS pipeline) [10,11]. Since we are working on large scale 3D reconstruction there is a very low possibility of fewer redundant images. The point cloud obtained on the bell dataset is shown in Fig. 4.

Since our objective was to work on large scale 3D reconstruction we experimented with our approach on large datasets like the Mahadeva Temple of Koppal which consists of 301 images, in which there were redundant. With our framework 226 images were selected and were able to generate a point cloud with texture

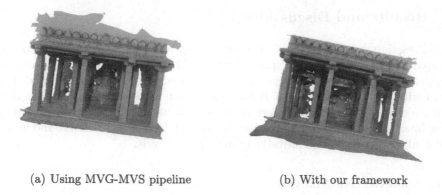

(a) Using MVG-MVS pipeline   (b) With our framework

Fig. 3. Point cloud of Sasivekalu Ganapati of Hampi.

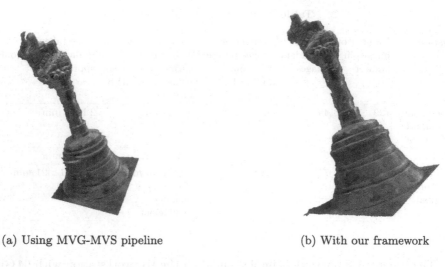

(a) Using MVG-MVS pipeline   (b) With our framework

Fig. 4. Point cloud of Bell dataset.

on the implemented system but, without our approach, point cloud with texture was not generated due to insufficient memory for rendering. Figure 5 shows the point cloud with and without our approach. Figure 5a shows the dense point cloud on Mahadeva Temple of Koppal without our framework. Figure 5b shows the dense point cloud on Mahadeva Temple of Koppal with our framework.

3.2 Qualitative Analysis

Figure 6 depicts the subjective analysis of the experimentation. The graph values indicate the number of people who were satisfied with the quality of the point cloud obtained with our approach or using state-of-art (MVG-MVS pipeline). The higher the value better is the quality of the result obtained. The survey was done with 100 people. It can be inferred from the graph that our approach has performed better.

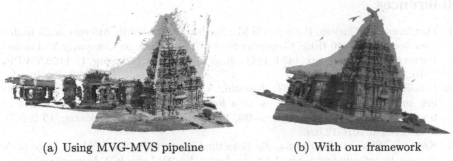

(a) Using MVG-MVS pipeline   (b) With our framework

Fig. 5. Point cloud of Mahadeva Temple of Koppal.

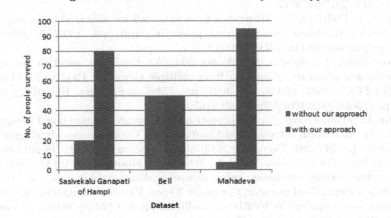

Fig. 6. Qualitative analysis

4   Conclusions

In this paper, we demonstrated the results in real-time for image selection for 3D reconstruction. We detected the similarity between images using two parameters and combined the parametric score of images being similar using DSCR (Dempster Shafer Combination Rule). We modeled 3D reconstruction as a combination of unique images. We have demonstrated the results of real-time heritage datasets. We have used the time taken for 3D reconstruction and the number of images selected for 3D reconstruction as a quantitative parameter and subjective analysis as a qualitative parameter to prove the superiority of the proposed method over the other algorithms.

References

1. Furukawa, Y., Curless, B., Seitz, S.M., Szeliski, R.: Towards internet-scale multi-view stereo. In: 2010 IEEE Computer Society Conference on Computer Vision and Pattern Recognition, pp. 1434–1441, June 2010. https://doi.org/10.1109/CVPR. 2010.5539802
2. Hosseininaveh, A., Yazdan, R., Karami, A., Moradi, M., Ghorbani, F.: Clustering and selecting vantage images in a low-cost system for 3D reconstruction of texture-less objects. Measurement **99**, 185–191 (2016). https://doi.org/10.1016/j. measurement.2016.12.026
3. Kato, T., Shimizu, I., Pajdla, T.: Selecting image pairs for SFM on large scale dataset by introducing a novel set similarity. In: 2017 6th ICT International Student Project Conference (ICT-ISPC), pp. 1–4, May 2017. https://doi.org/10.1109/ ICT-ISPC.2017.8075347
4. Repko, J., Pollefeys, M.: 3D models from extended uncalibrated video sequences: addressing key-frame selection and projective drift, pp. 150–157, July 2005. https://doi.org/10.1109/3DIM.2005.4
5. Thormählen, T., Broszio, H., Weissenfeld, A.: Keyframe selection for camera motion and structure estimation from multiple views. In: Pajdla, T., Matas, J. (eds.) ECCV 2004. LNCS, vol. 3021, pp. 523–535. Springer, Heidelberg (2004). https://doi.org/10.1007/978-3-540-24670-1_40
6. Yang, C., Zhou, F., Bai, X.: 3D reconstruction through measure based image selection. In: 2013 Ninth International Conference on Computational Intelligence and Security, pp. 377–381, December 2013. https://doi.org/10.1109/CIS.2013.86
7. Tabib, R.A., Patil, U., Ganihar, S.A., Trivedi, N., Mudenagudi, U.: Decision fusion for robust horizon estimation using dempster shafer combination rule. In: 2013 Fourth National Conference on Computer Vision, Pattern Recognition, Image Processing and Graphics (NCVPRIPG), Jodhpur, pp. 1–4 (2013). https://doi.org/10. 1109/NCVPRIPG.2013.6776247
8. Tabib, R.A., Patil, U., Naganandita, T., Gathani, V., Mudenagudi, U.: Dimensionality reduction using decision-based framework for classification: sky and ground. In: Sa, P.K., Sahoo, M.N., Murugappan, M., Wu, Y., Majhi, B. (eds.) Progress in Intelligent Computing Techniques: Theory, Practice, and Applications. AISC, vol. 519, pp. 289–298. Springer, Singapore (2018). https://doi.org/10.1007/978-981-10-3376-6_32
9. Patil, U., Tabib, R.A., Konin, C.M., Mudenagudi, U.: Evidence-based framework for multi-image super-resolution. In: Sa, P.K., Bakshi, S., Hatzilygeroudis, I.K., Sahoo, M.N. (eds.) Recent Findings in Intelligent Computing Techniques. AISC, vol. 709, pp. 413–423. Springer, Singapore (2018). https://doi.org/10.1007/978-981-10-8633-5_41
10. Moulon, P., Monasse, P., Perrot, R., Marlet, R.: OpenMVG: open multiple view geometry. In: Kerautret, B., Colom, M., Monasse, P. (eds.) RRPR 2016. LNCS, vol. 10214, pp. 60–74. Springer, Cham (2017). https://doi.org/10.1007/978-3-319-56414-2_5
11. OpenMVS. https://github.com/cdcseacave/openMVS
12. Lowe, D.G.: Distinctive image features from scale-invariant keypoints. Int. J. Comput. Vis. **60**(2), 91–110 (2004). https://doi.org/10.1023/B:VISI.0000029664.99615. 94
13. Bay, H., Ess, A., Tuytelaars, T., Van Gool, L.: Speeded-Up Robust Features (SURF). Comput. Vis. Image Underst. **110**(3), 346–359 (2008). https://doi.org/ 10.1016/j.cviu.2007.09.014

14. Rublee, E., Rabaud, V., Konolige, K., Bradski, G.: ORB: an efficient alternative to SIFT or SURF. In: Proceedings of the 2011 International Conference on Computer Vision (ICCV 2011), pp. 2564–2571. IEEE Computer Society, Washington, DC (2011). https://doi.org/10.1109/ICCV.2011.6126544

15. Leutenegger, S., Chli, M., Siegwart, R.Y.: BRISK: binary robust invariant scalable keypoints. In Proceedings of the 2011 International Conference on Computer Vision (ICCV 2011), pp. 2548–2555. IEEE Computer Society, Washington, DC (2011). https://doi.org/10.1109/ICCV.2011.6126542

Domain Decomposition Based Preconditioned Solver for Bundle Adjustment

Shrutimoy Das[✉], Siddhant Katyan, and Pawan Kumar

International Institute of Information Technology, 500032 Hyderabad, India
{shrutimoy.das,siddhant.katyan}@research.iiit.ac.in,
pawan.kumar@iiit.ac.in

Abstract. We propose Domain Decomposed Bundle Adjustment (DDBA), a robust and efficient solver for the bundle adjustment problem. Bundle adjustment (BA) is generally formulated as a non-linear least squares problem and is solved by some variant of the Levenberg-Marquardt (LM) algorithm. Each iteration of the LM algorithm requires solving a system of normal equations, which becomes computationally expensive with the increase in problem size. The coefficient matrix of this system has a sparse structure which can be exploited for simplifying the computations in this step. We propose a technique for approximating the Schur complement of the matrix, and use this approximation to construct a preconditioner, that can be used with the Generalized Minimal Residual (GMRES) algorithm for solving the system of equations. Our experiments on the BAL dataset show that the proposed method for solving the system is faster than GMRES solve preconditioned with block Jacobi and more memory efficient than direct solve.

Keywords: Computer vision · Bundle adjustment · Structure from motion · Generalized minimal residual · Preconditioning · Domain decomposition

1 Introduction

Many recent works in three dimensional ($3D$) reconstruction using Structure-from-Motion (SfM) algorithms has focused on building systems [1,9,19] that are capable of handling millions of images from unstructured internet photo collections. Given the feature matches between images, bundle adjustment (BA) [21] is a key component in most SfM systems. It is typically used as the last step in a $3D$ reconstruction pipeline. For large scale problems however, BA

© Springer Nature Singapore Pte Ltd. 2020
R. V. Babu et al. (Eds.): NCVPRIPG 2019, CCIS 1249, pp. 64–75, 2020.
https://doi.org/10.1007/978-981-15-8697-2_6

becomes very expensive computationally and thus, creates a bottleneck in the SfM systems. As a result, there has been a lot of interest in developing scalable large scale bundle adjustment algorithms [2,5,7,11,22].

The BA problem is typically formulated as the minimization of a nonlinear least squares problem, which can be done by using a classical algorithm such as the Levenberg-Marquardt (LM) algorithm. In each iteration of the LM algorithm, a solution to a linear system is required, which is the most computationally expensive step. A lot of research has been focused on making this step cheaper.

In [16], a direct method using Dense Cholesky factorization has been proposed. However, these methods do not scale well as the problem size increases. This has led to the application of iterative methods, specifically the Conjugate Gradient (CG) [18] method, for solving these systems. The convergence of these methods depend upon the condition number of the coefficient matrix. However, it has been observed that BA problems are very ill-conditioned. To solve this problem, preconditioning matrices or *preconditioners* [18] are applied to the system. They lower the condition number of the systems, which in turn speeds up the convergence of the iterative methods.

In this paper, we propose a new preconditioner which is based on the domain decomposition of the coefficient matrix. As it has been pointed out in [2]: "each point in the SfM problem is a domain, and the cameras form the interface between these domains". Using the domain decomposition method, we present a technique that can be used for approximating the global Schur complement of the matrix. We name this preconditioner as Mini Schur Complement (MSC) preconditioner. One of the advantages of using this preconditioner is that it is sparse, highly parallelizable and can be scaled up for very large problems. However, the preconditioned operator is unsymmetric. Thus, we use another iterative method known as restarted generalized minimal residual (GMRES). As the results show, solving the normal equations using GMRES preconditioned with MSC gives state-of-the-art performance on the BAL dataset.

The remaining part of the paper is organized as follows. Section 2 introduces the BA problem and also gives a review of the recent work on the use of preconditioned iterative methods. Section 3 gives a brief overview of domain decomposition methods and describes the design and implementation of the MSC preconditioner. Section 4 compares the results of our technique with direct solver and block Jacobi preconditioned GMRES solver. In Sect. 5, we conclude with a discussion.

2   Bundle Adjustment

Bundle adjustment tries to minimize the sum of reprojection errors between the 2D observations and the reprojected 2D points which are determined by the point and camera parameters. More information about this process can be found in [21].

Suppose that the scene to be reconstructed consists of p 3D points (or features), individually denoted as $y_i, i = 1, \ldots, p$, and these points are imaged in q cameras, whose individual parameters are denoted as $z_k, k = 1, \ldots, q$. Assume that the structure (point) and camera parameters to be estimated are taken in a large state vector $x \in \mathbb{R}^{(p+q)}$ which has the block structure $x = [y_1, \ldots, y_p, z_1, \ldots, z_q]^T$. Then, the reprojection error is defined as $f_k(x) = r_k(x) - m_{xk}$, for k $= 1, \ldots, $q. Given the mean reprojection error for each camera, the unknown 3D point and camera parameters can be estimated by minimizing the total reprojection error. Define $F(x) = [f_1(x), \ldots, f_q(x)]^T$ to be a q-dimensional function of the given parameter vector x. Then, the bundle adjustment problem can be stated as

$$x^* = \underset{x}{argmin} \frac{1}{2} \|F(x)\|_2^2. \tag{1}$$

In (1), the objective function is non-linear. For solving non-linear least squares problems of this form, the Levenberg-Marquardt (LM) algorithm [3,15,17] is applied. It is an iterative method where, in each iteration, an affine approximation of the cost function $F(x)$ in a neighbourhood of the current iterate x_t, is minimized. It is shown in [3] that the next iterate x_{t+1} can be computed as

$$x_{t+1} = x_t - (J^T J + \lambda^t \mathtt{diag}(J^T J))^{-1} J^T F(x_t). \tag{2}$$

Let $H_{LM} = J^T J + \lambda^t \mathtt{diag}(J^T J)$ and $g = J^T F(x_t)$. Here, J is the Jacobian of $F(x)$ at x_t and $\lambda^t > 0$ is a damping parameter which ensures that x_{t+1} lies in a neighbourhood of x_t. It should be noted that the definition of H_{LM} results in an approximation of the Hessian. Then, rearranging the terms in (2) gives

$$H_{LM} \Delta x = -g, \text{ where } \Delta x = x_{t+1} - x_t. \tag{3}$$

The Hessian H_{LM} is symmetric and positive definite (SPD). Thus, (3) can be solved as $\Delta x = -H_{LM}^{-1} g$ to get the exact solution. However, when the problem size becomes large, computing the inverse of H_{LM} becomes expensive. In these cases, an inexact solution of the system (3) can be computed by using an iterative method, such as GMRES. The convergence of the iterative methods depend on the condition number of the coefficient matrix, the Hessian in this case. For badly conditioned problems, such as bundle adjustment, the condition number can be improved with the help of a preconditioner [18]. This paper proposes the design and implementation of such a preconditioner, which exploits the special structure of the Hessian H_{LM}.

2.1   Structure of the Hessian

In the state vector x defined in Sect. 2, let s be the size of each point block and c be the size of each camera block. For the BAL dataset used in this paper, $c = 9$

and $s = 3$. Given these block sizes, the Jacobian J can be partitioned into a point part J_s and camera part J_c as $J = [J_s; J_c]$, which gives

$$H_{LM} = \begin{bmatrix} J_s^T J_s & J_s^T J_c \\ J_c^T J_s & J_c^T J_c \end{bmatrix} = \begin{bmatrix} D & L^T \\ L & G \end{bmatrix}. \tag{4}$$

Here, $D \in \mathbb{R}^{ps \times ps}$ is a block diagonal matrix with p blocks such that each block is of size $s \times s$ and $G \in \mathbb{R}^{qc \times qc}$ is a block diagonal matrix with q blocks such that each block is of size $c \times c$. The matrix $L \in \mathbb{R}^{qc \times ps}$ is a general block sparse matrix. Thus, we can rewrite (3) as a block structured linear system as follows

$$\begin{bmatrix} D & L^T \\ L & G \end{bmatrix} \begin{bmatrix} \Delta x_s \\ \Delta x_c \end{bmatrix} = \begin{bmatrix} g_s \\ g_c \end{bmatrix}, \tag{5}$$

where $\Delta x = [\Delta x_s; \Delta x_c]$, Δx_s and Δx_c correspond to point parameter blocks and camera parameter blocks of Δx, respectively, and $g = [g_s; g_c]$, g_s and g_c correspond to point and camera parameter blocks of g, respectively. Different approaches have been proposed for solving (5), which exploits the special structure of the Hessian.

2.2 Previous Work

For solving (5), direct methods have been well studied in literature [16,21]. In [4], the special structure of the Hessian is exploited to solve the system using a reduced camera system and a reduced structure system. A survey of various direct and iterative methods as well the use of various preconditioners can be found in [21]. Cholesky factorization is used for solving the reduced camera system in [16]. However, for large scale problems, this method does not scale satisfactorily.

An advantage of using iterative methods, such as CG, is that these methods require less memory compared to direct methods. This is because these methods require only matrix-vector products. However, since BA problems are very badly conditioned, recent research has focused on obtaining efficient preconditioners to speed up the convergence of these methods. In [2], several classical preconditioners have been implemented and their impact on large scale problems is shown. In [6], Preconditioned Conjugate Gradients (PCG) is used for solving (5) with an incomplete QR factorization based preconditioner. In [22], PCG is used for solving the reduced camera system with the bandwidth limited block diagonal of the Schur complement as the preconditioner. [7] exploits hardware parallelism on multicore CPUs as well as multicore GPUs to solve the BA problem by a new inexact Newton type method. Avanish et al. [14] utilizes the camera-point visibility structure in the scene to form block diagonal and block tridiagonal preconditioners. [11] explores a generalized subgraph preconditioning (GSP) technique which is based on the combinatorial structure of the BA problem. In [12], a preconditioner based on a deflated two grid methods is used with GMRES as the iterative method.

Usually for small to medium sized problems, direct methods converge faster than iterative methods. In this paper, we show that our method is more memory efficient than direct methods and faster than iterative methods preconditioned with block Jacobi, for small to medium problems, to converge to a comparable mean reprojection error. Also, it has been observed that the construction of the MSC preconditioner does not take much time.

3   Domain Decomposition Method

Domain decomposition (DD) methods refer to a class of divide-and-conquer techniques, that have been primarily developed for solving Partial Differential Equations over regions in two or three dimensions. However, the principles used in this techniques have also been exploited in other fields of scientific and engineering computational problems. The DD methods attempt to solve the problem on the entire domain from problem solutions to the subdomains. For more details, see [18, 20]. One of the most widely used non-overlapping DD methods is the Schur complement method, which is described below.

Consider the following block triangular factorization of H_{LM}:

$$H_{LM} = \begin{bmatrix} D & L^T \\ L & G \end{bmatrix} = \begin{bmatrix} I_D & 0 \\ LD^{-1} & I_G \end{bmatrix} \begin{bmatrix} D & L^T \\ 0 & S \end{bmatrix}$$

where $I_D \in \mathbb{R}^{ps \times ps}$ and $I_G \in \mathbb{R}^{qc \times qc}$, are identity matrices. Here, $S = G - LD^{-1}L^T$ is the *Schur complement* of D in H_{LM}. It has been observed that the construction of S for large problems becomes computationally expensive. Also, the Cholesky decomposition of S leads to dense factors, even though S remains sparse. Here, we present a technique for approximating the Schur complement and design a preconditioner using this approximation.

3.1   The Mini Schur Complement Preconditioner

In [13], several methods for approximation of the global Schur complement S have been mentioned. Here, we construct the Mini Schur Complements (MSC) using the MSC based on Numbering (MSCN) scheme, which is described below.

We consider the block 2×2 partitioned system in (4). The matrix H_{LM} is further partitioned as follows.

$$H_{LM} = \left[\begin{array}{cc|cc} D_{11} & D_{12} & L_{11}^T & L_{12}^T \\ D_{21} & D_{22} & L_{21}^T & L_{22}^T \\ \hline L_{11} & L_{12} & G_{11} & G_{12} \\ L_{21} & L_{22} & G_{21} & G_{22} \end{array} \right] \tag{6}$$

Now, a further approximation of the matrix in (6) is constructed by dropping the blocks D_{ij}, L_{ij}^T, L_{ij} and G_{ij} for which $i \neq j$. Thus the following approximation $\hat{H}_2$ is obtained.

$$
\hat{H}_2 = \left[\begin{array}{cc|cc}
D_{11} & & L_{11}^T & \\
& D_{22} & & L_{22}^T \\
\hline
L_{11} & & G_{11} & \\
& L_{22} & & G_{22}
\end{array}\right]
\tag{7}
$$

Here, the subscript 2 in $\hat{H}_2$ denotes the number of principal sub-matrices of the matrix G, namely, G_{11} and G_{22}. The matrix in (7) is further partitioned to get the following matrix

$$
\hat{H}_2 = \left[\begin{array}{cccc|cccc}
\hat{D}_{11} & \hat{D}_{12} & & & \hat{L}_{11}^T & \hat{L}_{12}^T & & \\
\hat{D}_{21} & \hat{D}_{22} & & & \hat{L}_{21}^T & \hat{L}_{22}^T & & \\
& & \hat{D}_{33} & \hat{D}_{34} & & & \hat{L}_{33}^T & \hat{L}_{34}^T \\
& & \hat{D}_{43} & \hat{D}_{44} & & & \hat{L}_{43}^T & \hat{L}_{44}^T \\
\hline
\hat{L}_{11} & \hat{L}_{12} & & & \hat{G}_{11} & \hat{G}_{12} & & \\
\hat{L}_{21} & \hat{L}_{22} & & & \hat{G}_{21} & \hat{G}_{22} & & \\
& & \hat{L}_{33} & \hat{L}_{34} & & & \hat{G}_{33} & \hat{G}_{34} \\
& & \hat{L}_{43} & \hat{L}_{44} & & & \hat{G}_{43} & \hat{G}_{44}
\end{array}\right]
\tag{8}
$$

Again, a sparse approximation of (8) is done by dropping the blocks $\hat{D}_{ij}, \hat{L}_{ij}^T, \hat{L}_{ij}$ and $\hat{G}_{ij}$ for which $i \neq j$, to obtain the following matrix

$$
\hat{H}_4 = \left[\begin{array}{cccc|cccc}
\hat{D}_{11} & & & & \hat{L}_{11}^T & & & \\
& \hat{D}_{22} & & & & \hat{L}_{22}^T & & \\
& & \hat{D}_{33} & & & & \hat{L}_{33}^T & \\
& & & \hat{D}_{44} & & & & \hat{L}_{44}^T \\
\hline
\hat{L}_{11} & & & & \hat{G}_{11} & & & \\
& \hat{L}_{22} & & & & \hat{G}_{22} & & \\
& & \hat{L}_{33} & & & & \hat{G}_{33} & \\
& & & \hat{L}_{44} & & & & \hat{G}_{44}
\end{array}\right]
$$

Here the subscript 4 in $\hat{H}_4$ denotes the number of principal sub-matrices of matrix G. Eliminating the blocks $\hat{L}_{ii}$ by using $\hat{D}_{ii}$ as a pivot, we obtain an approximation to the global Schur complement S by $\hat{S}_4 = \texttt{blkDiag}(S_{ii})$ where $S_{ii} = \hat{G}_{ii} - \hat{L}_{ii}\hat{D}_{ii}^{-1}\hat{L}_{ii}^T$.

The matrix S_{ii} is called a Mini Schur Complement (MSC). Here, for simplicity, we have partitioned the matrix recursively into a block 2×2 matrix. During implementation, by taking advantage of the sparsity structure of the Hessian H_{LM} and the information about the size of the blocks, we could directly identify the blocks $\hat{G}_{ii}, \hat{D}_{ii}, \hat{L}_{ii}^T$ and $\hat{L}_{ii}$, such that S_{ii} is computed as $S_{ii} = G_{ii} - L_{ii}D_{ii}^{-1}L_{ii}^T$, where $i = 1 : m$ and m is the number of MSCs desired.

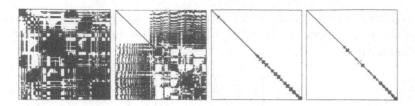

Fig. 1. The first two plots show the Schur complement of `ladybug-372` and `ladybug-885` respectively. The third and fourth plots show their respective MSC approximations ($m = 30$ blocks).

MSC Preconditioner: Let $\hat{S}_m$ denote the Schur complement approximation computed from m MSCs. Then we construct the MSC preconditioner as

$$P_{msc} = \left[\begin{array}{c|c} D & 0 \\ \hline L & \hat{S}_m \end{array}\right]$$

Here D and $\hat{S}_m$ have a block diagonal structure and also, D and L blocks are already available from the coefficient matrix H_{LM}. Thus, storing the required blocks of the MSC preconditioner does not require much extra memory. In Fig. 1, the Schur complement and the Mini Schur Complement approximation of two problems are shown. It can be seen that the MSC approximation has a lot more sparsity than the global Schur complement.

4   Experimental Evaluation

4.1   Implementation Details

For performing the experiments, we select block D such that the number of rows (and columns) of D is given by $3 \times$ (number of points) and block G such that the number of rows (and columns) is given by $9 \times$ (number of cameras). The information about the number of points and the number of cameras are available in the dataset. We construct the block Jacobi preconditioner as $P_{jac} =$ `blkdiag`(D, G) (as shown in [2]), where `blkdiag` forms a block diagonal matrix using the given blocks. For constructing the MSC preconditioner, the number of MSC blocks is taken as 30 blocks.

For the Levenberg-Marquardt algorithm, we use a freely available sparse C++ implementation (`SSBA`)[1], which has several cost functions that are used by the LM algorithm for the BA step. Out of these, we choose the `bundle_large_lifted_schur` cost function implemented in the `SSBA` package, which is discussed in detail in [23]. The LM algorithm runs for 100 iterations, or

---

[1] www.cvg.ethz.ch/research/chzach/opensource.html.

till the difference in norms of two consecutive residuals is not less than 10^{-12} in magnitude, whichever criterion is met first. For solving the *normal* equations in (3) using direct method, SSBA uses LDL factorization [10], which is a Cholesky like factorization method for sparse symmetric positive definite matrices. COLAMD is applied for appropriate column reordering. Both LDL and COLAMD have been adopted from the SuiteSparse package [8].

We experimented with Preconditioned Conjugate Gradient(PCG) as the iterative solver but the results we got using P_{jac} as a preconditioner were not encouraging. Hence, we implement an MSC preconditioned GMRES with restarts and warm starts [3, p. 393] as an iterative solver in the SSBA package, for solving (3). The restart parameter is taken as 40, thus forming a Krylov subspace of 40 vectors. The GMRES algorithm runs as long as the number of iterations is less than 100 or the norm of the relative residual is not less than 10^{-2} (as taken in [2]), whichever comes first. The GMRES method is implemented using the dfgmres routine available in the INTEL MKL library, version 2019.4.243. All of the experiments are performed on a subset of problems from the BAL dataset [2]. We run all of the experiments on a machine with Intel Pentium(R) processor and 8 GB of RAM. As all the problems from the BAL dataset cannot fit into memory, we select 8 problems for which the number of points varies from $7K$ to $226K$.

4.2   Results

We compare the direct solve, specifically, the LDL factorization method and the restarted GMRES preconditioned with two preconditioners: (1) block Jacobi preconditioner and (2) MSC preconditioner. The problems have been selected from the BAL dataset. We experimented with different number of MSC blocks and found that taking 30 blocks gave optimal results.

In Table 1, the time per LM iteration and the mean reprojection error for various methods are shown. As we have tested mostly on small to medium sized problems, we observe that direct solve is faster than iterative solve for these problems. However, as can be seen from Fig. 3, the memory requirement for direct solver increases with increase in problem size. Thus, iterative solvers are essential for very large problems. In Table 1, it can be seen that using MSC as a preconditioner results in faster computation time than using block Jacobi as a preconditioner.

Also, from Fig. 3 it can be seen that the MSC preconditioned GMRES is the most memory efficient of the three methods. In Fig. 3, as the number of cameras increases, the size of the L, D factors of block G also increases. Thus, doing an LDL factorization of block G during block Jacobi preconditioner solve requires more time compared to that of MSC, as seen in Fig. 4. Thus, for larger problems, using MSC as a preconditioner is a much better option for a memory constrained system (Fig. 3).

Table 1. Average time (in seconds) per iteration for the LM solver using the three methods on 8 problems from the BAL datasets using the bundle_large_lifted_schur cost function routine in SSBA. The time in bold represents the faster of the two preconditioners for iterative solve. The problems are prefixed as: L for LadyBug, TS for Trafalgar Square and D for Dubrovnik.

BAL Dataset Parameters			Direct Solve		Block Jacobi		MSC (30)	
Cameras	Points	Observations	Time	Error	Time	Error	Time	Error
L-49	7776	31843	0.1	0.73	**0.6**	0.96	**0.6**	0.65
L-138	19878	85217	0.4	0.89	**1.1**	0.82	1.6	0.88
TS-225	57665	208622	0.9	0.87	10.4	0.79	**9.5**	0.67
D-308	195089	1045197	8.2	0.71	29.4	0.71	**26.2**	0.72
D-356	226730	1255268	11	0.80	41.5	0.77	**30.6**	0.79
L-372	47423	204472	3.0	0.70	**11.9**	0.71	13.1	0.71
L-539	65220	277273	5.4	0.74	9.5	0.80	**6.7**	0.77
L-885	97473	434905	11.5	0.69	25.7	0.69	**17**	0.71

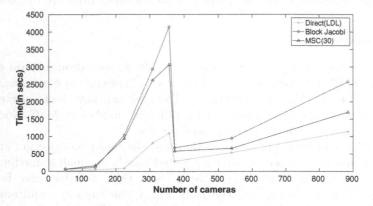

Fig. 2. Plot showing the total time taken for 100 iterations of the Levenberg Marquardt algorithm, using direct solve, block Jacobi preconditioned GMRES and MSC preconditioned GMRES.

5   Conclusions and Future Work

We proposed a technique for the approximation of the global Schur complement and used this approximation to design a preconditioner. We showed some preliminary results which were obtained by implementing our technique as a sequential

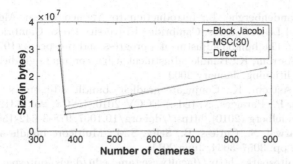

Fig. 3. Plot showing the memory requirement for the three methods for the 4 largest problems in our paper, as the number of cameras increases. We have plotted the memory for the three methods: L, D factors for direct solve, L, D factors of block G alongwith the Krylov subspace and the memory for storing the MSC block, its L, D factors as well as the Krylov subspace.

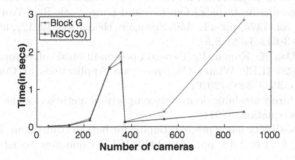

Fig. 4. Plot showing the time taken for LDL factorization of the G block and the MSC block.

code. As seen in Fig. 3, this solver has much less memory requirement than the other methods mentioned in the paper, and is also faster than using block Jacobi as a preconditioner. This makes using MSC as a preconditioner a much better choice. Also, since the MSC blocks are non-overlapping, they are independent of each other. Thus, one possible direction of future work is a parallel implementation of the proposed solver. Another direction would be to assess the robustness of the solver for very large scale problems.

References

1. Agarwal, S., et al.: Building rome in a day. Commun. ACM **54**(10), 105–112 (2011)
2. Agarwal, S., Snavely, N., Seitz, S.M., Szeliski, R.: Bundle adjustment in the large. In: Daniilidis, K., Maragos, P., Paragios, N. (eds.) ECCV 2010. LNCS, vol. 6312, pp. 29–42. Springer, Heidelberg (2010). https://doi.org/10.1007/978-3-642-15552-9_3

3. Boyd, S., Vandenberghe, L.: Introduction to Applied Linear Algebra -Vectors, Matrices, and Least Squares. Cambridge University Press, Cambridge (2018)
4. Brown, D.C.: The bundle adjustment - progress and prospects (1976)
5. Byröd, M., Åström, K.: Bundle adjustment using conjugate gradients with multi-scale preconditioning, January 2009
6. Byröd, M., Åström, K.: Conjugate gradient bundle adjustment. In: Daniilidis, K., Maragos, P., Paragios, N. (eds.) ECCV 2010. LNCS, vol. 6312, pp. 114–127. Springer, Heidelberg (2010). https://doi.org/10.1007/978-3-642-15552-9_9
7. Wu, C., Agarwal, S., Curless, B., Seitz, S.M.: Multicore bundle adjustment. In: CVPR 2011, pp. 3057–3064, June 2011
8. Davis, T.: Suitesparse. http://faculty.cse.tamu.edu/davis/suitesparse.html
9. Frahm, J.-M., et al.: Building rome on a cloudless day. In: Daniilidis, K., Maragos, P., Paragios, N. (eds.) ECCV 2010. LNCS, vol. 6314, pp. 368–381. Springer, Heidelberg (2010). https://doi.org/10.1007/978-3-642-15561-1_27
10. Golub, G.H., Van Loan, C.F.: Matrix Computations, 3rd edn. Johns Hopkins University Press, Baltimore (1996)
11. Jian, Y.-D., Balcan, D.C., Dellaert, F.: Generalized subgraph preconditioners for large-scale bundle adjustment. In: Dellaert, F., Frahm, J.-M., Pollefeys, M., Leal-Taixé, L., Rosenhahn, B. (eds.) Outdoor and Large-Scale Real-World Scene Analysis. LNCS, vol. 7474, pp. 131–150. Springer, Heidelberg (2012). https://doi.org/10.1007/978-3-642-34091-8_6
12. Katyan, S., Das, S., Kumar, P.: Two-grid preconditioned solver for bundle adjustment. In: 2020 IEEE Winter Conference on Applications of Computer Vision (WACV), pp. 3588–3595 (2020)
13. Kumar, P.: Purely algebraic domain decomposition methods for the incompressible navier-stokes equations (2011)
14. Kushal, A.: Visibility based preconditioning for bundle adjustment. In: CVPR 2012 Proceedings, CVPR 2012, pp. 1442–1449. IEEE Computer Society, Washington, DC (2012)
15. Levenberg, K.: A method for the solution of certain non-linear problems in least squares. Q. Appl. Math. 2(2), 164–168 (1944). http://www.jstor.org/stable/43633451
16. Lourakis, M.I.A., Argyros, A.A.: SBA: a software package for generic sparse bundle adjustment. ACM Trans. Math. Softw. 36(1), 2:1–2:30 (2009)
17. Marquardt, D.W.: An algorithm for least-squares estimation of nonlinear parameters. J. Soc. Ind. Appl. Math. 11(2), 431–441 (1963)
18. Saad, Y.: Iterative Methods for Sparse Linear Systems, 2nd edn. SIAM (2003)
19. Snavely, N., Seitz, S.M., Szeliski, R.: Modeling the world from internet photo collections. Int. J. Comput. Vis. 80(2), 189–210 (2008)
20. Toselli, A., Widlund, O.: Domain Decomposition Methods- Algorithms and Theory. Cambridge University Press, Cambridge (2005)
21. Triggs, B., McLauchlan, P.F., Hartley, R.I., Fitzgibbon, A.W.: Bundle adjustment — a modern synthesis. In: Triggs, B., Zisserman, A., Szeliski, R. (eds.) IWVA 1999. LNCS, vol. 1883, pp. 298–372. Springer, Heidelberg (2000). https://doi.org/10.1007/3-540-44480-7_21

22. Jeong, Y., Nister, D., Steedly, D., Szeliski, R., Kweon, I.: Pushing the envelope of modern methods for bundle adjustment. IEEE TPAMI **34**(8), 1605–1617 (2012)
23. Zach, C.: Robust bundle adjustment revisited. In: Fleet, D., Pajdla, T., Schiele, B., Tuytelaars, T. (eds.) ECCV 2014. LNCS, vol. 8693, pp. 772–787. Springer, Cham (2014). https://doi.org/10.1007/978-3-319-10602-1_50

Learning and Vision

Deep Dictionary Learning for Inpainting

K. Seemakurthy[1]($\boxtimes$), A. Majumdar[2], J. Gubbi[1], N. K. Sandeep[1], A. Varghese[1], S. Deshpande[1], M. Girish Chandra[1], and P. Balamurali[1]

[1] Embedded Systems and Robotics, TCS Research and Innovation, Bengaluru, India
karthik.seemakurthy@tcs.com
[2] Electronics and Communications Engineering, IIIT Delhi, New Delhi, India

Abstract. Sparse coding techniques have shown to perform well in solving the conventional inverse imaging problems like inpainting and denoising. In the recent past, the performance of deep learning architectures in solving these inverse imaging problems have exceeded the conventional approaches several times. The only limitation of these architectures is the requirement of large volumes of training data. Deep dictionary learning (DDL) is an emerging approach and has been shown to solve some important classification problems in the scenarios where there is a scarcity of training data. DDL framework effectively combines the advantages of sparse coding and deep learning. In this paper, DDL framework is adapted to solve the inverse imaging problem with specific focus on imaging inpainting. An alternating minimization (AM) approach is proposed to derive the dictionaries and their corresponding sparse coefficients at each level of the DDL framework. The aim of this work is to show that the multilevel dictionaries can be leveraged to derive the sparse representations without compromising on the restoration quality of streaked multispectral images. Inspite of being a conventional machine learning based technique, we show that the performance of our approach is better to the state-of-the-art deep learning approaches for multispectral image inpainting.

Keywords: Sparse coding · Deep dictionary learning

1 Introduction

Inverse imaging problems like denoising and inpainting play a very important role as a pre-processing step for many of the machine vision tasks. Traditionally, these problems were shown to be effectively solved by using compressive sensing (CS) techniques. The main aim of CS is to exploit the sparsity in natural images in the domain of standard basis like discrete cosine transform (DCT), wavelet, etc. Dictionary learning (DL) has shown the possibility of solving the inverse imaging problems by adaptively estimating the sparsifying basis rather than fixed basis

Electronic supplementary material The online version of this chapter (https://doi.org/10.1007/978-981-15-8697-2_7) contains supplementary material, which is available to authorized users.

R. V. Babu et al. (Eds.): NCVPRIPG 2019, CCIS 1249, pp. 79–88, 2020.
https://doi.org/10.1007/978-981-15-8697-2_7

as was done in CS. These are transductive learning techniques. Another class of techniques, which are gaining importance in the recent past are based on neural networks. These are inductive learning approaches, where the main assumption is that the training data itself can be used to learn generalized model, which in turn can predict the outcome of an unseen test sample. Here, large amounts of data is needed to build the model and can be easily applied for the case of natural images but not for other scientific data. Tariyal *et al.* [19] proposed a deep dictionary learning (DDL) framework which combines the advantages of both transductive and inductive nature of dictionary learning and deep learning, respectively, and is very well suited where there is a scarcity of training data. In some of the recent works, DDL was shown to be effective for classification problems [13–15], load monitoring [18], and speech recognition [17]. In this paper, the DDL framework is suitably modified to predict the intensity values in the missing regions in a single band of a multispectral image, which is basically a regression problem.

Every material in this world has its own unique spectral signature. However, human eye can record the signature only within red, blue, and green bands of the spectrum. Multispectral imaging can be used in scenarios where human eye might fail in distinguishing materials. Although this approach was predominantly used in satellite imaging, recently, it is finding multiple applications in biology and medicine [11], and agricultural applications [10]. A multispectral image is captured by using the sensors which are sensitive to different wavelengths beyond the visible light range *i.e.*, infrared and ultra-violet. For *e.g.*, LandSat7 has seven bands. One of the most important challenges in multispectral imaging is the malfunctioning of on-board sensors. This typically results in missing information and will appear as streaks in the acquired multispectral image. Filling the missing information in these images is popularly referred to as inpainting in the image processing literature.

Most of the classical inpainting techniques use the local or non-local information within the degraded image itself to perform inpainting. Efros *et al.* [5] proposed to fill the holes in the image by finding a similar texture in the same image. Some other techniques exploit the natural image priors such as statistics of patch off-sets [6], planarity [8], or low rank [7] to improve the efficiency of inpainting. All these techniques use the information from the input image itself to inpaint. When the missing information is large, then these single image inpainting techniques will fail to perform well. Another set of techniques that are emerging fast in the recent past are learning based approaches. Mairal *et al.* [12] proposed a dictionary learning based technique which is solved by using K-SVD. Xie *et al.* [20] proposed a method that combines the sparse coding and deep networks, which are pretrained by denoising auto-encoders to perform denoising as well as inpainting. Yeh *et al.* [21] proposed a deep generative network based approach to perform blind semantic inpainting. Zhang *et al.* [22] proposed a spatio-temporal based deep network architecture to address different kinds of streaks that might be present in multispectral images. However, the main limitation with any kind of deep network based technique is that they require large amounts of data for training. The prime advantage with DDL is that the training data needed for it will be very less when compared to the data needed to train deep networks. Hence, for multispectral imaging where the availability of public datasets is very less, DDL will be a better way to perform inpainting.

Yet another important challenge of multispectral images is the storage, due to their huge size. Sparse coding techniques have shown to perform well in obtaining the sparser representations which in turn will aid in effective storage of these images. In this paper, we show that the streaked multispectral image can be inpainted as well as sparsely represented with performance similar or better than the state-of-the-art inpainting techniques. The following are the main contributions of this paper:

- An alternating minimization methodology for DDL is proposed for addressing regression problems in image processing.
- The proposed DDL framework has been shown to be useful in inpainting multispectral images.
- We leverage the multi-level architecture to derive the sparse representations of multispectral images.
- The proposed method is experimentally validated and compared with state-of-the-art inpainting techniques.

2 Deep Dictionary Learning

In this section, the mathematical framework of deep dictionary learning is described, which was first proposed by [19] and it is adapted for regression problem in image processing like inpainting as explained in Sect. 3. The shallow (single layer) dictionary learning will provide the sparse representation of the input image. Let D_1 and Z_1 be the dictionary and sparse codes, respectively, for the input matrix X, where its columns indicate the lexicographically ordered input image patches. Mathematically, the relation between X, D_1, and Z_1 is expressed as $X = D_1 Z_1$. The multiple layer extension of the shallow dictionary learning is defined as deep dictionary learning. This is motivated from the concept of deep learning. If D_N and Z_N denotes the learnt dictionary and sparse codes, respectively at N^{th} layer, then the relation between X, D_N, and Z_N can be mathematically expressed as $X = D_1 \phi (D_2 \phi (D_3 \phi (... \phi (D_N Z_N))))$, where ϕ is the non-linear activation function. In this multi-level architechture, it is important to note that the sparse codes derived at one stage are passed onto next higher level. Since the higher level dictionaries are derived corresponding to sparse codes rather than intensity images itself, we show in Sect. 4.1 that the degree of sparsity in sparse codes estimated at final stage of proposed framework is much higher than when compared to the sparse codes derived from their single level counterparts.

3 Alternating Minimization Methodology

In this section, we describe the alternating minimization methodology followed to implement the DDL framework. The methodology for three layers is described.

The same can be extended for N number of layers. Let $\mathbf{Y}$ be the input data matrix where its columns are the lexicographically ordered streaked image patches, $\mathbf{R}$ is the mask indicating the streaks, and $\mathbf{X}$ is the data to be reconstructed, then

$$\mathbf{Y} = \mathbf{R} \odot \mathbf{X} \tag{1}$$

where, $\odot$ is a pixel wise multiplication operator. For a three layer DDL framework, the clean image $\mathbf{X}$ can be factorized as $\mathbf{X} = \mathbf{D_1}\phi\left(\mathbf{D_2}\phi\left(\mathbf{D_3}\mathbf{Z_3}\right)\right)$. The dictionary and the coefficient matrix at each layer can be estimated by minimizing the following cost function:

$$\min_{\mathbf{D_1},\mathbf{D_2},\mathbf{D_3},\mathbf{Z_3}} \quad \|\mathbf{Y} - \mathbf{R} \odot \mathbf{D_1}\phi\left(\mathbf{D_2}\phi\left(\mathbf{D_3}\mathbf{Z_3}\right)\right)\|_F^2 + \lambda_3\|\mathbf{Z_3}\|_1$$
$$\text{s.t} \qquad \mathbf{Z_2} = \phi\left(\mathbf{D_3}\mathbf{Z_3}\right), \mathbf{Z_1} = \phi\left(\mathbf{D_2}\mathbf{Z_2}\right) \tag{2}$$

The augmented lagrangian form [9] of Eq. 2 is given by:

$$\min_{\mathbf{D_1},\mathbf{D_2},\mathbf{D_3},\mathbf{Z_1},\mathbf{Z_2},\mathbf{Z_3}} \|\mathbf{Y} - \mathbf{R} \odot \mathbf{D_1}\phi\left(\mathbf{D_2}\phi\left(\mathbf{D_3}\mathbf{Z_3}\right)\right)\|_F^2 + \lambda_1\|\mathbf{Z_1}\|_1 + \lambda_2\|\mathbf{Z_2}\|_1$$
$$+ \lambda_3\|\mathbf{Z_3}\|_1 + \mu_1\|\mathbf{Z_1} - \phi\left(\mathbf{D_2}\mathbf{Z_2}\right)\|_F^2 + \mu_2\|\mathbf{Z_2} - \phi\left(\mathbf{D_3}\mathbf{Z_3}\right)\|_F^2 \tag{3}$$

where, λ_1, λ_2, λ_3, μ_1, and μ_2 are the regularization constants. Above cost function is non-convex in nature as all the unknowns are coupled together by a multiplication operator (see Section 1 of supplementary material for proof). Hence, we propose to solve by using an alternating minimization (AM) approach [2]. At the first layer of DDL framework, Eq. 3 can be simplified as follows:

$$\widehat{\mathbf{Z_1}} \leftarrow \min_{\mathbf{Z_1}} \|\mathbf{Y} - \mathbf{R} \odot \mathbf{D_1}\mathbf{Z_1}\|_F^2 + \mu_1\|\mathbf{Z_1} - \phi\left(\mathbf{D_2}\mathbf{Z_2}\right)\|_F^2 + \lambda_1\|\mathbf{Z_1}\|_1 \tag{4}$$

$$\widehat{\mathbf{D_1}} \leftarrow \min_{\mathbf{D_1}} \quad \|\mathbf{Y} - \mathbf{R} \odot \mathbf{D_1}\mathbf{Z_1}\|_F^2 \tag{5}$$

For the sake of mathematical convenience, we introduce $\mathbf{R}$ and $\mathbf{D_1}$ in the regularization term of Eq. 4 and can be modified as:

$$\widehat{\mathbf{Z_1}} \leftarrow \min_{\mathbf{Z_1}} \|\mathbf{Y} - \mathbf{R} \odot \mathbf{D_1}\mathbf{Z_1}\|_F^2 + \mu_1\|\mathbf{R} \odot \mathbf{D_1}\left(\mathbf{Z_1} - \phi\left(\mathbf{D_2}\mathbf{Z_2}\right)\right)\|_F^2 + \lambda_1\|\mathbf{Z_1}\|_1 \tag{6}$$

Equation 6 can be further simplified as

$$\widehat{\mathbf{Z_1}} \leftarrow \min_{\mathbf{Z_1}} \|\mathbf{R} \odot \mathbf{A_1}\mathbf{Z_1} - \mathbf{B_1}\|_F^2 + \lambda_1\|\mathbf{Z_1}\|_1 \tag{7}$$

where, $\mathbf{A_1} = \begin{bmatrix} \mathbf{D_1} \\ \sqrt{\mu_1}\mathbf{D_1} \end{bmatrix}$ and $\mathbf{B_1} = \begin{bmatrix} \mathbf{Y} \\ \sqrt{\mu_1}\mathbf{R}\odot\mathbf{D_1}\phi(\mathbf{D_2}\mathbf{Z_2}) \end{bmatrix}$. Similarly, at second layer Eq. 3 can be simplified as

$$\widehat{\mathbf{D_2}} \leftarrow \min_{\mathbf{D_2}} \quad \|\phi^{-1}(\mathbf{Z_1}) - \mathbf{D_2}\mathbf{Z_2}\|_F^2 \tag{8}$$

$$\widehat{\mathbf{Z_2}} \leftarrow \min_{\mathbf{Z_2}} \|\mathbf{A_2}\mathbf{Z_2} - \mathbf{B_2}\|_F^2 + \lambda_2\|\mathbf{Z_2}\|_1 \tag{9}$$

where $\mathbf{A_2} = \begin{bmatrix} \mathbf{D_2} \\ \sqrt{\mu_2}\mathbf{I} \end{bmatrix}$ and $\mathbf{B_2} = \begin{bmatrix} \phi^{-1}(\mathbf{Z_1}) \\ \sqrt{\mu_2}\phi(\mathbf{D_3Z_3}) \end{bmatrix}$, where $\mathbf{I}$ is the identity matrix. At third layer, Eq. 3 can be simplified as

$$\widehat{\mathbf{D_3}} \leftarrow \min_{\mathbf{D_3}} \|\phi^{-1}(\mathbf{Z_2}) - \mathbf{D_3Z_3}\|_F^2 \tag{10}$$

$$\widehat{\mathbf{Z_3}} \leftarrow \min_{\mathbf{Z_3}} \|\mathbf{D_3Z_3} - \phi^{-1}(\mathbf{Z_2})\|_F^2 + \lambda_3\|\mathbf{Z_3}\|_1 \tag{11}$$

Equations 7, 9, and 11 are similar to sparse coding stage of K-SVD algorithm [1] and we solve it by using standard orthogonal matching pursuit (OMP) [16] as we found it to be effective and simple to use. After obtaining the coefficients $\mathbf{Z_1}$, $\mathbf{Z_2}$, and $\mathbf{Z_3}$ we solve Eqs. 5, 8, and 10 by using the approach as was employed for dictionary update stage of K-SVD [1]. The final inpainted image can be reconstructed by using the following equation

$$\widehat{\mathbf{X}} = \widehat{\mathbf{D_1}}\phi\left(\widehat{\mathbf{D_2}}\phi\left(\widehat{\mathbf{D_3}}\widehat{\mathbf{Z_3}}\right)\right) \tag{12}$$

The alternating minimization approach used for proposed DDL framework is summarized in Algorithm 1.

Algorithm 1. AM framework for DDL to perform inpainting

Require: $NUM\_ITER = 1$, $MAX\_ITER = 1000$, $\mathbf{D_1} \leftarrow DCT_{64\times128}$, $\mathbf{D_2} \leftarrow DCT_{128\times200}$, $\mathbf{D_3} \leftarrow DCT_{200\times300}$
Ensure: $Reconstructed\_output$
1: **while** $NUM\_ITER < MAX\_ITER$ **do**
2:    Optimize $\mathbf{Z_1}$ in Eq. 7 using OMP [16].
3:    Optimize $\mathbf{D_1}$ in Eq. 5 using the dictionary update stage of KSVD [1].
4:    Optimize $\mathbf{Z_2}$ in Eq. 9 using OMP [16].
5:    Optimize $\mathbf{D_2}$ in Eq. 8 using the dictionary update stage of KSVD [1].
6:    Optimize $\mathbf{Z_3}$ in Eq. 11 using OMP [16].
7:    Optimize $\mathbf{D_3}$ in Eq. 10 using the dictionary update stage of KSVD [1].
8:    $NUM\_ITER + +$
9: **end while**
10: $Reconstructed\_output \leftarrow \widehat{\mathbf{D_1}}(\phi(\widehat{\mathbf{D_2}}(\phi(\widehat{\mathbf{D_3}}\widehat{\mathbf{Z_3}}))))$

It has to be noted in Algorithm 1, we have initialized $\mathbf{D_1}$, $\mathbf{D_2}$, and $\mathbf{D_3}$ as over-complete dictionaries. This is due to the fact that we impose sparsity at all the three levels. Even though our approach looks similar as proposed by [19], it differs from the original formulation in the following ways:

- The DDL framework developed by [19] is used for classification while our DDL is used for inpainting which is a regression problem.
- We use OMP at sparse coding stage while [19] use iterative soft thresolding algorithm [4], which we found to be slow in finding the dictionary coefficients.
- Unlike [19], we added the additional constraints on the dependency of the sparse codes on the previous layers which improved our restored results.

- They used 'tanh' as the non-linearity between the layers while we found 'tan' to be more appropriate as the range of sparse coefficient values is beyond the domain of 'tanh^{-1}' in our scenario.
- Tariyal *et al.* [19] imposes sparsity at the final stage of DDL while we impose at every stage which we found advantageous in obtaining the higher degree of sparsity without compromising on the reconstruction quality.

4   Experimental Results

In this section, the experimental results are presented on inpainting of multispectral images. We compare proposed technique with conventional exemplar based method [3], deep dictionary learning approach by [19], and state-of-the-art deep neural network technique [22]. Instead of working on the original streaked image, we synthetically generate the streaked observations from original clean images so as to do a quantitative analysis with state-of-the-art approaches. Patches of size 8×8 are extracted from the streaked image and then arranged lexicographically along the columns of $\mathbf{Y}$. For all our experiments, we found the optimal values for regularization constants as $\mu_1 = \mu_2 = 0.1$. The number of sparse coefficients at first, second, and third layers were empirically chosen as 20, 10, and 5 respectively. We have tried multiple non-linear activation functions and found that 'tangent' function suited the best for our experiments. We have included an experiment in Sect. refsec:ddl of supplementary material where the comparative study of the performance of proposed approach by using different non-linear functions is presented.

Figure 1 shows the results for LandSat7 dataset [22]. The first and the second rows represent the original and streaked images respectively. The output of [3] is presented in the third row of Fig. 1. It is to be noted that the output reconstructed by [3] has some boundary artifacts in the regions where the filling has been done. The main reason behind such artifacts might be due to the absence of smoothly varying regions in multispectral images. Restored result by [19] (in fourth row of Fig. 1) could not fill in the missing regions completely. This can be attributed to the reasons as mentioned in Sect. 2. The same is reflected in the quantitative analysis as was presented in Table 1. Finally, we also compare with a deep neural network approach [22]. The architecture proposed in [22] needs temporal observations as test input, where one of the observation is clean taken at a different time. Since all the competitive methods work on the single degraded observation, for fare evaluation, we give both the inputs to the architecture in [22] as the same streaked observation and the corresponding ouptuts are given in the fifth row of Fig. 1. It can be clearly seen that the streaks are not completely filled which affects the visual quality of the output. This might be due to the necessity of one clean observation among the test input given to its architecture. Also, the neural network architecture in [22] might lack the ability to generalize different kinds of degradations. The outputs of our approach are presented in the last row of Fig. 1. It can be seen that the reconstruction quality is much better than state-of-the-art qualitatively as well as quantitatively.

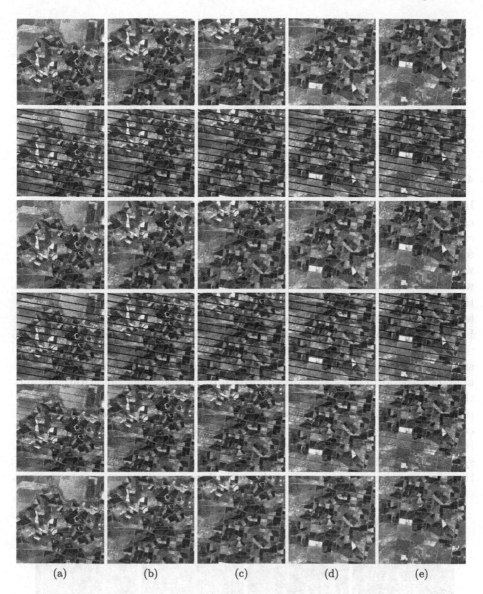

(a)   (b)   (c)   (d)   (e)

Fig. 1. Results of Inpainting: (a) Example 1, (b) example 2, (c) example 3, (d) example 4, and (e) example 5. First row: original image. Second row: streaked image. Third row: Output of [3]. Fourth row: Result of [19]. Fifth row: Restoration by [22]. Sixth row: Proposed approach.

Table 1. Quantitative analysis using PSNR.

	Example 1	Example 2	Example 3	Example 4	Example 5
Criminisi *et al.* [3]	26.3618	25.2753	25.2400	26.6653	27.3390
Tariyal *et al.* [19]	16.0605	16.5332	16.8917	16.1195	16.3779
Zhang *et al.* [22]	19.4899	20.0894	20.5723	19.7015	19.8901
Proposed approach	**29.4712**	**28.4403**	**28.1862**	**28.6552**	**29.2903**

4.1   Sparsifying the Sparsity

In this subsection, we present a synthetic experiment to show another interesting aspect of our proposed architechture with regards to its sparse representation capability. Figures 2(a) and (b) shows the clean and synthesized streaked images, respectively, of a single band in multispectral image from LandSat7 dataset. Here we compare the degree of sparsity that can be attained by proposed approach when compared to the single level dictionary learning technique in [1] without the loss in reconstrcution quality. The outputs of [1] and proposed approach (3 levels) with the constraint on the number of sparse coefficients as 5 is shown in Figs. 2(c) and (d), respectively. Quantitative analysis is mentioned in the caption of Fig. 2. It can be clearly seen that the output of [1] has lots of artifacts which significantly affects the visual quality. For the same degree of sparsity we were able to outperform the single level approach by several times quantitatively and the visual quality of our reconstructed output is much better than [1]. This was possible as the higher degree of sparsity is obtained by working on sparse latent codes (Z_1 and Z_2) domain rather than the intensity image domain as was done by a single level dictionary learning approach in [1]. This ability to produce sparse codes with higher degree of sparsity will help in the effective storage of these large multispectral images without the loss in quality.

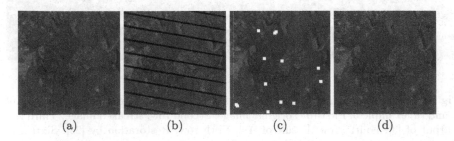

(a)   (b)   (c)   (d)

Fig. 2. Sparsifying the sparsity. (a) Clean image, (b) streaked observation. Output of: (c) Aharon *et al.* [1] with 5 non-zero coefficients (PSNR = 20.7288 dB), (d) proposed approach (PSNR = 36.3664 dB).

5   Conclusions and Future Work

In this paper, an alternate minimization based strategy for deep dictionary learning is proposed for addressing regression problems in image processing. The DDL framework is shown to be effective in terms of the sparsity while having a state-of-the-art performance. Even though we have taken inpainting as an application, the same framework can very well be used for other inverse problems like denoising where the size of the artifact is small when compared to the size of the patch used. Here, we inpainted the streaks in multi-spectral images. Compared to the traditional inpainting approaches, the drawback of the DDL method includes retraining the model for different scenarios. Further, the time taken by DDL is dependent on the number of layers and based on the formulation, it is clear that it takes more time than K-SVD. The main aim of this work was to achieve state-of-the-art performance with smaller model sizes. In future, we plan to address these issues by incorporating local neighborhood information within the DDL framework in addition to new methods for dictionary update. We would like to do further analysis on the image compression ability of proposed DDL framework. Also, we plan to incorporate spectral consistency priors and improve the reconstruction capability of the proposed technique with smaller model sizes.

References

1. Aharon, M., Elad, M., Bruckstein, A.: KSVD: an algorithm for designing overcomplete dictionaries for sparse representation. IEEE Trans. Signal Process. **54**(11), 4311–4322 (2006)
2. Boyd, S., Dattorro, J.: Alternating projections (2003)
3. Criminisi, A., Pérez, P., Toyama, K.: Region filling and object removal by exemplar-based image inpainting. IEEE Trans. Image Process. **13**(9), 1200–1212 (2004)
4. Daubechies, I., Defrise, M., De Mol, C.: An iterative thresholding algorithm for linear inverse problems with a sparsity constraint. Commun. Pure Appl. Math. **57**(11), 1413–1457 (2004)
5. Efros, A.A., Leung, T.K.: Texture synthesis by non-parametric sampling. In: Proceedings of International Conference on Computer Vision (ICCV), vol. 2, pp. 1033–1038. IEEE (1999)
6. He, K., Sun, J.: Statistics of patch offsets for image completion. In: Fitzgibbon, A., Lazebnik, S., Perona, P., Sato, Y., Schmid, C. (eds.) ECCV 2012. LNCS, vol. 7573, pp. 16–29. Springer, Heidelberg (2012). https://doi.org/10.1007/978-3-642-33709-3_2
7. Hu, Y., Zhang, D., Ye, J., Li, X., He, X.: Fast and accurate matrix completion via truncated nuclear norm regularization. IEEE Trans. Pattern Anal. Mach. Intell. **35**(9), 2117–2130 (2013)
8. Huang, J.B., Kang, S.B., Ahuja, N., Kopf, J.: Image completion using planar structure guidance. ACM Trans. Graph. (TOG) **33**(4), 129 (2014)
9. Jakovetić, D., Moura, J.M., Xavier, J.: Linear convergence rate of a class of distributed augmented lagrangian algorithms. IEEE Trans. Autom. Control **60**(4), 922–936 (2015)

10. Khanal, S., Fulton, J., Shearer, S.: An overview of current and potential applications of thermal remote sensing in precision agriculture. Comput. Electron. Agric. **139**, 22–32 (2017)
11. Levenson, R.M., Mansfield, J.R.: Multispectral imaging in biology and medicine: slices of life. Cytometry part A **69**(8), 748–758 (2006)
12. Mairal, J., Elad, M., Sapiro, G.: Sparse representation for color image restoration. IEEE Trans. Image Process. **17**(1), 53–69 (2008)
13. Majumdar, A., Singhal, V.: Noisy deep dictionary learning: application to Alzheimer's disease classification. In: Proceedings of International Joint Conference on Neural Networks (IJCNN), pp. 2679–2683. IEEE (2017)
14. Majumdar, A., Ward, R.: Robust greedy deep dictionary learning for ECG arrhythmia classification. In: Proceedings of International Joint Conference on Neural Networks (IJCNN), pp. 4400–4407. IEEE (2017)
15. Manjani, I., Tariyal, S., Vatsa, M., Singh, R., Majumdar, A.: Detecting silicone mask-based presentation attack via deep dictionary learning. IEEE Trans. Inf. Forensics Secur. **12**(7), 1713 (2017)
16. Pati, Y.C., Rezaiifar, R., Krishnaprasad, P.S.: Orthogonal matching pursuit: recursive function approximation with applications to wavelet decomposition. In: Proceedings of Asilomar Conference on Signals, Systems and Computers, pp. 40–44. IEEE (1993)
17. Sharma, P., Abrol, V., Sao, A.K.: Deep-sparse-representation-based features for speech recognition. IEEE Trans. Audio Speech Lang. Process. **25**(11), 2162–2175 (2017)
18. Singh, S., Majumdar, A.: Deep sparse coding for non-intrusive load monitoring. IEEE Trans. Smart Grid **PP**(99), 1 (2017)
19. Tariyal, S., Majumdar, A., Singh, R., Vatsa, M.: Deep dictionary learning. IEEE Access **4**, 10096–10109 (2016)
20. Xie, J., Xu, L., Chen, E.: Image denoising and inpainting with deep neural networks. In: Proceedings of Advances in Neural Information Processing Systems (NIPS), pp. 341–349. Curran Associates (2012)
21. Yeh, R., Chen, C., Lim, T.Y., Hasegawa-Johnson, M., Do, M.N.: Semantic image inpainting with perceptual and contextual losses. arXiv preprint arXiv:1607.07539 (2016)
22. Zhang, Q., Yuan, Q., Zeng, C., Li, X., Wei, Y.: Missing data reconstruction in remote sensing image with a unified spatial-temporal-spectral deep convolutional neural network. IEEE Trans. Geosci. Remote Sens. **99**, 1–15 (2018)

A Robust Pose Transformational GAN
for Pose Guided Person Image Synthesis

Arnab Karmakar[✉][iD] and Deepak Mishra

Indian Institute of Space Science and Technology,
Thiruvananthapuram 695547, Kerala, India
arnabkarmakar.001@gmail.com, deepak.mishra@iist.ac.in

Abstract. Generating photorealistic images of human subjects in any
unseen pose have crucial applications in generating a complete appearance
model of the subject. However, from a computer vision perspective, this
task becomes significantly challenging due to the inability of modelling
the data distribution conditioned on pose. Existing works use a complicated pose transformation model with various additional features such as
foreground segmentation, human body parsing etc. to achieve robustness
that leads to computational overhead. In this work, we propose a simple
yet effective pose transformation GAN by utilizing the Residual Learning
method without any additional feature learning to generate a given human
image in any arbitrary pose. Using effective data augmentation techniques
and cleverly tuning the model, we achieve robustness in terms of illumination, occlusion, distortion and scale. We present a detailed study, both
qualitative and quantitative, to demonstrate the superiority of our model
over the existing methods on two large datasets.

Keywords: Generative adversarial networks · Pose transformation ·
Image synthesis · Pose guided person image generation

1 Introduction

Given an image of a person, a pose transformation model aims to reconstruct
the person's appearance in another pose. While for humans it is very easy to
imagine how a person would appear in a different body pose, it has been a difficult problem in computer vision to generate photorealistic images conditioned
only on pose; given a single 2D image of the human subject. The idea of pose
transformation can help construct a viewpoint invariant representation. This
has several interesting applications in 3D reconstruction, movie making, motion
prediction or human computer interaction etc.

The task of pose transformation given a single image and a desired pose,
is achieved by any machine learning model in basically two steps: (1) learning
the significant visual features of the person-of-interest along with the background
from the given image, and (2) imposing the desired pose on the person-of-interest,
generate a photorealistic image while preserving the previously learned features.
Generative Adversarial Networks (GAN) [8] have been widely popular in this

© Springer Nature Singapore Pte Ltd. 2020
R. V. Babu et al. (Eds.): NCVPRIPG 2019, CCIS 1249, pp. 89–99, 2020.
https://doi.org/10.1007/978-981-15-8697-2_8

field due to its sharp image generation capability. While the majority of successful pose transformation models use different variation of GANs as their primary component, they give little importance to efficient data augmentation and utilization of inherent CNN features to achieve robustness. Recent developments in this field have been targeted to develop complex deep neural network models with the use of multiple external features such as human body parsing [4], semantic segmentation [1,4], spatial transformation [1,20] etc. Although this is helpful in some scenarios, there is accuracy issues and computational overhead due to each intermediate step that affects the final result.

In this work, we aim to develop an improved end-to-end model for pose transformation given only the input image and the desired pose, and without any other external features. We make use of the Residual learning strategy [9] in our GAN architecture by incorporating a number of residual blocks. We achieve robustness in terms of occlusion, scale, illumination and distortion by using efficient data augmentation techniques and utilizing inherent CNN features. Our results in two large datasets, a low-resolution person re-identification dataset Market-1501 [23] and high-resolution fashion dataset DeepFashion [13] have been demonstrated. Our contributions are two folds: First, we develop an improved pose transformation model to synthesize photorealistic images of a person in any desired pose, given a single instance of the person's image, and without any external features. Second, we achieve robustness in terms of occlusion, scale and illumination by efficient data augmentation techniques and utilizing inherent CNN features.

2   Related Work

There has been a lot of research in the field of generative image modelling using deep learning techniques. One line of work follow the idea of Variational Autoencoders (VAE) [5] which uses the reparameterization trick to maximize the lower bound of data likelihood [11]. VAEs have been popular for its image interpolation capability, but the generated images lack sharpness and high frequency details. GAN [8] models make use of adversarial training for generating images from random noise. Most works in pose guided person image generation make use of GANs because of its capability to produce fine details.

Amongst the large number of successful GAN architectures, many were developed upon the DCGAN [17] model that combines Convolutional Neural Network (CNN) with GANs. Pix2pix [10] proposed a conditional adversarial network (CGAN) for image-to-image translation by learning the mapping from condition image to target image. Yan et al. [22] explored this idea for pose conditioned video generation, where the human images are generated based on skeleton poses. GANs with different variations of U-Net [18] have been extensively used for pose guided image generation. The PG^2 [14] model proposes a 2-step process with a U-Net-like network to generate an initial coarse image of the person conditioned on the target pose and then refines the result based upon the difference map. Balakrishnan et al. [1] uses separate foreground and background synthesis using a spatial transformer network and U-Net based generator. Ma et al. [15] uses pose sampling using a GAN coupled with an encoder-decoder model. Dong et al.

[4] produces state-of-the-art results in pose driven human image generation and uses human body parsing as an additional attribute for Warping-GAN rendering. These additional attribute learning generates an overhead in computational capability and affects the final results. Other significant works for pose transfer in the field of person re-identification [16] [7] mostly deals with low resolution images and a complex training procedure. In this work, we propose a simplified end-to-end model for pose transformation without using additional feature learning at any stage.

3 Methodology

The proposed pt-GAN architecture is depicted in Fig. 1.

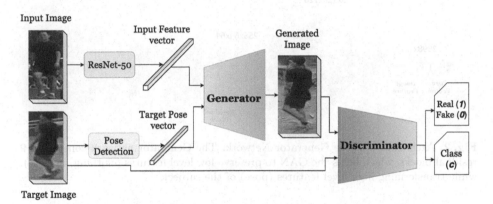

Fig. 1. Proposed architecture of the pose transformational GAN (pt-GAN). The idea is to transform the given person image to the desired pose. The additional classification branch of the Discrminator helps the Generator's learning to produce realistic images.

3.1 Pose Estimation

The image generation is conditioned on an input image and the target pose represented by a pose vector. In order to get the encoded pose vector, we use off-the-shelf pose detection algorithm OpenPose [2], which is trained without using either of the datasets deployed in this work. Given an input person image I_i, the pose estimation network OpenPose produces a pose vector P_i, which localizes and detects 25 anatomical key-points.

3.2 Generator

The Image generator (G_P) aims at producing the same person's images under different poses. Particularly, given an input person image I_i and a desired pose P_j, the generator aims to synthesize a new person image I_{P_j}, which contains the same identity but with a different pose defined by P_j. The image vector obtained using a pretrained ResNet-50 [9] model (ImageNet [3]), and the pose vector are concatenated and fed to the generator. The architecture is depicted in Fig. 2.

The generator consists of multiple Convolution and Transposed Convolution layers. The key element of the proposed Generator is the residual blocks. Each residual block performs downsampling using convolution followed by upsampling using transposed convolution and then re-using the input by addition (Fig. 3(b)). The motivation is to take advantage of Residual Learning ($y = F(x) + x$) that can be used to pass invariable information (e.g. clothing color, texture, background) from the bottom layers to the higher layers and change the variable information (pose) to synthesize more realistic images, achieving pose transformation at the same time.

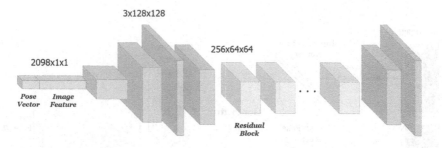

Fig. 2. Architecture of the Generator Network. The Generator network consists of 9 residual blocks, which helps the GAN to preserve low level features (clothing, texture), while transforming high level features (pose) of the subject.

3.3 Discriminator

In our implementation, the Discriminator (D_P) predicts the class label for the image along with the binary classification of determing whether the image is real or generated. Studies [12] show that incorporating classification loss in discriminator along with the real/fake loss, in turn increases the generator's capability to produce sharp images with high details. The Discriminator consists of stacked Conv-ReLU-Pool layer and the final fully connected layer has been modified to incorporate both binary loss and classification loss (Fig. 3(a)).

3.4 Data Augmentation

1. **Image Interpolation:** The input images have been resized to 256×256 before passing through ResNet. Market-1501 images (128×64) are resized to 256×128, and zero-padded to make 256×256. The images in DeepFashion are of the desired dimension by default.
2. **Random Erasing** [6]: Random erasing is helpful in achieving robustness against occlusion. A random patch of the input image is given random values while the reconstruction is expected to be perfect. Thus, the GAN learns to reconstruct (and remove) the occluded regions in the generated images.

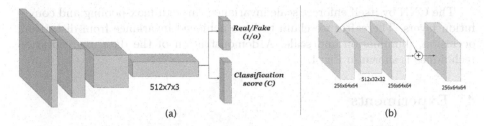

(a)   (b)

Fig. 3. (a) Architecture of the discriminator of pt-GAN. A classification task is added with the real/fake prediction. This simultaneously helps the Generator to produce more realistic images. **(b)** Architecture of the Residual Blocks used in the Generator. The Residual Learning strategy preserves low level features (color, texture) and learns high level features (pose) simultaneously.

3. **Random Crop:** The input image is randomly cropped and upscaled to the input dimension (256×256) to augment the cases where the human detection is inaccurate or only the partial body is visible.
4. **Jitter:** We use random jitter in terms of brightness, Contrast, Hue and Saturation (random jitter to each channel) to augment the effects of illumination variations.
5. **Random Horizontal Flip:** Inspecting the dataset, it is seen that most human subjects has both left-right profile images. Hence flipping the image left-right is a good choice for image augmentation.
6. **Random distortion:** We have incorporated random distortion with a grid size of 10, to compensate the distortion in the generated image as well as enforce our model to learn important features of the input image even in the presence of non-idealities.

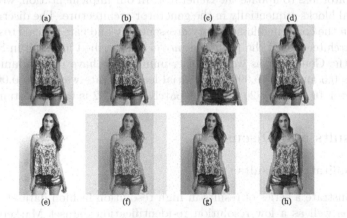

(a)   (b)   (c)   (d)

(e)   (f)   (g)   (h)

Fig. 4. The data augmentation techniques used in this work: (a) Original image, (b) Random erasing, (c) Random crop, (d) Random distortion, (e)–(g) Random jitter: (e) Brightness, (f) Contrast, (g) Saturation; (h) Random Flip

The CNN by itself enforces scale invariance through max-pooling and convolution layers. Thereafter we claim to have achieved invariance from distortion, occlusion, illumination and scale. A demonstration of the data augmentation techniques is shown in Fig. 4.

4   Experiments

4.1   Datasets

DeepFashion: The DeepFashion (In-shop Clothes Retrieval Benchmark) dataset [13] consists of 52,712 in-shop clothes images, and 200,000 cross-pose/scale pairs. The images are of 256×256 resolution. We follow the standard split adopted by [14] to construct the training set of 146,680 pairs each composed of two images of the same person but different poses.

Market-1501: We also show our results on the re-identification dataset Market-1501 [23] containing 32,668 images of 1,501 persons. The images vary highly in pose, illumination, viewpoint and background in this dataset, which makes the person image generation task more challenging. Images have size 128×64. Again, we follow [14] to construct the training set of 439,420 pairs, each composed of two images of the same person but different poses.

4.2   Implementation and Training

For image descriptor generation, We have used a pretrained ResNet-50 network whose weights were not updated during the training of the generator and discrimiator. The input image and the target image are of the same class with different poses. The reconstruction loss (MSE) is incorporated with the negative discriminator loss to update the Generator. In our implementation, we have used 9 Residual blocks sequentially in the generator architecture. The discriminator is trained on the combined loss (binary crossentropy and categorical crossentropy).

The architecture of the proposed model is described in detail in Sect. 3. For training the Generator as well as Discriminator we have used Adam optimizer with $\beta_1 = 0.5$ and $\beta_2 = 0.999$. The initial learning rate was set to 0.0002 with a decay factor 10 at every 20 epoch. A batch size of 32 is taken as standard.

5   Results and Discussion

5.1   Qualitative Results

We demonstrate a series of results in high resolution fashion dataset DeepFashion [13] as well as a low resolution re-identification dataset Market-1501 [23]. In both the datasets, by visual inspection, we can say that our model performs good reconstruction and is able to learn invariable information like the colour and texture of clothing, characteristics of make/female attributes such as hair and face while successfully performing image transformation into the desired pose. The results on DeepFashion is better due to good details and simple background, whereas the low resolution affects the quality of the generated images in Market-1501. The results are demonstrated in Fig. 5.

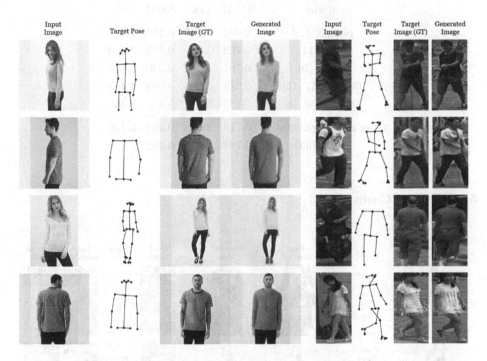

Fig. 5. Qualitative results on DeepFashion and Market-1501 datasets. The proposed model is able to reproduce good details, and also learn invariable information like the colour and texture of clothing, characteristics of make/female attributes such as hair and face while successfully perform image transformation into the desired pose.

5.2 Quantitative Results

We use two popular measures of GAN performance, namely Structural Similarity (SSIM) [21] and Inception Score (IS) [19] for verifying the performance of our model. We compare our work with the already existing methods based on SSIM and IS scores on both DeepFashion and Market-1501 datasets in Table 1. Our model achieves the best IS score in Market-1501 dataset while achieving second best results in SSIM score in both the datasets. However, the deviation from the state-of-the-art is ~1.5% in these cases which can be overcome through rigorous testing and hyperparameter tuning. We also inspect the improvement incorporated by data augmentation as seen in Table 1. The proposed augmentation methods give an average improvement of ~9%. This essentially strengthens our argument that a significant boost in performance can be gained by exploring effective training schemes, without changing the model parameters or loss function.

Table 1. Comparative study with existing methods in DeepFashion and Market-1501 datasets. The best and second best results are denoted in red and blue respectively.

Model	DeepFashion		Market-1501	
	SSIM	IS	SSIM	IS
pix2pix [10]	0.692	3.249	0.183	2.678
PG2 [14]	0.762	3.090	0.253	3.460
DSCF [20]	0.761	3.351	0.290	3.185
BodyROI7 [15]	0.614	3.228	0.099	3.483
Dong et al. [4]	0.793	3.314	0.356	3.409
Ours w/o augmentation	0.713	3.006	0.268	3.425
Ours (full)	0.781	3.238	0.302	3.488

5.3   Failure Cases

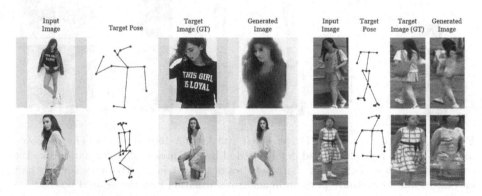

Fig. 6. Failure Cases in our pt-GAN model. If the input contains fine details (text, stripes) or the target pose is incomplete then the reconstruction is poor. The external attribute (handbag) learning is of limited success.

We analyse some of our failure cases in both the datasets to understand the shortcoming of our model. As seen in Fig. 6, the text in clothing as well as very fine patterns of clothing (stripes, dots) are not modelled properly. The external attribute features (e.g. the handbag in Fig. 6) are not learned properly as it is difficult to map external attributes to the output image when conditioned only on pose. The accuracy is also dependent on the completeness of the target pose. Finally, there is some limitation in cases where a rare complex pose is presented which has scarce training data. In Market-1501, the reconstruction of faces is not very good due to poor resolution.

5.4   Further Analysis

Along with the quantitative and qualitative results, we demonstrate a special case to show the improvement caused by data augmentation methods. As seen in Fig. 7, the occlusion in the input image is partially carried forward when the data augmentation methods are not used. With data augmentation the generated image is better in quality and the artifacts generated in the edges are less.

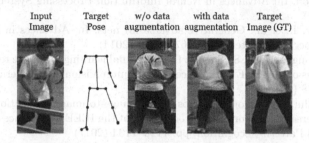

Input Image | Target Pose | w/o data augmentation | with data augmentation | Target Image (GT)

Fig. 7. Occlusion invariance using the proposed model. The occlusion is partially carried forward when data augmentation methods are not used. With data augmentation, the resultant image is free from the artifacts.

6   Conclusion

In this work, we proposed an improved end-to-end pose transformation model to synthesize photorealistic images of a given person in any desired pose without any external feature learning. We make use of the residual learning strategy with effective data augmentation techniques to achieve robustness in terms of occlusion, scale, illumination and distortion. For future work, we plan to achieve better results by utilising feature transport from the source image and conditioning the discriminator on both source image and target pose, alongwith using a perceptual (content) loss for reconstruction.

References

1. Balakrishnan, G., Zhao, A., Dalca, A.V., Durand, F., Guttag, J.: Synthesizing images of humans in unseen poses. In: Proceedings of the IEEE Conference on Computer Vision and Pattern Recognition, pp. 8340–8348 (2018)
2. Cao, Z., Simon, T., Wei, S.E., Sheikh, Y.: Realtime multi-person 2D pose estimation using part affinity fields. In: Proceedings of the IEEE Conference on Computer Vision and Pattern Recognition, pp. 7291–7299 (2017)
3. Deng, J., Dong, W., Socher, R., Li, L.J., Li, K., Fei-Fei, L.: ImageNet: a large-scale hierarchical image database. In: 2009 IEEE Conference on Computer Vision and Pattern Recognition, pp. 248–255. IEEE (2009)

4. Dong, H., Liang, X., Gong, K., Lai, H., Zhu, J., Yin, J.: Soft-gated warping-GAN for pose-guided person image synthesis. In: Advances in Neural Information Processing Systems, pp. 474–484 (2018)
5. Kingma, D.P., Welling, M.: Auto-encoding variational bayes. arXiv preprint arXiv:1312.6114 (2013)
6. Zhong, Z., Zheng, L., Kang, G., Li, S., Yang, Y.: Random erasing data augmentation. arXiv preprint arXiv:1708.04896 (2017)
7. Ge, Y., et al.: FD-GAN: pose-guided feature distilling GAN for robust person re-identification. In: Advances in Neural Information Processing Systems, pp. 1222–1233 (2018)
8. Goodfellow, I., et al.: Generative adversarial nets. In: Advances in Neural Information Processing Systems, pp. 2672–2680 (2014)
9. He, K., Zhang, X., Ren, S., Sun, J.: Deep residual learning for image recognition. In: Proceedings of the IEEE Conference on Computer Vision and Pattern Recognition, pp. 770–778 (2016)
10. Isola, P., Zhu, J.Y., Zhou, T., Efros, A.A.: Image-to-image translation with conditional adversarial networks. In: Proceedings of the IEEE Conference on Computer Vision and Pattern Recognition, pp. 1125–1134 (2017)
11. Karmakar, A., Mishra, D., Tej, A.: Stellar cluster detection using GMM with deep variational autoencoder. In: 2018 IEEE Recent Advances in Intelligent Computational Systems (RAICS), pp. 122–126. IEEE (2018)
12. Liu, J., Ni, B., Yan, Y., Zhou, P., Cheng, S., Hu, J.: Pose transferrable person re-identification. In: Proceedings of the IEEE Conference on Computer Vision and Pattern Recognition, pp. 4099–4108 (2018)
13. Liu, Z., Luo, P., Qiu, S., Wang, X., Tang, X.: DeepFashion: powering robust clothes recognition and retrieval with rich annotations. In: Proceedings of the IEEE Conference on Computer Vision and Pattern Recognition, pp. 1096–1104 (2016)
14. Ma, L., Jia, X., Sun, Q., Schiele, B., Tuytelaars, T., Van Gool, L.: Pose guided person image generation. In: Advances in Neural Information Processing Systems, pp. 406–416 (2017)
15. Ma, L., Sun, Q., Georgoulis, S., Van Gool, L., Schiele, B., Fritz, M.: Disentangled person image generation. In: Proceedings of the IEEE Conference on Computer Vision and Pattern Recognition, pp. 99–108 (2018)
16. Qian, X., et al.: Pose-normalized image generation for person re-identification. In: Proceedings of the European Conference on Computer Vision (ECCV), pp. 650–667 (2018)
17. Radford, A., Metz, L., Chintala, S.: Unsupervised representation learning with deep convolutional generative adversarial networks. arXiv preprint arXiv:1511.06434 (2015)
18. Ronneberger, O., Fischer, P., Brox, T.: U-net: convolutional networks for biomedical image segmentation. In: Navab, N., Hornegger, J., Wells, W.M., Frangi, A.F. (eds.) MICCAI 2015. LNCS, vol. 9351, pp. 234–241. Springer, Cham (2015). https://doi.org/10.1007/978-3-319-24574-4_28
19. Salimans, T., Goodfellow, I., Zaremba, W., Cheung, V., Radford, A., Chen, X.: Improved techniques for training GANs. In: Advances in Neural Information Processing Systems, pp. 2234–2242 (2016)
20. Siarohin, A., Sangineto, E., Lathuilière, S., Sebe, N.: Deformable GANs for pose-based human image generation. In: Proceedings of the IEEE Conference on Computer Vision and Pattern Recognition, pp. 3408–3416 (2018)

21. Wang, Z., Bovik, A.C., Sheikh, H.R., Simoncelli, E.P., et al.: Image quality assessment: from error visibility to structural similarity. IEEE Trans. Image Process. **13**(4), 600–612 (2004)
22. Yan, Y., Xu, J., Ni, B., Zhang, W., Yang, X.: Skeleton-aided articulated motion generation. In: Proceedings of the 25th ACM International Conference on Multimedia, pp. 199–207. ACM (2017)
23. Zheng, L., Shen, L., Tian, L., Wang, S., Wang, J., Tian, Q.: Scalable person re-identification: a benchmark. In: Proceedings of the IEEE International Conference on Computer Vision, pp. 1116–1124 (2015)

Structure Preserving Image Inpainting Using Edge Priors with Contextual Attention

Ashish Kumar Singh$^{(\boxtimes)}$, Praveen Agrawal, Ankit Dhiman, Rishav Raj, Pankaj Kumar Bajpai, and Yash Harbhajanka

Samsung R&D Institute Bangalore, Bangalore, India
ashish.23ks@samsung.com, ashish23ks@gmail.com

Abstract. Deep learning techniques have produced plausible results for both regular and irregular masks for challenging task of image inpainting. Few approaches make use of extra information like edge priors for generator network, which preserves the structure which is blurry and distorted. On the other hand, certain approaches use surrounding patches to flow information in the missing regions, which in some scenarios can lead to erroneous output. Motivated by these approaches, we propose a three-stage architecture, which consists of an Edge Generator, followed by a Multi-Branch Image Generator and a Contextual Attention layer to generate high quality plausible patches in the input hole image. We evaluate the proposed architecture on the ICME 2019 Image Inpainting challenge and places2 dataset. The proposed method out-performs state of the art both quantitatively and qualitatively. This model can process rectangular holes at arbitrary locations.

Keywords: Image inpainting · Deep learning

1 Introduction

Image Inpainting refers to the process of filling missing portions in images in a way that the filled portions are consistent, perceptually plausible and merge smoothly with the whole image. The filled portions also need to preserve the structures in the image and be semantically accurate. Image Inpainting has a wide range of applications like restoring damaged or deteriorated portions of images and video frames, removing unwanted objects and modifying undesired regions of images.

Traditional techniques, in the field of Image Inpainting, use image statistics and low level features from the remaining portion of the image to fill the missing regions [3–6]. A lot of diffusion based approaches like [4,6] propose propagating the information from neighbouring background regions to the missing regions while some patch-based methods like [3,5] use patches from the available region of image to fill the missing portions of the image. These techniques work well for repetitive structures but lack the ability to capture high-level semantics for

R. V. Babu et al. (Eds.): NCVPRIPG 2019, CCIS 1249, pp. 100–110, 2020.
https://doi.org/10.1007/978-981-15-8697-2_9

complex structures and non-repetitive regions. The major drawback of such traditional methods is the inherent assumption that the low level features or the patches in the missing regions are present in the available image regions, and hence, such methods lack the ability to imagine novel structures in the missing region.

Recent deep learning approaches [11,14,17–19] have shown the capability of Generative Adversarial Networks (GANs) to learn relevant semantics to generate coherent structures in missing regions. An illustrative work based on this model is by Pathak et.al. [14], which uses encoder-decoder network, trained with reconstruction and adversarial loss for imagining contents in missing region. Both Pathak et. al. [14] and Yang et. al. [17] assumes 64×64 missing region in the centre of 128×128 image. Iijuka et. al. [11] uses global and local discriminator to generate consistent and coherent patches in the missing regions. These methods often produce blurry boundaries and texture artifacts primarily, because of the lack of structural information.

Recently, two-stage methods [13,15,19] are proposed to overcome the issue of blurry boundaries and texture artifacts. These methods try to recover structural information in first stage and generate finer details in second stage. Song et. al. [15] predicts semantic segmentation label in missing regions and then recovers finer details. However, different structures can be present in same semantic label region. Nazeri et. al. [13] first completes edges in missing region and then use this information to inpaint the missing region. But, the edges can only provide structural guidance for the inpainting step. Yu et. al. [19] tries to refine the coarse output of first stage with an attention layer in second stage. However, there is no attempt for preserving the structure. This attention layer flows the information from surrounding regions based upon matching patches of coarsely completed image from the previous stage. But it doesn't know if any region of the neighborhood needs to be ignored while inpainting in case they do not belong to the same object that is being in-painted. This leads to erroneous filling in the missing region. To mitigate this issue, we provide an edge map to contextual attention layer, which serves as a segmentation guide. This forces this layer to give weightage to edge of the image, thus improving structure as well as color and texture in the missing regions.

Based on these insights, we propose a novel three-stage model for image inpainting. The model uses edge priors for preserving structure and guiding refinement. The proposed network consists of an edge generator, coarse image generator and a refinement network. The edge generator completes edge information in the missing regions to generate edge priors for next steps. It is based on GAN framework that contain a generator and a discriminator. The coarse image generator uses this edge prior to produce structure preserved coarse image with holes filled. It is based on multi-channel network which uses convolutional kernels with different kernel size to provide better receptive field for preserving structures. The refinement network then takes this coarse image to produce meaningful textures in missing regions. It is based on two branch attention network that uses attention layer to generate high level texture. We use edge prior as guidance in the refinement network. The proposed method achieves significantly high quality inpainting results on ICME [1] and places2 [20] dataset and out-performs previous state-of-art methods.

Contributions of the proposed method are as follows:

- Novel three-stage model for image inpainting which uses edge priors for preserving structure and guiding refinement.
- Edge generator which completes missing edges to generate edge prior.
- Coarse image generator which uses edge prior to produce structure preserved coarse image with holes filled.
- Refinement network which uses edge prior to produce meaningful textures.
- We conducted qualitative and quantitative comparison with several state-of-the-art methods to show that proposed method can achieve competitive results.

2 Method

The architecture of proposed inpainting network is shown in Fig. 1. The proposed network consists of three parts: edge generator G_e, coarse image generator G_i, and refinement network G_r. The edge generator G_e generates edge map $\hat{E}$ by predicting the edges in missing regions. The coarse image generator G_i uses the information from the predicted edge map $\hat{E}$ to output coarse inpainted image $\hat{I}_c$. The refinement network G_r, refines the coarse image $\hat{I}_c$ using guidance from edge map $\hat{E}$ to output the final inpainted image $\hat{I}$.

2.1 Edge Generator

Similar to recent methods [13,15,19], we try to recover structural information in first stage before filling the missing regions. The edge generator G_e is used to fill edges in missing regions which preserve structures in the image. Let I_{gt} be the ground truth image and E_{gt} be the ground truth edge map of I_{gt}. The working of edge generator can be expressed as,

$$\hat{E} = G_e(I_{gray}, E_{in}, M) \tag{1}$$

where M is a binary mask in which 1 represents hole region and 0 represent non-hole region, $E_{in} = E_{gt} \odot (1 - M)$ is the edge map of the input image $I_{in} = I_{gt} \odot (1 - M)$ and I_{gray} is the grayscale image of I_{in}. Here, $\odot$ represents element-wise product.

Furthermore, we apply generative adversarial framework [8] to train the edge generator with the help of discriminator network D_e. The adversarial loss of the network can be written as,

$$\mathcal{L}_{adv}^e = \mathbb{E}[logD_e(E_{gt}, I_{gray})] + \mathbb{E}[log(1 - D_e(\hat{E}, I_{gray}))] \tag{2}$$

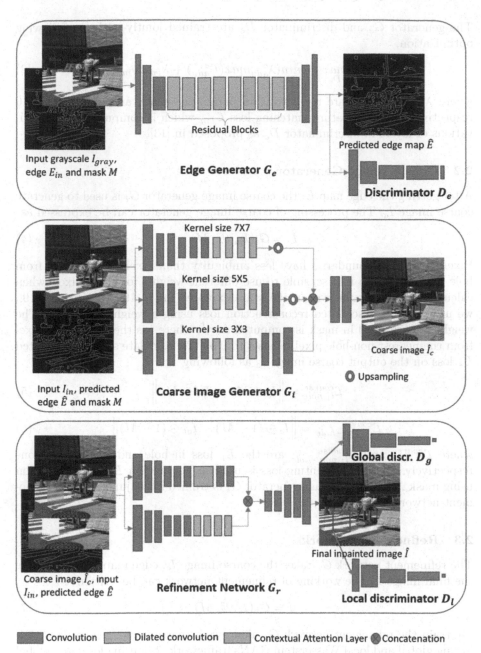

Fig. 1. Architecture of the proposed method

The generator G_e and discriminator D_e are trained jointly with the following optimization,

$$\min_{G_e}\max_{D_e} = min(\lambda_{adv}^e \max_{G_e}\max_{D_e}(\mathcal{L}_{adv}^e) + \lambda_{fm}\mathcal{L}_{fm}) \tag{3}$$

where λ_{adv}^e and λ_{fm} are regularization parameter which are set to 1 and 10 respectively. We use feature matching loss $\mathcal{L}_{fm}$ which is computed on the activations of layers in discriminator D_e as proposed in [13].

2.2 Coarse Image Generator

After getting the edge map $\hat{E}$, the coarse image generator G_i is used to generate coarse image $\hat{I}_c$. The processing of coarse image generator can be expressed as

$$\hat{I}_c = G_i(I_{in}, \hat{E}, M) \tag{4}$$

Pixels near hole boundaries have less ambiguity than pixels that are far from hole boundaries. So it is sensible to use different weights for these pixels when calculating loss. Similar weight ideas are explored in [14,19]. Inspired by [19], we use spatially discounted reconstruction loss using a weight mask M_w. The weight of each pixel in mask is computed as γ^l, where l is the distance of pixel from the nearest non-hole pixel. γ is set to 0.99. We calculate spatial discounted $L1$ loss on the output coarse image $\hat{I}_c$ as following

$$\mathcal{L}_{l_1,hole}^{coarse} = \left\| \hat{I}_c \odot M_w - I_{gt} \odot M_w \right\|_1 \tag{5}$$

$$\mathcal{L}_{l_1,non-hole}^{coarse} = \left\| \hat{I}_c \odot (1-M) - I_{gt} \odot (1-M) \right\|_1 \tag{6}$$

where $\mathcal{L}_{l_1,hole}^{coarse}$ and $\mathcal{L}_{l_1,non-hole}^{coarse}$ are the L_1 loss in hole and non-hole regions respectively. Spatial discounting loss is used in hole region L_1 loss calculation using mask M_w. Coarse image generator G_i is trained in conjunction with refinement network G_r.

2.3 Refinement Network

The refinement network G_r takes the coarse image $\hat{I}_c$, edge map $\hat{E}$ and outputs the final image $\hat{I}$. The working of refinement network can be written as

$$\hat{I} = G_r(\hat{I}_c, \hat{E}, M) \tag{7}$$

We train the refinement network G_r along with coarse image generator G_i following global and local Wasserstein GANs framework [2,9] using local and global discriminator D_l and D_g respectively. Inspired by [9,19] we use gradient penalty loss to both global and local outputs to enforce structural consistency.

Similar to Eqs. 5 and 6 we calculate $\mathcal{L}_{l_1,hole}^{refine}$ and $\mathcal{L}_{l_1,non-hole}^{refine}$ for final image $\hat{I}$. The full L_1 losses is computed as

$$\mathcal{L}_{l_1,hole} = \mathcal{L}_{l_1,hole}^{refine} + \lambda_{coarse}\mathcal{L}_{l_1,hole}^{coarse} \tag{8}$$

$$\mathcal{L}_{l_1,non-hole} = \mathcal{L}_{l_1,non-hole}^{refine} + \lambda_{coarse}\mathcal{L}_{l_1,non-hole}^{coarse} \quad (9)$$

Here, $\lambda_{coarse} = 1.2$ is a regularization parameter, $\mathcal{L}_{l_1,hole}$ and $\mathcal{L}_{l_1,non-hole}$ corresponds to the reconstruction loss in hole and non-hole region respectively for training G_i and G_r together. The adversarial loss including the gradient penalty [9] terms can be written as

$$\mathcal{L}_{adv}^{local} = \mathbb{E}[D_l(\hat{I}_{c,local})] - \mathbb{E}[D_l(I_{gt,local})] + \lambda_{gp}\mathbb{E}[(\left\|\nabla D_l(\hat{I}_{c,local})\right\|_2 - 1)^2] \quad (10)$$

$$\mathcal{L}_{adv}^{global} = \mathbb{E}[\lambda_{global}D_g(\hat{I}_c)] - \mathbb{E}[\lambda_{global}[D_g(I_{gt})] + \lambda_{gp}\mathbb{E}[(\left\|\nabla D_g(\hat{I}_c)\right\|_2 - 1)^2] \quad (11)$$

Here, $\lambda_{global} = 1$ and $\lambda_{gp} = 10$ are regularization parameters. $\hat{I}_{c,local}$ and $I_{gt,local}$ are the cropped images corresponding to the hole regions in mask M of $\hat{I}_c$ and I_{gt} respectively. We also compute well known Perceptual loss L_{perc} and style loss L_{sty} [7,12] using pretrained VGG weights. The full objective function of the W-GAN framework can be expressed as

$$\mathcal{L} = \mathcal{L}_{adv}^{local} + \mathcal{L}_{adv}^{global} + \lambda_h\mathcal{L}_{l_1,hole} + \lambda_{nh}\mathcal{L}_{l_1,non-hole} + \lambda_{perc}L_{perc} + \lambda_{sty}L_{sty} \quad (12)$$

For conducting experiments, we choose $\lambda_h = 6$, $\lambda_{nh} = 1$, $\lambda_{perc} = 0.5$ and $\lambda_{sty} = 250$.

3   Architecture and Training

The edge generator G_e follows encoder decoder architecture with residual blocks [10] in middle to process features. G_e contains an encoder that down-samples twice, followed by eight residual blocks and decoder that up-samples to the original size. The edge discriminator D_e is a simple five layer convolutional network that outputs whether the input edge image is real or fake. This architecture is similar to that proposed by Nazeri et al. [13]. Canny edges are used to generate incomplete edge input E_{in} which are fed to generator to hallucinate edges in missing areas. We used pre-trained weights provided by [13] for edge generator G_e to generate structural information in the missing regions.

The coarse image generator G_i contains three parallel branch with different size convolutional kernels to get information from different receptive fields. It also contains a merge layer to merge outputs of three branches together. This architecture is inspired by [16]. A five layer convolutional network based local discriminator D_l is used which takes only the mask regions input and outputs whether an image is real or not. The refinement network G_r contains two parallel branch and a merge layer to merge the outputs together. One of the branch uses Contextual Attention layer that uses patches from non-hole regions in image as kernels. The use of Contextual Attention layer is inspired by [19]. A five layer CNN architecture based global discriminator D_g is used which takes full image input and outputs whether an image is real or not. Figure 1 shows the proposed architecture, their sample inputs and outputs.

The proposed model is trained on places2 [20] and ICME [1] dataset. The network is trained using 256×256 images with batch size 16. The hole generated in mask M is rectangular in shape. The height and width of the hole is randomly selected from the range (32, 64) pixels. The generated hole is placed randomly to form the mask M with hole. Adam Optimizer is used with learning rate of 10^{-5}. The proposed edge generator (G_e) has a total of 10.8M parameters and takes 41.5 MB space. The proposed coarse and refinemnet generator ($G_i + G_r$) has 14.7M parameters and takes 56.3MB space. Pytorch framework is used for coding and training models. The models are trained on hardware with CPU Intel(R) Xeon(R) CPU E5- 2697 v3 (2.60 GHz) and 4 GPUs GTX 1080 Ti.

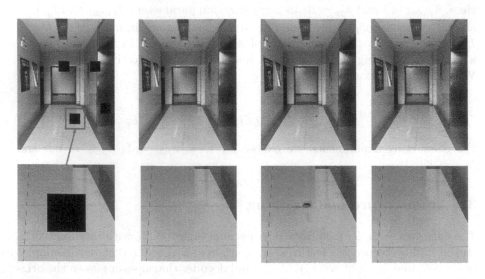

Fig. 2. Sample from ICME test dataset [1]: (left to right) damaged image, EdgeConnect [13], Contextual Attention [19], proposed approach. Bottom row: zoomed in version of a patch. In zoomed patch, the proposed method completes the line partitioning the tiles while keeping the two well segmented regions to be inpainted without any overflow from one region to the other. Whereas, Contextual attention method [19], fails to correctly complete the line as it has no information of the underlying structure.

4   Experiments and Results

We evaluated the proposed inpainting method on two datasets: Places2 [20] test dataset and ICME 2019 Inpainting challenge's test dataset [1]. We compare the output of proposed network with state-of-the-art methods [13,19].

For comparison on Places2 [20] test dataset, we used the pre-trained weights provided by authors of [13,19], trained on Places2 dataset. For comparing the results, we used images of resolution 256×256 with a hole at the image center of resolution 64 × 64. For comparison on ICME dataset, we fine-tune the pre-trained weights (trained on Places2 [20]) provided by both networks on ICME data [1]. We used regular masks with 4 rectangular holes provided in ICME [1] dataset. All images were resized to 256 × 256 for training and testing.

All the results reported are direct outputs from the trained models. No post-processing step is involved while reporting the results.

Qualitative Comparison. In Fig. 2 and 3, we show that the proposed three-stage model generates superior results than EdgeConnect [13] and Contextual Attention [19]. Proposed method uses edge as a prior information for contextual attention layer, this aids the contextual attention layer to fill right texture in the missing region.

Table 1. Results of PSNR and SSIM on ICME test dataset

Method	PSNR	SSIM
EdgeConnect [13]	31.3076	0.9781
Contextual attention [19]	30.7931	0.9784
Proposed method	**31.9059**	**0.9791**

Quantitative Comparison. We report peak signal-to-noise ratio (PSNR) and structural similarity (SSIM) [21] on ICME test data [1]. As shown in Table 1, proposed method outperforms the other two methods in the reported metrics. For comparison on Places2 [20] dataset, we report PSNR and SSIM metric on both the patch as well as the full image. As shown in Table 2, proposed method outperforms the other state-of-the-art methods.

Table 2. Results of PSNR and SSIM on Places2 test dataset

Method	Inpainted patch		Full image	
	PSNR	SSIM	PSNR	SSIM
EdgeConnect [13]	16.6757	0.3099	28.7107	0.9563
Contextual attention [19]	15.8059	0.2922	27.7868	0.9530
Proposed method	**16.7752**	**0.3181**	**28.8067**	**0.9569**

(a)   (b)   (c)   (d)   (e)

Fig. 3. Results on Places2 test dataset (a) ground truth image, (b) damaged image (c, d, e) Results (c) EdgeConnect [13], (d) Contextual Attention [19], and (e) Proposed method

5 Conclusion

We proposed a three-stage image completion network, which comprises of an edge generator, a multi-branch coarse image generator and refinement network with contextual attention layer. Also, we demonstrated how the edge information can be used to improve results of Contextual Attention Network. The proposed method outperforms state of the art methods on both qualtative and quantitative evaluation. The experimental results obtained, shows the feasibilty of the proposed method. For future work, we plan to experiment on better prior than Edges. We have observed that in textured regions, because of the spurious nature of output from edge completion network, output from the proposed method is not as expected. Furthermore, we would also like to extend this method for high-resolution images.

References

1. ICME 2019: Learning-Based Image Inpainting Challenge (2019). https://icme19inpainting.github.io/
2. Arjovsky, M., Chintala, S., Bottou, L.: Wasserstein GAN. arXiv e-prints arXiv:1701.07875, January 2017
3. Barnes, C., Shechtman, E., Finkelstein, A., Goldman, D.B.: PatchMatch: a randomized correspondence algorithm for structural image editing. ACM Trans. Graph. (ToG) **28**, 24 (2009)
4. Bertalmio, M., Sapiro, G., Caselles, V., Ballester, C.: Image inpainting. In: Proceedings of the 27th Annual Conference on Computer Graphics and Interactive Techniques, SIGGRAPH 2000, pp. 417–424. ACM Press/Addison-Wesley Publishing Co. (2000)
5. Darabi, S., Shechtman, E., Barnes, C., Goldman, D.B., Sen, P.: Image melding: combining inconsistent images using patch-based synthesis. ACM Trans. Graph. **31**(4), 82:1–82:10 (2012)
6. Efros, A.A., Freeman, W.T.: Image quilting for texture synthesis and transfer. In: Proceedings of SIGGRAPH 2001, pp. 341–346 (2001)
7. Gatys, L.A., Ecker, A.S., Bethge, M.: Image style transfer using convolutional neural networks. In: 2016 IEEE Conference on Computer Vision and Pattern Recognition (CVPR), pp. 2414–2423. IEEE Computer Society, June 2016
8. Goodfellow, I.J., et al.: Generative adversarial networks. arXiv e-prints arXiv:1406.2661, June 2014
9. Gulrajani, I., Ahmed, F., Arjovsky, M., Dumoulin, V., Courville, A.: Improved training of Wasserstein GANs. arXiv e-prints arXiv:1704.00028, March 2017
10. He, K., Zhang, X., Ren, S., Sun, J.: Deep residual learning for image recognition. arXiv e-prints arXiv:1512.03385, December 2015
11. Iizuka, S., Simo-Serra, E., Ishikawa, H.: Globally and locally consistent image completion. ACM Trans. Graph. (Proc. SIGGRAPH 2017) **36**(4), 107:1–107:14 (2017)
12. Johnson, J., Alahi, A., Fei-Fei, L.: Perceptual losses for real-time style transfer and super-resolution. arXiv e-prints arXiv:1603.08155, March 2016
13. Nazeri, K., Ng, E., Joseph, T., Qureshi, F., Ebrahimi, M.: EdgeConnect: generative image inpainting with adversarial edge learning. arXiv preprint arXiv:1901.00212 (2019)

14. Pathak, D., Krähenbühl, P., Donahue, J., Darrell, T., Efros, A.: Context encoders: feature learning by inpainting (2016)
15. Song, Y., Yang, C., Shen, Y., Wang, P., Huang, Q., Kuo, C.J.: SPG-net: segmentation prediction and guidance network for image inpainting. CoRR abs/1805.03356 (2018)
16. Wang, Y., Tao, X., Qi, X., Shen, X., Jia, J.: Image inpainting via generative multi-column convolutional neural networks. arXiv e-prints arXiv:1810.08771, October 2018
17. Yang, C., Lu, X., Lin, Z., Shechtman, E., Wang, O., Li, H.: High-resolution image inpainting using multi-scale neural patch synthesis. In: 2017 IEEE Conference on Computer Vision and Pattern Recognition (CVPR), pp. 4076–4084, July 2017
18. Yeh, R.A., Chen, C., Yian Lim, T., Schwing, A.G., Hasegawa-Johnson, M., Do, M.N.: Semantic image inpainting with deep generative models. In: The IEEE Conference on Computer Vision and Pattern Recognition (CVPR), July 2017
19. Yu, J., Lin, Z., Yang, J., Shen, X., Lu, X., Huang, T.S.: Generative image inpainting with contextual attention. In: Proceedings of the IEEE Conference on Computer Vision and Pattern Recognition, pp. 5505–5514 (2018)
20. Zhou, B., Lapedriza, A., Khosla, A., Oliva, A., Torralba, A.: Places: a 10 million image database for scene recognition. IEEE Trans. Pattern Anal. Mach. Intell. 40(6), 1452–1464 (2017)
21. Wang, Z., Bovik, A.C., Sheikh, H.R., Simoncelli, E.P.: Image quality assessment: from error visibility to structural similarity. IEEE Trans. Image Process. 13(4), 600–612 (2004)

Exploring Temporal Differences in 3D Convolutional Neural Networks

Gagan Kanojia[✉], Sudhakar Kumawat, and Shanmuganathan Raman

Indian Institute of Technology Gandhinagar, Gandhinagar, India
{gagan.kanojia,sudhakar.kumawat,shanmuga}@iitgn.ac.in

Abstract. Traditional 3D convolutions are computationally expensive, memory intensive, and due to large number of parameters, they often tend to overfit. On the other hand, 2D CNNs are less computationally expensive and less memory intensive than 3D CNNs and have shown remarkable results in applications like image classification and object recognition. However, in previous works, it has been observed that they are inferior to 3D CNNs when applied on a spatio-temporal input. In this work, we propose a convolutional block which extracts the spatial information by performing a 2D convolution and extracts the temporal information by exploiting temporal differences, i.e., the change in the spatial information at different time instances, using simple operations of shift, subtract and add without utilizing any trainable parameters. The proposed convolutional block has same number of parameters as of a 2D convolution kernel of size $n \times n$, i.e. n^2, and has n times lesser parameters than an $n \times n \times n$ 3D convolution kernel. We show that the 3D CNNs perform better when the 3D convolution kernels are replaced by the proposed convolutional blocks. We evaluate the proposed convolutional block on UCF101 and ModelNet datasets. All the codes and pretrained models are publicly available at https://github.com/GaganKanojia/SSA-ResNet.

Keywords: Deep learning · 3D convolution neural networks

1 Introduction

Lately, 3D convolutional neural networks are gaining popularity over the 2D CNNs when the task is to deal with 3D data representations which could be videos, shapes or other formats [6, 16]. This is because 2D CNN lack in exploiting the temporal information. 3D CNNs are more proficient than 2D CNNs in extracting temporal information and utilizing it to perform specific tasks. It has been shown that a 3D CNN of same depth as that of a 2D CNN performs better on tasks like action recognition [6, 17]. However, this proficiency comes with a cost in terms of the number of learnable parameters, memory requirements, and risks of overfitting. For example, 3D ResNet (18 layers) [6] has around 3 times more parameters than the 2D ResNet (18 layers) [7].

© Springer Nature Singapore Pte Ltd. 2020
R. V. Babu et al. (Eds.): NCVPRIPG 2019, CCIS 1249, pp. 111–121, 2020.
https://doi.org/10.1007/978-981-15-8697-2_10

In this work, our focus is on acquiring both spatial and temporal structure of the 3D data while reducing the cost in terms of trainable parameters. We propose a convolutional block which exploits both the spatial information and the temporal information by utilizing a 2D convolution and temporal differences, i.e., the change in the spatial information at different time instances, using simple operations of shift, subtract and add. We have also incorporated temporal max pooling in order to downsample the temporal depth of the feature maps along the depth of the network. None of the operations other than 2D convolution require trainable parameters which makes the number of trainable parameters of the proposed convolutional block equal to the 2D convolution kernel with same kernel size. The major contributions of the work are as follows. (a) We propose a novel convolutional block which captures spatial information by performing a 2D convolution and captures temporal information using simple operations of shift, subtract and add. (b) We reduce the number of parameters by n times by replacing the 3D convolution kernel of size $n \times n \times n$ with the proposed convolution block comprising a 2D convolution kernel of size $1 \times n \times n$. (c) We show that the proposed convolutional block helps the 3D CNNs to perform better while utilizing lesser parameters than the 3D convolution kernels.

2   Related Work

In recent years, 2D CNNs have been dominating several applications of computer vision like object detection [7] and image classification [7]. However, they lack in extracting the temporal information present in the spatio-temporal data [17]. There are works which extend the 2D CNNs on videos by processing the video frames individually and then combining the extracted information along the temporal dimension to obtain the output [5,24]. Recently, 3D CNNs have shown great potential in dealing with the spatio-temporal data or 3D CAD models as inputs [9,15,26]. It has been observed that 3D CNNs are much better in exploiting the temporal information than 2D CNNs [17]. However, 3D CNNs are computationally expensive and they are prone to overfit due to their large number of parameters. Hence, the researchers moved on to find better and more efficient ways of mimicking 3D convolutions. There has been notable advances in the separable convolutions in 2D CNNs to reduce the space-time complexity [2,21]. In many works, the idea of separable convolutions has been extended to 3D CNNs [11,14,17,22]. In [11], the authors proposed the idea of replacing the 3D convolution kernel by a 2D convolution kernel to capture the spatial information followed by a 1D convolution kernel to convolve along the temporal direction. They showed that the proposed technique has several advantages, like parameter reduction and better performance, over the 3D convolutions, which has been further explored in [17]. Temporal differences has been explored in few recent works [8,18]. Wang et al. [18] use difference in two frames as the approximation of motion information. Similarly, Lee et al. [8] propose a motion block which extracts features using spatial and temporal shifts. In this work, we only rely on the temporal differences. Instead of relying on only the adjacent frames, we compute aggregated temporal differences over several frames. The proposed SSA Layer does not involve any trainable parameter to extract temporal information via temporal differences. Our focus is to propose an efficient alternative to the 3D convolution filters which utilizes lesser parameters without compromising the performance.

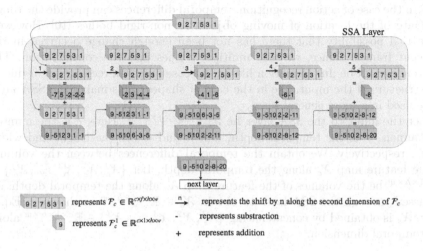

Fig. 1. An illustration of SSA layer

3 Proposed Approach

In this section, we discuss the proposed convolutional block which extracts both spatial and temporal information. The proposed convolutional block has three parts: 2D convolution kernel, SSA layer, and temporal pooling layer. Here, SSA stands for Shift, Subtract and Add. Let the input to the proposed convolutional block be $\mathcal{X} \in \mathbb{R}^{c \times f \times h \times w}$. Here, $\mathcal{X}$ is the output feature maps of the previous convolutional block or layer, c is number of channels, f corresponds to the temporal depth, and h and w are the height and width of $\mathcal{X}$, respectively.

2D Convolution. In traditional 3D CNNs, the feature maps are convolved with a 3D filter $\hat{g} \in \mathbb{R}^{c \times k \times k \times k}$ with c channels and kernel size $k \times k \times k$ [6]. In the proposed framework, first we obtain $\mathcal{X}_c = \mathcal{X} \star g$. Here, $\star$ stands for convolution, and g is a 2D filter of kernel size $1 \times k \times k$ and c channels. The purpose of the 2D convolution is to extract the spatial information present in the input feature maps [25]. We, then, pass $\mathcal{X}_c$ through the proposed SSA layer to obtain the temporal structure of the feature maps.

SSA Layer. SSA stands for Shift, Subtract and Add operations performed in the SSA layer. The purpose of the SSA layer is to extract the temporal information present in the spatio-temporal data. For example, in action recognition, motion features extracted from the videos can hold important information. In order to capture the motion information, optical flow techniques can be used [4]. However, capturing optical flow is in itself a computationally expensive task which can require a dedicated network [4]. In the proposed SSA layer, we rely on temporal differences, i.e., the change in the spatial information at different time instances, to extract the necessary temporal information present in the spatio-temporal data.In the case of action recognition, temporal differences can provide the rough extimate of the location of moving objects or non-rigid bodies [10]. However, there is a possibility that there has not been enough change occurred in the adjacent frames. Hence, we take multiple frames into the consideration. The difference could be due to motion like in the case of action recognition or due to the structure of the input, like in the case of shapes. This makes the SSA layer to be used in a more general sense.

Let the input to the SSA layer be $\mathcal{X}_c \in \mathbb{R}^{c \times f \times h \times w}$. Here, c is the number of channels, f is the temporal depth, and h and w are the height and width of $\mathcal{X}_c$, respectively. We obtain the temporal differences between the volumes of the feature map $\mathcal{X}_c$ along the temporal depth. Let $\{\mathcal{X}_c^1, \mathcal{X}_c^2, \mathcal{X}_c^3, \ldots, \mathcal{X}_c^f\} \in \mathbb{R}^{c \times 1 \times h \times w}$ be the volumes of the feature map $\mathcal{X}_c$ along the temporal depth. $\mathcal{X}_c$ is passed through the SSA layer to obtain $\mathcal{X}_s \in \mathbb{R}^{c \times f \times h \times w}$ as shown in Eq. 1. Here, $\mathcal{X}_s$ is obtained by concatenating $\{\mathcal{X}_s^1, \mathcal{X}_s^2, \mathcal{X}_s^3, \ldots, \mathcal{X}_s^f\} \in \mathbb{R}^{c \times 1 \times h \times w}$ along the temporal dimension.

$$\mathcal{X}_s^i = \mathcal{X}_c^i + \frac{1}{f} \sum_{k=1}^{i-1} \frac{f - (i - k)}{f} (\mathcal{X}_c^i - \mathcal{X}_c^k), \quad \forall i = 2, \ldots, f \tag{1}$$

Here, k is the shift and i is a location along the temporal direction. If $i = 1$, $\mathcal{X}_s^i = \mathcal{X}_c^i$. Since, the nearby frames can have more contextual relation, the term $\frac{f-(i-k)}{f}$ is to ensure that the larger shifts get smaller weights than smaller shifts. Instead of computing for each temporal volume separately, X_s can be computed in a cumulative manner as illustrated in Fig. 1. However, the mathematical formulation and the illustration shown in Fig. 1 lead to the same output. Since, $\mathcal{X}_c$ is a four dimensional volume, it would be hard to provide a clean illustration. We have also omitted the multiplicative constants from the illustration to keep it clean. Hence, we have used 1-D representation to illustrate its operations visually. In Fig. 1, each column refers to a single shift. It can be seen that the input feature map $\mathcal{X}_c$ is subtracted from its shifted version and then, the difference is added to it in the corresponding locations to obtain $\hat{\mathcal{X}}_s$. Then, we again shift the feature map $\mathcal{X}_c$ by one more step, subtract it from its original version and then add the difference to the corresponding locations of $\hat{\mathcal{X}}_s$. At the end of $f - 1$ steps, we obtain $\mathcal{X}_s$.

Temporal Pooling. As, we move along the depth of the 3D convolution networks, the temporal depth of the feature maps keeps reducing as we perform 3D convolutions of stride more than one. In our case, we are not performing convolution along the temporal depth. Hence, to reduce the temporal depth, we perform max pooling along the temporal direction whenever we want to reduce the temporal depth of the feature maps.

Parameter Analysis. A standard 3D convolutional kernel of size $n \times n \times n$ and c channels contains cn^3 parameters. The proposed convolution block comprises a standard 2D-convolution kernel, an SSA layer and temporal max pooling. A standard 2D-convolution kernel of size $n \times n$ and c channels contains cn^2 parameters and an SSA layer consists of shift, subtract and add operations which do not require any trainable parameters. Also, temporal max pooling does not require any trainable parameters. Hence, the overall number of trainable parameters used in the proposed convolution block is cn^2 which is n times less than the standard 3D convolution kernel.

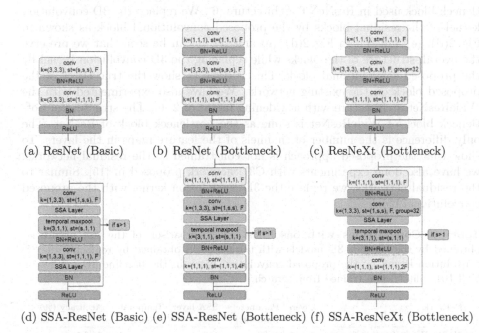

(a) ResNet (Basic) (b) ResNet (Bottleneck) (c) ResNeXt (Bottleneck)

(d) SSA-ResNet (Basic) (e) SSA-ResNet (Bottleneck) (f) SSA-ResNeXt (Bottleneck)

Fig. 2. (a) and (b) show the basic and bottleneck blocks used in 3D ResNet architecture [6]. (c) shows the bottleneck bock used in 3D ResNeXT architecture [6]. (d), (e) and (f) show the residual blocks in which 3D convolution kernel is replaced by the proposed convolutional block.

4 Experiments and Discussions

In this section, we show that the 3D CNNs perform better when the standard 3D convolution kernels are replaced by the proposed convolutional block. Our focus is mostly on the residual networks. We evaluate their performances on two types of 3D data: spatio-temporal image sequences and 3D CAD models.

4.1 Spatio-Temporal Image Sequences

Dataset. UCF101 [13] is a benchmark action recognition dataset containing complex real world videos which has been used in several works [3,15,16]. The videos of the dataset cover 101 action categories. We use UCF101 split-1 for all our experiments regarding spatio-temporal image sequences.

Network Architectures. We employ deep 3D residual networks to evaluate the proposed convolutional block [6]. Figure 2(a) and (b) show the basic and bottleneck block used in 3D ResNet architecture [6]. Figure 2(c) shows the bottleneck block used in ResNeXT architecture [6]. We replace the 3D convolution kernel of the residual blocks by the proposed convolutional block as shown in Fig. 2(d), (e) and (f). In Fig. 2(d), (e) and (f), it can be seen that we preserve the overall structure of the blocks while replacing the 3D convolution kernel by the proposed convolutional block. This is done to show the true effect of the proposed block on the existing networks. We have also experimented with the WideResNet architecture with a widening factor of 2 [6]. The structure of bottleneck block of WideResNet is same as the bottleneck block of ResNet. The only difference is the number of channels of the feature maps in the layers. To show that the proposed approach is not constrained to the residual networks, we have also done experiments with C3D network proposed in [15]. Similar to the residual networks, we replace the 3D convolution kernel with the proposed convolutional block.

Table 1. Comparisons with baselines. The comparison of the test accuracies obtained by the baseline 3D models with the networks obtained by replacing the 3D convolution kernel by the proposed convolution block in the baseline 3D models on UCF101 split-1 when trained from scratch.

Network	Layers	Parameters (millions)	SSA layer	Temporal pooling	Accuracy (%)
3D ResNet [6,16] (baseline)	18	≈ 33			45.6
SSA-ResNet (ours)	18	≈ 11		✓	52.8
SSA-ResNet (ours)	18	≈ 11	✓	✓	**55.7**
3D ResNeXT [6] (baseline)	50	≈ 26			49.3
SSA-ResNeXT (ours)	50	≈ 23		✓	54.9
SSA-ResNeXT (ours)	50	≈ 23	✓	✓	**56.9**
3D WideResNet [6] (baseline)	50	≈ 157			46.8
SSA-WideResNet(ours)	50	≈ 67		✓	50.7
SSA-WideResNet(ours)	50	≈ 67	✓	✓	**52.9**
C3D [15] (baseline)	5	≈ 18			44
SSA-C3D (ours)	5	≈ 14		✓	50
SSA-C3D (ours)	5	≈ 14	✓	✓	**51.6**
3D ResNet [3,6] (baseline)	101	≈ 88			46.7
SSA-ResNet (ours)	101	≈ 43		✓	52.1
SSA-ResNet (ours)	101	≈ 43	✓	✓	**54.4**

Comparisons with Baselines. We perform our experiments by training the networks from scratch on UCF101 split-1. The test accuracies of 3D ResNeXT and 3D WideResNet when trained from scratch on UCF101 split-1 are not available in the previous works [6]. So, we train these networks on UCF101 from scratch to obtain them. For the other baseline networks, we mention the accuracies reported in [3,6,16]. SSA-ResNet, SSA-WideResNet, SSA-ResNeXT, and SSA-C3D are obtained by replacing the 3D convolution kernels in ResNet, WideResNet, ResNeXT, and C3D [15] by the proposed convolutional block. We train these networks from scratch on UCF101 with same hyperparameter settings. Table 1 shows that the accuracies obtained by the baseline 3D models when trained from scratch on the split-1 of UCF101 dataset. It also shows the accuracies obtained by replacing the 3D convolution kernel by the proposed convolution block. It can be seen that the networks perform significantly better with the proposed convolutional block while utilizing lesser trainable parameters.

Table 2. Comparisons with the state-of-the-art. The comparison of the proposed approach with the state-of-the-art methods when trained from scratch on UCF101 dataset.

Network	Layers	Parameters (millions)	Model size (MB)	Accuracy
2D-ResNet [7,16]	18	≈11.2	–	42.2
2D-ResNet [7,16]	34	≈21.5	–	42.2
3D-ResNet [16]	18	≈33.2	254	45.6
3D-ResNet [16]	34	≈63.5	485	45.9
3D-ResNet [3]	101	≈86.06	657	46.7
3D STC-ResNet [3]	18	–	–	42.8
3D STC-ResNet [3]	50	–	–	46.2
3D STC-ResNet [3]	101	–	–	47.9
C3D [15]	5	≈18	139.6	44
R(2+1)D [17]	18	≈33.3	128	48.37
SSA-ResNet (ours)	18	≈11	88.5	55.7
SSA-ResNeXt (ours)	50	≈23	185.9	**56.9**

Comparisons with the State-of-the-Art. Table 2 compares the proposed approach with the state-of-the-art methods when trained from scratch on UCF101 dataset. The test accuracy of R(2+1)D [17] when trained from scratch on UCF101 is not available in the previous works. So, we trained the network on UCF101 split-1 from scratch to obtain it using the same hyperparameter settings as ours. It can be observed that SSA-ResNeXT performs significantly better than the previous approaches. SSA-ResNet (18 layers) utilizes approximately 11 million parameters which is roughly equal to the parameters used in 2D-ResNet [7] (18 layers). Inspite of having almost equal parameters, SSA-ResNet (18 layers) outperforms 2D-ResNet (18 layers) by 13.5 % in terms of classification accuracy. Also, SSA-ResNet (18 layers) utilizes approximately 3 times less parameters than 3D-ResNet (18 layers) [16], 3D STC-ResNet (18 layers) [3], and R(2+1)D (18 layers) [17] and still outperforms them by 10.1%, 12.9 %, and 7.33%, respectively.

Table 3. Analysis of different shifts and temporal pooling. The comparison of test accuracies obtained on UCF101 split-1 using SSA-ResNet (18 layers) (when trained-from-scratch) with varying number of shifts along with the effect of temporal pooling.

#Shift	Temporal pooling	Accuracy
0		46.3
0	✓	52.8
1	✓	52.6
2	✓	53.4
3	✓	53.9
f-1		51.3
f-1	✓	**55.7**

Analysis. In the proposed convolutional block, apart from a standard 2D convolution kernel, there are two components: SSA layer and Temporal pooling.

SSA Layer. As shown in Fig. 1, we perform the shift operation $f-1$ times, where f is the temporal depth of the input feature map. We perform the experiments on SSA-ResNet (18 layers) with different values of shifts. The results are shown in Table 3. It can be seen that as we increase the fixed number of shifts from 1 to 3, the test accuracy increases and we obtain the highest accuracy when we perform $f - 1$ shifts.

Temporal Pooling. In Table 3, it can be observed that by using 2D-convolution kernel and only max temporal pooling, the network outperforms the baseline case, i.e. with only 2D convolution kernels. The same pattern can be observed in Table 1, in which the baseline 3D models are replaced with the proposed convolution block without SSA layer (second row for each network) and the networks performed significantly better than the baseline 3D CNNs.

4.2   3D CAD Models

Dataset. ModelNet [20] is a collection of 3D CAD models of objects. It has two subsets: ModelNet10 and ModelNet40. ModelNet10 and ModelNet40 contains 10

Table 4. Comparisons with the state-of-the-art. The comparison of the SSA-ResNeXT8 with the state-of-the-art methods on the voxelized version of ModelNet40 and ModelNet10 datasets.

Network	Framework	Augmentation	Parameters (millions)	ModelNet40 (%)	ModelNet10 (%)
3D ShapeNets [20]	Volumetric	Az × 12	≈38	77	83.5
Beam Search [23]	Volumetric	Az × 12	≈0.08	81.26	88
3D-GAN [19]	Volumetric	Az × 12	≈11	83.3	91
VoxNet [9]	Volumetric	Az × 12	≈0.92	83	92
LightNet [26]	Volumetric	Az × 12	≈0.30	86.90	93.39
ORION [12]	Volumetric	Az × 12	≈.91	–	**93.8**
SSA-ResNeXT8 (ours)	Volumetric	Az × 12	≈3.38	**89.5**	93.3

and 40 classes of objects, respectively, which are manually aligned to a canonical frame. In our experiments, we use the voxelized version of size $32 \times 32 \times 32$ and augmentation with 12 orientations [9]. Similar to [1,9], we add noise, random translations, and horizontal flips for data augmentation to the training data. Similar to [1], we scale the binary voxel range from $\{0,1\}$ to $\{-1,5\}$.

Network Architecture. To avoid overfitting on ModelNet40 and ModelNet10, we use a smal network SSA-ResNext8 to evaluate our approach on 3D CAD models. We use the SSA-ResNeXT bottleneck block in the architecture of the network. Let us denote the SSA-ResNeXT bottleneck block with $SSAR(k, F, s)$, where $1 \times k \times k$ is the kernel size of the 2D convolution filter, F is the number of channels in the input feature map and s is the value of stride passed to the block. The architecture of SSA-ResNext8 is as follows: $Conv2D(3,1) \rightarrow MP(3,2) \rightarrow SSAR(3,64,1) \rightarrow SSAR(3,256,1) \rightarrow SSAR(3,256,2) \rightarrow SSAR(3,512,1) \rightarrow SSAR(3,512,2) \rightarrow SSAR(3,1024,1) \rightarrow GP \rightarrow FC$. Here, $Conv2D(3,1)$ is a 2D convolution kernel of size $1 \times 3 \times 3$ and stride of 1, followed by a batch normalization layer and ReLU, and $MP(3,2)$ is the max-pooling layer with kernel size of $3 \times 3 \times 3$ and stride of 2. GP and FC stands for global average pooling and fully connected layer, respectively.

Comparisons with the State of the Art. Table 4 shows the comparison of the SSA-ResNeXT8 with the state-of-the-art methods that use voxelized/volumetric ModelNet datasets as input. For fair comparison, we only consider volumetric frameworks. It can be observed that the network with the proposed convolutional block performs better than the state-of-the-art on ModelNet40 and comparable on ModelNet10 in the case when the networks are trained with shapes augmented with 12 orientations. This shows that the proposed convolution block is not restricted to videos and can be further exploited in shapes.

5   Conclusion

We propose a novel convolutional block which is proficient in capturing both spatial and temporal structure of the 3D data while utilizing lesser parameters than the 3D convolution kernel. It comprises three components: a 2D-convolution kernel to capture the spatial information, a novel SSA layer to capture the temporal structure, and a temporal pooling layer to reduce the temporal depth of the input feature map. We show that the 3D CNNs perform better when the 3D convolution kernels are replaced by the proposed convolutional block. SSA-ResNet (18 layers) outperforms the state-of-the-art accuracy on the UCF101 dataset split-1 while utilizing lesser parameters when networks are trained-from-scratch. We have also evaluated the proposed convolutional block on 3D CAD models and we outperform the state-of-the-art on ModelNet40 among the volumetric framework, when the training data is augmented with 12 rotations.

Acknowledgments. Gagan Kanojia and Sudhakar Kumawat were supported by TCS Research Fellowships. Shanmuganathan Raman was supported by SERB Core Research Grant and Imprint 2 Grant.

References

1. Brock, A., Lim, T., Ritchie, J.M., Weston, N.: Generative and discriminative voxel modeling with convolutional neural networks. arXiv preprint arXiv:1608.04236 (2016)
2. Chollet, F.: Xception: deep learning with depthwise separable convolutions. In: CVPR, pp. 1251–1258 (2017)
3. Diba, A., et al.: Spatio-temporal channel correlation networks for action classification. In: ECCV, pp. 284–299 (2018)
4. Dosovitskiy, A., et al.: FlowNet: learning optical flow with convolutional networks. In: ICCV, pp. 2758–2766 (2015)
5. Girdhar, R., Ramanan, D., Gupta, A., Sivic, J., Russell, B.: ActionVLAD: learning spatio-temporal aggregation for action classification. In: CVPR, pp. 971–980 (2017)
6. Hara, K., Kataoka, H., Satoh, Y.: Can spatiotemporal 3D CNNs retrace the history of 2D CNNs and ImageNet? In: CVPR, pp. 6546–6555 (2018)
7. He, K., Zhang, X., Ren, S., Sun, J.: Deep residual learning for image recognition. In: CVPR, pp. 770–778 (2016)
8. Lee, M., Lee, S., Son, S., Park, G., Kwak, N.: Motion feature network: fixed motion filter for action recognition. In: ECCV, pp. 387–403 (2018)
9. Maturana, D., Scherer, S.: VoxNet: a 3D convolutional neural network for real-time object recognition. In: IEEE IROS, pp. 922–928 (2015)
10. Park, D., Zitnick, C.L., Ramanan, D., Dollár, P.: Exploring weak stabilization for motion feature extraction. In: CVPR, pp. 2882–2889 (2013)
11. Qiu, Z., Yao, T., Mei, T.: Learning spatio-temporal representation with pseudo-3D residual networks. In: ICCV, pp. 5533–5541 (2017)
12. Sedaghat, N., Zolfaghari, M., Amiri, E., Brox, T.: Orientation-boosted voxel nets for 3D object recognition. In: BMVC (2017)
13. Soomro, K., Zamir, A.R., Shah, M.: UCF101: a dataset of 101 human actions classes from videos in the wild. arXiv preprint arXiv:1212.0402 (2012)
14. Sun, L., Jia, K., Yeung, D.Y., Shi, B.E.: Human action recognition using factorized spatio-temporal convolutional networks. In: ICCV, pp. 4597–4605 (2015)
15. Tran, D., Bourdev, L., Fergus, R., Torresani, L., Paluri, M.: Learning spatiotemporal features with 3D convolutional networks. In: ICCV, pp. 4489–4497 (2015)

16. Tran, D., Ray, J., Shou, Z., Chang, S.F., Paluri, M.: Convnet architecture search for spatiotemporal feature learning. arXiv preprint arXiv:1708.05038 (2017)
17. Tran, D., Wang, H., Torresani, L., Ray, J., LeCun, Y., Paluri, M.: A closer look at spatiotemporal convolutions for action recognition. In: CVPR, pp. 6450–6459 (2018)
18. Wang, L., et al.: Temporal segment networks: towards good practices for deep action recognition. In: Leibe, B., Matas, J., Sebe, N., Welling, M. (eds.) ECCV 2016. LNCS, vol. 9912, pp. 20–36. Springer, Cham (2016). https://doi.org/10.1007/978-3-319-46484-8_2
19. Wu, J., Zhang, C., Xue, T., Freeman, B., Tenenbaum, J.: Learning a probabilistic latent space of object shapes via 3D generative-adversarial modeling. In: NIPS, pp. 82–90 (2016)
20. Wu, Z., et al.: 3D shapenets: a deep representation for volumetric shapes. In: CVPR, pp. 1912–1920 (2015)
21. Xie, S., Girshick, R., Dollár, P., Tu, Z., He, K.: Aggregated residual transformations for deep neural networks. In: CVPR, pp. 1492–1500 (2017)
22. Xie, S., Sun, C., Huang, J., Tu, Z., Murphy, K.: Rethinking spatiotemporal feature learning: speed-accuracy trade-offs in video classification. In: ECCV, pp. 305–321 (2018)
23. Xu, X., Todorovic, S.: Beam search for learning a deep convolutional neural network of 3d shapes. In: IEEE ICPR, pp. 3506–3511 (2016)
24. Xu, Z., Yang, Y., Hauptmann, A.G.: A discriminative CNN video representation for event detection. In: CVPR, pp. 1798–1807 (2015)
25. Zeiler, M.D., Fergus, R.: Visualizing and understanding convolutional networks. In: Fleet, D., Pajdla, T., Schiele, B., Tuytelaars, T. (eds.) ECCV 2014. LNCS, vol. 8689, pp. 818–833. Springer, Cham (2014). https://doi.org/10.1007/978-3-319-10590-1_53
26. Zhi, S., Liu, Y., Li, X., Guo, Y.: LightNet: a lightweight 3D convolutional neural network for real-time 3D object recognition. In: Eurographics Workshop on 3D Object Retrieval, pp. 9–16 (2017)

PoshakNet: Framework for Matching Dresses from Real-Life Photos Using GAN and Siamese Network

Abhigyan Khaund$^{(\boxtimes)}$, Daksh Thapar, and Aditya Nigam$^{(\boxtimes)}$

Indian Institute of Technology, Mandi, India
{b16082,d18033}@students.iitmandi.ac.in, aditya@iitmandi.ac.in

Abstract. Online garment shopping has gained many customers in recent years. Describing a dress using keywords does not always yield the proper results, which in turn leads to dissatisfaction of customers. A visual search based system will be enormously beneficent to the industry. Hence, we propose a framework that can retrieve similar clothes that can be found in an image. The first task is to extract the garment from the input image (street photo). There are various challenges for that, including pose, illumination, and background clutter. We use a Generative Adversarial Network for the task of retrieving the garment that the person in the image was wearing. It has been shown that GAN can retrieve the garment very efficiently despite the challenges of street photos. Finally, a siamese based matching system takes the retrieved cloth image and matches it with the clothes in the dataset, giving us the top k matches. We take a pre-trained inception-ResNet v1 module as a siamese network (trained using triplet loss for face detection) and fine-tune it on the shopping dataset using center loss. The dataset has been collected inhouse. For training the GAN, we use the LookBook dataset [14], which is publically available.

Keywords: Deep learning · GAN · e-commerce · Siamese · Dress retrieval

1 Introduction

Clothes are like an extended body part of human beings. Every human being spends hours every day to make themselves look good in the best attire. To achieve this, we spent a lot of time buying clothes that we fancy. Recent years have seen a tremendous rise in e-commerce ventures and their sales. Clothes shopping has led these sales after electronics. This wave of online apparel shopping is due to the involvement of tech giants like Amazon, Flipkart, Myntra, and others. Users of these platforms generally search for clothes using some static and manually selected keywords that describe the shape or color of the dress. However, it is not always that searching through such keywords leads users directly to the desired dress.

© Springer Nature Singapore Pte Ltd. 2020
R. V. Babu et al. (Eds.): NCVPRIPG 2019, CCIS 1249, pp. 122–132, 2020.
https://doi.org/10.1007/978-981-15-8697-2_11

Motivation: More often than not, we tend to search for clothes that we see others wearing, and we find it challenging to frame that dress in terms of the available keywords. It is difficult to describe multi-colored apparel, and with so many new fashion designs hitting the market, it is sometimes confusing to pinpoint the dress type worn. These issues result in users not being able to search for the desired dress in the shopping sites and often getting unwanted results. This is the major drawback of any keyword based matching algorithms and can be solved if the products can be described using visual clues. We base our search model not on keywords but directly on the image content. We take a picture of the dress the user wants to find matches for and run a matching process to determine the closest matches to the dress from the shopping portal, reducing the dependence on being able to search and shop with exact keywords and textual descriptions.

Fig. 1. An example showing the end-to-end working of the street-to-shop problem.

Fig. 2. (a) Illustration of various challenges to content-based clothes retrieval. (b) Cropped picture from bounding box with unwanted body elements.

Challenges: How do we get a visual representation of the dress in a way that we can accurately do its matching with the available shopping products? If we directly use a person's picture for matching, it is bound to fail, as such photos have a varying background, inconsistent lighting, and different positions of the person's posture, which may lead to an obscured view of the dress. One easy solution to this problem is to crop the image using object detection to retrieve only the bounding box for the dress of the person from the image [15]. This approach is unable to remove certain unwanted portions like arms, hand, neck, or hair in the cropped portion. If the person is also at an angle that causes the dress to be not fully visible, this approach only gets the visible part of the dress due to object detection. These issues cause significant performance degradation and may ruin a user's shopping experience and leave them completely unsatisfied. To handle this problem, we should be able to generate the image of the dress directly from the image without any unwanted background or noise. That is, when the user provides an image of a person, a new image is produced consisting only of the dress of the person. The extraction should be independent of the posture of the person in the image, background, or any other noise.

Problem Statement: This work focuses on solving addressing above mentioned issues as a bi-phase problem and providing a single pipeline (shown in Fig. 2) that does an end-to-end work for solving this issue of street-to-shop. The proposal consists of two phases:

1. Content-Based Clothes Retrieval(CBCR) - Given an input street query photo with a single person in it, generate an image using a generative network with only the dress of the person worn in the input image.
2. Clothes Matching Network(CMN) - Use the generated image to find a match in the shopping products dataset using a matching convolution network and show the users top k matches.

Table 1. Summary of the work in relevant literature.

Clothes retrieval	Product similarity	Street to shop
Manual semantic attributes annotation, manual effort, dependent on correctness of semantic attributes [11]	Siamese Networks most popular to measure similarity of two images	Retrieving clothes from daily photos and matching similar looking (or identical) products is called Street to Shop
Deep learning models to handle cross-scenario variations, learn distinct features [1,4,5]	Fine-grained object retrieval matching with triplet based ranking loss [6,12]	Align body parts in the street photo with shop photo, works in constrained environment, distorted results in real-life scenarios [8]
Object detection to get dress's bounding box [3,7]	Face matching using triplet loss to train [9]	Use image annotation and a bounding box of the query product, lot of human interference required [3]
Generative Adversarial Nets(GAN) [2] generate clothes from person's picture [14,15]		Bounding box introduces unwanted human parts and background in the picture, contrast to clean shopping product image

Contributions: This paper addresses the Street to Shop problem as a bi-phase problem using deep learning methods. Clothes retrieval is considered the first phase and is approached by attempting to generate a new image of the clothes from the input image. This generation is independent of the human posture or background of the input image. Then, we explore siamese networks to establish similarity between the generated and shopping image. This invloves learning similarity in the clothing domain for the network.

Specific contributions are:

- Creation of a dataset, a shopping dataset that contains clean product images of the front view of the dress without any human part. Additionally, this dataset is classified based on fixed attributes manually. We will make the dataset publically available post-acceptance.
- Transfer learning of a siamese network trained on face dataset to the clothing domain using center loss. To the best of our knowledge, this is the first attempt where a siamese network has been fine-tuned to generate top recommendations of clean product images without any human or mannequin body similar to a query image.
- Exploring the utility of using a generative network for the clothes retrieval phase of the street to shop problem, constructing clean dress images invariant of the human pose, background, dress occlusion, and lighting in the input image.

The remaining paper is organized as: Sect. 2 describes the proposed methodology. Section 3 discuss the experimental analysis and Sect. 4 presents the conclusion and scope of future work.

2   Proposed Methodology

This section covers the detailed description of the methodology proposed in this work. Our methodology is divided into 2 phases, clothes retrieval, and product matching (Fig. 3).

2.1   Phase 1: Content-Based Clothes Retrieval(CBCR)

The first phase requires to generate an image of a dress from a street image containing a person wearing the dress. We propose a network that is invariant of the pose of the person and does not depend on the lighting conditions. It is also able to work if parts of the dress are occluded. The proposed idea is related to generative image models wherein we generate a final result as an image directly from an input image. There are two types of image-generative models, one with generative parametric approaches and one with adversarial approaches. In this work, we have used the adversarial approach. The adversarial approach was proposed by Goodfellow et al. as Generative Adversarial Nets (GAN) [2]. We want to use a GAN that works in the clothes domain and can generate clothes from the provided image. One approach to this is to do a pixel-level domain transfer in the GAN [14] on the clothes domain. We make use of [14] trained on the LookBook dataset. Using the generative network, we produce an image containing only the dress of size $64 \times 64 \times 3$.

The architecture proposed involved in [14] involves a converter network and a discriminator network. The converter is a network consisting of two parts

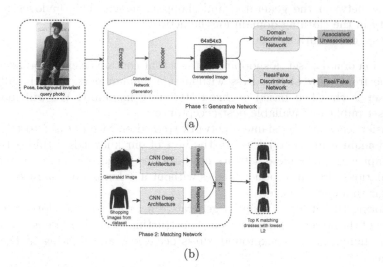

Fig. 3. (a) A generative network that is used generate the clean image of the product the person is wearing. (b) A matching network that matches the generated image with the images from the dataset.

Table 2. Network layers of the {encoder, real/fake discriminator, domain discriminator} of Generative Network [14].

Layers	Filters	Number of filters	Stride	Padding
Convolution 1	$5 \times 5 \times \{3, 3, 6\}$	128	2	2
Convolution 2	$5 \times 5 \times 128$	256	2	2
Convolution 3	$5 \times 5 \times 256$	512	2	2
Output Layer	$1 \times 1 \times 1024$	$\{64, 1, 1\}$	1	0

Table 3. Network layers of the decoder of Generative Network [14].

Layer	Filter	Number of filters	Stride
Convolution 1	$1 \times 1 \times 64$	$4 \times 4 \times 1024$	1
Conv2DTranspose 1	55512	1024	2
Conv2DTranspose 2	55256	512	2
Conv2DTranspose 3	55128	256	2
Conv2DTranspose 4	553	128	2

encoder and decoder. Both the encoder and decoder are composed of convolutional and transpose-convolutional layers, respectively. The encoder condenses the input to a 64-dimension capturing the semantic attributes, and the decoder then constructs the relevant target image from it. Table 2 and Table 3 describes the architectures of the encoder and decoder respectively. In the encoder network, the first four layers have L-ReLU as activation function, while the decoder network uses ReLU as the activation function in the first four layers.

On top of the converter network, it uses two discriminator networks, which behave as an adversary and guide the converter network. The first discriminator network D_R is used to differentiate between fake and real images, fake being the one generated by the converter, and real are the actual dataset images. The second is a domain discriminator D_A, which produces a scalar probability specifying whether the input image and the generated image are associated or not. In case of an unrealistic generated image, the real/fake discriminator backpropagates a loss while in case of a generated image irrelevant to the input, the domain discriminator backpropagates a loss.

The real/fake discriminator loss L_R is a binary cross entropy loss, defined as

$$L_R = -t \cdot log[D_R(I)] + (t - 1) \cdot log[1 - D_R(I)] \tag{1}$$

Here, t is 1 if I (input) is a real image from training set and 0 if I is a fake image drawn by the generator. The domain discriminator loss L_A is also defined similarly

$$L_A = -t \cdot log[D_A(I_S, I)] + (t - 1) \cdot log[1 - D_A(I_S, I)] \tag{2}$$

Here I_S is the source image and t is 1 if I (input) is a ground truth target and 0 if I is a irrelevant target or an inference from converter.

Considering both Eq. 1 and 2, the loss of the converter network L_C is defined as

$$L_C(I_S, I) = -\frac{1}{2}L_R(I) - \frac{1}{2}L_A(I_S, I), \tag{3}$$

where I is a random selection with equal probability among the ground truth, inference and irrelevant target.

2.2 Phase 2: Clothes Matching Network (CMN)

In this phase, we solve the matching problem using deep learning techniques. We use a pre-trained Inception ResNet v1 model [10], trained over face dataset using triplet loss function [9] and do transfer learning on top of it. The pre-trained model is capable of mapping an input image to a 128-d feature space, where each point lies on a unit radius hypersphere centered at the origin. Initially, it is trained to face datasets, but we have to retrain it in order to create a similarity measure for clothes. Hence, we fine-tuned the Inception ResNet v1 of Facenet using the shopping dataset (described in Sect. 3.1) we created. The fine-tuning is done on joint supervision of softmax loss and center loss function [13]. The center loss helps learn a center for the deep features of each class, moving the features of the same class to their centers. Softmax helps enlarge the inter-class difference and the center loss help reduce the intra-class feature distance.

The softmax loss L_S function is defined as,

$$L_S = -\sum_{i=1}^{m} log \frac{(e^{W_{y_i}^T x_i + b_{y_i}})}{\sum_{j=1}^{n} e^{W_j^T x_i + b_j}} \tag{4}$$

In Eq. 4, x_i denotes the ith deep feature from the yth class. W_j is the value of jth column of the weight matrix W of the last layer and b is the bias of that layer. m is the size of mini-batch and n denotes the number of classes.

To minimise intra-class variations of different classes, center loss [13] L_C is defined as,

$$L_C = \frac{1}{2} \sum_{i=1}^{m} ||x_i - c_{y_i}||_2^2 \tag{5}$$

Here, c_{y_i} is the y_i^{th} class center of the deep features. x_i and m are as defined for Eq. 4.

For joint supervision, the softmax loss (4) and center loss (5) are added to form the final loss to train the CNNs, $L = L_S + \lambda L_C$ where λ is a scalar for balancing the two loss functions. The model is fine-tuned for 10 epochs with λ value of 0.95. For extracting the products that are similar to the image generated in phase1, we use a siamese based matching framework. The trained inception-ResNet v1 model is used to create a feature embedding of the generated image. This embedding is then matched with the embeddings of all the images that are present in the dataset by computing $L2$ distance score. The output score for each pair of the input image and the products are sorted, and the top k results are shown as nearest to the input dress.

Justification: We want those products which are of different categories have their deep vectors away from each other. Within a category, we want closer matching among similar dresses and yet be able to differentiate among different designs. Using joint supervision of softmax and center loss over triplet loss helps us achieve distinction between different products within the same category as we could treat each product as a class of its own. Intuitively, the softmax loss forces the deep features of the different products and categories apart, while the center loss pulls the same product images to a common center.

3   Experimental Analysis

For validating the performance of our proposed approach, we have used two datasets. LookBook dataset [14] is used to train the image retrieval module, and the matching network is validated using our in house collected dataset. For validating the matching network, we have computed the precision in retrieving top k similar images.

Blue T-Shirts   Yellow T-Shirts   Bride Dress   Red Sweaters

Fig. 4. Collected shopping dataset examples.

3.1 Datasets Specification

GAN Dataset: For training the image retrieval system, we have utilized the LookBook dataset [14]. There are two categories of images in the dataset, one containing fashion models in different backgrounds and poses in a single dress, and the other is a corresponding product image with a clean background. The dataset consists of 84,748 images with 9,732 product images that are associated with 75,016 model images of the first category. Each model image on an average has eight pictures in different background and pose with the same product.

Shopping Dataset: We make a shopping dataset that contains images of products from the Amazon website. For every product, we take a product image with a clean background that contains the front view of the dress. We use data augmentation to generate eight other pictures of the same product. The products are of varied color and types. There are 326 products in the database. It means there are a total of 2,608 images. Five categories are used to classify the products. The categories are *Blue T-Shirts*, *Red Sweaters*, *Bridal Dress*, *Yellow T-Shirts* and *Others*. *Others* category consists of apparels that do not fall into any of the first four categories. We have used 80% data from all the categories for training the matching network and the rest 20% for testing. Figure 4 shows two examples from each of the categories in our dataset.

3.2 Performance Metrics

We follow ranking based evaluation criteria [8]. For an input image i, we are matching it to all the n images in the *shopping dataset*. The matches are ranked based on the score resulted from the matching network. The product with the lowest score is ranked the highest. We define a binary value $Res(r)$ which is the ground truth category relevance between i and the rth ranked image. Specifically, if the ground truth category of the input image i and the matched image are of the same category, then the Res value is 1. If the categories differ, the Res value takes 0.

We can evaluate a ranking of top k retrieved product images with respect to an input i by precision

$$Precision@k = \frac{\sum_r^k Rel(r)}{N} \tag{6}$$

where N is a normalization constant equal to k. This ensures that the correct ranking results in an precision score of 1.

3.3   Results and Analysis

Table 4. Precision of the system with k varying from 1 to 15.

k	1	2	3	4	5	6	7	8	9	10	11	12	13	14	15
Precision@k	0.846	0.846	0.820	0.811	0.793	0.764	0.742	0.713	0.687	0.667	0.646	0.625	0.608	0.596	0.576

Performance is measured in terms of *Precision@k* as described in Sect. 3.2. Table 4 depicts the result of a precision match with top k products for k values ranging from 1 to 15. Our approach yields a high precision of 0.84 when k is 1 and decreases gradually to 0.793, 0.667, and 0.576 for k values of 5, 10, and 15 respectively.

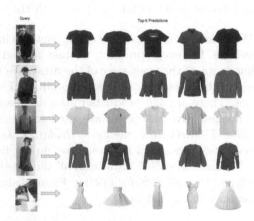

Fig. 5. Top 5 predictions of the framework from 5 sample query images.

Figure 5 shows the output produced by our proposed system. It is evident from the performance that the system works well in real-life scenarios as well, where there are significant challenges. Some of these beings pose variance, background clutter, and illumination variance. Moreover, the matching system can match the clothes on multiple attributes simultaneously. It can capture the type of garment as well as other attributes like color and sleeve length. Even the precision values indicate an excellent performance of the matching system, which is visible in Fig. 5.

However, the system still suffers some failures. Figure 6 shows two typical types of failures. The correct matching depends a lot on whether the required garment is in our database or not. If the garment is not in the database, then the system is not able to produce the correct results. The first failure in Fig. 6 shows one such example.

Fig. 6. Failure cases for the proposed system.

Moreover, since multiple attributes describe a garment, the network sometimes gives importance to some of the attributes than others. In the second failure case, the network can match the type of garment properly that is a half-sleeve t-shirt but is ignoring the color of the shirt. Hence, we need a system in which we could be able to control the priorities of different attributes during search time, also known as attribute matching.

4 Conclusion and Future Work

In this paper, we presented a new methodology to solve the street to shop problem of finding similar dresses to shop from different photo capturing scenarios. We also introduced a new dataset of clean images of dress shopping products on which we evaluated our proposed methodology. We proposed a methodology in two phases. First, using a GAN to generate clean dress images from daily query photos and then using the generated image as an input to a siamese network in the clothes domain for retrieving similar products. Future work involves expanding the collected dataset to more categories and do an attribute-based matching of products. The matching network should also be able to match generated images with clean product images that contain some parts of the human body part.

Acknowledgements. We wish to acknowledge and thank Pratyush Gaurav, Shashwat Garg and Sylvia Mittal, students of Indian Institute of Technology, Mandi for their work and contribution to the initial phases of idea and work.

References

1. Gajic, B., Baldrich, R.: Cross-domain fashion image retrieval. In: Proceedings of the IEEE Conference on Computer Vision and Pattern Recognition Workshops, pp. 1869–1871 (2018)
2. Goodfellow, I., et al.: Generative adversarial nets. In: Advances in Neural Information Processing Systems, pp. 2672–2680 (2014)
3. Hadi Kiapour, M., Han, X., Lazebnik, S., Berg, A.C., Berg, T.L.: Where to buy it: matching street clothing photos in online shops. In: Proceedings of the IEEE International Conference on Computer Vision, pp. 3343–3351 (2015)
4. Huang, J., Feris, R.S., Chen, Q., Yan, S.: Cross-domain image retrieval with a dual attribute-aware ranking network. In: Proceedings of the IEEE International Conference on Computer Vision, pp. 1062–1070 (2015)

5. Jiang, S., Wu, Y., Fu, Y.: Deep bi-directional cross-triplet embedding for cross-domain clothing retrieval. In: Proceedings of the 24th ACM international conference on Multimedia, pp. 52–56. ACM (2016)
6. Lai, H., Pan, Y., Liu, Y., Yan, S.: Simultaneous feature learning and hash coding with deep neural networks. In: Proceedings of the IEEE Conference on Computer Vision and Pattern Recognition, pp. 3270–3278 (2015)
7. Liang, X., Lin, L., Yang, W., Luo, P., Huang, J., Yan, S.: Clothes co-parsing via joint image segmentation and labeling with application to clothing retrieval. IEEE Trans. Multimed. 18(6), 1175–1186 (2016)
8. Liu, S., Song, Z., Liu, G., Xu, C., Lu, H., Yan, S.: Street-to-shop: cross-scenario clothing retrieval via parts alignment and auxiliary set. In: 2012 IEEE Conference on Computer Vision and Pattern Recognition, pp. 3330–3337. IEEE (2012)
9. Schroff, F., Kalenichenko, D., Philbin, J.: FaceNet: a unified embedding for face recognition and clustering. In: Proceedings of the IEEE Conference on Computer Vision and Pattern Recognition, pp. 815–823 (2015)
10. Szegedy, C., et al.: Going deeper with convolutions. In: Proceedings of the IEEE Conference on Computer Vision and Pattern Recognition, pp. 1–9 (2015)
11. Wan, J., et al.: Deep learning for content-based image retrieval: a comprehensive study. In: Proceedings of the 22nd ACM International Conference on Multimedia, pp. 157–166. ACM (2014)
12. Wang, J., et al.: Learning fine-grained image similarity with deep ranking. In: Proceedings of the IEEE Conference on Computer Vision and Pattern Recognition, pp. 1386–1393 (2014)
13. Wen, Y., Zhang, K., Li, Z., Qiao, Y.: A discriminative feature learning approach for deep face recognition. In: Leibe, B., Matas, J., Sebe, N., Welling, M. (eds.) ECCV 2016. LNCS, vol. 9911, pp. 499–515. Springer, Cham (2016). https://doi.org/10.1007/978-3-319-46478-7_31
14. Yoo, D., Kim, N., Park, S., Paek, A.S., Kweon, I.S.: Pixel-level domain transfer. In: Leibe, B., Matas, J., Sebe, N., Welling, M. (eds.) ECCV 2016. LNCS, vol. 9912, pp. 517–532. Springer, Cham (2016). https://doi.org/10.1007/978-3-319-46484-8_31
15. Zhang, S., Liu, S., Cao, X., Song, Z., Zhou, J.: Watch fashion shows to tell clothing attributes. Neurocomputing 282, 98–110 (2018)

Unsupervised Domain Adaptation for Remote Sensing Images Using Metric Learning and Correlation Alignment

Aniruddha Mahapatra[1](✉) and Biplab Banerjee[2]

[1] Indian Institute of Technology, Roorkee, India
amahapatra@cs.iitr.ac.in
[2] Indian Institute of Technology Bombay, Mumbai, India
bbanerjee@iitb.ac.in

Abstract. We address the problem of domain adaptation (DA) in the context of remote sensing (RS) image classification in this paper. By definition, the problem of unsupervised DA aims at classifying samples from a *target* domain which is strictly devoid of any label information while assuming that enough training data are available from a related yet non-identical (in terms of data distributions) *source* domain. A number of existing approaches in this regard are focused towards matching the underlying distributions of the data from both the domains in a shared latent space without explicitly considering: i) the discriminativeness of the embedding space, ii) the usefulness of a manifold distance is pulling the domains towards each other over the standard Euclidean measures. However, we argue the importance of both the aspects in learning the latent space, particularly for fine-grained classes. Our model jointly optimizes both the terms in an end-to-end fashion and the learned latent space is found to properly align the classes with high precision. Experimental results obtained on a hyper-spectral and a multi-spectral dataset confirm the superior performance of the approach over a number of techniques from the literature.

Keywords: Domain adaptation · Metric learning · Representation learning · Remote sensing.

1 Introduction

Remote sensing (RS) image analysis [1] is currently considered an active field of research, thanks to the ample amount of data acquired by a wide range of satellite-onboard sensors periodically. However many of the machine learning algorithms (predominantly supervised methods), that work on RS images inherently assume that the training and test samples are drawn from similar underlying distributions, which is often violated in analyzing multi-temporal RS images where the land-cover properties change due to seasonal effects, presence of cloud

© Springer Nature Singapore Pte Ltd. 2020
R. V. Babu et al. (Eds.): NCVPRIPG 2019, CCIS 1249, pp. 133–142, 2020.
https://doi.org/10.1007/978-981-15-8697-2_12

covers during the imaging process (considering passive sensors for data acquisition), man-made changes on ground, from one image to another.

Generation of training samples, in general, is a costly and time-consuming process and the challenges proportionately grow for the case of multi-temporal RS image sequences with many images. However considering that the labeled samples are available for some of the images in the sequence, the problem can now be formulated to classifying the images with no prior label information by judicious knowledge transfer from the images with available training data. Domain Adaptation (DA) [3] is a popular inductive transfer learning approach to handle such a critical classification framework.

DA techniques are used to build a classifier taking into consideration the mismatch in the distributions governing the training and test data. The training domain is generally termed as the *source* domain which is accumulated with an ample amount of labeled data (images with training samples) while the test domain is termed as the *target* domain. Note that the target domain may or may not contain any label information, based on which DA can further be classified as semi-supervised or unsupervised DA, respectively. Our focus is on the challenging unsupervised DA setup which tries to compensate for the degradation in classification performance by transferring knowledge from the labeled source domain to the unlabeled target domain.

Historically, machine learning literature is rich in DA techniques. There have been several endeavors towards feature adaptation (making the source and target features overlapping in some latent space) and classifier adaptation (making the classifier trained on the source domain samples to gradually adapt to the target domain properties). However, the classifier adaptation based techniques seldom suffer from the problem of *source forgetting* since the classifier iteratively finds its bias towards the target domain. The feature adaptation based approaches are resilient to such bottlenecks and have shown better performance in diverse scenarios including image, speech, text, to name a few.

Amongst the feature adaptation based approaches, the current trend to overcome the problem of domain mismatch by mapping the cross-domain samples on a shared subspace using deep neural network-based modules which make the entire process data-driven. This is generally achieved by minimizing some measure of domain variance, like the Maximum Mean Discrepancy (MMD) [7]. Likewise, a recently proposed Deep CORAL method [5] aligns second-order statistics of the source and the target distribution by constructing a differentiable loss function that minimizes the difference between the source and target correlations which the authors termed as the CORAL loss. However, to the best of our knowledge, the majority of such methods do not consider the discriminativeness of the learned embedding space, which nonetheless causes misclassification for fine-grained classes. Hence, the notion of learning a discriminative subspace is of prime interest for improved cross-domain classification.

Contributions: Inspired from the aforementioned discussions, we prose an end-to-end trainable neural network-based unsupervised DA module that learns a shared embedding space for the samples of both the domains which are also deemed to be discriminative. In particular, while a contrastive loss measure [6] is considered on the latent source domain labeled samples which is responsible to make the latent representations compact class-wise, simultaneously the domain difference is reduced in terms of minimizing the difference of the between-domain higher-order statistics. Experimental results obtained on two benchmark RS datasets showcase the superiority of the proposed DA module over several standard approaches.

2   Related Work

Unsupervised DA techniques are extensively applied in handling multi-temporal RS images on the ground captured at different time instances. Ad-hoc approaches for unsupervised DA usually consist of matching the feature distribution between the source and target domain [10,11] by exploring standard distance measures between distributions. These methods can generally be divided into two categories: (i) sample re-weighting [12,13] and (ii) feature space transformation [15,16], respectively. Besides, techniques based on metric learning [19], subspace alignment [20] and nonlinear transformation based on graph node matching [21] are explored in conjunction with different cross-domain RS images.

On the other hand, adaptive deep neural networks have recently been explored for unsupervised DA for image classification. For example, DLID [22] trains a joint source and target CNN architecture with two adaptation layers. Similarly, DDC [23] applies a single linear kernel to one layer to minimize the Maximum Mean Discrepancy (MMD). Deep CORAL applies CORAL loss to minimize the difference in learned feature covariances across source and target domain. Deep LogCORAL similar to the Deep CORAL method, proposes to use the Riemann distance, approximated by Log-Euclidean distance to replace the naive Euclidean distance in Deep CORAL.

We propose a metric learning-based approach that minimizes the feature covariances of the source and the target domain (using CORAL and LogCORAL losses separately) and at the same time form better clustering of similar images by Contrastive loss on labeled source data for better fine-grained classification of multi-temporal RS images.

3   Method

We consider the unsupervised DA situation where there are no labels associated with the target domain data distribution. Since the RS image data can be very challenging, like the Botswana dataset, with overlapping classes and very small feature vector for each image, we first try to learn a similarity-based classifier to obtain good clustering of data based on their respective classes to avoid overlap. For the second goal of reducing covariance between the source and target domain, we propose to minimize the difference in second-order statistics between the source and target feature activations, i.e. the CORAL/logCORAL loss. Figure 1 shows a sample architecture of our proposed model. The two losses are trained end-to-end.

This approach is based on the assumption that minimizing the difference between the second-order statics would bring the target domain to overlap with the source domain. Since cross-domain data point is inherently closer to their respective classes than of different classes of different domains, similarity-based learning on the source domain data would also make nice clusterings for target domain data points in the domain invariant feature space. Joint training with both the losses is likely to learn features that work well on the target domain:

$$L_{Total} = KL_{Source} + \lambda(1 - K)L_{CrossDomain} \tag{1}$$

where covariance loss denotes CORAL or logCORAL loss, $K = 1$ if pairs are from the same domain, $K = 0$ if pairs are from a different domain. λ is a trade off between domain adaptation and clustering accuracy on the source domain.

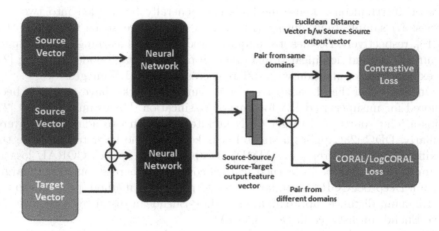

Fig. 1. Sample structure of our model. We determine whether the inputs are from same domain or not using the similarity labels of pair. If the input pairs are both from source domain, then we compute the Source Loss based on their class labels. Otherwise if one vector from source and other from target domain, we compute the Cross-Domain Loss.

3.1   Source Loss

For the purpose of finding a function that maps input patterns to the domain invariant space based on neighborhood relationship between samples, we use Contrastive Loss. The basis of the creation of clusters are the class labels of source domain data inputs. This loss function works on pairs of samples. Let $X_1, X_2 \in \mathbb{I}$ be a pair of input source domain vectors. Let Y be a binary label assigned to this pair. $Y = 0$ if X_1 and X_2 are deemed similar, and $Y = 1$ if they are deemed dissimilar. Define the parameterized distance function to be learned

D_W between $\boldsymbol{X_1}$ and $\boldsymbol{X_2}$ as the Euclidean distance between the outputs of G_W, where G_W is the output values of $\boldsymbol{X_1}$ and $\boldsymbol{X_2}$ from the network. That is,

$$D_W(\boldsymbol{X_1}, \boldsymbol{X_2}) = \|G_W(\boldsymbol{X_1}) - G_W(\boldsymbol{X_2})\| \qquad (2)$$

To shorten notation, $D_W(\boldsymbol{X_1}, \boldsymbol{X_2})$ is written D_W. Then the loss function in its most general form is:

$$\kappa(W) = \sum_{i=1}^{P} L(W, (Y, \boldsymbol{X_1}, \boldsymbol{X_2})^i) \qquad (3)$$

$$L(W, (Y, \boldsymbol{X_1}, \boldsymbol{X_2})^i = (1 - Y)L_S(D_W^i) + Y \max(0, m - L_D(D_W^i)) \qquad (4)$$

where $(Y, \boldsymbol{X_1}, \boldsymbol{X_2})^i$ is the ith labeled sample pair, L_S is the partial loss function for a pair of similar points, L_D is the partial loss function for a pair of dissimilar points, and P the number of training pairs (which may be as large as the square of the number of samples). m is the margin for dissimilar sample pair. The value of m for this experiment was taken as 1.0.

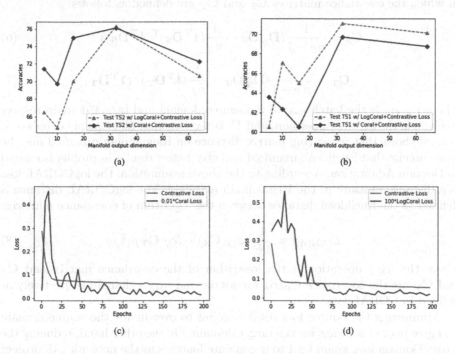

(a)   (b)

(c)   (d)

Fig. 2. Accuracy of model (a) Trained on TR1 (source) and TR2 (target) and Test on TS2, (b) Trained on TR2 (source) and TR1 (target) and Test on TS1 for different manifold output dimensions. (c) The loss curve for Contrastive and CORAL Loss, (d) Contrastive and LogCORAL Loss trained on TR2 (source) and TR1 (target) and test on TS1.

3.2 Cross-Domain Loss

Let us denote $\mathbf{D_S} = [\mathbf{x_1}, ..., \mathbf{x_{n_s}}]$ as the source domain features extracted from the last layer of the model as shown in the Fig. 1, where $\mathbf{x_i}$ is the ith source sample, and $\mathbf{D_T} = [\mathbf{u_1}, ..., \mathbf{u_{n_T}}]$ as the unlabeled target domain feature extracted from the final layer, where $\mathbf{u_i}$ is the ith training sample. To overlap the target source domain features with their corresponding source domain features, we try to reduce the covariance between them. For this purpose, we found that the most appropriate loss metrics to be CORAL and logCORAL loss and trained our model on them separately to compare performance.

CORAL loss [5] calculates the distance of second-order statics between the two domains. The covariance matrix of features is calculated from the output of the final layer for each domain which then minimizes the Euclidean distance of the covariance matrices of two domains. The CORAL loss is defined as follows:

$$L_{CORAL} = \frac{1}{4d^2}||\mathbf{C_S} - \mathbf{C_T}||^2 \tag{5}$$

in which the covariance matrices $\mathbf{C_S}$ and $\mathbf{C_T}$ are defined as follows:

$$\mathbf{C_S} = \frac{1}{n_S - 1}(\mathbf{D_S^T D_S} - \frac{1}{n_S}(\mathbf{1^T D_S})^T(\mathbf{1^T D_S})) \tag{6}$$

$$\mathbf{C_T} = \frac{1}{n_T - 1}(\mathbf{D_T^T D_T} - \frac{1}{n_T}(\mathbf{1^T D_T})^T(\mathbf{1^T D_T})) \tag{7}$$

where n_S, n_T is the batch size of the source domain and target domain respectively. d is the feature dimension, and 1^T is a vector that all elements equals to 1.

[28] shows that measuring matrix distance on Riemannian manifold may be more precise that Euclidean manifold and give better results in problems related to Domain Adaptation. According to the above assumption, the logCORAL loss is a distance measure in the Riemannian manifold. The logCORAL distance is defined as the Euclidean distance between the logarithm of covariance matrices:

$$L_{CORAL} = \frac{1}{4d^2}||log(\mathbf{C_S}) - log(\mathbf{C_T})||^2 \tag{8}$$

where the $log()$ operation is the logarithm of the covariance matrix and $\mathbf{C_S}$ and $\mathbf{C_T}$ are the covariance matrix for source and target domain respectively as defined in CORAL loss.

Minimizing the Source loss itself is going to over-fit for the source domain and give poor clusterings for the target domain. On the other hand, reducing the Cross-Domain loss would lead to degenerate features as the network will project all the source and target data to a single point leading to zero Cross-Domain loss. Jointly training the network on Cross-Domain loss with Source loss will make the network learn the desirable domain invariant mapping into feature space. We show that these two losses play counterparts and reach an equilibrium at the end of the training, where the final features are expected to work well on the target domain.

Table 1. Performance comparison with baseline models in domain adaptation. The first column gives test accuracy on TS2 with training on TR1 (source) + TR2 (target) while, second column gives test accuracy on TS1 with training on TR2 (source) + TR1 (target). The second last model uses CORAL w/ CONTRASTIVE Loss. The last model achieves state of the art result LogCORAL w/ CONTRASTIVE Loss.

Model	TR1 → TS2	TR2 → TS1
TCA	69.88	61.00
GFK	72.89	65.50
CORAL	54.54	47.36
SA	72.88	68.52
STK	75.28	70.20
BDA	62.52	50.72
Auto-encoder	67.46	62.69
Our (CORAL)	76.08	69.73
Our (LogCORAL)	**76.24**	**71.09**

4 Experiment

4.1 Dataset

We validate the proposed framework on commonly available but challenging Botswana hyper-spectral dataset acquired by the Hyperion sensor of the EO-1 satellite over a 1476 256 pixel study area located in the Okavango Delta, Botswana. 10 bands among the set of 145 bands are selected based on their discrimination capability using the method mentioned in [29]. Here, 14 land-cover classes are identified for two different spatially disjoint areas. There are a total of 4 sets in this data (2 for each domain). TR1 (train) and TS1 (test) for one domain and TR2 (train) and TS2 (test) for the second domain. We use all the labeled source data and all the target unlabeled data.

The second dataset contains two scenes acquired by the ROSIS sensor during a flight campaign over Pavia, northern Italy. The number of spectral bands is 102 for Pavia Centre and 103 for Pavia University. To make both of them of equal dimension, we use PCA to reduce the number of dimensions to 50. The geometric resolution is 1.3 m. Both image ground-truths differentiate 9 classes each out of which we use 7 classes common to both.

4.2 Model Specifications

In this experiment, we apply the Source loss and Cross-Domain loss from the features extracted from the last layer ($fc3$) of the model. In training for both losses, we set the batch size to 32, the learning rate to 10^{-3}, weight decay to 0. We train a small 3-layer fully-connected neural network on the features extracted from $fc3$ for source domain for classification purpose (Table 2).

Table 2. Performance comparison with our models with Auto-Encoder in domain adaptation. The first column gives test accuracy on PaviaU with training on PaviaCentre while, second column gives test accuracy on PaviaCentre with training on PaviaU. The second last model uses CORAL and CONTRASTIVE Loss. The last model achieves state of the art result LogCORAL w/ CONTRASTIVE Loss.

Model	PaviaC → PaviaU	PaviaU → PaviaC
Auto-Encoder	46.14	46.64
D-CORAL	47.72	45.86
D-LogCORAL	**47.81**	**56.32**

4.3 Choosing $fc3$ (final) Layer Dimension

To decide what is the optimal dimension of the $fc3$ layer for the Botswana and Pavia dataset, we train different networks with output dimension sizes of 5, 10, 16, 32 and 64. Based on the accuracies from the classifier applied to the output of $fc3$ for the domain shifts on both datasets, we get the maximum accuracy for the $fc3$ layer with dimension 32. In Fig. 2(a) and 2(b) we have plotted the accuracies from different output layer dimensions for the Botswana dataset.

4.4 Performance Between CORAL and LogCORAL Loss

We try using CORAL and logCORAL loss separately for reducing covariance across domains. From accuracy results, we find that logCORAL loss outperforms CORAL loss by a narrow margin of around 0.2%−0.3% (source TR2, target TR1, test TS1: CORAL accuracy-69.73%, logCORAL accuracy-71.09% and source TR1, target TR2, test TS2: CORAL accuracy-76.08%, logCORAL accuracy-76.24%) for Botswana Dataset and relatively a large margin of 9% on Pavia Dataset (source PaviaU, target PaviaC: CORAL accuracy-47.81%, logCORAL accuracy-56.32%).

4.5 Comparison with Popular da Techniques

We compare the generalization performance of the proposed framework with that of six popular and diverse unsupervised DA techniques from the literature as follows:

a) TCA [9]
b) Subspace alignment (SA) based DA [14]
c) GFK-based subspace projection [35]
d) CORAL with SVM
e) STL
f) BDA

GFK, SA, and TCA are manifold based methods that project the source and target distributions into a lower-dimensional manifold and are not end-to-end deep methods. In all the cases, we first project the data in the embedding space and further design a multiclass SVM classifier (with RBF kernel) in the new space exploiting the projected source domain training samples. The classifier is further evaluated on the projected target domain test samples. From Table 1 we see that our model achieves better performance for both domain shifts than the 6 baseline methods with a relative margin of 1–2%. We can see that even though Cross-Domain loss is not always decreasing, it gets to a relatively stable state after a few epochs.

5   Conclusion

In this paper, we propose a novel neural network architecture for unsupervised domain adaptation. We show that semantic similarity learning with the reduction in covariance between the source and target dataset can outperform the 'standard' convolution neural network in the domain adaptation problem. The method is feasible and simple. We demonstrate that this model achieves state-of-the-art performance on the Botswana dataset. Future works include using a similarity learning that adaptively assesses similarity based on distribution on representation space rather than penalizing individual pairs based on the notion of labels and with different domain discrepancy reduction algorithms (such as MMD and its variants). It will also be of interest to determine how this model performs on very high-resolution satellite images.

References

1. J. A. Richards and J. Richards, Remote Sensing Digital Image Analysis. Springer, Heidelberg (2013). https://doi.org/10.1007/978-3-642-30062-2_9
2. Donahue, J., Jia, Y., Vinyals, O., Hoffman, J., Zhang, N., Tzeng, E., Darrell, T.: Decaf: A deep convolutional activation feature for generic visual recognition. ICML, 2014
3. Patel, V.M., Gopalan, R., Li, R., Chellappa, R.: Visual domain adaptation: A survey of recent advances. IEEE Signal Process. Mag. **32**(3), 53–69 (2015)
4. A. Torralba and A. A. Efros. Unbiased look at dataset bias. In CVPR, 2011
5. Sun, Baochen, Saenko, Kate: Deep CORAL: Correlation Alignment for Deep Domain Adaptation. In: Hua, Gang, Jégou, Hervé (eds.) ECCV 2016. LNCS, vol. 9915, pp. 443–450. Springer, Cham (2016). https://doi.org/10.1007/978-3-319-49409-8_35
6. R. Hadsell, S. Chopra, and Y. LeCun. Dimensionality reduction by learning an invariant mapping. In CVPR, 2006
7. A. Gretton, K. Borgwardt, M. Rasch, B. Scholkopf, and A. Smola. A kernel two-sample test. JMLR, 2012
8. M. Long, H. Zhu, J. Wang, and M. I. Jordan. Deep transfer learning with joint adaptation networks. In ICML, 2017
9. Wang, Yifei, Li, Wen, Dai, Dengxin, Van Gool, Luc: Deep Domain Adaptation by Geodesic Distance Minimization. ICCV 2651–2657 (2017)

10. A. Gretton, A. Smola, J. Huang, M. Schmittfull, K. Borgwardt, and B. Scholkopf. Covariate shift and local learning by distribution matching. 2009
11. G. Csurka. A comprehensive survey on domain adaptation for visual applications. In Domain Adaptation in Computer Vision Applications. 2017
12. J. Jiang and C. Zhai. Instance weighting for domain adaptation in nlp. In ACL, 2007
13. J. Huang, A. Gretton, K. M. Borgwardt, P. B. Scholkopf, and A. J. Smola. Correcting sample selection bias by unlabelled data. In NIPS, 2007
14. B. Gong, K. Grauman, and F. Sha. Connecting the dots with landmarks: Discriminatively learning domain-invariant features for unsupervised domain adaptation. In ICML, 2013
15. S. J. Pan, I. W. Tsang, J. T. Kwok, and Q. Yang. Domain adaptation via transfer component analysis. Transactions on Neural Networks. 2017
16. R. Gopalan, R. Li, and R. Chellappa. Domain adaptation for object recognition: An unsupervised approach. In ICCV, 2011
17. M. Baktashmotlagh, M. T. Harandi, B. C. Lovell, and M. Salzmann. Unsupervised domain adaptation by domain invariant projection. In ICCV, 2013
18. B. Sun, J. Feng, and K. Saenko. Return of frustratingly easy domain adaptation. In AAAI, 2016
19. Geng, B., Tao, D., Xu, C.: DAML: Domain adaptation metric learning. IEEE Trans. Image Process. **20**(10), 2980–2989 (2011)
20. B. Fernando, A. Habrard, M. Sebban, and T. Tuytelaars. Unsupervised visual domain adaptation using subspace alignment. in Proc. IEEE Int. Conf. Comput. Vis., 2013
21. D. Tuia, J. Munoz-Mari, L. Gomez-Chova, and J. Malo. Graph matching for adaptation in remote sensing. IEEE Trans. Geosci. Remote Sens., vol. 51, no. 1, 2013
22. Chopra, S., Balakrishnan, S., Gopalan, R.: Dlid: Deep learning for domain adaptation by interpolating between domains. In: ICML Workshop, 2013
23. Tzeng, E., Hoffman, J., Zhang, N., Saenko, K., Darrell, T.: Deep domain confusion: Maximizing for domain invariance. 2014
24. O. Rippel, M. Paluri, P. Dollr, and L. D. Bourdev. Metric learning with adaptive density discrimination. In ICLR, 2015
25. R. Salakhutdinov and G. E. Hinton. Learning a nonlinear embedding by preserving class neighborhood structure. In AISTSTS, 2017
26. F. Siyahjani, R. Almohsen, S. Sabri, and G. Doretto. A supervised low-rank method for learning invariant subspaces. In ICCV, 2015
27. Pedro, O.: Pinheiro. Unsupervised Domain Adaptation with Similarity Learning, In CVPR (2017)
28. Z. Huang and L. Van Gool. A riemannian network for spd matrix learning. 2016
29. Bruzzone, L., Persello, C.: A novel approach to the selection of spatially invariant features for the classification of hyperspectral images with improved generalization capability. IEEE Trans. Geosci. Remote Sens. **47**(9), 3180–3191 (2009)
30. Pan, S.J., Tsang, I.W., Kwok, J.T., Yang, Q.: Domain adaptation via transfer component analysis. IEEE Trans. Neural Netw. **22**(2), 199–210 (2011)
31. B. Fernando, A. Habrard, M. Sebban, and T. Tuytelaars. Unsupervised visual domain adaptation using subspace alignment. In Proc. IEEE Int. Conf. Comput. Vis., 2013, pp. 2960–2967
32. B. Gong, Y. Shi, F. Sha, and K. Grauman. Geodesic flow kernel for unsupervised domain adaptation. In Proc. IEEE Conf. Comput. Vis. Pattern Recognit., 2012, pp. 2066–2073

Computationally Efficient Super-Resolution Approach for Real-World Images

Vishal Chudasama[1], Kalpesh Prajapati[1], and Kishor Upla[1,2(✉)]

[1] Sardar Vallabhbhai National Institute of Technology, Surat, India
[2] Norwegian University of Science and Technology (NTNU), Gjøvik, Norway
kishorupla@gmail.com

Abstract. Most of the existing single image super-resolution (SISR) methods are trained and evaluated on synthetic datasets in which the low-resolution (LR) images are synthesized with simple and uniform bicubic degradation. Those methods perform better on a synthesized testing dataset but fail to obtain better super-resolution (SR) results on real-world images. However, by stacking more convolution layer, the SR performance can be improved. But, such techniques increase the number of training parameters and hence offer heavy computational burden on resources which make them unsuitable for real-world applications. To solve this problem, we propose a computationally efficient SR approach called real-world super-resolution network (RSRN) to super-resolve the real-world images. In RSRN, we propose a novel residual block called densely connected parallel residual block (DPRB) which helps to extract more complex features of LR observations. To prove the effectiveness of the proposed RSRN method, we train the proposed model on real-world images as well as on synthetic dataset. We compare the SR performance of the proposed method with that of other existing SISR methods and observe that the proposed RSRN method obtains better SR performance with more high-frequency details than that of the recently proposed state-of-the-art SISR methods with significantly less number of training parameters.

Keywords: Super-resolution · Real-world image · Convolutional neural network · Densely connected parallel residual blocks

1 Introduction

SISR is one of the low-level computer vision tasks which can be applied in different fields such as medical imaging, surveillance and satellite imaging. The main idea behind the SISR task is to reconstruct the HR image from its corresponding LR counterpart. Recently, convolution neural network (CNN) have obtained improvements in SISR by designing new CNN architectures and loss functions [4,5,10–12,14,18,19]. These SISR methods are trained and evaluated

© Springer Nature Singapore Pte Ltd. 2020
R. V. Babu et al. (Eds.): NCVPRIPG 2019, CCIS 1249, pp. 143–153, 2020.
https://doi.org/10.1007/978-981-15-8697-2_13

(a) Bicubic   (b) RSRN(DF2K)   (c) RSRN(RealSR)   (d) Ground Truth
(24.8849 / 0.7852)   (27.3213 / 0.8335)   (29.3913 / 0.8810)

Fig. 1. The SR results of a single image of RealSR testing dataset [2]: (a) Bicubic (b) RSRN (trained on DF2K dataset), (c) RSRN (trained on RealSR dataset) and (d) Ground Truth. The corresponding PSNR and SSIM measures are mentioned in bracket along with SR result. (Zoomed-in for better visual.)

on simulated datasets in which the downsampled LR observations are prepared by applying known bicubic degradation. However, the SISR methods trained on such simulated datasets do not perform well in the case of real-world LR images where the degradations are blind. In Fig. 1(b), we display the SR results of real-world image obtained using the proposed method (named as RSRN) trained on a simulated dataset. In this result, one can observe that there are more degradations observed in the SR result.

Generally, there are three different low-level vision tasks named as image deblurring, image denoising and image super-resolution take place for SISR in real-world scenarios. Hence, it is a very complicated task to reconstruct HR image from real-world LR image. However, better SR results can be obtained by stacking more convolutional layers which increases the number of training parameters. But, such methods offer heavy burden on computational resources and hence they are not suitable for real-world applications. To do this, now-a-days in computer vision community, it is active research to propose an SR method which obtains better SR results with less number of training parameters.

In this paper, we propose a computationally efficient SR model called RSRN for real-world single image super-resolution for upscaling factor ×4. In order to learn different degradations of real-world images, we also train the proposed method, RSRN on RealSR training dataset [2] which consists of real-world HR-LR image pairs of the same scene produced by adjusting the focal length of a digital camera. The SR result of the proposed method RSRN trained using RealSR dataset is displayed in Fig. 1(c) where one can observe that the SR result has very low degradations and also it is close to ground truth image. The main contributions in this paper are as follow:

– We propose a new computationally efficient SR approach called RSRN which is capable to super-resolve the real-world LR images.
– In RSRN, we propose a novel residual network called densely connected parallel residual block (DPRB) inspired from Inception [3] and DenseNet [7] modules. This DPRB helps to learn more complex features of LR observations.

The rest of the paper is organized as follows. We discuss the brief review of different CNN based SISR methods in Sect. 2. In Sect. 3, the architecture design of the proposed method is discussed. We conduct experiments and its result analysis is discussed in Sect. 4. Finally, in Sect. 5, we conclude our work.

2   Related Work

Due to the availability of larger datasets and high power GPUs, deep learning based SISR methods obtains superior performance over traditional SISR methods. A detailed review of these methods has been investigated and discussed in [17]. A SRCNN was the first SISR method using deep learning proposed by Dong et al. [4]. After that many methods have been proposed in order to improve the SR performance such as VDSR [8], DRCN [9], SRResNet [10], EDSR [12], SRFeat$_M$ [14], MSRN [11], DBPN [5], RDN [19], RCAN [18]. The recently proposed EDSR [12], RDN [19] and RCAN [18] methods obtain better PSNR and SSIM measures among all other methods but they obtain their performance with the cost of large number of training parameters. Hence, these methods offer heavy burden on computational resources which make them unsuitable for real-world applications. However, the proposed RSRN model offers less number of training parameters (i.e., approximately 60–80% less training parameters than EDSR, RDN and RCAN models).

All the above SISR methods are trained on simulated training dataset where the LR images are synthesized by a simple and uniform bicubic degradation function. Such SISR methods may exhibit poor performance on real-world LR images where the degradation functions are unknown. Recently, Cai et al. [2] release a new benchmark dataset called RealSR which consists of HR-LR images of the same scenes captured by adjusting the focal length of a digital camera. They proposed a network named laplacian pyramid based kernel prediction network (LP-KPN) to recover the real-world HR images [2]. Inspired from this work, here we obtain the SR of real-world LR images.

3   Methodology

In this section, we discuss the overall network architecture of the proposed model for super-resolution of real-world images for upscaling factor ×4 which is illustrated in Fig. 2. Here, the network takes LR image (I_{LR}) as input and generates the corresponding SR image as output. The I_{LR} is first passed through a convolution layer which extracts the low-level features from the LR observation as

$$I_0 = F_0(I_{LR}), \tag{1}$$

where, F_0 is the convolution function which extracts the 64 number of feature maps from input I_{LR} observation. Here, I_0 is the extracted low-level features which are further passed through the feature extraction module in order to learn more complex abstract level features from the low-level feature informations.

$$I_1 = FEM(I_0), \tag{2}$$

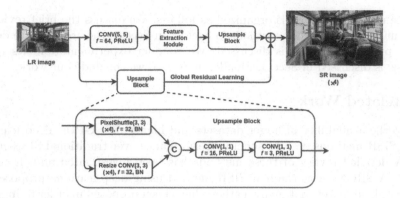

Fig. 2. The network architecture of the proposed RSRN model. Here, f indicates the number of feature maps.

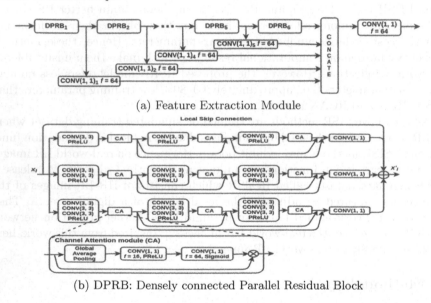

(a) Feature Extraction Module

(b) DPRB: Densely connected Parallel Residual Block

Fig. 3. The network design of (a) Feature extraction module and (b) DPRB: Densely connected parallel residual block.

where, FEM denotes the feature extraction module function. The design of feature extraction module is displayed in Fig. 3(a) which consists of 6 residual blocks. Inspired from Inception [3] and DenseNet [7] modules, we propose a novel residual block called densely connected parallel residual block (DPRB) in order to extract more complex features. The architecture design of DPRB is displayed in Fig. 3(b) which consists of several densely connected convolutional blocks in three parallel stacks. Each convolution block consists of convolution layers, a parametric ReLU (PReLU) [6] activation function and one channel attention (CA) module. The CA module (i.e., same module as described in RCAN [18] method) is used to adaptively re-scale the channel-wise feature maps by considering interdependencies between channels [18]. Here, we also adopt the local skip connection which helps the network to avoid vanishing as well as exploding gradient problem.

As shown in Fig. 3(a), the output of all DPRBs are concatenated via one convolution layer except the last DPRB and then the concatenated feature maps are passed through one convolution layer which is used to convert the concatenated feature maps to the desired number of feature maps. The output of the feature extraction module is passed through the upsample block which upsamples the feature maps to the desired level (see Fig. 2) which is represented as,

$$I_2 = F_{UP}(I_1). \tag{3}$$

Here, F_{UP} is the upsample block. We propose a new upsample approach with upscaling factor $\times 4$ as illustrated in Fig. 2 which consists of two different upsampling modules (i.e., one pixel-shuffle [15] and other resize convolution [13]) connected parallelly and then the output feature maps of both upsampling modules are concatenated and passed through two convolution layers.

Additionally, we also adopt the global residual learning (GRL) as suggested in VDSR [8] method where the input image and the output residual image are connected via global skip connection. Instead of using bicubic interpolation layer in GRL to maintain the size of input and output images, we use the proposed upsample block with upscaling factor $\times 4$ in GRL network. Such GRL helps the network to learn the identity function of input I_{LR}. GRL also stabilize the training process and reduce the color shifts in the output image. Finally, the output SR image (I_{SR}) is generated for upscaled factor $\times 4$ as,

$$I_{SR} = I_2 + F_{GRL}(I_{LR}), \tag{4}$$

where, F_{GRL} denotes the function of the proposed GRL network.

4   Result Analysis

In this section, we discuss the implementation details of the proposed RSRN model and present the analysis of the SR results obtained using the proposed along with the other state-of-the-art CNN based SR methods for upscaling factor of $\times 4$.

4.1   Training Details

We tested our proposed model on the five different testing benchmark datasets: Set5, Set14, BSD100, Urban100 and RealSR [2]. Here, we compare the SR performance of the proposed model RSRN with only those methods which have

Table 1. The quantitative comparison in terms of PSNR and SSIM measures for upscaling factor ×4. Here, the highest and second-highest values are mentioned with red and blue color fonts, respectively.

Methods	PSNR / SSIM			
	Set5	Set14	BSD100	Urban100
SRCNN [4]	30.48/0.7503	27.49/0.7503	26.90/0.7101	24.52/0.7221
VDSR [8]	31.35/0.8838	28.02/0.7678	27.29/0.7252	25.18/0.7525
DRCN [9]	31.53/0.8854	28.03/0.7673	27.24/0.7233	25.14/0.7511
SRResNet [10]	32.05/0.8910	28.53/0.7804	27.57/0.7354	26.07/0.7839
MSRN [11]	32.26/0.8960	28.63/0.7836	27.61/0.7380	26.22/0.7911
SRFeat$_M$ [14]	32.29/0.8957	28.72/0.7834	27.65/0.7371	26.26/0.7891
DBPN [5]	32.42/0.8975	28.75/0.7858	27.67/0.7389	26.38/0.7930
RSRN	32.40/0.8976	28.75/0.7856	27.65/0.7396	26.39/0.7959

less than 7M training parameters (except DBPN whose network has 10M number of training parameters). The SR results of these methods are obtained from the online available supplementary materials such as SRCNN [4][1], VDSR [8][2], DRCN [9][3], SRResNet [10][4], SRFeat$_M$ [14][5], MSRN [11][6] and DBPN [5][7]. In order to observe the effectiveness on real-world images, we reproduce the SR results of SRResNet [10] and SRFeat$_M$ [14] by training on RealSR dataset.

The PSNR and SSIM are used as metrics for quantitative comparison which are calculated after removing the boundary pixels of Y-channel images in YCbCr color space. We train the proposed model on two different datasets for different applications. In case of bicubic downsampled observations, the proposed model RSRN is trained on DF2K dataset (which is a combination of DIV2K [1] and Flickr2k [16] datasets) upto 10^6 number of iterations. While for real-world super-resolution, we train RSRN model on RealSR training dataset [2] upto 5×10^4 number of iterations. In both cases, the proposed model RSRN is trained using L_1 loss function and optimized it with Adam optimizer with an initial learning rate of 10^{-4}.

4.2 SR Results on Synthetic Data

Here, we discuss the quantitative and qualitative SR performance of the proposed and other state-of-the-art SR methods trained on a synthetic dataset. Table 1 shows the quantitative comparison in terms of PSNR and SSIM values obtained

---

[1] https://github.com/jbhuang0604/SelfExSR.

[2] http://cv.snu.ac.kr/research/VDSR/.

[3] http://cv.snu.ac.kr/research/DRCN/.

[4] https://twitter.app.box.com/s/lcue6vlrd01ljkdtdkhmfvk7vtjhetog.

[5] https://github.com/HyeongseokSon1/SRFeat.

[6] https://github.com/MIVRC/MSRN-PyTorch.

[7] https://github.com/alterzero/DBPN-Pytorch.

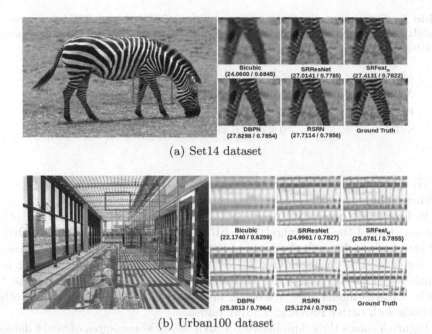

(a) Set14 dataset

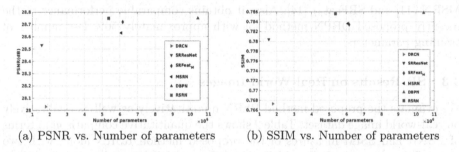

(b) Urban100 dataset

Fig. 4. The SR results obtained using the proposed methods along with the other SISR methods on Set14 and Urban100 dataset for upscaling factor ×4.

(a) PSNR vs. Number of parameters   (b) SSIM vs. Number of parameters

Fig. 5. The effect of PSNR and SSIM values of state-of-the-art SISR models along with the proposed RSRN model with respect to the number of training parameters on Set14 datasets.

using the proposed RSRN and other existing SR methods. In Table 1, we avoid comparing our SR results with that of EDSR [12], RDN [19] and RCAN [18] methods because these methods [12, 18, 19] require a huge number of training parameters in order to obtain better SR performance. From Table 1, one can notice that the proposed RSRN model outperforms to the recently proposed MSRN [11], SRFeat$_M$ [14] and DBPN [5] methods. Here, the proposed method RSRN obtains highest PSNR and SSIM measures than the other state-of-the-art methods except for

Table 2. The quantitative comparison in terms of PSNR and SSIM measures on RealSR testing dataset for upscaling factor ×4. Here, the highest value is indicated with bold font text.

Methods	Bicubic	SRResNet [10]	SRFeat$_M$ [14]	RSRN
Number of parameters	—	1,549k	6,166k	5,370k
PSNR	27.99	28.9408	28.9362	**29.1555**
SSIM	0.806	0.8161	0.8160	**0.8197**

PSNR measures of Set5 and BSD100 datasets and SSIM measure of Set14 dataset at where it obtains second-highest measures.

In Fig. 4, the qualitative results obtained using the proposed and the other existing state-of-the-art methods (i.e., SRResNet [10], SRFeat$_M$ [14] and DBPN [5]) are depicted for a single image of Set14, and Urban100 dataset for upscaling factor 4. The corresponding PSNR and SSIM of that SR image are also mentioned at the bottom of the SR results. Here, one can observe that the SR result of RSRN model preserves better high-frequency details than that of other methods with better PSNR and SSIM values.

Figure 5 shows the graph between PSNR & SSIM measures of Set14 dataset of different state-of-the-art SISR methods and number of training parameters required to train their network. One can observe from this Fig. 5 that the propose RSRN method obtains high PSNR and SSIM values than the recently proposed MSRN [11] and SRFeat$_M$ [14]. Also, it obtains comparable performance to the recently proposed DBPN method [5] with approximately 50% less number of training parameters.

4.3   SR Results on Real-World Images

We evaluate the proposed method RSRN quantitatively as well as qualitatively on real-world image dataset. Table 2 shows the quantitative comparison in terms of PSNR and SSIM measures of the proposed method RSRN along with two state-of-the-art methods (i.e., SRResNet [10] and SRFeat$_M$ [14]). We select these two methods as they are the most recent method which perform superior on the synthetic dataset. The number of training parameters used in those methods are also mentioned in the same table. From Table 2, one can observe that the proposed method RSRN outperforms than the recently proposed SRFeat$_M$ method with less number of training parameters. In addition to the quantitative comparison, Fig. 6 shows the qualitative comparison on the RealSR testing dataset [2] for upscaling factor ×4. The corresponding PSNR and SSIM measures are also mentioned at the bottom of SR results. From Fig. 6, one can observe that the proposed method RSRN obtains better results with more high-frequency details and better quantitative measures.

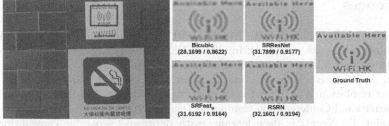

(a) Canon camera Image

(b) Nikon camera Image

Fig. 6. The qualitative comparison of SISR methods on RealSR testing dataset for upscaling factor ×4. The corresponding PSNR and SSIM values are also mentioned at the bottom of all SR results.

5 Conclusion

In this paper, we propose a computationally efficient SR approach called RSRN for real-world images for upscaling factor ×4. In RSRN, a novel densely connected parallel residual block (DPRB) is proposed which helps to learn more complex features from the LR observation. We compare the SR performance of the proposed RSRN method with the other existing SR methods and it shows that the proposed RSRN outperforms to the recently proposed state-of-the-art MSRN [11], SRFeat$_M$ [14] methods. However, it obtains similar performance than that of recently proposed state-of-the-art DBPN method [5] with approximately 50% less number of training parameters. We also compare the effectiveness of the proposed method on the real-world images and found that the proposed method obtains better SR results with more high-frequency details and better quantitative measures on real-world images.

References

1. Agustsson, E., Timofte, R.: NTIRE 2017 challenge on single image super-resolution: dataset and study. In: The IEEE Conference on Computer Vision and Pattern Recognition (CVPR) Workshops, vol. 3, p. 2 (2017)
2. Cai, J., Zeng, H., Yong, H., Cao, Z., Zhang, L.: Toward real-world single image super-resolution: a new benchmark and a new model. In: Proceedings of the IEEE International Conference on Computer Vision (2019)
3. Chollet, F.: Xception: deep learning with depthwise separable convolutions. In: Proceedings of the IEEE Conference on Computer Vision and Pattern Recognition, pp. 1251–1258 (2017)
4. Dong, C., Loy, C.C., He, K., Tang, X.: Image super-resolution using deep convolutional networks. IEEE Trans. Pattern Anal. Mach. Intell. **38**(2), 295–307 (2016)
5. Haris, M., Shakhnarovich, G., Ukita, N.: Deep back-projection networks for super-resolution. In: Proceedings of the IEEE Conference on Computer Vision and Pattern Recognition, pp. 1664–1673 (2018)
6. He, K., Zhang, X., Ren, S., Sun, J.: Delving deep into rectifiers: surpassing human-level performance on imagenet classification. In: Proceedings of the IEEE International Conference on Computer Vision, pp. 1026–1034 (2015)
7. Huang, G., Liu, Z., van der Maaten, L., Weinberger, K.Q.: Densely connected convolutional networks. 2017 IEEE Conference on Computer Vision and Pattern Recognition (CVPR), pp. 2261–2269 (2017)
8. Kim, J., Lee, J.K., Lee, K.M.: Accurate image super-resolution using very deep convolutional networks. In: The IEEE Conference on Computer Vision and Pattern Recognition (CVPR), pp. 1646–1654, June 2016
9. Kim, J., Lee, J.K., Lee, K.M.: Deeply-recursive convolutional network for image super-resolution. 2016 IEEE Conference on Computer Vision and Pattern Recognition (CVPR), pp. 1637–1645 (2016)
10. Ledig, C., et al.: Photo-realistic single image super-resolution using a generative adversarial network. In: Proceedings of the IEEE Conference on Computer Vision and Pattern Recognition, pp. 4681–4690 (2017)
11. Li, J., Fang, F., Mei, K., Zhang, G.: Multi-scale residual network for image super-resolution. In: Proceedings of the European Conference on Computer Vision (ECCV), pp. 517–532 (2018)
12. Lim, B., Son, S., Kim, H., Nah, S., Lee, K.M.: Enhanced deep residual networks for single image super-resolution. In: 2017 IEEE Conference on Computer Vision and Pattern Recognition Workshops (CVPRW), pp. 1132–1140 (2017)
13. Odena, A., Dumoulin, V., Olah, C.: Deconvolution and checkerboard artifacts. Distill **1**(10), e3 (2016)
14. Park, S.J., Son, H., Cho, S., Hong, K.S., Lee, S.: Srfeat: single image super-resolution with feature discrimination. In: Proceedings of the European Conference on Computer Vision (ECCV), pp. 439–455 (2018)
15. Shi, W., et al.: Real-time single image and video super-resolution using an efficient sub-pixel convolutional neural network. In: Proceedings of the IEEE Conference on Computer Vision and Pattern Recognition, pp. 1874–1883 (2016)
16. Timofte, R., Agustsson, E., Van Gool, L., Yang, M.H., Zhang, L.: NTIRE 2017 challenge on single image super-resolution: methods and results. In: Proceedings of the IEEE Conference on Computer Vision and Pattern Recognition Workshops, pp. 114–125 (2017)

17. Yang, W., Zhang, X., Tian, Y., Wang, W., Xue, J.H., Liao, Q.: Deep learning for single image super-resolution: a brief review. IEEE Trans. Multimedia **21**(12), 3106–3121 (2019)
18. Zhang, Y., Li, K., Li, K., Wang, L., Zhong, B., Fu, Y.: Image super-resolution using very deep residual channel attention networks. In: Proceedings of the European Conference on Computer Vision (ECCV), pp. 286–301 (2018)
19. Zhang, Y., Tian, Y., Kong, Y., Zhong, B., Fu, Y.: Residual dense network for image super-resolution. In: Proceedings of the IEEE Conference on Computer Vision and Pattern Recognition, pp. 2472–2481 (2018)

Accurate Damage Dimension Estimation in AI Driven Vehicle Inspection System

Adrita Barari, N. V. S. Abhilash(✉), Payanshi Jain, Ankit Sati, Karthik Sai Datta, and Chirag Jain

Data Science and Insights, Genpact, New York, USA
abhilash.nvs2@genpact.digital

Abstract. With the rise of Artificial Intelligence, research in Computer Vision and Deep Learning has made substantial advancement on understanding visual content. This has led industries across multiple sectors to upgrade and automate processes which require some visual understanding of the physical world. Damage assessment in vehicles is an important step for insurance claims and auto finance industry. The damage assessment involves granular part detection, damage localization and classification into different damage types such as dent, scratch, crush, tear, etc. Further, physical dimension estimation of the damages is required for computing cost to the customer. Currently, this process involves manual interventions, where an agent assesses the damages physically. This process leads to long turnaround time for the insurance majors and auto finance organizations. In this paper, we present a near real-time end-to-end solution which yields accurate damage detection and propose approaches for providing dimensions of the damages for accurate repair cost estimates for the vehicle. The solution further incorporates an ensemble of computer vision algorithms to calculate dimensions, generating bounding boxes, and consolidating the damage predictions to provide an overall damage estimate from multiple images captured by vehicle owner. Insurance majors and auto finance organizations can substantially reduce their turn around time for claims and charging penalties for damage incurred, respectively by integrating the developed solution in their existing process.

Keywords: Deep learning · Computer vision · Auto finance · Auto claims

1 Introduction

The current Auto Finance industry performs external damage assessment of the leased vehicle before taking it back from their customers. The assessment involves a granular analysis of the damages incurred to the body of the vehicle. The customer is charged based on the number and length of the damages present in each panel of the body. Currently, the assessment process is manual and time consuming. Many ongoing researches focus on to improve the process using automated computer vision systems to detect damages in the vehicle while providing accurate dimensions of the damage. An ideal damage detection system should be able to localize the damages in the vehicle accurately. However, designing a robust system is challenging as the images captured can have various lighting conditions, variable zoom, high reflective and shiny surfaces on vehicle's body, etc. The system should also provide an accurate estimation of the damage dimensions. Detecting the dimensions of the damages can also have challenges like lack of reference object, variable perspective at the corners of the vehicle, etc. In this paper, we extend our damage detection solution with accurate and efficient damage dimension estimation in vehicles to create an end to end pipeline. The concepts presented in this paper are transferable to other visual damage diagnosis systems as well.

2 Related Work

There have been previous efforts at damage detection in buildings using high resolution satellite images [1, 2]. For damage detection in cars, Jayawardena et al. [3] proposed a 3D model projection of an undamaged vehicle on that of a damaged vehicle to identify damages. Only recently have researchers started using deep learning approaches for solving damage detection. Patil et al. [4] have proposed a deep learning based approach for classifying different types of damages in cars. However, our proposed solution is different from [4] since our final objective is to perform damage estimation. The developed framework is a deep learning and computer vision based pipeline. For filtering out irrelevant images of the vehicle, Convolutional Neural Network (CNN) architectures such as ResNet50 [5, 6], Inception_v3 [7], Xception [8] were experimented with. Object detection algorithms were explored to localize the damages and classify the damage types into dents, scratches, tears, misalignments etc. For object detection, architectures such as Faster-RCNN [9] and 'You Look Only Once' (YOLO) [10] were assessed. However, to identify the accurate damage area, we finally use a semantic segmentation approach to predict the accurate segmentation maps of the damages. Deeplab [11] with Xception-65 backbone gives us the best performance for predicting accurate segmentation maps. The proposed solution in explained in details in the following section.

3 Proposed Solution

The proposed solution consists of three key modules, namely damage detection, damage dimension estimator and damage duplicity removal. The solution leverages multiple images of the damaged vehicle taken by the user from different viewing angles as input. In our previous work [12, 13], we described our damage detection pipeline which is a prerequisite for estimating dimension. The same has been captured below in Sect. 3.1. The damage detection module is treated as an object segmentation problem since we need to find the precise locations of the damages down to the pixel level. The localized damages are then fed into the dimension estimating module which predicts the dimensions of the detected damages in each image. Further, we pass the results obtained to a duplicity removal module which removes redundancy if the same damage is present in multiple images. Figure 1 illustrates the end-to-end pipeline on a high level.

3.1 Damage Detection

Our damage detection pipeline consists of three main sequential steps which are relevance filtering, vehicle part segmentation and vehicle damage segmentation. All the deep learning models were trained using a Nvidia Tesla M60 GPU with 8 GB RAM.

Fig. 1. Block diagram of the damage estimation pipeline

Relevance Filtering. This preprocessing step aims to increase the efficiency of the damage detection module by filtering out irrelevant images. Often the images captured by the customers include images irrelevant to visual damage detection such as images of vehicle documents, odometer readings, license plate etc. Customers may also capture images of car interiors which is out of scope of our current work. The relevance filtering model aims to filter out such images which are irrelevant to our damage analysis. A ResNet50 model trained on around 5000 hand-labelled images has been used for this image classification task. The model was trained for 50 epochs with a learning rate (lr) of 0.001. The accuracy achieved for this model was 91%.

Vehicle Part Segmentation. Parts segmentation plays an important role because Auto Finance companies usually calculate the cost by counting number of damages in each vehicle part. The vehicle part segmentation model was trained using DeepLabv3+ [11] architecture with TensorFlow backbone and segments 24 vehicle parts. The dataset used for this task is the open source PASCAL Parts dataset [17], along with some hand labelled dataset. The training ran for around 8 h for 30000 iterations with a lr of 0.0001. The mean Intersection over Union (mIOU) was 0.65 (Fig. 2).

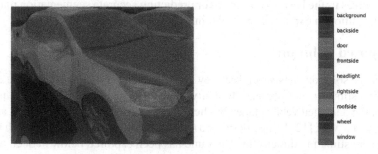

Fig. 2. Output of vehicle parts detection model

Vehicle Damage Segmentation. The vehicle damage segmentation model segments six different types of damages in the vehicle which are dents, scratches, misalignments, missing parts, crush/crumple and tear. This damage segmentation model helps to localize and classify the damages across the vehicle body. It should be noted that count of damage segments is intrinsic in this model, but scratches are a special case where detecting each line of the scratch is not practically possible by our deep learning model since the dataset was not labeled to incorporate such fine scratch lines. Thus, we use a Line Detection Algorithm, explained in the next section, which is used to overcome this problem specific to scratch damage types. Around 15000 images, annotated and verified by domain experts, were trained on a DeepLabv3+ [11] with Xception-65 architecture on Tensorflow backbone. The training used a batch size of 8 and a step lr with an initial lr of 0.001 and lr decay of 0.1 after every 10000 steps. The training ran for 30000 iterations over a span of 8 h. The mIOU was calculated per damage class as well as on the overall dataset. The overall mIOU achieved was 0.52. The final consolidation of outputs is done by performing intersection of the damage segmentation maps to the part segmentation maps. This module is helpful to provide damage count and dimension per damage per part of the vehicle.

Line Detection Algorithm. As discussed, above, the Vehicle Damage Segmentation Model detects the segmentation map of the detected damages. The output of this model can be used directly for damages such as dents, crush, crumple, tear, misalignments etc., where the customer charge out is calculated based on the damage area. However, for scratches, the focus is on scratch length rather than the total area. Hence, refinement is needed to further localize the scratch lines since the actual scratches are usually a small fraction of the larger detected scratch blob. Figure 3 shows the output of scratch lines refined from a scratch blob. A line detection algorithm is run on the retrieved scratch blobs. The line segment detector looks through the scratch blob and localizes the exact regions where the scratches are present so that the customer can be charged accurately based on scratch lengths. The OpenCV implementation of the probabilistic Hough Line algorithm [14, 15] with a minimum line length of 15 and maximum line gap of 5 is found to give the best performance on this dataset. Line detection algorithms detect straight lines only. Thus, for curved scratches, we take the summation of smaller line segments along the curved scratch lines.

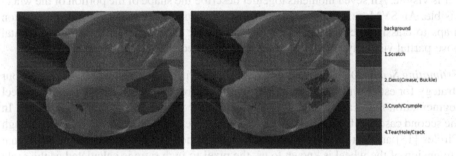

Fig. 3. (a) Output of damage detection (left) (b) Scratch lines from detected scratch blob (right)

3.2 Damage Dimension Estimation

Our dimension detection module contains multiple use case specific approaches to get the dimensions of the damages based on the view of the car visible. The main challenge to estimate the physical dimensions of any object from an image is to find a reference object with known dimensions in the image. Reference objects can then be used to find the scale which is defined as the pixel to inch ratio of the object. The scale can be then used to find the physical dimensions of the damage. The above steps, however, are under the assumption that both the object and the damage are in the same plane and the plane is orthogonal to the camera used to capture the image. This assumption can fail when the damages are present in the corner of the car, which is a point of intersection of two planes, and we address these issues below. We propose two algorithms to estimate the dimensions of the damages based on the reference object we chose, namely wheel and part as a reference object.

Wheel as a Reference Object. Wheels have a very distinct pattern irrespective of vehicle type. This allows the part detection model to detect it with high accuracy. Hence it is chosen to be a reference object in most of our scenarios. The physical dimensions of the wheel can be retrieved based on the car model information. However, challenges such as multiple wheel visibility at different locations, partial wheel visibility, tilted wheel, still exist. Below we enlist the various possibilities of wheel visibility and how we handle it to get the scale.

Detecting Wheel Pose and Visibility. To detect wheels, we use the output of the part segmentation model described in Sect. 3.1. The segment maps containing the wheel part is filtered for further use. We use shape descriptors to detect whether the wheel is partially or fully visible. We select HuMoments [16] as shape descriptors to identify the wheel pose and visibility. HuMoments are a set of seven numbers calculated using central moments of an image that are invariant to image transformations. The first six moments are invariant to translation, scale, and rotation, and reflection, while the seventh moment's sign changes for image reflection. We use OpenCV built-in HuMoments function to get the values of HuMoments for all the training samples in which any of the wheels of the car is visible. All seven moments together describe the shape of the portion of the wheel visible. An SVM model is trained on the HuMoment values of the wheel segmentation maps to classify them in the following categories: frontal pose-full visibility, frontal pose-partial visibility, tilted pose-full visibility, tilted pose-partial visibility.

Estimating Scale. Depending on the pose and the visibility of the wheel, we decide our strategy for estimating scale. In the first case, i.e. frontal pose-full visibility, the wheel segmentation map can be directly used to calculate the wheel dimensions in pixels. In the second case, i.e. frontal pose-partial visibility, we reconstruct the wheel using Hough Circles [13] and get the corresponding radius of the wheel in pixels. Since the actual dimension of the wheel is known to us, the pixel to inch ratio is calculated as the scale factor. The third case i.e. tilted pose-full visibility, occurs when the vehicle image is taken from non-frontal angles. In such a case, we apply perspective correction on the wheel segmentation map to transform it to a frontal pose and then get its accurate pixel dimensions. The last case i.e. tilted pose-partial visibility, is the most challenging of these cases. Here, we first use perspective correction on the wheel segmentation map and then reconstruct it using Hough Circles to get the scale factor.

Although, our algorithm performs well in the first three cases, the last case is subject to distortion due to perspective correction on the image. If the initial image is not captured in high resolution, it may be difficult to get enough features to correctly reconstruct the wheel from the perspective image owing to noise and distortion. Moreover, the Hough

Circle [13] reconstruction gives erroneous results for wheels which are less than 50% visible in the image. Work is in progress to address all wheel poses and visibilities and make the algorithm robust to distortion due to perspective correction.

Multiple Wheels Visibility. For a 4-wheeler passenger vehicle, we can safely assume that from any view angle of the vehicle at most two wheels are visible. However, both the wheels can have different scales if the plane of the wheels is not orthogonal to the point of view. So, if the damage is present in the plane as that of the wheels, the scale of the damage would be in between the scale of the two wheels. To overcome this, we incorporate perspective correction explained above, along with a simple approach based on weighted average. The scale factor of the damage is a weighted average of the scale of the two wheels detected, where the weight is inversely proportional to the distance of the damage to that wheel.

Part as a Reference Object. A fallback algorithm is used for images and planes where wheels are not visible or are not a reliable source for scale. Generally, such images involve zoomed-in images or images of front and rear end of the vehicle. In such cases, we cannot rely on wheel to retrieve a good scale estimate. For cases where front and rear end of the car is visible, we leverage the fact that we have the car width and the vehicle height information. Here, the scale is calculated from the physical dimensions of the car and its corresponding pixel width detected from part detection. The results of the different stages of the damage detection and estimation modules have been presented in Fig. 4.

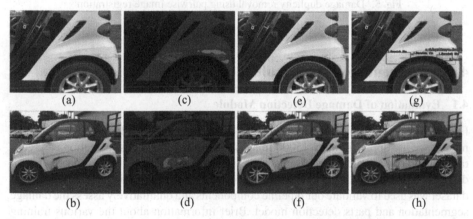

Fig. 4. Different stages of damage estimation pipeline. (a), (b) Two images of the same vehicle which focus on scratch and dents in different parts of the car body. (c), (d) Damage segmentation outputs where red indicates scratch and green indicates dent. (e), (f) Obtaining scale factor by reconstruction of partially visible wheel and multi wheel visibility. (g), (h) Damage lengths computed for the detected damages using the scale factor. (Color figure online)

3.3 Damage Duplicity Removal

As mentioned in earlier sections, we assume that customer captures multiple pictures of the vehicle and the damages. Since the image of a car is captured from multiple angles, there is a high probability that the same damage may be present in multiple images. Since our deep learning models are not trained to identify whether it is the same damage or a different one, we must incorporate post processing for damage duplicity removal. To address this issue, we use the approach of image stitching, going pairwise and finding damages which are the same across multiple images, as shown in Fig. 5. Once this is done, we stitch the relevant images together and map the damage information on the stitched image so that each unique damage is counted just once. This ensures that customers are not charged multiple times for the same damage.

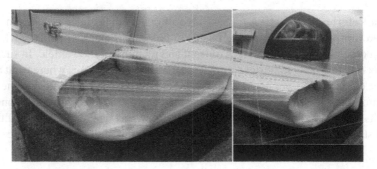

Fig. 5. Damage duplicity removal using pairwise image registration

4   Experimentation and Results

4.1   Evaluation of Damage Detection Module

For evaluation of vehicle parts segmentation and the vehicle damage segmentation model, we use approximately 15000 images. Each vehicle damage detection case contains around 16 images of the same vehicle. The images are generally taken from 8 different angles with approximately 45 degrees shift and with variable zoom. This rich dataset was used to validate our pipeline components and qualitatively assess the damage segmentation and parts detection model. Brief information about the various training datasets and evaluation metrics of the components of Damage Detection pipeline are provided below in Table 1.

4.2   Evaluation of Damage Estimation Module

Since there are no publicly available datasets which record damage lengths in vehicle damages, the evaluation of the damage estimation module was done through in-house data collection. Once collected, the damages were identified and the measured manually.

Table 1. Image dataset used for components in damage detection pipeline model training

Model name	Dataset size	Class names	Performance
Relevance filter	~5K Hand labeled dataset	Relevant, Irrelevant	Validation Accuracy - 91%
Parts segmentation	PASCAL Parts (Only Cars) + ~1K hand labeled image segmentation data [17]	24 part names from PASCAL Parts for Cars	Validation mIOU - 0.65
Damage segmentation	~15K Hand labeled image segmentation dataset	Scratch, Missing Dent, Crush, Tear, Misalignment	Overall Validation mIOU - 0.52

Scratch lengths were documented for around 50 samples. The same 50 samples were then given as an input to our damage estimation pipeline. The pipeline failed to perform on 4% of the cases due to challenges such as complex angles and zoom variations in the captured images. The reflection and dirt present on vehicle parts also lead to 21% of false positives.

5 Conclusion and Future Work

In this paper, we have shown that the current manual process of damage analysis in the Auto Finance industry, can be automated with our pipeline. We have also shown the importance of dimension measurement of the damages in calculating the charges to the customer. To address this, we have briefly presented our damage detection pipeline, and more importantly described our scaling strategy, i.e. using segmented wheels to get physical dimensions of the damages. We also demonstrated solutions to overcome challenges like partial wheel visibility with perspective tilts and multiple wheels visibility issues. Overall, the proposed approach provides insight to build a fast and accurate scaling system for damage analysis which can be of use with any of the damage analysis pipeline. Our solution is scalable across multiple domains and easily configurable for various business cases.

Possible ways of improvement of mIOU of our segmentation models include training our models with diverse and tightly annotated datasets. Experimentation with different semantic segmentation architectures with further hyperparameter tuning will also improve our semantic segmentation output. Ongoing work also targets to make the damage duplicity reduction module more accurate. Future work includes application of the developed techniques on live video streams so that damage estimates can be generated in real time.

Acknowledgment. The authors would like to sincerely thank Vikram Mahidhar, Sreekanth Menon, Amit Arora, Siva Tian, Krishna Dev Oruganty, Arun Pavuri and Rajat Katiyar for their help and support during the project development. We would also like to extend our thanks to the Genpact Product Engineering team and domain experts for helping in productizing the solution.

References

1. Samadzadegan, F., Rastiveisi, H.: Automatic detection and classification of damaged buildings, using high resolution satellite imagery and vector data. Int. Arch. Photogramm. Remote Sens. Spatial Inf. Sci. **37**, 415–420 (2008)
2. Kouchi, K., Yamazaki, F.: Damage detection based on object-based segmentation and classification from high resolution satellite images for the 2003 Boumerdes, Algeria earthquake. In: Proceedings of the 26th Asian conference on Remote Sensing, Hanoi, Vietnam (2005)
3. Jayawardena, S., et al.: Image based automatic vehicle damage detection. Ph.D. thesis, Australian National University (2013)
4. Patil, K., Kulkarni, M., Sriraman, A., Karande, S.: Deep Learning Based Car Damage Classification, pp. 50–54 (2017). https://doi.org/10.1109/icmla.2017.0-179
5. Krizhevsky, A., Sutskever, I., Hinton, G.: ImageNet classification with deep convolutional neural networks. In: NIPS (2012)
6. He, K., Zhang, X., Ren, S., Sun, J.: Deep residual learning for image recognition. In: 2016 IEEE Conference on Computer Vision and Pattern Recognition (CVPR), Las Vegas, NV, pp. 770–778 (2016)
7. Szegedy, C., Vanhoucke, V., Ioffe, S., Shlens, J., Wojna, Z.: Rethinking the inception architecture for computer vision. In: 2016 IEEE Conference on Computer Vision and Pattern Recognition (CVPR), Las Vegas, NV, pp. 2818–2826 (2016)
8. Chollet, F.: Xception: deep learning with depthwise separable convolutions. In: 2017 IEEE Conference on Computer Vision and Pattern Recognition (CVPR), Honolulu, HI, pp. 1800–1807 (2017)
9. Girshick, R.: Fast R-CNN. In: 2015 IEEE International Conference on Computer Vision (ICCV), Santiago, pp. 1440–1448 (2015)
10. Redmon, J., Divvala, S., Girshick, R., Farhadi, A.: You only look once: unified, real-time object detection. In: 2016 IEEE Conference on Computer Vision and Pattern Recognition (CVPR), Las Vegas, NV, pp. 779–788 (2016)
11. Chen, L.C., Papandreou, G., Kokkinos, I., Murphy, K., Yuille, A.L.: DeepLab: Semantic Image Segmentation with Deep Convolutional Nets, Atrous Convolution, and Fully Connected CRFs (2016)
12. Arun, P., Abhilash, N.V.S.: Deep learning and computer vision based damage analysis for auto insurance claims. In: ICBAI (2018)
13. Abhilash, N.V.S., Adrita, B., Ankit, S., Arun, P.: AI driven automatic vehicle damage assessment for auto insurance and auto finance industry. In: ICBAI (2019)
14. Cha, J., Cofer, R.H., Kozaitis, S.P.: Extended hough transform for linear feature detection. Pattern Recogn. **39**(6), 1034–1043 (2006)
15. Duan, D., Xie, M., Mo, Q., Han, Z., Wan, Y.: An improved hough transform for line detection. In: 2010 International Conference on Computer Application and System Modeling (ICCASM 2010) (2010)
16. Huang, Z., Leng, J.: Analysis of Hu's moment invariants on image scaling and rotation. In: Proceedings of 2nd International Conference on Computer Engineering and Technology (ICCET), vol. 7, pp. V7-476 (2010)
17. Chen, X., Mottaghi, R., Liu, X., Fidler, S., Urtasun, R., Yuille, A.: Detect What You Can: Detecting and Representing Objects using Holistic Models and Body Parts (2014)

A Deep Learning Based Framework for Distracted Driver Detection

Swadesh Kumar Maurya and Ayesha Choudhary[✉]

School of Computer and Systems Sciences,
Jawaharlal Nehru University, New Delhi, India
swades89_scs@jnu.ac.in, ayeshac@mail.jnu.ac.in

Abstract. In this paper, we propose a novel, real-time, deep learning-based framework for distracted driver detection for driver Advanced Driver Assistance Systems (ADAS). We assume that the camera is assumed to be mounted inside the vehicle such that the side view of the driver is in view. Distracted driving is a serious problem leading to a large number of serious and even fatal road accidents worldwide every year. We propose a deep learning architecture that takes as input the captured images of the driver and classifies and recognizes the various distracted driving behaviors. It also recognizes if the driver is not distracted and is alert. The experiments are performed on the publicly available State Farm Distracted Driver Detection (SFDDD) dataset [1] which has 9 classes of distracted driver behavior and one class of alert driving. The training time for the proposed framework is minimal and approach works in real-time. Our experimental results show that our proposed framework is robust and performs better than the state-of-the-art approaches on this dataset.

Keywords: Driver assistance · Distracted driver detection · Deep learning · Driver behavior · Smart vehicle · Road safety

1 Introduction

In this paper, we propose a novel, real-time framework for detecting distracted driving by placing a camera inside the vehicle such that the side view of the driver is visible. In recent years, there has been immense progress in the area of Intelligent Transportation System (ITS) that focuses on developing an Advanced Driver Assistance System (ADAS) to provide a safe driving environment. In this area, the problem of unexpected behavior and distracted driver on the road is very important since it may lead to serious and fatal accidents. According to the CDC motor vehicle safety division [2], one in five car accidents is caused by a distracted driver. Sadly, this translates to 425,000 people injured and 3,000 people killed by distracted driving every year across the US only.

There are three main types of driver distractions: (a) Visual: taking eyes off the road by the driver; (b) Manual: taking hands off the wheel that distracts

© Springer Nature Singapore Pte Ltd. 2020
R. V. Babu et al. (Eds.): NCVPRIPG 2019, CCIS 1249, pp. 163–173, 2020.
https://doi.org/10.1007/978-981-15-8697-2_15

Fig. 1. Distracted driver dataset sample visualization for all 10 classes (a–j), the classes detail of subfigure are (a) c0: Safe driving, (b) c1: Texting-right, (c) c2: Talking on the phone-right, (d) c3: Texting-left, (e) c4: Talking on the phone-left, (f) c5: Operating the radio, (g) c6: Drinking (h) c7: Reaching behind, (i) c8: Hair and makeup, (j) c9: Talking to passenger.

a driver's mind from driving; (c) Cognitive: taking the mind off from driving, leading to unattentive driving. Distracted driver detection is a major challenge to perform in an ADAS for improving driving conditions. In this work, we focus on visual and manual distractions and propose a Driver Assistance System that tracks the behavior of the driver while he is driving and alerts the driver if he/she does an unexpected task thereby increasing the chance of accidents. In autonomous driving systems, the driver needs to be well-prepared to take over the controls, whenever required. In such cases also, the distracted driver detection is an important issue and the driver should be alerted if he/she is distracted and not well-prepared to take control immediately in case the need arises.

There are various challenges in distracted driver detection such as illumination variation, occlusion, camera perspective may vary, day and night driving environments as well as the different clothing and the driver dependent physical characteristics. Based on the kind of distraction such as visual, manual or cognitive, different challenges arises. In our work, we focus on the visual and manual types of distractions of the driver.

We propose a deep learning-based novel architecture that builds upon a pretrained deep learning model, by further adding new layers to improve the performance. The deep learning models about the very large ImageNet dataset [7] are used to perform the training on the driver distraction dataset. We evaluate our approach and use different pre-trained models to compare and analyze the performance and convergence rate of individual models. This allows us to improve and find the optimal performance that requires the least amount of training and computation time. We use the State Farm Distracted Driver Detection Dataset [1], which has images of different drivers performing 9 classes of distracted behavior and 1 class of alert driving behavior (samples have shown in Fig. 1). We compare our proposed approach with the state of the art methods that exist on this dataset. The paper is structured as follows: In Sect. 2, the related work is discussed. We discuss our proposed work in Sect. 3 and the experimental results in Sect. 4. Finally, we conclude in Sect. 5.

2   Related Work

Detection of distracted driving is getting attention in the research community and the industry. Various vision and sensor-based approaches are proposed in this area. In this work, we focused on the techniques that use vision-based approaches. The detection of distracted driver behavior (i.e. driver drowsiness, lane departure, talking on phone, looking back, etc.) using a camera mounted inside the vehicle is an active area of research as Advanced Driver Assistance System (ADAS), various computer vision-based and machine learning-based methods are applied to extract features such as eye-tracking, driver posture, cellphone usage, etc. in driving images or video. The approaches proposed in [3,4] are focused on extracting features such as eye-tracking, driver posture, cellphone usage, etc. in driving image scene or video. These approaches are used in the distracted driving behavior analysis in the state of art.

The Convolutional Neural Networks (CNN) and deep learning approaches such as [5,6] are used in various work to perform the driver behavior analysis. In [8] the VGG-16 architecture is modified and used for the classification such that the system not only detects distracted driving behavior but also finds the type of distraction in the scene. Research in distracted driving behavior has also focused on the face and hand position of the driver in a naturalistic driving environment [9,11,12]. They focus on the detecting hand region to identifying the type of activities such as adjusting radio, mirror, operating gear.

Similarly, in Le et al. [10], identification of distracted driving is based on the position of the hand and cellphone usage. This uses multi-scale faster-RCNN for detecting objects such as cellphones, hands, steering wheel, etc. and classifies the behavior based on the position of objects. In [17], deep learning approach is used to classify the driver behaviour on the SFDDD dataset [1]. They have used AlexNet with Softmax and Triplet Loss to perform the classification task and achieved the 98.7% accuracy. Zhao et al. [13] proposed a distracted driver dataset with the side view of the driver having only four activities: safe driving, operating shift lever, eating and talking on the cellphone. In this paper, we propose a novel, real-time framework for the distracted driver detection and develop a new architecture that improves upon the feature extracted from a pre-trained network. We describe our proposed in the next proposed work section.

3   Proposed Work

In this work, we propose a novel architecture for classification using deep learning. The main challenge in classification is to be able to extract important features for better classification performance. For this, we use a pre-trained deep learning model as the base layer. In our implementation, we used the models and their pre-trained weights on ImageNet dataset [7] so that the optimal features can be learned from the images faster and with minimal training. Our proposed full model architecture is shown in Fig. 2 with all the layers, dropout, batch normalization, and other activation function structure.

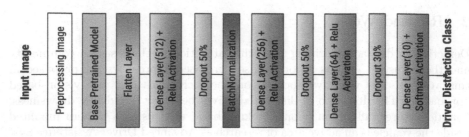

Fig. 2. Our proposed model architecture for distracted driver detection, where the Base Pre-trained Model layer can be replaced with any of the pre-trained model by Resnet50 [14], Inceptionv3 [14], InceptionResnetv2 [16] and Mobilenet [15].

As shown in Fig. 2, we define the following layers in our model. We consider the pre-trained network as the base layer, then add the 'Flatten layer' to ensure that all the features are converted into a single vector. The next layers are the 'Dense' layer with ReLu activation function followed by the 'Dropout' layer. We use dropout to ensure that generalized features are learned to overcome the problem of overfitting in the model. These 'Dense' layers and 'Dropout' are repeated with a reduced number of dense nodes as the number of features is also decreased from the top layers. We also perform Batch normalization after the first dense layer to ensure normalization of the features obtained from the initial layers.

The last output layer is meant to classify among K categories with a SoftMax activation function given by Eq. 3, that assigns conditional probabilities (given x) of each categories. We use the stochastic gradient descent (SGD) optimizer to train the model networks because new optimizers such as Adam and Nadam are not able to learn optimal weight at the time of training as compared to the SGD optimizer. The cross-entropy loss $\mathcal{L}$ used in the model to optimize the model weight and maximize the accuracy of the classification is given by Eq. 1.

$$\mathcal{L}\left(y_i, \hat{y}_i\right) = -\sum_{i=1}^{K} y_i \log\left(\hat{y}_i\right) \tag{1}$$

The each input batch sample is preprocessed as given in Eq. 2, initially it is mean centered on the average of the input batch and then normalized.

$$z = \frac{x - \mu}{\sigma}, \mu = \frac{1}{N} \sum_{j=1}^{N} (x_j), \ \sigma = \sqrt{\frac{1}{N} \sum_{j=1}^{N} (x_j - \mu)^2} \tag{2}$$

$$S_i = \frac{\exp(\mathbf{w}_i^\top \mathbf{x})}{\sum_{k=1}^{K} \exp(\mathbf{w}_k^\top \mathbf{x})} = \frac{\exp(Z_i)}{\sum_{k=1}^{K} \exp(Z_k)} \tag{3}$$

S_i defines the Softmax activation function on i^{th} class, w are the neuron connection's weight and x is the feature at dense layers.

We applied the early stopping criteria of 15 epoch patience to training whether it gets optimized or not. The technique 'Reduce on Plateau' is applied to get the advantage of reducing the learning rate by a factor of 0.95 once learning stagnates. This callback monitors a loss value and if no improvement is seen for patience or a specified number of epochs, the learning rate is reduced for future epochs. The pre-trained base model which we select as the base layer feature extraction, are ResNet50 [14],InceptionV3 [5], InceptionResnetv2 [16], and Mobilenet [15]. Each model is modified with the given architecture defined in Fig. 2 to improve classification and optimize the performance. The training results and all performance matrices are shown in Sect. 4 for each proposed model. If we consider the input image directly as input in the architecture, it may lead to an increase in computations as well as training time to learn the features, therefore, the input images are re-sampled and re-sized to fit in the base model architecture and meet the hardware requirements of the system. The image samples are then normalized by feature-wise mean centering, which sets the input means to 0 over the dataset feature-wise as shown in Eq. 2. The x here represents the complete set of images in a batch and μ is the mean of the complete data in the batch, and z is the final feature that is normalized and centered around the mean. The data augmentation significantly increases the diversity of data available and captures data invariance for training models. The data augmentation is performed with a rotation range of 30° and horizontal flip of the image so the scene can add diversity and variations in the dataset and consider the various cases of camera angle changes.

4   Experimental Results and Discussion

In our experiments, we use the State Farm Distracted Driver Detection(SFDDD) dataset [1]. It is publicly available with images taken in a car where the driver is acting on the set of activities such as texting, eating, talking on the phone, makeup, reaching behind, etc. The images are taken from a camera inside the vehicle such that the side view of the driver is visible. The dataset consists of 10 classes (Safe driving + 9 distracting behaviors) to predict and their performing actions are: c0: Safe driving; c1: Texting - right; c2: Talking on the phone - right; c3: Texting - left; c4: Talking on the phone - left; c5: Operating the radio; c6: Drinking; c7: Reaching behind; c8: Hair and makeup; c9: Talking to passenger(s). In our experiments, we perform the training with the large set of driver distraction dataset (Fig. 1), for which 22,000 labeled images are available. We have used 16,000 images in our experiments, out of which 10,000 images are

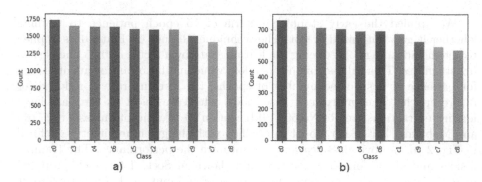

Fig. 3. Class distribution in the (a) training split data and (b) testing split data class distribution.

taken and split into training and validation set in the ratio of 70:30 such that 7000 images are taken for training and the rest 3000 images are for validation. The remaining 6000 images are reserved for testing to evaluate model performance. The reason to take the subset of 16000 images so that training time can be reduced and performance can be analyzed with this limited training set and evaluated on the large test set, with these limitations also the system performed accurately at testing phase, it shows that this amount of data is enough to learn this distracted driver classification task. The detailed class-wise training and testing data distribution are shown in Fig. 3.

The results are shown after the training and evaluation of the optimized model on the test data of 6000 images. The model with the best-achieved accuracy and loss are compared and the test data evaluation matrices are also shown with class-wise performance and number of support samples. The training and validation results of the different models as a comparison between the training and the validation accuracy and loss in performance with their corresponding epoch are shown in Fig. 5. Our experiments discover that even with large training datasets the proposed model with Resnet50 and Mobilenet models as base layers converge with only 49 and 46 epochs, respectively, with a very low number of trainable parameters. This is in comparison to our proposed model with Inceptionv3 and InceptionResnetv2 as base layers, in term of number of epoch to train and fit the model on the given training dataset, and also in terms of the number of trainable parameters in the model, as can be seen by the parameter analysis shown in Table 1.

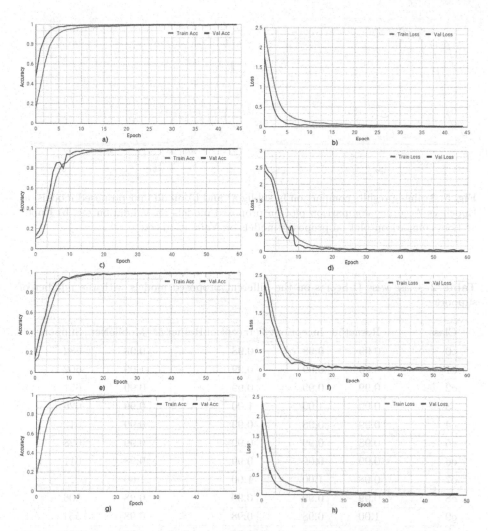

Fig. 4. Comparison of the training and validation accuracy and loss on each epoch, is shown in the figure, subfigure a) and b) shows the Resnet50 accuracy and loss plot, subfigure c) and d) shows the Inceptionv3 accuracy and loss plot, subfigure e) and f) shows the InceptionResnetv2 accuracy and loss plot, subfigure g) and h) shows the Mobilenet accuracy and loss plot.

Table 1. Model comparison and performance parameters

Proposed model using	#Parameter	Input Size	#Epoch	Accuracy	Loss	Test time(6000)
ResNet50	24,733,130	200 × 200	46	99.75	0.0094	104 s, 17 ms/sample
Inceptionv3	38,730,986	200 × 200	60	99.39	0.0413	73 s, 12 ms/sample
InceptionResnetv2	67,009,066	200 × 200	59	99.19	0.0491	75 s, 12 ms/sample
MobileNet	22,231,306	192 × 192	49	99.23	0.0410	34 s, 6 ms/sample

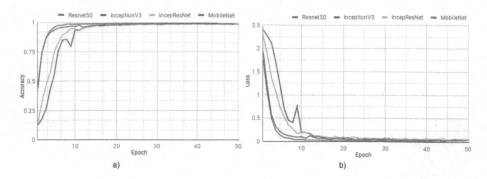

Fig. 5. Training results comparison in subfig a) and b) on all four proposed models. a) Epoch vs Accuracy comparison plot on proposed models on Validation set. b) Epoch vs Loss comparison plot on proposed models on Validation set.

Table 2. Class wise f1-Scores on the different proposed models with the number of support

Class	Resnet50	Inceptionv3	InceptionResnetv2	MobileNet	Support
c0	0.99	0.98	0.98	0.98	682
c1	0.99	0.99	0.99	1.00	602
c2	0.99	0.99	0.99	0.99	651
c3	0.99	1.00	1.00	0.99	626
c4	0.99	0.98	0.99	0.99	612
c5	0.98	0.99	0.99	0.99	628
c6	0.99	0.99	0.99	0.98	617
c7	0.98	1.00	1.00	1.00	522
c8	0.99	0.99	0.99	0.98	506
c9	1.00	0.98	0.98	0.98	554
micro-avg	0.99	0.99	0.99	0.99	6000
macro-avg	0.99	0.99	0.99	0.99	6000
weighted-avg	0.99	0.99	0.99	0.99	6000

Table 3. Summary of distracted driver detection results and comparison on State Farm Distracted Driver Detection dataset [1]

Model	Source	Accuracy%
AlexNet+Softmax Loss[17]	Original	96.8
AlexNet+Triplet Loss[17]	Original	98.7
Original VGG[8]	Original	94.44
VGG with Regularization[8]	Original	96.31
Modified VGG[8]	Original	95.54
Our proposed model using Resnet50	Original	99.75
Our proposed model using Inceptionv3	Original	99.39
Our proposed model using InceptionResnetv2	Original	99.19
Our proposed model using Mobilenet	Original	99.23

The individual model training results in terms of accuracy and loss values is shown in Fig. 4. The accuracy and loss plot of our proposed model using Resnet50 as the base layer is shown in Subfig. 4(a)–(b), of using Inceptionv3 as the base layer is shown in Subfig. 4(c)–(d), of using InceptionResnetv2 as the base layer is shown in Subfig. 4(e)–(f), and using Mobilenet as the base layer is shown in Subfig. 4(g)–(h). In terms of time on the test dataset, we perform the pre-processed test-set batch of 6000 samples already loaded in the memory, and with GPU mode, as mentioned in the Table 1. The last column 'Test time(6000)' shows the evaluation time on the complete 6000 samples are 104 s, 73 s, 75 s, 34 s on our proposed architecture with Resnet50, Inceptionv3, InceptionResnetv2, mobile net as base layers, respectively. This indicates that the performance of our architecture with the Mobilenet model as the base layers is much faster and more accurate as compared to the other three models. The micro-average f1-score on all four models is mentioned in Table 2 where the f1-score is given for each class separately, so we can analyze that not only overall classification performance is good but the individual classwise performance is also better for each trained models. The Fig. 6, shows the confusion matrix with all 10 classes of driver distraction for each model separately. The principal diagonal of the confusion matrix with dense values shows the better performance of our proposed model. The summary of distracted driver detection results and comparison with earlier approaches and our proposed approaches is shown in Table 3 shows better performance than other proposed models.

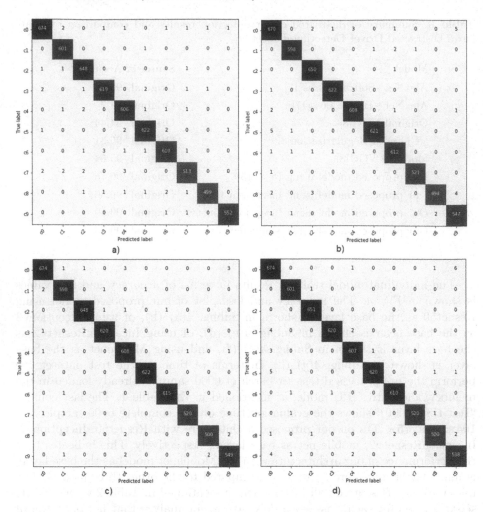

Fig. 6. Confusion matrix results on the test data by our four proposed models using different pretrained model as the base model. a) Resnet50 as base model, b) Inceptionv3 as base model, c) InceptionResnetv2 as base model, d) MobileNet as base model.

5 Conclusion

Driver distraction is a serious problem leading to a large number of road accidents worldwide. Hence, the detection of a distracted driver is important for the safety and security of the driver as well as the passengers. Our work focuses on the detection of the distracted driver from the scene captured from inside the vehicle. In this paper, we have proposed a deep learning-based classification model that uses the state of the art pre-trained deep learning models fine-tuned for distracted driver classification as the base layer. We use the publicly available State Farm Distracted Driver Detection dataset which has a large set of images for 10 classes. The training and testing results show that our proposed model has high classification performance, that is, up to 99.75% in different models. Our proposed architecture is robust and fast and works well in real-time scenarios.

References

1. State farm distracted driver detection. https://www.kaggle.com/c/state-farm-distracted-driver-detection
2. CDC motor vehicle safety division. https://www.cdc.gov/motorvehiclesafety/distracted_driving
3. Streiffer, C., et al.: Darnet: a deep learning solution for distracted driving detection. In: Proceedings of the 18th ACM/IFIP/USENIX Middleware Conference: Industrial Track. ACM (2017)
4. You, C.-W., et al.: Carsafe app: alerting drowsy and distracted drivers using dual cameras on smartphones. In: Proceedings of the 11th Annual International Conference on Mobile Systems, Applications, and Services. ACM (2013)
5. Szegedy, C., et al.: Rethinking the inception architecture for computer vision. In: Proceedings of the IEEE Conference on Computer Vision and Pattern Recognition (2016)
6. Szegedy, C., et al.: Going deeper with convolutions. In: Proceedings of the IEEE Conference on Computer Vision and Pattern Recognition (2015)
7. Deng, J., et al.: Imagenet: a large-scale hierarchical image database. In: 2009 IEEE Conference on Computer Vision and Pattern Recognition. IEEE (2009)
8. Baheti, B., Suhas, G., Sanjay, T.: Detection of distracted driver using convolutional neural network. In: Proceedings of the IEEE Conference on Computer Vision and Pattern Recognition Workshops (2018)
9. Das, N., Ohn-Bar, E., Trivedi, M.M.: On performance evaluation of driver hand detection algorithms: challenges, dataset, and metrics. In: 2015 IEEE 18th International Conference on Intelligent Transportation Systems. IEEE (2015)
10. Hoang Ngan Le, T., et al.: Multiple scale faster-RCNN approach to driver's cell-phone usage and hands on steering wheel detection. In: 2016 IEEE Conference on Computer Vision and Pattern Recognition Workshops (CVPRW). IEEE (2016)
11. Martin, S., et al.: Understanding head and hand activities and coordination in naturalistic driving videos. In: 2014 IEEE Intelligent Vehicles Symposium Proceedings. IEEE (2014)
12. Ohn-Bar, E., Trivedi, M.: In-vehicle hand activity recognition using integration of regions. In: 2013 IEEE Intelligent Vehicles Symposium (IV). IEEE (2013)
13. Zhao, C.H., et al.: Recognition of driving postures by contourlet transform and random forests. IET Intell. Transport Syst. 6(2), 161–168 (2012)
14. He, K., et al.: Deep residual learning for image recognition. In: Proceedings of the IEEE Conference on Computer Vision and Pattern Recognition (2016)
15. Howard, A.G., et al.: Mobilenets: efficient convolutional neural networks for mobile vision applications. arXiv preprint arXiv:1704.04861 (2017)
16. Szegedy, C., et al.: Inception-v4, inception-resnet and the impact of residual connections on learning. In: Thirty-First AAAI Conference on Artificial Intelligence (2017)
17. Okon, O.D., Meng, L.: Detecting distracted driving with deep learning. In: Ronzhin, A., Rigoll, G., Meshcheryakov, R. (eds.) ICR 2017. LNCS (LNAI), vol. 10459, pp. 170–179. Springer, Cham (2017). https://doi.org/10.1007/978-3-319-66471-2_19

RECAL: Reuse of Established *CNN* Classifier Apropos Unsupervised Learning Paradigm

Jayasree Saha$^{(\boxtimes)}$ (iD) and Jayanta Mukherjee

Indian Institute of Technology Kharagpur, Kharagpur 721302, West Bengal, India
jayasree.saha@iitkgp.ac.in, jay@cse.iitkgp.ac.in

Abstract. Recently, clustering with a deep network framework has attracted the attention of several researchers in the computer vision community. The Deep framework gains extensive attention due to its efficiency and scalability towards large-scale and high-dimensional data. In this paper, we transform supervised *CNN* classifier architecture into an unsupervised clustering model, called *RECAL* (https://arxiv.org/abs/1906.06480). It jointly learns discriminative embedding subspace and cluster labels. *RECAL* is made up of feature extraction layers that are convolutional, followed by unsupervised classifier layers which is fully connected. A multinomial logistic regression function (*softmax*) stacked on top of classifier layers. We train this network using stochastic gradient descent (*SGD*) optimizer. However, the successful implementation of our model is revolved around the design of loss function. Our loss function uses the heuristics that true partitioning entails lower entropy, given that the class distribution is not heavily skewed. This is a trade-off between the situations of "skewed distribution" and "low-entropy". To handle this, we have proposed classification entropy and class entropy, which are the two components of our loss function. In this approach, the size of the mini-batch should be kept high. Experimental results indicate the consistent and competitive behavior of our model for clustering well-known digit, multi-viewed object, and face datasets. Moreover, we use this model to generate unsupervised patch segmentation for multispectral *LISS-IV* images. We observe that it is able to distinguish built-up areas, wetland, vegetation and water-body from the underlying scene.

Keywords: Unsupervised classification · Entropy · Deep network

1 Introduction

Clustering of large scale data is an active area of research in deep learning and big-data domain. It has gained significant attention as labeling data is costly and anomalous in real-world data. For example, getting ground truths for satellite imagery is difficult. A few disaster management applications suffer from that. Nevertheless, clustering algorithms have been studied widely. But, its performance

© Springer Nature Singapore Pte Ltd. 2020
R. V. Babu et al. (Eds.): NCVPRIPG 2019, CCIS 1249, pp. 174–184, 2020.
https://doi.org/10.1007/978-981-15-8697-2_16

drops drastically when it encounters high dimensional data. Also, their time-complexity increases dramatically. To handle the curse of dimensionality, original data space is projected into low dimensional manifold and clustering is applied using them with standard algorithms on that new manifold. However, this approach fails when the number of samples reaches millions or billions. To cope up with the situation, several deep architecture based clustering approaches have been proposed in recent years. Most of them are *CNN* or *feed-forward* based autoencoder architecture [2,17,18], embedded with simple, *k-means* like, clustering algorithm. These models have the tendency of learning features of the dataset and their corresponding cluster labels jointly. They employ a heuristic for clustering and use it along with the reconstruction loss function for training the model. Therefore, the bottleneck is to get initial clusters to accommodate clustering objective function in the loss function. The intuitive choice for the above problem is to train the auto-encoder model with reconstruction loss to generate a new embedding subspace. Then, the best-known clustering algorithm is employed on that subspace to generate clusters [2]. Thereafter, the new model is ready to train using two components of the loss function. However, another choice is to employ *k-means* like algorithm to get initial cluster labels. Other than auto-encoders, there are stacked convolutional layer based deep architecture exist [6]. However, they pre-trained their model with a large-scale *ImageNet* dataset in order to use clustering objective function. It is to be noted that if the model architecture is similar to well-known classifiers architecture like *AlexNet* [7], *VGG* [13], *ResNet* [5], then learned parameters on those layers are eventually transferred. Pre-training can not fit the data distribution of the dataset under consideration appropriately. It requires fine-tuning the model with the new dataset. However, it proves better than the random initialization of the model parameters for the classification task in a new domain. Also, it is speeding up the convergence of iterations for real-time training. To put it in a nutshell, the existing unsupervised deep approaches have the following pitfalls: 1) training the network from scratch, and 2) obtaining initial cluster labels. To address the above-mentioned pitfalls, we propose a deep clustering algorithm that does not require any initial cluster labels. In this paper, we consider the following two issues:

1. Can we utilize features generated from well-known pre-trained deep networks to develop clustering algorithm such that computational cost and memory requirement be reduced?
2. Can we perform clustering of these feature vectors under the same deep learning framework in the absence of any information on the labeling of these data?

In recent years, *AlexNet* [7], *VGG* [13], *ResNet* [5] receive high popularity in *ImageNet* challenge. Thus, it motivates us to choose one of the networks which have the capability of extracting good feature representatives. However, these networks are supervised. Hence, they can not be used in a scenario where no label is present. In this paper, we propose a loss function that enables the unsupervised labeling of data using these networks. For illustration, we have chosen typically *VGG-16* with batch normalization in our experiments. Also, we replace all fully connected and following layers by a single fully connected layer followed by batch normalization and *ReLU* layers. Our loss function is formulated using the following entropy-based clustering heuristics:

1. For a true partitioning, low entropy is desirable. This demands highly skewed probability distribution for a sample to be assigned to a cluster.
2. Any random partitioning than the actual one should lead to higher entropy, given the class distribution is not heavily skewed. For example, when all the feature vectors form trivially a single cluster, the distribution becomes highly skewed. In this case, though the entropy is zero, it does not reflect any meaningful information regarding partitioning.

There is a trade-off between these two factors. We propose a loss function for the network, which takes into account these two factors for a given number of clusters. To summarize, the major contributions of our work are:

1. We propose a simple but effective approach to reuse well-known supervised deep architectures in an unsupervised learning paradigm.
2. We formulate an entropy-based loss function to guide clustering and deep representation learning in a single framework that can be transferred to other tasks and datasets.
3. Our experimental results show that the proposed framework is consistent and competitive irrespective of different datasets.
4. Finally, we use this network in remote sensing domain to provide segmentation for multi-spectral images.

2   Approach

2.1   Notation

We represent an image set with n images by $X = \{x_1, \cdots, x_n\}$ where each sample x_i represents an image of resolution $n_1 \times n_2$. The clustering task is to group image set X into K clusters $Y = \{y_1, \cdots y_K\}$. Using embedding function $f_\theta : X \to Z$, we transform raw image samples X into its embedding subspace $Z = \{z_1, \cdots, z_n\}$ where $z_i \in \mathbb{R}^d$. We estimate posterior probability $\mathbb{P}(Y|Z)$ and use Eq. 1 to assign each of the samples to one of K cluster labels.

$$\hat{k}_{x_i} = \arg\max_k \mathbb{P}(y_k|z) \tag{1}$$

However, we reuse well-known *CNN* network architecture to transform raw images into its embedded subspace. It is well-known that transfer learning expedites the process of learning new distribution. Hence, we may transfer the learned weights of those networks in the beginning. Additionally, *softmax* function is used to learn $\mathbb{P}(Y|Z)$. Section 3.4 describes detailed architecture of our model.

2.2   Unsupervised Training Criterion

Motivation: Designing a loss function for unsupervised classification is highly influenced by the concept of "structuredness" and "diversity" of the dataset. Data can be well predicted if it belongs to a uniform distribution. In information theory, this "structuredness" is quantified by low entropy. On the other hand, the multi-class environment is characterized by "diversity" in data, which increases the entropy of the dataset. A clustering algorithm becomes vulnerable when it produces a highly skewed partition. Thereby, it witnesses low entropy. Therefore, it is desirable that an algorithm should report low entropy for a partition only when it is non-skewed.

Deep Network Scenario: We discuss this issue in the context of deep architecture. In general, deep networks are trained by the dataset, which is divided into mini-batches. They accumulate losses incurred by each mini-batch and update the parameters of the network by incorporating the gradient of the loss function. We consider that data is well classified by the network when the probability that it corresponds to a particular class out of K classes, is near about 1. Therefore, it estimates low entropy. To accomplish it, classification entropy (H_Φ) is designed. However, skewed partitioning is reduced by enforcing "diversity" in the mini-batch. The underlying intuition is that the more the number of distinct representatives the architecture experiences in a mini-batch, the better it learns the grouping. To accomplish it, class entropy (H_Ψ) is designed. Therefore, the aim is to maximize the class entropy while minimizing classification entropy.

Mathematical Formulation: In our model, we have feature extraction layers and classification layers. Feature extraction layers provide the mapping from input image space to feature embedded space $f_{\theta_1} : X \to Z$. However, Classification layers provide the mapping of feature embedded space to cluster labels space, i.e. $f_{\theta_2} : Z \to R$. We are interested in knowing the probability that the mth sample belongs to l^{th} class, which is denoted as p_{ml}. i.e.

$$p_{ml} = P(y_m = l|Z) = P(y_m = l|R) = \frac{exp(r_{ml})}{\sum_{j=1}^{K} exp(r_{mj})} \quad (2)$$

We design our loss function (L) for unsupervised classification with aforesaid motivation as follows:

$$\begin{aligned}
L &= \lambda H_\Phi - H_\Psi \\
H_\Phi &= -\frac{1}{M}\sum_{m=1}^{M}\sum_{l=1}^{K} p_{ml} \log(p_{ml}) \\
H_\Psi &= -\sum_{l=1}^{K} p_l \log(p_l) \\
p_l &= \frac{\sum_{m=1}^{M}(p_{ml})}{\sum_{l=1}^{K}\sum_{m=1}^{M}(p_{ml})}
\end{aligned} \quad (3)$$

where λ weighs loss function L.

3   Experiments

In this section, we first compare *RECAL* with state-of-the-art clustering methods on several bench-mark image datasets. Then, we run the *k-means* clustering algorithm on our learned deep representations. Finally, we analyze the performance of the *RECAL* model on unsupervised segmentation tasks on multi-spectral *LISS-IV* images.

Algorithm 1: Joint optimization on y and θ

Input :
        X=Collection of Image Data
        K=Target number of cluster
        B= Batch Size
Output:
        Y^* : image labels
        θ^* : CNN parameters
1 Initialize θ, optimizer=$(SGD$, lr=0.0001$)$
2 **repeat**
3 | **foreach** *minibatch* **do**
4 | | Compute $\mathbb{P}(Y|Z)$ by forward propagation using θ.
5 | | compute $Loss= \lambda H_\Phi - H_\Psi$ using Eq. 3.
6 | | Update θ by back propagation.
7 | **end**
8 **until** *converged*;

3.1 Alternative Clustering Models

We compare our model with several baseline and deep models, including k-means, normalized cuts (NCuts) [11], self-tuning spectral clustering (SC-ST) [20], large-scale spectral clustering (SC-LS) [1], graph degree linkage-based agglomerative clustering (AC-GDL) [21], agglomerative clustering via path integral (AC-PIC) [22], local discriminant models and global integration (LDMGI) [19], NMF with deep model (NMF-D) [14], task-specific clustering with deep model (TSC-D) [15], deep embedded clustering (DEC)[17], joint unsupervised learning (JULE) [18] and deep embedded regularized clustering (DEPICT) [2] for unsupervised clustering.

3.2 Dataset

We have chosen different types of datasets to show the consistent behavior of our model towards accomplishing clustering: *MNIST-full* [8], *USPS*[1], *COIL-20* and *COIL-100* [9], *UMist* [4], *CMU-PIE* [12], *Youtube-Face (YTF)* [16].

3.3 Evaluation Metric

We follow the current literature which uses normalized mutual information (NMI) as evaluation criteria for clustering algorithms. *NMI* evaluates the similarity between two labels of the same dataset in normalized form (0,1). However, 0 implies no correlation, and 1 shows a perfect correlation between two labels. We use predicted labels (by the model) and the ground truth labels to estimate *NMI*.

---

[1] https://www.cs.nyu.edu/~roweis/data.html.

3.4   Implementation Details

We adopt feature extraction layers of *VGG16* [13] with batch normalization and use the weights of the original network trained with *ImageNet* as a starting point. However, we consider a fully connected layer followed by a batch-normalization and a *ReLU* layer for unsupervised labeling (equivalent classification layers). We stacked classification layers on top of feature extraction layers of *VGG16*. For *USPS* dataset, we decapitate feature layers of *VGG16* to get an output of size 1×1; otherwise, we use all feature layers of *VGG16*. Consequently, we normalize the image intensities using $\hat{x} = \frac{x-\mu}{\sigma}$ where (μ) and (σ) are the mean and standard deviation of the given dataset, respectively. Moreover, we use stochastic gradient descent (SGD) as our optimization method with the learning rate $= 0.0001$ and momentum $= 0.9$. The weights of fully connected layer is initialized by *Xavier* approach [3]. Pre-trained models may not generate useful features to obtain a good clustering for the target dataset. Hence, fine-tuning is required. Pre-trained models not only expedite the process of convergence in fine-tuning but, it helps to provide a global solution instead of a local one.

3.5   Quantitative Comparison

We show *NMI* for every method on various datasets. Experimental results are averaged over three runs. We borrowed the best results from either original paper or [18] if reported on a given dataset. Otherwise, we put dash marks (-) without reporting any result. We report our results in two parts: 1) the clustering labels predicted by our network after training it for several epochs; 2) the clustering results obtained by running *k-means* clustering algorithm on learned representation by our network. Table 1 reports the clustering metric, normalized mutual information *(NMI)*, of the comparative algorithms along with *RECAL* on the aforementioned datasets. We have transferred weights of feature layers of *VGG-16* (trained with *ImageNet*) to the feature layers of *RECAL* and classification layers are initialized with *Xavier*'s approach. As shown, *RECAL* perform competitively and consistently. It should be noted that hyperparameter tuning using labeled samples is not feasible always in real-world clustering task. *DEPICT* has already shown an approach of not using supervised signals. However, their approach is dependent on other clustering algorithm. Hence, our algorithm is an independent and significantly better clustering approach for handling real-world large scale dataset. Interestingly, clustering results on learned representatives produce better outcome, as shown in Table 2. It indicates that our method can learn more discriminative feature representatives compared to image intensity. Notably, our learned representation is much better than *JULE* [18] for multi-viewed objects and digit dataset where their clustering result by their model, produce perfect *NMI* on *COIL-20*. However, our method performs poorly on face datasets. We identified that *UMist* dataset contains the side face and the front face of individuals. Our model tends to group side faces of individuals in similar clusters. *CMU_PIE* dataset collects faces at different illumination conditions. Our model has a tendency for clustering faces of similar illumination conditions in one group. Also, Table 1 suggests that

Table 1. Clustering performance of different algorithms based on *NMI*.

Dataset	MNIST-full	USPS	COIL-20	COIL-100	U-Mist	CMU-PIE	YTF
k-means	0.500	0.447	0.775	0.822	0.609	0.549	0.761
N-cuts	0.411	0.675	0.884	0.861	0.782	0.411	0.742
SC-ST	0.416	0.726	0.895	0.858	0.611	0.581	0.620
SC_LS	0.706	0.681	0.877	0.833	0.810	0.788	0.759
AC-GDL	0.844	0.824	0.937	0.933	0.755	0.934	0.622
AC-PIC	0.940	0.825	0.950	0.964	0.750	0.902	0.697
LDMGI	0.802	0.563	–	–	–	–	–
NMF-D	0.152	0.287	0.648	0.748	0.467	0.920	0.562
TSC-D	0.651	–	–	–	–	–	–
DEC	0.816	0.586	–	–	–	0.924	0.446
JULE-SF	0.906	0.858	1.000	0.978	0.880	0.984	0.848
JULE-RC	0.913	0.913	1.000	0.985	0.877	1.000	0.848
DEPICT	0.917	0.927	–	–	–	0.974	0.802
RECAL	0.852	0.913	0.880	0.831	0.694	0.627	0.779

learned features are much distinctive compared to the features obtained by *V*GG-16 model trained with *I*mageNet. We have executed our code on a machine with *GeForce GTX 1080 Ti* GPU.

4   Multi-spectral Image Segmentation

For illustrating the usefulness of this approach, we consider the application of this method for unsupervised labeling of pixels in an image. We experiment with satellite multi-spectral images. We have observed that very tiny patches may be a representative of a pure class. With this assumption, we split the pre-processed satellite image into small patches (e.g., 32×32 or 16×16 or 8×8) with strides of k (e.g., 16 or 8) pixels. However, we decapitate the feature layers of *VGG-16* from its tail such that the size of the feature (not the output of the whole model) for an input patch of 8×8 is 1×1. Otherwise, there is no change in the network architecture. We do our experiments with other large size patches on this decapitated version of the network. Our multispectral-images (*LISS-IV*) have three channels that fit the *VGG-16* input channels. However, "Copy Initialization" [10] can be used when the number of channels is more than three.

4.1   Description of Dataset

For our experiments, we have used images captured by Linear Imaging Self Scanner *LISS-IV* sensor of *RESOURCESAT-2*. As field investigation is a crucial task and requires expertise, we have used Microsoft® BingTM maps for validation of our experiment.

Table 2. Performance *(NMI)* of *k-means* on learned representations by different models

Method	Model	MNIST-full	USPS	COIL-20	COIL-100	UMist	CMU_PIE	YTF
k-means	*RECAL*	0.885	**0.913**	**0.948**	**0.919**	0.675	0.715	0.809
	JULE	**0.927**	0.758	0.926	**0.919**	**0.871**	**0.956**	**0.835**
	VGG-16	0.182	0.014	0.769	0.792	0.576	0.302	0.167

4.2 Pre-processing of Dataset

In general, a sensor captures Earth's surface radiance, and this response is quantized into n-bit values. It is commonly called Digital Number (DN). However, to convert calibrated (DNs) to at-sensor radiance, two meta-parameters are used: known dynamic-range limits of the instrument and their corresponding pre-defined spectral radiance values. Meta files are provided by the satellite data provider. This radiance is then converted to the top-of-atmosphere (ToA) reflectance by normalizing for solar elevation and solar spectral irradiance.

4.3 Results

In this experiment, we separately trained the model with the patches from Scene-1 and Scene-2 for $K = 10$. Let's call it model-1 and model-2, respectively. We observe each segmented output from model-1 and model-2 (shown in Fig. 1) separately. However, we check the cross-dataset segmentation output, which measures the robustness of the network. i.e., We use model-1 to generate the segmentation for scene-2 and vice versa. Notably, the number of patches from Scene-1 and Scene-2 are approx. 0.2 million and 2.2 million, respectively. Models took nearly 1–1.5 days for training. For Scene-1, our model has detected the built-up area, vegetation, and water-body distinctively among 10 classes. However, model-2 identifies vegetation, water body, and wetland area. This is to be noted that model-2 predicts vegetation into three distinct classes. This result might be an indicator of three types of vegetation in that location. We measure the consensus of two models using *Jaccard similarity* score. Table 3 shows the *Jaccard similarity* score for various identified classes in scene-1 and scene-2, respectively.

Table 3. *Jaccard similarity* score for different classes for scene-1 and scene-2

	Scene-1						Scene-2				
	Model-2						Model-1				
	cV1S1	cV2S1	cB2S1	cB1S1	cWBS1		cV2S2	cV1S2	cV3S2	cWBS2	cWLS2
V1S1	0.545	0.004	0.004	0.002	0.004	V1S2	0.624	0.004	0.000	0.008	0.000
V2S1		0.299	0.015	0.014	0.001	V2S2		0.186	0.001	0.059	0.000
B1S1			0.243	0.105	0.007	V3S2			0.315	0.002	0.031
B2S1				0.211	0.004	WBS2				0.556	0.011
WBS1					0.721	WLS2					0.570

(Scene-1 rows labeled under Model-1; Scene-2 rows labeled under Model-2)

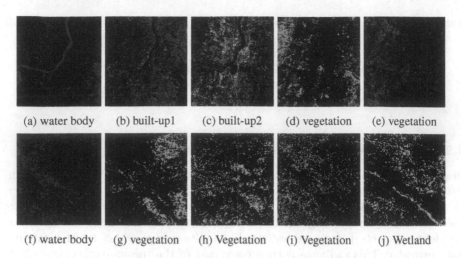

(a) water body   (b) built-up1   (c) built-up2   (d) vegetation   (e) vegetation

(f) water body   (g) vegetation   (h) Vegetation   (i) Vegetation   (j) Wetland

Fig. 1. First and second rows show segmentation results of scene-1 by model-1 and scene-2 by model-2 respectively.

5   Conclusion

In this paper, we have proposed an approach to transform supervised *CNN* classifier architecture into an unsupervised clustering model. We address "structuredness" and "diversity" of the dataset to migrate from supervised to unsupervised paradigm. Our model jointly learns discriminative embedding subspace and cluster labels. The major strength of this approach is: scalability and reusability. Experimental results show that *RECAL* performs competitively for real-world clustering task. However, it learns representation better compared to the existing approaches for non-face image datasets. We have shown segmentation as one of the applications by our proposed method in the remote sensing domain. To achieve this, we split the original image into small patches and get a label for each of them. Then, they are combined to get the segmentation of the whole image. We qualitatively observe that this model can detect vegetation, water-body, wet-land, built-up area separately. We also provide the power of transferring learned representation across separate scenes in this work. However, the built-up area has confusion with wetland and vegetation in the cross-dataset segmentation task. It is probably due to the similar characteristics among these classes, which is an innate problem in the underlying dataset. We also observe that training of the proposed network is fast. It took about roughly 30 h to process more than 2 million patches in our experiments in *GeForce GTX 1080 Ti GPU*. This strongly indicates the property of scalability for our model.

References

1. Cai, D., Chen, X.: Large scale spectral clustering via landmark-based sparse representation. IEEE Trans. Cybern. **45**, 1669–1680 (2015)
2. Dizaji, K.G., Herandi, A., Huang, H.: Deep clustering via joint convolutional autoencoder embedding and relative entropy minimization. In: IEEE International Conference on Computer Vision (ICCV), pp. 5747–5756 (2017)
3. Glorot, X., Bengio, Y.: Understanding the difficulty of training deep feedforward neural networks. In: International Conference on Artificial Intelligence and Statistics. Proceedings of Machine Learning Research, vol. 9, pp. 249–256 (2010)
4. Graham, D.B., Allinson, N.M.: Characterising Virtual Eigensignatures for General Purpose Face Recognition, pp. 446–456 (1998)
5. He, K., Zhang, X., Ren, S., Sun, J.: Deep residual learning for image recognition. CoRR abs/1512.03385 (2015)
6. Hsu, C., Lin, C.: CNN-based joint clustering and representation learning with feature drift compensation for large-scale image data. IEEE Trans. Multimedia **20**(2), 421–429 (2018)
7. Krizhevsky, A., Sutskever, I., Hinton, G.E.: Imagenet classification with deep convolutional neural networks. In: International Conference on Neural Information Processing Systems, vol. 1, pp. 1097–1105 (2012)
8. Lecun, Y., Bottou, L., Bengio, Y., Haffner, P.: Gradient-based learning applied to document recognition. Proc. IEEE **86**(11), 2278–2324 (1998)
9. Nene, S.A., Nayar, S.K., Murase, H.: Columbia object image library (coil-20. Technical report (1996)
10. Pan, B., Shi, Z., Xu, X., Shi, T., Zhang, N., Zhu, X.: Coinnet: copy initialization network for multispectral imagery semantic segmentation. IEEE Geosci. Remote Sens. Lett. **16**(5), 816–820 (2019)
11. Shi, J., Malik, J.: Normalized cuts and image segmentation. IEEE Trans. Pattern Anal. Mach. Intell. **22**(8), 888–905 (2000)
12. Sim, T., Baker, S., Bsat, M.: The CMU pose, illumination, and expression (PIE) database. In: IEEE International Conference on Automatic Face and Gesture Recognition, pp. 53–58 (2002)
13. Simonyan, K., Zisserman, A.: Very deep convolutional networks for large-scale image recognition. CoRR abs/1409.1556 (2014)
14. Trigeorgis, G., Bousmalis, K., Zafeiriou, S., Schuller, B.W.: A deep semi-NMF model for learning hidden representations. In: International Conference on Machine Learning (ICML), vol. 32, pp. II-1692–II-1700 (2014)
15. Wang, Z., Chang, S., Zhou, J., Huang, T.S.: Learning a task-specific deep architecture for clustering. CoRR abs/1509.00151 (2015)
16. Wolf, L., Hassner, T., Maoz, I.: Face recognition in unconstrained videos with matched background similarity. In: IEEE Conference on Computer Vision and Pattern Recognition (CVPR), pp. 529–534 (2011)
17. Xie, J., Girshick, R.B., Farhadi, A.: Unsupervised deep embedding for clustering analysis. CoRR abs/1511.06335 (2015)
18. Yang, J., Parikh, D., Batra, D.: Joint unsupervised learning of deep representations and image clusters. In: IEEE Conference on Computer Vision and Pattern Recognition (CVPR), pp. 5147–5156 (2016)
19. Yang, Y., Xu, D., Nie, F., Yan, S., Zhuang, Y.: Image clustering using local discriminant models and global integration. IEEE Trans. Image Process. **19**(10), 2761–2773 (2010)

20. Zelnik-Manor, L., Perona, P.: Self-tuning spectral clustering. In: International Conference on Neural Information Processing Systems, pp. 1601–1608 (2004)
21. Zhang, W., Wang, X., Zhao, D., Tang, X.: Graph degree linkage: agglomerative clustering on a directed graph. CoRR abs/1208.5092 (2012)
22. Zhang, W., Zhao, D., Wang, X.: Agglomerative clustering via maximum incremental path integral. Pattern Recogn. **46**(11), 3056–3065 (2013)

Pose Estimation of UAVs Using Stereovision

Samvram Sahu$^{(\boxtimes)}$, Harsha Simha, and Deepak Mishra

Department of Avionics Indian Institute of Space Science and Technology,
Thiruvananthapuram, India
samvram.iist@gmail.com, {harshasimhams,deepak.mishra}@iist.ac.in

Abstract. Pose of an UAV has been traditionally estimated by On Board Computers (OBCs) using Inertial Measurement Unit (IMU) sensor data as input. In this paper, the development of an architecture for estimating the pose of an UAV using popular Computer Vision based methods has bis proposed. Which consists of three sub modules, namely, Image Segmentation Block (IS), Perspective Transform (PT) and Pose Determination (PD) respectively. IS block uses segmentation to detect salient points from the image where as the PT block transforms image coordinates to world coordinates, finally the PD block uses camera parameters and object dimensions to provide Attitude and Translation matrix of the UAV. The proposed approach can adjust with change in environmental parameters. The system was characterized by observing the error in the estimated yaw and estimated depth. Analysis was made on the nature and variation of error with various experimental parameters. An in depth analysis of the paper was carried out. We were finally able to devise an algorithm for estimating the pose of a body without establishing any communication with the body.

Keywords: UAV · Pose · Computer Vision · Image processing

1 Introduction

The usage of Unmanned Aerial Vehicles (UAV) have gained importance over the last decade due to their subtle applications in surveillance and security. The growing applications of UAVs lead us to focus largely on UAV autonomy to improve manoeuvring capabilities. One important aspect of manoeuvring is docking, which requires fast and precise determination of attitude, altitude and motion. This paper proposes a simple and fast algorithm for determining the UAV attitude and distance from a pair of CCD cameras using stereovision. Given a pair of pictures from two spatially separated cameras, we would like to determine the pose by constructing rotation matrix and translation vector. We construct four markers on the UAV to solve for the pose matrix of the object. The primary assumption is that any three markers at any point of time is visible (which is true for Quadcopters) to construct two deterministic vectors and using our PT block algorithm on a minimum of 2 vector measurements.

© Springer Nature Singapore Pte Ltd. 2020
R. V. Babu et al. (Eds.): NCVPRIPG 2019, CCIS 1249, pp. 185–197, 2020.
https://doi.org/10.1007/978-981-15-8697-2_17

The significance of our work lies in the fact that in order to determine the pose, the sensors need not to be inside the vehicle. Also, we do not use any complicated marker pattern as the blobs can be constructed in an UAV using LEDs and the blob detection algorithm would still work with a significant accuracy. The primary experiments are developed on assuming a Quadcopter model and it is aimed at developing an efficient docking algorithm for nanosatellites.

2   Methodology

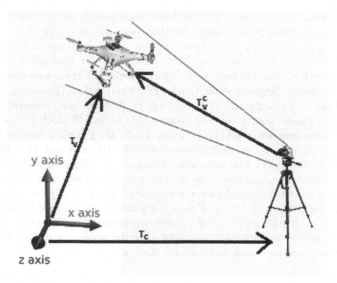

Fig. 1. Experimental setup: Camera fixed in inertial frame, UAV pose measured with respect to camera and then converted to pose in Inertial Frame

In Fig. 1 a camera can be seen observing the object, similarly a configuration of two cameras is used to observe an object in their common Field Of View (FOV).

Then the keypoints of both images are sent separately to the next block which is responsible for finding the real point of intersection in world frame using the data of the same keypoint from two different images. Since, the correspondence of keypoints in both images have to be maintained we place markers on the UAV which can be detected easily and then the correspondence can be found too.

As the relative position of the keypoints with respect to each other is known and how the image has deciphered them, using the above mentioned data the orientation is then calculated. The translation had been found in the previous block, and combining them both we get pose as the output of the system. Each of these blocks will be described in detail in the following chapters.

2.1 Advantages of the Method

This section is dedicated to listing all the benefits the proposed architecture in Fig. 2 provides over existing methods

- Modular - Each block is implemented independent of the other, however when cascaded they fulfil the objectives.
- Scalable - Each block has its own input for parameters which are subject to input or the problem we are dealing with.
- Reliable - While designing the functioning of each block it has been ensured that for trivial cases also, the solution exists.
- Optimized - We have optimized the system for computation time, which can then be utilized for real time applications.

2.2 Image Segmentation for Keypoint Detection

Image Segmentation is defined as the task of separating a foreground and background. Image Segmentation is an application specific task. This is one of the most crucial part of the system as it detects the keypoints from the image and based on this data pose is estimated.

Choice of Keypoints. The illumination from the LEDs causes the problem of shifting of the centroid. Hence, we choose the case of keypoint where coloured balls are mounted on the quadcopter which can be easily detected.

Algorithms. Algorithms developed for the project duration have been discussed below:

- RGB channel segmentation
  The output of using this method of segmentation is obtaining chroma centers, i.e., how we choose the center of blobs when it fits the required number of blob centers. We also apply certain filters:
  - Minimum Blob size = 50 px
  - Maximum Blob size = 10000 px
  - Minimum Circularity = 0.8

  Under these conditions, we find that the thresholds are allowed to change dynamically, however the presence of background noise renders this method inefficient. Also, this whole pipeline consumes more time as there is possibility of a loop while choosing threshold. The advantage of this type of segmentation is however user input free, i.e., manual input of threshold is not required for every run.

- HSV channel segmentation
  Unlike RGB, HSV separates luma, or the image intensity, from chroma or the color information. The separation of chroma or color information is very useful in many applications. This in theory will work regardless of lighting

changes in the value channel. In practice it is just a nice improvement. Even by singling out only the hue you still have a very meaningful representation of the base color that will likely work much better than RGB. The end result is a more robust color thresholding over simpler parameters.

- Classifying Blobs
  According to Fig. 4, we classify each center into the colour depending upon the way of classification. We only need to use this algorithm only if we use the RGB segmentation. With HSV segmentation this phase is done with hue classification alone. We have implemented HSV based segmentation as the Hue of the keypoint is an unique identity and can be easily mapped in HSV colour space.

- Streamlined Algorithm After a constant stream of refining from the above algorithms and adding better functionality in each step we come to the top-level algorithm in Fig. 5 is best suited for our purpose.
  This algorithm preserves modularity as well as provides us the scope to scale and generalize further.

Output. We provide output of the given block as a python dictionary with first letter of the colour as key. An example of output is shown below in Fig. 6.

2.3 Perspective Transform

The input to this block is the segmented blob center of each frame from both the cameras, this block takes into account the camera parameters and the position and orientation of camera and computes the real world position of the point in question. This computation makes use of perspective geometry and epipolar geometry.

Algorithm. Image Segmentation (IS) block takes input from cameras placed as shown in Fig. 7 and uses adaptive thresholding in all the three channels of the image to estimate x_{kc}^I, y_{kc}^I for each keypoint k for each camera c. These co-ordinates are pixel values in the image, where x and y are the co-ordinate values in the picture frame. I denote the co-ordinates are in Image Frame.

Perspective Transform (PT) block takes the x_{kc}, y_{kc} values as input and has access to information about the various camera parameters. Using the provided data and vector algebra, this block provides x_k^R, y_k^R, z_k^R for each keypoint k (super-script R signifies that these co-ordinates are in world frame). Using simple vector algebra, if we claim the camera co-ordinates to be x_c, y_c, z_c and the camera axis pointing along $[0, 0, 1]^T$ then a point p forms an image at x_p^I, y_p^I on the image plane which is only some finite distance f away. Now, using vector algebra we can write the equation for line joining center of camera and the point in image plane as

$$(x, y, z) = (x_c + s(x_p^I - x_c), y_c + s(y_p^I - y_c), z_c + s(z_p^I - z_c))$$

where s is a variable for extending the line and is called scale factor. Expanding the similar set of equation for a case of twin camera configuration, we assume that a single object represented as a point in two images would lie at intersection of two lines joining the respective camera centers and image of the objects. Using this concept we find that the value of,

$$s = \frac{x_{c1} + x_{c2}}{x_{c1} - x_{c2}} = \frac{y_{c1} + y_{c2}}{y_{c1} - y_{c2}} \tag{1}$$

Substituting the value of s in the determined set of equations we can get the values of x_p^R, y_p^R, z_p^R, provided the initial distance of z_p^I is calculated and stored beforehand from calibration of the camera. Also, it can further be trivially shown that when the denominator in the expression of s tends to zero the object is located farther away from the camera.

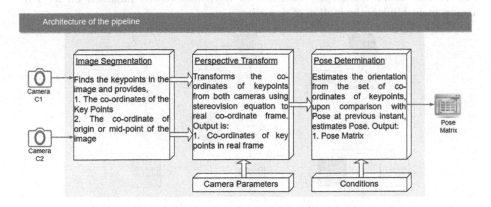

Fig. 2. Architecture of the proposed pose estimation pipeline

Output. The PT block renders the segmented image co-ordinates and translates to following real co-ordinates.

Unlike the output of Image Segmentation as in Fig. 8 which consists of 2D image co-ordinates of various keypoints for the case of Perspective Transform we have the output as 3D co-ordinates.

2.4 Pose Determination

This block essentially takes the x_k^R, y_k^R, z_k^R for each keypoint k, as input and has access to previous orientation (attitude) of these points in space. Using the position of these keypoints we construct two vectors namely v_1 and v_2 which after rotation becomes v_1^r and v_2^r respectively.

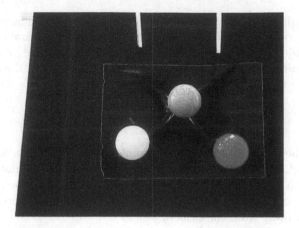

Fig. 3. The actual quadcopter mount with keypoints (balls) mounted on it. This arrangement hinders the motion of propellers

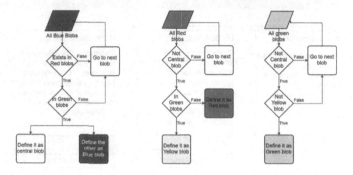

Fig. 4. Blob Classification based on Colour algorithm

However, for the case of translation vector determination, the use of stereovision approach allows us to determine the depth of individual point thus making a simple difference of the position of two vectors as the translational distance between them.

If the measurements are free of noise, we are bound to get accurate results as the method is deterministic and not probabilistic. However extensive simulation and experimentation suggests that errors in the previous stages (IS and PT blocks) cause the result of this block to diverge. We have implemented the following algorithms:

- TRIAD
- Asymmetric Triad
- Symmetric Triad
- Optimized Triad
- Wahba's Optimal Solution
- QUEST

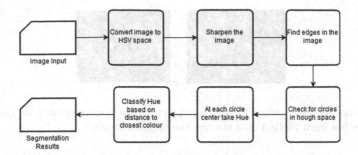

Fig. 5. Streamlined Image Segmentation Algorithm, after recurrent addition of advantages and removing bottlenecks

{'g': (250, 196), 'y': (374, 274), 'c': (390, 196), 'b': (419, 55), 'r': (531, 196)}

Fig. 6. Segmentation results as a Python dictionary containing image co-ordinate location of each keypoint

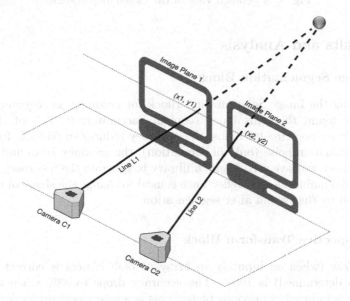

Fig. 7. Perspective transform: Camera positioning

3 Experimental Setup

Our proposed system is the featured part of the feedback system where the yaw of the system is measured and fed back to the system where the error is computed and based on it corrections are calculated by a PI controller and applied to the motors. The whole system representation can be found in Fig. 9.

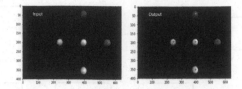

Fig. 8. Image segmentation: Output, as shown in previous section how each image co-ordinate has been plotted as a star on the original image.

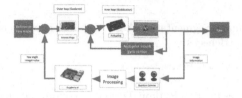

Fig. 9. A detailed view of the closed loop system

4   Results and Analysis

4.1   Image Segmentation Block

Upon testing the Image Segmentation Block for accuracy on segmenting blob centers, we found that this block segments accurately 92.33% of the time. On introducing non-circular blobs, the accuracy reduces to 66.66%, further on adding illumination noise (only in simulation), the accuracy is around 50%. In this simulation, we have used *vpython* library to generate the test cases in which the effect of illumination and reflectance is used to change the shape of the blobs as perceived by the system after segmentation.

4.2   Perspective Transform Block

The accuracy (when an input is an array of blob centers is correct and the position is determined) is 100%. The accuracy drops to 83% when measurement noise is induced in previous blobs. This is a case where errors in both the measurements can be modelled and then this metric can be improved.

4.3   Assembled System

First we shall discuss about the practical experiment results,**we were able to achieve steady state error of zero degrees**, for the experiment described in the previous chapter. However this has been only tested for the yaw case and still would be a great milestone for Computer Vision based pose estimation. Moreover the performance can be increased further by tuning the PI controller.

The performance of the assembled system as a whole will be reported here. The overall system reliability is 70% (Out of randomly oriented quadcopter's simulation scenes processed only 70 yield results).

In the Table 1 we can see how the system performs on different orientation shifts.

Table 1. Angular error table for different angles

Ang(^{o})	Pred Ang(^{o})	Err(^{o})	Abs Err(^{o})	Abs% Err(%)
0	0	0	0	nan
10	10.0543	0.0543	0.0543	0.0543
20	19.949	−0.051	−0.051	0.2549
30	30.1414	0.1414	0.1414	0.4713
40	40.5483	0.5483	0.5483	1.3708
50	49.9557	−0.0442	0.0442	0.0885
60	60.4334	0.4334	0.4334	0.7223
70	70.0509	0.0509	0.0509	0.0728
80	80.3862	0.3862	0.3862	0.4827
90	90.3525	0.3525	0.3525	0.3916

Out of 90 values, ten values covering the spread have been shown in the table. On the basis of this data where the first column describes the Yaw angle the system has, and the second column speaks of the result of the block. The mean error is 0.1114^o, and mean absolute error is 0.2653^o, and the mean absolute percentage error is 1.3581%.

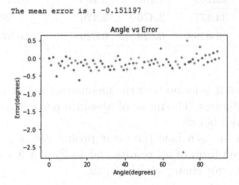

Fig. 10. Error profile (Angular), the error does not change too much with the change in true angle

In Fig. 10, we can see the plot describing how angular error changes with change in input angle; the Absolute Percentage Error (APE) profile can be seen in Fig. 11.

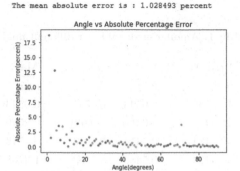

Fig. 11. Absolute % error profile (Angular), converges to 2%

The case of translatory motion shall be analyzed now. A similar experiment but with varying depth in the scene (using DTD). Table 2 shows the performance of the system with respect to translation.

Table 2. Translational error table for different depths

Dep.(uts)	Pred.(uts)	Err.(uts)	Abs Err(uts)	Abs% Err(%)
0	0.139	0.139	0.139	inf
10	11.232	1.232	1.232	12.327
20	22.105	2.105	2.105	10.542
30	33.477	3.476	3.476	11.592
40	46.629	6.629	6.629	16.5731

In this experiment it is found that the mean error is $1.85 units$, and the mean absolute error is $1.86 units$. The mean of absolute percentage error is 12%. The error profiles are given below:

In Fig. 12 it can be seen how the error profile varies as depth is changed, the table is condensed form of all results and in Fig. 13 it can be seen how the absolute percentage error changes with depth.

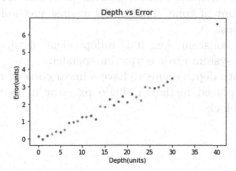

Fig. 12. Error profile (Depth), shows how the error increases with increase in true depth

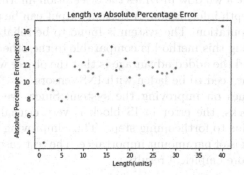

Fig. 13. Absolute % error profile (Translational), converges to 12 %

4.4   Analysis

Upon carefully analyzing the observed results we come to note the following:

- The IS block might make minor errors due to the rounding off, center of mass is truncated decimal value, which might contribute to error.
- Blobs of types where the centers are not on centroids, we face the issue of a non accurate evaluation.
- Illumination changes causes bias in the results, this shifts the center of mass drastically if the ball is closer.
- PT block is a straight forward calculative block and hence, an accurate input renders an accurate result. This concurs with our observation.
- For ground computations in PD block, absolute speed isn't all that important, since the estimation algorithm is only a part of the overall attitude determination data processing effort. Speed was more important in the past, when thousands of attitude solutions had to be computed by slower machines.
- For real-time processing in PD block, as for an attitude control system onboard a spacecraft, the longest time is more important than the average

time, because the attitude control system processor has to finish its task in a limited amount of time. This works against methods that may require sequential rotations.
- The yaw error is constant, i.e., it is independent of variation in the center which means our system error is yaw independent.
- However, error with depth seems to have a linear correlation which is natural, as the object is placed farther a single px error in IS will imply a larger deviation in PT block.

5   Conclusion

A real time system (where the system can detect the pose of the object and take action depending on it) implementation of the developed algorithm and architecture was done, where a window provides the orientation information and another window plots the depth information. A textual output can be programmed to be logged at each computation. The system is found to be reliable and robust. The overall accuracy using this method is comparable to the other available state of the art methods, and the added advantage is that the object whose pose is being determined does not need to be laden with INS sensors.

Here are few cues on improving the system: Since, we have a cascading arrangement of blocks, the error in IS block is very crucial, as a small error can get magnified due to forthcoming steps. Thus, improving the reliability and accuracy of IS block is of paramount importance. The test cases can be increased in simulation for more empirical results.

References

1. Markley, F.L.: Attitude determination using two vector measurements. In: Proceedings, Flight Mechanics Symposium, NASA Goddard Space Flight Center, Greenbelt, MD, NASA Conference Publication NASA/CP-19989-209235, pp. 39–52, May 1999
2. Newman, P., et al.: Navigating, recognizing and describing urban spaces with vision and lasers. Int. J. Robot. Res. 28(11–12), 1406–1433 (2009)
3. Konolige, K., Agrawal, M.: FrameSLAM: from bundle adjustment to real-time visual mapping. IEEE Trans. Robot. 24(5), 1066–1077 (2008)
4. Mondragón, I.F., et al.: 3D pose estimation based on planar object tracking for UAVs control. In: 2010 IEEE International Conference on Robotics and Automation (ICRA). IEEE (2010)
5. Santos, N.P., et al.: A ground-based vision system for UAV pose estimation. Int. J. Robot. Mech. 1(4), 138–144 (2014)
6. Warren, M., McKinnon, D., He, H., Upcroft, B.: Unaided stereo vision based pose estimation (2010)
7. Abdi, G., Samadzadegan, F., Kurz, F.: Pose estimation of unmanned aerial vehicles based on a vision aided multi-sensor fusion. In: The International Archives of the Photogrammetry, Remote Sensing and Spatial Information Sciences, vol. XLI-B6 (2016)

8. Sahu, S., Karmakar, A., Hari, P.: 3D Pose estimation of UAVs using stereovision. In: IEEE International Conference on Range Technology (ICORT), **2019**, pp. 630–635 (2019)
9. Su, W., Ravankar, A., Ravankar, A.A., Kobayashi, Y., Emaru, T.: UAV pose estimation using IR and RGB cameras. In: Proceedings of the 2017 IEEE/SICE International Symposium on System Integration
10. Li, F., Tang, D., Shen, N.: Vision-based pose estimation of UAV from line correspondences. Procedia Eng. **15**, 578–584 (2011)

U-RME: Underwater Refined Motion Estimation in Hazy, Cluttered and Dynamic Environments

Shilpi Gupta[1]([envelope]), Prerana Mukherjee[2], Santanu Chaudhury[3], and Brejesh Lall[1]

[1] Indian Institute of Technology, Delhi, India
Shilpi.Gupta@dbst.iitd.ac.in, brejesh@ee.iitd.ac.in
[2] Indian Institute of Information Technology, Sri City, Andhra Pradesh, India
prerana.m@iiits.in
[3] Indian Institute of Technology, Jodhpur, India
santanuc@iitj.ac.in

Abstract. Optical Flow is a popular method of computer vision for motion estimation. In this paper, we present a refined optical flow estimation method. Central to our approach is exploiting contour information as most of the motion lies on the edges. Further, we have formulated it as sparse to dense motion estimation. Proposed method has been evaluated on challenging real life image sequences of KITTI and Fish4Knowledge database. Results demonstrate that method performs well in case of low contrast, highly cluttered background, dynamic background, occlusion and illumination change.

Keywords: Optical flow · Marine ecosystem · Dense correspondence · Holistically nested edge detection

1 Introduction

Optical flow estimation is the primary block in multitude of computer vision applications involving motion information such as object segmentation, object detection and object tracking etc. Despite many research strides in this area, accurate estimation of optical flow is still an open problem due to challenges of real world videos. Traditional optical flow based approaches rely upon the energy minimization functions [9,16]. Due to the recent advancements in deep learning paradigms, optical flow estimation utilizing supervised deep learning based methods such as FlowNet2.0 [10], PWC-Net [24] etc. have outperformed traditional approaches. However, deep learning based supervised approaches are heavily dependent on the availability on ground truth data. In order to handle this, the networks are trained on synthetic data due to unavailability of ground truth on real scene sequences. There is high differences in the real and synthetic

We would like to thank the Ministry of Electronics and Information Technology Government of India and the Media Lab Asia for financial assistance to carry out research.

© Springer Nature Singapore Pte Ltd. 2020
R. V. Babu et al. (Eds.): NCVPRIPG 2019, CCIS 1249, pp. 198–208, 2020.
https://doi.org/10.1007/978-981-15-8697-2_18

images therefore existing approaches on synthetic data do not generalize on real images. Motivated by above reasons, researchers explored the direction of unsupervised Optical Flow estimation techniques like DD Flow [15] etc. But these approaches could not surpass the accuracy of supervised methods.

In recent years, there has been growing research interest to study the behavior of marine species due to its potential applications. Due to the complexity of the underwater environment and the limitations of human divers, underwater scenario is mainly explored by submarines, remotely operated vehicles (ROVs) and autonomous underwater vehicles (AUVs). Marine video surveillance is highly preferred over photography by divers or net-casting methods, since it provides a large amount of continuous data without effecting the fish behaviour. Detecting objects in underwater video is highly challenging task. The challenge posed is due to poor quality of vision data due to high turbidity, appearance variation with depth, light attenuation, suspended particles in the medium and dynamic environments due to movement in water particles and coral reefs as shown in Fig. 1. Objects are highly deformable, identical or very similar in appearance.

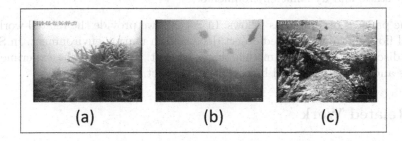

Fig. 1. Challenges in marine environment (a) Camouflage (b) Hazy environment (c) Clutter

In this paper, the objective is to find motion estimation of fishes in underwater videos using image processing and computer vision concepts. Hence, we propose Underwater Refined Motion Estimation (U-RME) in hazy, cluttered and dynamic environments. Recent efforts towards this problem assume availability of annotated datasets [10,19,24]. Most popular approach for object detection is to train a model by supervised learning. To achieve desirable accuracy, these methods require a large amount of annotated data, which is highly time consuming and requires human expertise to recognize fishes in cluttered background and high camouflage based marine conditions. In practical scenario, the datasets do not span over all possible classes of fish, limiting their effectiveness in analyzing underwater ecosystem, tracking fish population etc. while at the same time dampening utilization of such techniques in exploratory research for new applications of underwater imaging. Moreover, it is also important to note that, a large amount of images available over the web is not part of standard datasets. The pre-trained object detectors process individual frames of videos while completely ignoring the temporal information. Human visual system does not receive static images, it receives continuous video streams. Appearance cues provide limited information when videos are recorded in low light and hazy conditions. In such cases, motion is an important factor to get significant information about moving object in videos. Gestalt principle also states that "grouping forms the basis of human perception" [11]. Points moving together can be grouped together and they often belong to the same object. Motion based grouping appears early in the stages of visual perception than static grouping.

To this end, we introduce a refined end-to-end motion estimation technique. The key contributions in this paper can be summarized as,

- We have updated the pipeline by including a pre-processing block to handle highly illumination varying and hazy environment. Holistically nested edge detection and a median filtering based objective function is adopted to get better motion boundaries in cluttered and dynamic environments.
- To the best of our knowledge, we are the first to utilize dense optical flow for detecting motion of fish in real-life dataset of fish4knowledge.
- We have evaluated the proposed approach with several flow based techniques over static and dynamic environments.

The paper is organized as follows. In Sect. 2, we provide the related work on optical flow and motion based object detection in marine environment. In Sect. 3, we discuss the proposed methodology. In Sect. 4, we give the experimental results and analysis followed by conclusion in Sect. 5.

2   Related Work

Optical flow estimation has been studied as an important topic in computer vision for long. Research work done in this area can be broadly classified into various categories. Traditional methods are based on variational approaches [1, 9, 16]. In such methods, the aim is to optimize the function of brightness constancy and spatial smoothness. These methods are suitable for small displacements but fail in case of large displacement flows. Coarse to fine approaches have been proposed to tackle large displacements [3]. Later approaches integrate feature matching to tackle this issue. Specially, they find sparse feature correspondences to initialize flow estimation and further refine it in a pyramidal coarse-to-fine manner. SIFT FLOW performs dense matching between the Scale Invariant Feature Trasform (SIFT) feature matching between two images [14]. The seminal work of EpicFlow [21] interpolates dense flow from sparse matches and has been widely used for scene flow estimation in dynamic environments.

Recently, the success of deep learning has inspired researchers to solve flow estimation problem as optical flow learning problem. The pioneering work is FlowNet 2.0 [10], which is based on supervised learning and generates a dense optical flow map with two consecutive frame and a trained model. SpyNet introduces a spatial pyramid network in order to handle large displacements [19]. Recently, PWC-Net [24] has been proposed to warp extracted features learned by CNNs instead of warping images over different scales. Although these approaches show promising performance but the problem is that these methods require a large amount of labeled training data, which is particularly difficult to obtain for optical flow particularly in case of underwater scenarios. Synthetic dataset is used for training such models, while real images are very different from synthetic images. Due to this gap, these models do not always perform well with real data.

Another promising direction is to develop unsupervised learning approaches [20]. The idea is to warp the target image according to the predicted flow, the difference between the reference image and the warped image is optimized using a photometric loss. Most recent work of DDFlow generate annotations on unlabeled data using a model trained with a classical optical flow energy function, and then retrain the model using those extra generated annotations [15]. There is still a large gap if we compare the performance with supervised methods.

Due to these limitations of supervised and unsupervised deep learning based approaches, in this paper we propose an unsupervised approach to estimate flow in hazy, cluttered and dynamic environment of marine videos. The closest work to ours is EpicFlow [21]. However, we introduce non-local median filtering [8] in the optimization function. This allows the noise suppression and introduces brightness constancy term in the energy optimization function to mitigate the illumination variations. Since, there is light dispersion in the medium leading to shadow effects we also perform preprocessing measures.

3   Proposed Methodology

In this section, we detail the components of the proposed methodology. Figure 2 shows the pipeline of the proposed methodology.

3.1   Preprocessing

The primary focus is to get accurate optical flow estimation for complex environment where videos are of poor resolution quality, hazy in nature with uneven and rapidly changing illumination changes. There are two major causes of haze in surveillance videos: (i) Fog or Smog in aerial videos and (ii) Turbidity of water, light scattering in water particle in underwater videos. In order to handle this, we require the pre-processing step in such videos. We can improve the quality of images either by image enhancement techniques or image restoration techniques. For image enhancement, we used DehazeNet [4]. This is a CNN based deep architecture for haze removal. Network takes a hazy image as an input, and output is a haze free image. This method outperforms the existing haze removal techniques which are based on many prior assumptions. Another approach we have exploited is inspired by underwater particle physics [6]. In this paper [6], authors proposed Simultaneous localization and mapping (SLAM) to do object detection. In this work, Light Scattering Model produces better results when compared with DehazeNet in case of marine videos. The qualitative comparative results obtained by both methods are shown in Fig. 3. As can be seen, light

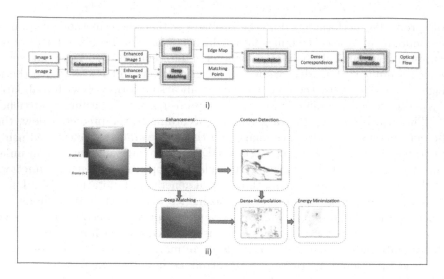

Fig. 2. i) Flowchart of proposed method. ii) Pipeline of the proposed flow method. Given two frames of the video, we first perform enhancement using Light scattering technique as proposed in [6]. Next, we use DeepMatching technique to get correspondence between two frames [22] and contours of the first frame (t) is computed using Holistic Nested Edges (HED) [26]. Finally, we combine these two cues to get dense interpolation image which enables computation of dense correspondence field. This is used to initialize the energy minimization framework of optical flow generation.

scattering is more in case of DehazeNet resulting in objects (fishes in this case) not being clearly visible.

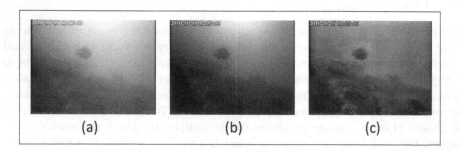

Fig. 3. (a) Original Image. Enhanced image by (b) DehazeNet [4] and (c) Light Scattering Model [6].

3.2 Contour Detection

Motion discontinuity mainly appears on edges [21]. The proposed method is heavily dependent on the conservation of motion boundaries. Conventional edge detection methods like Canny [5] rely on local intensity change. This results into a lot of spurious edges being generated as shown in Fig. 4(b). Structured edge detection (SED) utilizes random forest ensemble which spans over all the oriented edge combinations [7]. However, such hand crafted features are heavily dependent on the nature of images. To preserve the optimal set of object boundaries, we have resorted to deep learning based Holistically Nested Edge Detector (HED) [26]. In this approach, a deeply supervised fully convolutional neural network is used for multi-scale and multi-level edge feature learning. Figure 4 shows the comparative qualitative results of aforementioned methods. In case of hazy images, the object boundaries are not properly detected by SED as compared to HED. All the results have been generated before applying restoration techniques for fair evaluation and demonstrate the efficacy of HED over other compared edge detection methods even in hazy environments.

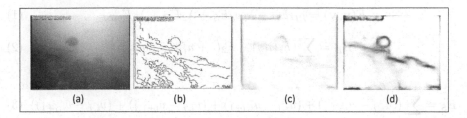

Fig. 4. (a) Original Image. Edges detected by (b) Canny [5], (c) SED [7] and (d) HED [26]

3.3 Energy Minimization

Energy minimization in a coarse to fine manner is a popular technique to obtain dense flow field. However, this approach suffers with a drawback of error propagation. Error at coarser level can propagate across scales. Obtaining the initial set of matches is quite costly in this manner. This can be estimated directly utilizing state of art matching methods. We utilize DeepMatch [22] to obtain matching points between two consecutive frames. It works on a deep convolutional architecture designed for matching images. Fishes and humans are highly deformable objects. DeepMatch can efficiently handle such non-rigid deformation and determine dense correspondences between images. Next step is to get dense matching points from the sparse list of matches obtained by DeepMatch. We have adopted edge aware sparse-to-dense interpolation method of Epic Flow. Nadraya-Watson estimation [25] method is utilized for interpolation. This method uses Geodesic Distance (GD) instead of Euclidean distance and cost map is obtained by edge detector. In the proposed method, cost is estimated by Holistically nested edge detection [26]. Since, GD estimation among pixels is time consuming thus authors have proposed a graph based approximation for this in [21].

It provides a smart heuristic for initialization of Optical Flow. Further, we perform variational refinement of dense optical flow map. We minimize the energy term defined by data term (E_D), smoothness term (E_S), coupling (E_C) and median term (E_{med}). Dequin Sun et al. [23] have justified that median filtering can significantly improve the result of optical flow field. They have incorporated the median filtering term in classical objective function and non-local coupling term to pertaining to the effect of data term. Flow updates are calculated by successive over relaxation method [27].

Given an image pair F_1 and F_2, such that $F_1, F_2 \in \mathbb{R}^{HXWX3}$ representing consecutive frames at time instants t and $t + 1$. The goal is to estimate the optical flow $\mathbf{V} = (u, v), \mathbf{V} \in \mathbb{R}^{HXWX2}$. The energy is defined as the weighted sum of data term (E_D), smoothness term (E_S) and non-local term (E_{NL}). The non-local term consists of the coupling term (E_C) and median term (E_{med}) proposed by Li and Osher [13]. It can be calculated as,

$$E(\mathbf{u}, \mathbf{v}) = \rho_D E_D + \lambda_1 \rho_s E_S + \lambda_2 E_C + \lambda_3 E_{med} \tag{1}$$

$$E_D = \sum_{i,j} (F_1(i,j) - F_2(i + u_{i,j}, j + v_{i,j})) \tag{2}$$

$$E_S = \sum_{i,j} ((u_{i,j} - u_{i+1,j}) + (u_{i,j} - u_{i,j+1}) + (v_{i,j} - v_{i+1,j}) + (v_{i,j} - v_{i,j+1})) \tag{3}$$

$$E_C = (\|\mathbf{u} - \hat{\mathbf{u}}\|^2 + \|\mathbf{v} - \hat{\mathbf{v}}\|^2) \tag{4}$$

$$E_{med} = \sum_{i,j} \sum_{(i',j') \in N_{i,j}} (\|\hat{u}_{i,j} - \hat{u}_{i',j'}\| + \|\hat{v}_{i,j} - \hat{v}_{i',j'}\|) \tag{5}$$

Equation 2 indicates the data term and ρ_D is the data penalty function. due to color constancy, we do not need to consider the change in RGB values between two images in the data term. λ_1, λ_2 and λ_3 are the regularization parameters. Equation 3 indicates the smoothness term and ρ_S is the smoothness/spatial penalty function. Charbonnier penalty function is used to penalize data and smoothness term. Equation 4 and Eq. 5 denote the coupling and median filtering term respectively. $\hat{\mathbf{u}}$ and $\hat{\mathbf{v}}$ denote the auxiliary flow field. $N_{i,j}$ denote the set of neighbors of pixel (i, j) [23].

4   Experimental Results and Analysis

In this section, we present the results obtained in evaluation of the proposed method. First, we describe the implementation and dataset details. Later, we discuss the empirical evaluation and analyze the test results.

4.1 Experimental Setup and Parameter Settings

All evaluations has been carried out on a machine with 32 GB RAM, Intel Core i7Xeon 1650 processor and Ubuntu 16 operating system. MATLAB 2017b was used as the programming platform. The values used for the different regularization parameters are $\lambda_1 = 1, \lambda_2 = 0.10$ and $\lambda_3 = 1$. Neighbourhood pixels $N_{i,j} = 5 * 5$ window.

4.2 Dataset

In the past, most of the research work has focused on flow estimation on synthetic images and other high quality datasets. While working on the proposed approach, our motive was to work with challenging images of real life underwater scenario. As per the best of our knowledge there does not exist any underwater dataset with ground truth. We have evaluated our method on complex and challenging image sequence of Fish4knowledge [12] dataset. This dataset does not have ground truth of optical flow. Due to lack of ground truth we will present qualitative results on this dataset. For quantitative evaluation, we have also tested our proposed method on popular optical flow dataset of KITTI [17].

KITTI Dataset: This dataset has been extensively used by researchers for quantitative evaluation of various optical flow methods. KITTI 2015 dataset consists of 200 training and 200 test scenes with moving camera and moving objects.

The Fish4knowledge Dataset: We have evaluated our results on this data set because this dataset comprises of real life data of ocean having challenges like moving background of coral reefs and movement in water, highly varying illumination due to light scattering in water particles, very low quality of videos, crowded scenes due to randomly moving fishes and camouflage. Videos are 10 min long with a resolution of 320×240 and a 24-bit color depth at a frame rate of 5 fps. Limitation of this data is that it does not have any ground truth of optical flow. For fair evaluation, we demonstrate qualitative results obtained on this data.

4.3 Quantitative Analysis

Most popular performance measure metrics for optical flow is the Angular Error [2] and Endpoint Error [18]. We have compared results with three kind of flow methods. First one is Feature based flow calculation methods like LDOF [3], SIFTFLOW [14]. Second one is sparse to dense method Epic Flow [21] and last one is Unsupervised deep learning based method like DD Flow [15]. DD Flow has already outperformed the other unsupervised flow methods. Focus of our proposed method is Underwater scenario. In most of the cases Angular Error is less than other flow computation methods, while End-point Error has marginal or no improvement (Table 1).

Table 1. Comparison between Average Angular Error (AAE) and Average Endpoint Error (AEE) for different optical flow methods on KITTI 2015 dataset

Methods	Proposed	DD flow	EPIC fLow	SIFT fLow	LDOF
Average Angular Error (AAE)	5.411669e+01	5.078307e+01	5.397299e+01	6.331552e+01	5.200370e+01
Average End Point Error (AEPE)	1.870108e+01	1.904110e+01	1.816318e+01	4.396911e-01	1.590453e+01

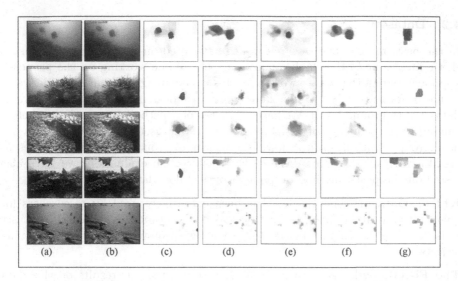

Fig. 5. Success cases: (a) Frame t (b) Frame t+1 (c) Proposed (d) DDFlow (e) EF (f) LDOF (g) SIFTFlow.

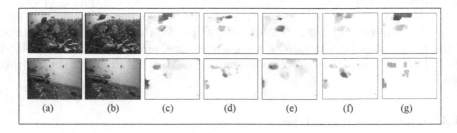

Fig. 6. Failure cases: (a) Frame t (b) Frame t+1 (c) Proposed (d) DDFlow (e) EF (f) LDOF (g) SIFTFlow.

4.4   Qualitative Analysis

In the absence of ground truth information, we present visual results to compare our method with competing methods on Fish4knowledge dataset. In Fig. 5 results of proposed technique is compared with existing methods, i.e., DDFlow [15], EPIC Flow [21], LDOF [3], and SIFT Flow [14].

These are the cases where our refined technique delineates the moving object accurately. We want to highlight that our approach is more robust to challenges such as occlusions, cluttered background, large illumination change, Low contrast, high water turbidity, crowded and fast moving and deformable objects like fish. In Fig. 5, row 1 shows the case of low contrast and high water turbidity. Middle rows presents the result under cluttered back-ground, deformable object, occluded fish and illumination change. Crowded and small fishes scenario is in the last row. Figure 6 has results of a few cases where our proposed method could not perform well. When we have analysed the intermediate results of these frames we found that there is need to refine the interpolation method to get more accurate results.

5 Conclusion

We proposed a refined optical flow estimation for challenging underwater video sequences. Motion information of objects is crucial for such low quality videos. We demonstrate how to effectively exploit the edge information of image to capture motion information. We have shown significant improvement for underwater videos and comparative results for dynamic environments on road sequences. The proposed flow estimation technique can be further extended to segment and track the objects in hazy, cluttered and dynamic environments.

References

1. Anandan, P.: A computational framework and an algorithm for the measurement of visual motion. Int. J. Comput. Vis. **2**(3), 283–310 (1989)
2. Barron, J.L., Fleet, D.J., Beauchemin, S.S.: Performance of optical flow techniques. Int. J. Comput. Vis. **12**(1), 43–77 (1994)
3. Brox, T., Malik, J.: Large displacement optical flow: descriptor matching in variational motion estimation. IEEE Trans. Pattern Anal. Mach. Intell. **33**(3), 500–513 (2010)
4. Cai, B., Xu, X., Jia, K., Qing, C., Tao, D.: Dehazenet: an end-to-end system for single image haze removal. IEEE Trans. Image Process. **25**(11), 5187–5198 (2016)
5. Canny, J.: A computational approach to edge detection. In: Readings in Computer Vision, pp. 184–203. Elsevier (1987)
6. Cho, Y., Kim, A.: Visibility enhancement for underwater visual slam based on underwater light scattering model. In: 2017 IEEE International Conference on Robotics and Automation (ICRA), pp. 710–717. IEEE (2017)
7. Dollár, P., Zitnick, C.L.: Structured forests for fast edge detection. In: Proceedings of the IEEE International Conference on Computer Vision, pp. 1841–1848 (2013)
8. Gilboa, G., Osher, S.: Nonlocal operators with applications to image processing. Multisc. Model. Simul. **7**(3), 1005–1028 (2008)
9. Horn, B.K., Schunck, B.G.: Determining optical flow. Artif. Intell. **17**(1–3), 185–203 (1981)
10. Ilg, E., Mayer, N., Saikia, T., Keuper, M., Dosovitskiy, A., Brox, T.: Flownet 2.0: evolution of optical flow estimation with deep networks. In: Proceedings of the IEEE Conference on Computer Vision and Pattern Recognition, pp. 2462–2470 (2017)

11. Johansson, G.: Visual perception of biological motion and a model for its analysis. Percept. Psychophys. **14**(2), 201–211 (1973)
12. Kavasidis, I., Palazzo, S., Di Salvo, R., Giordano, D., Spampinato, C.: A semi-automatic tool for detection and tracking ground truth generation in videos. In: Proceedings of the 1st International Workshop on Visual Interfaces for Ground Truth Collection in Computer Vision Applications, p. 6. ACM (2012)
13. Li, Y., Osher, S.: A new median formula with applications to PDE based denoising. Commun. Math. Sci. **7**(3), 741–753 (2009)
14. Liu, C., Yuen, J., Torralba, A.: Sift flow: dense correspondence across scenes and its applications. IEEE Trans. Pattern Anal. Mach. Intell. **33**(5), 978–994 (2010)
15. Liu, P., King, I., Lyu, M.R., Xu, J.: DDFlow: learning optical flow with unlabeled data distillation. arXiv preprint arXiv:1902.09145 (2019)
16. Lucas, B.D., Kanade, T., et al.: An Iterative Image Registration Technique With an Application to Stereo Vision (1981)
17. Menze, M., Geiger, A.: Object scene flow for autonomous vehicles. In: Conference on Computer Vision and Pattern Recognition (CVPR) (2015)
18. Otte, M., Nagel, H.-H.: Optical flow estimation: advances and comparisons. In: Eklundh, J.-O. (ed.) ECCV 1994. LNCS, vol. 800, pp. 49–60. Springer, Heidelberg (1994). https://doi.org/10.1007/3-540-57956-7_5
19. Ranjan, A., Black, M.J.: Optical flow estimation using a spatial pyramid network. In: Proceedings of the IEEE Conference on Computer Vision and Pattern Recognition, pp. 4161–4170 (2017)
20. Ren, Z., Yan, J., Ni, B., Liu, B., Yang, X., Zha, H.: Unsupervised deep learning for optical flow estimation. In: Thirty-First AAAI Conference on Artificial Intelligence (2017)
21. Revaud, J., Weinzaepfel, P., Harchaoui, Z., Schmid, C.: Epicflow: edge-preserving interpolation of correspondences for optical flow. In: Proceedings of the IEEE Conference on Computer Vision and Pattern Recognition, pp. 1164–1172 (2015)
22. Revaud, J., Weinzaepfel, P., Harchaoui, Z., Schmid, C.: Deepmatching: hierarchical deformable dense matching. Int. J. Comput. Vis. **120**(3), 300–323 (2016)
23. Sun, D., Roth, S., Black, M.J.: Secrets of optical flow estimation and their principles. In: IEEE Conference on Computer Vision and Pattern Recognition (CVPR), pp. 2432–2439. IEEE, June 2010
24. Sun, D., Yang, X., Liu, M.Y., Kautz, J.: PWC-net: CNNs for optical flow using pyramid, warping, and cost volume. In: Proceedings of the IEEE Conference on Computer Vision and Pattern Recognition, pp. 8934–8943 (2018)
25. Wasserman, L.: All of Statistics: A Concise Course in Statistical Inference. Springer, New York (2013). https://doi.org/10.1007/978-0-387-21736-9
26. Xie, S., Tu, Z.: Holistically-nested edge detection. In: Proceedings of the IEEE International Conference on Computer Vision, pp. 1395–1403 (2015)
27. Young, D.M.: Iterative Solution of Large Linear Systems. Elsevier (2014)

Emphasizing Similar Feature Representations to Defend Against Adversarial Attacks

Akhilesh Pandey[1], S. Balasubramanian[2(✉)], and Darshan Gera[2]

[1] KLA Tencor Software India Pvt. Ltd, Chennai, India
akhilesh.sssihl@gmail.com
[2] Sri Sathya Sai Institute of Higher Learning, Anantapur, Andhra Pradesh, India
{sbalasubramanian,darshangera}@sssihl.edu.in

Abstract. Deep Neural Networks (DNNs) are vulnerable to adversarial perturbations of the input data. For DNNs to be deployed in critical applications, they have to be made robust to such perturbations. In this work, we test an existing strategy and propose a new strategy based on autoencoders to defend DNNs against adversarial attacks. The first strategy is based on Contractive AutoEncoder (CAE). The second strategy is a Siamese network based AutoEncoder (SAE). Both CAE and SAE emphasize on similar feature representation for both the original sample and its adversarial counterpart. CAE reconstructs original sample from the adversarial input by imposing that the norm of the Jacobian of latent representation with respect to input should be minimum. SAE works with the pair of original sample and the adversarial input simultaneously, enforcing similarity in their representations at the level of layer granularity. We demonstrate the superlative performance of both the strategies in the presence of three popular attacks - The Fast Gradient Sign Method (FGSM), DeepFool (DF) and Universal Adversarial Perturbations (UAP). In particular, the proposed methods reduce the effectiveness of adversarial attacks by increasing the accuracy from 7% to 97% on the powerful DeepFool attack on MNIST dataset and from 18% to 67% on Universal Adversarial Perturbation on Fashion-MNIST dataset. We also show the superior performance of our methods over a recent method using Denoising AutoEncoder (DAE) (The PyTorch implementation of all the codes used in this work is made available at https://github.com/akhilesh-pandey/SAE).

Keywords: DNN · Siamese network · Contractive autoencoder · FGSM · DeepFool · Universal Adversarial Perturbations

1 Introduction

Deep Neural Networks (DNNs), by showing promising results, have made inroad into various fields such as natural language processing [13], bioinformatics [18],

© Springer Nature Singapore Pte Ltd. 2020
R. V. Babu et al. (Eds.): NCVPRIPG 2019, CCIS 1249, pp. 209–218, 2020.
https://doi.org/10.1007/978-981-15-8697-2_19

fraud detection in financial domain [4], malware detection, security and surveillance (biometric and facial recognition) [17] and many more. The high accuracy of DNNs can be attributed to the availability of large datasets, advanced computational hardware (GPUs) that reduces the training time, and improved open-source algorithms.

With the high accuracies shown by DNNs on test cases, we expect them to be robust to small noises. By robustness, we mean that addition of a small noise to the input should give rise to a small change in the output of the network. Specifically, in the case of image classification, robustness means that the addition of small noise to the input does not make the network misclassify the input. However, this is not the case in reality. Szegedy et al. [15] are the first to show that despite showing high accuracy on test cases, DNNs are vulnerable to adversarial examples. An adversarial example is an image obtained by adding to the clean (legitimate) image a carefully crafted noise that is almost imperceptible to the human visual system (HVS) but causes DNNs to successfully misclassify with high confidence. Figure 1 shows an example of a adversarial sample created using GoogleNet [14] on Imagenet [2] dataset. Moreover, these adversarial examples are transferable which means that the examples created to fool one network can be used to fool multiple networks. These properties make adversarial attacks very challenging. This has triggered interests among the researchers to find the reason behind the existence of adversarial examples and suggest suitable solutions to combat such attacks.

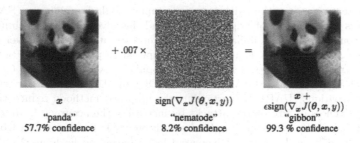

$$x$$
"panda"
57.7% confidence

$$\text{sign}(\nabla_x J(\theta, x, y))$$
"nematode"
8.2% confidence

$$x + \epsilon \text{sign}(\nabla_x J(\theta, x, y))$$
"gibbon"
99.3 % confidence

Fig. 1. Adversarial example: source [5]

2   Related Work

There are several methods to craft adversarial examples, popular among them being FGSM [5], JSMA [10], DF [9] and UAP [8]. [5] argues that vulnerability of DNNs to adversarial examples is due to the linear behaviour of DNNs in high dimensional spaces. Further, they craft adversarial examples by perturbing the input along the gradient direction that maximizes the loss. The problem with [5] is that all pixels in the input are perturbed. In [10], salient pixels are found using the Jacobian of the output with respect to the input. Salient pixels are those that would increase the misclassification rate when perturbed. This can be quantified using Jacobian. Unlike FGSM, JSMA is a targeted attack. The user needs to specify the target class and certain other information. A variant of JSMA called M-JSMA [16] is devoid of these extra requirements. While FGSM and JSMA create adversaries by perturbing the input, they do not explicitly minimize the amount of perturbation added. DF [9] makes sure that the amount of added perturbation is minimal to create an adversary, stressing the need for adversaries to be imperceptible to HVS. The adversarial example is computed iteratively by adding optimal perturbations to the input to push it outside the boundary of the discriminating surface of the classifier. FGSM, JSMA and DF create adversarial perturbation per image. UAP [8] creates a single universal perturbation per entire training data.

Literature on defense against the aforementioned attacks are scarce but slowly picking up recently. A general strategy is to train the model along with adversarial examples to improve its generalization capability. However, the model may not explicitly learn the similarity between the sample and its adversarial counterpart and therefore may still fail on unseen adversaries during test time. In [7], the effect of adversary on the input is attenuated by sparsifying the input with the intuition that HVS focuses on the most important features. In [1], the effect of adversary is mitigated by projecting the high dimensional input into a low dimensional space using Principal Components Analysis (PCA). In [12], a Denoising AutoEncoder (DAE) is used to reconstruct the original sample from the adversarial perturbation. Subsequently, low dimensional projection is employed to build the adversary resilient model. In addition to using DAE, [3] uses CAE to defend against low distortions. Further, for detecting L_0 adversarial perturbations, [19] employs inpainting and siamese architecture based processing. In this work, we test an existing strategy and propose a novel defense strategy to defend against adversary operating in a semi-white box environment. Our contributions are listed below.

2.1   Our Contributions

- Using Contractive AutoEncoder(CAE) [11] to mitigate the adversarial effect. The goal of CAE is to act as a pre-processor to reconstruct the original sample from the adversarial perturbation by emphasizing on similar feature representation between the two. It is to be noted that a similar defense based on CAE is proposed in [3]. Though the idea is similar in nature, we arrive at CAE by viewing defense as inverse of adversarial generation.
- A novel method to mitigate the adversarial effect using a Siamese architecture [6] based AutoEncoder(SAE). SAE also emphasizes on similar feature representation between the original sample and its adversarial perturbation but at a fine layer level granularity.
- Demonstration of the performance of our methods on MNIST and Fashion-MNIST datasets. Most of the few methods from literature quote results only on MNIST dataset. We also compared our defense strategies to a latest one [12] based on DAE from the literature.

The following section describes the proposed methods in detail. Subsequently, performance of the methods are demonstrated and conclusions are drawn.

3   Proposed Work

We test one strategy and propose another strategy to defend against adversarial attacks - former using CAE and the latter using SAE. First we describe the set up.

We have an adversary A and a defender D. A wants to attack the model M. It perturbs the input and supplies to M. M, instead of processing the adversarial input directly, deploys the defender D to pre-process the input and pass it to M. Subsequently M classifies the input. Our contribution is in the defender unit D. It is either CAE or SAE. We assume that A has access to trained M. A does not have access to D. That is, we assume a semi-white box environment for adversary. We will now describe CAE and SAE.

3.1   Contractive AutoEncoder (CAE)

We drew inspiration from JSMA [10] to test this defender. JSMA is a method to craft adversarial examples. It identifies salient pixels and perturbs them. Suppose our model M computes the probabilities $F(X)$ for the given input X. Say, we want M to misclassify X to a class t. For each pixel p, we check if the Jacobian (derivative) of F with respect to pixel p in X is positive and the cumulative derivative of F with respect to other pixels is negative or zero. If so, p is a salient pixel. Mathematically, if $S[p]$ denote the saliency score of the pixel p, then

$$S[p] = \begin{cases} 0, & if \frac{\partial F_t}{\partial X_p} < 0 \ or \ \sum_{j \neq t} \frac{\partial F_j}{\partial X_p} > 0 \\ \left(\frac{\partial F_t}{\partial X_p}\right) \mid \left(\sum_{j \neq t} \frac{\partial F_j}{\partial X_p}\right) \mid \end{cases}$$

where F_j denote the probability with respect to class j.

Effectively, JSMA looks for the influential derivatives of output with respect to the input. Inverting this idea, we can minimize the norm of the Jacobian (derivatives) of the input or its latent representation with respect to input. This is exactly the idea in CAE. It is to be noted that [3] also uses CAE to defend against small distortions. However, our view of arriving at deployment of CAE as inverse of adversarial generation process is novel. The architecture we used is similar to DAE [12]. It is a fully connected neural network with 5 hidden layers (784-256-128-64-128-256-784). The encoder (758-256-128-64) downsamples the adversarial image while the decoder(64-128-256-784) reconstructs the original image. The CAE loss to be minimized is given by:

$$L = L(X_{recons}, X_{clean}) + \lambda \|J_h(X)\|_{Fr}^2 \tag{1}$$
$$= \|X_{recons} - X_{clean}\|_2^2 + \lambda \|J_h(X)\|_{Fr}^2$$

It is the sum of squared error and a regularization term made up of squared Frobenius norm of Jacobian of the latent representation (hidden features h) of input with respect to the input. J can be written mathematically as:

$$\|J_h(X)\|_{Fr}^2 = \sum_{ij} \left(\frac{\partial h_i(X)}{\partial X_j}\right)^2 \tag{2}$$

λ is a hyper-parameter that controls the strength of regularization.

In effect CAE will enforce similar latent representation for the sample and its adversarial counterpart by imposing that the rate of change of latent representation with respect to small change in input is small, strictly small. This is in contrast to DAE used in [12] that does not emphasize on robustness with respect to change in the input. Further, CAEs are more effective than DAEs as elicited in [11]. We also demonstrate later that CAE performs better than DAE.

3.2   Siamese Network Based AutoEncoder (SAE)

Siamese networks [6] are popular for finding relationship (similarity) between two comparable things. Even though both adversarial samples and clean samples look very similar to the HVS, the network classifies them differently. We know that input to any hidden layer h_i is output of the hidden layer h_{i-1}. Further, the final set of features used by the DNN for classification is a function of the features learned by the hidden layers. The fact that the adversarial examples are assigned to a different class, this shows that the features learned by the hidden layers are different for clean and adversarial samples. Our goal is to make the network learn similar features for the sample and its adversarial counterpart. This motivates us to use the idea of Siamese network to design a defense strategy.

The input to the network is a pair of clean image X and its corresponding adversarial image $\widetilde{X}$. The network is shown in Fig. 2. The network downsamples the pair of images through 3 hidden layers(encoder part of the network)and subsequently upsamples them through another 3 layers(decoder part of the network) to original image size. The learnable weights are shared across both the images. We compute the loss as follows:

$$L(X,\widetilde{X}) = MSE(X_{recons}, X) + MSE(\widetilde{X}_{recons}, X)$$
$$+ MSE(X_{recons}, \widetilde{X}_{recons}) + \sum_{i=1}^{3} MSE(h_i(X), h_i(\widetilde{X})) \tag{3}$$

where $h_i(.)$ denote the output of the ith hidden layer of the encoder and MSE denote the mean-squared-error.

We emphasize that all the encoding features through the layers of the encoder part of the network must be similar for the image and its adversarial counterpart. This enforces similar encoding or feature representation for both the image and its adversarial perturbation. Therefore we can expect the adversarial counterpart to be reconstructed close to the original image by the decoder. Loss is further strengthened with MSE terms between all possible combinations of reconstructed pair and the input pair.

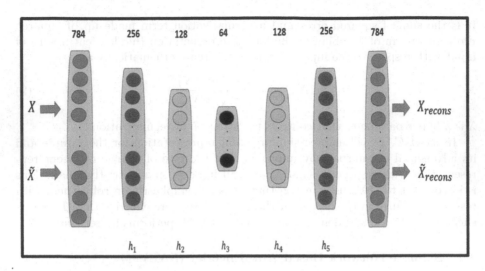

Fig. 2. SAE architecture

4 Experimental Set Up, Results and Analysis

First, we trained CAE and SAE. The datasets used are the standard benchmark datasets MNIST and Fashion MNIST. Each dataset has 60000 training images corresponding to 10 classes.

For CAE, we trained as follows. We generated using FGSM [5] one adversarial example per training image at $\epsilon = 0.25$. Thus we have a combined training set of 120000 images. Note that the groundtruth for unperturbed input in this set is itself, while for the perturbed one, it is the unperturbed input. We trained CAE on this set for 100 epochs using a batch size of 200 and Adam optimizer.

For SAE, we generated one adversarial image per training image as is done for CAE. However, during training, we pass a batch of pair of images - the clean image and its adversarial counterpart. Batch size is set to 256. Optimizer used is Adam optimizer. SAE is trained for 150 epochs.

The pre-trained defenders CAE and SAE protect the following base model in our experiments - a fully connected neural network with two hidden layers of 100 neurons each and an output layer containing 10 neurons corresponding to 10 classes. Each of the hidden layers uses ReLu non-linear activation and the output layer uses softmax activation. We train the base-model on 60000 MNIST or Fashion MNIST training images for 100 epochs with a batch size of 100. Optimizer used is Adam optimizer.

Figure 3 shows the accuracy of the base model without defense and with defense (CAE, SAE, DAE) on adversarial samples from MNIST data crafted using FGSM for $\epsilon \in [0, 1]$. From Fig. 3 it is clear that our proposed methods are more effective in mitigating the effect of adversarial attacks in comparison to DAE. A summary of the figure is also presented in the Table 1. Using CAE as a defense improves the accuracy from 0.0037 to 0.956 on FGSM attack with

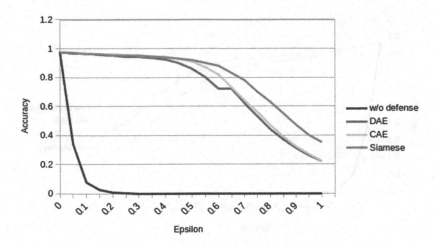

Fig. 3. Accuracy in the presence of various defense strategies on MNIST.

Table 1. Accuracy on MNIST after FGSM attack

ϵ	Without defense	DAE as defense	CAE as defense	SAE as defense
0.1	0.078	0.967	0.969	0.964
0.25	0.0037	0.945	0.956	0.95
0.5	0.00004	0.86	0.91	0.92
1	0	0.22	0.22	0.35

Table 2. Accuracy on DeepFool and Universal perturbation attack on MNIST

Attack	Without defense	DAE	CAE	SAE
DeepFool	0.07	0.9687	0.9689	0.97
Universal perturbation	0.31	0.75	0.87	0.67

$\epsilon = 0.25$ on MNIST dataset. Similarly SAE improves the accuracy to 0.95. As tabulated in Table 2, under DF attack and UAP attack on MNIST dataset, CAE and SAE again outperform DAE. For example, the accuracy increased from 0.07 to 0.97 for SAE under DF attack and from 0.31 to 0.87 for CAE under UAP attack. It is to be noted that under UAP attack, DAE performs better than SAE. A particularly interesting observation from Fig. 3 is that SAE outperforms all the other strategies for $\epsilon \geq 0.6$. For adversarial samples crafted using $\epsilon \geq 0.6$, SAE gives 15% better accuracy compared to others.

Figure 4 shows the accuracy of the base model without defense and with defense (CAE, SAE, DAE) on adversarial samples from Fashion MNIST data crafted using FGSM for $\epsilon \in [0, 1]$. CAE performs the best. DAE has outperformed SAE consistently for $\epsilon > 0.3$. However, under UAP attack, as depicted in Table 3, SAE significantly outperforms DAE and even CAE. It has reported

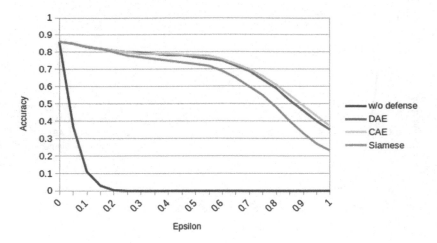

Fig. 4. Accuracy in the presence of various defense strategies of Fashion-MNIST

Table 3. Accuracy on DeepFool and Universal perturbation attack on Fashion-MNIST dataset

Attack	Without defense	DAE	CAE	SAE
DeepFool	0.069	0.862	0.863	0.855
Universal Perturbation	0.18	0.25	0.37	0.67

a jump from 0.18 to 0.67 while DAE improves only to 0.25. Under DF attack, the performance of all three methods are at par.

One general observation from the results reported is that both CAE and SAE defend the model very well. In most cases, the leap of accuracy from without defense to with defense using CAE or SAE is very high. A couple of cases where DAE has outperformed SAE could be due to the cascade of autoencoders and low dimensional projections used in DAE. However, note that CAE always outperformed DAE in all cases. This clearly shows that our intuition of minimizing the norm of the Jacobian of latent representation with respect to the input adds significant value in providing similar feature representation for both the clean image and its adversarial counterpart.

5   Conclusion and Future Work

In this work we tested an existing strategy based on CAE and proposed a novel defense strategy based on SAE to defend DNNs against adversarial attacks. We have shown that both methods defend the model very well across a variety of attacks including FGSM, DF and UAP. CAE based defender outperformed DAE. However, DAE showed superior performance over SAE in a couple of cases. Deriving cue from the performance of CAE, we plan to further strengthen the loss of SAE by incorporating Jacobian into it in the future. We expect an enhanced performance for SAE using this addition. Further, analysis on relative performance of SAE under UAP attack in comparison to its performance under DF attack could shed light on dependency of UAP on structure of data, including proportion of background in the image.

Dedication. We dedicate this work to the founder Chancellor of Sri Sathya Sai Institute of Higher Learning, Bhagawan Sri Sathya Sai Baba.

References

1. Bhagoji, A.N., Cullina, D., Sitawarin, C., Mittal, P.: Enhancing robustness of machine learning systems via data transformations. In: 2018 52nd Annual Conference on Information Sciences and Systems (CISS), pp. 1–5. IEEE (2018)
2. Deng, J., Dong, W., Socher, R., Li, L.J., Li, K., Fei-Fei, L.: Imagenet: a large-scale hierarchical image database. In: IEEE Conference on Computer Vision and Pattern Recognition, CVPR 2009, pp. 248–255. IEEE (2009)
3. Gu, S., Rigazio, L.: Towards deep neural network architectures robust to adversarial examples. arXiv preprint arXiv:1412.5068 (2014)
4. Hasan, A., Kalıpsız, O., Akyokuş, S.: Predicting financial market in big data: deep learning. In: 2017 International Conference on Computer Science and Engineering (UBMK), pp. 510–515. IEEE (2017)
5. Goodfellow, I.J., Shlens, J., Szegedy, C.: Explaining and harnessing adversarial examples. arxiv preprint arxiv:1412.6572 (2015)
6. Koch, G., Zemel, R., Salakhutdinov, R.: Siamese neural networks for one-shot image recognition. In: ICML Deep Learning Workshop, vol. 2 (2015)
7. Marzi, Z., Gopalakrishnan, S., Madhow, U., Pedarsani, R.: Sparsity-based defense against adversarial attacks on linear classifiers. In: 2018 IEEE International Symposium on Information Theory (ISIT), pp. 31–35. IEEE (2018)
8. Moosavi-Dezfooli, S.M., Fawzi, A., Fawzi, O., Frossard, P.: Universal adversarial perturbations. arXiv preprint (2017)
9. Moosavi-Dezfooli, S.M., Fawzi, A., Frossard, P.: Deepfool: a simple and accurate method to fool deep neural networks. In: Proceedings of the IEEE Conference on Computer Vision and Pattern Recognition, pp. 2574–2582 (2016)
10. Papernot, N., McDaniel, P., Jha, S., Fredrikson, M., Celik, Z.B., Swami, A.: The limitations of deep learning in adversarial settings. In: 2016 IEEE European Symposium on Security and Privacy (EuroS&P), pp. 372–387. IEEE (2016)
11. Rifai, S., Vincent, P., Muller, X., Glorot, X., Bengio, Y.: Contractive auto-encoders: explicit invariance during feature extraction. In: Proceedings of the 28th International Conference on International Conference on Machine Learning, pp. 833–840. Omnipress (2011)
12. Sahay, R., Mahfuz, R., Gamal, A.E.: Combatting adversarial attacks through denoising and dimensionality reduction: a cascaded autoencoder approach. arXiv preprint arXiv:1812.03087 (2018)
13. Sutskever, I., Vinyals, O., Le, Q.V.: Sequence to sequence learning with neural networks. In: Advances in Neural Information Processing Systems, pp. 3104–3112 (2014)
14. Szegedy, C., et al.: Going deeper with convolutions. In: Proceedings of the IEEE Conference on Computer Vision and Pattern Recognition, pp. 1–9 (2015)

15. Szegedy, C., et al.: Intriguing properties of neural networks. arXiv preprint arXiv:1312.6199 (2013)
16. Wiyatno, R., Xu, A.: Maximal jacobian-based saliency map attack. arXiv preprint arXiv:1808.07945 (2018)
17. Wright, J., Yang, A.Y., Ganesh, A., Sastry, S.S., Ma, Y.: Robust face recognition via sparse representation. IEEE Trans. Pattern Anal. Mach. Intell. **31**(2), 210–227 (2009)
18. Xiong, H.Y., et al.: The human splicing code reveals new insights into the genetic determinants of disease. Science **347**(6218), 1254806 (2015)
19. Zuo, F., Yang, B., Li, X., Zeng, Q.: Exploiting the inherent limitation of l0 adversarial examples. In: 22nd International Symposium on Research in Attacks, Intrusions and Defenses ($\{RAID\}$ 2019), pp. 293–307 (2019)

iSalGAN - An Improvised Saliency GAN

Kelam Goutam and S. Balasubramanian[✉]

Sri Sathya Sai Institute of Higher Learning, Prashanti Nilayam, Anantapur, India
kelamgoutam.sssihl@gmail.com, sbalasubramanian@sssihl.edu.in
http://sssihl.edu.in/

Abstract. Human visual system (HVS) is naturally attracted to the
salient regions that appear distinctly in the foreground of a scene. However, for a machine, automatically detecting the region of saliency is
a challenging problem. Recently, a generative model namely Saliency
GAN (SalGAN) discriminates if a pixel is salient or not by generating
the saliency map given the input image. The generator is guided by a
content loss and adversarial loss. However, the generated saliency maps
tend to be smooth lacking finer details. We propose an improvised generator called iSalGAN (improvised saliency GAN) that integrates both
low-level and high-level features to produce finer saliency maps. Our
iSalGAN is guided by a combination of multiple content losses and, the
adversarial loss. Our model is trained on MSRA10K dataset and tested
on ECSSD and DUT-OMRON datasets. Qualitative and quantitative
evaluation of our model shows the superior performance of our model
over state-of-the-art methods. Codes will be made publicly available.

Keywords: iSalGAN · Saliency GAN · SalGAN · Generator ·
Discriminator · Saliency

1 Introduction

The HVS receives about 10^8 to 10^9 bits of information every second. In order to
process such huge data in real time, HVS uses its ability to selectively focus on
different parts of the scene. Given an image, the nervous system selects part of the
scene for further detailed processing, while discarding the rest. It also prioritizes
the selected part such that the most relevant parts are processed first. This selection
and ordering process is known as selective attention or visual saliency [4].

The visual attention model aims to predict the salient regions of the image.
The salient region detection can save computational resources as only the relevant information is processed. It can also be used as a preprocessing step for
many other computer vision tasks such as object detection, object recognition
etc.

Deep learning (DL) models, particularly convolutional neural networks
(CNN) have achieved tremendous success in many of the computer vision tasks
such as image classification [5], image segmentation [12] etc. Hence, deployment

© Springer Nature Singapore Pte Ltd. 2020
R. V. Babu et al. (Eds.): NCVPRIPG 2019, CCIS 1249, pp. 219–228, 2020.
https://doi.org/10.1007/978-981-15-8697-2_20

of DL techniques for saliency prediction is a natural extension. The fully convolutional networks (FCN) being used to predict saliency maps achieves significant improvement over traditional approaches. However, these networks fail to produce sharp saliency maps. The saliency maps produced by these networks miss the fine details and, the boundaries are blurred.

In this work we improvise an adversarial training based architecture called SalGAN [14] to eliminate the blurriness at boundary pixels and produce a sharp saliency map for the given input image. We integrate both low-level and high-level features at the generator to produce low-level, high-level and combined saliency maps. By low-level we mean lower layer features and by high-level we mean higher layer features. The integration of low-level and high-level features has been inspired by [2]. We supervise the saliency maps using a loss function which is a combination of content loss at each level and, the adversarial loss. The discriminator decides the real vs fake between the ground truth saliency map and the combined saliency map produced by the generator. Our method is called as iSalGAN.

2 Related Work

Traditionally, saliency prediction is based on manually engineered features like texture, contrast etc. These methods lacked success as the manually engineered features could not capture the global semantics of the given input image. Presently, with a relatively significant volume of data available, it is a routine work for CNNs to capture global semantics and predict salient regions with higher accuracy than the traditional methods.

An early work in this direction is by Long et al. [12]. Subsequently, Liu et al. [11] designed a neural network consisting of two parts to predict the saliency map. The first subnet, a deep hierarchical saliency network (DHSNet), acts as an encoder network and predicts coarser global features. The coarser global features are then refined using the second subnet, a hierarchical recurrent convolutional neural network (HRCNN), to obtain finer local features. Kümmerer et al. [6] proposed the first transfer learning model for saliency prediction. Their model DeepGaze is a modification of AlexNet architecture [5]. DeepGaze omitted all of the fully connected layers and passed the features of the convolutional layers to a linear model as input to learn the weights. Huang et al. [3] introduced a deep neural network (DNN) model to reduce the semantic gap present between the predicted saliency map and the human's behavior. They redesigned an existing DNN for object recognition and used it for saliency prediction. Pan et al. [15] designed a shallow and a deep convolutional model, trained end-to-end, to detect the salient region in an image. The shallow network is trained from scratch and the deep network is trained using transfer learning.

Different loss functions have been used by different methods mentioned above. The definition of 'best' among them is debatable. To break the continuity of this exploration, instead of tailor making a loss function for the method, Pan et al. [14] proposed a adversarial training based saliency prediction called SalGAN.

Given an input image, the generator generates a saliency map with an aim to fool the discriminator that it is the real saliency map of the given image. Over a period of training guided by binary cross entropy (BCE) loss and adversarial loss, the generator produces accurate saliency maps. However, these saliency maps lack fine quality and are blurred. In this work we improvise SalGAN (iSalGAN) to eliminate the blurriness at boundary pixels and produce a sharp saliency map for the given input image. Our **contributions** are as follows:

- In iSalGAN, we integrate both low-level and high-level features at the generator to produce low-level, high-level and combined saliency maps. In contrast, SalGAN only works with a single layer output.
- In iSalGAN, we supervise these maps using a combination of content loss at each level and, the adversarial loss. In contrast, SalGAN uses only one content loss.
- Unlike VGG-16 used by SalGAN [14] for generator, we use ResNeXt-101. We gain a significant reduction in number of learnable parameters. The reason for this switch is further explained later.
- We compare iSalGAN with SalGAN and other state-of-the-art methods.

3   Proposed Method

Conventionally, in the CNN setting, only the final layers predict the saliency maps, independent of other layers. When an image passes through a neural network, the feature maps are constantly refined by the layers. The final layers use these enriched feature maps to make predictions about the salient objects in the image. Though CNN predict significantly better saliency maps compared to traditional approaches, making predictions independent of other layers does not take multi-scale semantics into consideration. SalGAN too uses a CNN in the generator that does not consider multi-scale semantics.

The proposed improvisation, iSalGAN, leverages on the salient features learned across multiple layers of the network.

3.1   iSalGAN Architecture

iSalGAN consists of a generator and a discriminator. Given an image to the generator, it extracts low-level and high-level features by passing the image through a feature extractor network. It then integrates all the low-level and high-level features respectively. Low-level features attend to fine details while high-level features capture the global semantics. The integrated low-level and high-level features are used to predict intermediate saliency maps respectively. The integrated feature maps are further fused to predict a combined high-resolution saliency map as output. The intermediate saliency maps are used to compute the content loss and the combined saliency map becomes the input to the discriminator for adversarial training. The discriminator attempts to differentiate between the synthesized high-resolution saliency map and the real saliency map which is the ground truth. Figure 1 illustrates the overall architecture of iSalGAN.

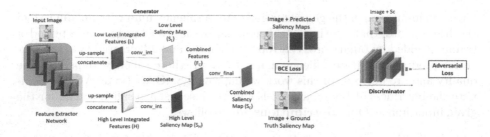

Fig. 1. The overall architecture of iSalGAN (Color figure online)

3.2 Generator

The generator in our iSalGAN network uses ResNeXt-101 [21] as the feature extractor. Given an image to the generator, the ResNeXt model yields a set of feature maps. These feature maps contain low-level as well as high-level semantic information of varying scales. The low-level features and the high-level features are extracted by the shallow layers (grouped in light blue in Fig. 1) and the deep layers (grouped in light yellow in Fig. 1) respectively. These features are up-sampled and concatenated to produce low-level integrated feature map, L (denoted in dark blue in Fig. 1) and high-level integrated feature map, H (denoted in dark yellow in Fig. 1) respectively. The low-level integrated feature, L, and the high-level integrated feature, H, are passed through a shallow convolutional network (denoted as conv_int) to produce low-level saliency map, S_L (denoted in light grey in Fig. 1) and high-level saliency map, S_H (denoted in dark grey in Fig. 1) respectively. The low-level integrated feature, L, and the high-level integrated feature, H, are further combined to produce a richer feature map, F_C (denoted in orange). The combined feature map, F_C, is then passed through another shallow convolutional network (denoted as conv_final) to produce a combined saliency map, S_C (denoted in red in Fig. 1). The generator therefore produces three saliency maps for each input image.

It is to be noted that SalGAN uses VGG-16 [18] as the feature extractor network in the generator. VGG-16 has 138 million learnable parameters. In order to reduce computation overload and memory footprint, SalGAN trades with accuracy by considering only last two groups of convolutional parameters for learning. For other parameters, weights are transfered from VGG-16 pre-trained for ImageNet challenge [16]. Recently, it has been shown that ResNeXt [21] significantly brings down the validation error on ImageNet. A ResNeXt block has varied number of residual paths, each with same topology with significantly less width. This helps in embedding the input into different subspaces thereby able to generalize well across variations. We do not want to trade with accuracy and so we train our iSalGAN model end-to-end. We use ResNeXt-101 that has roughly around 44 million parameters, less than VGG-16 by a factor of 3.

Figures 2 and 3 describe the detailed architecture of the shallow convolutional networks used to generate intermediate and final saliency maps respectively.

Layer	In-channels	Out-channels	Kernel	Activation
Conv1	256	128	3 x 3	PReLU
BatchNorm1	128	-	-	-
Conv2	128	128	3 x 3	PReLU
BatchNorm2	128	-	-	-
Conv3	128	1	1 x 1	sigmoid

Fig. 2. Architecture of conv_int which generates intermediate saliency maps

Layer	In-channels	Out-channels	Kernel	Activation
Conv1	2	128	3 x 3	PReLU
BatchNorm1	128	-	-	-
Conv2	128	128	3 x 3	PReLU
BatchNorm2	128	-	-	-
Conv3	128	1	1 x 1	sigmoid

Fig. 3. Architecture of conv_final which generates final saliency map

3.3 Discriminator

The discriminator network used is same as given in SalGAN [14]. It consists of six convolutional layers with a kernel size of 3×3. A ReLU layer follows each of the convolutional layer, and after every set of two convolutional layers, a maxpool layer follows which reduces the feature size by half. Finally, three fully connected layers follow the convolutional layers. Tanh is used as an activation function for the first two fully connected layers whereas the final fully connected layer uses sigmoid.

4 Training

Our iSalGAN network uses a combination of content loss and adversarial loss. The content loss in our model is computed by combining the losses of the intermediate saliency maps and the final saliency map with respect to the ground truth, respectively. The adversarial loss determines the discriminator's ability to distinguish the combined saliency map, S_C, as real or fake.

4.1 Content Loss

The content loss is defined as:

$$\mathscr{L}_{BCE} = BCE_{S_L} + BCE_{S_H} + BCE_{S_C}$$

where

$$BCE_{S_L} = -\frac{1}{N}\sum_{k=1}^{N}(S^k log(S_L{}^k) + (1 - S^k)log(1 - S_L{}^k))$$

$$BCE_{S_H} = -\frac{1}{N}\sum_{k=1}^{N}(S^k log(S_H{}^k) + (1 - S^k)log(1 - S_H{}^k))$$

$$BCE_{S_C} = -\frac{1}{N}\sum_{k=1}^{N}(S^k log(S_C{}^k) + (1 - S^k)log(1 - S_C{}^k))$$

Here, S^k and $S_i{}^k$, $i = \{L, H, C\}$ represent the probability of the kth pixel being salient in the ground truth and predicted saliency maps respectively and N is the number of pixels in the image. In summary, the content loss is computed by comparing the similarity between the predicted saliency maps with respect to the ground truth saliency map for every pixel.

4.2 Adversarial Loss

The loss function for the discriminator architecture is defined as:

$$\mathscr{L}_{Dis} = L(\mathscr{D}(I, S), 1) + L(\mathscr{D}(I, \tilde{S}), 0)$$

where L denotes BCE loss, the number 1 represents that target belongs to ground truth and 0 represents that it is predicted. $\mathscr{D}(I, \tilde{S})$ represent the probability of fooling the discriminator (i.e. given a predicted saliency map as input, the discriminator classifies it as real). $\mathscr{D}(I, S)$ represent the probability that given a ground truth saliency map, the discriminator predicts it as real. The loss function used in adversarial training is defined as:

$$\mathscr{L} = \alpha \times \mathscr{L}_{BCE} + L(\mathscr{D}(I, \tilde{S}), 1)$$

The loss function $\mathscr{L}$ aids in improving the convergence rate and stability of the adversarial training.

The training of iSalGAN happens in two phases:

1. Pretrain the generator for 15 epochs using only content losses.
2. Subsequently add discriminator and start the adversarial training.

During the adversarial training, the input to the iSalGAN is an RGB image of shape $256 \times 192 \times 3$. Input to the discriminator is an RGBS image of shape $256 \times 192 \times 4$. Generator and the discriminator are trained in alternative iterations. Weight decay is set to 1×10^{-4}. Learning rate is set to 3×10^{-4}. SGD is used as optimizer. Batch size is set to 8. A larger batch size would give better accuracy but due to limitation of resources we worked with batch size of 8. α is set to 5×10^{-3}. The entire network is trained for 120 epochs.

5   Results

In this section, we qualitatively and quantitatively report the results of our iSalGAN model for saliency prediction. The model is trained on MSRA10K dataset [1] and is tested on ECSSD [22] and DUT-OMRON [23] datasets. Parts a, b and c of Fig. 4 depict a sample of results of iSalGAN on MSRA10K, ECSSD and DUT-OMRON datasets. In the above mentioned figures, the first column consists of the query images, the second column consists of the ground truth saliency maps for the corresponding images and the third column shows the predicted saliency maps. Clearly, the results are impressive. Part d of Fig. 4 compares iSalGAN with SalGAN qualitatively. We can clearly emphasize on the sharpness of iSalGAN results over the blurry results produced by SalGAN. Even the minute variations have been reasonably picked up by iSalGAN while SalGAN completely averages them out.

Table 1. Comparison of iSalGAN with the state-of-the-art models for saliency prediction.

	ECSSD		DUT-OMRON	
	F-measure	MAE	F-measure	MAE
BSCA [17]	0.758	0.183	0.616	0.191
MC [24]	0.822	0.106	0.703	0.088
LEGS [19]	0.827	0.118	0.669	0.133
MDF [8]	0.831	0.108	0.694	0.092
ELD [7]	0.867	0.080	0.716	0.091
RFCN [20]	0.898	0.097	0.747	0.095
DS [10]	0.882	0.123	0.745	0.120
DCL [9]	0.898	0.071	0.757	0.080
DHSNet [11]	0.907	0.059	–	–
NLDF [13]	0.905	0.063	0.753	0.080
iSalGAN (ours)	**0.912**	**0.053**	**0.759**	**0.076**

We compared our iSalGAN model with 10 of the state-of-the-art models in literature, using the F-measure and mean absolute error (MAE) metrics. Table 1 shows that iSalGAN outperforms its competitors on both the ECSSD [22] and DUT-OMRON [23] datasets. Further, Table 2 illustrate that iSalGAN outperforms the SalGAN model. With respect to F-measure a significant jump of 8% is observed while the MAE has reduced by a factor of 10. To compare against SalGAN, we trained SalGAN on MSRA10K dataset for 120 epochs. The iSalGAN model is implemented using PyTorch framework. Both the qualitative and quantitative results clearly emphasize the importance of integration of both lower layer and higher layer features and also supervision at both levels.

(a) MSRA10K   (b) ECSSD

(c) DUT-OMRON   (d) SalGAN Vs. iSalGAN

Fig. 4. Qualitative results of iSalGAN on MSRA10K, ECSSD, DUT-OMRON datasets and SalGAN vs. iSalGAN

Table 2. Quantitative comparison of iSalGAN with the SalGAN model.

Method	MSRA10K	
	F-measure	MAE
SalGAN [14]	0.869	0.103
iSalGAN (ours)	**0.945**	**0.027**

6 Conclusion

The saliency maps generated using the SalGAN architecture have blurred boundaries and using them to segment the salient objects may either add a non-salient part to the segmented object or may ignore some part of the salient object. Such segmentation may affect the accuracy in case of applications like medical image analysis. In order to eliminate the blurriness of the boundary and retain the advantages provided by the SalGAN architecture, we designed an improvised SalGAN called iSalGAN to predict saliency map with clear boundaries. Our iSalGAN model considers both low-level features and high-level feature as equally important. The iSalGAN architecture performed better than 10 of the state-of-the-art models when compared using MAE and F-measure metrics. A future direction would be to extend iSalGAN to predict instance level saliency maps.

Acknowledgements. We would like to dedicate our work to founder chancellor of Sri Sathya Sai Institute of Higher Learning, Bhagawan Sri Sathya Sai Baba.

References

1. Cheng, M.M., Mitra, N.J., Huang, X., Torr, P.H., Hu, S.M.: Global contrast based salient region detection. IEEE Trans. Pattern Anal. Mach. Intell. **37**(3), 569–582 (2014)
2. Deng, Z., et al.: R3net: recurrent residual refinement network for saliency detection. In: Proceedings of the 27th International Joint Conference on Artificial Intelligence, pp. 684–690. AAAI Press (2018)
3. Huang, X., Shen, C., Boix, X., Zhao, Q.: Salicon: reducing the semantic gap in saliency prediction by adapting deep neural networks. In: Proceedings of the IEEE International Conference on Computer Vision, pp. 262–270 (2015)
4. Itti, L., Koch, C., Niebur, E.: A model of saliency-based visual attention for rapid scene analysis. IEEE Trans. Pattern Anal. Mach. Intell. **11**, 1254–1259 (1998)
5. Krizhevsky, A., Sutskever, I., Hinton, G.E.: Imagenet classification with deep convolutional neural networks. In: Advances in Neural Information Processing Systems, pp. 1097–1105 (2012)
6. Kümmerer, M., Theis, L., Bethge, M.: Deep gaze i: boosting saliency prediction with feature maps trained on imagenet. arXiv preprint arXiv:1411.1045 (2014)
7. Lee, G., Tai, Y.W., Kim, J.: Deep saliency with encoded low level distance map and high level features. In: Proceedings of the IEEE Conference on Computer Vision and Pattern Recognition, pp. 660–668 (2016)

8. Li, G., Yu, Y.: Visual saliency based on multiscale deep features. In: Proceedings of the IEEE Conference on Computer Vision and Pattern Recognition, pp. 5455–5463 (2015)
9. Li, G., Yu, Y.: Deep contrast learning for salient object detection. In: Proceedings of the IEEE Conference on Computer Vision and Pattern Recognition, pp. 478–487 (2016)
10. Li, X., et al.: Deepsaliency: multi-task deep neural network model for salient object detection. IEEE Trans. Image Process. **25**(8), 3919–3930 (2016)
11. Liu, N., Han, J.: Dhsnet: deep hierarchical saliency network for salient object detection. In: Proceedings of the IEEE Conference on Computer Vision and Pattern Recognition, pp. 678–686 (2016)
12. Long, J., Shelhamer, E., Darrell, T.: Fully convolutional networks for semantic segmentation. In: Proceedings of the IEEE Conference on Computer Vision and Pattern Recognition, pp. 3431–3440 (2015)
13. Luo, Z., Mishra, A., Achkar, A., Eichel, J., Li, S., Jodoin, P.M.: Non-local deep features for salient object detection. In: Proceedings of the IEEE Conference on Computer Vision and Pattern Recognition, pp. 6609–6617 (2017)
14. Pan, J., et al.: Salgan: visual saliency prediction with generative adversarial networks. arXiv preprint arXiv:1701.01081 (2017)
15. Pan, J., Sayrol, E., Giro-i Nieto, X., McGuinness, K., O'Connor, N.E.: Shallow and deep convolutional networks for saliency prediction. In: Proceedings of the IEEE Conference on Computer Vision and Pattern Recognition, pp. 598–606 (2016)
16. Russakovsky, O., et al.: Imagenet large scale visual recognition challenge. Int. J. Comput. Vision **115**(3), 211–252 (2015)
17. Shen, W., Liu, R.: Learning residual images for face attribute manipulation. In: Proceedings of the IEEE Conference on Computer Vision and Pattern Recognition, pp. 4030–4038 (2017)
18. Simonyan, K., Zisserman, A.: Very deep convolutional networks for large-scale image recognition. arXiv preprint arXiv:1409.1556 (2014)
19. Wang, L., Lu, H., Ruan, X., Yang, M.H.: Deep networks for saliency detection via local estimation and global search. In: Proceedings of the IEEE Conference on Computer Vision and Pattern Recognition, pp. 3183–3192 (2015)
20. Wang, L., Wang, L., Lu, H., Zhang, P., Ruan, X.: Saliency detection with recurrent fully convolutional networks. In: Leibe, B., Matas, J., Sebe, N., Welling, M. (eds.) ECCV 2016. LNCS, vol. 9908, pp. 825–841. Springer, Cham (2016). https://doi. org/10.1007/978-3-319-46493-0_50
21. Xie, S., Girshick, R., Dollár, P., Tu, Z., He, K.: Aggregated residual transformations for deep neural networks. In: Proceedings of the IEEE Conference on Computer Vision and Pattern Recognition, pp. 1492–1500 (2017)
22. Yan, Q., Xu, L., Shi, J., Jia, J.: Hierarchical saliency detection. In: Proceedings of the IEEE Conference on Computer Vision and Pattern Recognition, pp. 1155–1162 (2013)
23. Yang, C., Zhang, L., Lu, H., Ruan, X., Yang, M.H.: Saliency detection via graph-based manifold ranking. In: Proceedings of the IEEE Conference on Computer Vision and Pattern Recognition, pp. 3166–3173 (2013)
24. Zhao, R., Ouyang, W., Li, H., Wang, X.: Saliency detection by multi-context deep learning. In: Proceedings of the IEEE Conference on Computer Vision and Pattern Recognition, pp. 1265–1274 (2015)

Putting Jewellery and Accessories on a 3D Face Model Generated from 2D Image

Roshan Naik, Parth Singh$^{(\boxtimes)}$, and Prem Kalra

Indian Institute of Technology Delhi, New Delhi, India
parth.singh97@gmail.com

Abstract. Most of the work on adding accessories onto faces has been done in 2D. These methods use deep learning models and directly process the 2D images. In this paper, we perform this process in 3D space. This is done by converting 2D images into 3D face models and then placing the 3D model of the accessory on this face model. The automation has been done by using feature points and Procrustes analysis. We have also performed similar automation in Blender using the python API. The accessories include hats, glasses and Indian jewellery in various colours containing various diamonds and gemstones.

1 Introduction

Addition of accessories such as glasses is a very popular computer vision and graphics problem. A lot of private companies have developed their versions of solving this problem such as Lenskart, Try On Glasses that uses Ditto Technology and Glasses.com.

The method used in these technologies is partly Machine Learning based wherein a generic face model of the face is constructed from an input of face images. The method used by Ditto [1] takes a video of the person turning his head from left to right and then constructs a face model by detecting certain key positions of the face, such as points on the ear, eyes, nose and forehead. It then places a 3D model of the glasses onto the face mesh and then renders the frames with varying head positions with the glasses added.

The framework for our process involves a pipeline of three phases. The first phase is the generation of the Morphable face model from the input image. There are plenty of techniques available for the generation of 3D face models from a single input face image. For the pipeline, we have used Scalismo Morphable Model [2] to generate the 3D face. Once we have the generic face, we have to map the colours from the input image to the 3D mesh.

In the next phase, we attach a generic head to the constructed face. This process requires stitching and although there are methods to carry this out, we have developed our technique to stitch the face to the head. This step is necessary for the alignment of the accessories that comes next.

In the last phase, we add the 3D model of the accessory onto the 3D model of the complete face. For this we use Procrustes alignment, which we also perform in Blender via the API to make it automatic.

© Springer Nature Singapore Pte Ltd. 2020
R. V. Babu et al. (Eds.): NCVPRIPG 2019, CCIS 1249, pp. 229–238, 2020.
https://doi.org/10.1007/978-981-15-8697-2_21

The paper is structured as follows: Sect. 2 describes the theory behind Morphable Models and how we used it in our pipeline. Section 3 discusses stitching algorithm that we used for stitching the face to the generic head. Section 4 presents the alignment procedure that we used for automatically fitting accessory onto the face. Section 5 shows how this pipeline can be used as a try-on modelling tool for putting jewellery and other accessories onto a face given a single 2D image. It also demonstrates the working of the pipeline through various examples and results.

1.1 Related Work

Our paper builds upon the technologies and techniques developed by various authors in a lot of past research in Graphics and Vision such as 3D modelling, Morphable modeling, realistic rendering, 3D registration, stitching, alignment, etc.

The first phase of our pipeline works by constructing a 3D model of a face from a single 2D image [6–8]. This is a very popular problem and is a subclass of 3D reconstruction problem [2–5]. Some of these papers use more than just a single RGB image. We however are dealing with the problem of 3D model generation from a single 2D image, and within this problem, we are specifically targeting to reconstruct a face of a human. This problem has been solved in the literature by the help of Morphable Face Models. Machine Learning, Deep Learning techniques have been quite popular in solving this via Morphable Models [7,9].

In recently published work, the paper [11] deals with the same problem of adding accessories on the face, however, the paper focuses more on applying makeup and relighting the 3D face model, and less on adding accessories like glasses or hat, which are performed only in 2D. We borrow the first step of the pipeline in this paper for the generation of 3D face from 2D image. This step comes from [1,12] where it is discussed greatly. We develop novel techniques of our own to complete the addition of 3D accessories to a fully 3D reconstructed head.

2 3D Face Model

2.1 Morphable Model

To generate a 3D frontal face model from a given 2D image, we have used scalismo-faces. This tool uses Basel Face Models as a database of Gaussian Process Morphable Models. It uses Analysis by Synthesis approach to find the best model corresponding to the input image. This approach first synthesizes the model and then checks the likelihood of the model with the input image. It follows a Markov Chain Monte Carlo simulation to fit the Gaussian Process (i.e. the Morphable Models are modelled as a Gaussian Process) to the input image data [1].

The model generates, several parameters such as the shape of the Morphable Face Model (i.e. components of distortions that come from PCA of the population of distortions from the Basel Dataset), illumination, pose, distance from the camera, etc. are estimated and then the projected image of the model is compared with the input image for similarity, then a slight perturbation to the parameters is made according to the algorithm of Markov Chain Monte Carlo simulation to generate a new model which is compared with the input to see if it is a closer match. This process is repeated until the iteration count is met. The larger the iterations, the better is the fit that we obtain if the model is converging to the face. Sometimes however, the model doesn't converge which happens mostly because of a very bad initialization of the model.

All the final parameters from this approach are stored in the Render Parameter File. These Render Parameters are needed to synthesize an image of the Morphable Model and compare it with the input image.

2.2   2D Texture Mapping

Once the model is generated, we save it as a 3D mesh in '.ply' (Stanford Polygon Format) file. Now we need to map the texture of the original image onto this '.ply' mesh. The '.ply' file uses vertex colour. Also, since there is a correspondence between the rendered image of the Morphable Model and the input image, we simply replace the RGB values of the Morphable Model with the RGB values of the pixel corresponding to that vertex of that Morphable Model (Fig. 1).

Fig. 1. Scalismo generated model   **Fig. 2.** Texture mapping

3   Head Stitching

For the next step of the pipeline, we have to extend the face into a complete head. This is done by stitching a generic head model that is available in 'ply' format with the face model that is generated in Sect. 2 - the 3D Face Model.

Stitching of meshes has been an entire subject of it's own in other papers such as in [13,14]. The paper on Joint Alignment and Stitching of Non-Overlapping Meshes (JASNOM) [13] defines stitching as the process of joining two meshes say $M_1 = (V_1, E_1, F_1)$ & $M_2 = (V_2, E_2, F_2)$ which are 2-manifold meshes (i.e. have a $\mathbb{R}^2$ topology) with a boundary/hole. In this process a mesh $M_c = (V_{s1} \cup$

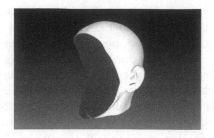

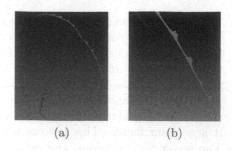

Fig. 3. The back-head model with the face carved out

Fig. 4. Back-head boundary contour

$V_{s2}, E_{stitch}, F_{stitch})$ is generated such that the resulting mesh $M = M_1 \cup M_2 \cup M_c$ is also a 2-manifold with $\mathbb{R}^2$ topology but without any boundary.

The connecting mesh M_c stitches the boundary of mesh M_1 with boundary of mesh M_2 seamlessly keeping the topology preserved. Since the connecting mesh doesn't introduce any new vertices it just includes V_{s1} which are the boundary vertices of M_1 and V_{s2} which are the boundary vertices of M_2 and connects all boundary vertices from one mesh to the other mesh. Also, each edge in E_{stitch} joins one vertex from V_{s1} to one vertex from V_{s2} and the edges don't cross over one another. There shouldn't be an edge that connects an interior vertex from any of the meshes, since then it would break the $\mathbb{R}^2$ topology of that mesh.

Although there is a developed algorithm [13] for automatically aligning two meshes appropriately and stitching them into a complete mesh, we have developed our own stitching algorithm for this special case of stitching a face mesh Fig. 2 with the back-head model Fig. 3 that obeys the constraints and specifications previously defined (Fig. 4).

The first step in the algorithm is to align the boundaries of the two meshes such that they are close to each other and don't intersect each other. The second step is to generate the connecting mesh M_c from the correspondences between vertices in V_{s1} and vertices in V_{s2}. The JASNOM algorithm [13] performs the first part by formulating a cost function for the distance between the contours of the two meshes and a cost function that measures the intersection of the meshes. It then tries to minimize the cost functions which is a non-convex optimization problem that is solved via an iterative method to give a local solution.

We however don't perform such optimization of cost functions, instead we do pre-processing on the back-head that ensures the alignment is reasonable. All face models generated from the prior phase are mostly similar in scale and position with minor variations in size and shape. Therefore in pre-processing, we align the back-head to a 'base' face manually so that the connecting mesh can be easily generated between corresponding points of the boundaries. Then, for any new face mesh coming from a different image, we compute the scale and translate required to transform the 'base' mesh such that it would roughly be aligned with the 'new' mesh. When we apply a transformation to the back-head based on these scale and translation values, it would also align the back-head appropriately, close to the 'new' mesh. This assumption is valid only when the scaling and translations are small.

The stitching by our algorithm has the following steps. We first select a 3D model of a complete generic head, that includes the ears, forehead, scalp & face. We then carve out the face portion meticulously using a 3D modeling software like Blender. The resulting model is called the back-head. Refer on Fig. 3.

The next stage is to extend the face mesh so that it smoothly merges with the back-head. For this, we extract the boundary points of the face and the back-head. We then iterate over each boundary point in the face mesh and extend it to the closest boundary point on the back-head contour, call it a matching point. For those points on the back-head contour which don't have a corresponding point that they are matched with on the face mesh boundary, an inverse matching point on the face mesh boundary is found. New edges and faces are then created such that all the vertices from both the boundaries are connected in an appropriate nearest-neighbor fashion and the resulting mesh has no boundary vertices. This is saved as a 'ply' file.

The final stage after creation of the new ply file is to polish it. This is done by performing some operations in Blender. In the edit mode, we perform "Remove Doubles" followed by "Recalculate Normals". Then we select the "smooth" shading instead of the "flat" shading in the Tools section for the purposes of better rendering in the software and Fig. 5 shows the results.

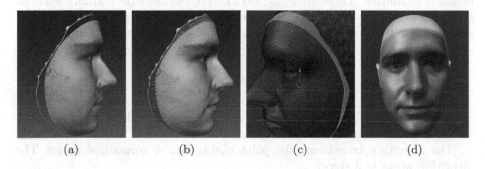

(a)   (b)   (c)   (d)

Fig. 5. Stitching results: (a)–(b) Side view of the face and back-head boundary before & after stitching, (c) Inter-connecting mesh, (d) Final render

4   Alignment of Accessories

4.1   Feature Points

Once we have the face mesh and the mesh of the accessory to be placed, we choose certain feature points. These feature points are chosen so that there is a one-one correspondence matching between the feature points of the face mesh and glasses mesh. We have used the points on the side temple and bridge of the nose as feature points in the case of glasses Fig. 6. Similarly, we use the points on the arms and nose support for the feature points on the glasses (Fig. 7).

Fig. 6. Feature points of glass model

Fig. 7. Glass aligned with the face model

4.2 Procrustes Analysis

To align the glasses and the face mesh, we use the Procrustes analysis algorithm [10]. The algorithm takes as input, two point clouds. These point clouds, in our case, are the points clouds composed of the feature points. The algorithm tries to find the best transformation matrix so that the distance between the points clouds is minimized. There are many ways we can calculate the distance between the meshes. One way is to sum the square of distances between each feature point and finally take the square root. This is referred to as Procrustes Distance.

$$d = \sqrt{\sum_{k=1}^{n}(x_k - u_k)^2 + (y_k - v_k)^2} \tag{1}$$

Where, (x_k, y_k), k = 1 to n are the points of the first cloud and (u_k, v_k), k = 1 to n are the points of the second cloud.

The algorithm transforms the point clouds into a normalized space. The algorithm works in 3 steps:

1. Translation is performed so as to bring the mean of both point clouds at the same point. For the normalized space that point is the origin.
2. Once the mean of the point clouds becomes the same, scaling is performed on the point clouds so that the variance of both the clouds becomes equal.
3. The algorithm then tries to minimize the angle between each pair of feature points by rotating the point clouds.

4.3   Correction Transformation

Our algorithm takes points on the face and accessories as feature points. This can sometimes act as a limitation to getting a good fit of the accessory. This is because the Procrustes algorithm will try to fit points on the meshes exactly touching each other. We found that this gives results where accessories collide and pass through each other. To overcome this, we apply one more 'Correction Transformation' to the accessory mesh. These corrections can be translational, rotational or scaling.

For example, in Fig. 8 (a), the cap is too small, so we apply a correction transformation to make the cap slightly bigger to improve the alignment.

This transformation can be generalized to any face mesh for a particular accessory, because the Procrustes alignment algorithm transforms the face mesh into a normalized space.

Scaling of accessory is necessary if we are dealing with accessories whose size does not match with the standard size of our head. But once we fix the accessory to be in the inventory, scaling would be done as a pre-processing step and size of the accessory should be fixed. However, the correction matrix can still be useful for making minute translational or rotational adjustments after Procrustes alignment (Fig. 9).

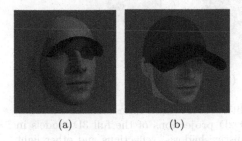

(a)   (b)

Fig. 8. Correction transformation

Fig. 9. Hat aligned with the face model

5   Results

The key advantage of having a 3D model of the face and stitching it to a complete head is that various accessories can be added to it in 3D and it can rendered onto a 2D screen realistically.

We have also coloured the back head of the model to match the colour of the skin of the face. This is achieved by a machine learning algorithm called K-Means Clustering. It is a clustering algorithm that clumps all the pixel colours found on the face into a certain fixed number of clusters and the colour of the cluster with the highest frequency is used to colour up the whole back head. Since, it is the most dominant colour on the face, it looks harmonious on the head (Fig. 10).

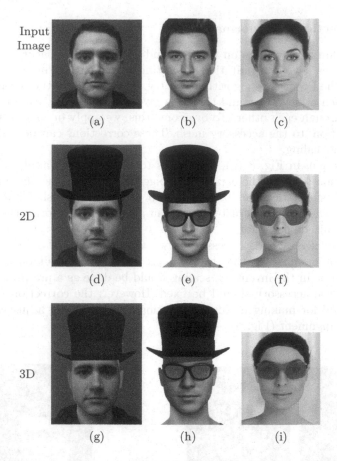

Fig. 10. Comparison of 3D accessories addition to 2D accessories addition. The 2D version in second row is just copy/paste of 2D projections of the full 3D models in the third row. The 3D version displays realistic shadows, reflections and other light properties, many of which is not observed in the 2D version. Some of the background has been manipulated using Photoshop for the sake of comparison with the original image in first row like the extension of the red background in (d), (g) and the copy of hair in (i) from (c) - there is no 3D model of hair.

5.1   Application as Try-On Tool

The whole pipeline can be used as a try-on tool. The user will give an input image of their face and would select an accessory from a repository of accessories which might include sunglasses, jewellery products, hats, caps and other facial accessories. For the purpose of demonstration, we have created our own repository of Indian jewellery. Jewellery can have multiple customization options such as choice of metal (gold, silver, etc.) and stones (ruby, diamond, emerald, etc.).

Given a 3D model of an accessory and some meta-data related to key points, the pipeline gives as output a photo-realistic rendering of the face with the accessory added on top in 3D.

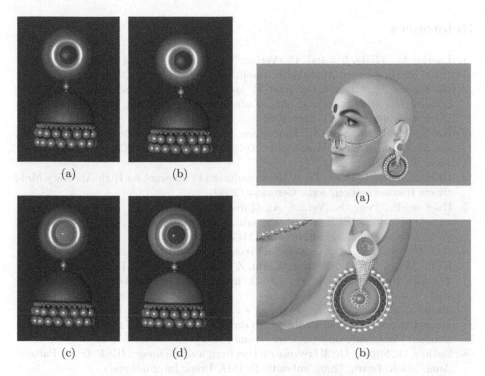

Fig. 11. The traditional earring jhumka in various colours, (a)–(c) purple hemisphere with (a) gold-ring, (b) silver-ring, (c) green center, (d) gold hemisphere with silver-ring and red center (Color figure online)

Fig. 12. Diamonds and other gemstones jewellery - (a) Full view with complete head, (b) Close up view of the jewellery rendered realistically at very high sampling rate and negligible artifacts.

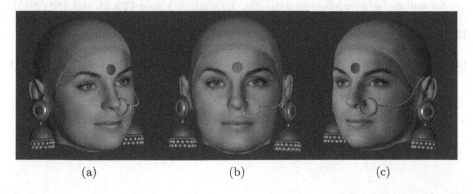

Fig. 13. Traditional Indian Jewellery on a full 3D model of a female face. Added accessories include earrings (jhumka), nose ring (nath) and bindi - (a) left view, (b) center view, (c) right view.

Our working demo consists of the following jewellery items - traditional Indian nose ring (nath), tradition Indian earrings (jhumka) of different colors and diamond/gemstones earrings (Figs. 11, 12 and 13).

References

1. Luethi, M., Gerig, T., Jud, C., Vetter, T.: Gaussian process morphable models. IEEE Trans. Pattern Anal. Mach. Intell. **40**(8), 1860–1873 (2018)
2. Goldluecke, B., Magnor, M.: Joint 3D reconstruction and background separation in multiple views using graph cuts. Madison, Wisconsin, USA, vol. 1, pp. 683–694. IEEE Computer Society, June 2003
3. Goldluecke, B., Magnor, M.: Space-time isosurface evolution for temporally coherent 3D reconstruction. Washington, D.C., USA, vol. 1, pp. 350–355, IEEE Computer Society, July 2004
4. Goldluecke, B., Cremers, D.: A Superresolution Framework for High-Accuracy Multiview Reconstruction, Jena, Germany (2009)
5. Haefner, B., Peng, S., Verma, A., Quéau, Y., Cremers, D.: Photometric depth super-resolution. IEEE Trans. Pattern Anal. Mach. Intell. **42**(10), 2453–2464 (2020). https://doi.org/10.1109/TPAMI.2019.2923621
6. Zou, C., Liu, J., Liu, J.: Precise 3D reconstruction from a single image. In: Lee, K.M., Matsushita, Y., Rehg, J.M., Hu, Z. (eds.) ACCV 2012. LNCS, vol. 7727, pp. 271–282. Springer, Heidelberg (2013). https://doi.org/10.1007/978-3-642-37447-0_21
7. Jackson, A.S., Bulat, A., Argyriou, V., Tzimiropoulos, G.: Large pose 3D face reconstruction from a single image via direct volumetric CNN regression. In: International Conference on Computer Vision (2017)
8. Rother, D., Sapiro, G.: 3D reconstruction from a single image. IEEE Trans. Pattern Anal. Mach. Learn. (2009, submitted). IMA Prepr International
9. Tran, A.T., Hassner, T., Masi, I., Medioni, G.G.: Regressing Robust and Discriminative 3D Morphable Models with a very Deep Neural Network (2016)
10. Gower, J.C.: Generalized procrustes analysis. Psychometrika **40**(1), 33–51 (1975)
11. Parihar, R., Dashpute, A., Kalra, P.: Scene adaptive cosmetic makeup transfer. In: ICVGIP (2018)
12. Schönborn, S., Egger, B., Morel-Forster, A., Vetter, T.: Markov chain Monte Carlo for automated face image analysis. Int. J. Comput. Vision **123**(2), 160–183 (2016). https://doi.org/10.1007/s11263-016-0967-5
13. Brandão, S., Costeira, J., Veloso, M.: Effortless scanning of 3D object models by boundary aligning and stitching. In: VISAPP (2014)
14. Turk, G., Levoy, M.: Zippered polygon meshes from range images. In: SIGGRAPH 1994, New York, NY, USA. ACM (1994)

Motion-Constrained Generative Adversarial Network for Anomaly Detection

Anitha Edison(✉) and C. V. Jiji

College of Engineering Trivandrum, Thiruvananthapuram, Kerala, India
{anithaedison,jijicv}@cet.ac.in

Abstract. Increased volume of video data made human monitoring impossible and necessitated automated abnormal event detection system. Abnormal event detection involves learning normal patterns and identifying any deviation as abnormal. In this paper, we propose a generative adversarial network (GAN) based abnormal event detection system. GAN is trained to generate normal frames, and fails to generate the frames with abnormal events. Usually adversarial loss and appearance loss are used to train GANs. In this paper, we propose to impose motion constraint using optical flow and acceleration during generator training. Our experiments on standard datasets prove that motion is an important cue for abnormal event detection.

Keywords: Abnormal event detection · Generative adversarial network (GAN) · Motion constraint

1 Introduction

Automated anomaly detection in videos is getting increased attention of computer vision community ever since video surveillance became a crucial part of public safety. Evolution of solid state technology resulted in cheaper cameras and surveillance equipments; there by increasing the volume of surveillance videos. This boom has made automated anomaly detection a greater necessity than before. Anomaly detection in videos aims to find any event deviating from the normal pattern. The case of anomaly detection is not a typical classification problem, since it is not possible to train using all negative samples. Common trend is to learn the normal patterns from training videos and identify any deviation as abnormal.

A combination of hand-crafted features and sparse reconstruction methods provided applaudable performance for abnormal event detection in surveillance videos [2,12]. In spite of the advantages of these methods, deep learning based reconstruction methods always had an edge in terms of accuracy. Reconstruction of videos using autoencoders was used for anomaly detection. Autoencoders trained on normal videos result in large error while reconstructing videos of

© Springer Nature Singapore Pte Ltd. 2020
R. V. Babu et al. (Eds.): NCVPRIPG 2019, CCIS 1249, pp. 239–249, 2020.
https://doi.org/10.1007/978-981-15-8697-2_22

irregular events. Abnormal event detection using convolutional autoencoders proposed by Hasan et al. was the pioneer work in this category [7]. Long-short term memory (LSTM) networks were used in autoencoders to encode sequential information in videos thereby improving anomaly detection capabilities [1,16]. The accuracy was further improved by the use of generative networks like generative adversarial networks (GAN) [11] and variational autoencoders [8].

In this paper, we propose a GAN-based algorithm for anomaly detection. GANs are usually trained using adversarial loss and appearance loss. But we believe that motion is an important cue that can differentiate abnormal and normal events. The contribution of the paper is the use of motion constraints for training a GAN to generate frames of normal events. We use optical acceleration constraint in addition to constraints on optical flow for training GANs.

2   Proposed Method

Generative adversarial network (GAN) introduced by Goodfellow et al. [6] is used to generate images from random noise. Recently, GANs were used for predicting future frames in videos [15] and for anomaly detection [11]. We use normal videos to train the GAN to predict future frames. During testing, prediction of future frames result in error in case of abnormal frames. The peak signal to noise ratio (PSNR) between the original and predicted frame is used to detect anomaly.

2.1   Generative Adversarial Networks

GAN consists of two neural network models, a generator and a discriminator. Generator learns the distribution of train data and discriminator classifies the train data and generated data as real or fake.

Suppose x is the train data sampled from random variable X and z is sampled from random noise Z with predefined prior $p_Z(z)$. Generator learns a mapping, $G_{\theta_g}(z)$ from z to data space. G_{θ_g} is differentiable function implemented using multi layer perceptron (MLP) with weights θ_g. The second network, discriminator (D_{θ_d}) with parameters θ_d takes in train data x and generated data $G_{\theta_g}(z)$ and outputs probability that each of them is real or fake.

Generator and discriminator are trained simultaneously. The discriminator is trained to correctly label real data and generated data, whereas the generator is trained to produce data that cannot be distinguished by discriminator. Generator tries to maximise $D_{\theta_d}(G_{\theta_g}(z))$ and minimize $D_{\theta_d}(x)$, while discriminator tries to minimize $D_{\theta_d}(G_{\theta_g}(z))$ and maximise $D_{\theta_d}(x)$. Taking these into account, the objective function of GAN [6] is expressed as

$$\min_{\theta_g} \max_{\theta_d} E_{x \sim p_X(x)}[log(D_{\theta_d}(x))] + E_{z \sim p_Z(z)}[log(1 - D_{\theta_d}(G_{\theta_g}(z)))] \qquad (1)$$

where $E_{x \sim p_X(x)}[log(D_{\theta_d}(x))]$ is the average log probability of discriminator predicting original data as real and $E_{z \sim p_Z(z)}[log(1 - D_{\theta_d}(G_{\theta_g}(z)))]$ is the average log probability of discriminator predicting generated data as fake.

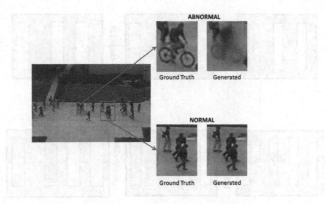

Fig. 1. Illustration of error during prediction of abnormal frames

2.2   Anomaly Detection Using GAN

We use future frame prediction using GANs for abnormal event detection. Generator is trained to predict the future frame given a sequence of normal frames. Since the generator is trained to predict normal future frames, the generated frames will be blurred in case of some abnormal/out-of-context events as shown in Fig. 1. This error can be leveraged for abnormal event detection.

In our algorithm generator learns mapping from a sequence of frames, $Z = \{I_{t-n}, ..., I_{t-2}, I_{t-1}, I_t\}$ to future frame, $X = \{I_{t+1}\}$. Discriminator assigns correct label to both x and $G_{\theta_g}(z)$. We use U-Net autoencoder architecture [17] for our generator and deep convolutional generative adversarial networks (DCGAN) discriminator architecture [19] for our discriminator. Discriminator and generator were trained simultaneously to solve the adversarial min-max problem. In addition to adversarial loss, an appearance loss and motion loss are used to train the generator.

Generator: The task of the generator is to predict the future frame from a sequence of previous frames. Video frames are resized to 256×256 and a set of consecutive frames, $Z = \{I_{t-n}, ..., I_{t-2}, I_{t-1}, I_t\}$, are concatenated and given as an input to the generator. The output of the generator is a single future frame, $G_{\theta_g}(z) = \{I'_{t+1}\}$.

The architecture of our generator network is shown in Fig. 2a. Generator is an encoder-decoder network with skip connections from encoder to decoder [17]. The encoder path consist of 4 encoder modules and each encoder module has two 3×3 convolutional layers followed by a rectified linear unit (ReLU) activation and a 2×2 max pooling operation. In each successive module, the number of filters (feature dimension) is increased two times and output is downsampled by 2 using max pooling layer. The last encoder module does not have max pooling layer. The decoder consist of upsampling the features by 2 followed by concatenating the upsampled features with the corresponding ones from encoder module. The concatenated features are passed through 2D convolutional layer

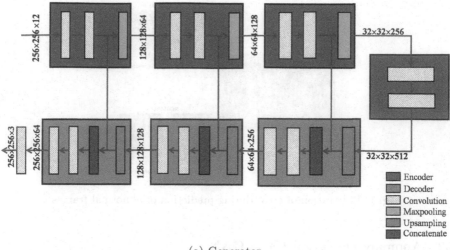

(a) Generator

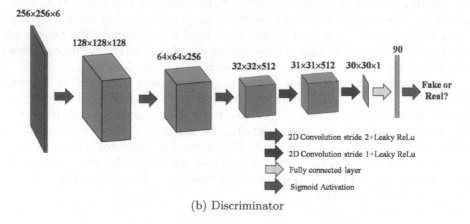

(b) Discriminator

Fig. 2. Network architecture

with filter size 3×3. The number filter in each successive decoder is reduced as a fraction of 2. The residual connections from encoder to decoder reduces the vanishing gradient problem.

Discriminator: The task of the discriminator is to correctly label the original frame, $X = \{I_{t+1}\}$ and the generated frame, $G_{\theta_g}(z) = \{I'_{t+1}\}$. The inputs to discriminator network is the concatenated original frame and generated frame and output is a label assigned to each input.

The flow diagram of the discriminator is shown in Fig. 2b. Discriminator uses convolutional layers with 3×3 filter size, followed leaky ReLU activation [19]. In subsequent layers, the number of features is increased from 64 to 512 by a factor of 2 and feature map size decreased by a factor of 2. Instead of max pooling, strided convolutions are used to reduce the feature map size. All convolutional layers except the last two layers use two-strided convolutions. Convolutional layers are followed by a fully connected layer and a sigmoid layer.

Training: Generator and discriminator are trained in alternating manner. As depicted in Fig. 3a, generator is trained to predict the future frame such that discriminator cannot distinguish the real frame and the generated frame, while the discriminator is trained to assign correct labels to real and generated frame. This min-max problem is similar to the one in Eq. 1. We use the variant of Eq. 1 put forward by Mao et al. for training least square GANs [14]. Our adversarial training involves minimizing the mean square errors in Eq. 2 and Eq. 3 by disciminator and generator respectively

$$\min_{\theta_d} L^d_{adv} = \frac{1}{2}E_{x \sim p_X(x)}[(D_{\theta_d}(x) - 1)^2] + \frac{1}{2}E_{z \sim p_Z(z)}[(D_{\theta_d}(G_{\theta_g}(z)) - 0)^2] \quad (2)$$

$$\min_{\theta_g} L^g_{adv} = \frac{1}{2}E_{z \sim p_Z(z)}[(D_{\theta_d}(G_{\theta_g}(z)) - 1)^2] \quad (3)$$

In addition to adversarial loss, we use appearance loss and motion loss to train the generator. Appearance loss limits the intensity and gradient of intensity of the generated frame to be close to the ground truth. Motion loss constraints optical flow and optical acceleration computed using the generated frames to be close to ground truth.

Appearance loss for a frame of size $W \times H$ is the sum of intensity and gradient loss given by Eqs. 4 and 5 respectively [9]. Intensity loss is the euclidean distance between pixel intensities of the generated and original frame at time $t + 1$. It ensures that the intensity of the generated pixel match that of the original frame. In addition to intensity, another important feature of an image is the edge. Gradient loss ensures that the edges are properly formed so that the generated frame is as sharp as the original frame.

$$L_{intensity} = \frac{1}{W \times H} \sum_{i}^{W} \sum_{j}^{H} (G_{\theta_g}(z)(i,j) - x(i,j))^2 \quad (4)$$

$$L_{gradient} = L_{gradient_x} + L_{gradient_y} \quad (5)$$

$$L_{gradient_x} = \frac{1}{W \times H} \sum_{i}^{W} \sum_{j}^{H} (|G_{\theta_g}(z)(i,j) - G_{\theta_g}(z)(i-1,j)| - |x(i,j) - x(i-1,j)|)^2 \quad (6)$$

$$L_{gradient_y} = \frac{1}{W \times H} \sum_{i}^{W} \sum_{j}^{H} (|G_{\theta_g}(z)(i,j) - G_{\theta_g}(z)(i,j-1)| - |x(i,j) - x(i,j-1)|)^2 \quad (7)$$

Motion is an important parameter in videos and we use velocity and acceleration information contained in the video frames to train the generator. Motion loss is the sum of acceleration loss and flow loss. To estimate acceleration loss, the absolute difference of optical acceleration computed using generated frame and real frame is taken. Similarly the difference of flow computed using generated and real frame gives flow loss [11].

Flow loss is given by the sum of losses in x and y direction.

$$L_{flow} = L_{flow_x} + L_{flow_y} \tag{8}$$

where L_{flow_x} and L_{flow_y} are given by Eqs. 9 and 10.

$$L_{flow_x} = \frac{1}{W \times H} \sum_i^W \sum_j^H |u(G_{\theta_g}(z), I_t)(i,j) - u(x, I_t)(i,j)| \tag{9}$$

$$L_{flow_y} = \frac{1}{W \times H} \sum_i^W \sum_j^H |v(G_{\theta_g}(z), I_t)(i,j) - v(x, I_t)(i,j)| \tag{10}$$

where (u, v) is the Farneback optical flow vector [4].

Similarly, acceleration loss is the sum of losses in horizontal and vertical component of acceleration

$$L_{acceleration} = L_{accn_x} + L_{accn_y} \tag{11}$$

where L_{acc_x} is given by

$$L_{acc_x} = \frac{1}{W \times H} \sum_i^W \sum_j^H |a(G_{\theta_g}(z), I_t, I_{t-1})(i,j) - a(x, I_t, I_{t-1})(i,j)| \tag{12}$$

and L_{acc_y} is given by

$$L_{acc_y} = \frac{1}{W \times H} \sum_i^W \sum_j^H |g(G_{\theta_g}(z), I_t, I_{t-1})(i,j) - g(x, I_t, I_{t-1})(i,j)| \tag{13}$$

where (a, g) is the Farneback optical acceleration vector [3].

Combining the appearance losses and motion losses with the adversarial loss, the objective function for generator can be written as

$$\min_{\theta_d} L^g = \lambda_d L^g_{adv} + \lambda_a L_{intensity} + \lambda_a L_{gradient} + \lambda_m L_{flow} + \lambda_m L_{acceleration} \tag{14}$$

Anomaly Detection: We train the GAN using normal videos and it is assumed that generation of abnormal frames results in error. When generator tries to predict an abnormal frame, there will be comparatively large difference between generated and real frame and hence PSNR between these frames will be low. A frame is assumed to be abnormal if the PSNR is low. We use the abnormal score in [11] for detecting abnormal frames. The flow diagram of abnormal event detection using GAN is shown in Fig. 3b.

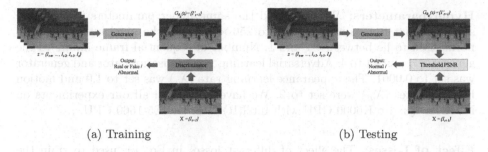

(a) Training   (b) Testing

Fig. 3. Flow diagram of training and testing GAN for abnormal event detection

3 Experiments and Discussions

This section describes the details of experiments performed to test our algorithm for abnormal event detection. We experimentally demonstrate that using motion information including velocity and acceleration improves anomaly detection performance.

Datasets: The performance of the descriptor was evaluated using standard abnormal event detection datasets: UCSD anomaly detection dataset and Avenue dataset. UCSD Anomaly Detection Dataset [10] consists of videos divided into two scenarios: Peds1 and Peds2. U In UCSD Peds1 dataset, 34 normal samples and 36 video samples with some abnormal events are available for training and testing. UCSD Peds2 dataset contains 16 normal training video samples and 12 testing video samples with some irregular events. Peds1 dataset has a spatial resolution of 158×238 pixels while the resolution of Peds2 dataset is 240×360. Avenue dataset [12] contains 16 normal videos for training and 21 testing video clips with some abnormal activity. It contains a total of 30,652 frames (15,328 training and 15,324 testing) of resolution 360×640. Frame-level annotations are available for all datasets.

Evaluation Measures: Using our algorithm, a frame is classified as normal or abnormal and hence we use frame-level criteria in [10] for quantitative analysis of the performance of the proposed algorithm. Similar to performance analysis of any binary classification problem, we compute the false positive rate (FPR) and true positive rate (TPR). FPR is a measure of false alarms generated by the detector and TPR measures detector's ability to classify abnormal events correctly. Performance evaluation includes plotting receiver operating characteristics (ROC) of FPR versus TPR and obtaining area under the curve (AUC) from it. EER is the common error rate obtained when FPR is equal to false negative rate (miss rate).

Hyper-parameters: We have used the same hyper parameters in [11]. The size the input frames were resized to 256×256 and the pixel intensities were normalised to lie between -1 and 1. Number of sequential frame inputs to the generator n was set to 4. Adversarial learning rate of discriminator and generator was set to 0.0001. The appearance learning rate (λ_a) was set to 1.0 and motion learning rates (λ_m) were set to 2. We have performed all our experiments on NVIDIA Quadro K6000 GPU with Intel(R) Xeon(R) E5-1660 CPU.

Effect of Losses: The effect of different losses in Eq. 14, used to train the generator, were evaluated adding each of them sequentially. These experiments were carried on Avenue dataset and Table 1 shows the results. As shown in the table, the addition of motion constraints improved the results considerably. Our contribution was the use of acceleration to train the generator and the use of acceleration had positive impact in the results as expected.

Table 1. Effect of losses on training the generator

Trial	Losses					
	Intensity	Gradient	Adversarial	Flow	Acceleration	AUC
Trial 1	✓					82.0%
Trial 2	✓	✓				82.6%
Trial 3	✓	✓	✓			83.7%
Trial 4	✓	✓	✓	✓		85.1%
Trial 5	✓	✓	✓	✓	✓	86.2%

Comparison with State-of-the-Art: We compare our GAN based algorithm with the deep learning algorithms in the literature. AUC and EER of some recent methods are listed in Table 2. Earlier works in anomaly detection used reconstruction of videos using autoencoders. The trend of using deep learning for anomaly detection started with convolutional autoencoders [7] and it gave commendable performance on standard datasets. From then on, autoencoder based methods have improved significantly and the use of sequential information using deep networks like convolutional LSTM autoencoders [1] and sRNN [13] had a profound impact. The use of generative networks improved the results further [11]. We use optical acceleration in addition to optical flow and appearance features to train the generator in GAN. As shown in Table 2, our method outperforms most of the existing methods in the literature. Our method processes an average 25.6 frames per second, which makes it useful for real-time video monitoring.

Table 2. Comparison of Frame Level AUC and EER of our anomaly detection method with existing algorithms in the literature (AUC (%)/EER (%))

Descriptor	Peds1	Peds2	Avenue
TSC [13]	-/-	91.03/-	80.56/-
sRNN [13]	-/-	92.21/-	81.71/-
ConvAE [7]	81/27.9	90.0/21.7	70.2/25.1
ConvLSTMAE [1]	89.9/12.5	87.4/12.0	80.3/20.7
VAE [8]	63.0/-	72.0/-	78.0/-
CAE [8]	66.0/-	65.0/-	83.0/-
R-ConvVAE [18]	75.0/32.4	91.0/15.5	79.6/27.5
HOFM-AE [5]	78.0/29.49	91.0/15.78	-/-
GAN [11]	83.1/-	95.4/-	85.1/-
Proposed Method	83.15/23.14	95.7/10.8%	86.17/18.59

Cross Database Testing: We did a cross database testing on UCSD pedestrian dataset to evaluate the generalization ability of our algorithm. We considered two scenarios. Model trained using Peds1 was tested using Peds2 and vice versa. Table 3 shows the comparison of cross and same database testing and generalisation results are satisfactory.

Table 3. Cross database testing (AUC/EER(%))

Train	Test	
	Peds1	Peds2
Peds1	83.15%/23.14%	89.78%/19.07%
Peds2	76.26%/29.95%	95.7%/10.8%

4 Conclusion

We have developed a deep learning based algorithm for anomaly detection, an application of action recognition. Our method uses GAN for detecting abnormal frames. Acceleration loss computed using our optical acceleration algorithm is used along with optical flow loss and appearance loss to train the generator. Generator is trained to predict future frames using normal videos and during testing, the PSNR between predicted frame and original ground truth is thresholded to detect anomaly. If the PSNR is high, then it is potentially a normal frame, otherwise it is an abnormal frame. This algorithm gave better AUC compared to existing methods in the literature.

References

1. Chong, Y.S., Tay, Y.H.: Abnormal event detection in videos using spatiotemporal autoencoder. In: Cong, F., Leung, A., Wei, Q. (eds.) ISNN 2017. LNCS, vol. 10262, pp. 189–196. Springer, Cham (2017). https://doi.org/10.1007/978-3-319-59081-3_23
2. Cong, Y., Yuan, J., Liu, J.: Sparse reconstruction cost for abnormal event detection. In: Proceedings of IEEE Conference on Computer Vision and Pattern Recognition, pp. 3449–3456 (2011)
3. Edison, A., Jiji, C.V.: Optical acceleration for motion description in videos. In: Proceedings of IEEE Conference on Computer Vision and Pattern Recognition Workshops, pp. 1642–1650 (2017)
4. Farnebäck, G.: Two-frame motion estimation based on polynomial expansion. In: Proceedings of Scandinavian Conference on Image Analysis, pp. 363–370 (2003)
5. George, M., Jose, B.R., Mathew, J., Kokare, P.: Autoencoder-based abnormal activity detection using parallel-piped spatio-temporal region. IET Comput. Vis. **13**(1), 23–30 (2018)
6. Goodfellow, I., et al.: Generative adversarial nets. In: Proceedings of the Advances in Neural Information Processing Systems, pp. 2672–2680 (2014)
7. Hasan, M., Choi, J., Neumann, J., Roy-Chowdhury, A.K., Davis, L.S.: Learning temporal regularity in video sequences. In: Proceedings of IEEE Conference on Computer Vision and Pattern Recognition, pp. 733–742 (2016)
8. Kiran, B.R., Thomas, D.M., Parakkal, R.: An overview of deep learning based methods for unsupervised and semi-supervised anomaly detection in videos. arXiv preprint arXiv:1801.03149 (2018)
9. Ledig, C., et al.: Photo-realistic single image super-resolution using a generative adversarial network. In: Proceedings of the IEEE Conference on Computer Vision and Pattern Recognition, pp. 4681–4690 (2017)
10. Li, W., Mahadevan, V., Vasconcelos, N.: Anomaly detection and localization in crowded scenes. IEEE Trans. Pattern Anal. Mach. Intell. **36**(1), 18–32 (2014)
11. Liu, W., Luo, W., Lian, D., Gao, S.: Future frame prediction for anomaly detection-a new baseline. In: Proceedings of the IEEE Conference on Computer Vision and Pattern Recognition, pp. 6536–6545 (2018)
12. Lu, C., Shi, J., Jia, J.: Abnormal event detection at 150 fps in Matlab. In: Proceedings of IEEE International Conference on Computer Vision, pp. 2720–2727 (2013)
13. Luo, W., Liu, W., Gao, S.: A revisit of sparse coding based anomaly detection in stacked RNN framework. In: Proceedings of IEEE International Conference on Computer Vision, pp. 341–349 (2017)
14. Mao, X., Li, Q., Xie, H., Lau, R.Y.K., Wang, Z., Paul Smolley, S.: Least squares generative adversarial networks. In: Proceedings of the IEEE International Conference on Computer Vision, pp. 2794–2802 (2017)
15. Mathieu, M., Couprie, C., LeCun, Y.: Deep multi-scale video prediction beyond mean square error. arXiv preprint arXiv:1511.05440 (2015)
16. Medel, J.R., Savakis, A.: Anomaly detection in video using predictive convolutional long short-term memory networks. arXiv preprint arXiv:1612.00390 (2016)
17. Ronneberger, O., Fischer, P., Brox, T.: U-Net: convolutional networks for biomedical image segmentation. In: Navab, N., Hornegger, J., Wells, W.M., Frangi, A.F. (eds.) MICCAI 2015. LNCS, vol. 9351, pp. 234–241. Springer, Cham (2015). https://doi.org/10.1007/978-3-319-24574-4_28

18. Yan, S., Smith, J.S., Lu, W., Zhang, B.: Abnormal event detection from videos using a two-stream recurrent variational autoencoder. IEEE Trans. Cogn. Dev. Syst. **12**, 30–42 (2018)
19. Yu, Y., Gong, Z., Zhong, P., Shan, J.: Unsupervised representation learning with deep convolutional neural network for remote sensing images. In: Zhao, Y., Kong, X., Taubman, D. (eds.) ICIG 2017. LNCS, vol. 10667, pp. 97–108. Springer, Cham (2017). https://doi.org/10.1007/978-3-319-71589-6_9

Performance Analysis and Optimization of Serialization Techniques for Deep Neural Networks

Akshay Parashar[✉], Payal Anand, and Arun Abraham

Samsung Research Institute, Bangalore, India
{aks.parashar, payal.anand, arun.abraham}@samsung.com

Abstract. Deep Neural Networks (DNN) are being increasingly used to solve complex problems. While exciting research efforts are ongoing to improve the inference performance, other concerns such as the model loading time and memory usage of DNN models have taken a backseat. Use of an efficient data serialization library is necessary for tackling these concerns, especially for heavy DNNs like VGG, which requires around 550 MB just for storage. This paper analyses the effects of prominent DNN framework serialization libraries like FlatBuffers and Protocol Buffers on model loading time and memory consumption. Our comparative analysis demonstrates that using FlatBuffers in Caffe framework results up to 75% improvement in model loading time and up to 48% peak memory usage reduction (dependent on the size of model used) as compared to default Protocol Buffers. Further, we propose memory optimized and embedded device oriented layout for Protocol Buffers specifically for neural network use-cases. This layout significantly reduces the model loading time and memory consumption of Protocol Buffers and achieve similar results as produced by the state-of-the-art FlatBuffers. We achieve around 67% improvement in model loading time and 47.6% peak memory usage reduction with the proposed Protocol Buffer layout. We show that the superiority of Proposed Protocol Buffers in data mutation i.e. serialization plus deserialization performance for on-device training use-cases gives it an edge over existing FlatBuffers.

Keywords: Data serialization [2] · FlatBuffers [3] · Protocol Buffers [4] · Deep Neural Networks [5] · Caffe [1]

1 Introduction

Deployment of Deep Neural Network on smartphones and embedded devices poses challenges of memory and computing power restrictions. Thus, there is growing demand for efficient deployment of DNNs on such devices. Optimizations are required at each possible step of DNN inferencing and training. This paper focuses on Data serialization aspect of the above process. Deciding a better on-device DNN inference serialization library depends on two factors: the nature of neural network use-cases and the embedded device limitations.

© Springer Nature Singapore Pte Ltd. 2020
R. V. Babu et al. (Eds.): NCVPRIPG 2019, CCIS 1249, pp. 250–260, 2020.
https://doi.org/10.1007/978-981-15-8697-2_23

The nature of neural network use-case can be either for only inference (the network is fixed and is used for only forward propagation) or for both training and inference (a common network architecture is deployed on device and is personalized via repeated learning). For inference only use-case, no modification to the network is required and only the data de-serialization (reading) step needs to be efficient. For both training and inference case, both serialization (write) and de-serialization (read) methods need to be efficient. For embedded devices memory and time are two important limitations. These devices have limited memory and real time use case demands model loading to be as fast as possible. Thus, the time taken to de-serialize the models and the memory footprint of the procedure should be as low as possible. Keeping above restrictions for embedded device inference, we explore existing popular data serialization techniques and propose modifications on Protocol Buffers for better inference.

Each DNN framework has its own set of data serialization libraries. Famous DNN frameworks such as Caffe [1] and TensorFlow [6] uses Protocol Buffers, whereas TensorFlowLite [7] uses FlatBuffers. Both of these serialization libraries have their own set of advantages and disadvantages.

Protocol Buffers [4] is language neutral, platform independent and needs to be cross-compiled for usage on other architectures. In order to read Protocol Buffer binary, the object tree needs to be parsed first. This reading of binary is sequential and at best Protocol Buffer object has to be parsed until the required field is discovered (partial parsing). Data cannot be accessed directly without parsing it. Additional memory is required for the secondary representation of the parsed Protocol Buffer object. FlatBuffers is a low memory footprint technique [8] and unlike Protocol Buffers, it does not requires the creation of parsed object, thereby reducing the extra memory overhead of secondary representation. Time to load data is reduced since everything can be accessed directly from binary file. Random memory reads are possible in FlatBuffers. In this paper, we explore the memory advantages and efficient model loading of FlatBuffers over the Protocol Buffers. We utilize the random access property of FlatBuffers in Caffe framework to further reduce the memory footprint by directly accessing the data from serialized binary.

One disadvantage with FlatBuffers is that it is inefficient for data manipulation/modifications and needs full data to be re-written in the binary file in case of even a small modification. We propose a memory optimized and embedded device oriented layout for Protocol Buffers specifically for neural network use-cases. By changing the model structure and arrangement of weights, we achieve results comparable to the industrial standard i.e. FlatBuffers, while maintaining developer friendliness of Protocol Buffers.

2 Background and Related Work

There is a requirement for storing trained models in specific data format for future inference purposes. Each DNN framework has its own way of storing data and reading it back from stored object called this process is called as Data Serialization. Data Serialization plays a key role in storing the trained neural network models on different devices and platforms. Same technique is also used to de-serialize already trained models for inference purposes. During de-serialization, network is parsed from binary and this network data is then copied into the framework structure. The time taken to parse a serialized binary into object is called model parsing time and the time taken to parse the object and then load it into framework is called model loading time.

There is an increasing demand for DNN use-cases on Mobile phones like Intelligent Camera, Virtual Reality, Augmented Reality and Voice to text applications. These applications require model loading to be as fast as possible to provide quick response to the user. Also, the shift of context between these DNN applications loads and unloads the DNN network. To ensure swift and responsive shift between DNN applications, the model loading time needs to be efficient. So, context of model loading remains critical for our exploration of different serialization techniques.

There has been a lot of research works differentiating various data serialization libraries. Many surveys are done on different perspectives like [2] which tries to compare various techniques on qualitative (readability of serialized objects, multiple programming language support) and quantitative (size of the serialized object) aspects of data serialization. Evaluations presented in [9] tries to compare data formats like XML, JSON and binary formats including Protocol Buffers on above mentioned parameters. An attempt to evaluate Protocol Buffer as an incremental data serialization update over XML standard is explored in [10]. These papers do not include the new FlatBuffers concept which is widely known and has become an industrial standard.

S.Popic tries to explore the performance of Protocol Buffers over JSON and BSON in IOT communication [11]. It compares the data formats on basis of network load (length of the message to be transferred). Future scope of this paper is to take into consideration serialization and de-serialization processing time as another important factor for analysis which are included in this paper.

Our work evaluates data serialization specifically for Deep Neural Network (DNN) use-cases for embedded devices. In contrast to the background research, both memory footprint and model processing time in DNN inference context are evaluated in this paper. Comparison between the latest trends of data serialization i.e. Protocol Buffers and FlatBuffers is drawn. Optimization on Protocol Buffers is done by storing weights and bias in byte string format instead of storing it in array format in order to achieve similar parsing results as state-of-the-art FlatBuffers.

3   Experimental Setup

We demonstrate the comparison between Protocol Buffers and FlatBuffers by simulating environment similar to on device Deep Neural Network Framework inference. We design data schema containing a list of elements with each element consisting of 10 million float values (structure similar to neural networks with each layer having weights array). We calculate the time taken to modify the existing contents in the file (both read and write) by FlatBuffers and Default Protocol Buffers on an embedded device. As showcased in Table 1, FlatBuffers are better than Protocol Buffers for both read and write performance. It is because there is no requirement of data parsing in FlatBuffers during data read while Default Protocol Buffers de-serializes millions of array values one by one and then store them into the parsed array object thereby overhead of both memory and performance.

Table 1. Comparison for read/write performance of the proposed protocol buffer layout

S no.	Timings (calculated in milliseconds)			
	Process	Protocol buffers	Flat buffers	Proposed protocol buffer layout
1	Serialization (Write)	1468	827	121
2	De-serialization (Read)	252	0.00075	54
3	Modification of binary (Both Read + Write)	1720	~827	175

So, we experiment by changing the data arrangement in Protocol Buffers. Since the time taken to parse the repeated data type (array) in Protocol Buffers is evidently more than that of simple byte string, we propose a layout in which arrays are stored as byte string (float values stored one after the other in raw format). We showcase that the proposed design is better than state-of-the art FlatBuffers when both serialization and de-serialization timings are considered (in case of use-cases with on-device training along with inference). It is approximately 10x better than Default Protocol Buffers and 4.7x better than the FlatBuffers for the experimental data as presented in Table 1. Provided that even a simple neural network contains millions of parameters for example AlexNet contains as high as 62 million parameters, the above property is exploited to store the neural network weights as byte string rather than float arrays.

The above experiments also showcases the framework independence of the proposed Protocol Buffer layout for on-device DNN frameworks. To align with industrial standards, Caffe framework has been used to verify above results on the actual DNN framework. Caffe comes with in-built Protocol Buffers implementation. We utilize Caffe framework for inference purposes and thus the Caffe experiments include data de-serialization timings of above serialization techniques.

Caffe Network [13] contains layers and each layer contains blobs. These blobs contain the actual model weights and bias as explained in Fig. 1. The caffemodel file is loaded into memory and is de-serialized to get the actual weights. This data is then copied inside Caffe framework network into their corresponding layers and blobs. We explore above mentioned data serialization techniques keeping in mind model loading time and memory footprint. Experimentation analysis is done on the Caffe framework with the below setup.

Samsung Exynos 9820 mobile device with Octa-core CPU (2 × 2.73 GHz Mongoose M4 & 2 × 2.31 GHz Cortex-A75 & 4 × 1.95 GHz Cortex-A55) has been used for experimentation. Caffe library has been cross compiled for arm64-v8a architecture. The Caffe library has been benchmarked with prominent open-source neural networks for the model loading time and memory footprint. During the benchmark, multiple iterations of model parsing is done and the average model loading time and memory impact is calculated. To avoid any caching impact, loaded model is deleted from memory in between iterations. For each serialization technique, below are the preprocessing steps required to plug-in the technique to the framework and to generate the models in the correct format.

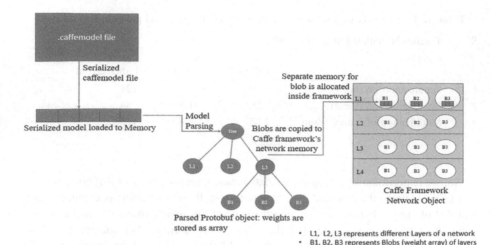

Fig. 1. Protocol Buffers with Caffe – default implementation

3.1 Original Protocol Buffers

Caffe comes with built-in Protocol Buffers implementation Fig. 1. Here the weights and bias are stored as array (defined by repeated data type) inside the Protocol Buffer binary. There is an additional copy of data from the parsed object to the framework due to which the memory shoots to double the actual size of the model during the copy of last layer data.

3.2 FlatBuffers

Migrating Flatbuffers to Caffe framework requires some additional work. A tool that converts already trained Protocol Buffer models (caffemodel file) to FlatBuffers format is created. The tool converts the Protocol Buffer binary to FlatBuffers format via JSON. Protocol Buffer provides APIs to convert the model file into intermediate JSON format. FlatBuffers compiler provides APIs to convert the JSON file to FlatBuffers binary. FlatBuffers does not require parsing of the serialized object. We can directly use the data present inside the FlatBuffers binary and refer this array for data access. Due to this property, there is elimination of the secondary memory representation, unlike in Protocol Buffers, thereby making it memory efficient. This property of FlatBuffers has been explored further and experimented to get the memory benefits for DNN use-cases.

FlatBuffers data de-serialization (read) methods are plugged into Caffe framework. Since FlatBuffers data is stored relative to each other in raw format, direct pointers to the FlatBuffer blobs array are used to read the data directly. Further memory footprint is reduced by directly using this Flatbuffer array for blobs data instead of copying data into new allocated arrays in framework (as done in Caffe by default). Since the location of weights data pointer for each layer inside the FlatBuffers array is known, the reference to this data can be stored inside Caffe layer's blobs. As explained in Fig. 2, this direct access further reduces the memory requirement due to elimination of memory allocations (malloc) in framework. We demonstrate the working of FlatBuffers in Caffe framework with improvement in model load timings (2x improvement) and memory footprint (dependent on size of the model) without any impact on accuracy of models.

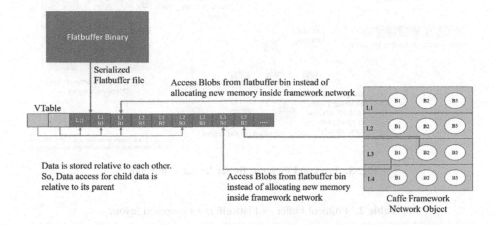

Fig. 2. FlatBuffers implementation with Caffe

3.3   Proposed Protocol Buffers Layout

We customize the Protocol Buffer specifically for neural network use-cases as explained above. By default weights and bias are stored as array (repeated data type) in Default Protocol Buffers.

The experimentation includes pre-processing the Protocol Buffer binary to store array present inside blobs as string. The weights data from array is appended one after the other as a byte string. For reading this data into Caffe network object, a pointer to data is used rather than doing malloc and copying data into this newly allocated memory one by one as explained in Fig. 3. Thus this direct pointer access to Protocol Buffer binary results in memory optimization. After changing the implementation from array to string in Protocol Buffers, model loading time comes closer to FlatBuffers (Table 2) while preserving the advantages of data mutation of Protocol Buffers.

4   Experimentation Results

4.1   Model Loading Time

Here we present the experimental data for the famous open-source Caffe trained models using different data serialization libraries. We calculate the model loading time (data de-serialization plus framework network generation) for different models. In case of FlatBuffers, since data parsing is not there, the timing includes time to create Caffe net

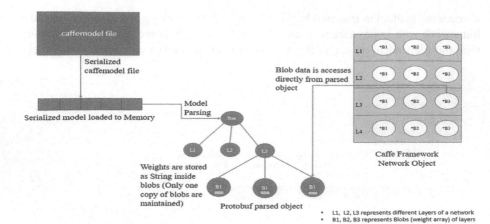

Fig. 3. Proposed Protocol Buffer layout with Caffe

Table 2. Protocol buffer vs FlatBuffers vs proposed layout

S no.	Model loading time (calculated in milliseconds)					
	Model name	Protocol buffer	FlatBuffers	Proposed protocol buffer layout	Percentage improvement of FlatBuffers over default protobuf	Percentage improvement of proposed layout over default protobuf
1	Squeezenet	39.26	29.85	31.00	23.96	19.22
2	Mobilenet v2	101.11	78.09	95	22.76	17.86
3	Mobilenet v1	120.25	85.54	95.40	28.86	17.00
4	GoogleNet	311.95	119.94	124.00	61.55	60.25
5	Inception-v3	433.48	255.37	284.05	41.10	28.93
6	Alexnet	778.87	201.72	253.00	74.10	68.36
7	VGG19	1787.31	471.85	596.00	73.59	67.77
8	VGG16	1821.47	420.13	571.00	76.93	68.94

object from FlatBuffers binary. We observe approximately 24% improvement for lighter models like SqueezeNet and around 75% improvement for heavier models like VGG and AlexNet in terms of load time with FlatBuffers as shown in Table 2. The results with FlatBuffers are much better as compared to default Protocol Buffers.

The proposed Protocol Buffer layout for embedded device technique yields comparable results as that of FlatBuffers. Table 2 shows load time improvements of various models over default Protocol Buffer. There is 19% improvement for SqueezeNet model and around 67% for heavier VGG model. We could successfully demonstrate that similar results can be achieved in Protocol Buffers with our suggested optimizations for DNN related use-cases. The advantages of easy mutability gives our proposed layout an edge over FlatBuffers.

4.2 Memory Impact

Here, we showcase the memory impact of the above discussed serialization techniques on Caffe model loading. The memory data is captured using valgrind memory profiler tool to detect memory allocations done during Caffe model loading. In the graphs represented in Fig. 4, the x-axis represents time and the y-axis represents the memory heap size. The area under the graph represents the amount of memory that was used by the use-case for the period of time. We gather memory data for VGG network and it is observed that the time taken by FlatBuffers is less (nearly half) than the time taken by Protocol Buffers and FlatBuffers consume less memory for this shorter duration (Fig. 4). Since there is no secondary representation of parsed data in FlatBuffers and time consumed is less and the area under the graph of Flatbuffers is almost one-fourth of the area under default Protocol Buffers (combining both memory-time effects). We observed that heavier the model, more significant are the memory and load timing reductions. The time-memory graph area reduction for FlatBuffers for all the models are approximated to be more than 50% for heavier models like VGG and AlexNet and more than 25% for lighter models like SqueezeNet. These memory reductions are proportional to the model size. There is reduction in memory for proposed Protocol Buffers due to optimizations for using parsed data directly instead of additional memory allocation and copy in DNN framework. These reductions are proportional to the model size since the redundant copy of weights and bias are avoided.

We also verify the valgrind results by calculating the peak memory usage in the above methods by checking the memory available on the mobile device at any point of time. Our aim is to check the peak memory usage in both of the methods. We observe that in case of Protocol Buffers, the peak memory usage is almost double the case of FlatBuffers (Fig. 5 diagram on right side). The maximum memory utilized is gathered by checking the deepest trough during model loading. We observe results consistent with the ones reported by valgrind profiling tool.

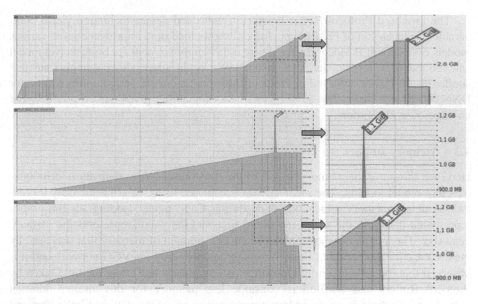

Fig. 4. Valgrind memory plot for VGG Network with Default Protocol Buffer (on top), FlatBuffers (in middle) and Proposed Protocol Buffers layout (bottom).

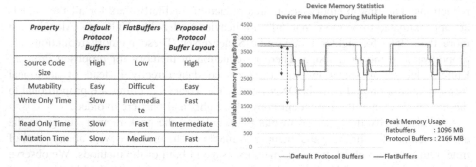

Property	Default Protocol Buffers	FlatBuffers	Proposed Protocol Buffer Layout
Source Code Size	High	Low	High
Mutability	Easy	Difficult	Easy
Write Only Time	Slow	Intermediate	Fast
Read Only Time	Slow	Fast	Intermediate
Mutation Time	Slow	Medium	Fast

Fig. 5. Overall comparison of different serialization techniques (left) and Peak Memory utilization in case of FlatBuffers and Protocol Buffers (right)

5 Conclusion and Future Work

Use of FlatBuffers and proposed Protocol Buffers provide similar improvement in Caffe inference performance. We observed that by using FlatBuffers there is significant improvement in model loading time (up to 76%) as well as memory footprint (depends to the size of model) as compared to default Protocol Buffer technique. Plugging into the Protocol Buffer optimization of storing weights as a string having weights array gave 30–60% load time improvement over default layout that is comparable with Flatbuffers. Directly accessing the parsed data instead of malloc lead to memory footprint reductions of both Proposed Protocol Buffers and FlatBuffers.

Sample experimentation done shown in Table 1 proves that these optimizations of Protocol Buffer technique by changing weights storage layout can be applied to other DNN frameworks as well. In Fig. 6, Comparison of the model load timing of all the three techniques for prominent neural network architectures has been plotted. It is evident that with increase in the model size, the advantages are more prevalent.

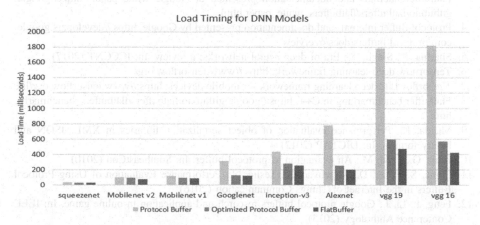

Fig. 6. Load Timings for famous Neural Networks (model size increases from left to right).

The use of suitable library depends on the use case. FlatBuffers bins are difficult to be changed and modification in some part of binary results in rewriting the whole binary again. Protocol Buffers on the other hand are mutable and easy to change data inside it.

If we can achieve similar performance with Protocol Buffers as compared to FlatBuffers, the decision to use which serialization technique depends on other differentiating factors between the two (Fig. 5 left side). When we consider the write timings, we observe the proposed Protocol Buffer layout is faster than FlatBuffers. Combining both read and write timings, Proposed Protocol Buffers is 4x better than FlatBuffers and 10x better than default Protocol Buffers. The Proposed Protocol Buffers layout can be extended to use-cases where huge data is transferred over the wire in form of arrays such as gaming applications [12] and applications where on-device learning is applied (personalized learning).

Future scope of this paper is to include backward propagation timing on caffe framework and check the combined effects of forward (read time) and backward inference (read and write time) of serialization libraries. Further, the advantages of Proposed Protocol Buffers can be applied to other fields where huge amounts of data like gaming applications.

References

1. Jia, Y., et al.: Caffe: Convolutional Architecture for Fast Feature Embedding, arXiv preprint arXiv: 1408.5093 (2014)
2. Maeda, K.: Comparative Survey of Object Serialization Techniques and the Programming Supports (2011)
3. Flatbuffer internals and documentation presented at Google white paper. https://google.github.io/flatbuffers/flatbuffers_white_paper.html
4. Protocol Buffer internals and documentation presented by Google. https://developers.google.com/protocol-buffers/docs/overview
5. Sharma, P., Singh, A.: Era of deep neural networks: a review. In: ICCCNT (2017)
6. Tensorflow deep learning framework. https://www.tensorflow.org/
7. TensorflowLite deep learning framework for mobile devices. https://www.tensorflow.org/lite
8. Flatbuffer benchmarking in C++. https://google.github.io/flatbuffers/flatbuffers_benchmarks.html
9. Maeda, K.: Performance evaluation of object serialization libraries in XML, JSON and binary formats. In: DICTAP (2012)
10. Kaur, G., Faud, M.: An evaluation of protocol buffer. In: SoutheastCon (2010)
11. Popić, S., Pezer, D., Mrazovac, B., Teslić, N.: Performance Evaluation of Using Protocol Buffers in the Internet of Things Communication (2016)
12. Feng, J., Li, J.: Google protocol buffers research and application in online game. In: IEEE Conference Anthology (2013)
13. Caffe framework network definition present at net.cpp. https://github.com/BVLC/caffe/blob/master/src/caffe/net.cpp

Learning to Generate Atmospheric Turbulent Images

Shyam Nandan Rai[✉] and C. V. Jawahar

IIIT Hyderabad, Hyderabad, India
shyam.nandan@research.iiit.ac.in, jawahar@iiit.ac.in

Abstract. Modeling atmospheric turbulence is a challenging problem since the light rays arbitrarily bend before entering the camera. Such models are critical to extend computer vision solutions developed in the laboratory to real-world use cases. Simulating atmospheric turbulence by using statistical models or by computer graphics is often computationally expensive. To overcome this problem, we train a generative adversarial network which outputs an atmospheric turbulent image by utilizing less computational resources than traditional methods. We propose a novel loss function to efficiently learn the atmospheric turbulence at the finer level. Experiments show that by using the proposed loss function, our network outperforms the existing state-of-the-art image to image translation network in turbulent image generation. We also perform extensive ablation studies on the loss function to demonstrate the improvement in the perceptual quality of turbulent images.

Keywords: Generative adversarial network · Atmospheric turbulence · Loss function

1 Introduction and Related Work

The performance of computer vision algorithms drastically decreases when deployed in varying weather conditions [12,13]. Especially in applications like autonomous navigation and aerial imaging, the atmospheric condition adversely affects the performance of the underlying vision algorithm. The problem of computer vision models adapting to changing weather could be solved by collecting data for all the weather conditions and training vision algorithms on them. But, collecting data for each weather condition would require a huge cost and time. Hence, we propose a deep learning-based approach, which particularly models the hot weather conditions among all weather conditions. We also show that the computational time taken to generate hot weather images by our method was less than the traditional methods. The phenomena of geometrical distortion caused by extremely hot weather are termed as atmospheric turbulence.

The primary cause of atmospheric turbulence is the heterogeneous nature of the atmosphere between the camera and the object. The heterogeneity in the medium is caused by the time-space varying changes in temperature, air pressure,

© Springer Nature Singapore Pte Ltd. 2020
R. V. Babu et al. (Eds.): NCVPRIPG 2019, CCIS 1249, pp. 261–271, 2020.
https://doi.org/10.1007/978-981-15-8697-2_24

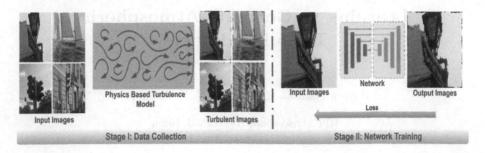

Fig. 1. Illustration of the overall pipeline to generate a turbulent image. *Stage I*: In this stage, we create a turbulent dataset using [16] method to train our network. *Stage II*: Training of our generative adversarial network using the created turbulent dataset. After training, turbulent images can be generated by simply passing the corresponding non-turbulent image through the network.

wind speed and humidity, which results in the introduction of geometrical distortion as well as a decrease in perceptual information of an imaged object. Several methods have been proposed to model the nature of atmospheric turbulence and render images with the help of these models. Turbulence modeling methods can be divided into two major approaches: Ray tracing in computer graphics [4,17] and image distortion simulation [7,16]. Initial approaches in computer graphics either used curved ray tracing [17] or solved physically-based differential equations [4,14] to estimate the parameters of atmospheric turbulence based on real turbulent images, which help in describing the trajectory of light. Another approach to model atmospheric turbulence is to statistically model the turbulence and distort images using those models. Earlier methods used light propagation through multiple phase screens [7] for this purpose. Later methods model turbulence as a simple Gaussian function [22] or derived a physics-based method [16] by which turbulent fields were generated efficiently. However, these methods are computationally expensive, which requires a large amount of computational time to generate a large dataset. Recently, Deep learning [8] has become a powerful framework to generate complex non-linear data such as images, speech, and videos. In particular, Generative Adversarial Networks (GANs) are widely used for the generation of images as it directly learns the empirical data distribution from the data samples. Application of GANs include images-to-image translation tasks such as super-resolution [9], style transfer [2], and synthetic data generation [18].

Leveraging the advantages of GANs, we train a deep adversarial network that takes an input image and gives out the corresponding turbulent image. While training, our GAN tries to learn the natural image distribution of the turbulent image. GANs provides the flexibility of sampling infinite samples from the learned distribution by simply feed-forwarding input samples into the network. Hence after training, using our trained GAN, we can generate large datasets of turbulent images at inference which would take few milliseconds to generate a turbulent image on an average GPU enabled device. Hence, we solve the problem of high computational issues encountered with traditional methods by using

(a)   (b)

Fig. 2. (a) and (b) are the samples turbulent images generated by our network. Red boxes show the magnified patches of the input image and green boxes shows the turbulent patches. (Color figure online)

GAN. Additionally, we introduce a novel loss function specifically intended to improve the quality of output turbulent images. To train the adversarial network, we require a substantial number of turbulent and non-turbulent image pairs. Since there was no public dataset available for training, we build a dataset by generating turbulent fields using [16], method and then we randomly placed the turbulent field onto the non-turbulent images to generate the corresponding turbulent image. Figure 1 illustrates the overall pipeline of our approach for generating turbulent images. We quantitatively and qualitatively show that the turbulent images generated by our network are close to natural turbulent images. Figure 2 shows the sample turbulent image generated by our model. These generated turbulent images can be further used as turbulent datasets in building restoration networks. Also, it increases the accuracy of various computer vision algorithms such as classification and semantic segmentation in a turbulent environment.

The major contributions of this paper are:

1. We propose a deep generative network for the generation of turbulent images by taking lesser computational time than traditional methods. To the best of our knowledge, it is the first approach to generate turbulent images using deep learning.
2. We propose a novel loss function by which deep network efficiently learns to transfer atmospheric turbulence into the non-turbulent natural images. An extensive ablation study is reported to demonstrate the effectiveness of the loss function.
3. To train our network, we constructed a large scale dataset consisting of turbulent and non-turbulent image pairs.

2   Proposed Model

Generative models are widely used for generating samples from a data distribution. GAN is one of the models among all the generative models. Consider, two

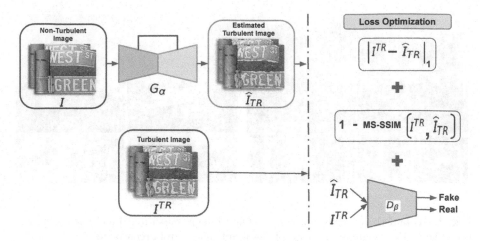

Fig. 3. Overview of our proposed generative adversarial network. While training the network, a non-turbulent image I is passed through generator G_α with learnable parameter α which gives the estimated turbulent image $\hat{I}^{TR}$. I^{TR} and $\hat{I}^{TR}$ are passed through loss optimization block to minimize the L1 loss, MS-SSIM loss and adversarial loss between them.

differential function generator G_α and D_β where α and β are learnable parameters. The generator creates fake samples that are intended to be closer to the training data distribution. The discriminator is a classifier where it examines whether the given samples belong to training data distribution or not. The generator tries to generate fake samples by adjusting its α to fool the discriminator. On the other hand, the discriminator learns to discriminate between real and fake samples. In this way the generator and discriminator their parameters α and β. This framework can be viewed as a mini-max game where the generator tries to minimize the probability of its samples to be fake whereas discriminator tries to maximize it. Formally, we assume G_α and D_β to be a deep neural network.

In our problem setting, we train a generative adversarial network that aims to estimate a turbulent image $\hat{I}^{TR}$ from a non-turbulent image I. Here, I^{TR} is the turbulent image corresponding to a non-turbulent image I. Our goal is to train a generator G_α with learnable parameter α, which can generate turbulent images by minimizing loss function and can fool the discriminator D_β. Here, D_β is a classification network which classifies between estimated non-turbulent turbulent and non-turbulent images with learnable parameter β. Figure 3 shows the overall outline of our proposed network architecture. In the subsequent subsections, we describe the architecture of our generative adversarial network along with the new loss function, which is particularly formulated to improve the quality of the turbulent image generation process.

Network Architecture: The generative adversarial network is divided into two networks: generator and discriminator. Our generator mainly follows the architecture of U-Net [15]. The architecture of our generator is divided into two paths: contracting path and expanding path. The contracting path downsamples the input image into the feature space. It consists of four contracting blocks, where, each block contains two 4×4 convolutional layer of stride 2 and padding 1. Each convolutional layer is followed by a LeakyReLU layer and a batch normalization layer. After, each contracting block, we double the depth of the feature maps. For each contracting block, we have a corresponding expanding block in the expanding path. An expanding block contains two 4×4 transpose convolutional layer of stride 2 and padding 1. Each transpose convolutional layer is followed by a ReLU layer and a batch normalization layer. Each expanding block concatenates the cropped feature from its contracting block. The depth of the feature map decreases to half after each contracting block. The activation function of the outer most convolution layer in the expanding path is tanh as our input image pixel value ranges from −1 to 1. The contracting path and expanding path are joined by a bottleneck. The bottleneck consists of a convolution layer with LeakyReLU as activation and a transpose convolution layer with ReLu as activation. The discriminator follows the standard architecture of [1] which is used in most of the GANs architecture.

Loss Functions: Least absolute deviations (L1 loss) is widely used as a loss function for many deep networks. However, the minimization of L1 loss for generation tasks results in blurry output images lacking in high-frequency details. Hence, we add adversarial loss to our generator encourages it to produce images that lie in natural image manifold with sharp textures. We use LS-GAN [11] over vanilla GAN for better stability and faster convergence. We also use MS-SSIM loss [20] to improve the generation of turbulence at the finer level. The final loss function of our generator network is a weighted linear combination of L1 loss, MS-SSIM loss and adversarial loss which is:

$$L_{generator} = \lambda_1 L_1 + \lambda_2 L_{Adverserial} + \lambda_3 L_{MS-SSIM} \tag{1}$$

$$L_{generator} = \lambda_1 |I^{TR} - G_\alpha(I)|_1 + \lambda_2 [D_\beta(G_\alpha(I)) - 1]^2 + \lambda_3 (1 - MS\text{-}SSIM(I^{TR}, G_\alpha(I))) \tag{2}$$

where, λ_1, λ_2 and λ_3 are the hyper-parameter of the generator loss function. Similarly, the loss of our discriminator network would be:

$$L_{discriminator} = D_\beta(G_\alpha(I))^2 + (D_\beta(I^{TR}) - 1)^2 \tag{3}$$

Training Description: We train our network end-to-end by following the training methodology from [10] and [9]. To optimize our network, we use Adam [6] optimizer with $\beta_1 = 0.5$ and $\beta_2 = 0.999$ for computing running average of gradient and its squares. The value of λ_1, λ_2, and λ_3 were found to be 100, 1, and 5, respectively. We first train our network for 10,000 iterations with a learning rate of $1e - 4$ and then decrease the learning rate to $5e - 5$ for another 15,000 iterations with a batch size of 16. For each iteration, the discriminator and generator are updated only once.

3   Experimentation

Dataset: We use physics-based method [16] for synthesizing our turbulent dataset. The virtual camera parameters used while imaging in the turbulence

Fig. 4. (a) and (c) show the sample turbulent images of the training dataset. (b) and (d) shows the enlarged patches in red boxes. (Color figure online)

Table 1. Quantitative results of various turbulence models. Our method outperforms baseline methods by using the proposed loss function.

Methods	PSNR	SSIM	MSE
Encoder-Decoder (L1 loss) [3]	12.1040	0.1071	461.8092
Encoder-Decoder (MSE loss) [3]	14.9994	0.2423	333.6431
CycleGAN [21]	14.0471	0.2803	402.6070
Pix2Pix [5]	17.8422	0.4412	254.0445
Encoder-Decoder with skip connections (L1-loss) [10]	15.4503	0.2905	320.6347
Encoder-Decoder with skip connections (MSE loss) [10]	15.5124	0.2925	318.4140
Ours	**18.2321**	**0.5211**	**234.9368**

environment is: focal distance $= 300\,\mathrm{mm}$ having the lens diameter of $\approx 5.57\,\mathrm{cm}$ and a pixel size of $4 \times 10^{-3}\,\mathrm{mm}$. The placement of the virtual camera is at an elevation of $5\,\mathrm{m}$ with object distance of $3\,\mathrm{km}$. The value for structure constant C_n^2 which expresses the atmospheric turbulent strength is $3 \times 10^{-13}\,\mathrm{m}^{-2/3}$. Using the above parameters, we rendered turbulent images by applying simulated turbulent field on ImageNet dataset. The dataset consists of 100,000 of turbulent and non-turbulent image pairs for training and the validation is performed on ImageNet validation dataset. Figure 4 shows sample turbulent images.

Evaluation Metrics: To measure the structural and perceptual similarity between the estimated turbulent image and ground-truth turbulent image, we use Peak-Signal-To-Noise-Ratio (PSNR), Structural Similarity [19] (SSIM) and Mean Squared Error (MSE). We use SSIM and PSNR as they calculate structural similarity and perceptual quality between two images. These evaluation metrics are applied to various generated turbulent images and ground-truth turbulent images to give a qualitative comparison.

Results: We compare our results of final turbulence generation model with the image-to-image translation networks: Pix2Pix [5], CycleGAN [21], Encoder-Decoder [3], and Encoder-Decoder with skip connections [10]. Our final turbulence generation model shows significant quantitative improvement over the other aforementioned methods as shown in Table 1. In Table 1, we observe that methods with MSE loss as a loss function give better results on evalua-

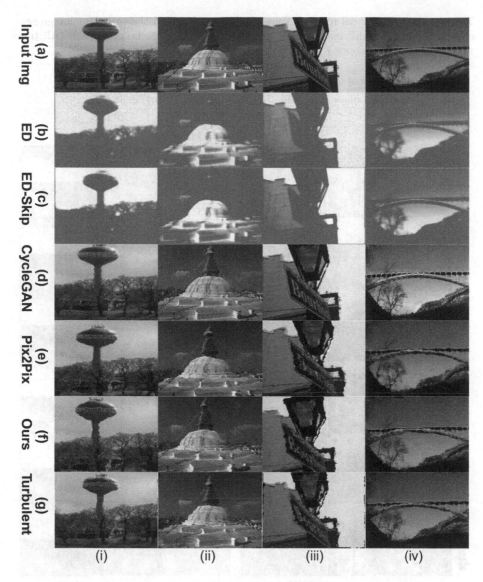

Fig. 5. Qualitative results of various turbulence models. Row a: Input Img is the non-turbulent input image to the network. Row b: ED is the Encoder-Decoder network output. Row c: ED-Skip is the Encoder-Decoder with a skip-connections network output. Row d: CycleGAN network output. Row e: Pix2Pix network output. Row f: Our network output. Row g: Turbulent is the Ground-truth turbulent image. *(Best view when zoomed)*

tion metrics over the L1 loss. The quantitative performance of Pix2Pix is better than CycleGAN as Pix2Pix learns from paired images whereas CycleGAN learns from unpaired images, which makes the generation of turbulent images difficult. Qualitative results of turbulent image generation on ImageNet images by various

Table 2. Computational resource time comparison between the turbulent image generation methods on different number of turbulence images to be generated. (All time values reported in seconds.)

Number of images	1	100	500	1000
Schwartzman *et al.* [16]	184.367	197.357	280.472	389.559
Ours	0.018	0.979	5.243	10.646

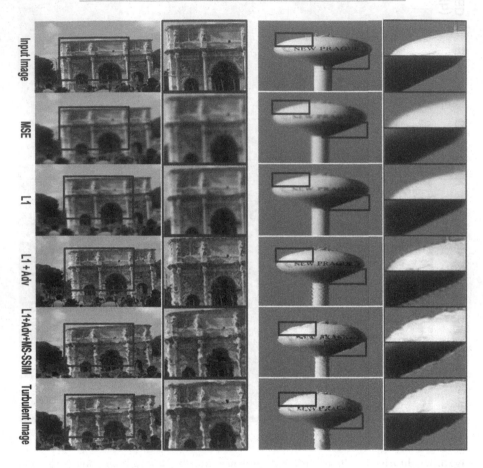

Fig. 6. Qualitative results of the ablative study on the various loss function. Row 1: Input image to the network. Row 2: MSE loss output. Row 3: L1 loss output. Row 4: L1 + Adv is the output of the combined output of L1 loss and adversarial loss. Row 5: L1 + Adv + MS-SSIM is the output of the combined output of L1 loss, MS-SSIM, and adversarial loss. Row 6: Ground-truth turbulent image. Red boxes show the zoomed image patch. *(Best viewed when zoomed)*

Table 3. Ablation study results of our loss function.

Loss function	PSNR	SSIM	MSE
L1 loss	16.7413	0.3523	293.5724
MSE loss	17.0215	0.3915	273.3178
L1 loss + Adversarial loss	17.5243	0.4215	259.2911
L1 loss + MS-SSIM loss + Adversarial loss	**17.6515**	**0.4402**	**256.5432**

methods are shown in Fig. 5. In Fig. 5, we infer that CycleGAN and Pix2Pix struggle to generate larger geometrical distortion compared to our method. Moreover, Pix2Pix suffers from color artifacts which could be seen in Fig. 5 (column e) (iii) (iv). Encoder-Decoder and Encoder-Decoder with skip connections failed to generate turbulent images with sharp details. Although encoder-decoder suffers from the checkerboard effect which is eliminated by skip connections. Table 2 shows the comparison between the computational time taken by Schwartzman *et al.* [16] and our method to generate atmospheric turbulent images. We can observe from the table that our approach requires a small fraction of computational time to generate turbulent images.

Ablation Study: We perform an ablation study on our loss function to show its advantages qualitatively and quantitatively. The ablative study is performed by training our generator architecture individually on L1 loss, MSE loss, L1 loss + Adversarial Loss, and L1 loss + Adversarial loss + MS-SSIM loss. We use L1 loss instead of MSE loss as it leads to sharper images. All the networks were trained for 10,000 iterations with the learning rate of $1e-4$ and batch size of 16. From Table 3, we observe that adding MS-SSIM loss into the total loss leads to higher PSNR and SSIM which implies that it improves the structural as well as perceptual information of the generated image. Figure 6 shows the qualitative results of the ablation where we can observe in Fig. 6(row 5) the output generated by ours looks more realistic. Although in Fig. 6(row 4) the output looks more promising when zoomed, it looks more like a uniform artifact.

4   Conclusion

In this paper, we proposed a turbulent image generation model by training a deep adversarial network. Unlike, the traditional turbulent image generation methods which rely on a statistical model, our approach uses data to learn the parameters of the generative adversarial network, which transforms a non-turbulent image into a turbulent image. We proposed a novel loss function that encourages the learning of finer turbulence fields. To support our claim, we performed extensive ablation studies on the loss function.

References

1. Radford, A., Metz, L., Chintala, S.: Unsupervised representation learning with deep convolutional generative adversarial networks. In: International Conference on Learning Representations (ICLR) (2016)
2. Azadi, S., Fisher, M., Kim, V.G., Wang, Z., Shechtman, E., Darrell, T.: Multi-content GAN for few-shot font style transfer. In: Proceedings of the IEEE Conference on Computer Vision and Pattern Recognition, pp. 7564–7573 (2018)
3. Badrinarayanan, V., Kendall, A., Cipolla, R.: Segnet: a deep convolutional encoder-decoder architecture for image segmentation. IEEE Trans. Pattern Anal. Mach. Intell. **39**(12), 2481–2495 (2017)
4. Gutierrez, D., Seron, F.J., Munoz, A., Anson, O.: Simulation of atmospheric phenomena. Comput. Graph. **30**(6), 994–1010 (2006)
5. Isola, P., Zhu, J.Y., Zhou, T., Efros, A.A.: Image-to-image translation with conditional adversarial networks. In: Proceedings of the IEEE Conference on Computer Vision and Pattern Recognition, pp. 1125–1134 (2017)
6. Kingma, D.P., Ba, J.: Adam: a method for stochastic optimization. arXiv preprint arXiv:1412.6980 (2014)
7. Lane, R., Glindemann, A., Dainty, J., et al.: Simulation of a Kolmogorov phase screen. Waves Random Media **2**(3), 209–224 (1992)
8. LeCun, Y., Bengio, Y., Hinton, G.: Deep learning. Nature **521**(7553), 436 (2015)
9. Ledig, C., et al.: Photo-realistic single image super-resolution using a generative adversarial network. In: Proceedings of the IEEE/CVPR Conference on Computer Vision and Pattern Recognition, pp. 4681–4690 (2017)
10. Mao, X., Shen, C., Yang, Y.B.: Image restoration using very deep convolutional encoder-decoder networks with symmetric skip connections. In: Advances in Neural Information Processing Systems, pp. 2802–2810 (2016)
11. Mao, X., Li, Q., Xie, H., Lau, R.Y., Wang, Z., Paul Smolley, S.: Least squares generative adversarial networks. In: Proceedings of the IEEE International Conference on Computer Vision, pp. 2794–2802 (2017)
12. Nayar, S.K., Narasimhan, S.G.: Vision in bad weather. In: Proceedings of the Seventh IEEE International Conference on Computer Vision, vol. 2, pp. 820–827. IEEE (1999)
13. Purohit, K., Mandal, S., Rajagopalan, A.N.: Multilevel weighted enhancement for underwater image dehazing. J. Opt. Soc. Am. A: **36**(6), 1098–1108 (2019)
14. Riley, K., Ebert, D.S., Kraus, M., Tessendorf, J., Hansen, C.D.: Efficient rendering of atmospheric phenomena. Rendering Tech. **4**, 374–386 (2004)
15. Ronneberger, O., Fischer, P., Brox, T.: U-Net: convolutional networks for biomedical image segmentation. In: Navab, N., Hornegger, J., Wells, W.M., Frangi, A.F. (eds.) MICCAI 2015. LNCS, vol. 9351, pp. 234–241. Springer, Cham (2015). https://doi.org/10.1007/978-3-319-24574-4_28
16. Schwartzman, A., Alterman, M., Zamir, R., Schechner, Y.Y.: Turbulence-induced 2D correlated image distortion. In: 2017 IEEE International Conference on Computational Photography (ICCP), pp. 1–13. IEEE (2017)
17. Seron, F.J., Gutierrez, D., Gutiérrez, G., Cerezo, E.: Implementation of a method of curved ray tracing for inhomogeneous atmospheres. Comput. Graph. **29**(1), 95–108 (2005)
18. Tripathi, S., Chandra, S., Agrawal, A., Tyagi, A., Rehg, J.M., Chari, V.: Learning to generate synthetic data via compositing. In: Proceedings of the IEEE Conference on Computer Vision and Pattern Recognition, pp. 461–470 (2019)

19. Wang, Z., Bovik, A.C., Sheikh, H.R., Simoncelli, E.P., et al.: Image quality assessment: from error visibility to structural similarity. IEEE Trans. Image Process. **13**(4), 600–612 (2004)
20. Zhao, H., Gallo, O., Frosio, I., Kautz, J.: Loss functions for image restoration with neural networks. IEEE Trans. Comput. Imaging **3**(1), 47–57 (2016)
21. Zhu, J.Y., Park, T., Isola, P., Efros, A.A.: Unpaired image-to-image translation using cycle-consistent adversarial networks. In: Proceedings of the IEEE International Conference on Computer Vision, pp. 2223–2232 (2017)
22. Zhu, X., Milanfar, P.: Removing atmospheric turbulence via space-invariant deconvolution. IEEE Trans. Pattern Anal. Mach. Intell. **35**(1), 157–170 (2012)

Rejection-Cascade of Gaussians: Real-Time Adaptive Background Subtraction Framework

B. Ravi Kiran[1], Arindam Das[2], and Senthil Yogamani[3(✉)]

[1] Navya, Paris, France
ravi.kiran@navya.tech
[2] Detection Vision Systems, Valeo, Chennai, India
arindam.das@valeo.com
[3] Valeo Vision Systems, Galway, Ireland
senthil.yogamani@valeo.com

Abstract. Background-Foreground classification is a well-studied problem in computer vision. Due to the pixel-wise nature of modeling and processing in the algorithm, it is usually difficult to satisfy real-time constraints. There is a trade-off between the speed (because of model complexity) and accuracy. Inspired by the rejection cascade of Viola-Jones classifier, we decompose the Gaussian Mixture Model (GMM) into an adaptive cascade of Gaussians (CoG). We achieve a good improvement in speed without compromising the accuracy with respect to the baseline GMM model. We demonstrate a speed-up factor of 4–5× and 17% average improvement in accuracy over Wallflowers surveillance datasets. The CoG is then demonstrated to over the latent space representation of images of a convolutional variational autoencoder (VAE). We provide initial results over CDW-2014 dataset, which could speed up background subtraction for deep architectures.

Keywords: Background subtraction · Rejection cascade · Real-time

1 Introduction

Background subtraction is critical component of surveillance applications (indoor and outdoor), action recognition, human computer interactions, tracking, experimental chemical procedures that require significant change detection. Work on background subtraction started since the 1970s and even today it is an active open problem. There have been a host of methods which have been developed and below is a short review which will serve to aid understanding our algorithm. A survey by [5] provides an overview of common methods which includes Frame differencing (FD), Running Gaussian average (RGA), Gaussian Mixture Model (GMM) and Kernel Density Estimation (KDE). We employ these basic methods in a structured methodology to develop our algorithm.

© Springer Nature Singapore Pte Ltd. 2020
R. V. Babu et al. (Eds.): NCVPRIPG 2019, CCIS 1249, pp. 272–281, 2020.
https://doi.org/10.1007/978-981-15-8697-2_25

A survey of variants of GMM, issues and analysis are presented in [2]. In our work, we focus on solving the variable-rate adaptation problem and improving the performance. Abstractly, our work tries to fuse several algorithms to achieve speed and accuracy and we list similar methods here. Similar attempts have been made by the following researchers. [7] and [3] used a Hierarchical background subtraction method that operates in different scales over the image: namely pixel, region and image level, while their models themselves are not hierarchical. Authors [14] switch between GMM and RGA models, while choosing a complex model for complicated backgrounds and simple model for simpler backgrounds. They use an entropy based measure to switch between the different models. We briefly describe our observations and improvement over the standard GMM from [6]. We observe in most cases, background subtraction is an asymmetric classification problem with probability of foreground pixel being much lesser than that of background. This assumption fails in the case of scenes like highways, a busy street, etc. In our work, we focus mainly on surveillance scenarios where there is very low foreground occupancy. Our framework exploits this fact and at the same time handles variable rate changes in background and improves accuracy. Our key contributions in this paper include: 1. Decomposition of GMM to form an adaptive cascade of classifiers - Cascade of Gaussians (CoG) which handles complex scenes in an efficient way to obtain real-time performance. 2. A confidence estimate for each pixel's classification which would be used to vary the learning rate and thresholds for the classifiers and adaptive sampling. 3. Learning a time windowed KDE from the training data-set which would act as a prior to the Adaptive Rejection Cascade and also help the confidence estimate.

The decomposition of the GMM into the cascade is similar to the increasing true positive detection rate inspired by the Viola Jones Rejection Cascade [9]. Authors [8] provided an optimized lookup for highly probable colors in the incoming background pixels thus providing speedup in the access.

2 Components of the Cascade

This section describes the different components of the rejection cascade and how they were determined. The rejection cascade is accompanied by the confidence measure to make an accurate background classification at each level of the cascade.

Scene Prior in Background Model: The process of distinguishing linearly varying background and noisy pixels is a challenge and critical since the background subtraction model intrinsically has no additional attribute to separate them. For this scenario, in our approach we introduce a prior probability for every pixel (Eq. 1). The non-parametric probability distribution for the pixels assuming independent R, G, B channels is now given too. The Scene prior basically provides an non-parametric estimate of pixel-values value over N frames during training. The choice of N is empirical and depends on how much dynamic background and foreground is present in the training frames. To obtain complete variability we choose as large N as possible. Henceforth we refer to Scene Prior as the prior. In the training phase we estimate the underlying temporal distribution of pixels by calculating the kernel function that approximates the said distribution. Our case primarily concentrates on long surveillance videos with sufficient information (minimal foreground) available in the training sequence that decides N. For the standard GMM model (assuming the covariance matrix is diagonal) the updates of the parameters include:

$$P(I_n(x,y)) = \sum_{i=1}^{K} \omega_{i,n} * \eta(I_n(x,y), \mu_{i,n}, \sigma_{i,n},$$

$$\omega_{n+1,k}(x,y) \longleftarrow (1-\alpha)\omega_{n,k}(x,y) + \alpha(M_{i,n+1}) \tag{1}$$

$$\mu_{n+1,k}(x,y) \longleftarrow (1-\rho)\mu_{n,k}(x,y) + \rho I_n(x,y)$$

$$\sigma_{n+1,k}^2(x,y) \longleftarrow (1-\rho)\sigma_{n,k}^2(x,y) + \rho I_n(x,y)$$

Where K_σ, represents the gaussian kernel and σ the scale or bandwidth. This Kernel function is calculated to provide the modes of the different pixels. Where η represents the pixel mode distribution obtained in Eq. 1, where ω_i represents the ratio of the component i in the distribution of pixel $I_n(x,y)$, and μ_i, σ_i are the parameters of the component, M represents 0 or 1 based on a component match and finally α represents the learning rate of the pixel model. The α is initialised for all pixels usually, there has been work in adapting it based on the pixel entropy. We use the pixel gradient value distribution to do the same.

Determining Learning Rate Hyper-Parameters: Besides the kernel density, we also estimate the dynamic nature of the pixels in the scene. This is obtained by the clustering the residue between consecutive frames into 3 categories: into static/drifting, oscillating and dynamic pixels (Fig. 1 top right). This helps resolve a pixel drift versus a pixel jump as shown in example below in figure. Once we have the residue $R_n(x,y) = I_n(x,y) - I_{n-1}(x,y), n \in [1,N]$, we evaluate the normalized histogram over the residue values. We select bins intervals to extract the 3 classes based on the dynamic nature of pixels. A peaky first bin implies near zero residue, thus a drift or static pixels. A peaky second bin implies oscillating pixels and the other cases are considered as dynamic pixels. Based on these values we choose the weights for the confidence measure (explained in the next section). This frequency over each bin sets the learning rate for the pixel. The process of obtaining the right learning rates(confidence function) from the normalized binned histogram values to determine α, β and γ test for the learning rates have determined empirically by shape matching the histograms.

Clustering Similar Background - Spatio-Temporal Grouping: The next step in the training phase is to determine background regions of pixels, in the frame that behave similarly in terms of adapted variance, number of modes, and optimally use fewer parameters and lesser instructions to update this specific region's, pixel models. The problem definition can be formalized as: We are given $Nx(framesize)$ pixels and for each pixel $I_n(x,y)$ we have a set of matches of the form $(I_n(x,y), I_n(x',y'))_{t_n}$, which means that pixel $I_n(x,y)$ correlated with pixel $I_n(x', y')$ at frame number n. From these N matches, we construct a discrete time series $x_i(t)$ by clustering pixel F_x, y^n at time interval t frames. A time series of the pixel $I_n(x, y)$ values at frame n_0. Intuitively, x_i measures the correlation in behavior of pixels over time window t. For convenience we assume that time series x_i have the same length. We group together pixel value time series so that similar behavior is captured by similarity of the time series $x_i(t)$. This way we can infer which pixels have a similar temporal pattern variances and modalities, and we can then consider the center of each cluster as the representative common pattern of the group. This helps us cluster similar behaving pixels together. This is can be seen a spectral clustering problem as described in [1]. We try a simpler approach here first by clustering the adapted pixel variances (matrix V) and weights (matrix R) of first dominant mode of pixels within a mixture model.

1. Get N frames & estimate pixel-wise $\mu(t), \sigma(t), \omega(t)$
2. Form matrix whose rows are adapted variance and ranked weight observations, while columns are variables V and R, $V(t_k, i) = I(t_k), k = 1 : N$
3. Obtain covariance matrices $R_{cov} = Cov(R), V_{cov} = Cov(V)$
4. Perform K-means clustering with K=3 (for temporal pixel residue due to dynamic, oscillating, or drifting BG).
5. Threshold for pixels within $0.7 - 0.5\sigma$
6. Calculate the KDE of given cluster & the joint occurrence distribution and associated weight ω_1, μ_1 and σ_1

where μ_1 is first dominant common cascade level at grouped pixels. This suffers from the setback that the variances chosen temporally do not correspond to mean values associated with the maximum eigen value as obtained in case of Spectral Clustering. So we have the pixel variance and adapted weight (dominant mode) covariance matrices $R(x_i, y_i) = Cov(Var(I_n(x_i, y_i)))$ and $W(x_i, y_i) = Cov(Var(W_n(x_i, y_i)))$. A single gaussian is fit over thresholded covariance matrices (Adapted variance and first dominant mode weight).

$$r_n = \mu_{\text{advar}} - \sigma_{\text{advar}} < var(R_{cov}) < \mu_{\text{advar}} + \sigma_{\text{advar}}$$
$$w_n = \mu_{\text{adw}} - \sigma_{\text{adw}} < var(W_{cov}) < \mu_{\text{adw}} + \sigma_{\text{adw}}$$
$$(2)$$

The parameters $\mu_{\text{advar}}, \sigma_{\text{advar}}$ and $\mu_{\text{adw}}, \sigma_{\text{adw}}$ represent the mean and standard deviation of the cluster of pixel variances and adapted weights of the first dominant modes. The fundamental clustering algorithm requires Data set R_cov and V_cov, number of clusters - quantization of the adapted weights or variances, Gram matrix [1]. One critical point to note here is that, when we do not choose to employ spatio-temporal grouping, and reduce the number of parameters and consequent updates, we can use the Scene Prior covariance estimation to increase the accuracy of the foreground detection. This is very similar to the background subtraction based on Co-occurrence of Image Variations.

Confidence Measure: The confidence measure is a latent variable use to aid the Rejection Cascade to obtain a measure of fitness for the classification of a pixel based on various criteria. The Confidence $C_n(x, y)$ for a pixel $I_n(x, y)$ is given by $C_n(x, y) = \alpha P(x, y) + \beta(\Delta_n I(x, y) + \gamma M(I_n(x, y)))$.

Here, $M()$ represents the difference between the current pixel value $I_n(x, y)$ and the parameters of the model occurring at the top of the ordered Rejection cascade described below, while $\Delta_n I(x, y) = I_n(x, y) - I_{n-1}(x, y)$. As seen in the ordered tree, the first set of parameters would be the first dominant mode - $(\mu_1 + \sigma_1, \mu_1 - \sigma_1)$. This is carried out based on the level in which the pixel gets successfully classified. $P()$ represents the probability of occurrence of the pixel from the KDE. The values of α β and γ are determined by the normalized temporal residue distribution (explained above). The physical significance and implications of α β and γ- α says how confident the region is and regions that are stable (for example from the segments from clustering adapted variances and weights of training phase pixel models) would have high α values. While the value of β determines how fast the pixel would need to adapt to new incoming values and this would mean a lower effect of the prior distribution. The final parameter γ determines the consistency of the pixel belonging to a model and this would change whenever the pixels behavior is much more dynamic (as opposed to a temporal residue weighting it).

Confidence Based Temporal Sampling: Applying multiple modes of background classifiers and observing the consistency in their model parameters (mean, variance, and connectivity) we predict the future values of these pixels. A threshold on confidence function value determined by using stable regions (using region growing) as a reference is used to select the pixels both spatially and temporally. The pixels with low confidence reflect regions R over the frame with activity and thus a high probability of finding pixels whose label are in transition (FG-BG). Thus by thresholding the confidence function we sub-sample the incoming pixels spatio-temporally. This intuition is when pixel values arriving now are within the first dominant mode's 0.7σ region, and even more so within the CHP level for a large number of frames, the confidence value saturates. The Region $R(x_i, y_i) = C_n(x_i, y_i) > C_{ScencePrior}(x_i, y_i)$ is just a thresholded binary map of this confidence value. This is demonstrated in the analysis in Sect. 3.

Cascade of Gaussians CoG: The proposed method can be viewed as a decomposition of the GMM in an adaptive framework so as to reduce complexity and improve accuracy using a strong prior to determine the scenarios under which said gains can be achieved. The prior is used to determine the modality of the pixels distribution and any new value is treated as a new mean with variance model. The Cascade can be seen to consist of K Gaussians which are ordered based on the successful classification of the pixel. During steady state the ordered cascade conforms to the Viola Jones Rejection Cascade with decreasing positive detection rates.

The cascade is first headed by a Consistent Hypothesis Propagation (CHP) classifier which basically repeats the labeling process on the current pixel if its value is equal to the previous value (previous frame). This CHP classifier is then followed by an ordered set of Gaussians $\omega_i . \eta(\mu_i, \sigma_i)$ including the spatio-temporally grouped parameters. The tree ordering is different for different pixel and the order is decided based on the prior distribution (KDE) of the pixel and the temporal consistency of the pixel in the different levels. When the pixel

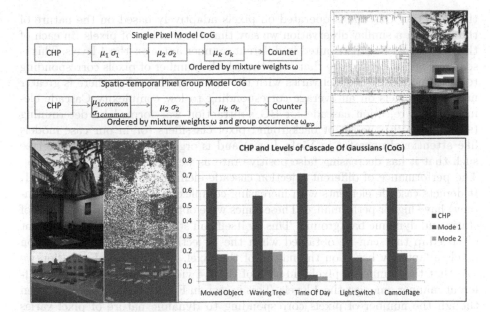

Fig. 1. Top-left: Elements of CoG: CHP, first and second modes of gaussians and spatio-temporal window of CoG. **Top-right**: Dynamic Pixel Vs Oscillation Vs Pixel Drift, **Bottom**: 1. Pixels in CHP (red), Mode 1 (green), Mode 2 (blue), Mode 3 (violet), Foreground (white) 2. Normalized pixel count over elements of Cascade of Gaussians CHP, first and Second modes of Gaussians. (Color figure online)

values do not belong to any of the dominant modes based on the prior, we have scenario where the beta weight and gamma weight only considered and alpha is rejected (Prior Nullified).

The rejection cascade assumes that the frequency of occurrences of foreground detections is lesser than that of the background. This idea was first introduced in the classic Viola-Jones paper [9]. For the rejection cascade the training phase produces a sequence of features with decreasing rates of negative rejections. In our case we arrange the different classifiers in increasing complexity to maximize the speed. We observe in practice that, this cascade would also produce decreasing rates of negative rejections. The critical difference in this rejection cascade is that the classifier in each level of the cascade is evolving over time. To make adaptation efficient we adapt only the active level of the cascade, thus resulting in only one active update at a time, and during a transition the parameters are updated.

The performance of different rejection cascade elements is depicted in Fig. 1. It depicts cascade elements with increasing complexity (and consequently accuracy) have higher performance. These times were obtained over 4 videos from the wallflowers data set by [7] of different types of dynamic background. This by itself can stand for the possible amount of speedup that can be obtained when the Rejection Cascade is operated on pixels adaptively based on the nature of the pixel. In a similar observation we saw that the number of pixels (in each of these 4 videos) was distributed in different manner amongst the 4 levels. This is seen in Fig. 1. Thus we see that even though the number of pixels corresponding to dynamic nature of pixel varies with the nature of the video, there is greater number of pixels on an average corresponding to low complexity Cascade elements. The rejection cascade for BG subtraction was formed by determining (same as in [9]) the set of background pixel classifiers (or in our case models like attentional operator in Viola Jones) and is organized as a degenerate tree such that it has decreasing false positive rate as we proceed down the cascade. The performance of different rejection cascade elements are depicted in Fig. 1. It depicts cascade elements with increasing complexity (and consequently accuracy) have higher performance. These times were obtained over different types of static and dynamic background. This by itself can stand for the possible amount of speedup that can be obtained when the Rejection Cascade is operated on pixels adaptively based on the nature of the pixel. In a similar observation we saw that the number of pixels (in each of these 4 videos) was distributed in different manner amongst the 4 levels. This is seen in Fig. 1. Thus we see that even though the number of pixels corresponding to dynamic nature of pixel varies with the nature of the video, there is greater number of pixels on an average corresponding to low complexity Cascade elements. The learning rate for the model is calculated as a function of the confidence measure of the pixels. The abrupt illumination change is detected in the final level of the rejection cascade, by adding a conditional counter. This counter measures the number of pixels that are not modeled by the penultimate cascade element. If this value is above a threshold we can assume an abrupt illumination change scenario. This threshold is around seven tenth of the total number of pixels in the frame [7].

3   Analysis and VAE-COG

3.1   Scene Prior Analysis

Here we discuss the Scene Prior and its different components. First with regard to the clustering pixels based on their dynamic nature similarity, we show results of various clustering methods and their intuitions. The first model considers the time series of variances of said pixels in the N frames of training. The covariance matrix is calculated for the variances of the pixels. This can loosely act as the affinity matrix for the describing similar behavior of a pair of pixels. The weight of the first dominant mode is also considered to form the affinity matrix.

3.2   Cascade Analysis

The CoG is faster on two accounts: Firstly it is cascade of simple-to-complex classifiers, CHP to RGA, and averaging over the performance (seen in figure), we see an improvement in speed of operation, since the simpler cases of classification

Fig. 2. The CoG rejection cascade over the latent space representation of the convolutional-VAE. The filters are all size 3×3.

outweigh the complex ones. Secondly it models the image as a spatio-temporal group of super pixels that needs a single set of parameters to update, even more so, when the confidence of the pixel saturates, the Cascade updates are halted, providing huge speedups. Though it is necessary to mention that the window of sampling is chosen empirically and in scale with the confidence saturation values. The average speedup of the rejection tree algorithm is calculated as: $\frac{I(x,y)}{\sum_i s_i n_i}$ where x, y go over all indices of image, n_i refers the ratio of background pixels labeled mean or mean with variance w.r.t the total number of background pixels in the image, s_i is the normalized ratio of the time it takes for level i BG model to evaluate and label a pixel as background. The values of n and s were profiled over various videos for different durations. Also we show the distribution of the CHP pixels as well as the first 3 dominant modes within different frames of Waving tree and Time of Day videos with 40 frames of training each. We can see a huge occupancy of Red (CHP) for both background and foreground pixels. Here we explain the confidence measure and effect on accuracy of the GMM model. We obtain a speedup of $2\times$–$3\times$ with the use of the Adaptive Rejection cascade based GMM. This speedup goes up at the effectiveness of accuracy of confidence based spatio-temporal sampling to 4–$5\times$. This is evident in the Cascade level population (in Fig. 1). We observe a 17% improvement in accuracy over the baseline model because of adaptive modelling to handle difficult scenarios explicitly using scene priors (Fig. 2).

3.3   Latent Space CoG with VAEs

CNNs have become become the state-of-the-art models for various computer vision tasks. Our proposed framework is generic and can be extended to CNN models. In this section, we study a possible future extension of the Rejection cascade to the Variational AutoEncoder (VAE). There has been recent work on using auto-encoders to learn dynamic background for the subtraction task [11]. Rejection cascades have also been employed within convolutional neural networks architectures for object detection [12]. VAEs one of the most interpretable deep generative models.

VAEs are deep generative models that approximate the distribution for high-dimensional vectors **x** that correspond to pixel values in the image domain. Like a classical auto-encoder. VAEs consists of a probabilistic encoder $q_\phi(\mathbf{x}|\mathbf{z})$ that reduces the input image to latent space vector **z** and enforces a Gaussian prior, and a probabilisic decoder $p_\theta(\mathbf{x}|\mathbf{z})$ that reconstructs these latent vectors back to the original images. The loss function constitutes of the KL-Divergence

Fig. 3. The input-output pairs and absolute value of residue between input-output pairs from a Convolutional VAE: top half without foreground bottom half with foreground. We remark that the dynamic background such as the snow has been removed. The right column demonstrates the 2d-Histogram over the latent space **z** of the CVAE (top) and the histogram over the temporal residue over **z** for the same test sequence.

regularization term, and the expected negative reconstruction error with an additional KL-divergence term between the latent space vector and the representation with a mean vector and a standard deviation vector, that optimizes the variational lower bound on the marginal log-likelihood of each observation [4]. The classical cascade: CHP, ordered sequence of modes of GMM (μ_i, σ_i), can now be envisaged in the latent space for a multivariate 1-Gaussian $\mathcal{N}(\mathbf{z}, \mathbf{0}, I)$. The future goal would be to create Early rejection classifiers as in [13] for classification tasks, where within each layer of the probabilistic encoder we are capable of measuring the log-likelihood of being foreground. Storing previous latent space vectors for the CHP test would require addition memory aside that assigned to the latent space mean and variance vectors. VAEs are an ideal extension to the rejection cascade since the pixel-level tests in CoG are now performed by the VAE in the latent space, over which a likelihood can be evaluated. We also gain the invariance to positions, orientations, pixel level perturbations, and deformations in mid-level features due the convolutional architecture. A convolutional VAE with latent space of 16 dimensions was trained on the CDW-2014 datasets [10], preliminary results are show in Fig. 3.

4   Conclusion

The CoG was evaluated on the wallflower dataset, as well as its autoencoder counterpart VAE-CoG on the CDW-2014 datasets. We observed a speedup of 4–5×, over the baseline GMM, with an average improvement of 17% in the misclassification rate. This study has demonstrated conceptually how a GMM can be re-factored optimally into a prior scene based pixel density and rejection cascade constituent of simpler models ordered based on the probability of occurrences of each level of the cascade, the accuracy (and complexity) of each model in the cascade level.

References

1. Azran, A., Ghahramani, Z.: Spectral methods for automatic multiscale data clustering. In: 2006 IEEE Computer Society Conference on Computer Vision and Pattern Recognition, vol. 1, pp. 190–197, December 2006. https://doi.org/10.1109/ICDM.2008.88
2. Bouwmans, T., Baf, F.E., Vachon, B.: Background modeling using mixture of gaussians for foreground detection - a survey. Recent Patents Comput. Sci. **1**(3), 219–237 (2008)
3. Javed, O., Shafique, K., Shah, M.: A hierarchical approach to robust background subtraction using color and gradient information. In: Proceedings of Workshop on Motion and Video Computing, pp. 22–27, December 2002. https://doi.org/10.1109/MOTION.2002.1182209
4. Kiran, B.R., Thomas, D.M., Parakkal, R.: An overview of deep learning based methods for unsupervised and semi-supervised anomaly detection in videos. J. Imaging **4**(2), 36 (2018)
5. Piccardi, M.: Background subtraction techniques: a review. In: 2004 IEEE International Conference on Systems, Man and Cybernetics, vol. 4, no. 1, pp. 3099–3104 (2004). https://doi.org/10.1109/ICSMC.2004.1400815
6. Strauffer, C., Grimson, W.: Adaptive background mixture models for real-time tracking. In: Proceedings of the IEEE Computer Society Conference on Computer Vision and Pattern Recognition (1999)
7. Toyama, K., Krumm, J., Brumitt, B., Meyers, B.: Wallflower: principles and practice of background maintenance. In: The Proceedings of the Seventh IEEE International Conference on Computer Vision, vol. 1, no. 1, pp. 255–261 (1999)
8. Valentine, B., Apewokin, S., Wills, L., Wills, S.: An efficient, chromatic clustering-based background model for embedded vision platforms. Comput. Vis. Image Underst. **114**(11), 1152–1163 (2010). https://doi.org/10.1016/j.cviu.2010.03.014
9. Viola, P., Jones, M.: Robust reabouwmansl-time object detection. Int. J. Comput. Vision **57**(2), 137–154 (2004). https://doi.org/10.1023/B:VISI.0000013087.49260.fb. Supplied as additional material tr.pdf
10. Wang, Y., Jodoin, P.M., Porikli, F., Konrad, J., Benezeth, Y., Ishwar, P.: CDNET 2014: an expanded change detection benchmark dataset. In: Proceedings of the IEEE Conference on Computer Vision and Pattern Recognition Workshops, pp. 387–394 (2014)
11. Xu, P., Ye, M., Li, X., Liu, Q., Yang, Y., Ding, J.: Dynamic background learning through deep auto-encoder networks. In: Proceedings of the 22nd ACM International Conference on Multimedia, pp. 107–116. ACM (2014)
12. Yang, F., Choi, W., Lin, Y.: Exploit all the layers: fast and accurate CNN object detector with scale dependent pooling and cascaded rejection classifiers. In: Proceedings of the IEEE Conference on Computer Vision and Pattern Recognition, pp. 2129–2137 (2016)
13. Zhang, K., Zhang, Z., Wang, H., Li, Z., Qiao, Y., Liu, W.: Detecting faces using inside cascaded contextual CNN. In: Proceedings of the IEEE International Conference on Computer Vision, pp. 3171–3179 (2017)
14. Zuo, J., Pan, Q., Liang, Y., Zhang, H., Cheng, Y.: Model switching based adaptive background modeling approach. Acta Automatica Sinica **33**(5), 467–473 (2007)

Hybrid Resection-Intersection Method for Real-Time Bundle Adjustment on Mobile Devices

Ashish Kumar Singh[✉], Karthik Srinivasan, and Venkat Ramana Peddigari

Samsung R&D Institute Bangalore, Bangalore, India
ashish.23ks@samsung.com, ashish23ks@gmail.com

Abstract. In Augmented Reality systems, Bundle Adjustment (BA) is commonly used for simultaneously optimizing poses for multiple camera frames. BA is essentially a large non-linear optimization problem which consume a significant amount of time and computation power. In this paper, we propose a modified version of Resection Intersection (RI) algorithm for BA with better damping heuristics and conditional line search to obtain an average reduction of 67% in execution time. We also propose a hybrid algorithm using the proposed modified version of RI algorithm for reduction of 17% in reprojection error with trade-off in execution time. Both the algorithms have been tested on a collection of 130+ samples from various datasets and the results are compared with state-of-the-art algorithms on mobile devices.

Keywords: Bundle adjustment · Resection intersection · Levenberg Marquardt · Reprojection error · Line search

1 Introduction

Estimating camera poses and 3D scene points location accurately, from a collection of images obtained from cameras is a well known problem in computer vision, known as structure from motion (SfM) [13,17]. In navigation systems, the problem of constructing a map of an unknown environment while simultaneously tracking agent's location is known as simultaneous localization and mapping (SLAM) [6]. Optimizing for scene points and camera parameters using corresponding feature points in images, known as Bundle Adjustment (BA) is an essential component of SfM and SLAM [2,8,13,15,17,19]. BA is the problem of refining visual reconstruction to obtain *jointly optimal* parameters for 3D points and camera poses [19]. *Optimal* implies that parameters are estimated while minimizing a cost function (re-projection error) that quantifies model fitting error and *jointly* refers that the solution is simultaneously optimal for perturbations in both structure and camera parameters [2,19].

B. Triggs et al. [19] provides an extensive summarization about bundle adjustment. The classical BA algorithms are based on Levenberg-Marquardt (LM)

© Springer Nature Singapore Pte Ltd. 2020
R. V. Babu et al. (Eds.): NCVPRIPG 2019, CCIS 1249, pp. 282–291, 2020.
https://doi.org/10.1007/978-981-15-8697-2_26

methods [20], which are slow due to its computational complexity [2–4,7,19]. S. Liu et al. [18] proposed a first order Resection-Intersection (RI) method by iteratively solving points and camera parameters equations separately. It reduces computational complexity with a trade-off in accuracy [16,18]. But even with the increasing computation power of recent mobile devices, RI methods are not suitable for performing any application requiring BA on mobile devices. The motivation of our work is to modify available BA algorithms to make them suitable for running on mobile devices.

In this paper, we propose a modified RI method for running real-time BA and a hybrid algorithm for running offline BA on mobile devices. LM methods are iterative methods [12,20] which requires dynamic damping parameter strategies for ensuring its convergence [2]. Nielsen et al. [14], gives an extensive overview of damping parameter update for LM methods. In contrast, different damping parameter strategies for two steps in RI algorithm are proposed. R. Lakemond et al. [16] considers triangulation for stable behaviour in Intersection step of RI algorithm. For faster execution and stability, linear damping increment startegy for Intersection step is proposed. Michot et al. [11] explores new line search method for finding optimal step length in an iteration. However, finding optimum will require many iterations for line search. To reduce redundant line searches and speed execution, working with near-optimum step length is proposed. To verify the usability of proposed modifications, we conducted experiments on a large collection of 130+ samples of varying number of cameras, number of points and number of observations. The results obtained, shows faster execution time with similar convergence error of proposed modified RI compared to vanilla RI methods. The proposed hybrid algorithm outperforms RI methods in terms of reprojection error. The results demonstrate the feasibility of running real-time and offline BA on mobile devices.

Contributions of the work presented in this paper are as follows:

- Proposed modified RI algorithm for running real-time BA on mobile devices
  - Introduced different parameter strategies for two steps in RI algorithm
  - Proposed conditional line search to achieve real-time execution
- Accurate and efficient hybrid algorithm compared to LM
- Detailed experimental results to highlight the feasibility of proposed methods

2   Classical Methods

Bundle adjustment is inherently just a large geometric parameter estimation problem. Classically, it is formulated as non-linear least square problem that minimizes the sum of squared error. Triggs et al. [19] outlines various implementation strategies for bundle adjustment algorithms including second order method and first order methods.

$$f(x) = \frac{1}{m}\sqrt{\sum_i \Delta z_i(x)^T \Delta z_i(x)} \tag{1}$$

Reprojection error $f(x)$ is the cost function, here $\Delta z_i(x) = z_i - z_i(x)$, z_i is the vector of given observations (2D point locations) in the ith image, $z_i(x)$ is the observation obtained by the estimated parameters, m is the total number of observations and x is the vector of parameters of the model.

2.1 Second Order Methods

Using the Taylor Series, cost function can be approximated as:

$$f(x + \delta x) \approx f(x) + g^T \delta x + \frac{1}{2} \delta x^T H \delta x \qquad (2)$$

Here, $g \equiv \frac{df}{dx}(x)$ is the gradient vector and $H \equiv \frac{d^2 f}{dx^2}(x)$ is the Hessian matrix. Setting derivative of the cost function to zero we get, $\delta x = -H^{-1}g$ (Normal equation). Now, x is updated iteratively till it converges. Levenberg-Marquardt uses a damping term μ for step control. Thus, the normal equation becomes:

$$(H + \mu I)\delta x = -g \qquad (3)$$

In this case, the parameter update is accepted only if error (cost function) is reduced otherwise parameter update is rejected and μ is increased. Non-linear cost metric is linearized using Jacobian, $J = \frac{dz}{dx}$, $g = J^T \Delta z$, $H \approx J^T J$. Now the problem is reduced using Schur compliment method and solved through Cholesky/LDL^T decomposition [5,9]. Complete implementation details are given in (Lourakis et al.)[10].

2.2 First Order Methods

Calculating Hessian inverse for solving Newton update equations is computationally expensive [2,19]. First order method uses approximations or iterations to avoid solving the full Newton Update equations. Since the full Newton step is not calculated, First Order Methods only achieve linear asymptotic convergence whereas Second Order Methods achieve quadratic asymptotic convergence [2,19]. First Order Methods takes less time per iteration than Second Order Methods to execute but still cannot be executed real-time on mobile devices due to limited computation power. In this paper, we propose modifications to Resection Intersection algorithm which improve its execution time three fold without compromising with the convergence error.

2.3 Resection Intersection Algorithm

Resection-Intersection is a linear implementation of bundle adjustment that minimizes the error by independently refining camera parameters (resection) and 3D points (intersection). In this algorithm, it is assumed that each camera is independent of other cameras and each point is independent of other points (R Lakemond et al. [16]). These two steps are iterated one after another until they converge. Levenberg-Marquardt is used for refinement in both steps. Solving Hessian inverse becomes less compute intensive because either camera or points parameters are kept constant in each step. Algorithm 1 shows the psuedo code.

Algorithm 1: Resection Intersection Algorithm Overview

Load initial estimates of points and camera parameters
while *significant changes occur* **do**
    Apply LM algorithm to camera parameters   *frame equations*
    Update camera parameters
    Apply LM algorithm to point parameters   *point equations*
    Update point parameters
end

---

3 Modified Resection Intersection

Although RI algorithm has an advantage of reduced time spent on each iteration, its main disadvantage is that the convergence rate is slow, primarily because of interactions between variables (camera and point parameters) that were assumed to be independent. Also the changes in camera parameters can make the previous iteration changes in point parameters redundant. In this paper, we propose modifications to increase the convergence rate by reducing the redundancies between two steps. Following major modifications were done in Linear Resection-Intersection to improve its execution time and convergence rate:

- Usage of proportional damping
- Heuristics for damping parameter μ increment
- Line search for both frame and points parameters
- Conditional Line search

3.1 Usage of Proportional Damping

Using $\mu diag(H)$ as damping in normal equation (3) gives better results than using μI. This is well-known in non-linear least squares optimisation and in fact is the basis of the improvements that Marquardt added to Levenberg's original method [20]. We found that the use of $\mu diag(H)$ is also useful while solving for point and frame equations in Resection-Intersection method. This is due to the fact that μI increments every diagonal entry of Hessian equally assuming that diagonal entries of Hessian are comparable. This assumption is often wrong and in reality there can be huge difference in order of magnitude between the diagonal entries of Hessian. This may lead to non positive definite Hessian. Also as an extra step, preconditioning will be required if we intend to use μI. On the other hand, using $\mu diag(H)$ will increment every diagonal entry of Hessian in proportion to its value and no preconditioning is required.

μI in normal equation (3) is the regularization factor, also called the Tikhonov Matrix. We are chosing a better Tikhonov Matrix based on the structure of our problem. Another advantage of using $\mu diag(H)$ is the lesser number of iterations required to converge. It may not affect the convergence error but it will improve the convergence rate. This will have a direct impact on execution time. The results in the next section comply with the arguments provided above.

Algorithm 2: Modified Resection Intersection Algorithm

Load initial estimates of points and camera parameters
while *significant changes occur* **do**
    Compute point and frame jacobians A,B
    Compute Hessians U,V from jacobians
    while *error not reduced* **do**
        Solve for camera parameters update using $\mu_a diag(U)$
        if *error reduced* **then**
            if *error reduced is greater than threshold* **then**
                Line search to find better update without recomputing U
                Update camera parameters
            else
                Decrease μ_a
            end
        else
            Increase μ_a exponentially
        end
    end
    while *error not reduced* **do**
        Solve for point parameters update using $\mu_b diag(V)$
        if *error reduced* **then**
            if *error reduced is greater than threshold* **then**
                Line search to find better update without recomputing V
                Update points parameters
            else
                Decrease μ_b
            end
        else
            Increase μ_b linearly
        end
    end
end

3.2 Heuristics for Damping Parameter μ Increment

In RI algorithm, 3D points and camera parameters are solved repeatedly using LM method one after the other. Hence we maintain two damping parameters, μ_a for frame equations and μ_b for points equations (refer to Algorithm 1, 2). We propose to use exponential increment for μ_a and linear increment for μ_b i.e. if in an iteration the parameter update causes the cost function to increase, the iteration is discarded and μ_a is multiplied by exponentially increasing β or μ_b is multiplied by a constant γ. On the other hand, if in an iteration the parameter update causes the cost function to decrease, the update is accepted and μ_a and β or μ_b and γ are reset to their initial value. Algorithm 2 shows the psuedo-code of the proposed modifications.

The exponential increment benefits in threefold manner. First, it reduces the step size. Second, it moves closer to steepest descent direction. Finally, it improves the convergence rate by decreasing inner iterations. In the Intersection (points equation solving) step, having a large update on points parameter can result in unstable convergence behaviour as camera parameters have a huge impact on points parameters. R. Lakemond et al. [16] proposes to use repeated triangulation of points. We instead propose to use linear increment in damping parameter μ_b while solving points equation. This in turn will ensure a small and stable update in points parameters.

3.3   Line Search for both Frame and Points Parameters

Modifying the parameters immediately with an update that decreases the cost function does not guarantee optimal local minima in the overall convergence behaviour. We propose to do line search for both camera parameter solving (resection) and point parameters solving (intersection) step. Performing a line search near the original update can potentially help us in identifying a better parameter set corresponding to the optimal local minima. This will ensure that the updates are in correct direction and also reduce the redundancy between the Intersection and Resection steps. Also, performing a Line search will increase the number of inner iteration but due to faster convergence the global solution will be reached earlier.

3.4   Conditional Line Search

Resection-Intersection only achieves first order (linear) asymptotic convergence i.e. initially the algorithm can have large error reduction but asymptotically the error reduces by a constant. Line search is useful if large decrease in cost function is possible than what the equation solving provides. Thus, line search is only useful during the initial part of the algorithm and not in the later part. To quantify it, a metric: error reduction in previous iteration is used. If the metric value is greater than a heuristic threshold we use line search for optimal local minima, else we avoid the use of line search. For our experiments, we set the threshold to be 0.1. Hueristically, this threshold should be two or three orders of magnitude higher than the convergence criteria. In order to reduce the search redundancy, we limit the maximum number of line search operations in a particular iteration.

4   Hybrid Algorithm

We propose a Hybrid 1.5^{th} order algorithm for Bundle Adjustment. The objective is to develop an algorithm with lower reprojection error than state-of-the-art first order algorithms with real-time execution. We will use the modified first order Resection-Intersection algorithm proposed in this paper and classic second order Levenberg-Marquardt algorithm.

First of all, we refine the parameters using modified Resection-Intersection algorithm till we move towards the direction of steepest descent. This also take cares of the problem of bad initial estimate of parameters by providing a good initial estimation for the subsequent part of the algorithm.

Next, we continue to refine the parameters using the classic Levenberg-Marquardt method for correction of descent direction. The initial estimate will come from the previous step which is guaranteed to be a good estimate. Levenberg-Marquardt method will start converging the solution rapidly, but it can't be used for many iterations due to its time complexity. We incorporate a threshold for minimum reduction in error required to iterate again. This step updates the parameters in the right direction of convergence.

Finally, we use modified Resection-Intersection algorithm until the solution converges. The proposed algorithm will give better reprojection error than first order methods for trade off with execution time.

5 Results

5.1 Datasets and System

The algorithms (Modified Resection Intersection (ours), Resection Intersection, Levenberg Marquardt and Hybrid (ours)) were tested on a large collection of samples. This collection includes samples from $CastleP19$, $CastleP20$, $EntryP10$, $fountainP11$, $HerzJesusP25$, $HerzJesusP8$ datasets [1]. Table 1 and Fig. 1 compare the results. We have considered number of observations as the indicator for the complexity of a particular dataset sample across which the comparisons are done. Results are compared on execution time, reprojection error and average number of inner/outer iterations. Results are obtained by running an executable android app on a mobile device with cores running at up to 2.9 GHz.

Table 1. Results of proposed modified algorithms compared with their basic version

Algorithm	Avg. Execution Time (in sec)	Avg. Final Re-projection Error	Avg. Outer iterations	Avg. Inner per Outer iterations
Initial Error	–	16.08	–	–
RI	1.60	3.58	90.98	9.00
Modified RI	0.53	3.48	33.92	8.17
LM	182.72	2.76	–	–
Hybrid	55.75	2.97	–	–

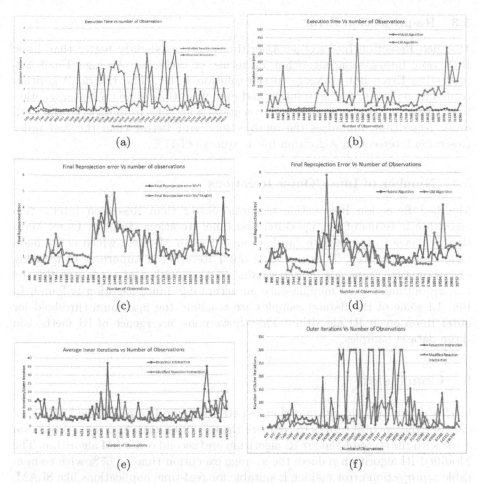

Fig. 1. Execution Time comparison between Resection Intersection and Modified Resection Intersection (a), Hybrid Algorithm and Levenberg Marquardt Algorithm (b). Final Re-projection Error comparison between Resection Intersection and Modified Resection Intersection (c), Hybrid Algorithm and Levenberg Marquardt Algorithm (d). Average inner (e) and outer (f) iterations comparison between Resection Intersection and Modified Resection Intersection

5.2 Execution Time

From Fig. 1, we can observe that Modified Resection Intersection performs better than original Resection Intersection algorithm by an average of 67%. Hybrid Order Algorithm executes three times faster than second order Levenberg Marquardt Algorithm in terms of execution time with comparable reprojection error.

5.3   Re-projection Error

Modified Resection Intersection Algorithm performs slightly better than basic Resection Intersection algorithm in terms of reducing Average Final Reprojection Error but converge to the solution faster. The Hybrid Algorithm trade-offs between optimal solution and execution time giving a better solution than linear algorithms in practical execution time. The proposed Hybrid 1.5th order Algorithm minimizes the reprojection error better than the first order Resection Intersection Algorithm by an average of 17%.

5.4   Number of Inner/Outer Iterations

Modified Resection Intersection performs better than Resection Intersection algorithm in terms of average Outer and Inner iterations. In every Outer iteration, we have to re-compute Jacobian and Hessian Matrices which is the main time consuming step. Thus, reducing outer iteration is important in reducing execution time. Line search helps reducing the number of outer iteration by finding optimum local minima once an acceptable inner iteration is found. In Fig. 1.f some of the dataset samples are reaching the maximum threshold for outer iteration in RI algorithm. This shows non-convergence of RI method in those dataset samples.

6   Conclusion

In this paper, two algorithms (Modified RI and hybrid) are proposed with conclusive experimental results to compare the execution time and the reprojection error with the state-of-the-art RI algorithm and second order LM algorithm. The Modified RI algorithm reduces the average execution time by 67% with comparable reprojection error making it suitable for real-time applications like SLAM, SfM, 3D reconstruction. The hybrid algorithm reduced the average reprojection error by 17% in comparison with the first-order Resection Intersection algorithm making it suitable for applications that demand high accuracy and faster execution of Bundle Adjustment.

References

1. http://documents.ep.ch/groups/c/cv/cvlab-unit/www/data/multiview/denseMVS.html
2. Agarwal, S., Snavely, N., Seitz, S.M., Szeliski, R.: Bundle adjustment in the large. In: Daniilidis, K., Maragos, P., Paragios, N. (eds.) ECCV 2010. LNCS, vol. 6312, pp. 29–42. Springer, Heidelberg (2010). https://doi.org/10.1007/978-3-642-15552-9_3
3. Agarwal, S., Snavely, N., Simon, I., Seitz, S.M., Szeliski, R.: Building Rome in a day. In: ICCV (2009)

4. Byröd, M., Åström, K.: Conjugate gradient bundle adjustment. In: Daniilidis, K., Maragos, P., Paragios, N. (eds.) ECCV 2010. LNCS, vol. 6312, pp. 114–127. Springer, Heidelberg (2010). https://doi.org/10.1007/978-3-642-15552-9_9
5. Chen, Y., Davis, T., Hager, W., Rajamanickam, S.: Algorithm 887: Cholmod, supernodal sparse cholesky factorization and update/downdate. ACM Trans. Math. Softw. **35**, 1–14 (2008)
6. Dissanayake, M.W.M.G., Newman, P., Clark, S., Durrant-Whyte, H.F., Csorba, M.: A solution to the simultaneous localization and map building (slam) problem. IEEE Trans. Robot. Autom. **17**(3), 229–241 (2001). https://doi.org/10.1109/70. 938381
7. Frahm, J.-M., et al.: Building Rome on a cloudless day. In: Daniilidis, K., Maragos, P., Paragios, N. (eds.) ECCV 2010. LNCS, vol. 6314, pp. 368–381. Springer, Heidelberg (2010). https://doi.org/10.1007/978-3-642-15561-1_27
8. Hartley, R., Zisserman, A.: Multiple View Geometry in Computer Vision, 2nd edn. Cambridge University Press, New York (2003)
9. Krishnamoorthy, A., Menon, D.: Matrix inversion using cholesky decomposition. In: 2013 Signal Processing: Algorithms, Architectures, Arrangements, and Applications (SPA), pp. 70–72 (2011)
10. Lourakis, M.I.A., Argyros, A.A.: SBA: a software package for generic sparse bundle adjustment. ACM Trans. Math. Softw. **36**(1), 2:1–2:30 (2009)
11. Michot, J., Bartoli, A., Gaspard, F.: Algebraic line search for bundle adjustment (2009). https://doi.org/10.5244/C.23.44
12. Moré, J.J.: The Levenberg-Marquardt algorithm: implementation and theory. In: Watson, G.A. (ed.) Numerical Analysis. LNM, vol. 630, pp. 105–116. Springer, Heidelberg (1978). https://doi.org/10.1007/BFb0067700
13. Mouragnon, E., Lhuillier, M., Dhome, M., Dekeyser, F., Sayd, P.: Generic andreal-time structure from motion using local bundle adjustment. Image Vis. Comput. **27**(8), 1178–1193 (2009). https://doi.org/10.1016/j.imavis.2008.11.006
14. Nielsen, H.B.: Damping parameter in marquardt's method (1999)
15. Pereira, F., Luft, J., Ilha, G., Susin, A.: A novel resection-intersection algorithm with fast triangulation applied to monocular visual odometry. IEEE Trans. Intell. Transp. Syst. **19**, 1–10 (2018). https://doi.org/10.1109/TITS.2018.2853579
16. Ruan Lakemond, C.F., Sridharan, S.: Resection-intersection bundle adjustment revisited. ISRN Machine Vision (2013). https://doi.org/10.1155/2013/261956
17. Schönberger, J.L., Frahm, J.: Structure-from-motion revisited. In: 2016 IEEE Conference on Computer Vision and Pattern Recognition (CVPR), pp. 4104–4113, June 2016. https://doi.org/10.1109/CVPR.2016.445
18. Shigang, L., Jiancheng, S., Jianwu, D.: A linear resection-intersection bundle adjustment method. Inf. Technol. J. **7**, 220–223 (2008). https://doi.org/10.3923/ itj.2008.220.223
19. Triggs, B., McLauchlan, P.F., Hartley, R.I., Fitzgibbon, A.W.: Bundle adjustment – a modern synthesis. In: Triggs, B., Zisserman, A., Szeliski, R. (eds.) Vision Algorithms: Theory and Practice, pp. 298–372. Springer, Berlin, Heidelberg (2000)
20. Wright, S.J., Holt, J.N.: An inexact levenberg-marquardt method for large sparse nonlinear least squres. ANZIAM J. **26**, 387–403 (1985)

DocDescribor: Digits + Alphabets + Math Symbols - A Complete OCR for Handwritten Documents

Ridhi Aggarwal[1], Hiteshi Jain[1], Gaurav Harit[1(✉)], and Anil Kumar Tiwari[2]

[1] Department of Computer Science and Engineering, Indian Institute of Technology Jodhpur, Jodhpur, Rajasthan, India
{pg201384012,jain.4,gharit,akt}@iitj.ac.in
[2] Department of Electrical Engineering, Indian Institute of Technology Jodhpur, Jodhpur, Rajasthan, India

Abstract. This paper presents an Optical Character Recognition (OCR) system for documents with English text and mathematical expressions. Neural network architectures using CNN layers and/or dense layers achieve high level accuracy in character recognition task. However, these models require large amount of data to train the network, with balanced number of samples for each class. Recognition of mathematical symbols poses challenges of the imbalance and paucity of training data available. To address this issue, we pose the character recognition problem as a Distance Metric Learning problem. We propose a Siamese-CNN Network that learns discriminative features to identify if the two images in a pair contain similar or dissimilar characters. The network is then used to recognize different characters by character matching where test images are compared to sample images of any target class which may or may not be included during training. Thus our model can scale to new symbols easily. The proposed approach is invariant to author's handwriting. Our model has been tested over images extracted from a dataset of scanned answer scripts collected by us. It is seen that our approach achieves comparable performance to other architectures using convolutional layers or dense layers while using lesser training data.

Keywords: Distance metric learning · Ensemble methods · Siamese network · Mathematical symbols · Characters · Digit · Handwritten documents

1 Introduction

Optical Character Recognition (OCR) is widely used in many applications such as signature verification, cheque processing, form processing, converting scanned documents to machine-text form, etc. Handwritten documents can consist of character lines, digits, mathematical expressions and figures. In this work we

© Springer Nature Singapore Pte Ltd. 2020
R. V. Babu et al. (Eds.): NCVPRIPG 2019, CCIS 1249, pp. 292–301, 2020.
https://doi.org/10.1007/978-981-15-8697-2_27

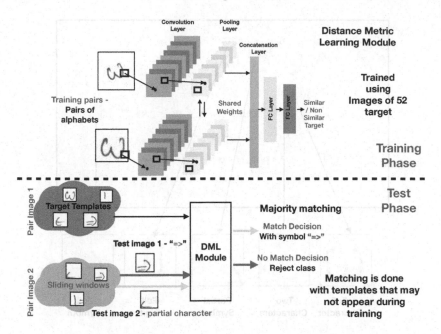

Fig. 1. Alpha-symbol recognition framework

focus towards recognizing characters, digits and symbols from a handwritten document.

The integrated OCR for printed [15] and online handwritten mathematical documents [11] are already well developed. In contrast, the task of offline handwritten mathematical symbol recognition is relatively unexplored. Offline formula recognition and structure parsing of isolated expressions is recently addressed in the Competition on Recognition of Online Handwritten Mathematical Expressions (CROHME) 2019 [8]. However, the task of recognizing digits and math symbols in a complete handwritten document image has not been addressed in the past.

The design of an OCR for documents involves three steps: 1) segmentation step that involves isolating the characters from each other, 2) designing a classification system for possible target classes and a decision function that allows assigning a character image to predefined class 3) finally, the verification strategy that uses the global decision module and allows the rejection or acceptance of the processed image.

Handwritten documents pose various challenges like touching characters, non-uniform sized words and slanted/unaligned writing patterns unlike printed documents that have non-touching individual characters mostly uniform in size. Thus segmentation of a handwritten document is a difficult task and a sliding window mostly used for segmentation can result into partial characters, twin characters or whole characters, as shown in Fig. 2 for one of our document

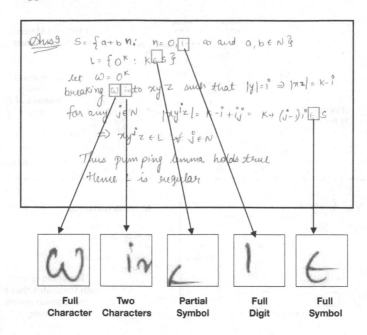

Fig. 2. Sliding windows of a document image highlighting various possible different ways of characters present in a window

images. In this work we address the classification steps and the decision making step.

Neural network architectures using convolutional layers (CNN)/dense layers have emerged as a replacement of traditional techniques of handwritten character recognition that used hand-crafted features [4,5,9,12,14]. These networks can extract visual features from images using different filters such that the learned features are invariant to shift, size and noise.

Training a good model requires a large training dataset with equal number of samples for all target classes. Further, prediction of these models is limited to classes used during training and learning a new category requires retraining the models.

Building a character recognition model to identify mathematical symbols like $\leq, \in, \sum$ in presence of alphabets and digits faces a problem of *Dataset Imbalance*. Math symbols such as $\leq, \sum, \in$ or greek alphabets like α, β rarely occur in documents. Thus there are too few samples of such characters in the training data as compared to alphabets and digits. As an example, Kaggle dataset contains 2692 samples of $\sum$ and 11197 samples for letter a. This dataset imbalance leads to a alphabet/digit biased training.

To solve the problem of dataset imbalance, image transformation techniques can be used that can help increase the samples of rarely occurring characters in the dataset. Rotation, translation, scaling and shearing are few of such transformations used in past to increase the dataset size [1,3,6,7].

In the decision step, a test image that does not belong to any of the trained target class is classified as a novel class/reject-class/anomaly based on a probability threshold i.e. if for a test image the probability of recognition is less than a threshold the image is classified as a reject class [2,10]. The difficulty here remains - how to choose the right threshold?

Few questions arise: Can we design a classification framework that can leverage only few target class labels and use this to identify new unseen (not seen during training) but known target character classes? Further, can a framework be designed to make a decision of the target class without using a threshold?

A recent paper [13] has addressed this problem and proposed a Siamese-CNN model that uses the contrastive loss to maximize Euclidean distance between the representations of dissimilar pairs and minimize the distance between similar ones. In contrast, we pose the similarity learning task with match/mismatch targets. This allows the CNN layers to learn representations of inputs such that the fully connected layer can learn to map similar/dissimilar inputs to match/mismatch targets. Unlike [13], our network is able to learn the distance metric without the use of Euclidean distance between learned representations.

Our Alpha-Symbol Recognition framework (Fig. 1) works in two phases: 1) Distance Metric Learning between two characters using Siamese-CNN network. This module learns to identify if two images in a pair are similar or dissimilar. This module is trained using image pairs taken from alphabets only. 2) Decision module that evaluates a match/non-match decision using the learned distance metric learning (DML) module where one image in the pair is the sliding window for which the target label needs to be evaluated and the other image is a candidate template of a candidate target class. These target classes may or may not be included in the training phase.

Our model is seen to overcome the problem of dataset imbalance as it has only been trained with the balanced Kaggle alphabet dataset and does not require re-training of the network for new symbols. Further, the decision of rejection is based on a match-mismatch decision of DML module and does not depend on any threshold. The framework has been tested for sliding windows extracted from examination answer scripts that have been collected by us. It is seen that our approach gives comparable or better performance compared to alternative architectures trained to do classification using dense, convolutional or Gated-CNN layers, with softmax classification layer.

2 Alpha-Symbol Recognition Framework

To recognize alphabets and mathematical symbols, we pose the recognition problem as Distance Metric Learning problem. As a first step, the Siamese-CNN Network is designed to identify if the pair of images containing characters are similar or dissimilar. Once the network learns to identify the similarity and dissimilarity between two images through distance metric learning, we use this network to compare the test sliding windows with images of known symbols to predict the label for the image. We explain the two steps in detail here:

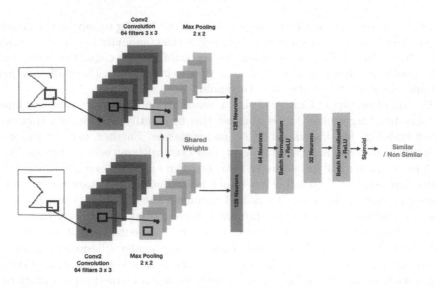

Fig. 3. Siamese network for similarity metric learning and identify input pair as match/mismatch

2.1 Distance Metric Learning Module

The goal of this module is to learn if two images are similar or dissimilar. For this we propose a Siamese-CNN Network that takes symbol image pairs as input and learns similarity between them. The network is as shown in Fig. 3. The input images are individually passed to separate but similar networks comprising a single layer CNN with 64 3×3 filters and a 128 unit dense layer. The weights of the two individual branches are shared. Thus the two CNN networks take an image pair as input and produce two output vectors O_p and $O_q \in R_N$ (here $N = 128$). The outputs are concatenated and fed to a Multi Layer Perceptron with a final sigmoid layer to give 0/1 output label, i.e. match/non-match label.

2.2 Label Prediction for Sliding Windows

Till now, the Similarity-CNN Network has been able to mark the input pairs as similar and dissimilar. The learned metric of image similarity is used to find the matching labelled images. The label of the matched image is adopted as the label of the test image. As an input to the learned Similarity-CNN network, we give the test image as one input to the network and a template with a known label as the other input. One by one we compute the similarity of the test image with the template images of the target classes. The class for which there are maximum number of matched templates with the sliding window is assigned as the label to the window. If there is no match found from the template images, the sliding window is said to belong to a reject-class.

This technique of Distance Metric Learning for handwritten character recognition provides multiple advantages:

1. If a test image is a partial character or a touching character, i.e. belongs to the reject class, the Similarity-CNN Network predicts the reject class label without any threshold requirements.
2. Such a network provides an advantage that it can be trained with a few classes and during test time it can be used to find similarity with even the templates belonging to new labels i.e. symbols not seen during training. The reason for this being that the network has learned to discriminate if a pair is similar or dissimilar. Thus, irrespective of the type of input images provided at the test time it can identify if the input images match or not and thus provide an appropriate label. The network now is not required to be retrained every time for a new character type. Further, it can be trained with a few symbol classes only, like the Kaggle alphabet dataset. Use of datasets like Kaggle or MNIST for training the Siamese makes the system learn features which are invariant to handwriting.

In the next section we discuss the experimental settings and results where we show the capabilities of our model and compare it with a few character recognition methods.

3 Experiments

Our task is to identify the different characters, digits, and mathematical symbols that are there in the examination scripts collected by us. Character hypotheses are generated with a sliding window approach. The sliding window approach comes with the inherent drawback of the windows containing partial as well as touching characters which need to be classified by the network to a reject class.

The documents that we consider contains 106 character types including 10 digits, 26 alphabets (uppercase and lowercase) and mathematical symbols like $\alpha, \beta, \sum$, etc. Some of the sample sliding windows are as shown in Fig. 4.

We consider the following baselines for comparison.

1. Dense Neural Network: In the dense neural networks (Fig. 5), the input images are flattened and passed to a single dense layer (128 neuron) network followed by a dropout layer with drop probability of 0.2. The final layer is the softmax layer used for multi-class classification.

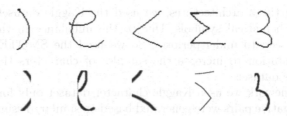

Fig. 4. Sliding windows of the documents with sample partial and full characters

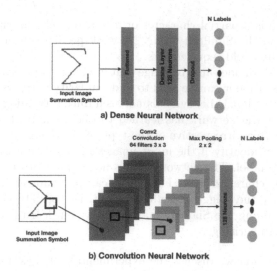

Fig. 5. Dense Neural Network and Convolution Neural Network (CNN) architectures used for character recognition

2. Convolution Neural Network: A popular technique to use deep learning to classify images is to build a convolutional neural network (CNN). A convolution multiplies a matrix of pixels with a filter matrix or kernel and sums up the multiplication values. Then the convolution slides over to the next pixel and repeats the same process until all the image pixels have been covered. We use 64 kernels of size 3 × 3 followed by Max-Pooling with filters of size 2 × 2 to reduce the image output size. Finally the images are flattened and passed as an input to the 128 dimension dense layer. The output of the layer is passed to the softmax layer for the final multi-class classification (Fig. 5).

3. Gated Convolution Neural Network: In the gated convolution network, 2-dimensional convolution layer is used. We use 32 kernels of size 3 × 3 followed by gated convolution block. Then Max-Pooling with filters of size 2 × 2 is used followed by dropout layer with drop probability 0.25. It is flattened and passed to a single dense layer (128 neurons) network followed again by dropout layer with drop probability 0.5 and single dense layer of 106 neurons. The final layer is softmax layer used for multi-class classification.

For training the 3 architectures, we used the Kaggle dataset of alphabets, digits, and mathematical symbols. Due to the imbalance in the dataset, the networks were seen to under-perform. So we used the SMOTE technique for dataset augmentation to increase the samples of characters that were rarely occurring in the dataset.

For our framework we used Kaggle character dataset only for training. The positive and negative pairs were generated based on similar/dissimilar characters in the images. Table 1 gives the details of the count of samples used for training and testing. The network has been tested for 52 document images that have been

Table 1. Number of Samples used for training

Comparison techniques	Number of training samples	
	Before augmentation	After augmentation
CNN, DenseNN, GCNN	Variable samples Class with min sample = 21 Class with max samples = 33997 Total Samples = 639113	2500 samples for each class (Alphabets, Symbols, Digits) Total samples = 265000 (Balanced dataset)
Siamese-CNN Model	2500 samples of digits and alphabets. (Balanced dataset, but symbols were not used for training)	

Table 2. Accuracy for isolated instances of Symbols, Characters and Digits. Note that the last row shows results when symbols were not used for training

Model	Train	Test Accuracy (%)					
		Alphabets		Symbols		Digits	
	Train data	Before augment	After augment	Before augment	After augment	Before augment	After augment
DenseNN	Digits + Alphabets + Symbols	78.9	89.6	66	81	81.8	78
CNN	Digits + Alphabets + Symbols	81.2	84.3	67.55	84.9	81.8	80.8
GCNN	Digits + Alphabets + Symbols	88.7	88.9	68.55	84.9	81.8	81.8
[13]	Digits	54.72		29.77		82.6	
Proposed	Digits	56.8		32.2		90	
	Alphabets	76		45.8		78.9	
	Digits + Alphabets	86.9		61.7		88.6	

collected by us from answer scripts of students. A sample image of the document is shown in Fig. 2. The accuracy of these models on isolated digits, symbols and alphabets recognition are as shown in Table 2.

The recognition accuracy, averaged over all classes, of the different architectures for classifying sliding windows in test documents are as shown in Table 3. A candidate window was classified to the reject class if the highest probability attributed to a class by the softmax classification layer was below a threshold. For the proposed technique, a candidate window was classified to the reject class if it could not match with enough (majority) number of templates of any of the classes.

From both Table 2 and Table 3, we can see that though our model does not outperform the models like CNN, Dense-NN and GCNN, however, with limited training data and without the use of instances from symbol classes for training it performs close to these models.

Table 3. Recognition accuracy (%) of different models over test dataset of handwritten documents

	Before data augmentation	After data augmentation
Dense-NN	75.6	82.82
CNN	76.85	83.33
Gated CNN	79.66	85.2
Proposed	79.06	

4   Conclusion and Discussion

In this paper we have introduced an OCR system to recognize math symbols, along with alphabets and digits, for a handwritten document image. We use a distance metric learning approach to learn discriminative features such that two similar characters are drawn nearer to each other in the representation space and the dissimilar ones are moved apart. Such a network can be trained on fewer classes and tested for unseen character recognition using match or no-match decision. The network has been trained for digits and characters and still can be used to identify symbols. This helps in handling the class imbalance problem that occurs because of few training samples available for rarely used symbols. The network is seen to perform comparable to the traditional neural network architectures using dense layers, convolutional layers, or gated convolutional layers, with a softmax classification layer. The classification stage takes time because a candidate window needs to be compared for match/no-match with a number of templates belonging to all classes. However, retraining of the model to classify a new symbol gets avoided. A drawback of sliding windows technique is that some sliding windows containing a partial character or two touching characters do not get classified into the reject class. Common problems, e.g., are, a window with a partial alphabet 'B' matches to digit '3', partial alphabets 'D', 'L', 'M', 'N', 'P' often match to digit '1', partial symbols 'α', 'X', 'K', match to 'a', 'Y', '<', respectively. Future work would consider refining the possible misclassifications by using language models.

References

1. Brown, W.M., Gedeon, T.D., Groves, D.I.: Use of noise to augment training data: a neural network method of mineral-potential mapping in regions of limited known deposit examples. Nat. Resour. Res. **12**(2), 141–152 (2003). https://doi.org/10.1023/A:1024218913435
2. Chalapathy, R., Menon, A.K., Chawla, S.: Anomaly detection using one-class neural networks. arXiv preprint arXiv:1802.06360 (2018)
3. Cireşan, D.C., Meier, U., Masci, J., Gambardella, L.M., Schmidhuber, J.: High-performance neural networks for visual object classification. arXiv preprint arXiv:1102.0183 (2011)

4. Gunawan, T.S., Noor, A.F.R.M., Kartiwi, M.: Development of English handwritten recognition using deep neural network. Indonesian J. Electric. Eng. Comput. Sci. **10**(2), 562–568 (2018)
5. He, W., et al: Context-aware mathematical expression recognition: an end-to-end framework and a benchmark. In: 2016 23rd International Conference on Pattern Recognition (ICPR), pp. 3246–3251. IEEE (2016)
6. LeCun, Y.: The mnist database of handwritten digits. http://yann.lecun.com/exdb/mnist/ (1998)
7. LeCun, Y., Bottou, L., Bengio, Y., Haffner, P., et al.: Gradient-based learning applied to document recognition. Proc. IEEE **86**(11), 2278–2324 (1998)
8. Mahdavi, M., Zanibbi, R., Mouchere, H., Garain, U.: ICDAR 2019 CROHME+ TFD: competition on recognition of handwritten mathematical expressions and typeset formula detection. In: Proceedings ICDAR (2019)
9. Maitra, D.S., Bhattacharya, U., Parui, S.K.: CNN based common approach to handwritten character recognition of multiple scripts. In: 2015 13th International Conference on Document Analysis and Recognition (ICDAR), pp. 1021–1025. IEEE (2015)
10. Marchi, E., Vesperini, F., Eyben, F., Squartini, S., Schuller, B.: A novel approach for automatic acoustic novelty detection using a denoising autoencoder with bidirectional LSTM neural networks. In: 2015 IEEE International Conference on Acoustics, Speech and Signal Processing (ICASSP), pp. 1996–2000. IEEE (2015)
11. Mouchère, H., Viard-Gaudin, C., Zanibbi, R., Garain, U.: ICFHR 2016 CROHME: competition on recognition of online handwritten mathematical expressions. In: 2016 15th International Conference on Frontiers in Handwriting Recognition (ICFHR), pp. 607–612. IEEE (2016)
12. Simard, P.Y., Steinkraus, D., Platt, J.C., et al.: Best practices for convolutional neural networks applied to visual document analysis. In: ICDAR, vol. 3 (2003)
13. Sokar, G., Hemayed, E.E., Rehan, M.: A generic OCR using deep siamese convolution neural networks. In: 2018 IEEE 9th Annual Information Technology, Electronics and Mobile Communication Conference (IEMCON), pp. 1238–1244. IEEE (2018)
14. Suryani, D., Doetsch, P., Ney, H.: On the benefits of convolutional neural network combinations in offline handwriting recognition. In: 2016 15th International Conference on Frontiers in Handwriting Recognition (ICFHR), pp. 193–198. IEEE (2016)
15. Suzuki, M., Tamari, F., Fukuda, R., Uchida, S., Kanahori, T.: INFTY: an integrated OCR system for mathematical documents. In: Proceedings of the 2003 ACM Symposium on Document Engineering, pp. 95–104. ACM (2003)

Non-contextual Long-Term Person Re-ID Under Sudden Illumination Conditions

B. Yogameena[1,2,3]($\boxtimes$), K. Menaka[1,3], and S. Saravana Perumaal[1,2,3]

[1] Department of ECE, Thiagarajar College of Engineering, Madurai, India
{ymece,sspmech}@tce.edu, ece.menaka@gmail.com
[2] Department of ECE, V.S.B. Engineering College, Karur, India
[3] Department of Mechanical Engineering, Thiagarajar College of Engineering, Madurai, India

Abstract. Person Re-ID (Re-ID) has been an emerging topic and there is a need for non-contextual, long term person Re-ID algorithm since most of the crimes occur in public places such as airports, railway stations where the video is recorded for a long duration across arbitrary camera views. The proposed work comprises of two fusion frameworks. First, the people detection is accomplished by fusing Histogram of Oriented Gradients (HOG) and extended Center Symmetric Local Binary Pattern (XCS-LBP) features which overcomes several disadvantages like missing detection and false detection due to sudden illumination, and near/far field of view changes. Next, each body part of the tracked person is learned using Deformable Part Model (DPM) which is robust to different viewpoints. Secondly, the feature level fusion of Gabor (appearance feature) and Skeleton Recurrent Motion Image (SRMI Gait biometric feature) is proposed to overcome the homogeneity issue of distinguishing people when both the texture and color of the people attire are similar. Finally, person Re-ID is achieved by relevance metric learning method with list wise constraints (RMLLCs). The performance measure, Cumulative Matching Curve (CMC) Rate shows the improved matching accuracy compared to other state-of-the-art algorithms with benchmark datasets.

Keywords: Person Re-identification · Long-term · Skeleton recurrent motion image sudden illumination · Gait and appearance features

1 Introduction

Deployment of large networks of cameras is drastically increasing in public places like airports, railway stations and office buildings. Fascinatingly, automated analysis of huge video data can improve the quality of surveillance by processing the video faster. Such automated analysis is more useful for high-level surveillance tasks like suspicious activity detection or undesirable event prediction for timely alerts or behaviors or events of interest. These tasks can only be inferred from a long term analysis of the target person across the camera network. It is inferred from the literature that till now there is a lack of research in non-contextual long term person Re-ID where multiple cameras have been employed [1]. Since most of the crimes occur in public places like airports, railway stations where the video is recorded for a long duration, this paper aims to

© Springer Nature Singapore Pte Ltd. 2020
R. V. Babu et al. (Eds.): NCVPRIPG 2019, CCIS 1249, pp. 302–311, 2020.
https://doi.org/10.1007/978-981-15-8697-2_28

provide a framework for non-contextual long term person Re-ID. It includes four phases like people detection, tracking, identification and Re-ID across multiple camera views.

2 Related Work

Contextual methods rely on external contextual information which considers camera geometry as well as camera calibration as context of a single static camera for feature extraction [1]. Non-contextual methods rely on dissimilar context information across arbitrary cameras and view. Short term person Re-ID utilizes the video taken only for few hours and the external factors influencing the scenario is less. Nevertheless, the appearance features such as Symmetry Driven Accumulation of Local Features (SDALF) and HOG possibly will fail due to varying illumination, occlusions and noise. Hence, these features are not suitable for long term person Re-ID which utilizes videos recorded in a day, week or a month which is the main focus of the proposed framework. Existing non contextual, long term Re-id methods in literature are categorized into color calibration, descriptor learning and metric learning methods. Color calibration category consists of direct and indirect approaches and claimed Weighted Brightness Transfer Function (WTBF) outperforms than Brightness Transfer Function (BTF) and Cumulative BTF [2]. Recently the authors in [3, 4] have adopted calibration methods to be robust against uncalibrated images and less space constraints. However, background clutter, large pose variations still remains as a major challenge. Descriptor learning type consists of Shape Context [5], Re-id with attributes [6] and Re-id by saliency. The closed set Re-ID problem has been solved by the endeavor of recent state-of-the-art methods [1, 7]. Moreover, various approaches using appearance descriptors for person Re-ID with their merits and demerits have been reviewed [8]. Amongst these appearance descriptors, it is recommended to utilize Gait biometric for long term Re-ID and most of the recent research is concentrated on non-contextual methods [1]. HoG [5] is used for shape and appearance based person detection and they had achieved only 82% of matching accuracy. HOG performs poorly when the background is cluttered with noisy edges and the detection rate decreases further in sudden illumination conditions. An attempt has been done by fusing HoG [9] and LBP features [10] to improve the detection rate since both HOG and LBP individually revealed bigger achievement in person detection applications. Also LBP filters the noisy background. However, the false positives which occurs more frequently in sudden illumination conditions is not addressed. Later, XCS-LBP [11] has been proposed and it is robust to sudden illumination changes. Hence, a framework which considers the non-contextual and long-term person Re-ID issues by adapting Gait as well as the appearance features is needed. Moreover, to obtain the correct match against query is another major challenge. Distance metric learning includes Dynamic Time Warping, Distance Metric, Set Based Discriminative Ranking (SBDR), Mahanolobis Metric Distance Learning [12], and Probabilistic Relative Distance Learning (PRDC) [13]. It is inferred from the literature that distance metric learning methods pay no attention to geometry information as well as sensitive to outliers especially Mahalanobis distance metric learning. More recently in [14, 15], asymmetric metric learning is used to eradicate the issues such as similar appearance, motion and actions in video representations. Even though, methods based on metric learning lack adequate feature representation and efficiency.

Gait Energy Image (GEI) proposed by Liu et al. in [16] requires perfect alignments of the silhouettes for comparison and it is sensitive to segmentation errors too especially in real-world applications. Recently, Chen et al. [17] proposed RMLLC (R) model to solve the person Re-ID problem based on cross view gait recognition. As per the survey of various human detection algorithms, till now there is no algorithm which is robust to detect persons even in cluttered background and sudden illumination changes. The authors well known that the traditional methods are obsolete as compared with recent deep learning methods. However, recent deep learning algorithms need larger dataset for training is obvious. Traditional approaches characterizes a rapid and effective method for processing computer vision algorithms, whereas CNN need lakhs of training samples of known objects for effective training. The benchmark person Re-ID dataset under sudden illumination conditions is very few [18]. The recent datasets Market1501, MARS, Duke MTMC, MSMT17 are larger dataset, lacks challenging conditions like sudden illumination changes. Hence, the traditional approach, the combination of HoG and XCS-LBP descriptor, is proposed and attempted for further validation with deep learning. Re-ID datasets such as ETH and PETS 2009 have sudden illumination variations. However, these datasets are insufficient to implement with deep learning algorithms. Taking this idea into consideration, in this paper, the fusion of appearance and gait biometric (Skeleton Recurrent Motion Image (SRMI)) with relevance metric learning for non-contextual long term person Re-ID is proposed. It is detailed in Sect. 3. The discussion is elaborated with results and discussion is conferred in Sect. 4. Finally, the work is summarized in Sect. 5.

3 Proposed Method

First, the person is detected by combining HOG and XCS-LBP feature vectors. Subsequently, tracking of multiple persons is carried out across multiple cameras using Kalman filter [20]. Followed that, the images of tracked persons are automatically cropped and saved. DPM [19] is used to model each body part of a tracked person. Further, the Gabor feature descriptor [21] is extracted from each body part. The fusion of appearance (Gabor feature) and Gait (Skeleton RMI) features are proposed for long term person Re-ID. Finally, the correct match of the given query image against Gallery is achieved by relevance metric learning approach [16]. The overall methodology of the proposed framework is illustrated in Fig. 1.

3.1 Person Detection by Fusing HOG and XCS-LBP and Multiple Person Tracking

The first and the foremost step is to detect multiple persons across multiple views. Hence, the fusion of HOG and XCS-LBP features is proposed since HOG provides person shape information and XCS-LBP is illumination invariant as well as provides texture information. Extension of Centre Symmetric Local Binary Pattern (CS-LBP) operator is performed by comparing the gray values of center symmetric pixel pair which is quite sensitive to quick illumination variations. It is expressed as:

$$XCS - LBP_{P,R}(C) = \sum_{i=0}^{(p/2)-1} s(g_1(i, c) + g_2(i, c))2^i \tag{1}$$

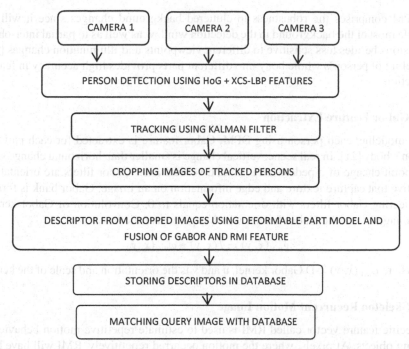

Fig. 1. The proposed methodology for person Re-ID for sudden illumination conditions.

$$XCS - LBP = s((g_0 - g_4) + g_c + (g_0 - g_c)(g_4 - g_c))2^0 + s((g_1 - g_5) + g_c + (g_1 - g_c)(g_5 - g_c))2^1 +$$
$$s((g_2 - g_6) + g_c + (g_2 - g_c)(g_6 - g_c))2^2 + s((g_3 - g_7) + g_c + (g_3 - g_c)(g_7 - g_c))2^3 + \ldots\ldots$$

Where g_c is the center pixel and $g_0, g_1\ldots\ldots g_7$ are the neighborhood pixels. Subsequent to the detection of multiple persons, Kalman filter is used for tracking the labelled persons. It estimates and up-dates the new observation with minimum prediction (estimation) error [20]. At time k, each target has state and observation,

$$x_k = F_k x_{k-1} + w_k \tag{2}$$

Where $w_k \sim N(0, Q_k)$ F_k is the state transition model which is applied to the previous state X_{k-1}; W_k is the process noise which is assumed to be drawn from a zero mean multivariate normal distribution with covariance Q_k.

$$y_k = H_k x_k + v_k \tag{3}$$

where, H_k is the observation model which maps the true state space into the observed space and V_k is the observation noise which is assumed to be zero mean Gaussian white noise with co-variance R_k.

3.2 Deformable Part Model

Subsequently, the image regions of tracked persons are only considered for further process. DPM [19] is adopted for modeling each part of the person's body. The advantages of DPM comprises the robustness to cluttered background changes since it will not include most of the background in the detection window as well as to partial inter-object occlusions besides less sensitive to different viewpoints and illumination changes [19]. Modeling of person's whole body into different parts provides high accuracy in feature extraction.

3.3 Gabor Feature Extraction

After modeling each person using DPM, Gabor feature is extracted for each part of a person's body [21]. In real scene, vertical change is smaller than horizontal change since viewpoint change of a pedestrian is around vertical axis. Gabor filters are orientation-sensitive that capture texture and edge information on an image. Gabor bank is formed by selecting Gabor filters with orientation equals to 0. Convolution of Gabor kernels with image I form the Gabor feature which is given as follows:

$$g_{u,v}(x, y) = I(x, y) * \varphi_{u,v}(x, y) \tag{4}$$

Where $\varphi_{u,v}(x, y)$ 2-D Gabor kernel, u and v is the orientation and scale of the kernel.

3.4 Skeleton Recurrent Motion Image

A specific feature vector called RMI is used to estimate repetitive motion behavior of moving objects. At pixels, where the motion occurred repetitively, RMI will have high values whereas at pixels with little or no motion occurred, RMI constitutes low values. Using (2) and (3), RMI is computed to determine the areas of moving object's silhouette with repetitive changes.

$$DS_a(x, y, t) = S_a(x, y, t - 1) \oplus S_a(x, y, t) \tag{5}$$

$$RMI_a = \sum_{k=0}^{T} DS_a(x, y, t - k) \tag{6}$$

Where S_a is a binary silhouette for object at frame t, DS_a is a binary image which indicates areas of motion for object a between frame t and $t - 1$ and $t - k$ is the RMI for object a calculated over T frames. Subsequently, to compute the average recurrence for each block, RMI is partitioned into N equal-sized blocks.

Hence, the fusion of appearance feature (Gabor) and Gait feature (Skeleton RMI) is proposed for long term person Re-ID across multiple cameras.

3.5 Relevance Metric Learning

After that, the framework utilizes person Re-ID algorithm, Relevance Metric Learning method with List wise Constraints (RMLLC) proposed by Chen et al. [17]. This algorithm treats the person Re-ID as an image retrieval task, and measures the similarity of two feature vectors by using their inner product, or, relevance, which is angle between two vectors. To overcome sparse pairwise limitations, similarity score list [17] is predefined for every probe image x_i and gallery set x_j through their inner product and initializing binary numbers for similar and dissimilar pairs.

4 Results and Discussion

Experimentations are carried out using benchmark datasets and the results are evaluated using Matlab 2018a. The PETS2009 dataset comprises multi-sensor sequences. This scenario contains one group who navigate around a stationary group. Here, PETS2009-S3-View 5, View 6, and View 7 datasets (Flow Analysis and Event Recognition) as well as VIPER, ETHZ, i-LIDS, CAVIAR4REID and TRECVid 2008 dataset are used for the evaluation of person Re-ID. The specifications of benchmark datasets in terms of frame rate, scenario with place, people size, and number of cameras employed are depicted in Table 1.

Table 1. Specifications of various benchmark dataset

Dataset	Image/Video	Frame rate	Place	People size	No. of cameras
VIPER	Still images	–	Outdoor surveillance	128×48	1
ETHZ	Video	15	Moving cameras on city street	13×30 to 158×432	1
i-LIDS	Video	25	Collection from different scenarios	21×53 to 176×326	5
Choke	Video	25	Corridor	Normal	1
CAVIAR4REID	Still images	–	Shopping centre	17×39 to 72×144	2
TRECVid 2008	Video	25	Gatwick International Airport –London	21×53 to 176×326	5
PETS2009	Video	7	Outdoor surveillance	26×67 to 57×112	8

Initially, HOG feature is used for person detection in PETS 2009 dataset. But, few shortcomings like when the person is just entering the field of view, the algorithm fails to detect that person. Also, 'false positives' occur in sudden illumination changing conditions. Such failure cases are illustrated in Fig. 2a and Fig. 2c respectively. These shortcomings overcome by the proposed framework and it is depicted in Fig. 2b and Fig. 2d. Subsequently, the appearance features (Gabor texture) are extracted from the DPM of the detected persons. The output of Gabor feature extraction is shown in Fig. 3 (d). The fusion of appearance (Gabor) and Gait (Skeleton RMI) features is done for long term person Re-ID across multiple cameras. It is illustrated in Fig. 3 (a, b, c, and d). Re-ID process is carried out by matching the probe image with the gallery images using RMLLC with rectification (RMLLC (R)) [16] by adopting list wise similarities, which consist of the similarity list of each image with respect to all remaining images.

The appearance features fail in case if a person wears different attire or two persons wear same color attire and it is illustrated in Fig. 4. From Fig. 4 (a) it is inferred that,

(a)   (b)

(c)   (d)

Fig. 2. Detection of multiple person across multiple views by fusion of HOG and XCS-LBP (a) Camera 1, (b) Camera 1 (c), Camera 2 (d) Camera 2.

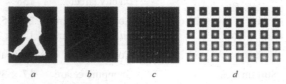

a   b   c   d

Fig. 3. (a) Silhouette sequence of person 1 in View - 1 (b) Skeleton features (c) Partitioned RMI of skeleton features (d) Gabor filter banks used and the output of Gabor feature extraction

(a)   (b)

Fig. 4. (a) 'Correct match' in case of person-23 in gallery image and person-23 in query image (Same color clothes) in i-LIDS dataset. (b) Re-ID of person-1 with gallery image (View-1) and person-2 with query image (View-2) is 'Wrong match' in i-LIDS dataset.

'Correct match' is correctly indicated in case of person-23 in gallery image of camera 1 and person-23 in query image of camera 2 are wearing same clothes for i-LIDS dataset using the proposed framework. Figure 4 (b) shows the performance of using Gabor feature under challenging scenarios and it displays 'Wrong match' for i-LIDS dataset. This shows the advantage of the proposed long term Re-ID using Gait features and fusing it with Gabor.

The performance metric widely used for person Re-ID is the Cumulative Matching Characteristics (CMC) rate. This metric is adopted where each image in the database is ranked based on its comparison to the query image. Various existing algorithms such as SDALF, Re-ID by Saliency and the proposed work are evaluated on benchmark datasets, given in Table 1 and the results obtained is depicted in Fig. 5. It is inferred that proposed framework with rank 20 provides better accuracy as compared with the state-of-the-art algorithms. The CMC rate obtained for the person Re-ID using GEI, Gabor, RMI, GEI + Gabor, SDALF, context-based methods and the proposed fusion framework of Gabor + Skeleton RMI on i-LIDS is illustrated in Table 2. The CMC rate obtained for person Re-ID compared with non-contextual state-of-the-art methods is depicted in Table 3. It is inferred that, the proposed framework significantly provides better performance than the state-of-the-art methods.

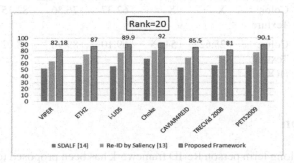

Fig. 5. CMC rate for the proposed person Re-ID framework and the state-of-the-art non contextual methods.

Table 2. The CMC rate obtained for person Re-ID using GEI, Gabor, RMI, GEI + Gabor and proposed RMI + Gabor for i-LIDS

Rank	r = 1	r = 5	r = 10	r = 15	r = 20
(2009) Context-based method [9]	16.15	39.71	48.12	54.52	60.13
(2013) SDALF	17.43	41.44	50.00	56.72	63.35
(2012) RMI	16.30	35.90	52.50	62.30	70.29
(2015) GEI + Gabor [17]	22.11	51.32	64.37	75.42	82.18
(2015) Gabor [17]	19.32	46.31	62.27	73.15	80.45
(2015) GEI [17]	13.27	31.52	49.15	58.55	67.18

Apart from this validation, the ablation study has been carried out with HOG, XCS-LBP, DPM, Gabor and Skeleton RMI. The entire proposed system is experimented with only HOG for person detection. Unfortunately, missing detection and false detection rate is high in sudden illumination conditions and near/far field of views and it is illustrated in Fig. 2a and Fig. 2c respectively. It has been overcome by the proposed fusion framework and it is illustrated in 2b and Fig. 2d. This experimentation validates the fusion of XCS-LBP and HOG as well as Gabor and skeleton RMI features for person detection and Re-ID.

Table 3. The CMC rate, Training Time (TT (ms)) and Testing Time (TS (ms)) for the proposed person Re-ID framework and the state-of-the-art non contextual methods for i-LIDS

Passive Approach	Features	Rank in % (Accuracy)				Computational Time	
		1	5	10	20	TT	TS
(2011) CPS [5]	Color	21.84	X	57.21	X	70.12	0.010
(2013) SDALF [14]	Color, Texture	X	X	X	50-60	80.18	0.012
(2012) Re-ID Attributes [10]	Color, Texture	15-32	43-53	36-63	X	90.03	0.017
(2013) Re-ID by Saliency [13]	Color, Texture	X	X	62.37	76.36	82.15	0.029
Proposed framework	Color, Texture, HOG	25.62	54.55	69.10	89.90	68.02	07.34

5   Conclusion

Non-contextual long term person Re-ID framework has been proposed to re-identify the person across multiple camera views under sudden illumination conditions. The combination of HOG and XCS-LBP improved the accuracy of person detection under sudden illumination conditions and at the same time it reduces the false positives. Subsequently DPM has been used on the detected persons. Afterwards, fusion of Appearance (Gabor) and Gait (Skeleton-RMI) features is proposed to overcome the homogeneity issue of distinguishing people even the texture and color of their attire are similar. When considering long term person Re-ID, possibility of wearing similar color and textured clothes by different persons is high. Hence, fusion of appearance and Gait features has been proposed. Even though deep learning booms, the limited dataset under the challenging conditions like sudden illumination encourages to h with traditional features. The future work aims to create such dataset in high dense crowd and to use deep learning to overcome severe occlusions.

References

1. Bedagkar-Gala, A., Shah, S.K.: A survey of approaches and trends in person re-identification. Image Vis. Comput. **32**(4), 270–286 (2014)
2. Datta, A., Brown, L.M., Feris, R., Pankanti, S.: Appearance modeling for person re-identification using Weighted Brightness Transfer Functions. In: International Conference on Pattern Recognition, Tsukuba, Japan, pp. 2367–2370 (2012)
3. Chen, L., Chen, H., Li, S., et al.: Person re-identification by color distribution fields. J. Chi. Comput. Syst. **38**(6), 1404–1408 (2017)
4. Yang, M., Wan, W., Hou, L., et al.: Person re-identification using human salience based on multi-feature fusion. In: International Conference on Smart and Sustainable City and Big Data, Shanghai, China, pp. 1–5 (2016)

5. Wang, X., Doretto, G., Sebastian, T., Rittscher, J., Tu, P.H.: Shape and appearance context modeling. In: International Conference on Computer Vision, Rio de Janiero, pp. 1–8 (2007)
6. Layne, R., Hospedales, T.M., Gong, S.: Towards person identification and re-identification with attributes. In: European conference on Computer Vision, Florence, Italy, pp. 402–412 (2012)
7. Vezzani, R., Balteiri, D., Cucchiara, R.: People reidentification in surveillance and forensics: a survey. ACM Comput. Surv. 46(2), 29 (2013)
8. Satta, R.: Appearance descriptors for person re-identification: a comprehensive review. In: International Conference on Computer Vision and Pattern Recognition, CoRR abs/1307.5748 (2013)
9. Dalal, N., Triggs, B.: Histograms of oriented gradients for human detection. In: Computer Society Conference on Computer Vision and Pattern Recognition, San Diego, CA, USA, pp. 886–893 (2005)
10. Ma, Y., Chen, X., Chen, G.: Pedestrian detection and tracking using HOG and oriented-LBP features. In: International Conference on Network and Parallel Computing, Changsha, China, pp. 176–184 (2011)
11. Silva, C., Bouwmans, T., Frelicot, C.: An eXtended center-symmetric local binary pattern for background modeling and subtraction in videos. In: International Joint Conference on Computer Vision, Imaging and Computer Graphics Theory and Applications, Berlin, Germany, pp. 1–8 (2015)
12. Yang, L., Jin, R.: Distance metric learning: a comprehensive survey. Technical report, Michigan State University (2006)
13. Zheng, W.S., Gong, S., Xiang, T.: Person re-identification by probabilistic relative distance comparison. In: International Conference on Computer Vision and Pattern Recognition, Washington, DC, pp. 649–656 (2011)
14. Yu, H.X., Wu, A., Zheng, W.S.: Symmetry-driven accumulation of local features for human characterization and re-identification. Comput. Vis. Image Underst. 117(2), 130–134 (2013)
15. Chen, J., Wang, Y., Qin, J., et al.: Fast person re-identification via cross-camera semantic binary transformation. In: IEEE Conference on Computer Vision and Pattern Recognition, Hawaii, USA, pp. 3873–3882 (2017)
16. Liu, Z., Zhang, Z., Wu, Q., Wang, Y.: Enhancing person re-identification by integrating gait biometric. Neurocomputing 168, 1144–1156 (2015)
17. Chen, J., Zhang, Z., Wang, Y.: Relevance metric learning for person re-identification by exploiting listwise similarities. IEEE Trans. Image Process. 24(12), 1657–1662 (2015)
18. Li, W., Zhao, R., Xiao, T., et al.: Deepreid: deep filter pairing neural network for person re-identification. In: IEEE Conference on Computer Vision and Pattern Recognition, Columbus, OH, USA, pp. 152–159 (2014)
19. Felzenszwalb, P.F., Girshick, R.B., McAllester, D., Ramanan, D.: Object detection with discriminatively trained part based models. IEEE Trans. Pattern Anal. Mach. Intell. 32(9), 1627–1645 (2010)
20. Li, X., Wang, K., Wang, W., Li, Y.: A multiple object tracking method using Kalman filter. In: International Conference on Information and Automation, Harbin, pp. 1862–1866 (2010)
21. Liu, C., Wechsler, H.: Gabor feature based classification using the enhanced fisher linear discriminant model for face recognition. IEEE Trans. Image Process. 11(4), 467–476 (2002)

Artificially Intelligent Game Framework Based on Facial Expression Recognition

Itisha Patidar, Karan Sanjay Modh, and Chiranjoy Chattopadhyay(✉)

Indian Institute of Technology Jodhpur, Jodhpur, India
{patidar.1,modh.1,chiranjoy}@iitj.ac.in

Abstract. During gameplay, a player experiences emotional turmoil. In most of the cases, these emotions directly reflect the outcome of the game. Adapting game features based on players' emotions necessitates a way to detect the current emotional state. Researchers in the area of "video game user research" has studied biometric data as a way to address the diverse characteristics of players, their individual preferences, gameplay expertise, and experiences. Identification of the player's current state is fundamental for designing a game, which interacts with the player adaptively. In this paper, we present an artificially intelligent game framework with smart features based on automatic facial expression recognition and adaptive game features based on the gamer's emotion. The gamer's emotions are recognized at run-time during gameplay using Deep Convolutional Neural Networks (CNN), and the game is adapted accordingly to the emotional condition. Once identified, these features directly modify critical parameters of the underlying game engine to make the game more exciting and challenging.

Keywords: Facial expression recognition · Deep learning · CNN · Game engine · User experience · Game interface

1 Introduction

Articial Intelligence (AI) has seen tremendous progress in recent years. It is a prosperous research field containing a cumulative number of vital research areas, as well as an essential technology for a growing number of application areas. AI in games was started with board games, and then slowly graduated into video games, where researchers are making a significant contribution in terms of developing new algorithms for the game engine, rendering, human-computer interaction, etc. As a result, video games, in their present form, have become intelligent. Analyzing game statistics and learning the critical performance parameters have been the area of interest to many AI researchers. In the literature there has been efforts to combine biometry based feedback for making the game engaging. For facial expression recognition works like [8,10,14,15,17] have demonstrated significant contribution. Also there were efforts to create a dataset [6] solely based on the expressions of the player while playing the game. Apart from emotional

© Springer Nature Singapore Pte Ltd. 2020
R. V. Babu et al. (Eds.): NCVPRIPG 2019, CCIS 1249, pp. 312–321, 2020.
https://doi.org/10.1007/978-981-15-8697-2_29

states, efforts were made to capture the gamer's psychological and physiological states in the area of user experience research based on biometry and also game-user research through biometry [9,11]. In [1], a facial expression based game personalizing technique was proposed. Bio-feedback in games is another area where very recently researchers have started looking into and made significant contributions [4,7,13,16].

In this paper, we provide an artificially intelligent game framework that adapts to the users emotional status by analyzing the facial expression during game play. We hypothesize that a user will be happy on winning points bonus in the game. On the other hand, the user will be in a sad mood if the performance in the game is not well. Under this assumption, to make the game more engaging and to keep the gamer motivated, by introducing two key features. They are: (1) if the user is happy (i.e., the facial expression reflects happiness), then the game automatically adapts to itself and makes it more challenging, (2) for sad facial expression, we introduce reward for the gamer and thereby makes it engaging. One thing to be noted here is that we do not change the level of the game, which is by default is more challenging. We change the difficulty of the game in the same level by updating the critical parameters and features of game by interacting directly with the game engine.

The paper is organized in the following way: Section 2 presents the proposed framework in details. In Sect. 3, we present the details of the experimental studies. Finally Sect. 4 concludes the paper.

2   Proposed Framework

Figure 1 depicts the flow diagram of the proposed framework. There are three critical components in the framework, namely (i) Player's Emotion Recognition, (ii) Game Engine, (iii) Adaptation Rules. In the following subsections, we present the details of the proposed artificially intelligent game framework.

2.1   Player's Emotion Recognition

We leveraged the *Mememoji* [3] model to extract the facial emotions of the user in real time, and adapted it as per the requirements. Figure 2 depicts the overall facial expression recognition framework. OpenCV was used for face detection in the image. Detection of objects in an image using Haar feature-based cascade classifiers has proven to be an effective method. In this work, we have used the Viola-Jones Face Detection technique [12] to detect and crop the face of the gamer from the input video stream. Next, to ensure that all the face images are of the same dimension, the cropped regions are converted into 48×48 sized grayscale images. The resultant matrix is linearized into an array of dimension $1 \times 48 \times 48$ and fed into the input layer. The input vector goes through the Convolution2D layer. The filters in the convolutional layer is a small matrix of size 3×3, which are convolved with the original image and yields a feature map.

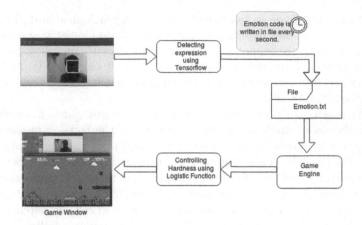

Fig. 1. Schematic representation of the proposed game framework.

The next processing stage is Pooling (in our case, Max Pooling is used) to reduce the dimension and results in computational efficiency. In this work, a $(2,2)$ pooling windows is used that scans through the feature map and keeps the maximum pixel value. The next processing stage is the dense layer or fully connected layers. It takes a large number of input features and transforms features through layers connected with trainable weights. These weights are trained by forwarding propagation of training data then backward propagation of its errors. The final segment in the network is the output layer, where the Softmax activation function is used. This output presents itself as a probability for each emotion class. To finalize the configuration of the network, we have conducted several experiments, and empirically determined the number of each type processing layers. In the end, the final neural network architecture that yielded the best performance has 9 convolution layers, and after three consecutive convolution layer, there is one max-pooling layer.

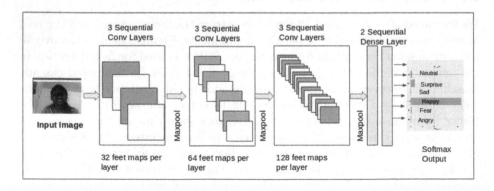

Fig. 2. Architecture of the convolutional neural network.

2.2   Game Engine

We consider the classical video game "SUPER MARIO BROS" and have made further enhancements to its game engine, and thereby making it adaptive to the individual player concerning experienced challenge applying PCG (Procedural Content Generation) [5]. The goal of our approach is to generate online game spaces such that the spaces optimize player to challenge for the individual player, by modeling the parameters like speed attributes, number of enemies, changing the abilities of the player, etc.

The working structure of the game is a huge Matrix, in which a map is loaded first based on the level which the user is playing. The map consists of blocks/bricks placed at individual squares of matrices, and also all enemies are loaded at the beginning and are called based on their position as a square of the matrix. A check on the state of the player is kept at every square of the matrix through which it passes, which responds whether the player is alive or dead. So we analyzed this structure and implemented the dynamic change of the game on each square of the matrix (where it checks for player state) and applied an algorithm to alter the attributes with the help of 'mathematical modeling' (discussed in Sect. 2.3) whenever the physiological states (emotions) of the players' changes. A key contribution of this work is that game personalization techniques can leverage novel computer vision-based techniques to infer player experiences automatically based on facial expression analysis unobtrusively.

2.3   Mathematical Modelling

Mathematical functions are used for personalizing the various parameters (listed in Table 1) of game depending on classifications of the user's facial expression – to the end of tailoring the affective game experience to the individual user. To dynamically change the game attributes we require a function which can regulate personalization such that the game remains playable and players' could remain engaged. To regulate the challenge level a *hardness parameter* (x) is used which at the start of game is set to zero. Player's emotions are then tracked using facial expression recognition model through out the entire duration of the game session, which are further used for sampling the hardness parameter. This is then applied on a mathematical function to give personalized game features depending on emotions.

Algorithm 1 is currently used for personalizing game features. The FER model gives percentage of distinct emotions, namely (0) angry, (1) fear, (2) happy, (3) sad, (4) surprise, and (5) neutral in an array, depending on the progress of the player through the Mario game. The index of expression with maximum percentage is taken as the expression code β. These expression code are then used for sampling hardness parameter x, which further optimizes game. The Algorithm 1 is called for every frame. For every 10th frame we take the decision and update the game, as shown in line no. 6 to 12. The sampling parameter shown in line no. 9 is taken as 2.5 for logistic function and 0 for linear function

Algorithm 1. Optimising game using Linear Function

```
1: procedure PERSONALIZE(E)                    ▷ E: Emotions array
2:     x ← 0
3:     α ← max(E)                              ▷ Maximum probability of an emotion
4:     β ← index(α, E)                         ▷ β: Expression code
5:     E.append(β)                             ▷ E: Expression array
6:     if E.Length = 10 then
7:         β ← mode(E)
8:     if β = 0 ∨ β = 1 ∨ β = 3  then
9:         x ← x − γ                           ▷ γ: Sampling parameter
10:    if β = 2 ∨ β = 4 then
11:        x ← x + γ
12:    map ← OPTIMIZEGAME(x)
```

Table 1. Various game parameters and their update rule.

List of Parameter		
Parameter	On positive valence	On negative valence
Speed on enemies	Increased	Decreased
Number of enemies	Increased	Decreased
Frequency of power Ups	Decreased	Increased

Linear Function. In this approach, linear functions were used to map classifications of the human player's facial expressions to appropriate in-game challenge levels. It was employed for optimising the challenge levels in the game such that the human interactions yield increased hardness level for positive valence (i.e., happiness, surprise), while decreasing hardness level for negative valence (i.e., fear, sad, anger) and no change for neutrality. Algorithm 2 optimizes the game based on the hardness parameter calculated from users affective states. This approach failed when emotional activity giving positive valence increases rapidly. The minions in game attains such a high speed that their trajectories do not even lie within the game frame. Also the number of minions increases very rapidly which flood the game frame making diversions which are uncontrollable.

Algorithm 2. Optimising game using Linear Function

```
1: procedure OPTIMIZEGAME(x)                   ▷ x: Hardness parameter
2:     if x > 0 then
3:         γ ← 1.5 × x                         ▷ γ: Challenge Level
4:     if x < 0 then
5:         γ ← 0.8 × x
6:     UPDATEGAME(γ)                           ▷ Update game parameters
```

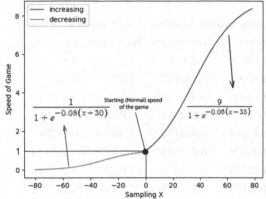

Fig. 3. Logistic functions for game personalization.

Logistic Function. The excessively high challenge levels imposes an unpleasant experience on game players. In order to avoid player abandonment resulting from an inappropriately high challenge level, a **logistic function** was formulated. This helped to remove the flaws of linear function by getting saturated after certain values of hardness parameter. Additionally, it also provided a cushion, in the form of graceful increase/decrease. We not only take into consideration player assessments made during actual play of the game, but also the playable conditions of the game as we observed during observational period many game players express high emotional activity, which could lead to extreme increase of speed or flood the game with enemies. To avoid such scenarios logistic function is useful by streamlining and controlling the flow from point of entry to the end of game. The logistic functions formulated for the algorithm as:

$$f(x) = \frac{1}{1 + e^{-}0.08(x + 30)} \tag{1}$$

The above function (Eq. 1) decreases the challenge levels in the face of user anger, while the following (Eq. 2) increases the challenge levels in the face of

---

Algorithm 3. Optimising game using Logistic Function

1: **procedure** OPTIMIZEGAME(x)   ▷ x: Hardness parameter
2:     **if** $x < 0$ **then**
3:         $\gamma \leftarrow \frac{1}{1 + e^{-}0.08(x + 30)}$ ▷ γ: Challenge Level
4:     **if** $x \geq 0$ **then**
5:         $\gamma \leftarrow \frac{9}{1 + e^{-}0.06(x - 35)}$
6:     UPDATEGAME(γ)   ▷ Update game parameters

Table 2. Comparative analysis of logistic and linear functions.

Using logistic function		Using linear function	
Increasing	Decreasing	Increasing	Decreasing
2.12098	0.90025	1.5	0.8
2.27666	0.880797	2.25	0.64
2.44998	0.858149	3.375	0.512
2.64183	0.832018	5.0625	0.4096
2.85283	0.802184	7.59375	0.32768
3.08328	0.768525	11.3906	0.262144
3.33303	0.731059	17.0859	0.209715
3.60145	0.689974	25.6289	0.167772
3.88739	0.645656	38.4434	0.134218
4.18909	0.598688	57.665	0.107374

user neutrality or happiness.

$$g(x) = \frac{9}{1 + e^{-}0.06(x - 35)} \tag{2}$$

Thereby, the online personalizing method operates as expected. Algorithm 3 optimizes game based on the hardness parameter calculated from users affective states. Graphs for these functions are shown in the Fig. 3. Table 2 shows how challenge level changes using both the functions, hence one can observe the need to discard the idea of linear function. The *updateGame* function call at line number 6 in Algorithm 2 and 3 updates the critical parameters of the game.

3   Experiments

Experiments were conducted on a computer having Ubuntu 18.04 with Intel i5 processor, and 8 GB memory. The entire programming was done on OpenCV, Keras and TensorFlow for face expression recognition, while SDL2 and CMake packages were used for the Mario game engine [2].

3.1   Methodology

We analyzed our system on the age group of 15–20 where participants interacted with the game under controlled experimental conditions like proper lighting, face exposed to the web cam for the entire duration, game starting at neutral hardness level. Our hypothesis is that the game would change its hardness level in correspondence to the emotional state of the user. We observed that the maximum

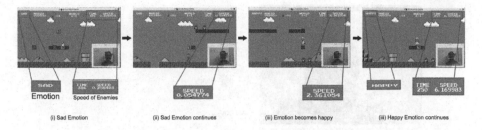

Fig. 4. Schematic representation of variation of speed based on user's emotion. (i) As the user is Sad, the speed is less than normal i.e. 1. (ii) User continues to remain sad and hence the speed even decreases more. (iii) User becomes happy and the speed increases above the normal level i.e. 1. (iv) User remains happy and speed keeps increasing.

facial expressions were changed with 15–18 age group while with participants of higher ages the maximum observed emotion was sad and game decreased gradually. We observe the general trend where the algorithm decreases the hardness levels in the face of user anger, sad or fear and increases the hardness levels in the user's emotion of surprise or happiness, hence validating our approach. Thereby, the mathematical model along with FER algorithm operates as expected. Also the framework maintains the levels in neutral face.

3.2 Qualitative Results

The mostly observed pattern showed that hardness is initially decreased because of "sad" levels. However, later in the game, high "neutral" and "happy" levels cause a increase in the hardness level. When lastly the "happy" emotion disappears, the hardness level becomes stable as well. Furthermore, we observe that the mathematical model appears stable in the face of classification noise, i.e. when the human player suddenly expresses a "mix" of emotions; denoting, in practise, that the player is talking or moving too much. As expected, the associated hardness level remains stable in the face of this noise from the facial expression classifier. This phenomenon is also in unison with our hypothesis.

Figure 4 shows the series of frames depicting the speed of enemies and emotion of the player. The facial expression is shown as inset to the frame. It can be observed from Fig. 4 (i) and (ii) that when the emotion continues to be sad for sometime, the speed parameter (that controls the speed of the enemies) is reduced to make the game easy, and thereby allowing the gamer to avoid the enemies and collect the bonus points. On the other hand, in Fig. 4 (iii) and (iv) depicts the situation when the gamer is happy. Here, the enemy speed is increased to make the game more challenging.

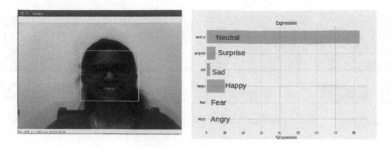

Fig. 5. Expression being wrongly recognized.

3.3 Failure Cases

As per the current model, the failure cases includes the following cases: (i) expression being recognized wrongly and (ii) expression not being recognized at all. For (i), expression recognized is not the correct expression. For example, the actual expression is 'happy', however, it being recognized as 'neutral'. In such a scenario, our model would work according to the expression recognized, which is not expected (ideally). The solution to such scenario is design of a better by improving the efficiency of FER module. For he later scenario, there will be no effect on the game since no expression is detected. Case (ii) occurs when the player is (a) not in-front of the camera, (b) at a distance of more that 60 cm from the camera, or (c) in dark room/low lighting area. In terms of game, our Linear model failed since it increased or decreased the game speed to such an extent such that it is not playable, hence owing to this failure we came up with Logistic Model to control the hardness of the game. Moreover, if the game is exposed to multiple faces at the same time with different expressions, then the model recognizes multiple expressions at the same time and hence the result is not favorable. This issue can be resolved using single-face FER detection model. Figure 5 shows the failure case when the expression 'happy' is wrongly recognised as 'Neutral'.

4 Conclusion and Future Work

In this paper, we presented a framework for changing the properties of a game when played based on classifications of the user's facial expression. A significant contribution of this paper is that the proposed technique unobtrusive in nature, and does not required the game player to be conscious about it. In this paper, we augmented the Mario game engine and manipulate its features through Facial Emotions recognition. For future work, we will investigate how to make the framework more robust by learning the game engine features, and trying to generalize the method of game personalization.

References

1. Blom, P.M., et al.: Towards personalised gaming via facial expression recognition. In: AAAI, pp. 30–36 (2014)
2. Jakowski, L.: umario. https://github.com/jakowskidev/uMario_Jakowski
3. Jostine, H.: Mememoji. https://github.com/JostineHo/mememoji
4. Leahy, A., Clayman, C., Mason, I., Lloyd, G., Epstein, O.: Computerised biofeedback games: a new method for teaching stress management and its use in irritable bowel syndrome. J. R. Coll. Physicians Lond. **32**(6), 552–556 (1998)
5. Lelis, L.H.S., Reis, W.M.P., Gal, Y.: Procedural generation of game maps with human-in-the-loop algorithms. IEEE T-G **10**(3), 271–280 (2018)
6. Li, W., Abtahi, F., Tsangouri, C., Zhu, Z.: Towards an "In-the-Wild" emotion dataset using a game-based framework. arXiv e-prints (2016)
7. Lobel, A., Gotsis, M., Reynolds, E., Annetta, M., Engels, R.C., Granic, I.: Designing and utilizing biofeedback games for emotion regulation: the case of nevermind. In: CHI EA, pp. 1945–1951 (2016)
8. Lopes, A.T., de Aguiar, E., Souza, A.F.D., Oliveira-Santos, T.: Facial expression recognition with convolutional neural networks: coping with few data and the training sample order. PR **61**, 610–628 (2017)
9. Mirza-Babaei, P., Nacke, L., Fitzpatrick, G., White, G., McAllister, G., Collins, N.: Biometric storyboards: visualising game user research data, May 2012
10. Mollahosseini, A., Chan, D., Mahoor, M.H.: Going deeper in facial expression recognition using deep neural networks. In: WACV, pp. 1–10 (2016)
11. babaei Pejman, M., Sebastian, L., Emma, F.: Understanding the contribution of biometrics to games user research. In: DiGRA International Conference: Think Design Play, January 2011
12. Viola, P., Jones, M.J.: Robust real-time face detection. IJCV **57**(2), 137–154 (2004)
13. Weerdmeester, J., van Rooij, M., Harris, O., Smit, N., Engels, R.C., Granic, I.: Exploring the role of self-efficacy in biofeedback video games. In: CHI PLAY, pp. 453–461 (2017)
14. Bai, Y., Guo, L., Jin, L., Huang, Q.: A novel feature extraction method using pyramid histogram of orientation gradients for smile recognition. In: ICIP (2009)
15. Yao, A., Shao, J., Ma, N., Chen, Y.: Capturing au-aware facial features and their latent relations for emotion recognition in the wild. In: ICMI (2015)
16. Zafar, M.A., Ahmed, B., Al-Rihawi, R., Gutierrez-Osuna, R.: Gaming away stress: using biofeedback games to learn paced breathing. IEEE T-AC **11**, 519–531 (2018)
17. Zhang, J., Huang, K., Yu, Y., Tan, T.: Boosted local structured hog-lbp for object localization. In: CVPR, pp. 1393–1400 (2011)

A Performance Evaluation of Loss Functions for Deep Face Recognition

Yash Srivastava, Vaishnav Murali, and Shiv Ram Dubey[✉]

Computer Vision Group, Indian Institute of Information Technology,
Chittor, Sri City, A.P., India
{srivastava.y15,murali.v15,srdubey}@iiits.in

Abstract. Face recognition is one of the most widely publicized feature in the devices today and hence represents an important problem that should be studied with the utmost priority. As per the recent trends, the Convolutional Neural Network (CNN) based approaches are highly successful in many tasks of Computer Vision including face recognition. The loss function is used on the top of CNN to judge the goodness of any network. In this paper, we present a performance comparison of different loss functions such as Cross-Entropy, Angular Softmax, Additive-Margin Softmax, ArcFace and Marginal Loss for face recognition. The experiments are conducted with two CNN architectures namely, ResNet and MobileNet. Two widely used face datasets namely, CASIA-Webface and MS-Celeb-1M are used for the training and benchmark Labeled Faces in the Wild (LFW) face dataset is used for the testing.

Keywords: Deep learning · CNN · Loss functions · Face recognition

1 Introduction

Unconstrained face recognition is one of the most challenging problems of computer vision. With numerous use cases like criminal identification, attendance systems, face-unlock systems, etc., face recognition has become a part of our day to day lives. The simplicity of using these recognition tools is one of the major reasons for its widespread adoption in industrial and administrative use. Many scientists and researchers have been working on various techniques to obtain an accurate and robust face recognition mechanism as its use will increase exponentially in coming years.

In 2012, the revolutionary work presented by Krizhevsky et al. [9] with Convolutional Neural Networks (CNN) was one of the major breakthroughs in the image recognition area and won the ImageNet Large Scale Challenge. Various CNN based approaches have been proposed for the face recognition task in the past few years. Most of the techniques dealt with including all the complexities and non-linearities needed for the problem and thus obtaining more generalized features and achieving state-of-the-art accuracies over major face datasets like LFW [8], etc. Since 2012, many deep learning based face recognition frameworks

© Springer Nature Singapore Pte Ltd. 2020
R. V. Babu et al. (Eds.): NCVPRIPG 2019, CCIS 1249, pp. 322–332, 2020.
https://doi.org/10.1007/978-981-15-8697-2_30

like DeepFace [20], DeepID [18], FaceNet [16], etc. have come up, easily surpassing the performance obtained via hand-crafted methods with a great margin.

The rise in the performance in image recognition was observed along with the line of increasing depth of the CNN architectures such as GoogLeNet [19] and ResNet [6]. Whereas, it is found that after certain depth, the performance tends to saturate towards mean accuracy, i.e., more depth has almost no effect over performance [6]. At the same time, large scale application of face recognition would be prohibitive due to the need of high computational resources for deep architectures. Thus, in recent years, researchers are also working over the other aspects of the CNN model like loss functions, nonlinearities, optimizers, etc. One of the major works done in this field includes the development of suitable loss functions, specifically designed for face recognition. Early works towards loss functions include Center Loss [23] and Triplet Loss [16] which focused on reducing the distance between the current sample and positive sample and increase the distance for the negative ones, thus closely relating to human recognition. Recent loss functions like Soft-Margin Softmax Loss [10], Congenerous Cosine Loss [13], Minimum Margin Loss [22], Range Loss [27], L_2-Softmax Loss [15], Large-Margin Softmax Loss [11], and A-Softmax Loss [12] have shown promising performance over lighter CNN models and some exceeding results over large CNN models.

Motivated by the recent rise in face recognition performance due to loss functions, this paper provides an extensive performance comparison of recently proposed loss functions for deep face recognition. Various experiments are conducted in this study to judge the performance of different loss functions from different aspects like effect of architecture such as deep and light weight and effect of training dataset. The results are analyzed using the training accuracy, test accuracy and rate of convergence. This paper is divided into following sections. Section 2 gives a comparative overview of the popular loss functions. Section 3 describes the CNN architectures used. Section 4 discusses the training and testing setup. Section 5 presents the results. Section 6 concludes the paper.

2   Loss Functions Used

As discussed in the earlier section, loss functions play an important role in CNN training. In this study, we discuss the widely used loss functions in face recognition. We have considered five loss functions, namely, Cross-Entropy Loss [18], Angular-Softmax Loss [12], Additive Margin Softmax Loss [21], ArcFace Loss [2], and Marginal Loss [3]. Some loss functions like Angular-Softmax Loss and Additive Margin Softmax Loss etc. are proposed specifically for the face recognition task.

Cross-Entropy Loss: The cross-entropy loss is one of the most widely used loss functions in deep learning for many applications [4], [9]. It is also known as softmax loss and has been proven quite effective in eliminating outliers in face recognition task as well [14], [18]. The cross-entropy loss is given as,

$$\mathcal{L}_{CE} = -\frac{1}{N} \sum_{i=1}^{N} \log \frac{e^{W_{y_i}^T x_i + b_{y_i}}}{\sum_{j=1}^{n} e^{W_j^T x_i + b_j}}, \tag{1}$$

where W is the weight matrix, b is the bias term, x_i is the ith training sample, y_i is the class label for i^{th} training sample, N is the number of samples, W_j and W_{y_i} are the jth and y_i^{th} column of W, respectively. The loss function has been used in the initial works done for face recognition tasks like the DeepID2 [18], which has formed the foundation for current work in the domain.

Angular-Softmax Loss: Liu et al. in 2017 published one of the many modifications to softmax function to introduce margin based learning. They proposed the Angular-Softmax (A-Softmax) loss that enables CNNs to learn angularly discriminative features [12]. It is defined as,

$$\mathcal{L}_{AS} = -\frac{1}{N} \sum_{i=1}^{N} \log \left(\frac{e^{\|x_i\| \psi(\theta_{y_i,i})}}{e^{\|x_i\| \psi(\theta_{y_i,i})} + \sum_{j \neq y_i} e^{\|x_i\| \cos(\theta_{j,i})}} \right) \tag{2}$$

where x_i is the ith training sample, $\psi(\theta_{y_i,i}) = (-1)^k \cos(m\theta_{y_i,i}) - 2k$ for $\theta_{y_i,i} \in [\frac{k\pi}{m}, \frac{(k+1)\pi}{m}]$, $k \in [0, m-1]$ and $m \geq 1$ is an integer that controls the size of angular margin. The performance of this function has been impressive, which has given a base for various margin based loss functions including CosineFace [21] and ArcFace [2].

Additive-Margin Softmax Loss: Motivated from the improved performance of SphereFace using Angular-Softmax Loss, Wang et al. have worked on an additive margin for softmax loss and given a general function for large margin property [21], described in following Equation,

$$\psi(\theta) = cos\theta - m. \tag{3}$$

Using this margin, the authors have proposed the following loss function,

$$\mathcal{L}_{AM} = -\frac{1}{N} \sum_{i=1}^{N} \log \frac{e^{s \cdot (cos\theta_{y_i} - m)}}{e^{s \cdot (cos\theta_{y_i} - m)} + \sum_{j=1, j \neq y_i}^{c} e^{s \cdot cos\theta_j}} \tag{4}$$

where a hyper-parameter s as suggested in [21] is used to scale up the cosine values.

ArcFace Loss: Based on the above loss functions, Deng et al. have proposed a new margin $\cos(\theta + m)$ [2], which they state to be more stringent for classification. The angular margin [2] represents the best geometrical interpretation as compared to SphereFace and CosineFace. The ArcFace Loss function using angular margin is formulated as,

$$\mathcal{L}_{AF} = -\frac{1}{N} \sum_{i=1}^{N} \log \frac{e^{s \cdot (\cos(\theta_{y_i} + m))}}{e^{s \cdot (\cos(\theta_{y_i} + m))} + \sum_{j=1, j \neq y_i}^{n} e^{s \cdot \cos\theta_j}}, \tag{5}$$

where s is the radius of the hypersphere, m is the additive angular margin penalty between x_i and W_{y_i}, and $cos(\theta + m)$ is the margin, which makes the class-separations more stringent. The ArcFace loss function has shown improved performance over the LFW dataset. Its performance is also very promising over the large-scale MegaFace dataset for face identification.

Marginal Loss: In 2017, Deng et al. proposed the Marginal Loss function [3] which works simultaneously to maximize the inter-class distances as well as to minimize the intra-class variations, both being desired features of a loss function. In order to do so, the Margin Loss function focuses on the marginal samples. It is given as,

$$\mathcal{L}_{\mathrm{M}} = \frac{1}{N^2 - N} \sum_{i,j,i \neq j}^{N} \left(\xi - y_{ij} \left(\theta - \left\| \frac{x_i}{\|x_i\|} - \frac{x_j}{\|x_j\|} \right\|_2^2 \right) \right) \qquad (6)$$

The term $y_{ij} \epsilon \{\pm 1\}$ indicates whether the faces x_i and x_j are from the same class or not, θ is the distance threshold to distinguish whether the faces are from the same person or not, and ξ is the error margin besides the classification hyperplane [3]. The final Marginal Loss function is defined as the joint supervision with regular Cross-Entropy (Softmax) Loss function and is given as,

$$\mathcal{L}_{\mathrm{ML}} = \mathcal{L}_{\mathrm{CE}} + \lambda \mathcal{L}_{\mathrm{M}} \qquad (7)$$

where $\mathcal{L}_{\mathrm{CE}}$ is the cross-entropy (Softmax) Loss (Eq. 1). The hyper-parameter λ is used for balancing the two losses. Usage of cross-entropy loss provides separable features and prevents the marginal loss from degrading to zeros [3].

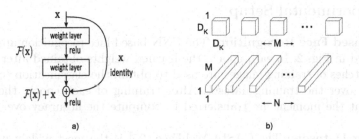

Fig. 1. (a) Basic residual block used in ResNet [6] which is a function where X is the input and $F(x)$ is the function on X and X is added to the output of $F(X)$. (b) MobileNet uses two different convolution to reduce the computation. Here, D_k is the filter size and M is the input dimension. Next, N filters of 1×1 dimension with M depth are used to get output of the same dimension of D_k output with depth on N. The Figures are taken from their respective papers.

3   Network Architectures

The CNNs have shown great performance for face recognition. We use the ResNet and MobileNet models to test over high performance and mobile platform scenarios.

ResNet Model: He et al. proposed a novel ResNet architecture which won the ImageNet challenge in 2015. The ResNet architecture is made with the building blocks of residual units. The Fig. 1(a) demonstrate a residual unit. The ResNet unit learns a mapping between inputs and outputs using residual connections [17]. This approach eliminates the problem of vanishing gradient as the identity mapping provides a clear pathway for the gradients to pass through the network. ResNet has proven to be a quite effective for a wide variety of vision tasks like image recognition, object detection and image segmentation. Hence, it makes the architecture one of the pioneer ensembles for face recognition tasks as visible from its many variants including ResNeXt [24] and SphereFace [12]. In this paper, ResNet50 is used by keeping in mind the primary objective of evaluating efficiency of loss functions on standard architectures.

MobileNet: In 2017, Howard et al. presented a class of efficient architectures named MobileNets. These CNN models were designed with the primary aim of achieving efficient performance for mobile vision applications. This model uses the depth-wise separable convolutions as proposed by Chollet for the Xception architecture [1]. The building blocks for MobileNet are portrayed in Fig. 1(b). The MobileNet architecture facilitates to build a light weight deep learning model. This model has shown the promising results over various vision based applications like object detection, face attributes and large scale Geolocalization with an efficient trade-off between latency and accuracy.

4   Experimental Setup

CNN based Face Recognition: The CNN based face recognition approach is illustrated in Fig. 2. In each epoch, the learned weights obtained after training on all batches of training images are used to obtain the classification scores and accuracy over the training dataset. After training of each epoch, the trained weights at the moment are transferred to compute the accuracy over the test dataset.

Training Datasets: The CASIA-WebFace [25] is the most widely used publicly available face dataset. It contains 4,94,414 face images belonging to 10,575 different individuals. The original MS-Celeb-1M dataset [5] consists of 100k face identities with each identity having approximately 100 images resulting in about 10M images, which are scraped from public search engines. We have used a refined high-quality subset based on the clean list released by ArcFace [2] authors. Finally, we obtained the MS-Celeb-1M dataset which contains 350k images with 8750 unique identities.

Testing Dataset: Labeled Faces in the Wild (LFW) images [8] are used as the testing dataset in this study. The LFW dataset contains 13,233 images of faces collected from the web. This dataset consists of the 5749 identities with 1680

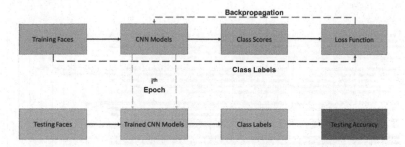

Fig. 2. Training and testing framework for performance evaluation of loss functions using CNN's. The ith epoch represents the transfer of the trained model after i^{th} epoch's for testing.

people with two or more images. By following the standard LFW evaluation protocol [7], we have reported the verification accuracies on 6000 face pairs.

Input Data and Network Settings: We have used MTCNN [26] to detect facial landmarks to align the face images, similar to [2,3,12]. Each pixel in these images is normalized by subtracting 127.5 and then being divided by 128. We have set the batch size as 64 with the initial learning rate as 0.01. The learning rate is divided by 10 at the 8th, 12th and 16th epoch. The model is trained up to 20 epochs. The number of epochs is less because the number of batches in an epoch is very high. The SGD optimizer with momentum is used for the optimization. The momentum and weight decay are set at 0.9 and $5e^{-4}$, respectively.

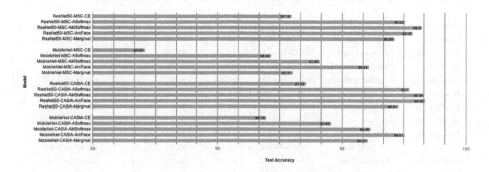

Fig. 3. Highest test accuracies obtained over LFW dataset for different models under consideration in this study. These models have been trained on two datasets as described in the paper. The naming convention is as follows: Model Name-Training Dataset-Loss Function. Here, 'CASIA' refers to CASIA-Webface and 'MSC' refers to MS-Celeb-1M face datasets. For loss functions, 'CE' refers to Cross Entropy loss, 'ASoftmax' refers to the Angular Softmax loss and 'AMSoftmax' refers to Additive Margin Softmax loss.

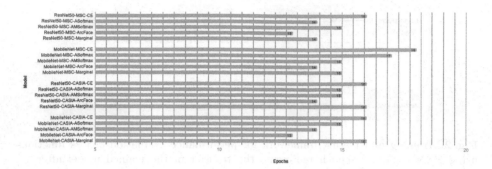

Fig. 4. The minimum number of epochs taken to obtain the best model for a given loss function. The best model of a loss function gives the highest accuracy on LFW dataset. The naming convention is same as Fig. 3.

Table 1. The training accuracies and testing accuracies obtained over LFW dataset performance comparison over two CNN architectures: ResNet50 and MobileNetv1 when trained on CASIA-Webface and MS-Celeb-1M datasets. The column 'Training Accuracy' represents the accuracy obtained after training the model till 20th epoch. The term 'Epochs' in the table signify the number of epochs at which we obtain the best model accuracy on LFW. The loss function AM Softmax refer to Angular-Margin Softmax. The last column, 'Mean', denotes the mean of the test accuracies between the 10th and 20th epoch with the standard deviation in the same interval.

Base model	Loss function	Training dataset	Train Acc	Test Acc	**Epochs**	Mean accuracy
ResNet 50	Cross entropy	CASIA-Webface	93.51	97.42	16	95.86 ± 1.262
ResNet 50	Cross entropy	MS-Celeb-1M	92.43	97.19	16	95.84 ± 1.254
ResNet 50	Angular softmax	CASIA-Webface	94.01	99.10	15	98.51 ± 0.625
ResNet 50	Angular softmax	MS-Celeb-1M	93.33	99.02	14	98.28 ± 0.839
ResNet 50	AM softmax	CASIA-Webface	94.37	99.34	15	98.65 ± 1.044
ResNet 50	AM softmax	MS-Celeb-1M	93.68	99.3	15	98.13 ± 1.643
ResNet 50	ArcFace	CASIA-Webface	94.54	99.35	14	99.01 ± 0.305
ResNet 50	ArcFace	MS-Celeb-1M	92.34	99.15	13	98.06 ± 1.532
ResNet 50	Marginal loss	CASIA-Webface	93.87	98.91	16	96.43 ± 1.401
ResNet 50	Marginal loss	MS-Celeb-1M	91.57	98.84	14	97.86 ± 0.669
MobileNet v1	Cross entropy	CASIA-Webface	93.42	96.78	16	95.59 ± 1.030
MobileNet v1	Cross entropy	MS-Celeb-1M	93.91	94.83	18	93.03 ± 1.539
MobileNet v1	Angular softmax	CASIA-Webface	92.47	97.83	15	96.34 ± 1.120
MobileNet v1	Angular softmax	MS-Celeb-1M	93.45	96.86	17	95.80 ± 0.803
MobileNet v1	AM softmax	CASIA-Webface	95.12	98.46	14	97.48 ± 0.913
MobileNet v1	AM softmax	MS-Celeb-1M	94.10	97.65	15	96.47 ± 1.165
MobileNet v1	ArcFace	CASIA-Webface	92.31	99.01	13	97.33 ± 0.477
MobileNet v1	ArcFace	MS-Celeb-1M	94.61	98.43	14	97.33 ± 1.086
MobileNet v1	Marginal loss	CASIA-Webface	93.15	98.41	16	97.10 ± 1.428
MobileNet v1	Marginal loss	MS-Celeb-1M	93.81	97.21	15	95.90 ± 1.504

5 Performance Evaluation and Observations

The loss functions as described in Sect. 2 are used with ResNet50 and MobileNetv1 CNN architectures to perform the training over MS-Celeb-1M and CASIA-Webface datasets and testing over LFW dataset. Here, we give a comparison of results based on test accuracies, rate of convergence and training and testing results.

5.1 Test Accuracy Comparison

The different models have shown diverse performance when evaluated on the LFW dataset for face recognition. As evident from Fig. 3, the two CNN architectures, ResNet50 and MobileNetv1 when trained on two face datasets, namely MS-Celeb-1M and CASIA-Webface show a varied performance of face recognition tasks. The best performing model obtained during the experiments is the ResNet50 model when trained on CASIA-Webface dataset using the ArcFace loss with an accuracy of 99.35% on LFW dataset. The observed performance of ArcFace also resonates with its results when obtained with MobileNet architecture. It can be observed that the highest accuracies of 99.01% and 98.43% using MobileNetv1 are obtained using the ArcFace loss function when trained over CASIA-Webface and MS-Celeb-1M datasets, respectively. However, when ArcFace loss is used with ResNet50 and trained with the MS-Celeb-1M dataset, its accuracy of 99.15% over LFW is slightly edged out by the Additive-Margin Softmax where we observed an accuracy of 99.30%, the third best performing model obtained in our experiments.

In view of loss functions, the overall performance observed is in the following decreasing order: ArcFace, Additive Margin Softmax, Angular Softmax, Marginal Loss and Cross Entropy (Softmax). The Angular Softmax and Marginal loss almost have a similar performance with the first performing better with ResNet50 model while the latter showing better results with MobileNet model. The performance of Cross-Entropy Loss is not as good when compared to other losses. It can be justified as other four losses are proposed as the improvements over the Cross-Entropy Loss. The Additive Margin softmax Loss performed close to ArcFace Loss when observed with ResNet50 architecture, but lagged behind when MobileNet architecture is used.

The performance difference observed for ArcFace Loss in ResNet and MobileNet architectures can be attributed to the base architecture itself. The ResNet 50 architecture used in our analysis is deep with 50 convolutional layers and residual modules. Whereas, the MobileNet architecture, has less number of convolutional layers and uses Depth Wise Separable Convolutions which tend to increase computation efficiency (for mobile devices) with certain tradeoffs. Moreover, the performance of other losses such as Angular Softmax, AM Softmax and Marginal loss is slightly lower than ArcFace due to the different ways of incorporating the margins.

Now coming to training datasets, we observed a distinct pattern when we evaluated models on LFW. The results that we obtained on both CNN architectures when trained on CASIA-Webface were comparatively better as compared to the same architectures trained on MS-Celeb-1M. One possibility for this observation stems out from the fact that MS-Celeb-1M contains more variations and even after extensive cleaning of the dataset as described in Sect. 4, there might be some existing noise as compared to CASIA-Webface.

5.2 Convergence Rate Comparison

In this paper, we define convergence rate in terms of the minimum number of epochs taken for a particular model to achieve it's highest test accuracy over LFW dataset. As discussed in the last section, a similar pattern of results is observed when we compare the convergence rate of loss functions for a same set of CNN architectures and training datasets. A comparison of convergence rate can be seen in Fig. 4. Again, the ArcFace loss has showed the fastest rate of convergence in all the models considered in this experiment. The ResNet architecture when trained on the MS-Celeb-1M dataset using ArcFace converged at 13th epoch, the lowest epoch value seen in our tests. The same result is also observed with ArcFace when using MobileNet with CASIA-Webface training dataset.

Considering the two CNN architectures, ResNet50 and MobileNet, we observed a distinct pattern in terms of convergence rate when both the architectures are trained on the MS-Celeb-1M dataset. The ResNet model converged faster when compared to the MobileNet model with most of the loss functions, with the exception of Additive Margin Softmax Loss which converged on the 15th epoch for both the architectures. On the other hand, when the performance of architectures is observed over CASIA-Webface training dataset, a similar rate of convergence was observed for almost all the models based on ResNet and MobileNet using test dataset.

5.3 Training and Testing Results Comparison

The training and testing accuracies obtained during the experiments are summarized in Table 1. The training accuracies reported in the table are obtained after training the model till the 20th epoch, that means after complete training of the model with the specified training dataset. Comparing the training accuracies, the highest accuracy of 95.12% is obtained with the Additive Margin Softmax Loss when used with MobileNetv1 architecture and trained on CASIA-Webface dataset.

We have also computed the mean and standard deviation of testing accuracies obtained between the 10th and the 20th epoch to obtain the more generic performance of the loss functions discussed in Sect. 2. These results also help us to observe the deviations of results between epochs as well as the convergence of the loss functions towards a saturation point. The highest mean accuracy of 99.01% was observed for the ArcFace Loss when trained over CASIA-Webface dataset using the ResNet50 architecture with the standard deviation of 0.305. It is also observed that the above standard deviation is the lowest obtained over all the models considered in the experiments. Such a low standard deviation reaffirms the better performance of the ArcFace Loss over the epochs when compared to other loss functions discussed before in this study. The above observation resonates with other results like test accuracies and rate of convergence that we noticed in the previous sections, hence solidifying our computation of results obtained during the experiments.

6 Conclusion

In this paper, we have presented a performance evaluation of recent loss functions with Convolutional Neural Networks for face recognition tasks. Recent loss functions like Angular-Softmax, Additive-Margin Softmax, ArcFace and Marginal Loss are compared and evaluated along with Cross-Entropy Loss. The ResNet50 and MobileNetv1 are used in our performance studies. Publicly available datasets like CASIA-Webface and MS-Celeb-1M are used for training the models. The performance is evaluated on the Labeled Faces in the Wild (LFW) dataset. The results are computed in terms of the training accuracy, test accuracy, and convergence rate. The ArcFace loss emerged as the best performing loss function with highest accuracy of 99.35% over CASIA-Webface dataset. We evaluated the state-of-the-art losses for deep face recognition, which can help to the research community to choose among the different loss functions.

Acknowledgment. This research is funded by Science and Engineering Research Board (SERB), Govt. of India under Early Career Research (ECR) scheme through SERB/ECR/2017/000082 project fund. We also gratefully acknowledge the support of NVIDIA Corporation with the donation of the GeForce Titan X Pascal GPU for our research.

References

1. Chollet, F.: Xception: deep learning with depthwise separable convolutions. CoRR abs/1610.02357 (2016)
2. Deng, J., Guo, J., Zafeiriou, S.: Arcface: additive angular margin loss for deep face recognition. arXiv preprint arXiv:1801.07698 (2018)
3. Deng, J., Zhou, Y., Zafeiriou, S.: Marginal loss for deep face recognition. In: IEEE CVPR Workshop on Faces "in-the-wild" (2017)
4. Goodfellow, I., Bengio, Y., Courville, A., Bengio, Y.: Deep Learning, vol. 1. MIT Press, Cambridge (2016)
5. Guo, Y., Zhang, L., Hu, Y., He, X., Gao, J.: MS-Celeb-1M: a dataset and benchmark for large-scale face recognition. In: Leibe, B., Matas, J., Sebe, N., Welling, M. (eds.) ECCV 2016. LNCS, vol. 9907, pp. 87–102. Springer, Cham (2016). https://doi.org/10.1007/978-3-319-46487-9_6
6. He, K., Zhang, X., Ren, S., Sun, J.: Deep residual learning for image recognition. In: IEEE CVPR, pp. 770–778 (2016)
7. Huang, G.B., Learned-Miller, E.: Labeled faces in the wild: updates and new reporting procedures. Department Computer Science University Massachusetts Amherst, Amherst, MA, USA, Technical report, pp. 14–003 (2014)

8. Huang, G.B., Mattar, M., Berg, T., Learned-Miller, E.: Labeled faces in the wild: a database for studying face recognition in unconstrained environments. In: Workshop on Faces in 'Real-Life' Images: Detection, Alignment, and Recognition (2008)
9. Krizhevsky, A., Sutskever, I., Hinton, G.E.: Imagenet classification with deep convolutional neural networks. In: NIPS, pp. 1097–1105 (2012)
10. Liang, X., Wang, X., Lei, Z., Liao, S., Li, S.Z.: Soft-margin softmax for deep classification. In: Liu D., Xie S., Li Y., Zhao D., El-Alfy ES. (eds) Neural Information Processing. ICONIP 2017. LNCS, vol. 10635. Springer, Cham (2017). https://doi.org/10.1007/978-3-319-70096-0_43
11. Liu, W., Wen, Y., Yu, Z., Yang, M.: Large-margin softmax loss for convolutional neural networks. ArXiv e-prints (2016)
12. Liu, W., Wen, Y., Yu, Z., Li, M., Raj, B., Song, L.: Sphereface: deep hypersphere embedding for face recognition. In: IEEE CVPR, vol. 1, p. 1 (2017)
13. Liu, Y., Li, H., Wang, X.: Learning deep features via congenerous cosine loss for person recognition. CoRR abs/1702.06890 (2017)
14. Parkhi, O.M., Vedaldi, A., Zisserman, A., et al.: Deep face recognition. In: BMVC (2015)
15. Ranjan, R., Castillo, C.D., Chellappa, R.: L2-constrained softmax loss for discriminative face verification. CoRR abs/1703.09507 (2017)
16. Schroff, F., Kalenichenko, D., Philbin, J.: Facenet: a unified embedding for face recognition and clustering. CoRR abs/1503.03832 (2015)
17. Srivastava, R.K., Greff, K., Schmidhuber, J.: Highway networks. CoRR abs/1505.00387 (2015)
18. Sun, Y., Chen, Y., Wang, X., Tang, X.: Deep learning face representation by joint identification-verification. In: NIPS, pp. 1988–1996 (2014)
19. Szegedy, C., Vanhoucke, V., Ioffe, S., Shlens, J., Wojna, Z.: Rethinking the inception architecture for computer vision. CoRR abs/1512.00567 (2015)
20. Taigman, Y., Yang, M., Ranzato, M., Wolf, L.: Deepface: closing the gap to human-level performance in face verification. In: IEEE CVPR, pp. 1701–1708, June 2014
21. Wang, F., Cheng, J., Liu, W., Liu, H.: Additive margin softmax for face verification. IEEE SPL 25(7), 926–930 (2018)
22. Wei, X., Wang, H., Scotney, B.W., Wan, H.: Minimum margin loss for deep face recognition. CoRR abs/1805.06741 (2018)
23. Wen, Y., Zhang, K., Li, Z., Qiao, Yu.: A discriminative feature learning approach for deep face recognition. In: Leibe, B., Matas, J., Sebe, N., Welling, M. (eds.) ECCV 2016. LNCS, vol. 9911, pp. 499–515. Springer, Cham (2016). https://doi.org/10.1007/978-3-319-46478-7_31
24. Xie, S., Girshick, R.B., Dollár, P., Tu, Z., He, K.: Aggregated residual transformations for deep neural networks. CoRR abs/1611.05431 (2016)
25. Yi, D., Lei, Z., Liao, S., Li, S.Z.: Learning face representation from scratch. arXiv preprint arXiv:1411.7923 (2014)
26. Zhang, K., Zhang, Z., Li, Z., Qiao, Y.: Joint face detection and alignment using multitask cascaded convolutional networks. IEEE SPL 23(10), 1499–1503 (2016)
27. Zhang, X., Fang, Z., Wen, Y., Li, Z., Qiao, Y.: Range loss for deep face recognition with long-tail. CoRR abs/1611.08976 (2016)

Image Processing and Document Analysis

Document Image Binarization Using U-Net

Dhara Kotecha(✉) and Manjunath V. Joshi

Dhirubhai Ambani Institute of Information and Communication Technology,
Gandhinagar, India
kotechadhara6@gmail.com, manjunath.joshi@gmail.com

Abstract. In this paper, we propose an algorithm to binarize the degraded document images. We incorporate U-Net for the task at hand. We model document image binarization as a classification problem wherein we generate an image which is a result of classification of each pixel as text or background. Optimizing the cross entropy loss function, we translate the input degraded image to the corresponding binarized image. Our approach of using U-Net ensures low level feature transfer from the input degraded image to the output binarized image and thus it is better than using a simple convolution neural network. Our method tries to obtain the desired results with suitable generalization. The results obtained are significantly better than the state-of-the-art techniques and the approach is simpler than other deep learning approaches for document image binarization.

Keywords: U-Net · Document Image Analysis · Image binarization · Deep learning.

1 Introduction

Document image analysis includes a set of techniques and algorithms to extract content from the document images. This content should be in a computer readable format. Graphics recognition, word spotting, document segmentation, Optical Character Recognition (OCR), etc. are few of the examples of document image analysis techniques. In the world of digitization, there has been an extensive amount of research on documents digitization. OCR is a very important step towards digitizing the documents. The main goal of OCR is to convert a document image into text which can be interpreted by a computer. The two main stages of OCR are text segmentation and character recognition. The scanned document images usually contain degradation such as dark background, stains, non-uniformity in the background, ink spreads, watermarks, logo in the background and non-uniformity in the illumination. In order to improve the performance of both these stages of OCR, the scanned documents are processed in order to enhance the content in the document. One of the pre-processing steps in document image analysis corresponds to document image binarization. This

© Springer Nature Singapore Pte Ltd. 2020
R. V. Babu et al. (Eds.): NCVPRIPG 2019, CCIS 1249, pp. 335–343, 2020.
https://doi.org/10.1007/978-981-15-8697-2_31

refers to identifying the text and the background pixels and converting the given document image into a binary image. It can also be considered as a form of text segmentation.

In the past, the proposed approaches on binarization included computing local or global thresholds based on image statistics [11,20]. However, in such techniques, the shape around the pixel is not taken into consideration. The techniques based on edge detection, Markov Random Field (MRF) modeling, connected components, etc. take into account the shape of the foreground. Fully Convolutional Neural Networks (FCN) classify the background and the foreground pixel based on the training data. Since these networks heavily downsample the images, they cannot be used directly for image to image translation task. We therefore propose to use a U-Net architecture [19] which has skip connections between layers. These skip connections promote direct transfer of features between layers.

2 Related Work

Statistical approaches such as applying global and local thresholds [11,20] on image statistics to binarize degraded document images were some of the earliest methods proposed for binarization. In such methods, based on the ground truth, a pixel intensity is considered as threshold and each pixel is classified as text or background based on this threshold. Global threshold method considers a single threshold value for the entire image while the approach based on local threshold has adaptive value depending on the surrounding pixels. Howe's method [4] uses Laplacian of the image to differentiate the foreground and the background. Here, the binarization problem is modeled as a MRF and the Laplacians contribute to the unary energy terms. The edge discontinuities are incorporated into smoothness terms and canny edge detection is incorporated to determine the pairwise connections. The energy function is then minimized with the help of min-cut/max-flow algorithms. Many variants of this method have been introduced with successful results.

A few classification approaches have also been explored. In [3], Hamza use Multi Layer Perceptron (MLP) for classification of pixels. The gray level intensities that represent the foreground components are identified by clustering technique called Self Organizing Maps (SOM) [7]. For a color image, SOM is trained on a part of the image. The neurons are then labeled using k-means clustering technique. After that, the labeled neurons are classified using MLP. In [1], Afzal propose document image binarization using Long Short-Term Memory (LSTM) in which the image is modeled as a 2D sequence of pixels to classify each pixel as a background or text component. The method considers local features initially and then propagates these features globally. J. Pastor-Pellicer incorporated a Convolution Neural Network (CNN) to classify the image pixels as background or foreground depending on it's 19 × 19 neighborhood pixels [12].

Wu trained a randomized tree classifier to classify the pixel. They used a variety of statistical features for training [23]. Long [8] proposed Fully Convolution

Neural Network (FCN) for solving semantic segmentation problem on natural images. However, because FCNs heavily down-sample images, content is lost and hence they cannot be directly incorporated for document image binarization. To take care of this, Tesmeyer propose an FCN that is operated on multiple image scales [21]. They also propose to use relative darkness feature in addition to the degraded image as an input to the network. This feature helps in improving the performance of the FCN network significantly. As pointed out already, down-sampling in CNNs degrades the performance in image to image translation as all the features from the initial layers are not used in the layers towards the end. Hence, we propose to use U-Net in our approach.

3 Proposed Method

We model document image binarization as image to image translation task (where the output image contains the class label of each pixel in the input degraded image) and propose a method to perform binarization using U-Net. The important text features in documents are low level features which need to be transferred from the input degraded image to the output binarized image. Hence, in order to encourage the transfer of low level features, we propose to use a U-Net architecture which takes a degraded image as input and outputs a binarized image. The U-Net is a convolutional neural network with two modules, the encoder part and the decoder part. In the encoder part, there are convolutional layers which down-sample the input image at every layer and extracts a feature vector. The extracted feature vector is then given as an input to the decoder part that generates an image by using transposed convolution layers by up-sampling the input feature vector. The U-Net has skip connections between layers i and n−i where n is the total number of layers. Thus the output at layer i is stacked with the output of layer n−i and given as an input to the layer n−i + 1. Our U-Net takes an input of size 256 × 256 × 3 as shown in Fig. 1. The blocks denote the Convolutional (C) and Transposed Convolutional (CT) layers. It can be seen that the output from the encoder layers are also used as

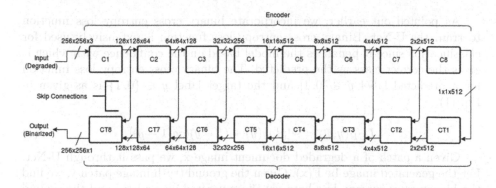

Fig. 1. Block schematic of U-Net.

an input to the decoder layers and thus the features are directly used from the encoder layers while decoding. Each layer is followed by a batch normalization [5] and a non-linearity layer. Note that, we have used Leaky ReLU and ReLU for non-linearity in the encoder and decoder layers respectively. We use ReLU in the decoder layer because the function of the decoder is to generate image and hence negative values are not desired. The last convolution layer in the decoder is followed by a sigmoid layer since the binarized image needs to have a value between 0 and 1 which indicates the probability of a pixel belonging to one of the two classes. The binarized output is an image of size $256 \times 256 \times 1$.

Table 1. U-Net Architecture [19]

Layer name	Input depth @ h x w	Filter N - depth @ h x w	Stride	Zero Padding	Result depth @ h x w
C1	3 @ 256 × 256	64 − 3 @ 4 × 4	2	1	64 @ 128 × 128
C2	64 @ 128 × 128	128 − 64 @ 4 × 4	2	1	128 @ 64 × 64
C3	128 @ 64 × 64	256 − 128 @ 4 × 4	2	1	256 @ 32 × 32
C4	256 @ 32 × 32	512 − 256 @ 4 × 4	2	1	512 @ 16 × 16
C5	512 @ 16 × 16	512 − 512 @ 4 × 4	2	1	512 @ 8 × 8
C6	512 @ 8 × 8	512 − 512 @ 4 × 4	2	1	512 @ 4 × 4
C7	512 @ 4 × 4	512 − 512 @ 4 × 4	2	1	512 @ 2 × 2
C8	512 @ 2 × 2	512 − 512 @ 4 × 4	2	1	512 @ 1 × 1
CT1	512 @ 1 × 1	512 − 512 @ 4 × 4	2	1	512 @ 2 × 2
CT2	1024 @ 2 × 2	512 − 1024 @ 4 × 4	2	1	512 @ 4 × 4
CT3	1024 @ 4 × 4	512 − 1024 @ 4 × 4	2	1	512 @ 8 × 8
CT4	1024 @ 8 × 8	512 − 1024 @ 4 × 4	2	1	512 @ 16 × 16
CT5	1024 @ 16 × 16	256 − 1024 @ 4 × 4	2	1	256 @ 32 × 32
CT6	512 @ 32 × 32	128 − 512 @ 4 × 4	2	1	128 @ 64 × 64
CT7	256 @ 64 × 64	64 − 256 @ 4 × 4	2	1	64 @ 128 × 128
CT8	128 @ 128 × 128	1 − 128 @ 4 × 4	2	1	1 @ 256 × 256

As pointed out earlier, we incorporate binary cross entropy loss function to train the U-Net. Binary cross entropy loss function is extensively used for classification since it penalizes the model based on the confidence with which it gives the correct class as the predicted. The binary cross entropy loss function for a predicted label $\hat{y} \in [0,1]$ and the target label $y \in \{0,1\}$ is as given in Eq. (1).

$$L_{CE}(y,\hat{y}) = -[y log(\hat{y}) + (1-y)log(1-\hat{y})] \tag{1}$$

Given a patch of a degraded document image x, we pass it through U-Net. Let the generated image be F(x). Given the ground truth image patch y, we find the binary cross entropy loss between the generated image F(x) and the ground truth image y. The loss is calculated as mentioned in Eq. (1) where $\hat{y}$ is our predicted label F(x) and y is the target. Thus, the loss function for the network is as given in Eq. (2). The total loss is found out by taking expectation of loss over all the image patches in the dataset.

$$L_{U-Net} = \mathbb{E}_x[L_{CE}(y, F(x))] \tag{2}$$

We adopt the U-Net architecture from [19], the details of which are as given in Table 1. In the table, C indicates the convolution layer for down-sampling and CT indicates transposed convolution layer for up-sampling. The third column mentions the number of filters (N) in that layer and shape of each filter, depth indicates the number of channels and h and w indicate the height and width, respectively. The numbers given in second and the last column indicate the dimensions of the input and output of each layer. The fourth and fifth columns denote the amount of stride and zero padding, respectively.

To train the U-Net, patches of size 256 × 256 with an overlap of 128 are extracted from both, the degraded and the ground truth images. There were a total of 2000 image patches. These patches were used for training after normalisation. The binary cross entropy loss function as mentioned in Eq. (2) is minimized using ADAM [6] optimization technique with a batch size of 1. The learning rate is chosen as 0.0002 and β_1 and β_2 (constants for ADAM optimization) are selected as 0.5 and 0.999, respectively. The network is trained for 20 epochs.

After training the network, to binarize a test image, patches are extracted and binarized using the proposed approach. The binarized patches are then stitched together to obtain a complete binarized document image.

4   Experiments

The network has been trained on images of the Document Image Binarization Competition (DIBCO) datasets [2,10,13–16,18]. These datasets consist of both, hand-written and machine printed document images. The images have all types of degradations since they represent the benchmark datasets for the competition and they constitute a total of 97 degraded and ground truth image pairs of varying sizes. Patches of size 256 × 256 with an overlap of 128 were extracted from the degraded and the ground truth images for experiments. We use the H-DIBCO 2016 dataset [17] as test data for evaluating the performance of our method. This dataset consists of 10 handwritten document images.

We compare our results with the approach that uses FCN [21]. This method is recently proposed and is the state-of-the-art technique and it performs better than other methods. Hence, results are compared with their approach only. The qualitative comparison is as shown in Fig. 2. Here, we show three examples of the degraded image and the corresponding binarized images obtained using FCN approach and our approach. The corresponding ground truth images are also displayed. Figure 2(a) shows degraded images. In Fig. 2(b) and 2(c), we show the binarized images from the FCN approach and our method, respectively. Looking at Fig. 2(b) and 2(c), we see that in the first image, our method retains

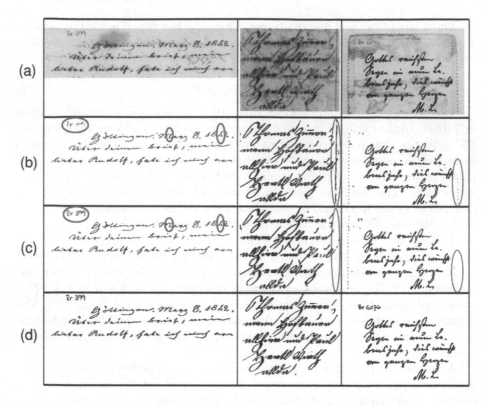

Fig. 2. Qualitative comparison with other approaches. (a) Degraded document images, (b) binarization using FCN [21], (c) binarization using our method, (d) ground truth.

the content that is marked in red which has lighter shade in the degraded image. However, the FCN method fails to retain the same. In the second and the third images, our method successfully eliminates the dark background while the other method fails to do so. We evaluate the quantitative performance of our approach on the basis of three benchmark criteria often used in evaluating the document image binarization methods. These quantitative measures include F-measure, Pseudo F-measure and Peak Signal to Noise Ratio (PSNR). Considering the text as the positive class and the background as negatives, the F-measure can be given as

$$FM = \frac{2 \times Precision \times Recall}{Recall + Precision}, \tag{3}$$

where, FM represents F-measure and

$$Recall = \frac{TP}{TP + FN}, Precision = \frac{TP}{TP + FP}.$$

Here, TP represents true positives while FP and FN represent the false positives and negatives, respectively.

Table 2. Quantitative comparison with other approach.

Metric	Our method	Best competition system [17]	FCN [21]	FCN with relative darkness [21]
FM	**98.92**	88.72	89.52	–
pFM	**98.95**	91.84	93.76	97.15
PSNR	18.30	18.45	**18.67**	–

Pseudo F-Measure (pFM) was proposed in [9] specifically for evaluating the performance of document image binarization methods. It aims to evaluate the model based on the skeleton of the text in the binarized image. This metric penalizes the classifier less if the skeletons are correctly formed. Thus, the pixels wrongly classified as text pixels significantly away from the actual text (false positives much away from true positives) are penalized less than those near the actual text. For that, the ground truth (real) image is skeletonized first. Let skeletonized image of size MxN at location (x,y) be denoted as SG(x,y), which can be written as

$$SG(x, y) = \begin{cases} 0, & \text{if background.} \\ 1, & \text{if foreground.} \end{cases} \tag{4}$$

Pseudo Recall ($pRecall$) is defined as the proportion of the skeletonized ground truth image SG that is detected in the generated binary image B. It is defined as given in Eq. (5) as

$$pRecall = \frac{\sum\limits_{x=1,y=1}^{x=M,y=N} SG(x,y) \times B(x,y)}{\sum\limits_{x=1,y=1}^{x=M,y=N} SG(x,y)}. \tag{5}$$

Using Eq. (5), pFM is defined as

$$pFM = \frac{2 \times Precision \times pRecall}{pRecall + Precision}. \tag{6}$$

PSNR is a measure of the closeness of one image to another. Therefore, the higher the value of PSNR, the higher the similarity of the two $M \times N$ images is. We consider that the difference between foreground and background equals to C. The PSNR can be calculated as

$$PSNR = 10 \log \frac{C^2}{MSE}, \tag{7}$$

where,

$$MSE = \frac{\sum\limits_{x=1}^{M} \sum\limits_{y=1}^{N} (I(x,y) - I'(x,y))^2}{MN}.$$

To measure the performance of our approach quantitatively, we compare our results with the FCN method [21] and the best competition performance for each criteria in H-DIBCO 2016 [17]. The comparison is also shown for FCN with relative darkness included. We compare these metrics for the performance on H-DIBCO 2016 dataset. The scores are as shown in Table 2. Note that "–" entries in the last column of Table 2 indicates non-availability of those metric values.

Our method outperforms the others in terms of F and pF measures. It can be clearly observed from the above Table 2 that two of the scores, FM and pFM of our method are significantly better than the state-of-the-art technique that has been proposed recently. We also see that our approach outperforms the FCN method with relative darkness. PSNR is also comparable to the FCN method. It has been mentioned in [22] that PSNR is not a good metric to evaluate image qualities. Hence we conclude that with less complexity and simpler approach, our method is clearly better in binarizing degraded document images.

5   Conclusion

In this paper, we proposed a method for document image binarization using a U-Net. Since we model this as a problem of classification, we train the U-Net by optimizing the binary cross entropy loss function between the ground truth image and the binarized image. Our method achieves significantly better results than the state-of- the-art technique that has been recently proposed. It is comparatively simpler and performs better than other deep learning approaches incorporated for document image binarization. It fails at places where the background is very dark and prominent.

References

1. Afzal, M.Z., Pastor-Pellicer, J., Shafait, F., Breuel, T.M., Dengel, A., Liwicki, M.: Document image binarization using LSTM: a sequence learning approach. In: Proceedings of the 3rd International Workshop on Historical Document Imaging and Processing, pp. 79–84. ACM (2015)
2. Gatos, B., Ntirogiannis, K., Pratikakis, I.: ICDAR 2009 document image binarization contest (DIBCO 2009). In: 10th International Conference on Document Analysis and Recognition, 2009. ICDAR 2009, pp. 1375–1382. IEEE (2009)
3. Hamza, H., Smigiel, E., Belaid, E.: Neural based binarization techniques. In: Proceedings of Eighth International Conference on Document Analysis and Recognition 2005, pp. 317–321. IEEE (2005)
4. Howe, N.R.: Document binarization with automatic parameter tuning. Int. J. Doc. Anal. Recog. (IJDAR) 16(3), 247–258 (2013)
5. Ioffe, S., Szegedy, C.: Batch normalization: accelerating deep network training by reducing internal covariate shift. arXiv preprint arXiv:1502.03167 (2015)
6. Kingma, D.P., Ba, J.: Adam: a method for stochastic optimization. arXiv preprint arXiv:1412.6980 (2014)
7. Kohonen, T.: The self-organizing map. Neurocomputing 21(1–3), 1–6 (1998)

8. Long, J., Shelhamer, E., Darrell, T.: Fully convolutional networks for semantic segmentation. In: Proceedings of the IEEE Conference on Computer Vision and Pattern Recognition, pp. 3431–3440 (2015)
9. Ntirogiannis, K., Gatos, B., Pratikakis, I.: An objective evaluation methodology for document image binarization techniques. In: The Eighth IAPR International Workshop on Document Analysis Systems, 2008. DAS 2008, pp. 217–224. IEEE (2008)
10. Ntirogiannis, K., Gatos, B., Pratikakis, I.: ICFHR 2014 competition on handwritten document image binarization (H-DIBCO 2014). In: 2014 14th International Conference on Frontiers in Handwriting Recognition (ICFHR), pp. 809–813. IEEE (2014)
11. Otsu, N.: A threshold selection method from gray-level histograms. IEEE Trans. Syst. Man Cybern. **9**(1), 62–66 (1979)
12. Pastor-Pellicer, J., España-Boquera, S., Zamora-Martínez, F., Afzal, M.Z., Castro-Bleda, M.J.: Insights on the use of convolutional neural networks for document image binarization. In: Rojas, I., Joya, G., Catala, A. (eds.) IWANN 2015. LNCS, vol. 9095, pp. 115–126. Springer, Cham (2015). https://doi.org/10.1007/978-3-319-19222-2_10
13. Pratikakis, I., Gatos, B., Ntirogiannis, K.: ICDAR 2011 document image binarization contest (DIBCO 2011). In: 2011 International Conference on Document Analysis and Recognition, pp. 1506–1510 (2011)
14. Pratikakis, I., Gatos, B., Ntirogiannis, K.: H-DIBCO 2010-handwritten document image binarization competition. In: 2010 International Conference on Frontiers in Handwriting Recognition (ICFHR), pp. 727–732. IEEE (2010)
15. Pratikakis, I., Gatos, B., Ntirogiannis, K.: ICFHR 2012 competition on handwritten document image binarization (h-dibco 2012). In: 2012 International Conference on Frontiers in Handwriting Recognition (ICFHR), pp. 817–822. IEEE (2012)
16. Pratikakis, I., Gatos, B., Ntirogiannis, K.: ICDAR 2013 document image binarization contest (DIBCO 2013). In: 2013 12th International Conference on Document Analysis and Recognition (ICDAR), pp. 1471–1476. IEEE (2013)
17. Pratikakis, I., Zagoris, K., Barlas, G., Gatos, B.: ICFHR 2016 handwritten document image binarization contest (H-DIBCO 2016). In: 2016 15th International Conference on Frontiers in Handwriting Recognition (ICFHR), pp. 619–623. IEEE (2016)
18. Pratikakis, I., Zagoris, K., Barlas, G., Gatos, B.: ICDAR 2017 competition on document image binarization (dibco 2017). In: 2017 14th IAPR International Conference on Document Analysis and Recognition (ICDAR), vol. 1, pp. 1395–1403. IEEE (2017)
19. Ronneberger, O., Fischer, P., Brox, T.: U-Net: convolutional networks for biomedical image segmentation. In: Navab, N., Hornegger, J., Wells, W.M., Frangi, A.F. (eds.) MICCAI 2015. LNCS, vol. 9351, pp. 234–241. Springer, Cham (2015). https://doi.org/10.1007/978-3-319-24574-4_28
20. Sauvola, J., Pietikäinen, M.: Adaptive document image binarization. Pattern Recogn. **33**(2), 225–236 (2000)
21. Tensmeyer, C., Martinez, T.: Document image binarization with fully convolutional neural networks. arXiv preprint arXiv:1708.03276 (2017)
22. Wang, Z., Bovik, A.C.: Mean squared error: Love it or leave it? a new look at signal fidelity measures. IEEE Sign. Process. Mag. **26**(1), 98–117 (2009)
23. Wu, Y., Natarajan, P., Rawls, S., AbdAlmageed, W.: Learning document image binarization from data. In: 2016 IEEE International Conference on Image Processing (ICIP), pp. 3763–3767. IEEE (2016)

Towards Faster Offline Handwriting Recognition Using Temporal Convolution Networks

Annapurna Sharma[✉], Rahul Ambati, and Dinesh Babu Jayagopi

Multimodal Perception Lab, International Institute of Information Technology,
Bangalore, India
{annapurna.sharma,rahul.ambati}@iiitb.org, jdinesh@iiitb.ac.in

Abstract. The problem of unconstrained handwriting recognition is quite challenging in the field of document analysis and recognition. The state of the art models utilize Recurrent Neural Networks (RNN) and its variants to extract the features with Connectionist Temporal Classification (CTC) as the cost function. Because of the recurrent connections these models are extremely slow to train and test but enable the recognition of the handwritten text images with high accuracy at character and word level. In this work, we present a faster system for handwritten text recognition which takes the input as a handwritten text line image and outputs the text transcription of the same. The model uses convolution structure based on Temporal Convolution Network (TCN) and CTC cost function at the output layer. The model shows a comparable Character Error Rate (CER) of 9.6% with respect to state of the art models on IAM handwritten lines dataset. Since our model is a TCN based architecture, it can effectively use the parallelism offered by GPUs. Our baseline model takes $52s$ per epoch to train and $3ms$ per image to test which is a significant improvement as compared with the existing models for the same task. It has comparatively lesser number of parameters. This makes our model suitable to use for real life applications and to be deployed on smart phone devices. To the best of our knowledge, ours is the first work which uses TCN based model for the task of transcribing the text of handwritten line images.

Keywords: Offline handwriting recognition · Dilated TCN

1 Introduction

Handwriting recognition has been seen as a classical research problem in machine learning. Recent deep learning approaches have shown many promising results by considering the image of the handwritten text as a sequential data and incorporating the context for the purpose of recognition of handwritten characters

Supported by Visvesvaraya PhD Scheme for Electronics and IT, MEITY, Government of India.

[4,11,12,14]. These approaches enabled the transcriptions of the text images to be done at the word and line level as opposed to traditional approaches which worked on handwriting recognition at character level. With the promising results, a number of applications have been proposed which can make use of transcriptions received from the handwriting recognition system. Not only the accuracy but the number of parameters and the speed (both training and testing) of the handwriting recognition systems can thus be important for the performance of the overall system as well as for designing real time applications. In this work, we propose a model architecture for handwriting recognition of line images which uses fully convolution based system which can be trained faster and has less parameters as opposed to the current state of the art architectures which are based on Long Short Term Memory (LSTM) and its variants.

Lea et al. [8] proposed Temporal Convolution Network (TCN) and showed that these networks are able to capture long-range dependencies, and are over a magnitude faster to train than competing LSTM-based Recurrent Neural Networks. They considered the task of action segmentation and detection in video dataset.

In this work, we propose a faster neural network compared with the existing models. The network is based on convolutions and TCN for feature extraction and Connectionist Temporal Classification (CTC) for sequence learning at the output layer. Figure 1 shows an overview of the system where the input is a line image of the handwritten text and output is the transcription of the text.

The main contributions of our work are as follows: 1) A TCN based network

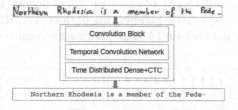

Fig. 1. An overview of the proposed model. The input to the model is the line image of handwritten text and the expected output is the transcription of the text.

architecture is proposed for handwriting recognition with less number of parameters which makes it suitable to deploy on ubiquitous smart phone devices. We show the network is faster to train and test as compared to the state of the art models based on LSTM and its variants. 2)We show empirically that the use of preprocessing like denoising of the images does help while deslanting alone does not help in getting better recognition results with our model architecture. Augmenting the training data (raw line images) by including the denoised images and deslanted images further improves the handwriting recognition results.

2   Related Works

The recent works in handwriting recognition use sequential models with CTC output layer. These sequential models are mostly RNNs and various variants of RNN with combination of convolution layers. Graves et al. [3,4] proposed Multidimensional RNN structure, which they call as Multidimensional Long Short Term Memory (MDLSTM) network, for feature extraction and CTC for sequence learning task. Subsequently, different models were proposed with MDLSTM in combination with convolution and different regularization techniques. The results created new milestones in handwriting recognition techniques. Pham et al. [11] trained a handwriting recognition model with alternating convolution and MDLSTM layers and showed that dropout at different layers results in improvement of the handwriting recognition model.

Voigtlaender et al. [14] showed the empirical results with different model structures using MDLSTM and convolution layers. The authors also used slant corrected handwriting images for training the model and showed empirically that it improves the performance slightly as compared to model trained on raw line images. The results were shown on two popular datasets IAM and RIMES which are English and French handwritten lines dataset, respectively. Puigcerver [12] trained a handwriting recognition model with convolution and BLSTM layers. The model showed the state of the art recognition results on both the IAM and RIMES dataset. The model had high number of parameters and needed less training time per epoch for training the model as compared to the model given by Voigtlaender et al. [14].

Krishnan et al. [6] used Spatial Transformer Network (STN) followed by residual convolution and LSTM blocks with CTC output layer. They trained the base network with synthetic handwriting dataset, i.e., IIIT-HWS dataset [7] and fine-tuned their network on IAM handwriting recognition dataset.

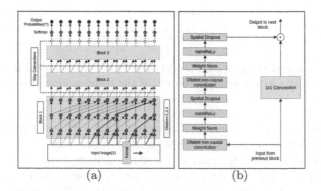

Fig. 2. Schematic representation of TCN. (a) TCN block and layer structure, (b) Residual block structure for a non causal TCN.

Recently Lea et al. [8] proposed TCN for capturing action compositions, segment duration, and long-range dependencies, which are over a magnitude faster to train than the LSTM-based Recurrent Neural Networks. The TCNs use a hierarchy of temporal convolutions to perform fine-grained action segmentation or detection. These networks use 1-D convolutions in residual blocks as the basic unit which are further structured in layers and blocks. A schematic of Dilated TCN is shown in Fig. 2. The effective receptive field of the network can be adjusted with the depth of layers and blocks. TCNs are faster to train and used for modeling the sequence learning tasks where input sequences are of variable length.

Bai et al. [2] presented a systematic evaluation of generic convolutional and recurrent architectures for sequence modeling tasks. The results indicated that a simple convolution architecture outperforms canonical recurrent networks such as LSTMs across a diverse range of tasks and datasets, while demonstrating longer effective memory. The models were evaluated across a broad range of standard tasks that are commonly used to benchmark recurrent networks. They experimented on sequential MNIST task which is a handwritten digit recognition task on images.

A recent work by Iwana et al. [5] propose the use of local distance based features determined by Dynamic Time Warping was shown with Unipen online handwritten character datasets.

In this work, we show an end to end trainable handwriting recognition model which uses convolution and dilated TCN layers (with dilation factor 2) for feature extraction, and CTC for sequence learning task. As opposed to character recognition task considered by Bai et al.[2] and Iwana et al. [5], our model is designed and trained to transcribe the handwritten line images. The comparison is shown with Character Error Rate (CER) as the metric for evaluation, number of parameters for the size of the network and the time required to train the model. As compared to LSTM based models our model is significantly faster to train while achieving comparable CER. The next section presents a brief description of the dataset and the preprocessing techniques that we have used on this dataset to experiment under different settings. The subsequent section shows the model architecture and implementation details followed by the experiments we carried out in this work along with comparison of the results with different works in the literature.

3   Dataset

We show our results on two popular handwriting datasets, i.e., IAM lines dataset and RIMES lines dataset [1,9].

3.1   Dataset Description

IAM lines handwriting dataset is composed of handwritten lines which are further divided into 6161, 976, 2915 line images as the training, validation and testing set. There are a total of 79 different characters in the dataset.

RIMES lines dataset is a French handwriting dataset with 11333 and 778 lines images for training and testing. We have used the same training, validation and testing lines partition as used by Puigcerver et al. [12] and hence we have

10203, 1130 and 778 lines for training, validation and testing, respectively. There are a total of 99 different characters in the dataset. All the line images in the dataset are not of the same height, width or aspect ratio. The line images in the training partition of the IAM dataset have a maximum height of 342 pixels and a maximum width of 2260 pixels. The line images in the training partition of the RIMES dataset have an average height of 113 pixels and average width of 1658 pixels.

Subsection-3.2 shows the details of the resizing and preprocessing used for the images in the dataset before being used as the input to the model.

3.2   Preprocessing

The images in the IAM lines dataset have varied height and width. In order to reduce the computational costs without compromising on accuracy, all the images are resized to half of its original size. To cater with the different heights of images, all the images are padded vertically to the maximum height of the resized images, i.e., 171 pixels. All the images are padded along the width axis to the maximum width of the resized images, i.e., 1130 pixels. We further added a padding of 5 pixels along width axis on both sides. All images are input to the model after normalizing the pixel intensity values to the range (0, 1).

To counter the effect of image capturing hardware on the overall task, we performed noise removal. The images are binarized using Sauvola image binarization technique [13]. We will refer to these images as denoised images in this paper. A sample raw image and a corresponding binarized image is shown below in the Fig. 3.

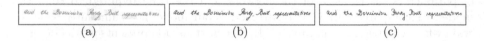

(a)   (b)   (c)

Fig. 3. Preprocessing steps used in our work. (a) Raw Image, (b) Image after binarization, (c) Image after slant correction

Slant correction is used to normalize the text writing (when the writer writes at an angle with respect to the baseline), making the text upright. We have adopted the de-slanting strategy as mentioned by Zeeuw [15]. A sample image and the corresponding denoised slant corrected image is shown in Fig. 3. We will refer to these images as denoised-deslanted images in later sections.

4   Model

Figure-4 shows the architecture of the model that we have used in this work for the task of handwriting recognition of line images. The model is composed of convolution and TCN blocks followed by CTC output layer. The input to the network is single channel image of handwritten text line and output is the text transcription. The following subsections will show the details of the architecture and training of the handwriting recognition model followed by the implementation details.

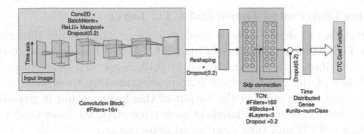

Fig. 4. The Network architecture for handwriting recognition.

4.1 Architecture

The input image is first passed through five 2-D convolution layers which form the convolution block. The output of convolution layers is passed through a TCN followed by a time distributed dense layer with *numClass* hidden units and softmax activation function, where *numClass* is the number of class labels to be predicted by the model. It includes characters in the dataset and CTC blank label. The description of each module is given below.

Convolution Block. The convolution block, as shown in Fig.-4, composed of a series of 2-D convolution layers. The structure is derived from the model proposed by Puigcerver [12]. Each 2-D convolution layer is followed by batch normalization during training. We further used ReLU [10] activation function on the batch normalized output. A maxpooling operation is used for better generalization with less number of parameters. A Max pool of 2×2 kernel has been used without overlap after the first convolution operation and 2×1 kernel after all other convolutions in the convolution block. We have used $16n$ filters in 2-D convolution layers; where n is the layer number from starting of the convolution block. We have used the same kernel size of 5×5 for all convolution layers. No dropout has been used for first two layers while a dropout of 0.2 has been used for all the subsequent layers in convolution block. The 3-D output of convolution block is reshaped by merging the height and depth dimension. We refer to this as feature dimension *numFeatures* for the TCN. The width dimension (time axis) has been kept as is. So, the input to the TCN is of dimension *numFeatures* × *timesteps*.

TCN. TCN network block contains a dilated TCN network with four blocks of three layers each. Each layer is composed of a residual block with two 1-D convolution operation with a residual connection with input to the residual block. We have used a dilation factor of 2 for all the experiments in this paper. The number of filters in all layers is set equal to *numFeatures*. In our experiments with IAM dataset *numFeatures* = 160. A kernel size of 3 has been used for all 1-D convolution operations in TCN block. We have also used a spatial dropout of 0.2 in TCN and skip connections between layers as shown in [8]. Further, since we are using offline handwriting recognition task, we use noncausal 1-D convolutions to get the context from both left and right directions to enable better recognition performance.

4.2 Time Distributed Dense and CTC Layer

A time distributed dense layer is used to convert the feature dimension output from TCN block to the class labels for CTC loss function, i.e., $numClass$. The time distributed layer allows to apply fully connected dense layer on every temporal slice of the input and get output separated by time steps [1]. We used softmax activation function at the output of this layer so that it gives the probability distribution over class labels at each time step. We have used a dropout of 0.2 between TCN and time distributed dense layer.

4.3 Network Training

For training the model, we use a CTC cost function which marginalizes the probability of a label over all alignments. This objective function does not explicitly need the time aligned labels as the ground truth.

CTC scores are used with the back-propagation algorithm to update the neural network weights with Adam optimizer. We have used a batch size of 32 and learning rate=0.001 with time inverse decay with decay rate =0.0001. The output of the model shown in Subsect. 4.1 gives the probability distribution over class labels at each time step. We are using beam search decoding with beam width of 100 for decoding these probability distributions of the CTC output.

We have used CER as the criterion for evaluating the performance of the model. The CER is computed by taking the mean of the edit distance, between the ground truth transcription and the transcription given by model, over all the example images. The training is stopped when the CER over validation set does not change for 20 epochs.

5 Experiments and Results

We trained the model architecture presented in Sect. 4.1 with raw line images of the lines dataset. We refer this as our baseline model. The corresponding validation and testing results are shown in Table 1. We show our results with CER, WER and WER results enhanced by lexicon model on both validation and test set.

We further experiment with different preprocessing settings of the line images to show if the preprocessing of the dataset helps in a better trained model. We first considered deslanting the images(shown in Sect. 3.2) independently and trained the model. The results corresponding to this setting are shown in the second row of the Table 1. The deslant operation does not improve the recognition results and in fact the model shows very poor recognition rate in terms of both CER and WER as compared to the baseline model. This is in contrast to MDLSTM based models where Voigtlaender et al. [14] showed that deslanting the image dataset helps in a better trained model and shows improvements in CER of the testing set. This could be because the variabilities in the handwritings are reduced by the deslanting operation as compared to raw data which may have different slants by different writers. The denoising of the images helps to

---

[1] https://www.tensorflow.org/api_docs/python/tf/keras/layers/TimeDistributed.

improve the handwriting recognition results significantly as compared to baseline model. This setting shows better recognition performance on both CER and WER than the baseline model.

The next set of experiments include images with denoising followed by deslanting for training the model. This setting performs poorer than both the baseline and denoise settings. Further the results of this pipeline show lower CER and WER as compared to the deslanted image dataset as shown in row-2 of the Table 1. In the next setting, we have created a combined training dataset with raw images, denoised images and deslanted images. The results of above experiments show that our model is able to give the best results on both validation and test set when trained on this combined dataset.

Table 1. Experiment set-up and corresponding results for IAM handwritten lines dataset.

System	VAL			Test		
	CER	WER	WER with Lexicon	CER	WER	WER with Lexicon
Baseline	7.1	25.1	19.1	10.3	33.0	25.0
+deslant	12.3	35.4	29.1	14.7	41.7	33.9
+denoise	6.9	24.5	19.0	10.1	32.6	24.7
+denoise+deslant	10.9	33.3	26.4	13.9	40.7	32.3
+Combined	**6.4**	**23.4**	**18.1**	**9.6**	**30.6**	**23.6**

Table 2 shows a comparative analysis of the CER and WER as reported on IAM lines dataset by different research groups and ours. Some research groups report the raw results while others use various lexicon and language models (LM) over the transcriptions received from their model and report the results as final transcriptions. The second column of the Table mentions whether the model uses Lexicon/ Langauge model for transcription. The third column of the Table shows the number of parameters required to train and save the model. The next column shows the approximate total training time required to train the model for 80 epochs. Both the works by Voigtlaender et al. [14] and Puigcerver [12] reported the CER and WER values at epoch 80. The lower this time is, the less is the time required to train the overall model. Some of the research groups have not mentioned the number of parameters and average training time per epoch. The last column of the Table shows the CER as reported by different research groups. The last row shows our results without any language model. For a fairer comparison with respect to training time, we have put the model trained for 80 epochs in here.

As shown in the Table 2, the CER of the models (by Pham et al. [11] and Puigcerver [12]) improves significantly by using the lexicon/ language model. Our reported CER here is better than Pham et al. [11] while 0.4% worse than Krishnan et al. [6]. A comparison of the result with Puigcerver [12] shows our results are poorer on CER but there is a huge difference in number of parameters in the model and training time. We further noted that the testing time for our model is approximately $3ms$ per test image. This is significantly less than the testing time of approximately $400ms$ per test image by the model given by Voigtlaender et al. [14]. With this significant difference in training and inference time TCN based architectures can be further be explored for the task of handwriting recognition.

We further trained our baseline model on RIMES lines dataset. The results are compared with state of the art architectures in Table 3. Our baseline model is trained on raw images and can be further improved by training on combined dataset. It can further be fine tuned to adjust the receptive field for a specific dataset as Bai et al. [2] pointed out that TCNs need a potential change in hyperparameters for different datasets.

Table 2. Comparison of handwriting recognition results on IAM lines test set. ** indicates that this model is trained on the combined dataset.

Results by	Lexicon/LM Model	# Parameters	Total trainingtime	Testing time per image	CER
Pham et al. [11]	Yes	-	-	-	5.1
Voigtlaender et al. [14]	Yes	2.6M	32.4 hrs	$400ms$	4.8
Puigcerver [12]	Yes	9.3M	31.66 hrs	$10ms$	4.4
Pham et al. [11]	No	-	-	-	10.8
Puigcerver et al. [12]	No	9.3M	$31.66hrs$	$10ms$	**5.8**
Krishnan et al. [6]	No	-	-	-	9.7
Ours (**Baseline**)	No	**1.5M**	**1.15 hrs**	$3ms$	10.3
*Ours*** (**best model**)	No	1.5M	$3.45hrs$	$3ms$	9.6

Table 3. Comparison of CER on RIMES test dataset. The results calculated with lexicon model are marked with*.

Results by	# Parameters	CER
Pham et al. [11]	-	6.8
Voigtlaender et al. [14]	2.6M	2.8*
Puigcerver [12]	9.6M	**2.3**
Ours(baseline)	1.58M	7.5

6   Conclusion and Future Works

In this work, we presented a TCN based model for handwriting recognition task which is fast to train and test. The model does not have recurrent connections and can utilize the parallelism offered by GPU. This makes the model suitable for the applications which use handwriting recognition model at the back end for the overall task performance. The model has less number of parameters as compared to the other existing models for handwriting recognition task. The work showed the preprocessing that we have used to get a slant corrected handwriting image. The simple network architecture that we have used achieves CER of 9.6% which is comparable with existing state of the art results. The model takes only $52s$ to train each epoch which is a very less time as compared to the state of the art architectures which use RNN based models for handwriting recognition. The testing time is 3 ms for each image which makes the model suitable for designing real time applications. We have presented our results with and without the lexicon model to show the raw transcription performance of the model. The future directions include experimenting with dataset of different languages to show the efficacy of the model on both the speed and the performance of recognition task.

References

1. Augustin, E., Carré, M., Grosicki, E., Brodin, J.M., Geoffrois, E., Prêteux, F.: Rimes evaluation campaign for handwritten mail processing. In: International Workshop on Frontiers in Handwriting Recognition (IWFHR 2006), pp. 231–235 (2006)
2. Bai, S., Kolter, J.Z., Koltun, V.: An empirical evaluation of generic convolutional and recurrent networks for sequence modeling. CoRR abs/1803.01271 (2018)
3. Graves, A., Fernández, S., Gomez, F., Schmidhuber, J.: Connectionist temporal classification: labelling unsegmented sequence data with recurrent neural networks. In: Proceedings of the 23rd international conference on Machine learning, pp. 369–376. ACM (2006)
4. Graves, A., Schmidhuber, J.: Offline handwriting recognition with multidimensional recurrent neural networks. In: Advances in Neural Information Processing Systems, pp. 545–552 (2009)
5. Iwana, B.K., Mori, M., Kimura, A., Uchida, S.: Introducing local distance-based features to temporal convolutional neural networks. In: 2018 16th International Conference on Frontiers in Handwriting Recognition (ICFHR), pp. 92–97. IEEE (2018)
6. Krishnan, P., Dutta, K., Jawahar, C.: Word spotting and recognition using deep embedding. In: 2018 13th IAPR International Workshop on Document Analysis Systems (DAS), pp. 1–6. IEEE (2018)
7. Krishnan, P., Jawahar, C.: Generating synthetic data for text recognition. arXiv preprint arXiv:1608.04224 (2016)
8. Lea, C., Flynn, M.D., Vidal, R., Reiter, A., Hager, G.D.: Temporal convolutional networks for action segmentation and detection. In: The IEEE Conference on Computer Vision and Pattern Recognition (CVPR), July 2017
9. Marti, U.V., Bunke, H.: The IAM-database: an English sentence database for offline handwriting recognition. Int. J. Doc. Anal. Recogn. **5**, 39–46 (2002)
10. Nair, V., Hinton, G.E.: Rectified linear units improve restricted boltzmann machines. In: Proceedings of the 27th international conference on machine learning (ICML-10), pp. 807–814 (2010)
11. Pham, V., Bluche, T., Kermorvant, C., Louradour, J.: Dropout improves recurrent neural networks for handwriting recognition. In: 2014 14th International Conference on Frontiers in Handwriting Recognition (ICFHR), pp. 285–290. IEEE (2014)
12. Puigcerver, J.: Are multidimensional recurrent layers really necessary for handwritten text recognition? In: 2017 14th IAPR International Conference on Document Analysis and Recognition (ICDAR), vol. 01, pp. 67–72, November 2017. https://doi.org/10.1109/ICDAR.2017.20
13. Sauvola, J., Pietikäinen, M.: Adaptive document image binarization. Pattern Recogn. **33**(2), 225–236 (2000)

354   A. Sharma et al.

14. Voigtlaender, P., Doetsch, P., Ney, H.: Handwriting recognition with large multidimensional long short-term memory recurrent neural networks. In: 2016 15th International Conference on Frontiers in Handwriting Recognition (ICFHR), pp. 228–233. IEEE (2016)
15. de Zeeuw, F.: Slant correction using histograms. Undergraduate Thesis. http://www.ai.rug.nl/~axel/teaching/bachelorprojects/zeeuw_slantcorrection.pdf (2006)

Recognition of Gurmukhi Signboard Image Classes Based on Static and Dynamic Feature Sets

Jasleen Kaur Bains[1]([✉]), Sukhdeep Singh[2], and Anuj Sharma[1]

[1] Department of Computer Science and Applications, Punjab University,
Chandigarh, India
{jasleen,anujs}@pu.ac.in
[2] D. M. College, Moga, Punjab, India
sukha13@ymail.com
https://sites.google.com/view/anujsharma/

Abstract. The efficient feature extraction technique plays a pivotal role in the text recognition systems. A stable and an effective feature set can help to achieve benchmarked accuracy in text recognition systems. In the present study, we aim to recognize the Gurmukhi signboard image classes using the dynamic, static and hybrid feature sets. The static features consist of the zoning and diagonal features, while dynamic features are based on the recovery of drawing order technique. The hybrid feature set comprises both static and dynamic features. An in-house dataset of the Gurmukhi characters has been developed from 820 real-time Gurmukhi signboard images as no benchmarked Gurmukhi signboard dataset is available publicly. 43 distinct classes are obtained for Gurmukhi middle zone characters having 9,544 strokes. The stroke recognition has been performed using the Support Vector Machine and Conv1D deep learning method. Best overall recognition accuracy using a hybrid feature set have been achieved using the Support Vector Machine and Conv1D deep learning method as 91.37% and 93.39% respectively. The primary objective of the proposed study is to present a comparison of the static, dynamic and hybrid features based recognition scheme for various image classes obtained from the Gurmukhi signboard images. This work can be extended for other Indic scripts as it is suitable for real-life applications.

Keywords: Gurmukhi signboard · Hybrid features · Recovery of drawing order · Offline text recognition · Indic script · SVM · Deep learning

1 Introduction

With the advent of new technology, the field of pattern recognition has seen an upsurge in the available feature extraction techniques for effective text recognition. The feature extraction techniques differ according to the kind of data

© Springer Nature Singapore Pte Ltd. 2020
R. V. Babu et al. (Eds.): NCVPRIPG 2019, CCIS 1249, pp. 355–364, 2020.
https://doi.org/10.1007/978-981-15-8697-2_33

being dealt with by the text recognition system, as online text or offline text. The online text refers to the data which is captured using a stylus on tablet or PDA and offline text refer to the text present in scanned documents and digital images. The proposed study is based on the offline text present in real-time Gurmukhi signboard images. As the offline text does not carry any dynamic information like pen pressure or trajectory information therefore, most of the offline text recognition systems use static properties for text recognition which are generally based on structural features. These derived features are classified using an appropriate classifier such as the Support Vector Machine (SVM), hidden markov model or deep learning methods. Some of the recent studies use these classifiers for text recognition. Nag et al. [1] have used CNN and bidirectional long short term memory deep leaning methods for recognition of information regarding Indic script extracted from scene text containing address information. Tian et al. [2] proposed two feature descriptors Co-occurrence HOG(Co-HOG) and Convolutional Co-HOG(ConvCo-HOG) for accurate recognition of scene texts in English, Chinese and Bangla language. They have used SVM classifier for recognition and obtained a recognition accuracy of 81.7%, 71% and 92.2% for English, Chinese and Bangla characters. Narang et al. [3] have used the part-based model to identify Devanagari characters from scene text. The corner points of the extracted character serve as parts of the proposed part model. The part-based model classified the test data into appropriate classes. They have identified 40 classes of Devanagari script. The handwritten dataset DSHnd-30 K and the machine printed dataset DSMP-28 K was taken as training data. They tested their model on the DSIW-2 K dataset containing images of street scenes. They have obtained a recognition accuracy of 56.1%(DSMP-28 K) and 42.33%(DSHnd-30 K) respectively. Fraz et al. [4] proposed an end to end system for text recognition. They have emphasized that proper utilization of color information and using low-level image processing operations for text enhancement, can increase the recognition accuracy. They computed the histogram of gradient features of candidate images and classified them using multiclass SVM. Character recognition accuracy ranging from 81% to 83% have been reported. Park et al. [5] described a system for automatic detection, recognition, and translation of Korean text into the English language. For recognition of a Korean character, a shape-based statistical feature has been used for character recognition. A character recognition accuracy ranging from 60.92% to 85.97% is reported. Coates et al. [6] have proposed a scalable feature learning algorithm based character recognition system for scene images. They have shown through experiments that the recognition accuracy increases when we train the classifier with an increased number of features. For 1500 features, recognition accuracy ranging from 81.7% to 85.5% has been reported. The present study presents a comparison of the static, dynamic and hybrid features based stroke recognition scheme for signboard images in the Gurmukhi script. The hybrid feature set comprises static and dynamic features, where the static features are computed on the basis of zonal and diagonal features, while dynamic features are based on the recovery of drawing order method. The recovery of drawing order technique helps to compute the trajectory of stroke, thus making the otherwise missing dynamic information available for offline stroke images. The dynamic information is available in the form of trajectory points and computed chain codes. The present study is based on strokes obtained from 820 real-time Gurmukhi signboard images as shown in Fig. 1. The outline of the present work is as follows. This paper includes five sections including this section. Section 2 gives an overview of the proposed system, Sect. 3 gives details of computing static, dynamic and hybrid features, Sect. 4 discusses the experimental results and Sect. 5 gives a conclusion.

Fig. 1. Illustration for the Gurmukhi signboard images

2 Overview of the Proposed System

The proposed system has been implemented in three phases, Fig. 2 depicts the various phases and the major activities performed in each phase of the proposed system. Phase I is the data acquisition and preprocessing phase. It works as follows, first the real-time image is captured and fed as an input to the proposed system. Then the user is prompted to select the Region Of Interest(ROI) which should contain the Gurmukhi text to be recognized. The ROI is cropped and then considered for preprocessing. In the image preprocessing phase, all the tasks are performed step by step such as, image smoothing using the median filter for eliminating noise from the image and then image binarization based on the threshold is performed for carrying on various text extraction techniques which work well on the binarized image. The proposed study works on images with both light and dark backgrounds, therefore the binarized image has foreground in white pixels and background in black pixels. Then skew detection and correction is done. Then image thinning is carried out for implementing segmentation techniques. Image is further refined by removing the unconnected components or pixels having very small size and later text area is determined through automatic cropping of ROI. This is implemented by considering the information of boundary pixels. All these tasks aid in achieving better segmentation results. Phase II is the text extraction phase and it comprises three steps as text segmentation, zone-wise clustering of strokes and determination of static and dynamic features. Text segmentation helps to obtain the strokes from selected text region. Zone-wise clustering of the strokes is performed using the k-means clustering method using the Hartigan-Wong method [9]. As a result of clustering a total of 56 classes

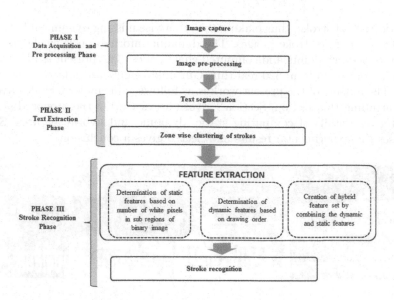

Fig. 2. Proposed system overview

have been formed. The upper zone consists of 10 classes, middle zone consists of 43 classes and lower zone consists of 3 classes as shown in Fig. 3. A total of 13,039 segmented strokes were obtained out of which 609 strokes belonged to lower zone, 2,876 strokes belonged to upper zone and middle zone had 9,544 strokes. As the middle zone consists of a maximum number of stroke as 9,544, therefore we have considered it for stroke recognition.

3   Feature Extraction

3.1   Static Feature Set

The static features have been determined by computing the zonal and diagonal features present in various sub-regions of binary stroke images. All these images have been resampled to 130×130 pixels size. Some of the stroke images have been present in skeletonized form after resampling, as the preprocessing step rendered them skeletonized for text segmentation technique. In order to have uniformity in the width of the stroke, the binary image of the stroke has been preprocessed using dilation operation. This helps in effective computation of static features as shown in Fig. 5. After dilating the image, the static features have been computed for the Gurmukhi signboard stroke image as presented in the study by Sharma [8]. For computing the zonal features, the stroke image has been divided into 169 zones each of 10×10 pixels. The total number of white pixels in various zones have been calculated to form the zonal features. The total number of white pixels in ten horizontal sub-regions each of size 13×130 and ten vertical sub-regions each of size 130×13 have been calculated. In addition

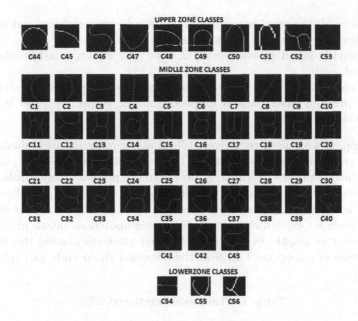

Fig. 3. Zone-wise representation of classes

to it, white pixels present in the 20 regions of right as well as 20 regions of left aligned diagonals have also been calculated. Figure 4 shows the structure of the static feature set.

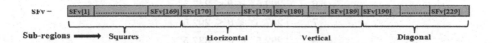

Fig. 4. Structure of the static feature set

3.2 Dynamic Feature Set

The 9,544 strokes belonging to the middle zone have been used for the calculation of dynamic features based on the recovery of drawing order technique. To perform the recovery of drawing order technique the strokes are skeletonized first. The recovery of drawing order technique helps to calculate the trajectory of a stroke. Using these trajectory points we can compute the chain code features belonging to eight directions. The recovery of drawing order has been performed as per the algorithms explained in the study conducted by Sharma [7] for digits(0–9). Following assumptions based on expert writer feedback and on Sharma [7,8] have been used for obtaining the drawing order in the present study, as the images contain no dynamic information:

1. The sub-regions close to the origin of the image are selected first.

2. For traversal, the pixel in sub-region with only one neighbor and closest to the origin is selected first as the beginning point.
3. If no pixel is found in assumption 2, then the left top pixel is selected for traversal.
4. In the case of more than two neighbor pixels to traverse, the direction close to the previous pixel path is followed and the respective pixel is selected iteratively.

Assumptions 1–4 are used recursively till all non-zero pixels are visited. A pixel in an image can be only visited once. The pixels are resampled to place them at equidistance from the neighboring pixels. In the present study, strokes belong to the Gurmukhi script whereas the algorithm by Sharma [7] has been developed for digits(0–9) only. To obtain the chain code features of the stroke image, the chain code for eight directions have been computed as shown in Table 1. A feature vector of length 48 has been obtained after calculating the frequency of occurrence of directions 1 to 8 in the obtained chain code as explained by Sharma [7].

Table 1. Chain code directions(CCD)

CCD	Scope in degrees
1	$337.5° < \theta \leq 22.5°$
2	$22.5° < \theta \leq 67.5°$
3	$67.5° < \theta \leq 112.5°$
4	$112.5° < \theta \leq 157.5°$
5	$157.5° < \theta \leq 202.5°$
6	$202.5° < \theta \leq 247.5°$
7	$247.5° < \theta \leq 292.5°$
8	$292.5° < \theta \leq 337.5°$

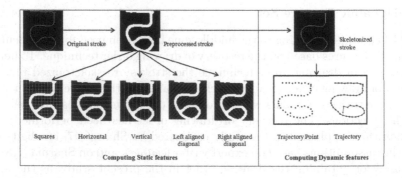

Fig. 5. Pictorial representation of computing static and dynamic features

3.3   Hybrid Feature Set

A hybrid feature set comprising of dynamic and static features has been created for recognition of the Gurmukhi stroke. Figure 6 shows the structure of the proposed hybrid feature set HFv, it has a feature length of 373 where first 96 elements are the (x,y) trajectory coordinates(TP), the next 48 elements are the chain codes(CC) and the last 229 elements are the static features(SF) obtained in Sect. 3.1.

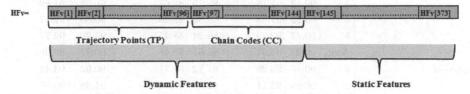

Fig. 6. Structure of the hybrid feature set

4   Experimental Results

For stroke recognition, two classifiers SVM and deep learning method Conv1D have been used. SVM is a suitable classifier for stroke recognition where data is distributed among multiple classes. The present study is based on 9,544 middle zone strokes of the Gurmukhi character set which have been obtained from 820 real-time Gurmukhi signboard images. These middle zone strokes are distributed among 43 classes. The hybrid feature vector consists of data in a continuous and categorized way. Therefore, SVM is best suitable for training such a kind of data. Separate files consisting of a random train and test data have been created in the LIBSVM format as instructed by Chang and Lin [10]. Tests were run using the LIBSVM tool created by Chang and Lin [10] which implements C-SVC for multi classes. Nowadays, deep learning methods have gained enormous attention due to the benchmarked text recognition accuracy reported by using these methods. We have used the Conv1D method proposed by Gan et al. [11] as it performs computationally well, requires less amount of data for training, works well with spatial and temporal information of data and gives overall good recognition accuracy.

In all, 150 experiments have been conducted for stroke recognition, using only static features, only dynamic features and hybrid feature set comprising of both static and dynamic features. For each set of a train and test data five experiments(run) have been performed. Table 2 shows the comparative recognition results of the same. The dynamic feature set is of length 144 and comprises trajectory points(TP) and chain codes(CC). The average recognition accuracy across all datasets using only dynamic features with SVM and Conv1D classifier is 87.3% and 89.86%, using only static features it is 90.86% and 93.01% and using the hybrid feature set it is 91.37% and 93.39% respectively. The hybrid feature set shows the best average recognition accuracy as compared to static and dynamic feature sets. It is stable, efficient and computationally effective due

Table 2. Comparative analysis of the stroke recognition accuracy using static, dynamic and hybrid feature sets

DATASET (Train% and Test%)	Run	Static Feature Set SF		Dynamic Feature Set TP+CC		Hybrid Feature Set TP+CC+SF	
		SVM	Conv1D	SVM	Conv1D	SVM	Conv1D
50–50	1	90.38	92.39	86.63	88.63	90.9	92.45
	2	89.89	92.41	85.61	88.47	90.23	92.60
	3	90.13	91.18	86.79	88.67	90.38	91.89
	4	90.22	91.08	86.30	88.20	90.89	92.17
	5	90.47	92.79	86.24	88.45	91.20	92.77
	Avg.	90.22	91.97	86.31	88.48	90.72	92.38
60–40	1	90.80	93.26	87.72	89.71	90.93	93.42
	2	90.66	92.11	86.86	89.14	91.38	93.07
	3	90.69	93.46	85.89	89.44	91.20	93.52
	4	90.55	92.45	87.72	89.16	90.96	93.12
	5	90.66	92.79	86.78	89.77	90.69	93.15
	Avg.	90.67	92.81	86.99	89.44	91.03	93.26
65–35	1	90.69	93.81	87.21	89.99	91.15	93.83
	2	91.26	93.26	86.96	89.31	91.42	93.49
	3	90.94	92.81	87.76	90.23	91.14	93.37
	4	90.43	92.75	87.15	89.74	90.87	92.97
	5	91.04	92.59	87.3	90.31	91.88	93.24
	Avg.	90.87	93.04	87.82	89.92	91.29	93.38
70–30	1	90.07	93.12	85.86	90.51	91.95	93.69
	2	91.96	93.18	87.53	89.72	92.10	93.84
	3	90.85	93.67	86.96	90.36	91.77	94.02
	4	91.07	92.89	87.71	89.14	91.66	93.19
	5	91.40	93.49	87.71	90.51	91.81	93.66
	Avg.	91.07	93.27	87.15	90.05	91.86	93.68
80–20	1	91.71	92.98	88.93	90.87	91.85	93.82
	2	91.71	94.72	88.98	91.89	93.02	94.73
	3	90.66	93.10	88.71	90.97	90.74	93.98
	4	91.66	94.71	88.29	91.13	91.85	94.09
	5	91.66	94.33	88.87	92.10	92.17	94.63
	Avg.	91.48	93.96	88.76	91.39	91.93	94.25

to smaller feature length of 373. Moreover, it can be trained using a smaller dataset. Thus, it is suitable for use in real-life applications.

As there is no benchmark dataset available of Gurmukhi signboard images, a comparison of the present study cannot be done directly with an existing dataset. But, in order to validate the recognition accuracy with existing similar studies

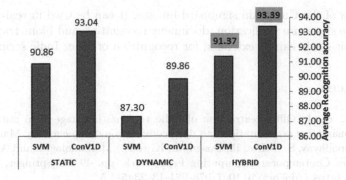

Fig. 7. Comparative analysis of the average stroke recognition accuracy, across various train and test datasets shown in Table 2 for the static, dynamic and hybrid feature sets computed using SVM and Conv1D methods

in Indic script a comparative Table 3 is presented to show that this work is at par literature. The static, dynamic and hybrid features in the proposed study can be adapted to be used with the other Indic scripts such as Devanagari and Bangla.

Table 3. Comparison with the recognition of scene text in the other Indic scripts

References	Script	Method	Accuracy
Proposed study	Gurmukhi	Recovery of drawing order and static features	**93.39**%
Nag et al. [1]	Devanagari	MaxOut CNN and Bidirectional LSTM	0.81 precision & 0.78 recall
Narang et al. [3]	Devanagari	Part-based model	56.1%(DSMP-28 K)
Narang et al. [3]	Devanagari	Part-based model	42.33%(DSHnd-30 K)
Tian et al. [2]	Bangla	Co_HOG	91.3%
Tian et al. [2]	Bangla	ConvCo-HOG	92.2%

5 Conclusion

In the present study, we have focused on comparing the performance of static, dynamic and hybrid features for recognizing the stroke belonging to classes obtained from the Gurmukhi signboard images. The dynamic features are based on the recovery of drawing order technique which helps to compute vital information regarding the trajectory of the stroke which is otherwise missing in the offline text. Further, this trajectory information can be used to create a dynamic feature set based on chain codes. The static feature set is stable and robust, it is based on zonal and diagonal features. It is evident from experimental results that the hybrid feature set is the most stable, consistent and efficient for the stroke recognition of the Gurmukhi signboard images. It can be used in real-life applications like signature verification, document recognition and biometric systems. The present study can be extended for recognition of other Indic scripts.

References

1. Nag, S., et al.: Offline extraction of indic regional language from natural scene image using text segmentation and deep convolutional sequence. In: Mandal, J.K., Mukhopadhyay, S., Dutta, P., Dasgupta, K. (eds.) Methodologies and Application Issues of Contemporary Computing Framework, pp. 49–68. Springer, Singapore (2018). https://doi.org/10.1007/978-981-13-2345-4_5
2. Tian, S., et al.: Multilingual scene character recognition with co-occurrence of histogram of oriented gradients. Pattern Recogn. **51**, 125–134 (2016). https://doi.org/10.1016/j.patcog.2015.07.009
3. Narang, V., Roy, S., Murthy, O.V.R., Hanmandlu, M.: Devanagari character recognition in scene images. In: Proceedings of 12th International Conference on Document Analysis and Recognition, USA. IEEE (2013). https://doi.org/10.1109/ICDAR.2013.184
4. Fraz, M., Sarfraz, M.S., Edirisinghe, E.A.: Exploiting colour information for better scene text detection and recognition. Int. J. Document Anal. Recogn. (IJDAR) **18**(2), 153–167 (2015). https://doi.org/10.1007/s10032-015-0239-x
5. Park, J., Lee, G., Kim, E., Lim, J., Kim, S., Yang, H., et al.: Automatic detection and recognition of Korean text in outdoor signboard images. Pattern Recogn. Lett. **31**, 1728–1739 (2010). https://doi.org/10.1016/j.patrec.2010.05.024
6. Coates, A., et al.: Text detection and character recognition in scene images with unsupervised feature learning. In: Proceedings of the International Conference on Document Analysis and Recognition, China, pp. 440–445. IEEE (2011). https://doi.org/10.1109/ICDAR.2011.95
7. Sharma, A.: Recovery of drawing order in handwritten digit images. In: Proceedings of the 2013 IEEE Second International Conference on Image Information Processing, India. IEEE (2013). https://doi.org/10.1109/ICIIP.2013.6707630
8. Sharma, A.: A combined static and dynamic feature extraction technique to recognize handwritten digits. Vietnam J. Comput. Sci. **2**(3), 133–142 (2015). https://doi.org/10.1007/s40595-014-0038-1
9. Hartigan, J.A., Wong, M.A.: Algorithm as 136: a k-means clustering algorithm. J. R. Stat. Soc. Ser. C (Appl. Stat.) **1**(28), 100–108 (1979). https://doi.org/10.2307/2346830
10. Chang, C.C., Lin, C.J.: LIBSVM: a library for support vector machines. J. ACM Trans. Intell. Syst. Technol. (TIST) **2**(3), 1–27 (2011). https://doi.org/10.1145/1961189.1961199
11. Gan, J., Wang, W., Lu, K.: A new perspective: recognizing online handwritten chinese characters via 1-dimensional CNN. Inf. Sci. **478**, 375–390 (2019). https://doi.org/10.1016/j.ins.2018.11.035

Segmentation and Enhancement of Mammograms for the Detection of Cancer Using Gradient Weight Map and Decorrelation Stretch

B. V. Divyashree[✉] and G. Hemantha Kumar

Department of Studies in Computer Science, University of Mysore, Manasagangotri, Mysore 570006, Karnataka, India
divyashreenivas@gmail.com

Abstract. To deal with computer aided detection of breast cancer in mammograms, an efficient automated preprocessing stage is the most vital step which assists radiologist's decision. The approach proposes a model for the segmentation and enhancement of the breast region. The proposed method includes gradient weight map followed by region property-based extraction and morphological operations for background suppression and artifacts removal. Intensity adjustment and Otsu's thresholding methods were adopted for breast region extraction. Finally, enhancement of the breast region is accomplished by Contrast-Limited Adaptive Histogram Equalization (CLAHE) and Decorrelation stretch. Experimentation conducted on mini Mammographic Image Analysis Society (miniMIAS) dataset shows segmentation accuracy of about 97.64%. Enhancement contributes with better feature discrimination with high Peak Signal Noise Ratio (PSNR) and low Root Mean Square Error (RMSE).

Keywords: Mammograms · Segmentation · Gradient weight · Otsu's threshold · Contrast-Limited Adaptive Histogram Equalization (CLAHE) · Decorrelation stretch

1 Introduction

Breast cancer is a deadly disease among women crossed 40 years. Early detection is the only way to reduce the mortality rate [1, 2]. Mammography is a successful screening tool, used to detect breast cancer in the early stage. Mammographic image provides possibility of discovering abnormalities enclosed by dense and overlapping breast tissues [3]. The major parts of mammographic images are background region, the pectoral region and breast region shown in Fig. (1). Since the mammographic images are of low contrast, accurate detection of masses and calcification in the breast region needs proper segmentation and enhancement technique. Segmentation of breast region can be accomplished by separating the foreground regions (breast region plus pectoral region) from background regions and by the removal of pectoral muscle. Various artifacts, high intensity labels,

© Springer Nature Singapore Pte Ltd. 2020
R. V. Babu et al. (Eds.): NCVPRIPG 2019, CCIS 1249, pp. 365–374, 2020.
https://doi.org/10.1007/978-981-15-8697-2_34

low intensity labels, orientation labels and inflammatory folds are available as noise in the background of the mammographic image. They have similar intensities as the dense tissues in the breast and pectoral parenchyma tissues. Hence, to avoid further complications in analyzing the breast region accurately, background suppression, pectoral muscle removal and highlighting the features of masses are to be accomplished [4].

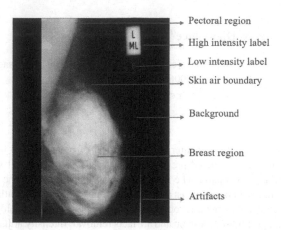

Fig. 1. Mammographic image

The existing state of the art on preprocessing techniques adopted for mammograms are discussed in this section. Ferrari et al. [5] proposed a contour-based method for breast boundary detection. Their method worked good for interrupted boundaries and with reduced time for selecting the initial contour. But the average processing time taken was not optimal. Marti et al. [6] adopted a combination of methods like edge detection, scale space concepts and the growing active contour to extract the breast line boundary. The method was robust but, difficult to segment images having more noise and there were segmentation errors. Fast Marching methods were used by Yapa and Harada [7] to accurately identify the breast line boundary. They evolved with a robust model for different breast tissue densities and the model was able to detect the nipple partially. Their method was not popular as it needs user involvement to select an initial seed point. The combination of global image thresholding, multilevel Otsu's thresholding methods were adopted by Czaplicka and Włodarczyk [8] to estimate the breast line. The authors improved the accuracy level, but experimented on selected images in the dataset. Shi et al. and Gonzalez et al. [9, 10] proposed a gradient weight map method followed by line fitting methods to detect skin air boundary. The authors concentrated on performance evaluation of pectoral muscle segmentation and calcification detection but not evaluated the breast line boundary segmentation. Wonghanavasu and Tanvoraphonkchai adopted the Otsu's thresholding for pectoral muscle segmentation. However, their method faced difficulty to segment pectoral muscle in dense breasts and tested on small datasets [11]. Kwok et al. [12] presented the iterative thresholding and cliff detection method, Weidong and Shunren proposed the iterative thresholding on the selected region [13]. Makandar and Halalli proposed segmentation technique using morphological thresholding followed by the region growing method and discussed various filtering techniques and contrast adjustment techniques [14].

In view of the limitations in the state of art, the proposed method concentrates on background suppression, removal of pectoral muscle and enhancement of breast region. Background suppression is carried out using the gradient weight map, region properties and morphological opening operations. For pectoral muscle removal, combination of intensity adjustment, Otsu's thresholding and morphological closing operation with median filters are applied. Then, breast region is enhanced to improve the visibility using Contrast-Limited Adaptive Histogram Equalization (CLAHE) and Decorrelation stretch. Experimentation is performed on mini Mammographic Image Analysis Society (miniMIAS) datasets considering parameters like sensitivity, specificity, correctness, Jaccard and dice similarity index for segmentation. Further Peak Signal Noise Ratio (PSNR) and Root Mean Square Error (RMSE) parameters were used for the evaluation of enhancement [15]. The methods adopted in the proposed work for the segmentation and enhancement achieved promising results.

2   Materials and Method

The proposed method focuses on suppression of background, removal of pectoral muscle and enhancement of the breast region. The framework to accomplish the proposed work is shown in Fig. (2).

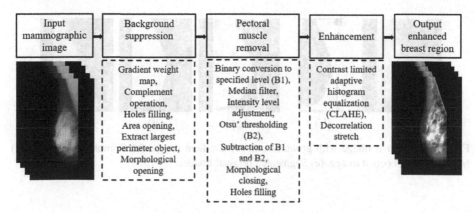

Fig. 2. Framework of the proposed method

2.1   Background Suppression Using Gradient Weight and Region Properties

In the first step, the gradient weight map is applied to the input mammographic image, wherein the weights are calculated using 3x3 windows for each pixel based on gradient magnitude. The weight of a pixel is inversely proportional to the gradient magnitude. Sharp image gradients are available at the edges between the foreground and background regions. Vertical and horizontal directional gradients are combined at each location to separate the higher intensity areas from the lower intensity areas. To compute the image gradient, standard deviation is used as σ for deriving Gaussian derivative. The proposed method assumes σ value as 4.5. The resultant gradient image obtained is shown in Fig. (3(b)).

To enhance the dark foreground regions of the image, complement operation is performed where the dark regions become lighter and light regions become darker as shown in Fig. 3(c). Then, to reduce the processing time, the complemented images are converted to binary. However, in the proposed method binary conversion is only meant for segmentation of the Region Of Interest (ROI) and hence it will not lose information in the breast region.

The binary image obtained has a set of background pixels, which are not filled in the background region from the image edge. These pixels are removed by changing its intensity value to white/light color. Then, to remove all invalid connected components that are less than the threshold, the area opening operation is adopted. Further, object with the largest perimeter is extracted which is the breast region and pectoral region. For the final refinement in the background region morphological opening operation is performed with a square shaped structuring element to take away the small invalid regions (square and rectangular regions) lesser than a threshold 'O' using (1). The resultant image is shown in Fig. 3(d).

$$ROI \bullet O = (ROI \ominus O) \oplus O \tag{1}$$

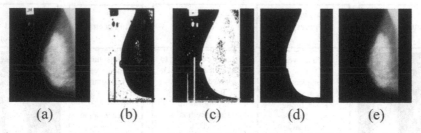

Fig. 3. (a) Original image with ground truth, (b) Gradient image, (c) Complement image, (d) Morphological opened image, (e) Segmented original image.

2.2 Pectoral Muscle Removal Using Intensity Level Adjustment and Otsu's Thresholding

Pectoral muscle region needs to be suppressed to obtain the breast region for further analysis. Removal of pectoral muscle is one of the difficult tasks as they vary in their shape, size, and orientation. The background suppressed image then undergoes a series of steps to remove pectoral muscle. Firstly, the image is binarized to a specified thresholding factor (T) considering the luminance of the pixels (depicted in image B1) (Fig. 4(b)).

$$I(x, y) = \begin{cases} 1, & \text{if } I(x, y) > T \\ 0, & \text{otherwise} \end{cases} \tag{2}$$

Next, the original background suppressed image is filtered using the median filter using 3 × 3 window which removes the noises like salt and pepper, Gaussian noises by maintaining the sharpness of the image.

Then, the contrast of the image is increased twice by adjusting the intensity values to new contrast values that are chosen empirically.

Further, an optimal global segmentation method called Otsu's thresholding method is adopted in the proposed model. It works in an unsupervised scenario for the selection of threshold. Based on the global characteristics of the histogram, the method finds the maximum and minimum values of the input data and divides the image into two classes using optimal threshold (the image obtained is depicted as B2) (Fig. 4(c)).

Later, the difference operation is computed between B1 and B2 to remove pectoral muscle and extract only the breast region which is the Region Of Interest (ROI) (Fig. 4(d)). Along with the pectoral muscle some dense areas in the breast regions were also removed in the previous step. Hence, to fill the minor discontinuities morphological closing operation with disk structuring element and holes filling operations are performed to extract the entire breast region (Fig. 4(e)).

$$ROI \bullet C = (ROI \oplus C) \ominus C \tag{3}$$

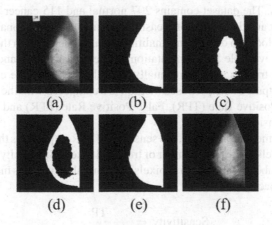

Fig. 4. (a) Original image with ground truth, (b) Binary image, (c) Otsu's thresholded image, (d) Subtracted image, (e) Holes filled image, (f) Segmented breast region

2.3 Enhancement Using CLAHE and Decorrelation Stretch

Finding the malignancy in the breast region is a challenging task as the mammograms are mild energy X-rays with invisible abnormal tissues that reside in the dense tissues. Hence, image enhancement plays one of the major roles to increase the sensitivity of the visibility and to improve the rate of detection of breast cancer. The combination of contrast limited adaptive histogram equalization and decorrelation stretch has improved the visibility of the image to find the abnormal tissues as shown in Fig. 5(b, c, e, f). CLAHE enriches the contrast and edge information, decorrelation stretch increases the visual interpretation. This exaggeration builds feature discrimination easier.

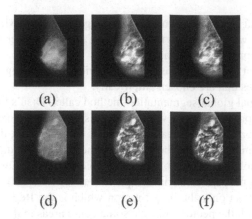

Fig. 5. (a)&(d) Original image, (b)&(e) CLAHE image, (c)&(f) Decorrelation stretch image

3 Results and Discussion

The proposed algorithm has been tested on mini MIAS dataset that contains 322 mammographic images. The dataset contains 207 normal and 115 cancer images including fatty, the glandular and dense type of breast density images. Additional information like severity, class and location of the abnormalities are also contained in the dataset. Ground truth data are not available for segmentation of the breast region and pectoral region. Hence the ground truth is marked manually with the advice of the expert radiologist. The segmented outputs of the proposed method are compared with the ground truth. For evaluation, True Positive Rate (TPR), False Positive Rate (FPR) and Accuracy (ACC) parameters are considered.

In terms of segmentation of ROI, the sensitivity (TPR) represents the ratio of number of true positive pixels to the total number of true ROI pixels. Specificity (FPR) represents the ratio of the number of false positive pixels to the number of pixels marked as non-ROI pixels in the true background.

$$\text{Sensitivity} = \frac{\text{TP}}{(\text{TP} + \text{FN})} \tag{4}$$

$$\text{Specificity} = \frac{\text{FP}}{(\text{FP} + \text{TN})} \tag{5}$$

The Accuracy is defined as the sum of correctly classified ROI pixels and correctly identified non-ROI pixels to the total number of pixels in the images.

$$\text{ACC} = \frac{\text{TP} + \text{TN}}{\text{TP} + \text{FP} + \text{TN} + \text{FN}} \tag{6}$$

Further, Jaccard and Dice similarity indexes are also considered for evaluation of segmentation of ROI (Table 1). Diversity and similarity between ROI segmentation results and ground truths are measured using Jaccard index, Dice coefficient measures similarity between them. For calculating the similarity index, metrics are defined for simplicity as follows, Ss for segmented output of the proposed method and Sg for the ground truth image.

$$Jaccard = \frac{|Ss \cap Sg|}{|Ss \cup Sg|} \tag{7}$$

$$Dice = 2\frac{|Ss \cup Sg|}{|Ss| + |Sg|} \tag{8}$$

Table 1. Performance for segmentation of ROI (breast region plus pectoral region).

Number of images	Sensitivity	Specificity	Correctness	Accuracy (%)	Dice similarity	Jaccard similarity
322	**0.9872**	0.0711	0.9277	**97.64%**	0.921	**0.974**

Table 2. Performance for segmentation of ROI (breast region).

Number of images	Sensitivity	Specificity	Correctness	Accuracy (%)	Dice similarity	Jaccard similarity
322	0.8900	0.0295	0.9398	**95.95%**	0.902	0.840

The proposed method outperformed better for segmentation of ROI (breast region + pectoral region) compared to segmentation of ROI (breast region) with an accuracy of about 97.64%. Sensitivity and specificity achieved is about 0.98 and 0.07 respectively. The accuracy recorded for segmentation of breast region is 95.95%, sensitivity = 0.89, specificity = 0.0295. The result drop occurred due to errors in segmentation and removal of pectoral muscle. Dice and Jaccard similarity indexes have performed well as tabulated in Table 2. Jaccard similarity and sensitivity observed for ROI (breast region plus pectoral muscle) is maximum compared to the state of the art.

For measuring the performance of the enhancement, PSNR and RMSE parameters are considered (Table 3). PSNR defines the relationship between maximum powers a signal has and the noise power. RMSE is an error metric parameter.

$$RMSE = \sqrt{\frac{1}{MN}\sum_{i=1}^{M}\sum_{j=1}^{N}(x(i,j) - y(i,j))^2} \tag{9}$$

$$PSNR = 10\log\frac{(2^n - 1)^2}{RMSE} \tag{10}$$

The enhancement results show minimum RMSE values that help for further analysis with better feature discrimination for the detection of abnormalities in the breast regions.

Table 4 shows comparison with the state-of-the-art methods with respect to accuracy of ROI where (B+P) is the breast region plus the pectoral region and B is the breast region.

Table 3. Performance of enhancement of breast region (ROI)

Image Number	PSNR (CLAHE)	RMSE (CLAHE)	PSNR (DECORR STRETCH)	RMSE (DECORR STRETCH)
mdb001	22.99	0.8548	20.86	0.2893
mdb002	22.42	0.0730	16.03	0.0728
mdb003	23.69	0.0833	18.49	0.0001
mdb004	23.39	0.0833	16.16	0.0001
mdb005	23.42	0.3240	21.03	0.4822
mdb006	22.98	0.5291	20.08	0.5291
mdb007	22.11	0.2982	15.27	0.2982
mdb008	22.49	0.0001	15.27	0.0001
mdb009	25.37	0.0001	14.54	0.0001
mdb0010	22.19	0.0273	13.37	0.0451

Table 4. Performance comparison with the state of art method

Proposed by	Dataset and detected boundary	Accuracy (%)
Ferrari et al. [5]	MIAS (84 images) (B+P)	96
Martí et al. [6]	MIAS (65 images) (B+P)	97
Wirth and Stapinski [16]	MIAS (25 images) (B+P)	97
Peng Shi et al. [9]	MIAS (322 images) (B+P)	N/A
Chen and Zwiggelaar [17]	MIAS (322 images) (B)	92.8
Maitra et al. [18]	MIAS (322 images) (B)	95.7
Proposed method	**MIAS (322 images) (B+P)**	**97.64**
Proposed method	**MIAS (322 images) (B)**	**95.95**

By comparing the accuracies obtained in the existing literature, the proposed method has performed better with an improvement of accuracy of 0.64% for (B+P) and 0.25% for (B). The authors in the state of art used contrast enhancement techniques for the enhancement of breast region, but in the present work along with the contrast enhancement each pixel is discriminated for the feature using decorrelation stretch for further interpretation.

Conclusion: In computer-based detection of breast cancer in mammography, segmentation of ROI and enhancement of the low contrast image are the important steps needed for further analysis. In the proposed work, we have presented an approach for background suppression and the artifacts removal using gradient map and the region property. Segmentation of the breast region is accomplished by intensity adjustments and Otsu's thresholding method. To highlight the hidden abnormalities, enhancement of breast regions is performed using CLAHE and decorrelation stretch. The proposed method produced promising results and helps in distinction between cancer and normal tissues. Future scope is to explore the proper features from the enhanced breast region for accurate breast cancer detection and test with other standard datasets.

Acknowledgements. The authors would like to thank Dr Deepashree Basavalingu, Consultant Radiologist, Blackpool Teaching Hospitals, NHS Foundation Trust, United Kingdom for her certification of ground truths, valuable help and comments in carrying out this work. The first author would like to thank the Ministry of Tribal Affairs, The Government of India for awarding the National Fellowship (201718-NFST-KAR-00159) to carry out this research work.

References

1. DeSantis, C., Ma, J., Bryan, L., Jemal, A.: Breast cancer statistics, 2013. CA Cancer J. Clin. **64**(1), 52–62 (2014)
2. Oeffinger, K.C., Fontham, E.T.H., Etzioni, R.: Breast cancer screening for women at average risk: 2015 guideline update from the American Cancer Society. JAMA **314**(15), 1599–1614 (2015)
3. American Cancer Society, USA. https://www.cancer.org/cancer/breast-cancer/about/how-common-is-breast-cancer.html
4. Moghbel, M., Ooi, C.Y., Ismail, N., Hau, Y.W., Memari, N.: A review of breast boundary and pectoral muscle segmentation methods in computer-aided detection/diagnosis of breast mammography. Artif. Intell. Rev. **53** (2019). https://doi.org/10.1007/s10462-019-09721-8
5. Ferrari, R.J., Rangayyan, R.M., Desautels, J.E.L.: Identification of the breast boundary in mammograms using active contour models. Med. Biol. Eng. Comput. **42**(2), 201–208 (2004)
6. Martí, R., Oliver, A., Raba, D., Freixenet, J.: Breast skin-line segmentation using contour growing. In: Martí, J., Benedí, J.M., Mendonça, A.M., Serrat, J. (eds.) IbPRIA 2007. LNCS, vol. 4478, pp. 564–571. Springer, Heidelberg (2007). https://doi.org/10.1007/978-3-540-72849-8_71
7. Yapa, R.D., Harada, K.: Breast skin-line estimation and breast segmentation in mammograms using fast-marching method. Int. J. Biol. Biomed. Med. Sci. **3**(1), 54–62 (2008)
8. Czaplicka, K., Wodarczyk, H.: Automatic breast-line and pectoral muscle segmentation. SchedaeInformaticae **20**, 195–209 (2011)
9. Shi, P., Zhong, J., Rampun, A., Wang, H.: A hierarchical pipeline for breast boundary segmentation and calcification detection in mammograms. Comput. Biol. Med. (2018). https://doi.org/10.1016/j.compbiomed.2018.03.011
10. Gonzalez, R.C., Woods, R.E., Eddins, S.L.: Digital Image Processing Using MATLAB: and Mathworks, MATLAB Sim SV 07. Gatesmark Publishing (2009)
11. Wongthanavasu, S., Tanvoraphonkchai, S.: Cellular automata-based identification of the pectoral muscle in mammograms. In: The proceedings of the 3rd International Symposium on Biomedical Engineering, pp 294–298 (2008)
12. Kwok, S.M., Chandrasekhar, R., Attikiouzel, Y.: Automatic pectoral muscle segmentation on mammograms by straight line estimation and cliff detection. In: The seventh Australian and New Zealand intelligent information systems conference, pp 67–72. IEEE (2001)
13. Weidong, X., Shunren, X.: A model based algorithm to segment the pectoral muscle in mammograms. In: Proceedings of the 2003 International Conference on Neural Networks and Signal Processing, Nanjing, vol 2, pp. 1163–1169 (2003)
14. Makandar, A., Halalli, B.: Threshold based segmentation technique for mass detection in mammography. J. Comput. **11**(6), 472–478 (2016)

15. Suckling, J., et al.: The mammographic image analysis society digital mammogram database. In: Proceedings of the 2nd International Workshop on Digital Mammography, pp. 375–378 (1994)
16. Wirth, M.A., Stapinski, A.: Segmentation of the breast region in mammograms using active contours. In: Visual Communications and Image Processing, pp. 1995–2006. International Society for Optics and Photonics, Lugano (2003)
17. Chen, Z., Zwiggelaar, R.: A combined method for automatic identification of the breast boundary in mammograms. 5th International Conference on Biomedical Engineering and Informatics (BMEI). pp. 121–125. IEEE (2012)
18. Maitra, I.K., Nag, S., Bandyopadhyay, S.K.: Technique for preprocessing of digital mammogram. Comput. Methods Program. Biomed. **107**(2), 175–188 (2012)

LR-HyClassify: A Low Rank Based Framework for Classification of Degraded Hyperspectral Images

Sourish Sarkar[✉] and Rajiv R. Sahay

Department of Electrical Engineering, Indian Institute of Technology,
Kharagpur, India
sourish.sarkar@iitkgp.ac.in, rajiv@ee.iitkgp.ernet.in

Abstract. We propose a novel framework for the classification of hyperspectral data corrupted by severe degradation. We propose an optimization framework for extracting discriminative features from noisy hyperspectral data which are then passed onto a simple classifier which exploits both the spatial and spectral correlations in the data. Instead of directly extracting the features from the noisy input data, we learn a basis matrix from the underlying clean data using a combination of non-negative matrix factorization and nuclear-norm minimization. The input degraded data are then projected onto the basis vectors to obtain features. We use structural incoherence to maximize the discriminative ability of the features, which, to the best of our knowledge, is being used for the first time in hyperspectral image processing literature. We show the deterioration in the performance of classification algorithms with the progressive addition of noise while demonstrating the robustness of our algorithm. We evaluate the performance of our algorithm on three well known datasets, namely, Botswana, Salinas and Indian Pines, obtaining state-of-the-art results that validate the efficacy of our algorithm.

Keywords: Hyperspectral image classification · Structural incoherence · Non-negative matrix factorization · Nuclear-norm minimization

1 Introduction

Hyperspectral image (HSI) classification has been an area of active research since over 20 years where the task is to assign each pixel in a HSI to its respective class. HSI classification is a challenging task due to the high data dimensionality, availability of very few labelled samples and the presence of noise. The presence of noise damages both the spatial and spectral information available in the data, thereby degrading the performance of classification algorithms drastically. This motivates us to devise a novel technique which can achieve impressive classification accuracies even in the presence of significant amount of noise. Algorithms

© Springer Nature Singapore Pte Ltd. 2020
R. V. Babu et al. (Eds.): NCVPRIPG 2019, CCIS 1249, pp. 375–384, 2020.
https://doi.org/10.1007/978-981-15-8697-2_35

used in the earlier days of research in HSI classification considered only the spectral signatures which did not provide satisfactory classification results. However, recent works [4, 8, 9] acknowledge the contribution of the spatial information contained in HSI in addition to the spectral information. The importance of spatial information stems from the simple hypothesis that nearby pixels in a HSI belong to the same class with high probability. In [12], the authors address the problem of robust face recognition in the presence of data corrupted due to occlusion and disguise. They incorporate a constraint of structural incoherence in order to make the bases learnt for different classes independent. This leads to the achievement of a higher discriminating ability resulting in an impressive classification performance. Inspired by their approach, in this work, we aim to exploit both the spectral and spatial information and classify a severely degraded HSI by learning discriminative features. Instead of learning these features from the corrupted data, we learn them from the underlying clean data which leads to state-of-the-art classification results.

2   Prior Work

Several methods which perform a pixelwise classification of HSIs have been proposed [10, 14, 23]. Sparse representation based classifiers have been used for HSI classification in [5, 6]. A combination of low rank and sparsity for HSI classification can be found in [8, 19, 21]. Collaborative representation based classifiers have been used in [9, 11]. In [1], extended morphological profiles were used for HSI classification. The authors in [22] used conditional random fields for HSI classification. The random forest framework was investigated for HSI classification in [7]. Owing to the excellent performance in classification of images and videos, deep learning based methods have been extensively investigated for HSI classification. Stacked auto encoders (SAEs) [16], convolutional neural networks (CNNs) [13], deep belief networks (DBNs) [4] and deep recurrent neural networks (RNNs) [15] have been used for HSI classification. Recently, generative adversarial networks (GANs) have been introduced for the purpose of HSI classification [24]. However, these models are data hungry and are prone to overfitting due to the scarcity of available labelled samples. Hence, most of the recent research with deep models deals with finding new techniques to mitigate this problem.

3   Proposed Methodology

In this work, we present a novel framework wherein we combine non-negative matrix factorization (NMF), nuclear norm minimization (NNM) and structural incoherence to learn discriminative features from a degraded HSI. Given a HSI of size $m \times n \times b$, the training samples are the b-dimensional spectral vectors. Let $\mathbf{Y} \in \mathcal{R}^{b \times N}$ denote a matrix formed by stacking together all the N available training samples. Hence, for a HSI with C classes, $\mathbf{Y} = [\mathbf{Y}_1, \mathbf{Y}_2, \ldots, \mathbf{Y}_C]$ where $\mathbf{Y}_i = [\mathbf{y}_1^i, \mathbf{y}_2^i, \ldots, \mathbf{y}_{n_i}^i] \in \mathcal{R}^{b \times n_i}$ $(i = 1, 2, \ldots, C)$ denotes the training samples belonging to class i and n_i is the number of available training samples from class i so that $N = Cn_i$. We model the data as:

$$\mathbf{Y} = \mathbf{L} + \mathbf{S} + \mathbf{N} \tag{1}$$

where $\mathbf{L} = [\mathbf{L}_1, \mathbf{L}_2, \dots, \mathbf{L}_C] \in \mathcal{R}^{b \times N}$ is a low rank matrix, $\mathbf{S} = [\mathbf{S}_1, \mathbf{S}_2, \dots, \mathbf{S}_C] \in \mathcal{R}^{b \times N}$ is the matrix of sparse noise and $\mathbf{N} = [\mathbf{N}_1, \mathbf{N}_2, \dots, \mathbf{N}_C] \in \mathcal{R}^{b \times N}$ denotes additive Gaussian noise. We aim to combine non-negative matrix factorization and nuclear norm minimization to simultaneously denoise the available data and learn a basis matrix for classification. We wish to solve the following optimization problem:

$$\min_{\mathbf{L},\mathbf{S},\mathbf{U}\geq 0,\mathbf{V}\geq 0} \alpha\|\mathbf{L}\|_* + \beta\|\mathbf{S}\|_1 + \gamma\sum_{j\neq i}\|\mathbf{L}_j^T\mathbf{L}_i\|_F^2 + \delta\|\mathbf{L} - \mathbf{UV}\|_F^2$$

$$s.t. \|\mathbf{Y} - \mathbf{L} - \mathbf{S}\|_F^2 \leq \epsilon \tag{2}$$

where $\|\cdot\|_F$ and $\|\cdot\|_*$, respectively, denote the Frobenius norm and the nuclear norm of a matrix, α, β, γ, δ are positive parameters and ϵ is a small constant whose value is fixed to 0.001. It is noteworthy that the basis matrix $\mathbf{U}$ is being learnt from the underlying clean data $\mathbf{L}$ and not directly from the degraded training data $\mathbf{Y}$. The third term in Eq. (2) corresponds to the structural incoherence [17] which measures the similarity between the derived low-rank matrices of different classes. Hence, minimizing this term separately for every class tends to make these derived matrices incoherent and enhances their discriminating ability. Hence, for the ith class, we wish to solve:

$$\min_{\mathbf{L}_i,\mathbf{S}_i,\mathbf{U}\geq 0,\mathbf{V}\geq 0} \alpha\|\mathbf{L}_i\|_* + \beta\|\mathbf{S}_i\|_1 + \gamma\sum_{j\neq i}\|\mathbf{L}_j^T\mathbf{L}_i\|_F^2 + \delta\|\mathbf{L}_i - (\mathbf{UV})_i\|_F^2$$

$$s.t. \|\mathbf{Y}_i - \mathbf{L}_i - \mathbf{S}_i\|_F^2 \leq \epsilon \tag{3}$$

We use the method of augmented Lagrangian multipliers (ALM) [18] to solve the above problem. To this end, we first introduce an auxiliary variable $\mathbf{Z}_i$ as follows:

$$\min_{\mathbf{L}_i,\mathbf{S}_i,\mathbf{U}\geq 0,\mathbf{V}\geq 0,\mathbf{Z}_i} \alpha\|\mathbf{L}_i\|_* + \beta\|\mathbf{S}_i\|_1 + \gamma\sum_{j\neq i}\|\mathbf{L}_j^T\mathbf{Z}_i\|_F^2 + \delta\|\mathbf{Z}_i - (\mathbf{UV})_i\|_F^2$$

$$s.t. \|\mathbf{Y}_i - \mathbf{L}_i - \mathbf{S}_i\|_F^2 \leq \epsilon, \; \mathbf{Z}_i = \mathbf{L}_i \tag{4}$$

The augmented Lagrangian is as follows:

$$\mathcal{L}(\mathbf{L}_i, \mathbf{S}_i, \mathbf{U} \geq 0, \mathbf{V} \geq 0, \mathbf{Z}_i \geq 0, \mathbf{M}_1, \mathbf{M}_2; \mu) = \alpha\|\mathbf{L}_i\|_* + \beta\|\mathbf{S}_i\|_1$$

$$+\gamma\sum_{j\neq i}\|\mathbf{L}_j^T\mathbf{Z}_i\|_F^2 + \delta\|\mathbf{Z}_i - (\mathbf{UV})_i\|_F^2 + \langle\mathbf{M}_1, \mathbf{Y}_i - \mathbf{L}_i - \mathbf{S}_i\rangle$$

$$+\langle\mathbf{M}_2, \mathbf{Z}_i - \mathbf{L}_i\rangle + \frac{\mu}{2}[\|\mathbf{Y}_i - \mathbf{L}_i - \mathbf{S}_i + \frac{\mathbf{M}_1}{\mu}\|_F^2 + \|\mathbf{Z}_i - \mathbf{L}_i + \frac{\mathbf{M}_2}{\mu}\|_F^2] \tag{5}$$

where $\mathbf{M}_1$, $\mathbf{M}_2$ are Lagrange multipliers, μ is a positive parameter and $\langle\cdot,\cdot\rangle$ denotes the inner product. We now provide the updation rules for each of the variables.

– Computing $\mathbf{L}_i$ with other variables fixed:

With some algebraic manipulations, the $\mathbf{L}_i$-subproblem can be obtained from Eq. (5) as follows:

$$\min_{\mathbf{L}_i} \frac{\alpha}{2\mu}\|\mathbf{L}_i\|_* + \frac{1}{2}\|\mathbf{L}_i - (\mathbf{Y}_i - \mathbf{S}_i + \mathbf{Z}_i + \frac{\mathbf{M}_1}{\mu} + \frac{\mathbf{M}_2}{\mu})\|_F^2 \qquad (6)$$

Eq. (6) can be solved using singular value thresholding [3].

– Computing $\mathbf{S}_i$ fixing others:

The $\mathbf{S}_i$-subproblem can be obtained from Eq. (5) as follows:

$$\min_{\mathbf{S}_i} \frac{\beta}{\mu}\|\mathbf{S}_i\|_1 + \frac{1}{2}\|\mathbf{S}_i - (\mathbf{Y}_i - \mathbf{L}_i + \frac{\mathbf{M}_1}{\mu})\|_F^2 \qquad (7)$$

Eq. (7) can be solved using the soft shrinkage operation.

– Computation of $\mathbf{Z}_i$:

In order to achieve factorization of $\mathbf{Z}_i$, the non-negativity constraint on $\mathbf{Z}_i$ must be satisfied. To this end, we first introduce an indicator function as follows:

$$l_+(\mathbf{Z}_i) = \begin{cases} 0, & Z_{i_{m,n}} \geq 0 \quad \forall m, n \\ \infty, & otherwise \end{cases} \qquad (8)$$

where, $Z_{i_{m,n}}$ denotes the $(m,n)^{th}$ element of $\mathbf{Z}_i$. The $\mathbf{Z}_i$ sub-problem is then obtained from Eq. (5) as follows:

$$\min_{\mathbf{Z}_i} \gamma \sum_{j \neq i} \|\mathbf{L}_j^T \mathbf{Z}_i\|_F^2 + \delta\|\mathbf{Z}_i - (\mathbf{UV})_i\|_F^2 + \frac{\mu}{2}\|\mathbf{Z}_i - \mathbf{L}_i + \frac{\mathbf{M}_2}{\mu}\|_F^2 + l_+(\mathbf{Z}_i) \quad (9)$$

To solve this, we use the alternating direction method of multipliers (ADMM) [2]. To do so, we first introduce an auxiliary variable in order to make the objective function separable:

$$\min_{\mathbf{Z}_i} \gamma \sum_{j \neq i} \|\mathbf{L}_j^T \mathbf{Z}_i\|_F^2 + \delta\|\mathbf{Z}_i - (\mathbf{UV})_i\|_F^2 + \frac{\mu}{2}\|\mathbf{Z}_i - \mathbf{L}_i + \frac{\mathbf{M}_2}{\mu}\| + l_+(\mathbf{C}_i)$$

$$\text{s.t. } \mathbf{C}_i = \mathbf{Z}_i \qquad (10)$$

The above equation is solved iteratively by updating one of the variables and keeping the other fixed until convergence. The update equations are:

$$\mathbf{Z}_i = [(\delta + \frac{\mu}{2} + \frac{\rho}{2})\mathbf{I} + \gamma \sum_{j \neq i} \mathbf{L}_j \mathbf{L}_j^T]^{-1}[\delta(\mathbf{UV})_i + \frac{\mu \mathbf{L}_i}{2} - \mathbf{M}_2 - \mathbf{T} + \rho \mathbf{C}_i] \quad (11)$$

$$\mathbf{C}_i \leftarrow \max(\mathbf{Z}_i + \frac{\mathbf{T}}{\rho}, 0) \qquad (12)$$

$$\mathbf{T} \leftarrow \mathbf{T} + \rho(\mathbf{Z}_i - \mathbf{C}_i) \qquad (13)$$

$$\rho \leftarrow \min(\kappa\rho, \rho_{max}) \qquad (14)$$

where, $\mathbf{I}$ denotes the identity matrix of appropriate size, $\mathbf{T}$ is the Lagrange multiplier and $\rho > 0$, $\kappa > 0$, ρ_{max} are parameters.

– Computation of $\mathbf{U}$ and $\mathbf{V}$:

$$\min_{\mathbf{U} \geq 0, \mathbf{V} \geq 0} \|\mathbf{Z}_i - (\mathbf{UV})_i\|_F^2 \tag{15}$$

The above optimization problem can be solved directly using any of the existing NMF solvers.

– The final step is to update the multipliers and μ:

$$\mathbf{M}_1 \leftarrow \mathbf{M}_1 + \mu(\mathbf{Y}_i - \mathbf{L}_i - \mathbf{S}_i) \tag{16}$$

$$\mathbf{M}_2 \leftarrow \mathbf{M}_2 + \mu(\mathbf{Z}_i - \mathbf{L}_i) \tag{17}$$

$$\mu \leftarrow \min(\psi\mu, \mu_{max}) \tag{18}$$

Once we obtain the basis matrix $\mathbf{U}$ learnt from the underlying clean data $\mathbf{L}$, we project all the degraded training and testing data onto $\mathbf{U}$ to obtain discriminative features which are subsequently used for classification. For any spectral vector $\mathbf{y}$, we obtain its feature vector as follows:

$$\mathbf{f} = \mathbf{U}^\dagger \mathbf{y} \tag{19}$$

where $\mathbf{U}^\dagger$ denotes the pseudoinverse of $\mathbf{U}$. We propose to use a very simple classifier to classify these obtained features with high accuracy. For a test feature $\mathbf{f}_{test}$ and the training features $\mathbf{f}_i, i = 1, 2, \ldots, N$, let the spatial positions of the test and training features (corresponding to the test and training spectral vectors, respectively) be denoted by $\mathbf{p}_{test} = [x, y]^T$ and $\mathbf{p}_i = [x_i, y_i]^T$, respectively. Let $d_1 = dist(\mathbf{p}_{test}, \mathbf{p}_i)$ and $d_2 = dist(\mathbf{f}_{test}, \mathbf{f}_i)$, where $dist(\mathbf{a}, \mathbf{b})$ denotes the squared Euclidean distance between the vectors $\mathbf{a}$ and $\mathbf{b}$. Then we propose to define

$$d_i \triangleq \alpha_1 d_1 + \alpha_2 d_2 \tag{20}$$

as the dissimilarity between the test feature $\mathbf{f}_{test}$ and the training feature $\mathbf{f}_i$. The test sample is then classified to the class of the training sample with which this dissimilarity metric is minimum. d_1 simply takes into account the spatial correlation acknowledging the fact that pixels close to each other belong to the same class with a high probability while d_2 corresponds to the Euclidean distance between the test and training features. Note that setting α_1 to zero leads to the nearest neighbour classifier.

4   Experimental Results

In order to assess the performance of our algorithm, we use three HSI datasets. We synthetically corrupt these datasets by adding Gaussian noise of 0.05 standard deviation. Note that the spectral vectors are normalized to [0–1]. We also add impulse noise and stripes to bands 61 to 70 in all the three datasets. We randomly choose 10 per cent of labelled samples from each class for training and use the rest for testing. We compare our algorithm with SVM [14], SRC [20] and CRNN [11]. The classification performance is measured by the overall accuracy

---

Algorithm 1. Proposed algorithm for obtaining discriminative features

---

Input: Training dataset: $\{\mathbf{Y}_i\}$, i=1,2, ..., C; parameters $\alpha, \beta, \gamma, \delta$ in Eq.(3) and number of basis vectors r

Output: Learnt basis matrix $\mathbf{U}$

  1: Initialise $\kappa > 0, \rho > 0, \mu_{max} = 10^5, \rho_{max} = 10^5, \epsilon = 0.001, \mathbf{U}$=random matrix with positive elements of appropriate size.

  2: **for** $i = 1$ to C **do**

  3:    Initialise $\mu > 0, \psi > 0, \mathbf{M}_1 = \mathbf{0}, \mathbf{M}_2 = \mathbf{0}, \mathbf{Z}_i = \mathbf{0}, \mathbf{S}_i > \mathbf{0}, \mathbf{V}$=random matrix with positive elements of appropriate size.

  4:    **while** $\|\mathbf{Y}_i - \mathbf{L}_i - \mathbf{S}_i\|_F^2 / \|\mathbf{Y}_i\|_F^2 < \epsilon$ **do**

  5:      Update $\mathbf{L}_i$ by Eq. (6)

  6:      Update $\mathbf{S}_i$ by Eq. (7)

  7:      Update $\mathbf{Z}_i$ by Eq. (11)

  8:      Update $\mathbf{C}_i$ by Eq. (12)

  9:      Update $\mathbf{T}_i$ by Eq. (13)

10:      Update ρ_i by Eq. (14)

11:      Update $\mathbf{U}$ and $\mathbf{V}$ by Eq. (15)

12:      Update multipliers and penalty parameter μ using Eqs. (16,17 and 18)

13:    **end while**

14: **end for**

(OA) which is defined as the ratio between the number of correctly predicted pixels to the total number of test pixels. The robustness of our algorithm to noise is analysed by gradually increasing the amount of noise added and monitoring its effect on the class accuracies as compared to the other algorithms. The parameters $\alpha, \beta, \gamma, \delta, \alpha_1$ and α_2 are tuned to obtain the best results.

4.1   Datasets

The datasets used are Indian Pines, Botswana and Salinas. The Indian Pines dataset has a size of $145 \times 145 \times 200$ and has 16 classes. The Botswana dataset has a size of $1476 \times 256 \times 145$ and has 14 classes. The third dataset is the Salinas dataset which has a size of $512 \times 217 \times 204$ and 16 classes. The Botswana dataset has only 326 labelled training samples and hence is particularly more challenging among these datasets due to the scarcity of training samples.

4.2   Classification Performance

The performance of the classifiers on the three synthetically corrupted datasets is demonstrated in Tables 1, 2 and 3. We find that our algorithm achieves accuracies of 97.39%, 99.85% and 98.28% on the Botswana, Salinas and Indian Pines datasets respectively, outperforming the other methods. In the Salinas dataset, CRNN achieves the next best accuracy of 90.42% while SVM achieves the next best accuracies of 30.15% and 52.03% in the Botswana and the Indian Pines datasets, respectively. Note that our algorithm outperforms other state-of-the-art methods in these two datasets by a very large margin. Figure 1 depicts

Table 1. Classification accuracy (%) for the Botswana dataset

Class	SVM	SRC	CRNN	Proposed approach
Water	88.89	34.57	46.50	100
Hippo grass	3.30	4.40	5.49	100
Floodplain grasses 1	23.01	10.62	12.39	86.28
Floodplain grasses 2	10.36	2.60	7.25	100
Reeds 1	22.31	15.70	21.49	100
Riparian	26.86	12.40	6.20	98.76
Firescar 2	30.90	17.17	17.17	81.55
Island interior	37.70	12.02	24.04	99.45
Acacia woodlands	16.96	7.77	6.36	100
Acacia shrublands	19.73	9.42	8.07	100
Acacia grasslands	35.40	27.73	35.40	100
Short mopane	22.70	8.59	11.66	100
Mixed mopane	17.01	9.96	5.40	100
Exposed soils	74.12	24.70	72.94	100
OA (%)	**30.15**	**14.54**	**18.41**	**97.39**

Table 2. Classification accuracy (%) for the Salinas dataset

Class	SVM	SRC	CRNN	Proposed approach
Brocoli green weeds 1	97.34	98.34	99.56	100
Brocoli green weeds 2	97.67	95.68	99.85	100
Fallow	75.42	0	99.10	100
Fallow rough plow	98.72	98.88	98.96	98.17
Fallow smooth	96.47	99.34	97.80	99.05
Stubble	99.04	99.80	99.75	99.78
Celery	99.25	99.35	99.60	99.97
Grapes untrained	95.63	81.47	79.54	100
Soil vinyard develop	98.76	98.73	99.25	100
Corn senesced green weeds	75.38	79.02	95.73	99.97
Lettuce romaine 4wk	0	0	98.86	99.79
Lettuce romaine 5wk	95.50	93.54	99.60	99.71
Lettuce romaine 6wk	97.81	97.94	98.06	99.76
Lettuce romaine 7wk	90.13	90.34	93.87	99.27
Vinyard untrained	9.92	46.72	66.43	100
Vinyard vertical trellis	79.15	75.52	98.95	100
OA (%)	**80.82**	**80.02**	**90.42**	**99.85**

Table 3. Classification accuracy (%) for the Indian Pines dataset

Class	SVM	SRC	CRNN	Proposed approach
Alfalfa	0	0	4.88	100
Corn-notill	34.44	36.96	33.85	96.19
Corn-mintill	1.07	2.28	4.82	97.86
Corn	0.94	0.94	0.47	96.71
Grass-pasture	10.80	4.14	9.19	98.16
Grass-trees	88.28	86.15	75.19	99.70
Grass-pasture-mowed	0	0	0	96.00
Hay-windrowed	96.51	97.67	73.25	100
Oats	0	0	0	100
Soybean-notill	7.66	12.11	11.31	95.66
Soybean-mintill	89.09	85.56	75.37	98.73
Soybean-clean 5wk	0.19	4.31	5.06	98.50
Wheat	33.70	27.17	28.26	99.46
Woods	97.89	99.21	94.20	100
Buildings-Grass-Trees-Drives	6.92	1.73	2.59	99.71
Stone-Steel-Towers	80.95	85.71	69.05	100
OA (%)	**52.03**	**51.77**	**46.68**	**98.28**

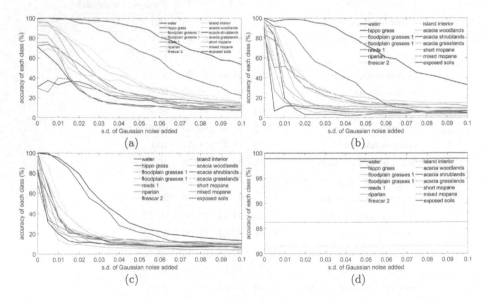

Fig. 1. Effect of progressive addition of noise on individual class accuracies on the Botswana dataset: (a) SVM, (b) SRC, (c) CRNN and (d) proposed approach

the sensitivity of the classifiers to noise. We progressively increase the standard deviation of Gaussian noise using increments of 0.005 upto 0.1 and examine the effect on class specific accuracies obtained by the algorithms. From Fig. 1, we infer that our algorithm is robust to noise in the data since the class specific accuracies do not drop and remain fairly constant while the performance of all the other methods deteriorates sharply with the increase in noise levels.

5   Conclusion

A novel algorithm for the classification of degraded hyperspectral data is proposed. A combination of nuclear norm minimization and non-negative matrix factorization is used to exploit the low rank nature of the data. A basis matrix is learnt from the underlying clean data which is used to extract features from the input degraded data. The discriminative ability of the underlying clean data is exploited using structural incoherence, which to the best of our knowledge, is being introduced for the first time in the hyperspectral image processing literature. Both the spatial and spectral information are exploited for classification which lead to state-of-the-art results.

References

1. Benediktsson, J.A., Palmason, J.A., Sveinsson, J.R.: Classification of hyperspectral data from urban areas based on extended morphological profiles. IEEE Trans. Geosci. Remote Sens. **43**(3), 480–491 (2005)
2. Boyd, S., Parikh, N., Chu, E., Peleato, B., Eckstein, J., et al.: Distributed optimization and statistical learning via the alternating direction method of multipliers. Found. Trends Mach. Learn. **3**(1), 1–122 (2011)
3. Cai, J.F., Candès, E.J., Shen, Z.: A singular value thresholding algorithm for matrix completion. SIAM J. Opt. **20**(4), 1956–1982 (2010)
4. Chen, Y., Zhao, X., Jia, X.: Spectral-spatial classification of hyperspectral data based on deep belief network. IEEE J. Sel. Topics Appl. Earth Observ. Remote Sens. **8**(6), 2381–2392 (2015)
5. Chen, Y., Nasrabadi, N.M., Tran, T.D.: Hyperspectral image classification using dictionary-based sparse representation. IEEE Trans. Geosci. Remote Sens. **49**(10), 3973–3985 (2011)
6. Chen, Y., Nasrabadi, N.M., Tran, T.D.: Hyperspectral image classification via kernel sparse representation. IEEE Trans. Geosci. Remote Sens. **51**(1), 217–231 (2012)
7. Ham, J., Chen, Y., Crawford, M.M., Ghosh, J.: Investigation of the random forest framework for classification of hyperspectral data. IEEE Trans. Geosci. Remote Sens. **43**(3), 492–501 (2005)
8. Jia, S., Zhang, X., Li, Q.: Spectral-spatial hyperspectral image classification using $\ell_{1/2}$ regularized low-rank representation and sparse representation-based graph cuts. IEEE J. Sel. Topics Appl. Earth Observ. Remote Sens. **8**(6), 2473–2484 (2015)
9. Jiang, J., Chen, C., Yu, Y., Jiang, X., Ma, J.: Spatial-aware collaborative representation for hyperspectral remote sensing image classification. IEEE Geosci. Remote Sens. Lett. **14**(3), 404–408 (2017)

10. Li, J., Bioucas-Dias, J.M., Plaza, A.: Semisupervised hyperspectral image segmentation using multinomial logistic regression with active learning. IEEE Trans. Geosci. Remote Sens. **48**(11), 4085–4098 (2010)
11. Li, W., Du, Q., Zhang, F., Hu, W.: Collaborative-representation-based nearest neighbor classifier for hyperspectral imagery. IEEE Geosci. Remote Sens. Lett. **12**(2), 389–393 (2015)
12. Lu, Y., Yuan, C., Zhu, W., Li, X.: Structurally incoherent low-rank nonnegative matrix factorization for image classification. IEEE Trans. Image Process. **27**(11), 5248–5260 (2018)
13. Makantasis, K., Karantzalos, K., Doulamis, A., Doulamis, N.: Deep supervised learning for hyperspectral data classification through convolutional neural networks. In: Proceedings IGARSS, pp. 4959–4962. IEEE (2015)
14. Melgani, F., Bruzzone, L.: Classification of hyperspectral remote sensing images with support vector machines. IEEE Trans. Geosci. Remote Sens. **42**(8), 1778–1790 (2004)
15. Mou, L., Ghamisi, P., Zhu, X.X.: Deep recurrent neural networks for hyperspectral image classification. IEEE Trans. Geosci. Remote Sens. **55**(7), 3639–3655 (2017)
16. Ozdemir, A., Gedik, B., Cetin, C.: Hyperspectral classification using stacked autoencoders with deep learning. In: Proceedings WHISPERS, pp. 1–4. IEEE (2014)
17. Ramirez, I., Sprechmann, P., Sapiro, G.: Classification and clustering via dictionary learning with structured incoherence and shared features. In: Proceedings CVPR, pp. 3501–3508. IEEE (2010)
18. Rockafellar, R.T.: Augmented lagrange multiplier functions and duality in nonconvex programming. SIAM J. Contr. **12**(2), 268–285 (1974)
19. Sun, W., Yang, G., Du, B., Zhang, L., Zhang, L.: A sparse and low-rank near-isometric linear embedding method for feature extraction in hyperspectral imagery classification. IEEE Trans. Geosci. Remote Sens. **55**(7), 4032–4046 (2017)
20. Wright, J., Yang, A.Y., Ganesh, A., Sastry, S.S., Ma, Y.: Robust face recognition via sparse representation. IEEE Trans. Pattern Anal. Mach. Intell. **31**(2), 210–227 (2009)
21. Zhao, Y., Yang, J.: Hyperspectral image denoising via sparse representation and low-rank constraint. IEEE Trans. Geosci. Remote Sens. **53**(1), 296–308 (2015)
22. Zhong, P., Wang, R.: Learning conditional random fields for classification of hyperspectral images. IEEE Trans. Image Process. **19**(7), 1890–1907 (2010)
23. Zhong, Y., Zhang, L.: An adaptive artificial immune network for supervised classification of multi/hyperspectral remote sensing imagery. IEEE Trans. Geosci. Remote Sens. **50**(3), 894–909 (2012)
24. Zhu, L., Chen, Y., Ghamisi, P., Benediktsson, J.A.: Generative adversarial networks for hyperspectral image classification. IEEE Trans. Geosci. Remote Sens. **56**(9), 5046–5063 (2018)

Detection and Recognition

Neighbourhood Projection Embedding Based Image Tampering Detection and Localization

Anjali Diwan[✉], Purvi A. Koringa, Anil K. Roy, and Suman K. Mitra

Dhirubhai Ambani Institute of Information and Communication Technology,
Gandhinagar, India
{201521013,201321010,anil_roy,suman_mitra}@daiict.ac.in

Abstract. Image tampering detection is a well developed field that not only analyzes the authenticity of image but restores credibility of it. Motive of image tampering is to create false notion about an image in viewers prospective. Image can be forged by modifying various features of image or by adding or eliminating part of it. Copy-move tampering can be defined as the process of inserting or deleting image region from an image such that no proof of alteration is visible. In this paper we propose to use Neighbourhood Projection Embedding (NPE) with regard to detection of copy-move tampering. Neighbourhood information preserving property of NPE can effectively detect and localize tampering in the presence of various post-processing operations like, additive Gaussian noise, JPEG compression, brightness change, colour reduction and blur images effectively.

Keywords: Digital image · Image forgery · Tampering detection · Copy-move tampering · Passive technique · Block features · Neighbourhood projection embedding · Forgery localization

1 Introduction

With boom in digital technology and tools manipulated images have become indistinguishable part of digital images available on various platforms. Copy-move tampering is one of the most commonly used image manipulation techniques. In copy-move tampering, a part of image is copied and pasted in the same image. As tampered part belongs to the same image, detection of tampering becomes more challenging. To restore trust on image, researchers are working and coming-up with variegated detection methods. Two most explored methods for copy-move tampering detection are keypoint based and block feature based methods.

In keypoint feature based method each keypoint have some unique discriminatory feature which can be used [1]. Edges of objects in an image are used as keypoint. Likewise there are corners and blobs that are also used for getting keypoint [2]. Main concern in this method is uniqueness of image keypoints,

© Springer Nature Singapore Pte Ltd. 2020
R. V. Babu et al. (Eds.): NCVPRIPG 2019, CCIS 1249, pp. 387–396, 2020.
https://doi.org/10.1007/978-981-15-8697-2_36

where many keypoints have close or similar characteristics which lead to create a false matching. These limitations can be overcome by block based technique. Block- based method works on block features, considering all pixels of the block. Hence, block based method are able to deal with images having various textural properties like smooth or high texture regions. In block based method images are divided into overlapping or non overlapping blocks and block feature of each block is calculated. Here all pixels are examined, which increases accuracy of this method [3].

Its worth mentioning here that in recent past, researchers have worked on block based method for copy move tampering detection. Some of them are discussed here. Hosny et al. [4] have used PCET(Polar Complex Exponential Transform) for feature extraction. Fadl et al. [5] used polar coordinate transformation with one dimensional FFT. Mahmood et al. [6] have applied SWT and DCT. Bi et al. [7] introduced the use of enhanced coherency sensitive hashing (CSH) for tampering detection. Wang et al. [8] have labeled images using LBP and find SVD coefficient for further process. Dixit et al. [9] have used SWT and SVD for detecting tampering is blur images. Bi et al. [7] have used RGB colour features as descriptor. Detection of tampering and localization are two aspect of tampering detection, accurate localization adds more meaning to the tampering detection process [10].

Proposed block based copy-move tampering detection algorithm can detect and localize simple copy-move in digital images. Here simple copy-move implies for copy-move without any transformation. The algorithm should satisfy two main properties: Sensitivity and Robustness.

- **Sensitivity:** Algorithm should be able to detect any small tampered region.
- **Robustness:** Algorithm should be able to detect and localize tampering in the presence of various kind of post-processing in images.

In proposed algorithm NPE [11] has been use for block feature extraction. Inherent property of NPE enable us to get sorted feature vectors and simplify further process, in addition it increases effective localization of detected regions. The remainder of the paper is organized as follows. In Sect. 2, brief introduction of NPE is discussed. Proposed copy-move tampering detection is discussed in Sect. 3. Section 4 presents experimental setup. Results and discussion is in Sect. 5. Short conclusion is drawn in Sect. 6.

2   Neighbourhood Preserving Embedding

Neighbourhood preserving embedding (NPE) is a linear dimensionality reduction technique which works on similarity preserving approach. It preserves similarity by preserving neighbourhood information of the data. This neighbourhood information aims to discover the local structure of the data. The basic idea is to approximate each data point by weighted linear combination of its neighbourhood. There are three basic algorithmic steps on which NPE works.

- **Define neighbourhood:** Approximation of the data point is defined by neighbourhood of that data point. It is done by creating adjacency graph. There are two ways by which this graph is created first is k-nearest neighbour search and second is by ϵ neighbourhood search.
- **Computing weight for reconstruction:** Weights are computed by minimizing the reconstruction error of a data point and linear combination of its neighbour.

$$min \sum_i ||X_i - \sum_j W_{i,j} X_i||^2, \tag{1}$$

With constraints

$$\sum W_{i,j} = 1, \; j = 1, 2, ..., m \tag{2}$$

Here W denotes weight matrix, for data point X_i weight corresponding to it is $W_{i,j}$

- **Representation in Transformation Space:** In this step lower dimensional representation is constructed form high dimensional input data. It is assumed that the same weight along the same neighbour will reconstruct the lower dimensional representation. The basis vector can be found by minimizing the reconstruction error in lower dimensional space. Following generalized eigenvalue problem is solved for minimizing error.

$$XMX^T a = \lambda XX^T a \tag{3}$$

Where $X = (x_1, ..., x_m)$, $M = (I - W)^T(I - W)$ and I is diagonal matrix.

3 Proposed Method

In this section details of the proposed copy-move tampering detection is discussed. There are three main steps in finding tampering in an image: in first step block are extracted; second step is taking care of offset based feature matching process and in the final step tampering localization and detection is done.

3.1 Feature Extraction

Selection of feature plays key role in copy-move tampering detection, therefore it is very important to choose effective block features, which can detect and localize tampering in diverse conditions. As shown in Fig. 1 sometimes tampered images are pre-processed before using it. This pre-processing is an optional step and depends on the feature extraction approach. In the proposed algorithm we are converting test images in the form of YCbCr color space and Y component of the image is used in the further steps.

Image of size $M \times N$ is divided in overlapping block of size $b \times b$. In proposed algorithm stride of one pixel is taken for the movement of block. Blocks are arranged in the raster scanning order. In this process movement of block starts from left most upper corner to right most bottom corner of the image. Total blocks created in this way are C and ranges as follows:

$$C = 1 \text{ to } (M - b + 1)(N - b + 1)$$

After getting all possible blocks, each block is vectorized and used as column element of matrix X. Matrix X is having R rows where $(b \times b = R)$ and total column of X is total number of block generated from that image i.e C. Finally we get a matrix X of dimension $R \times C$.

Dimentionality reduction approach learns a transformation matrix that are used to map data from original space to the new subspace. A point to be noted, the set of data point in our algorithm are set of all possible extracted blocks. Now this X is data matrix to be given to NPE. As discussed in Sect. 2 NPE preserves local structure of the data, by local structure it is meant to be linear combination of neighbours of the data point (in our case the block). We get the feature matrix Y that is subspace representation of X with the help of NPE algorithm.

3.2   Feature Matching and Tampering Detection

Now we have a subspace matrix Y with information of all blocks. Because of inherent property of NPE, very few (in our observation only 5) similar blocks are enough to do offset computation. Offsets are calculated for all matching blocks b_is. To accomplish this, first find location $[x_i, y_i]$ of the block and locations of all its nearest neighbors b_j, i.e., $[x_j, y_j]$. This is followed by calculating offset (dx, dy) of all such possible pairs for $[x_i, y_i]$. Offset calculation is done in Eq. 4.

$$(dx, dy) = [(x_i - x_j), (y_i - y_j)] \tag{4}$$

Since blocks associated with duplicated region of image are similar, offset between block b_i and b_j is same as it's consecutive blocks. So, all blocks associated with copy-move region have same offset which leads to creation of high peak of histogram. Based on highest occurring peak of offset histogram are selected and blocks associated with those offsets are traced back in the image. The process of tampering detection by proposed algorithm is shown in Fig. 1.

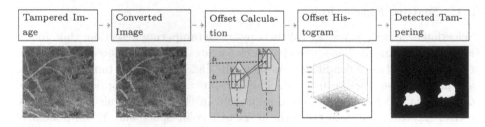

Fig. 1. Process flow of proposed copy-move tampering detection using offset calculation

4   Experimental Setup

In this section we discuss about the datasets used, statistically evaluated metrics and parameter selection.

4.1   Datasets and Evaluation

Six different datasets have been used for the evaluation of proposed algorithm. They are CMFD dataset [12], GRIP dataset [13], CoMoFoD dataset [14], MICC F600 [15] and CVIP dataset [16].

To evaluate effectiveness of algorithm with some more difficulty level we have created dataset of high dimensional images, it has 95 single and multiple copy-move images saved in PNG format. As edges are more prone to reveal tampering on an image. In our test datasets we have many images with processed edges like, creation of fused edges and blend edges which reduces similarity between copy-moved regions. In our test datasets we have many images with processed edges as mentioned above.

Experiments are performed on pixel level so as to get effective evaluation of tampering. Calculation done by evaluation metrics are also based on pixel level. Following metrics have been used for evaluation of proposed method and comparison with other methods: True positive (TP), False positive (FP), False negative (FN), Precision (P) and Recall (R). F1-Score: It is a measure to detect test's accuracy. It is measured as harmonic mean of precision and recall. Their value ranges from 1 to 0.

$$P = \frac{TP}{TP + FP}, \; R = \frac{TP}{TP + FN}, \; F_1 = 2\frac{P \cdot R}{P + R} \tag{5}$$

4.2   Parameter Selection

Selection of threshold play key role to make an algorithm sensitive and robust. In the proposed algorithm threshold selection is done on the basis of image information and extensive experiment based on it. First parameter in block based method is to determine the size of the block. Size of the block is important, as, in block based method, the block size should be smaller than tampered region. It is significant to mention, that block size affects sensitivity of the algorithm. An algorithm is considered sensitive if it can detect smallest meaningful tampering in a digital image. We have done experiments for different block size on all the test images. These images have wide variety of tampered region with various size. On the basis of this we concluded that for tampering detection, block size should be less than one third of the tampered region.

The second most important parameter in proposed algorithm is threshold T_h. Selection of this affects localization and accuracy of the algorithm. Threshold T_h is the range of offset histogram peak which we ignore. In images due to inter pixel similarity nearby blocks of the image contribute in the histogram peak having low offset value. We have performed extensive experiment to study effects of detection accuracy and localization with respect to T_h. As shown in Fig. 2 A, ignoring histogram peaks form 0 to 20 gives highest detection accuracy in all the 5 datasets. Having said that it can be added here that in GRIP dataset we are getting best result when ignoring peaks for 0 to 25. This happens due to image texture of GRIP dataset, here many images have self similar texture like smooth images (sky, desert etc.) and monuments with fine carving.

Algorithm 1. Multi peak Copy-Move Detection Algorithm

1: Create all possible overlapping blocks of size bxb
2: Convert each block into b^2 dimensional vector. Resulting in data matrix **A** having each block vector as one column
3: Find LPP basis V using data **A**.
4: Project data matrix **X** to low dimensional space **Y**.
5: Find k-Nearest Neighbor of data point
6: Find location $[x_i, y_i]$ of the b_i block and locations of all its nearest neighbors b_js i.e. $[x_j, y_j]$
7: Calculate offset of all such pairs [dx, dy] = $[(x_i-x_j),(y_i-y_j)]$
8: Identify blocks which give maximum occurring offset
9: Plot 2-D histogram of offset
10: Identify highest peak of histogram considering it as 100%
11: Consider peaks under certain percent of highest peak

5   Results and Discussion

Average results of tampering detection and localization are discussed on the following basis: first is for simple copy-move tampered images without any post-processing and second tampered images with post-processing.

5.1   Copy-Move Detection Algorithm

As discussed in Sect. 4, block feature is extracted and feature matching processes are done. In the first algorithm at the detection step offset between all blocks are calculated and based on these offsets, 2-D histogram is prepared. The highest peak of histogram generally belongs to copy-move tampered region and it is used for tampering detection and localization. Results of single copy-move tampered images are shown in Fig. 2 B. There are images in which a part of image is copied and moved at multiple parts of the same image or multiple parts of the images are copied and moved. In such cases offset between copy-move blocks are not same and hence they contribute on different peak of histogram. Selecting highest peak will not detect tampered region belonging to subsequent peaks. To overcome this problem algorithm was modified and multiple peak of histogram was selected for tampering detection.

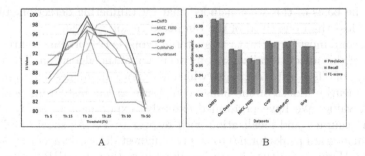

| A | B |

Fig. 2. Average F1-Score of T_h (Threshold) for images of all the datasets shown in fig. A, Results of single copy-move tampering detection by single peak selection is shown in fig. B

As shown in Algorithm 1 to address single as well as multiple copy-move tampering in images selection of histogram peak is modified. Here at the detection step we are considering highest peak as 100% and then all peak under certain percentage of it is selected. This percent depends on type of multiple copy-move. We have taken a large number of sample multiple copy-move images and found, that peaks up to 50% of highest peak are adequate to detect and localize tampering in single and multiple copy-move images where copied and moved regions have diverse distances. In this way, selecting multiple peaks leads to effective detection of single as well as multiple copy-move regions. Average detection result is shown for all the datasets in Fig. 3 For some tampered images, the ground truth along with detected image are shown in Fig. 5. Results of all the dataset have been reported in Table 1.

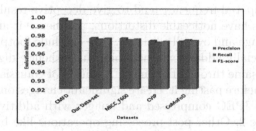

Fig. 3. Average result of single and multiple copy-move tampering detection on CMFD, Our dataset, MICC F600, CVIP, Grip and CoMoFoD dataset

Table 1. Comparison of CMFD, Our dataset, MICC F600, and Grip dataset results with recent algorithm results

Dataset	Chen2018 [17]	Bi2018 [7]	Li2019 [2]	Proposed
CMFD	93.92	92.87	98.91	99.76
Grip	95.33	92.98	100	96.73
MICC F600	–	–	91.50	97.39

5.2   Detection Result Against Different Post-processing Attacks

Robustness of any algorithm largely depends on how effectively it can ignore various post-processing operations and detect tampering. Different post-processing operations like JPEG compression, Added Gaussian noise, colour reduction or enhancement, brightness change and blur are used for hiding footprint of tampering. In this process, images go through changes which affect block features. Proposed algorithm effectively detects and localizes tampering in such images.

Table 2. Average values of precision, recall, F1 score of tampered images with JPEG compression and Gaussian noise

Parameter	P	R	F1	Parameter	P	R	F1
JPEG100	98.96	98.66	98.81	Noise20	99.97	99.47	99.72
JPEG70	96.40	93.49	94.46	Noise40	96.40	95.91	96.15
JPEG50	92.81	92.31	92.56	Noise60	94.83	94.44	94.63
JPEG20	85.67	83.61	84.51	Noise100	94.79	94.37	94.57

JPEG compression is one of the most commonly used operation applied on a digital image. JPEG compression preserves more information about low spatial frequency than high spatial frequency. Hence, structural images and images with abrupt change in spatial frequency tend to give deceptive result. We know that, compressed images have noticeable distortions, and hence it affects localization of the detected image and overall efficiency. One can hide footprint of tampering in images by artificially adding external noise. In authentic digital images, level of noise should be same through the image. Addition of Gaussian noise on copied part of the image before pasting it, create significant changes on the image pixels. Average results of JPEG compressed and images with additive Gaussian noise are shown in Table 2. Other post-processing operations like brightness change, blur, colour reduction and colour enhancement are used for hiding copy-move tampering are evaluated using proposed algorithm and result is shown in Fig. 4. To detect transformed copy-move tampering detection Orthogonal vertion of NPE i.e. MONPE [18] can be explored.

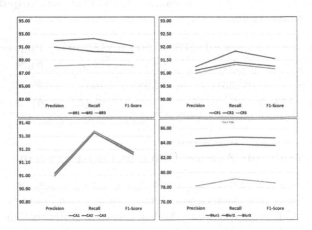

Fig. 4. Average result of Precision, Recall and F1-Score for various level of post-processing (1) Contrast adjustment,(2) Colour reduction, (3) Brightness change and (4) Blur image for CoMoFoD dataset [14]

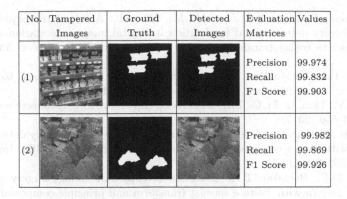

No.	Tampered Images	Ground Truth	Detected Images	Evaluation Matrices	Values
(1)				Precision	99.974
				Recall	99.832
				F1 Score	99.903
(2)				Precision	99.982
				Recall	99.869
				F1 Score	99.926

Fig. 5. Some examples of images from dataset where we can localize and detect tampering

6 Conclusion

In this work, we aim to address detection and localization of digital image attacked with copy-move tampering. We have focused on making an algorithm which is sensitive enough to address smallest tamper region and robust enough to address tampered images attacked with various kind of post-processing. It is achieved due to effective use of similarity preserving property of NPE and accurate threshold selection.

Proposed algorithm can effectively detect and localize tampering in images with various kind of post-processing operations. In the presence of noise also we can effectively detect tampering, however with increase in noise level the localization decreases slightly. Proposed algorithm is designed for images without transformation. In future work we would address tampered images with transformation like rotation and scaling.

References

1. Lin, C., Lu, W., Huang, X., Liu, K., Sun, W., Lin, H.: Region duplication detection based on hybrid feature and evaluative clustering. Multimedia Tools Appl. **78**(15), 20739–20763 (2019). https://doi.org/10.1007/s11042-019-7342-9
2. Li, Y., Zhou, J.: Fast and effective image copy-move forgery detection via hierarchical feature point matching. IEEE Trans. Inf. Forensics Secur. **14**(5), 1307–1322 (2019)
3. Teerakanok, S., Uehara, T.: Copy-move forgery detection: a state-of-the-art technical review and analysis. IEEE Access **7**, 40550–40568 (2019)
4. Hosny, K.M., Hamza, H.M., Lashin, N.A.: Copy-move forgery detection of duplicated objects using accurate PCET moments and morphological operators. Imaging Sci. J. **66**(6), 330–345 (2018)
5. Fadl, S.M., Semary, N.A.: Robust copy-move forgery revealing in digital images using polar coordinate system. Neurocomputing **265**, 57–65 (2017)

6. Mahmood, T., Mehmood, Z., Shah, M., Saba, T.: A robust technique for copy-move forgery detection and localization in digital images via stationary wavelet and discrete cosine transform. J. Vis. Commun. Image Represent. **53**, 202–214 (2018)

7. Bi, X., Pun, C.-M.: Fast copy-move forgery detection using local bidirectional coherency error refinement. Pattern Recogn. **81**, 161–175 (2018)

8. Wang, Y., Tian, L., Li, C.: LBP-SVD based copy move forgery detection algorithm. pp. 553–556 (2017)

9. Dixit, R., Naskar, R., Mishra, S.: Blur-invariant copy-move forgery detection technique with improved detection accuracy utilising SWT-SVD. IET Image Proc. **11**(5), 301–309 (2017)

10. Jwaid, M.F., Baraskar, T.N.: Detection of copy-move image forgery using local binary pattern with discrete wavelet transform and principle component analysis. In 2017 International Conference on Computing, Communication, Control and Automation (ICCUBEA), pp. 1–6. IEEE (2017)

11. He, X., Cai, D., Yan, S., Zhang, H.-J.: Neighborhood preserving embedding. In: Tenth IEEE International Conference on Computer Vision (ICCV 2005) Volume 1, vol. 2, pp. 1208–1213. IEEE (2005)

12. Christlein, V., Riess, C., Jordan, J., Riess, C., Angelopoulou, E.: An evaluation of popular copy-move forgery detection approaches. IEEE Trans. Inf. Forensics Secur. **7**(6), 1841–1854 (2012)

13. Cozzolino, D., Poggi, G., Verdoliva, L.: Copy-move forgery detection based on patchmatch. In: 2014 IEEE International Conference on Image Processing (ICIP), pp. 5312–5316. IEEE (2014)

14. Tralic, D., Zupancic, I., Grgic, S., Grgic, M.: Comofod-new database for copy-move forgery detection. In: Proceedings ELMAR-2013, pp. 49–54. IEEE (2013)

15. Amerini, I., Ballan, L., Caldelli, R., Del Bimbo, A., Serra, G.: A sift-based forensic method for copy-move attack detection and transformation recovery. IEEE Trans. Inf. Forensics Secur. **6**(3), 1099–1110 (2011)

16. Ardizzone, E., Bruno, A., Mazzola, G.: Copy move forgery detection by matching triangles of keypoints. IEEE Trans. Inf. Forensics Secur. **10**(10), 2084–2094 (2015)

17. Chen, B., Yu, M., Su, Q., Shim, H.J., Shi, Y.-Q.: Fractional quaternion zernike moments for robust color image copy-move forgery detection. IEEE Access **6**, 56637–56646 (2018)

18. Koringa, Purvi A., Mitra, Suman K.: L1-norm orthogonal neighbourhood preserving projection and its applications. Pattern Anal. Appl. **22**(4), 1481–1492 (2018). https://doi.org/10.1007/s10044-018-0745-9

DeepPFCN: Deep Parallel Feature Consensus Network for Person Re-identification

Shubham Kumar Singh$^{(\boxtimes)}$, Krishna P. Miyapuram$^{(\boxtimes)}$,
and Shanmuganathan Raman$^{(\boxtimes)}$

Indian Institute of Technology Gandhinagar, Palaj 382355, Gujarat, India
{shubham.singh,kprasad,shanmuga}@iitgn.ac.in

Abstract. Person re-identification aims to associate images of the same person over multiple non-overlapping camera views at different times. Depending on the human operator, manual re-identification in large camera networks is highly time consuming and erroneous. Automated person re-identification is required due to the extensive quantity of visual data produced by rapid inflation of large scale distributed multi-camera systems. The state-of-the-art works focus on learning and factorize person appearance features into latent discriminative factors at multiple semantic levels. We propose Deep Parallel Feature Consensus Network (DeepPFCN), a novel network architecture that learns multi-scale person appearance features using convolutional neural networks. This model factorizes the visual appearance of a person into latent discriminative factors at multiple semantic levels. Finally consensus is built. The feature representations learned by DeepPFCN are more robust for the person re-identification task, as we learn discriminative scale-specific features and maximize multi-scale feature fusion selections in multi-scale image inputs. We further exploit average and max pooling in separate scale for person-specific task to discriminate features globally and locally. We demonstrate the re-identification advantages of the proposed DeepPFCN model over the state-of-the-art re-identification methods on three benchmark datasets - Market1501, DukeMTMCreID, and CUHK03. We have achieved mAP results of 75.8%, 64.3%, and 52.6% respectively on these benchmark datasets.

Keywords: Person re-identification · Deep learning · Architecture

1 Introduction

Person re-identification detects whether a person of interest has been observed in another place (time) by a different camera [20]. In many scenarios, people appearing in one camera do not necessarily appear in another camera and sometimes the camera view may include people that have never appeared in any other camera as well. Therefore, it is better to treat person re-identification as a verification problem [6]. Person re-identification is a naturally challenging task because

© Springer Nature Singapore Pte Ltd. 2020
R. V. Babu et al. (Eds.): NCVPRIPG 2019, CCIS 1249, pp. 397–407, 2020.
https://doi.org/10.1007/978-981-15-8697-2_37

correctly matching two images of the same person is difficult under extensive appearance changes, such as human pose, illumination, occlusion, background clutter, (non)uniform clothing, and camera view-angle [6]. It has applications in tracking a particular person across these cameras, tracking the trajectory of a person, real time surveillance, and forensic and security applications.

In this paper, we propose Deep Parallel Feature Consensus Net (DeepPFCN) a novel network architecture that learns multi-scale person appearance features using convolutional neural networks (CNN) [2] and factorizes the visual appearance of a person into latent discriminative factors at multiple semantic levels [1]. DeepPFCN is a combination of the above mentioned two architectures, which are orthogonal to each other as mentioned in [1]. DeepPFCN focuses on fusing both automated discovery of latent appearance factors and fusing image resolutions. DeepPFCN deploys a multi-loss concurrent supervision mechanism. This allows enforcing and improving scale-specific feature learning.

DeepPFCN is evaluated on three person re-identification benchmark datasets - Market1501 [20], DukeMTMCreID [21], CUHK03 [12]. Extensive experiments and ablation study have been conducted on these datasets. In particular, we achieve the mAP scores of 75.8%, 64.3%, and 52.6% on the above mentioned benchmark datasets, which is observed to be better than the state-of-the-art methods by 1.5%, 1.5% and 3.4%, respectively.

This paper is organized as follows. In Sect. 3, we describe the components of DeepPFCN architecture - (a) modified multi-level factor net as base model and (b) multi-scale consensus learning with back-propagation. We combine these methods, which achieves the state-of-the-art performance for person re-identification. In Sect. 4, we work with the following datasets: Market1501 [20], DukeMTMCreID [21] and CUHK03 [12] and explain the evaluation metrics, data augmentation, training and evaluation in detail. In Sect. 5, we describe the experiments and present the ablation study conducted on these datasets. Finally, Sect. 6 concludes the paper.

2   Related Work

Person re-identification is considered as an important task in the field of computer vision. Several researchers have attempted to find effective and efficient person re-identification solution. Existing methods can be either traditional methods [3,10,14] or deep learning based methods [1,2,12,13]. Recently, deep learning based person re-identification models have obtained excellent performance. In practice, two types of models are used for person re-identification: verification model and identification model.

For verification model, a Siamese neural network [9] or triplet loss is exploited to make feature vector similar for a pair of images with same identity and dissimilar for different identities [1,4,12]. For the identification model in [18], a discriminative representation of the given input image is learned and it is generally observed to perform better than the verification model. However, existing re-identification methods typically consider only one resolution scale of person appearance which is potentially not considered as an useful information on another scale and it also loses the correlated complementary advantage across different scales appearance.

Multi-Level Factorization Net (MLFN) [1] come up with a discriminative latent factor with no secondary supervision. Multi-level factors are shared by all network blocks rather than overloading the final layer. However, all the existing methods with one resolution scale of person appearance does not only drop the potential useful information of other scales, but also lose the correlated complementary advantage across appearance scale. Deep Pyramidal Feature Learning (DPFL) [2] deploys a multi-loss concurrency for improving scale-specific feature individuality learning. Softmax classification loss is used in this method for reducing model training complexity and improve the model learning scalability when a large, different scale data is provided.

Our approach is aimed to combine both the orthogonal architectures into one single model called DeepPFCN. DeepPFCN not only learns discriminative scale-specific features and maximize multi-scale feature fusion selections in multi-scale image inputs, but also exploits average and max pooling in separate scales for person-specific task to discriminate features globally and locally.

Our Contributions are as follows. (1) DeepPFCN is self-reliant to discover discriminative and view-invariant appearance features at multiple scales without secondary supervision. (2) We exploit average and max pooling in separate scales for person-specific task to discriminate features globally and locally. We obtain the state-of-the-art results on three large person re-identification benchmark datasets - Market1501 [20], DukeMTMCreID [21], and CUHK03 [12].

3 Model Architecture

This section describes the problem statement and structure of Deep Parallel Feature Consensus Network (DeepPFCN) architecture. DeepPFCN architecture has the following components: (a) modified multi-level factorization network as base model and (b) multi-scale consensus learning network with back-propagation. We combine these components, which achieves new state-of-the-art results in person re-identification.

3.1 Problem Statement

Consider a set of n training images $I = \{I_i\}_{i=1}^{n}$ with the corresponding identity class labels $\gamma = \{y_i\}_{i=1}^{n}$. These training images capture the visual appearance and the variation of n_{id} (where $y_i \in [\ 1, \ldots, n_{id}]$) different people under multiple non-overlapping camera views.

A re-identification model needs to learn from these image-identity corresponding relations and use the learned knowledge to recognize other unseen person identities. We have formulated a DeepPFCN model that aims to extract discriminative appearance information about person identity from multiple resolution scales under significant viewing condition changes across distinct locations.

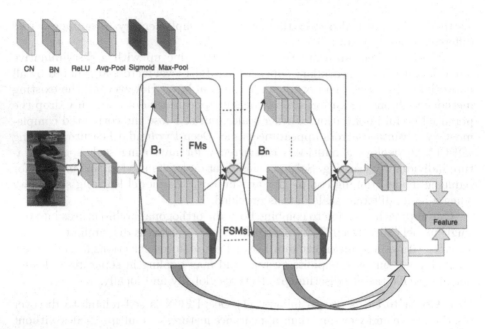

Fig. 1. Illustration of Multi-Level Factorisation Network (MLFN) Architecture.[1]

3.2   Parallel Feature Consensus Learning

The overall network design of the proposed DeepPFCL model is depicted in Fig. 2. This DeepPFCL model has $(m + 1)$ feed-forward sub-network branches: (1) m branches of scale-specific sub-networks with an identical structure for learning the most discriminative visual features for each individual pyramid scale of person bounding box images, (2) One fusion branch responsible for learning the discriminative feature selection and optimal integration of m scale-specific representations of the same images and average and max pooling in separate scale for person-specific task to discriminate features globally and locally. We describe the architecture components below: (i) modified multi-level factor net as base model and (ii) multi-scale consensus learning with back-propagation.

Multi-level Factorisation Network: The work by [1] aims to automatically discover latent discriminative factors at multiple semantic levels and dynamically identify their presence in each input image. As shown in Fig. 1, N blocks are stacked to model N semantic levels. For person re-identification task, within each block, 32 Factor Modules (FMs) and 1 Factor Selection Module (FSM) are used and 16 blocks are let up in MLFN. Let B_n denotes the nth block, $n \in 1, \ldots, N$ and within each B_n, there are two key components: FMs and a FSM. FMs help the model to learn a latent factor at the corresponding level indexed by n. FSM handles the case where multiple discriminative latent factors are required simultaneously to explain the visual appearance of the input image. MLFN fuses the deep feature computed from the final block B_N and the Factor Signature

Table 1. Comparison of Multi-scale resolution to MLFN model.

Dataset	Market1501		DukeMTMCreID	
Metric (%)	Rank-1	mAP	Rank-1	mAP
(192×96)	88.8	73.4	81.4	62.0
(256×128)	90.4	75.8	82.0	63.4
(384×192)	91.1	75.9	81.1	63.9

(FS). The final output representation of MLFN is computed by averaging the two projected features. A final fully connected layer is added that projects it to a dimension matching the number of training classes.

Multi-scale Consensus Learning: We perform multi-scale consensus learning on person identity classes from m scale-specific branches. In PFCL instantiation by modified MLFN, we achieve the feature fusion by the operation of concatenation. The loss at final layer is added with scale-specific loss and back-propagated in each scale respective. The proposed DeepPFCN model uses a kind of knowledge transfer dynamically in an interactive manner. The entire feature learning by multi-scale person identity consensus is a close-loop. We further propagate the consensus as extra feedback information to regularize the batch learning of all scale-specific branches concurrently as shown in Fig. 2. For person re-identification tasks, in single scale MLFN 32-D FSM output vector is generated and FS becomes 32 FM $\times$ 16 blocks = 512. As a result, each MLFN output is combination of FM's and FMS's output. The final feature dimension of parallel feature consensus net is set to twice of the MLFN feature vector.

We perform an experiment on three different scale resolution as 192×96, 256×128, and 384×192 on the state-of-the-art for Market1501 and DukeMTMCreID datasets as shown in Table 1. We exploit m = 2 resolution scale for input image: 384×192 and 256×128, based on the better results obtained on the respective datasets.

4   Experiments

4.1   Datasets

The following three person re-identification benchmarks - Market1501 [20], Duke MTMCreID [21], CUHK03 [12]. Each of the above mentioned individual datasets are used for testing. **Market1501** [20] has 12,936 training, 3368 query and 15913 gallery images with 1501 identities in total from 6 cameras. Deformable Part Model(DPM) [5] is used for person detection. **DukeMTMCreID** [21] comprises of 16522 training, 2228 query and 17661 gallery images with 1404 identities in total from 8 cameras. Manually labelled pedestrian boxes are provided for person detection. **CUHK03** [12] contains 7365 training, 1400 query and 5332 gallery images with 1467 identities in total from 2 cameras. Both manually labelled and DPM detected person bounding boxes are provided.

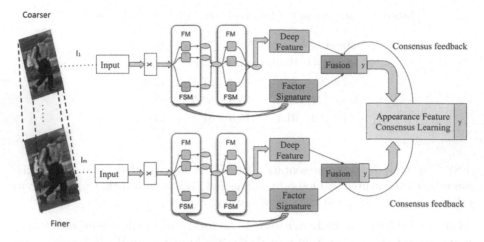

Fig. 2. Overview of the proposed Deep Parallel Feature Consensus Learning (DeepPFCL). The feature representations learned by DeepPFCN are more robust as: (a) we learn discriminative scale-specific features and maximize multi-scale feature fusion selections in multi-scale image inputs and (b) we exploit average and max pooling in separate scales for person-specific task to discriminate features globally and locally.

4.2 Evaluation Metrics

Cumulated Matching Characteristics (CMC) curve and mean Average Precision (mAP) as suggested in [20] are used to evaluate the performance of re-identification methods. We only report the CMC and mAP for rank-1 in tables rather than plotting the actual curves. All results described in this paper is under single query and does not use post-processing re-ranking by [22].

4.3 Data Augmentation

We use five data augmentation techniques during training, such as, random cropping [11], random erasing [23], flipping [16], color jitter, and color augmentation. Random cropping [11] is used to reduce the contribution of the background. Random erasing [23], which randomly select a rectangle region in an image and erases its pixels with random values. Left-right flip [16] augmentation is used so that an image should be equally recognizable as its mirror image. Color jitter randomly changes brightness, contrast, and saturation. Color augmentation randomly alters the intensities of RGB channels. No data augmentation is used for testing.

4.4   Training and Evaluation

All the person re-identification models are fine tuned on ImageNet [4] pre-trained networks. The Adam [8] optimizer is used with a mini-batch size of 16. We use initial learning rate of 0.0005 in CUHK03 with setting 2 [22] and 0.0003 for the remaining two datasets. Momentum terms are $\beta_1 = 0.5$, $\beta_2 = 0.999$. The number of training iterations is 80 epochs for all the person re-identification datasets. Cross-Entropy loss is used during training.

5   Result

5.1   Comparison with the State-of-the-Art Methods

Results on Market1501. Comparison between DeepPFCN and the state-of-the-art approaches on Market1501 [20] are shown in Table 2. The results show that our DeepPFCN achieves the best performance with the mAP of 75.8% and Rank-1 accuracy 90.6 %, which outperform all the existing works by more than 1.5% and 0.6%, respectively. No post-processing operation (e.g. the re-rank algorithm [22]) is used here. Results on Market1501 dataset can be observed in the first two rows of Fig. 3.

Results on DukeMTMCreID. Table 2 shows the results on DukeMTMCreID [21]. This dataset contains person boundary box of varying size across different camera view. This challenge is best suited for our multi-scale architecture. Without any post-processing, DeepPFCN achieves the result of mAP, 64.3 and Rank-1 accuracy as 82.1 %. This is better than the state-of-the-art methods by 1.5% and 1.1% respectively. Results can be shown on DukeMTMCreID dataset corresponding to third and fourth rows of Fig. 3 with two distinct example.

Results on CUHK03. Person re-identification results on CUHK03 [12] are given in Table 2 with setting 2 when detected person boundary boxes are used for both training and testing. Our DeepPFCN performs better in terms of the mAP (52.6%) and Rank-1 accuracy (56.7 %) on this dataset, which surpasses all existing works more than 3.4% and 2.0 % respectively. We can see the results on DukeMTMCreID dataset corresponding to fifth and sixth rows of Fig. 3 with two distinct example.

5.2   Ablation Study

Recall that our DeepPFCN determines the scale-specific feature learning and optimize discriminative feature selection from multi-scale representation of re-identification, by aggregating modified MLFN with identical structures within each scale. **DeepPFCN**: Multi-Scale full model with average and max pooling use in separate scale. **MLFN**: Single scale DeepPFCN using average polling [1]. **MLFN-Fusion**: MLFN using dynamic factor selection without FS feature. **ReNeXt**: All FMs are always active and FSMs are eliminated from MLFN so

Table 2. Comparison of the proposed method with the state-of-the-art on Market1501, DukeMTMCreID and CUHK03.

Method	Market1501		DukeMTMC		CUHK03	
	R1	mAP	R1	mAP	R1	mAP
SVDNet [17]	82.3	62.1	76.7	56.8	41.5	37.3
ACRN [15]	83.6	62.6	72.6	52.0	–	–
JLML [13]	83.9	64.4	–	–	–	–
LSRO [21]	84.0	66.1	–	–	–	–
DPFL [2]	88.9	73.1	79.2	60.6	40.7	37.0
MLFN [1]	90.0	74.3	81.0	62.8	54.7	49.2
DeepPFCN (Ours)	**90.6**	**75.8**	**82.1**	**64.3**	**56.7**	**52.6**

Table 3. Ablation Results on three Person re-identification datasets. CUHK03 results were obtained under Setting 2.

Datasets	Market1501		DukeMTMC		CUHK03	
Methods	R1	mAP	R1	mAP	R1	mAP
ResNet [7]	84.3	66.0	71.6	48.6	41.7	37.9
ResNeXt [19]	88.0	69.8	75.7	54.1	43.8	38.7
MLFN-Fusion[1]	87.9	70.8	78.7	58.4	47.1	42.5
MLFN [1]	90.0	74.3	81.0	62.8	54.7	49.2
DeepPFCN	**90.6**	**75.8**	**82.1**	**64.3**	**56.7**	**52.6**

then it becomes ResNeXt [19]. **ResNet**: When the sub-network at each level are replaced with one large holistic residual module which is ResNet [7].

A comparison of these models on all three person re-identification dataset is shown in Table 3. We can see that DeepPFCN consistently outperforms the other models on all the datasets, and each component contributed to the final result. DeepPFCN and MLFN shows the benefit of adding multi-scale architecture. MLFN and MLFN Fusion emphasize the importance of including the latent factor descriptor FS. MLFN-Fusion and ResNeXt display the priority of dynamic module selection.

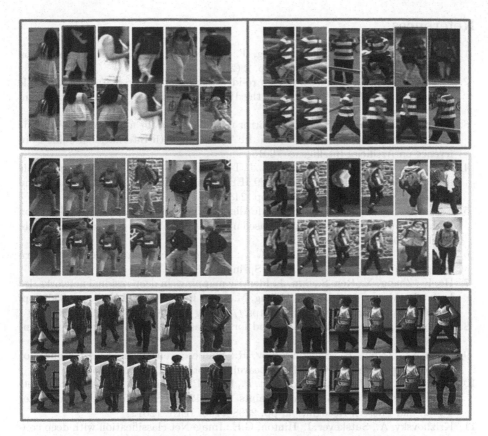

Fig. 3. Visualising person re-identification performance by MLFN [1] (Upper row) and DeepPFCN (lower row). For three groups of images from Market1501 [20], DukeMTM-CreID [21] and CUHK03 [12] benchmark datasets respectively, first image of each example shows the probe person image, followed by upto Rank-5 gallery images by respective methods with red box indicating false matches.

6   Conclusion

We have proposed a simple but effective Deep Parallel Feature Consensus Net (DeepPFCN) approach for person re-identification. Experimental results with comparisons to other representative methods are provided, which indicate that the proposed approach outperforms other ensemble based person re-identification approaches, and achieves better than the state-of-the-art performance. Ablation study validates combination of modified MLFN with multi-scale consensus learning on improving performance.

References

1. Chang, X., Hospedales, T.M., Xiang, T.: Multi-level factorisation net for person re-identification. In: CVPR, vol. 1, p. 2 (2018)
2. Chen, Y., Zhu, X., Gong, S.: Person re-identification by deep learning multi-scale representations. In: Proceedings of the IEEE International Conference on Computer Vision, pp. 2590–2600 (2017)
3. Chen, Y.C., Zheng, W.S., Lai, J.: Mirror representation for modeling view-specific transform in person re-identification. In: Twenty-Fourth International Joint Conference on Artificial Intelligence (2015)
4. Deng, J., Dong, W., Socher, R., Li, L.J., Li, K., Fei-Fei, L.: ImageNet: a large-scale hierarchical image database. In: 2009 IEEE Conference on Computer Vision and Pattern Recognition, CVPR 2009, pp. 248–255. IEEE (2009)
5. Felzenszwalb, P.F., Girshick, R.B., McAllester, D., Ramanan, D.: Object detection with discriminatively trained part-based models. IEEE Trans. Pattern Anal. Mach. Intell. **32**(9), 1627–1645 (2010)
6. Gong, S., Cristani, M., Yan, S., Loy, C.C.: Advances in computer vision and pattern recognition person re-identification, Springer (2014)
7. He, K., Zhang, X., Ren, S., Sun, J.: Identity mappings in deep residual networks. In: Leibe, B., Matas, J., Sebe, N., Welling, M. (eds.) ECCV 2016. LNCS, vol. 9908, pp. 630–645. Springer, Cham (2016). https://doi.org/10.1007/978-3-319-46493-0_38
8. Kingma, D., Ba, J.: Adam: a method for stochastic optimization. arXiv preprint arXiv:1412.6980 (2014)
9. Koch, G., Zemel, R., Salakhutdinov, R.: Siamese neural networks for one-shot image recognition. In: ICML Deep Learning Workshop, vol. 2 (2015)
10. Koestinger, M., Hirzer, M., Wohlhart, P., Roth, P.M., Bischof, H.: Large scale metric learning from equivalence constraints. In: 2012 IEEE Conference on Computer Vision and Pattern Recognition, pp. 2288–2295. IEEE (2012)
11. Krizhevsky, A., Sutskever, I., Hinton, G.E.: ImageNet classification with deep convolutional neural networks. In: Advances in Neural Information Processing Systems, pp. 1097–1105 (2012)
12. Li, W., Zhao, R., Xiao, T., Wang, X.: DeepReid: deep filter pairing neural network for person re-identification. In: Proceedings of the IEEE Conference on Computer Vision and Pattern Recognition, pp. 152–159 (2014)
13. Li, W., Zhu, X., Gong, S.: Person re-identification by deep joint learning of multi-loss classification. arXiv preprint arXiv:1705.04724 (2017)
14. Li, X., Zheng, W.S., Wang, X., Xiang, T., Gong, S.: Multi-scale learning for low-resolution person re-identification. In: Proceedings of the IEEE International Conference on Computer Vision, pp. 3765–3773 (2015)
15. Schumann, A., Stiefelhagen, R.: Person re-identification by deep learning attribute-complementary information. In: Proceedings of the IEEE Conference on Computer Vision and Pattern Recognition Workshops, pp. 20–28 (2017)
16. Simonyan, K., Zisserman, A.: Very deep convolutional networks for large-scale image recognition. arXiv preprint arXiv:1409.1556 (2014)
17. Sun, Y., Zheng, L., Deng, W., Wang, S.: SVDNet for pedestrian retrieval. In: Proceedings of the IEEE International Conference on Computer Vision, pp. 3800–3808 (2017)
18. Xiao, T., Li, H., Ouyang, W., Wang, X.: Learning deep feature representations with domain guided dropout for person re-identification. In: Proceedings of the IEEE Conference on Computer Vision and Pattern Recognition, pp. 1249–1258 (2016)

19. Xie, S., Girshick, R., Dollár, P., Tu, Z., He, K.: Aggregated residual transformations for deep neural networks. In: Proceedings of the IEEE Conference on Computer Vision and Pattern Recognition, pp. 1492–1500 (2017)
20. Zheng, L., Shen, L., Tian, L., Wang, S., Wang, J., Tian, Q.: Scalable person re-identification: a benchmark. In: Proceedings of the IEEE International Conference on Computer Vision, pp. 1116–1124 (2015)
21. Zheng, Z., Zheng, L., Yang, Y.: Unlabeled samples generated by GAN improve the person re-identification baseline in vitro. In: Proceedings of the IEEE International Conference on Computer Vision, pp. 3754–3762 (2017)
22. Zhong, Z., Zheng, L., Cao, D., Li, S.: Re-ranking person re-identification with k-reciprocal encoding. In: 2017 IEEE Conference on Computer Vision and Pattern Recognition (CVPR), pp. 3652–3661. IEEE (2017)
23. Zhong, Z., Zheng, L., Kang, G., Li, S., Yang, Y.: Random erasing data augmentation. arXiv preprint arXiv:1708.04896 (2017)

Motion Classification in *Bharatanatyam* Dance

Himadri Bhuyan(✉) , Mousam Roy , and Partha Pratim Das

IIT Kharagpur, Kharagpur 721302, West Bengal, India
himadribhuyan@gmail.com , mousam05@gmail.com , ppd@cse.iitkgp.ac.in

Abstract. The paper presents a method to classify the unique motions in *Bharatanatyam* dance videos. Unlike the motions in our daily activities, the motions involved in the dance is rather complex in nature. Looking at the state of art, there is a new scope of the motion classification in the domain of dance. During dance performance, the number of frames in each motion may vary, which leads to the variable feature lengths. This variability, makes comparisons of motions difficult for classification and adds to challenges of the current work. We use the velocities of the skeleton joints as a feature. The joint coordinates are captured by Kinect 1.0. Dynamic Time Warping (DTW) and kNN algorithm are used for classification. The DTW is used to measure the similarity between two motions using skeleton joint velocities and the extracted similarity measure is supplied to the kNN algorithm to identify similar motions. The paper adopts two techniques while measuring the similarity of the joint velocities; i) *Non-Weighted Joints* ii) *Weighted Joints*. To optimize the joint weights, Particle Swarm Optimization (PSO) algorithm is used. We also compare the result of the two techniques and highlight the pros and cons of each. The proposed approach is simple and very effective and eventually achieves an accuracy of more than 85%. Finally motion classification in Indian Classical Dance (ICD) can help in digital heritage, design of dance tutoring system, dance synthesis application, and the like.

Keywords: Bharatanatyam · Key posture · Adavu · DTW · kNN

1 Introduction

Despite several efforts in motion classification for daily tasks such as cooking, walking, running etc., there is little attempt for motion classification in Indian Classical Dance (ICD). *Bharatanatyam* is one of the ancient forms of ICD that is widely popular in India. It is characterized by well-defined poses (momentarily stationary body postures, called *Key Postures* [1]), hand gestures, facial expressions, and fluidic body movements. These basic units follow a certain pattern called *Adavu* of *Bharatanatyam*. The *Adavu*s are used to train the dancers. Each *Adavu* is a sequence of a fixed set of *Key Postures* that are synchronized with musical beats and interleaved with body motions. Consider a particular

© Springer Nature Singapore Pte Ltd. 2020
R. V. Babu et al. (Eds.): NCVPRIPG 2019, CCIS 1249, pp. 408–417, 2020.
https://doi.org/10.1007/978-981-15-8697-2_38

performance P in which the *Key Postures* (not all of them may be distinct) are performed in a sequence, say, $K_1, K_2, ..., K_n$ and the interleaved motions occur as $M_1, M_2, ..., M_{(n-1)}$. This leads to the performance sequence P given by $K_1, M_1, K_2, M_2, K_3, M_3, ..., K_{(n-1)}, M_{(n-1)}, K_n$. It may be noted that it is not sufficient to merely identify clusters of repeating motions. The exact nature of each distinct motion must be identified. For example, M_1 may be *Advance right leg* while M_2 may be *Retract right leg*. M_1 and M_2 will be labeled accordingly.

Our objective in this paper is to label each motion in an RGB-D video (captured by Microsoft Kinect 1.0 [2]), given a reference set of labeled motions known a priori. The challenges involved in this work include:

- Unavailability of benchmark data sets of *Bharatanatyam* dance videos.
- Unavailability of a reference set of manually labeled (annotated) videos.
- While the motion information (velocity, acceleration) from skeleton joints, as estimated by Kinect, can provide useful information for overall motion; ill-formed skeletons often adversely affect the result. Ill-formed skeletons are caused due to various factors including the dress of the dancers, occlusions during motion etc.
- The number of frames in a motion sequence is not uniform across motions. So while comparing two motions, the feature lengths of the motions need to be normalized.

We start with creating our own data set captured by Kinect 1.0. The skeleton joint is used to compute the joint velocities during a motion. Dynamic Time Warping (DTW) [3] is used to measure the similarity between two motion sequences though the number of frames are different. The kNN [4] algorithm takes the similarity measure as an input and compute how far the motions are similar and takes a decision on best matching.

In the rest of the paper we first discuss the related work in Section 2. Section 3 describes the data set. The methodology is explained in the Sect. 4. Section 5 deals with the experimental results and discussion. We conclude in Sect. 6.

2   Related Work

In recent years, substantial volume of research has been directed at motion classification, synthesis and segmentation. Schulz and Woerner [5] introduced a method for automatically segmenting joint-angle trajectories and applied it to articulated human motion. They emphasised on a distinction between resting phases and phases of movement. Wang and Shi [6] presented a method to segment temporal structure based on kinetic and potential energies of the human 3D skeleton. Tokmakov et al. [7] used fully convolutional networks to determine whether an object is in motion, irrespective of camera motion.

Specifically in dance motion classification, Aymeric et al. [8] attempt to recognise body movements in *Salsa* dance. They use body joint trajectories and foot tapping impact (from piezoelectric sensors). With the help of Hidden Markov Model they achieve the classification accuracy of 74%. Likewise Romano et al. [9]

implements Dance Coach, an application to support the practice of dancing steps in *Salsa*. They used skeleton joint motions captured by Kinect 2.0. Shinoda et al. [10] build a system to study the classification of dance movements using motion of the center of gravity. Shiratori et al. [11] segment the dance motion by auto detecting the musical rhythm. Kitsikidis et al. [12] propose a method to partition the dance sequences into multiple periods and motion patterns using skeletal data. They use multiple sensors to extract the skeletal feature. Samanta et al. [13] classify ICD using the pose descriptor (based on the fact that the set of poses of one dance form is different from the other)generated by Histogram of Optical Flow (HOOF). Similarly Kishore et al. [14] classifies ICD actions on the basis of the dance *Mudras* (poses) using convolutional neural networks (CNN). They achieved 93.33% recognition rate. However, the authors [13,14] do not address aspects of motion. Kim et al. [15] design an efficient ReLU-based ELMC which takes six joint angles obtained from Kinect data set to classify the dance movements for Korean pop (K-pop) dances. However, there is little work in ICD related to motion classification.

3   Data Set Generation and Annotation

Since no benchmark data set is available for *Bharatanatyam Adavus*, we first attempt to record and annotate a data set. Microsoft Kinect 1.0 is used as the capture device in a controlled environment as in [16]. Though in this paper, Kinect captures synchronized Audio, RGB, Depth, and Skeleton streams, we use only the skeleton stream during analysis[1]. Every skeleton frame has 20 joint points in the human body as shown in Fig. 1(a). 4 of these joints are located within the body (*HipCenter*, *Spine*, *ShoulderCenter* (*Neck*), and *Head*), and the remaining 16 joints are located on the limbs – 4 joints on each limb (2 legs and 2 hands). The (x, y, z) coordinate of each joint is available in each skeleton frame.

3.1   Data Recording and Key Posture Annotation

In *Bharatnatyam* there are 58 variants of 15 *Adavus*. To build the data set, 7 trained dancers performed each variant thrice. Momentarily stationary *Key Frames* (expectedly containing *Key Postures*) were then annotated in each video by *Bharatanatyam* experts. A part of this data set [17] is available for public use. In this paper, we use 8 variants of *Natta Adavus*. Statistics about the used data set is shown in Table 1(a) and the manual annotation[2] for *Key Frames* is given in Table 1(b). Every row in this annotation represents a *Key posture* (KP) identified by a KP ID (comprising the variant of *Adavu*, Dancer#, Audio beat# and KP#) and Start & End Frame#s denoting the duration of the KP. For example, KP ID = N1D6B1P02 encodes N1: *Adavu Natta-1*, D6: Dancer-6, B1: Audio beat# 1, P02: KP# 02.

---

[1] Audio and RGB streams, however, are used during the manual annotation process.
[2] In future, we intend to adopt automated annotation schemes like the one in [20].

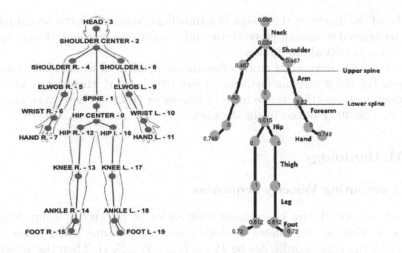

Fig. 1. Kinect joints in Schematic & Data. (a) Joint map from *msdn.microsoft.com* (Version 1.0). (b) Joint weights as obtained from PSO (Sect. 4.3)

Table 1. Data set & annotation file

(a) *Used Data Set* (b) *Sample annotation*

Adavu	# of frames in Performance			Total motions	# of unique motions
	#1	#2	#3		
Natta-1	1546	1590	1532	32	4
Natta-2	1557	1522	1545	32	4
Natta-3	2680	2698	2760	64	8
Natta-4	5537	5531	5504	128	8
Natta-5	2580	2728	2748	64	10
Natta-6	2781	2764	2729	64	12
Natta-7	2828	3022	2706	64	14
Natta-8	2710	2811	2752	48	11
Overall	22,219	22,666	22,276	496	71

KP ID	Start frame	End frame
N1D6B1P02	139	170
N1D6B2P01	186	218
....	....	....
....	....	....
....	....	....
N1D6B16P01	1436	1466

3.2 Motion Annotation

As motions and *Key Postures* are alternatingly interleaved in a *Bharatanatyam* video, a motion M_i can be marked by the pair of *Key Postures* (P_k, P_{k+1}) within which it occurs. As we have already annotated the KPs (Table 1(b)), we collect the motions by considering all possible such pairs. It may be noted that in *Bharatanatyam* there is always a unique motion between any two specific KPs that may occur consecutively in an *Adavu*. So, it may appear that one can obviate the need for motion recognition by just recognizing the KPs and considering their pairs. However, in general, it is possible that between the same pair of KPs the actual motions (trajectory paths) are different for different *Adavus*. Also, the analysis of the dance, or the design of a tutoring system needs the actual motion to be recognized to guarantee syntactic and semantic correctness. Hence, motion recognition is critical for *Adavus*.

Next, for the purpose of motion classification, we need to manually label the motions. For the 8 variants for *Natta Adavu* (Table 1(a)), the experts identified 71 unique motions (that is, we have 71 classes or labels). These were manually annotated on 496 motions in the data set.

4   Methodology

4.1   Computing Velocity Sequences

We first convert all joint coordinates information to velocity by computing difference of position coordinates between consecutive frames[3]. For frame i and joint k, let the joint coordinates be $P_{k,i} = (X_{k,i}, Y_{k,i}, Z_{k,i})$. Then the velocity of the joint is $V_{k,i} = (V_{X_{k,i}}, V_{Y_{k,i}}, V_{Z_{k,i}}) = P_{k,i} - P_{k,i-1}$. Considering one joint at a time, every motion M (with n frames) essentially reduces to a sequence of velocities $V_1, V_2, ..., V_{n-1}$. We then use DTW [3] to calculate the distance between a pair of motions $M1$ and $M2$. The cost function used is Euclidean distance as given in Eq. 1.

$$d_{Euclidean}((V_{X1_{M1}}, V_{Y1_{M1}}, V_{Z1_{M1}}), (V_{X2_{M2}}, V_{Y2_{M2}}, V_{Z2_{M2}})) =$$
$$\sqrt{(V_{X1_{M1}} - V_{X2_{M2}})^2 + (V_{Y1_{M1}} - V_{Y2_{M2}})^2 + (V_{Z1_{M1}} - V_{Z2_{M2}})^2} \quad (1)$$

As input, we have two velocity-sequences V_{M1} and V_{M2} for a joint J (corresponding to motions $M1$ and $M2$), and the DTW returns a single value d, which denotes the distance between the two motions. The lower the value, the higher is the similarity between the two motions, with respect to joint J in use. For every unknown motion M, we compute its distance from each of the pre-labeled motions M_a, M_b, M_c etc. The pre-labeled motion which has least distance from M is most similar to M, with respect to joint J in use.

4.2   Computing the *Best* Motion Match

Once we have joint-wise distances or *best matches between the unknown motion and pre-labeled motions*, we need to compute the final match over all (or most significant) joints. This can be done in one of the two ways (*Approach 1 and 2*) decided by the order of *computing* the aggregation of the joint-wise distances and *choosing* the nearest neighbor (using 1NN).

Approach 1 (Without Joint Weightage) – Compute-Then-Choose: For 20 skeletal joints, we get a vector of 20 joint-wise distances computed by Eq. 1. To combine these joint-wise distances into a single value, we first **compute** a norm

---

[3] The actual velocity would differ by a constant factor, but it suffices for our purpose.

of this vector (using either sum (d_s), sum-of-squares (d_{ss}) or sum-of-square-roots (d_{ssr})) and then use this norm as a metric for **choosing** the nearest neighbor. Let d_i denote distance with respect to joint i. Using different norms, we get different metrics for choosing the nearest neighbor.

- *Sum:* $d_s = d_1 + d_2 + d_3 + ... + d_{20}$
- *Sum of squares:* $d_{ss} = d_1^2 + d_2^2 + d_3^3 + ... + d_{20}^2$
- *Sum of square roots:* $d_{ssr} = \sqrt{d_1} + \sqrt{d_2} + \sqrt{d_3} + ... + \sqrt{d_{20}}$

Finally we choose the nearest neighbor (1NN) M_x of M and assign the label of M_x to M. The pros and cons of this approach are as follows:

- **Pros:**
  - This is intuitive, simple to understand and implement.
  - In the absence of any prior knowledge regarding the nature of the dance form, this is a quick approach that is reasonably effective.
- **Cons:**
  - Here every joint is treated equally (with the same weight). However, in *Bharatanatyam*, body joints usually have much less motion as compared to the limb joints. This fact is not utilized.
  - This approach is not amenable to data-driven optimization.

Approach 2 (With Joint Weightage) – Choose-then-Compute: Now we first **choose** a nearest neighbor each with respect to every joint. We then use a second metric, called *score*, to **compute** the *best* from the joint-wise nearest neighbors.

A simple *score function* would be to use *voting* to choose the nearest neighbor motion that occurs with maximum number of joints. However, this again treats all joints as equally significant and does not exploit the ground truth of *Bharatanatyam* that some joints have more motion than others. Thus we need to assign **weights** to joints – higher weights for joints that are more significant in motion. For example, the weight can be (using the notation from Fig. 1(a)):

- **Body**: 1-1-0-1, **Hands**: 1-4-3-4, **Legs**: 1-4-3-4, or
- **Body**: 1-1-1-1, **Hands**: 1-2-3-4, **Legs**: 1-2-3-4

where **Body** $\equiv$ *HipCenter–Spine–ShoulderCenter (Neck)–Head*, **Hand** $\equiv$ *Shoulder–Elbow–Wrist–Hand (Palm)*, and **Leg** $\equiv$ *Hip–Knee–Ankle–Foot* with *Left* (**L**) and *Right* (**R**) variants for **Hand** and **Leg** symmetrically assigned. We define the *score* for a particular labeled motion M_i as the sum of the weights of all joints for which M_i happens to be the joint-wise nearest neighbor.

This aggregation approach too has a caveat. It ignores all distance values apart from the lowest distance for every joint. So we modify the score calculation to include fractional weight contributions from joints with respect to which M_i is not the nearest neighbor.

$$Score(M_i) = \sum_{k=1}^{20} w_k \times \frac{d_{k,min}}{d_{k,M_i}} \qquad (2)$$

where w_k = weight of joint k, $d_{k,min}$ = minimum distance of any motion M_i from M with respect to joint k, and d_{k,M_i} = distance of M_i from M with respect to joint k. The fraction evaluates to 1 for joints with respect to which M_i is indeed the nearest neighbor, and it is less than 1 for all other joints. The pros and cons of this approach are as follows:

- **Pros**:
  - Knowledge about an ICD form is used to assign weights (for example, in a foot-heavy dance like *Kathak*, higher weights can be assigned to feet).
  - Black-box optimization approaches can be used to iteratively tweak the weights to obtain high accuracy. We attempt in Sect. 4.3.
- **Cons**:
  - With score function, this is more complex to understand and implement.
  - Programmatic optimization of weights is an iterative, slow process.

4.3 Optimization of Weights

Particle Swarm Optimization (PSO). [18,19] is a black-box optimization approach that tries to maximize an objective function by iteratively tweaking its parameters. In our case, the parameter is the **weight vector** $(J_1, J_2, ..., J_{20})$ of 20 joints and the objective function is the overall accuracy of the classification of motion over the dataset. As needed by PSO for tweaking, we use 0 and 1 respectively as lower and upper bounds for every joint parameter. The optimal computed weight after 24 iterations is shown in the Fig. 1(b).

5   Experimental Results

For motion classification in a video, we first use the annotated *Key Frame* information to segment the video into a sequence of motions. We then manually label the first occurrence of each unique motion in the sequence (also available from annotation). Finally, we engage the classification algorithm to label the remaining occurrences of the motions in the video. For example, if a video comprises motion sequence $M_1, M_2, M_3, M_4,$ M_1, M_5 $, M_4, M_1, M_5, M_4, M_1, M_2$, then we pre-label and create $M_1, M_2, M_3, M_4, \_, M_5, \_, \_, \_, \_, \_, \_$ as the input sequence for our classifier. The number of unlabeled motions in this case is 7. The accuracy of classification is determined by the number of unlabeled motions correctly labeled by the algorithm. For example, if 5 out of the 7 motions are labeled correctly, the accuracy is $\frac{5}{7} \times 100\% = 71.43\%$. The classification accuracy over the data set is shown in Table 2(a) & (b) for *Approach-1* & *Approach-2* respectively.

From the tables, we observe as follows:

- **Trend of decreasing accuracy from *Natta*-1 to 8**:
  The best performing *Adavus* are *Natta*-1, 2, 3 with near-perfect accuracy whereas the worst performing *Adavus* are *Natta*-4 and 7 where accuracy hovers around 70%. This can be attributed to various factors:

Table 2. Classification Accuracy (in %) by *Approach-1* and *2* (Sect. 4.2)

(a) *Approach-1*

Adavu	Norm to combine joint-wise distances		
	Sum (d_s)	Sum of sqr (d_{ss})	Sum of sqrt (d_{ssr})
Natta-1	96.00	98.67	96.00
Natta-2	96.00	96.00	95.00
Natta-3	99.33	81.00	97.33
Natta-4	72.33	65.00	66.33
Natta-5	88.00	86.00	90.00
Natta-6	93.67	79.67	95.00
Natta-7	66.00	62.67	68.67
Natta-8	87.00	82.33	90.00
Overall	**84.43**	**77.41**	**83.37**

(b) *Approach-2*

Adavu	Wts. to compute scores of potential NNs		
	Static (wt_1)	Static (wt_2)	Optimal (PSO, wt_3)
Natta-1	95.00	92.33	96.29
Natta-2	88.67	83.33	95.05
Natta-3	94.83	87.33	96.85
Natta-4	68.92	70.67	75.77
Natta-5	91.82	84.67	88.00
Natta-6	93.87	85.00	93.87
Natta-7	70.00	66.00	76.00
Natta-8	90.47	86.00	89.52
Overall	**81.89**	**79.88**	**86.05**

wt_1: 1101–1434–1434
wt_2: 1111–1234–1234
wt_3: 0.150 0.000 0.024 0.098–
0.467 0.820 0.000 0.749–
0.000 1.000 0.812 0.720

- **Complexity of motions**: As motions become more complex, the quality of skeletons (and their joints) degrades. Also, certain types of joint motions, such as rotatory motions, do not produce significant changes in joint coordinates.
- **Fast motions**: Some motions in the more complex *Adavus* are rather fast, lasting less than 15 frames. The DTW computation is vulnerable to producing unstable results when one of the input sequences becomes too short.
- **Occlusion**: At times, the dress worn by the performer *occludes* or hides the locations of critical joints, rendering the data of joint coordinate useless. This has been found to be especially true when the performer wears a *Saree* or similar clothing that drapes loosely around the body.
- **Approach 2 performs better than Approach 1**: The overall accuracy obtained using *Approach 2* is 86.05%, which is marginally better than the accuracy 84.43% obtained using *Approach 1*. This reassures us that the optimization used to iteratively tweak weights is indeed worthwhile.
- **Optimal weights are concentrated towards outer limbs**: The weights reported by the optimization algorithm (wt_3 in Table 2(b)) are biased towards the limbs in contrast to the body. Indeed, the weights assigned to 4 body joints are negligible, whereas the *Ankle*, *Foot*, *Knee*, *Hand*, and *Elbow* joints get high weights, closer to the maximum of 1. This observation is largely in accordance with our expectations based on an intuitive understanding of the *Natta Adavu* and assignment of heuristic weights wt_1 and wt_2 in Table 2(b). The motions

are largely driven by limbs, while core body movements are relatively less frequent.

6   Conclusions

The paper attempts to classify the motions involved in the *Bharatanatyam Adavus*. The solution is provided through two approaches where *Approach-2* emerges as a marginal winner.

The current method performs fairly well given the manual labeling of the first occurrence of unique motions as it reduces the variability of matching across dancers. However, as rightly pointed out by a reviewer, such an evaluation does not conform to the idea of evaluating on test sequences that have not been seen during training. So, we need to automate this step and allow these occurrences to be machine-classified as well to make the process robust across various dancers, and alleviate the need for such *hand-holding* of the recognizer. At the same time, instead of using manual annotations to extract motion frames, we may use auto-segmented motion frames which could be a good addition to overall automation.

Further, acceleration may be considered, in addition to velocity, to compute the measures of similarity between the motions. This possibly can make the classification more accurate and robust. Approaches based on RGB video need due consideration too.

We have considered only eight variations of *Bharatantaym Adavus*, and classified each unknown motion into one of the known motion labels from this set. In future, we would like to scale our data set and analyze the performance of the existing algorithm on all (over 50) *Adavus*. It is likely that new approaches may be necessary as more variations in motion are put to considerations.

Finally the same approach can also be applied to other ICD or non-ICD forms to classify the motions whenever some method based on Key-Posture or other has rightly segmented the motions[4]. The same may also be used for the inter– and intra–ICD classification taking motion type into consideration. This can improve the quality of the applications like digital heritage, dance tutoring system [16], dance transcription and dance synthesis.

References

1. Mallick, T., Das, P.P., Majumdar, A.K.: Characterization, detection, and synchronization of audio-video events in *Bharatanatyam Adavus*. In: Chanda, B., Chaudhuri, S., Chaudhury, S. (eds.) Heritage Preservation, pp. 241–268. Springer, Singapore (2018). https://doi.org/10.1007/978-981-10-7221-5_12
2. Zhang: Microsoft Kinect Sensor and Its Effect, Microsoft Research. IEEE Multimed. **19**(2) (2012)
3. Berndt, D.J., Clifford, J.: Using dynamic time warping to find patterns in time series. In: Workshop on Knowledge Discovery in Databases. AAAI (1994)

---

[4] All ICD forms, however, may not have well-defined Key-Postures for segmentation.

4. Laaksonen, Oja, Classification With Learning k-nearest Neighbors, IEEE International Conference on Neural Networks, 1996
5. Schulz, W.: Automatic motion segmentation for human motion synthesis. In: AMDO (2010)
6. Wang, S.: Human activities segmentation and location of key frames based on 3D skeleton. In: Chinese Control Conference (2014)
7. Tokmakov, P., Alahari, K., Schmid, C.: Learning Motion Patterns in Videos (2017). arXiv: 1612.07217v2
8. Aymeric, M., Essid, S., Richard, G.: Multimodal classification of dance movements using body joint trajectories and step sounds. In: 2013 14th International Workshop, WIAMIS 2013, pp. 1–4. IEEE (2013)
9. Romano, G., Schneider, J., Drachsler, H.: Dancing salsa with machines-filling the gap of dancing learning solutions. Sensors **19**(17), 3661 (2019)
10. Shinoda, Y., Mito, Y., Ozawa, T., Mizutani, Y., Watanuma, R., Marumo, M.: Consideration of classification of dance movements for Nihon Buyo using motion capture system. In: 2012 Proceedings of SICE Annual Conference (SICE), pp. 1025–1028. IEEE (2012)
11. Takaaki, S., Nakazawa, A., Ikeuchi, K.: Detecting dance motion structure through music analysis. In: 2004 Sixth IEEE International Conference on Automatic Face and Gesture Recognition, Proceedings, pp. 857–862. IEEE (2004)
12. Kitsikidis, A., Boulgouris, N.V., Dimitropoulos, K., Grammalidis, N.: Unsupervised dance motion patterns classification from fused skeletal data using exemplar-based HMMs. Int. J. Herit. Digit. Era **4**(2), 209–220 (2015)
13. Samanta, Soumitra, Pulak Purkait, and Bhabatosh Chanda. Indian classical dance classification by learning dance pose bases. In 2012 IEEE Workshop on the Applications of Computer Vision (WACV), pp. 265–270. IEEE, 2012
14. Kishore, P.V., et al.: Indian classical dance action identification and classification with convolutional neural networks. Adv. Multimed. (2018)
15. Kim, D., Kim, D.-H., Kwak, K.-C.: Classification of K-Pop dance movements based on skeleton information obtained by a kinect sensor. Sensors **17**(6), 1261 (2017)
16. Aich, A., Mallick, T., Bhuyan, H.B.G.S., Das, P.P., Majumdar, A.K.: *NrityaGuru*: a dance tutoring system for *Bharatanatyam* using kinect. In: Rameshan, R., Arora, C., Dutta Roy, S. (eds.) NCVPRIPG 2017. CCIS, vol. 841, pp. 481–493. Springer, Singapore (2018). https://doi.org/10.1007/978-981-13-0020-2_42
17. Mallick, T., Bhuyan, H., Das, P.P., Majumdar, A.K.: Annotated Bharatanatyam Data Set (2017). http://hci.cse.iitkgp.ac.in
18. Kennedy, E.: Particle swarm optimization. In: IEEE International Conference on Neural Networks (1995)
19. PYSWARMS: Research Toolkit for Particle Swarm Optimization (PSO) in Python. https://pyswarms.readthedocs.io/en/latest/
20. Mallick, T., Das, P.P., Majumdar, A.K.: Posture and sequence recognition for Bharatanatyam dance performances using machine learning approach. arXiv preprint arXiv:1909.11023 (2019)

CS-ONPP: Class Similarity Based ONPP for the Modular Facial Expression Recognition

Sujata$^{(\boxtimes)}$, Purvi A. Koringa, and Suman K. Mitra

Dhirubhai Ambani Institute of Information and Communication Technology,
Gandhinagar, India
{201521003,201321010,suman_mitra}@daiict.ac.in

Abstract. Facial expression recognition is a big problem in the field of Human behavioral analysis. Much work has been done in this field where local texture, features have been extracted and used in the classification. Due to the very local nature of this information, the dimension of the feature vector achieved for the full image is very high, posing computational challenges in real-time expression recognition. In recent times, Dimensionality Reduction methods have been successfully used in image recognition tasks. Though being high dimensional data, natural images such as face images lie in low dimensional subspace, and Dimensionality Reduction methods try to learn this underlying subspace to reduce the computational complexity involved in classification stage of image recognition task. This paper proposes the Orthogonal Neighborhood Preserving Projection with Class Similarity-based neighborhood for expression recognition. The extensive experiment has been performed on three well-known Facial Expression Databases. The proposed techniques achieve similar recognition performance at very low dimensions compared to local feature extraction based methods.

Keywords: Facial expression recognition · Dimensionality reduction · ONPP

1 Introduction

Facial expressions, poses, and gestures are the non-verbal cues, which are an essential part of our daily communication where the face is the most prominent. Facial expression through expressing feelings common means of human communication, it indicates their agreement or disagreement, express intentions, interacting with others as well as environment [1]. Thus, many research is being done in the field of automated expression recognition. Numerous approaches for facial expression recognition have been suggested in the literature, which can be broadly classified into feature-based techniques and appearance-based techniques [2]. Local image descriptors like SIFT(Scale Invariant Feature Transform) [3] has been extensively examined and has assumed a predominant job in FER applications. SIFT has achieved the best overall performance as local image descriptors in the literature. It improves effectiveness while diminishing

© Springer Nature Singapore Pte Ltd. 2020
R. V. Babu et al. (Eds.): NCVPRIPG 2019, CCIS 1249, pp. 418–428, 2020.
https://doi.org/10.1007/978-981-15-8697-2_39

the memory prerequisites. Impressed by the SIFT [4] presented Speed Up Robust Features (SURF). Instead of using the gradient information like SIFT descriptor does, SURF computes responses of Haar Wavelet and exploits integral images to save computational cost. As a result, it runs faster than SIFT. Dalal and Triggs [5] introduced the Histogram of Oriented Gradient (HOG) descriptor. For a long time, Gabor wavelet [6] have been comprehensively utilized in face feature extrication. It is capable of extracting the multi-direction and multi-scale statistics from the given face image. It is able to extract the multi-orientation and multi-scale information from the given face image. Gabor features has the huge feature dimensions, so it is not useful for the real time applications. [7] proposed Local Binary Patterns (LBP) for texture classification, and such a descriptor encodes texture information by comparing the central pixel and its neighborhood. It was successfully applied in the task of face recognition [8] and object categorization [9]. LBP is sensitive to local illumination variations. It does not correctly identify the texture of facial muscles and other types of local deformations, thus not very robust for FER applications. Another local feature based method based on Histogram of Second order Gradient (HSOG) [10].

Above mentioned work basically works based on local texture information, the local texture of face image is extracted with various image processing procedures, followed by histogram pooling by various block sizes. These approaches usually results in the feature vector length of order 10^5 making classification step computationally complex. To overcome problem of high dimensionality, in recent times many Dimensionality Reduction (DR) techniques are proposed, these techniques are proved to be very efficient in image recognition tasks. In this article, we are using one state of the art DR method - ONPP for facial expression recognition. The paper mainly proposes a variant of ONPP suitable for facial expression recognition. The main advantage achieved in the DR based method is computational complexity reduction in the classification. Using ONPP, the image is represented using feature vector 100s of dimensions instead of the feature vector having 10^5 dimensions. The performance of proposed method is tested on three bench-mark databases: CK+, Jaffe and Video database. Proposed method achieves similar recognition accuracy with comparatively very low dimensions than that of local feature based methods.

Remaining part of the study is held as follows. Section 2 explains dimensionality reduction methods employed successfully in image recognition tasks, followed by detailed discussion on Orthogonal Neighborhood Preserving Projection in Sect. 3. Section 4 documents expression recognition experiments performed on well-known facial expression databases, followed by the conclusion in Sect. 5.

2   Dimensionality Reduction for Image Recognition

Natural images are considered as very high-dimensional data, but as proved in [11], they usually reside on relatively low dimensional linear or non-linear manifold. The fundamental idea of dimensionality reduction is to seek this linear/non-linear manifold where data representation is compact and more meaningful, in the sense that the learned low dimensional representation reveals the variability of the data more clearly. During last two decades many dimensionality reduction methods are employed in image recognition.

Among these methods appearance based DR methods consider the image of size $m \times n$ as a mn-dimensional data point in $\mathcal{R}^{mn}$ and learn the low dimensional image manifold $\mathcal{M} \in \mathcal{R}^d$ where $d << mn$. DR methods are broadly classified in two categories: Non-linear DR methods and Linear DR methods. Linear Embedding (LE) [11], Laplacian Embeddings (LE) are non-linear DR methods. The mapping of data points achieved by these methods are non-explicit thus making recognition of an *out-of-sample* image data impossible. The solutions to overcome non-explicit mapping are proposed in Locality Preserving Projections (LPP) [12], Neighborhood Preserving Projections (NPP) where training samples are used to learn a projection matrix which can be used to project *out-of-sample* test data on the learned projection space. These linear methods have performed very well in image recognition tasks, but in recent times, orthogonal variants of these DR methods are proposed in OLPP [13] and ONPP [14] have been proved superior to their non-orthogonal counterparts and considered state-of-the-art in appearance based image recognition. Over the time, various discriminating and/or 2-dimensional variants of OLPP and ONPP are proposed and used in the image recognition tasks, too.

In this article, ONPP technique with class similarity based neighborhood is used to perform expression recognition and the performance is compared with conventional ONPP approach [14] and Modified ONPP approach [15]. The article also compares the performance of DR based expression recognition approach with local feature descriptor based state-of-the-art approaches.

3   Expression Recognition Using ONPP and Class Similarity Based Neighborhood

3.1   Data Preparation for Modular Expression Recognition

Appearance based DR methods consider an $m \times n$ image as a data point in mn-dimensional space where each image is vectorized either by columns or by rows. Let $\mathbf{x_1}, \mathbf{x_2}, ..., \mathbf{x_N}$ be the N data points of given training images, so the data matrix $\mathbf{X}$ can be defined as $\mathbf{X} = [\mathbf{x_1}, \mathbf{x_2}, ..., \mathbf{x_N}] \in \mathbf{R}^{mn \times N}$. As discussed in Sect. 2 it is expected that the similar images will be projected in the same neighborhood in the projected space. It is proven in that area between eyebrows, eyes, area containing nose and lips plays major role in expressing emotions while the rest of the facial area does not provide any significant information for expression recognition. The modular approach considers only these areas while recognizing expressions, thus the each data vector $\mathbf{x_i}$ corresponding to image i is prepared considering above mentioned four areas from the image. Each significant area is cropped from the whole image and vectorized, these four vectors of facial region are then concatenated to make l-dimensional vector $\mathbf{x_i}$ as shown in Fig. 1. Note that the size of these regions across all face images should be same so that the resulting vector representation be a point in $\mathcal{R}^l$.

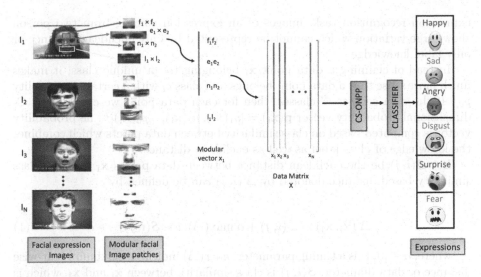

Fig. 1. Conversion of Facial expression image data into modular vectorized data: each l-dimensional vector $\mathbf{x_i} \in \mathbf{X}$ represents face image $\mathbf{I_1}$

3.2 ONPP with Class Similarity Based Neighborhood

Let X be the data matrix of training images such that $\mathbf{X} = [\mathbf{x_1}, \mathbf{x_2}, ..., \mathbf{x_N}] \in \mathbf{R}^{l \times N}$ for N modular vector representing face images. ONPP is a three step procedure where in the first step defines the neighborhood of each data point $\mathbf{x_i}$, the next step expresses each data point as a linear combination of its neighbors $\mathbf{x_j}s$. The last step finds projection bases $\mathbf{V} \in \mathcal{R}^{l \times d}$ of an ONPP space using training data $\mathbf{X}$ that can be used to embed test image $\mathbf{x_t}$ in the ONPP space for recognition step.

Step 1: Finding Nearest Neighbors: For every data point $\mathbf{x_i}$, neighborhood $\mathcal{N}_{x_i}$ is defined. The choice of neighborhood can be defined in several ways, the simple choice can be made using k neighbors are chosen by Nearest Neighbor (NN) method where k is a reasonably picked parameter. In another way, neighbors could be chosen which are inside ε radius from the data point. Let $\mathcal{N}_{x_i}$ be the set of k neighbors of $\mathbf{x_i}$. Both these approaches do not consider the available knowledge of class labels, thus known as unsupervised approach. In an alternative approach - supervised approach - data points belonging to same class are considered neighbors of each other.

Both the methods have their own shortcomings. Unsupervised methods consider only euclidean distance which essentially describes similarity between data points regardless of discriminating information based on class labels. Supervised methods decide the neighborhood neglecting the similarity between data points those are not in the same class. Both of these approaches are suitable for face recognition application where the difference between two images stems only from occlusions, illumination, expression and pose variations. On the other hand, in expression recognition task, images of an expression coming from two person show large variation which cannot be represented by only euclidean distance or only label knowledge.

Instead of claiming a data point $\mathbf{x_i}$ belonging to an unique class, it makes much more sense that a data point belongs to a class c_i with a certain probability p_{c_i}. If the data set has C classes, then for each data point we can build a C-dimensional probability vector $\mathbf{p}(\mathbf{x_i}) = [p_1(\mathbf{x_i}), p_2(\mathbf{x_i}), ...p_c(\mathbf{x_i})]^T$. he probability vector is computed based on class similarity between data points which combines the knowledge of class label as well as euclidean distance.

Let $\Delta(i, j)$ be the euclidean distance between data points $\mathbf{x_i}$ and $\mathbf{x_j}$. Class similarity based distance denoted by $\Delta'(i, j)$ can be defined by

$$\Delta'(\mathbf{x_i}, \mathbf{x_j}) = \Delta(i, j) + \alpha \max(\Delta)(1 - \mathcal{S}(i, j)) \tag{1}$$

where, $\alpha \in [0, 1]$ is a tuning parameter. $max(\Delta)$ indicates maximum pair-wise distance or data diameter. $\mathcal{S}(i, j)$ is class similarity between $\mathbf{x_i}$ and $\mathbf{x_j}$, which is defined as,

$$\mathcal{S}(i, j) = \begin{cases} 1; & \mathbf{x_i} = \mathbf{x_j} \\ \mathbf{p}(\mathbf{x_i})^T \mathbf{p}(\mathbf{x_j}); & \mathbf{x_i} \neq \mathbf{x_j} \end{cases} \tag{2}$$

We used Logistic Discrimination (LD) to find probability of each data point $\mathbf{x_i}$ belonging to class c_i. Performing LD on high dimensional data causes huge computational burden, thus lower dimensional representation is sought using PCA. Let $\mathbf{z_i}$ be a lower dimensional representation of $\mathbf{x_i}$, to find probability vector $\mathbf{p}(\mathbf{x_i})$. The cth element of $\mathbf{p}(\mathbf{x_i})$ corresponding to class c can be computed by

$$p_c(\mathbf{x_i}) = \frac{\pi(\mathbf{z_i}; \alpha_c, \beta_c)}{\sum_{c=1}^{C} \pi(\mathbf{z_i}; \alpha_c, \beta_c)} \tag{3}$$

where the function, $\pi(\mathbf{z_i}; \alpha_c, \beta_c) = \dfrac{\exp(\alpha_c + \beta_c{}^T \mathbf{z_i})}{1 + \exp(\alpha_c + \beta_c{}^T \mathbf{z_i})}$

The neighbors for each data point $\mathbf{x_i}$ will be chosen based on class similarity based distance given in Eq. (1).

Step 2: Calculating Reconstruction Weight: In this step, the neighborhood $\mathcal{N}_{x_i}$ is expressed as a linear combination of neighbors with reconstruction weight $w_{ij}s$ as $\sum_{j=1}^{k} w_{ij}\mathbf{x_j}$. The weight w_{ij} are computed by minimizing the reconstruction error i.e. error between $\mathbf{x_i}$ and linear combination of $\mathbf{x_j} \in \mathcal{N}_{x_i}$.

$$\arg\min \mathcal{E}(W) = \arg\min_{\mathbf{W}} \sum_{i=1}^{N} \parallel \mathbf{x_i} - \sum_{j=1}^{k} w_{ij}\mathbf{x_j} \parallel^2 \tag{4}$$

subject to $\sum_{j=1}^{k} w_{ij} = 1$.

For each data point x_i, optimization problem given in (4) can be modeled as a least square problem $(X_{N_i} - x_i e^T) w_i = 0$ with a constraint $e^T w_i = 1$. Here, X_{N_i} is a matrix having x_j as its columns, where $x_j \in N_{x_i}$. Note that X_{N_i} includes x_i as its own neighbor making it a matrix of dimension $l \times k + 1$. Solving the least square problem results in a closed form solution for w_i given by Eq. (5).

$$w_i = \frac{G^{-1}e}{e^T G^{-1}e} \tag{5}$$

Here, e is a vector of ones having dimension $k \times 1$ same as w_i. $G \in \mathcal{R}^{k \times k}$ is a Gramiam matrix, each entry of G is given by $g_{pl} = (x_i - x_p)^T (x_i - x_l)$, $for \; \forall x_p, x_l \in N_{x_i}$.

Step 3: Finding Projection Matrix: Last step is dimensionality reduction or finding the projection matrix V that explicitly maps l-dimensional data point x_i to d-dimensional representation y_i assuming that the neighborhood relationship among N_{x_i} with corresponding weights w_{ij} will be preserved in lower dimensional space, too.

The optimization problem to achieve such mapping can be formed as minimization of the sum of squares of reconstruction errors in lower dimensional space. The cost function is given by

$$\arg \min \mathcal{F}(Y) = \arg \min_{Y} \sum_{i=1}^{N} \| y_i - \sum_{j=1}^{k} w_{ij} y_j \|^2 \tag{6}$$

subject to orthogonality constraint, $V^T V = I$.

Solving the optimization problem results in eigenvalue problem $XMX^T V = \lambda V$. Here, columns of V are eigen-vectors that corresponding to the smallest d eigen-values. The matrix $M = (I - W)(I - W^T)$. Note that XMX^T is symmetric and positive semi-definite. ONPP explicitly maps X to Y, which is of the form $Y = V^T X$, i.e. each test sample x_t can now be projected to lower dimension by just a matrix-vector product $y_t = V^T x_t$.

Considering the under-sampled size issue where the number of samples N is less than dimension l. In such situation, the matrix $XMX^T \in R^{l \times l}$ will have maximum rank $N - c$, where c is number of classes. To ensure that the resulting matrix M be non-singular, one may utilize an initial PCA projection that reduces the dimensionality of the data vectors to $N - c$. If V_{PCA} is the projection matrix of PCA, then on performing the ONPP the resulting dimensionality reduction matrix is given by $V = V_{PCA} V_{ONPP}$. Note that the PCA projection is most common pre-processing applied in many dimensionality reduction methods and in this article we are using it in our advantage to define new distance measure for local neighborhood.

Following Table 1 gives procedure to find Class-similarity based ONPP subspace and mechanism to recognize expression of the test image.

Table 1. Procedure for expression recognition using Class-Similarity based ONPP

Input: Dataset $\mathbf{X} \in R^{l \times N}$ representing N facial expression images in modular format and number of reduced dimension d

Output: Lower dimension representation $\mathbf{Y} \in \mathcal{R}^{d \times N}$

1: Find low dimensional representation $\mathbf{z_i}$ of data by projecting on d_{pca} dimensional space using PCA $(\mathbf{z_i} = V_{pca}^T \mathbf{x_i})$

2: Use Logistic Regression on $\mathbf{z_i}$ to find class probability vector $\mathbf{p_i}$

3: Calculate modified distance for all data point pairs $\Delta'(\mathbf{x_i}, \mathbf{x_j})$ using equation (1)

2: Compute NN $\mathcal{N}_{\mathbf{x_i}}$ with modified distance$\Delta'(\mathbf{x_i}, \mathbf{x_j})$

3: Compute the weight W for each neighbor data point $\mathbf{x_j} \in \mathcal{N}_{\mathbf{x_i}}$ as given in equation (5)

4: Compute Projection matrix $V \in \mathcal{R}^{l \times d}$ whose column vectors are smallest d eigenvectors of matrix $\mathbf{XMX^T}$

5: Compute Embedding on lower dimension by $\mathbf{Y} = \mathbf{V^T X}$

6: Project test facial expression image represented as modular vector $\mathbf{x_t}$ on learned ONPP space to get low dimensional representation $\mathbf{y_t}$

7: Use 1-NN classifier to identify the class label for test image

---

4   Experiments

To approve the hypothetical conclusion of the proposed framework, experiments were performed on the four facial datasets. 1) JAFFE database [16] having 213 facial images of 10 Japanese female models of 7 facial expressions (6 basic facial expressions + 1 neutral). Out of 213 images, random 140 images were chosen for the training and the remaining 73 were used for testing. 2) The Video database [17] has videos of 11 persons. The single video contains four different facial expressions: Smiling, Angry, Open mouth and Normal. Out of 6668 images, randomly 70% images were chosen for training and remaining 30% images used as testing 3) In CK+ [18] there are 593 sequences across 123 persons giving 8 facial expressions. Table 2 reports average and best recognition result of 20 such iterations.

Comparison of performance of ONPP [14] and CS-ONPP on facial expression databases in the light of recognition score (in %) with corresponding subspace dimensions are reported in Table 3. Where as Table 4 reported the comparison between the MONPP [15] and CS-ONPP. CS-ONPP are reported along with tuning parameter Alpha and PCA dimension (d_pca).

Table 5 compares recognition results of the proposed technique with that of few State-of-the-art Local feature based facial expression recognition techniques. As can be seen from the comparison that for JAFFE database , similar performance is achieved with proposed method but with feature vector of only 110 dimensions. For CK+ data, best recognition is achieved at 510 dimensions,

Table 2. Best recognition Accuracy (%) achieved with proposed method of three benchmark databases along with related parameters: PCA subspace dimension (dpca), Number of Nearest Neighbors (k), tuning parameter α and ONPP subspace dimensions

Database	Recognition accuracy (%)	ONPP dimensions	dpca	alpha α	Number of nearest neighbors (k)
JAFFE	94.54	100	24	0.25	7
Video	94.76	110	20	0.50	13
CK+	86.76	510	22	0.25	5

Table 3. Comparison of performance of ONPP and CS-ONPP on facial expression databases in the light of recognition score (in %) with corresponding subspace dimensions. CS-ONPP are reported along with tuning parameter Alpha and PCA dimension (d_pca).

Databases	ONPP		CS-ONPP				
	RecAcc	Subspace dim	RecAcc	Subspace dim	d_pca	Alpha	NN_k
JAFFE	93.62	155	94.54	100	24	0.25	7
VIDEO	94.12	175	94.76	110	20	0.5	13
CK+	85.66	705	86.76	510	22	0.25	5

Table 4. Comparison of performance of MONPP and CS-ONPP on facial expression databases in the light of recognition score (in %) with corresponding subspace dimensions. CS-ONPP are reported along with tuning parameter Alpha and PCA dimension (d_pca).

Databases	MONPP		CS-ONPP				
	RecAcc	Subspace dim	RecAcc	Subspace dim	d_pca	Alpha	NN_k
JAFFE	93.76	145	95.35	85	20	0.25	9
VIDEO	94.4	170	95.66	105	20	0.5	14
CK+	87.14	675	87.88	485	18	0.5	9

which is not superior to other methods, but provides an advantage in terms of reduced feature vectors. Table 6 repeats the comparisons given in [23] for Local features based Facial Expression Recognition methods along with the dimensions of feature vectors for the given method.

Table 5. Comparison with Recognition Accuracy reported in some State-of-the-Art facial expression methods

DataBase	Existing methods	Classifiers	Accuracy
JAFFE	2D Geometry	NN with	90.00%
	&Gabor Wavelet	PROP	
	Gabor Filter [19]	ANN	88.75%
	HSOG [10]	1-NN	94.15%
	EPCA [20]	1-NN	89.01%
	DBN	Adaboost	91.8%
	WMDNN[21]	–	92.89%
	Proposed: ONPP using CS	1-NN	**94.54%**
CK+	DCV [22]	HMM	88.00%
	Gabor filter [19]	ANN	88.94%
	HSOG [10]	1-NN	92.54%
	CNN+loss layer	–	90.66%
	CNN, RBM	SVM	92.05%
	EPCA [20]	1-NN	91.72%
	Proposed: ONPP using CS	1-NN	86.76%

Table 6. Comparison of proposed method with Local feature based methods in the light of Feature vector length for JAFFE dataset for 256×256

Holistic approaches		
Method	Feature length	Recognition accuracy (%)
Local Binary Pattern (LBP)	65536	89.42
Local Gradient Code (LGC)	65536	90.38
Histogram of Gradients (HOG)	20736	85.71
Local Directional Pattern (LDP)	14337	85.20
Modular approaches		
Method	Feature length	Recognition accuracy (%)
Histogram of 2nd Order Gradient (HSOG)	38582	94.15
Proposed ONPP with CS	11541	94.56

5   Conclusion

Though, Local Features based methods have been successfully applied to Facial Expression Recognition problems, the resulting feature vector lengths usually are of order 10^5 which slow down classification process. The article proposes a Dimensionality Reduction based method which can be employed in FER.

Basically, state-of-the-art DR method ONPP is used and a novel approach of neighborhood selection based on class similarity is proposed to suit FER application. Proposed method is tested on three benchmark databases and proved to be gaining huge margin in terms of feature vector length while maintaining same recognition accuracy.

References

1. Sandbach, G., Zafeiriou, S., Pantic, M., Yin, L.: Static and dynamic 3D facial expression recognition: a comprehensive survey. Image Vis. Comput. **30**(10), 683–697 (2012)
2. Pantic, M., Rothkrantz, L.J.: Automatic analysis of facial expressions: the state of the art. IEEE Trans. Pattern Anal. Mach. Intell. **22**(12), 1424–1445 (2000)
3. Lowe, D.G.: Distinctive image features from scale-invariant keypoints. Int. J. Comput. Vis. **60**(2), 91–110 (2004)
4. Bay, H., Tuytelaars, T., Van Gool, L.: SURF: speeded up robust features. In: Leonardis, A., Bischof, H., Pinz, A. (eds.) ECCV 2006. LNCS, vol. 3951, pp. 404–417. Springer, Heidelberg (2006). https://doi.org/10.1007/11744023_32
5. Dalal, N., Triggs, B.: Histograms of oriented gradients for human detection. In: 2005 IEEE Computer Society Conference on Computer Vision and Pattern Recognition, CVPR 2005, vol. 1, pp. 886–893. IEEE (2005)
6. Zhang, B., Shan, S., Chen, X., Gao, W.: Histogram of gabor phase patterns (HGPP): a novel object representation approach for face recognition. IEEE Trans. Image Process. **16**(1), 57–68 (2007)
7. Ojala, T., Pietikainen, M., Maenpaa, T.: Multiresolution gray-scale and rotation invariant texture classification with local binary patterns. IEEE Trans. Pattern Anal. Mach. Intell. **24**(7), 971–987 (2002)
8. Ahonen, T., Hadid, A., Pietikäinen, M.: Face recognition with local binary patterns. In: Pajdla, T., Matas, J. (eds.) ECCV 2004. LNCS, vol. 3021, pp. 469–481. Springer, Heidelberg (2004). https://doi.org/10.1007/978-3-540-24670-1_36
9. Zhu, C., Bichot, C.-E., Chen, L.: Multi-scale color local binary patterns for visual object classes recognition. In: 2010 20th International Conference on Pattern Recognition (ICPR), pp. 3065–3068. IEEE (2010)
10. Sujata, Mitra, S.K.: A modular approach for facial expression recognition using IISOG. In: Proceeding of 9th International Conference on Advances in Pattern Recognition (ICAPR 2017). IEEE (2017)
11. Roweis, S.T., Saul, L.K.: Nonlinear dimensionality reduction by locally linear embedding. Science **290**(5500), 2323–2326 (2000)
12. He, X., Niyogi, P.: Locality preserving projections. In Advances in Neural Information Processing Systems, pp. 153–160 (2004)
13. Cai, D., He, X., Han, J., Zhang, H.-J.: Orthogonal Laplacian faces for face recognition. IEEE Trans. Image Process. **15**(11), 3608–3614 (2006)
14. Kokiopoulou, E., Saad, Y.: Orthogonal neighborhood preserving projections: a projection-based dimensionality reduction technique. IEEE Trans. Pattern Anal. Mach. Intell. **29**(12), 2143–2156 (2007)
15. Koringa, P., Shikkenawis, G., Mitra, S.K., Parulkar, S.K.: Modified orthogonal neighborhood preserving projection for face recognition. In: Kryszkiewicz, M., Bandyopadhyay, S., Rybinski, H., Pal, S.K. (eds.) PReMI 2015. LNCS, vol. 9124, pp. 225–235. Springer, Cham (2015). https://doi.org/10.1007/978-3-319-19941-2_22

16. Lyons, M., Akamatsu, S., Kamachi, M., Gyoba, J.: Coding facial expressions with Gabor wavelets. In: 1998 Proceedings of Third IEEE International Conference on Automatic Face and Gesture Recognition, pp. 200–205. IEEE (1998)
17. Shikkenawis, G., Mitra, S.K.: On some variants of locality preserving projection. Neurocomputing **173**, 196–211 (2016)
18. Kanade, T., Cohn F.J., and Tian Y.: Comprehensive database for facial expression analysis. In Automatic Face and Gesture Recognition, 2000. Proceedings. Fourth IEEE International Conference on, pages 46–53. IEEE, 2000
19. Saabni, R.: Facial expression recognition using multi radial bases function networks and 2-D Gabor filters. In: 2015 Fifth International Conference on Digital Information Processing and Communications (ICDIPC), pp. 225–230. IEEE (2015)
20. Trivedi, M., Mitra, S.K., et al.: A modular approach for facial expression recognition using Euler principal component analysis (E-PCA). In: 2018 IEEE Applied Signal Processing Conference (ASPCON), pp. 204–208. IEEE (2018)
21. Yang, B., Cao, J., Ni, R., Zhang, Y.: Facial expression recognition using weighted mixture deep neural network based on double-channel facial images. IEEE Access **6**, 4630–4640 (2018)
22. Wang, Y.-K., Huang, C.-H.: Facial expression recognition with discriminative common vector. In: 2007 Third International Conference on Intelligent Information Hiding and Multimedia Signal Processing, IIHMSP 2007, vol. 2, pp. 431–434. IEEE (2007)
23. Kumari, J., Rajesh, R., Pooja, K.M.: Facial expression recognition: a survey. Procedia Comput. Sci. **58**, 486–491 (2015)

Compressive Sensing Based Privacy for Fall Detection

Ronak Gupta[1]($\boxtimes$), Prashant Anand[1], Santanu Chaudhury[1,2], Brejesh Lall[1], and Sanjay Singh[3]

[1] Department of Electrical Engineering, Indian Institute of Technology Delhi, New Delhi, India
ronakgupta143@gmail.com
[2] Indian Institute of Technology Jodhpur, Jheepasani, India
[3] Cognitive Computing Group, CSIR-CEERI, Pilani, India

Abstract. Fall detection holds immense importance in the field of healthcare, where timely detection allows for instant medical assistance. In this context, we propose a 3D ConvNet architecture which consists of 3D Inception modules for fall detection. The proposed architecture is a custom version of Inflated 3D (I3D) architecture, that takes compressed measurements of video sequence as spatio-temporal input, obtained from compressive sensing framework, rather than video sequence as input, as in the case of I3D convolutional neural network. This is adopted since privacy raises a huge concern for patients being monitored through these RGB cameras. The proposed framework for fall detection is flexible enough with respect to a wide variety of measurement matrices. Ten action classes randomly selected from Kinetics-400 with no fall examples, are employed to train our 3D ConvNet post compressive sensing with different types of sensing matrices on the original video clips. Our results show that 3D ConvNet performance remains unchanged with different sensing matrices. Also, the performance obtained with Kinetics pre-trained 3D ConvNet on compressively sensed fall videos from benchmark datasets is better than the state-of-the-art techniques.

Keywords: Fall detection · Human privacy · Compressive sensing · 3D Convolutional Neural Network · Human activity recognition

1 Introduction

As per WHO report [12], India is the second most populous country in the world with more than 75 million people lying in the age group of more than 60 years. Human fall is a serious problem concerning people with this age group and is considered as one of the "Geriatric Giants" [12]. Therefore, to address this issue, the need for intelligent monitoring system of the elderly people has risen over the past years. The precise objective for these systems is to automatically detect falls while minimizing false negatives and then to intimate the caregivers/family members.

© Springer Nature Singapore Pte Ltd. 2020
R. V. Babu et al. (Eds.): NCVPRIPG 2019, CCIS 1249, pp. 429–438, 2020.
https://doi.org/10.1007/978-981-15-8697-2_40

Several deep learning based fall detection techniques [3,8,17,19] have been presented and for generalization few depend on large action recognition datasets for pre-training. In [17] authors proposed a scheme for fall detection through ambient camera, where they employed 3D convolutional neural network (3D CNN) to obtain coarse spatio-temporal features, This was followed by Long short-term memory (LSTM) based visual attention mechanism to extract the motion information encoded within the region of interest from coarse spatio-temporal features of the video sequence. The kinetic database Sports-1M which does not have fall data was used for training the 3DCNN. In [3] fall events are detected as a series of sequential change in human pose and these different poses are recognized using CNN. They tried different input image combinations of RGB, Depth, background subtracted RGB to name a few as input to the CNN. Their focus was on human silhouette extracts for recognizing human pose for fall detection.

In this paper, we propose 3D ConvNet architecture which consists of 3D Inception modules for the task of fall detection. The architecture takes spatio-temporal input in compressed domain, rather than spatio-temporal input in image domain as done in Inflated 3D (I3D) architecture. The compressive sensing captures the measurements which are then used for performing classification as a fall or other daily activities (labelled as non fall). In visual systems, while training the fall data is usually generated by simulated falls under a variety of circumstances, that makes it difficult to obtain large quantity of training instances and thus trained classifier has high chance of overfitting the training data. Also, since both the fall dataset used for experiments do not have sufficient training samples, we pre-train the architecture on action recognition datasets for learning better representation of the input videos. This significantly improves the generalization of the deep neural network by giving good detection rates [5,26].

The authors adopt compressive sensing step in the recognition framework which render the compressive samples visually imperceptible. This is essential in circumstances where one might prefer a system which doesn't disclose their identity and capturing all personal activities/details via visual systems/cameras used for detecting falls poses a serious threat to one's privacy. Compressive sensing demonstrates that a signal that is K-sparse in one basis called sparsity basis can be recovered or classified from K linear projections onto a second basis. The latter is called measurement basis which is incoherent with the first. While the measurement process is linear, the reconstruction or classification process has to be done through non linear transformations. It is also a well known fact that the compressive samples of images/video frames containing personal information can essentially be used to achieve privacy. This is because CS transformation is viewed as a symmetric cipher resulting in computational secrecy when the secret sensing matrix is unknown to the adversary [10,20,21].

Although, several privacy based intelligent systems for fall detection have been designed in the past [18]. These systems employ action recognition algorithms which run directly on the camera monitoring the person thus enhancing privacy. Their deployment is done in such a manner that only the fall alarms are transmitted but the video frames are not. Other popular systems [19] are usually based on thermal heat- maps although capable of masking the person's identity effectively but are an expensive option. The earlier in-house implementation will be problematic to update when new instances are available [18]. In contrast to the aforementioned approaches, compressive sensing field suggests that a small group of linear projections of a compressible signal contains enough information for reconstruction, classification and processing [6,9,13–15,27,28].

2 Related Works

Existing non-deep learning fall detection techniques depends on extracting the person (foreground) first, which is highly influenced by image noise (background), illumination variation and occlusion. In [23] authors presented the fall detection by quantifying human shape deformation. For human shape change analysis, they extract and compare two consecutive silhouettes of a person. The landmarks/edge points extracted from silhouette are then matched through video sequence to quantify the silhouette deformation. They compare the mean matching cost of silhouette landmarks and the full Procrustes distance [7] as body shape deformation measures. Based on these shape deformation measures during the fall followed by a lack of significant movement after the fall are fed to Gaussian Mixture Model (GMM) to classify the different activities as fall or not. In [18] the authors presented a fall detection system that uses silhouette area as a feature. Their approach works irrespective of the direction of the movement of the person with respect to the camera. They present a mathematical analysis to confirm the relation between silhouette area and a fall event. The classification is done separately based on the variations of silhouette area as features for SVM classifier.

In [8] authors have proposed a spatial-temporal fall detection method, which can present specific spatial and temporal locations of fall events in complex scenes. In their method, an object detector YOLO v3 [22] is used for person detection, later a deep learning based method for multi-object tracking is used. The features from the tracker are fed to an attention guided LSTM model to detect specific fall events. In [19] the authors presented the use of thermal camera for fall detection which is privacy preserving as it effectively masks the identity of those being monitored. They formulated the fall detection problem as an anomaly detection problem and used Convolutional LSTM Autoencoders to identify unseen falls.

In compressive sensing, random Gaussian matrix or random Bernoulli matrix has been widely used to generate linear measurements of natural images, frames of video, etc. [9]. In practice there are several problems with GRM such as GRM is non-sparse and complicated, and hence highly computational complex and highly difficult in hardware implementation. The other issue is that the measurements generated by GRM are random, neither are data-driven nor adjacent measurements have enough correlation. In literature other measurement matrices have been proposed to solve the above issues. In [6], the authors proposed structural measurement matrix (SMM) to achieve a better Rate-Distortion performance in CS based image coding, in which the image is sampled by small blocks for better measurement coding while CS recovery can be performed in large blocks for better quality of recovered images. Their method of measurement coding with SMM, helps exploit the spatial correlation in measurement domain, which is represented by directional pixel behaviour (i.e object edges), that improves measurement prediction scheme and reconstructed with large blocks spliced from small correlated blocks improves CS recovery. In [9], the authors proposed a novel local structural measurement matrix (LSMM) for block-based CS coding of natural images by utilizing the local smooth property of images. Their proposed LSMM is a highly sparse matrix and the adjacent measurement elements generated by LSMM have high correlation that has been shown to improve the coding efficiency of spatial information.

Outline of the paper is as follows: Section 3 introduces methodology to solve the problem and the proposed architecture. Section 4 presents experimental results to show the effectiveness of the framework and Sect. 5 concludes the paper.

3 Methodology

We use 3D ConvNet which includes submodules designed from Inception-V1 network architecture for fall detection. The submodules present in Inception-V1 architecture are inflated as done in I3D Convolutional neural network [5] to construct 3D ConvNet. The inflated Inception-V1 modules are found to be more effective in action recognition compared to VGG-style 3D CNN [5]. There are four inflated Inception submodules in our 3D ConvNet architecture. For fall detection, our 3D ConvNet takes compressed measurements of video sequence as spatio-temporal input, obtained from compressive sensing framework (as shown in Fig. 1), rather than video sequence as input, as in the case of I3D convolutional neural networks. Here, the compressed measurements for RGB frames of given video sequence are stacked together along the color (RGB) channel dimension. Figure 2 shows the fall detection architecture.

We adopt a compressive sensing step in the recognition framework which render the compressive samples visually imperceptible, a necessity for privacy. When block based compressive sensing is performed over video frame, we get compressed measurements for the corresponding block. If the dimension of block is $N(= B^2)$ and when it is multiplied with a sensing matrix of size $M \times N$, we get M measurements and the compression ratio is defined as $r = \frac{N}{M}$. The compressed measurement vectors obtained for corresponding blocks in a frame, are arranged across channel dimension as shown in figure before given as input to fall detection architecture. Hence, when compressive sensing is applied to the frame at block level, the output compressed representation will have spatial dimension depending on the number of blocks in video frame and the channel dimension depending on the compression ratio. Similar rearrangement of images or video frame is also performed in the inverse pixel shuffling operation present in sub-convolutional layer of image or video super-resolution frameworks [24]. The difference between their inverse pixel shuffling operation is that it does not involve dimensionality reduction. Moreover, the linear transformation involved in CS of the video frame blocks into compressed measurements makes rearrangement of the measurements back to the input frame difficult compared to pixel shuffling in sub-convolutional layer.

We show that our CS based privacy for fall detection architecture can work with different compressive sensing matrices. Random Gaussian matrix or random Bernoulli matrix has been used to generate random linear measurements of the video frame blocks. We have also used structural measurement matrix and local structural measurement matrix which exploits intra-block correlation in spatial domain.

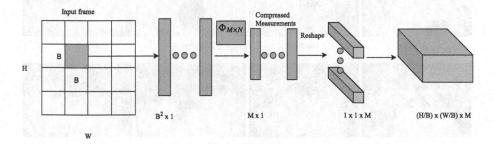

Fig. 1. Compression technique

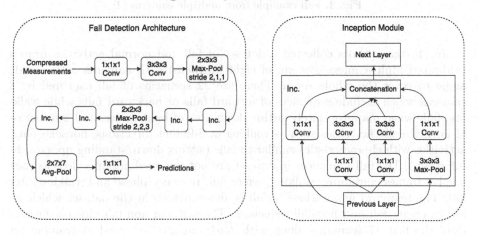

Fig. 2. Fall detection architecture

4   Experimental Results

In this section we report performance of our framework over action recognition
and fall datasets with a wide variety of sensing matrices. Once our 3D ConvNet is
trained on action recognition dataset, we fine-tune the network for fall detection
dataset.

4.1   Fall and Action Datasets

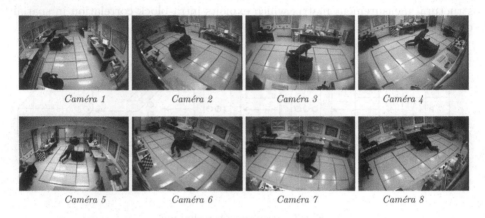

Caméra 1   Caméra 2   Caméra 3   Caméra 4

Caméra 5   Caméra 6   Caméra 7   Caméra 8

Fig. 3. Fall example from multiple cameras [4]

In [4], the authors collected a dataset of fall and normal activities from a
calibrated Multi-camera system, of eight inexpensive IP cameras with a wide
angle to cover the whole room. There are 22 scenarios of fall captured by 8
cameras which include sequences of forward falls or backward falls while walking, falls when inappropriately sitting down, loss of balance etc. and 2 scenarios
of normal daily activities such as walking in different directions, housekeeping,
activities with characteristics similar to falls (sitting down/standing up, crouch-
ing down). The fall sequences in dataset are not trimmed action videos as they
involve frames containing walking before fall, recovery phase and walking after
fall. The temporal annotations of fall is also provided in the dataset which we
use to create fall and non-fall sequences. The fall and non-fall video sequences
from the first 17 scenarios along with 23rd scenario, are used as training set
while the video sequences from 18th to 22nd along with 24th scenario, are used
as test set (Fig. 3).

In [16], the authors collected dataset containing 70 videos, comprising of 30
fall videos and 40 videos with activities of daily living. Fall and daily activities
sequences were recorded with Microsoft Kinect cameras in form of RGB and
depth data. Here we create the learning set containing 70 fall and 642 non-fall

sequences with temporal strides. Fall sequences from first 24 fall videos and non-fall sequences from first 32 non-fall videos are used as training set and the rest are used as test set.

For pretraining our 3D CovNet, we create a learning set by randomly selecting 10 classes* from Kinetics-400 dataset [5]. The actions involved in these 10 classes from Kinetics-400 are archery, belly dancing, cheerleading, dodgeball, high jump, playing cello, push up, swimming backstroke, tying tie and washing hair. This subset is composed of around 8K clips of YouTube videos. Each video includes only one actions. The training set, validation set and test set is divided as given in Kinetics-400 dataset.

Table 1. Accuracy on test split of Kinetics dataset with different deep learning architectures

Dataset	Method	Accuracy
Kinetics-400	I3D network (ImageNet pre-trained)	71.1%
Kinetics-10*	I3D network (ImageNet pre-trained)	92.3%
Kinetics-10	I3D network (scratch)	79.73%
Kinetics-10	**3D ConvNet (scratch)**	**78.98%**

Table 2. Accuracy on test split of Kinetics-10* with our 3D ConvNet architecture

Sensing matrix type	Compression ratio			
	4	16	32	64
Random Gaussian Matrix	77.07	77.22	**78.48**	**78.26**
Random Bernoulli Matrix	75.50	75.28	77.22	76.99
Structural Measurement Matrix (SMM) [6]	**78.63**	78.11	77.81	75.58
Local Structural Measurement Matrix [9]	74.98	75.13	77.74	76.99
Convolutional CS Measurement Matrix [25]	77.96	**78.78**	76.62	75.23

Table 1, shows the accuracy performance on test split of Kinetics dataset with different deep learning architectures. Table 2 shows the accuracy results over 10 classes of Kinetics dataset with random Gaussian, random Bernoulli, structural measurement matrix, local structural measurement matrix and Convolutional CS measurement matrix at different compression ratios. We train separately, from scratch, the 3D ConvNet for different compression ratios and different measurement matrices. The performance of 3D ConvNet is more or less similar for the reported measurement matrices. If we train I3D [5] network from scratch over the given classes from Kinetics dataset, the performance comes out to be 79.73% and the performance of our 3D ConvNet comes out to be 78.98%. Since there is small difference in performance between I3D and our 3D ConvNet with compressive sensing, it is safe to say our 3D ConvNet is sufficient to learn actions for the reported action recognition dataset.

Table 3. Performance of various techniques over Multi-camera fall dataset and UR fall dataset

Method	Compression ratio	Pre-trained on Dataset	Multi-camera fall dataset	UR fall dataset [16]
Full Proscrustes distance [23]	1 (No privacy)	–	96.20%	–
3DCNN [17]	1 (No privacy)	Sports-1M [11]	99.73%	–
Visual Attention Guided 3DCNN [17]	1 (No privacy)	Sports-1M [11]	99.36%	99.27%
Proposed framework (SMM+ 3DConv Inception Network)	1 (No privacy)	Kinetics-10	100%	100%
	4	Kinetics-10	100%	100%
	16	Kinetics-10	100%	100%
	32	Kinetics-10	100%	100%
	64	Kinetics-10	100%	100%

In Table 3, we report the performance on fall detection dataset using pre-trained 3D ConvNet (over reported action recognition dataset) with structural measurement matrix at different compression ratios. Since fall detection is a binary classification problem, we report 100% accuracy with pre-trained 3D ConvNet. We found that our 3D ConvNet architecture performs better than 3D CNN from [17] for fall detection.

4.2 Implementation Details

All action sequences (including fall and non-fall), were resized to 224×320 before compressed using measurement matrix. We train our model using ADAM optimizer with initial learning rate of 10^{-3} which is reduced by a factor of 10 when validation loss doesn't decrease for 10 consecutive epochs and training is terminated when validation loss doesn't decrease for 22 consecutive epochs. We implemented all the models in TensorFlow [2] and trained and evaluated them on nvidia-docker [1] for Tensorflow on NVIDIA DGX-1.

5   Conclusion

A compressive sensing based fall detection framework has been presented in the paper that also enables privacy preserving since it is a huge concern for patients being monitored through regular cameras. Our deep learning architecture performs similar to I3D network [5], when trained from scratch, in accuracy for reported action recognition dataset, even with wide variety of compressive sensing measurement matrices. Experimental results on Multi-camera fall dataset and UR-Fall dataset were presented to show the effectiveness of the framework at different compression ratios.

Acknowledgment. The NVIDIA DGX-1 for experiments was provided by CSIR-CEERI, Pilani, India

References

1. Nvidia GPU cloud tensorflow. https://ngc.nvidia.com/catalog/containers/nvidia:tensorflow, nVIDIA offers GPU accelerated containers via NVIDIA GPU Cloud (NGC) for use on DGX systems
2. Abadi, M., et al.: TensorFlow: large-scale machine learning on heterogeneous systems (2015). http://tensorflow.org/
3. Adhikari, K., Bouchachia, H., Nait-Charif, H.: Activity recognition for indoor fall detection using convolutional neural network. In: 2017 Fifteenth IAPR International Conference on Machine Vision Applications (MVA), pp. 81–84. IEEE (2017)
4. Auvinet, E., Rougier, C., Meunier, J., St-Arnaud, A., Rousseau, J.: Multiple cameras fall dataset. DIRO-Université de Montréal, Tech. Rep 1350 (2010)
5. Carreira, J., Zisserman, A.: Quo vadis, action recognition? A new model and the kinetics dataset. In: 2017 IEEE Conference on Computer Vision and Pattern Recognition (CVPR), pp. 4724–4733. IEEE (2017)
6. Dinh, K.Q., Shim, H.J., Jeon, B.: Measurement coding for compressive imaging using a structural measurement matrix. In: 2013 IEEE International Conference on Image Processing, pp. 10–13. IEEE (2013)
7. Dryden, I.L.: Shape analysis. Statistics Reference Online, Wiley Stats Ref (2014)
8. Feng, Q., Gao, C., Wang, L., Zhao, Y., Song, T., Li, Q.: Spatio-temporal fall event detection in complex scenes using attention guided LSTM. Pattern Recogn. Lett. **130**, 242–249 (2018)
9. Gao, X., Zhang, J., Che, W., Fan, X., Zhao, D.: Block-based compressive sensing coding of natural images by local structural measurement matrix. In: 2015 Data Compression Conference, pp. 133–142. IEEE (2015)
10. Hu, G., Xiao, D., Xiang, T., Bai, S., Zhang, Y.: A compressive sensing based privacy preserving outsourcing of image storage and identity authentication service in cloud. Inf. Sci. **387**, 132–145 (2017)
11. Karpathy, A., Toderici, G., Shetty, S., Leung, T., Sukthankar, R., Fei-Fei, L.: Large-scale video classification with convolutional neural networks. In: Proceedings of the IEEE Conference on Computer Vision and Pattern Recognition, pp. 1725–1732 (2014)
12. Krishnaswamy, B., Usha, G.: Falls in older people
13. Kulkarni, K., Lohit, S., Turaga, P., Kerviche, R., Ashok, A.: Reconnet: Non-iterative reconstruction of images from compressively sensed measurements. In: Proceedings of the IEEE Conference on Computer Vision and Pattern Recognition. pp. 449–458 (2016)
14. Kulkarni, K., Turaga, P.: Recurrence textures for human activity recognition from compressive cameras. In: 2012 19th IEEE International Conference on Image Processing (ICIP), pp. 1417–1420. IEEE (2012)

15. Kulkarni, K., Turaga, P.: Reconstruction-free action inference from compressive imagers. IEEE Trans. Pattern Anal. Mach. Intell. **38**(4), 772–784 (2016)
16. Kwolek, B., Kepski, M.: Human fall detection on embedded platform using depth maps and wireless accelerometer. Comput. Methods Programs Biomed. **117**(3), 489–501 (2014)
17. Lu, N., Wu, Y., Feng, L., Song, J.: Deep learning for fall detection: three-dimensional CNN combined with LSTM on video kinematic data. IEEE J. Biomed. Health Inf. **23**(1), 314–323 (2019)
18. Mirmahboub, B., Samavi, S., Karimi, N., Shirani, S.: Automatic monocular system for human fall detection based on variations in Silhouette area. IEEE Trans. Biomed. Eng. **60**(2), 427–436 (2013)
19. Nogas, J., Khan, S., Mihailidis, A.: Fall detection from thermal camera using convolutional LSTM autoencoder. In: 2nd Workshop on AI for Aging, Rehabilitation and Independent Assisted Living at IJCAI (2018)
20. Orsdemir, A., Altun, H.O., Sharma, G., Bocko, M.F.: On the security and robustness of encryption via compressed sensing. In: MILCOM 2008–2008 IEEE Military Communications Conference, pp. 1–7. IEEE (2008)
21. Rachlin, Y., Baron, D.: The secrecy of compressed sensing measurements. In: 2008 46th Annual Allerton Conference on Communication, Control, and Computing, pp. 813–817. IEEE (2008)
22. Redmon, J., Farhadi, A.: YoloV3: an incremental improvement. arXiv preprint arXiv:1804.02767 (2018)
23. Rougier, C., Meunier, J., St-Arnaud, A., Rousseau, J.: Robust video surveillance for fall detection based on human shape deformation. IEEE Trans. Circuits Syst. Video Technol. **21**(5), 611–622 (2011)
24. Shi, W., et al.: Real-time single image and video super-resolution using an efficient sub-pixel convolutional neural network. In: Proceedings of the IEEE Conference on Computer Vision and Pattern Recognition, pp. 1874–1883 (2016)
25. Shi, W., Jiang, F., Zhang, S., Zhao, D.: Deep networks for compressed image sensing. In: 2017 IEEE International Conference on Multimedia and Expo (ICME), pp. 877–882. IEEE (2017)
26. Tran, D., Bourdev, L., Fergus, R., Torresani, L., Paluri, M.: Learning spatiotemporal features with 3D convolutional networks. In: Proceedings of the IEEE International Conference on Computer Vision, pp. 4489–4497 (2015)
27. Wakin, M.B., e al.: An architecture for compressive imaging. In: 2006 IEEE International Conference on Image Processing, pp. 1273–1276. IEEE (2006)
28. Xu, K., Ren, F.: CSvideoNet: a real-time end-to-end learning framework for high-frame-rate video compressive sensing. In: 2018 IEEE Winter Conference on Applications of Computer Vision (WACV), pp. 1680–1688. IEEE (2018)

Indian Plant Recognition in the Wild

Vamsidhar Muthireddy(✉) and C. V. Jawahar

IIIT Hyderabad, Hyderabad, India
vamsidhar.muthireddy@research.iiit.ac.in, jawahar@iiit.ac.in

Abstract. Conservation efforts to protect biodiversity rely on an accurate identification process. In the case of plant identification, traditional methods used are manual, time-consuming and require a degree of expertise to operate. As a result, there is an increasing interest today for an automated plant identification system. Such a system can help in aiding plant-related education, promoting ecotourism, creating a digital heritage for plant species among many others. We propose a solution using modern convolutional neural network architectures which achieves state-of-the-art performance for plant classification in the wild. An exhaustive set of experiments are performed to classify 112 species of plants from the challenging Indic-Leaf dataset. The best performing model gives Top-1 precision of 90.08 and Top-5 precision of 96.90.

1 Introduction

Diversity is an important trait of biological life that helps in sustaining itself. This biodiversity is decreasing across the world due to indirect or direct human interventions [16]. Conservation efforts employed to sustain biodiversity involve geographical mapping of species for better monitoring. These efforts rely on an accurate identification process which is almost always time-consuming. Take, for example, the case of plant species that form a significant portion of biodiversity. The traditional process for identifying them involves an expert who is required to identify qualitative morphological characteristics of a plant and compare them with discriminatory features of known plants to arrive at a species. This process is very long and tedious requiring the involvement of domain experts. Traditional plant species identification is challenging even for people like gardeners, farmers or conservationists whose daily jobs involve dealing with plants. Moreover, it cannot be used by nature enthusiasts since many of them are not equipped with domain knowledge. Thus, the process of plant species identification along with being accurate also needs to be robust and simple enough for the general public to use.

There are more than 3,00,000 [7] estimated plant species that inherit this world. It might not be possible for an experienced expert to identify all these plant species. They can be supplemented with a simple computational system that can identify these species. For this purpose, a recognition system based on images is considered a promising approach [5]. The image data captured for the said system should contain necessary features needed to recognise the plant

© Springer Nature Singapore Pte Ltd. 2020
R. V. Babu et al. (Eds.): NCVPRIPG 2019, CCIS 1249, pp. 439–449, 2020.
https://doi.org/10.1007/978-981-15-8697-2_41

species such as its leaves. Leaves are the most abundant part of a plant that can be used for visual identification. They contain important visible features such as shape, texture, veins, colour, edge, and leaf type. Images of these leaves can be used in developing methods for plant species classification. It is crucial to create such image datasets tagged by different geographical locations. Keeping this in view, we created Indic-Leaf dataset composed of some of the plant species found in India.

1.1 Motivation

Plants play a crucial role in Indian culture. Among their many uses, some are described here. Our indigenous medicine uses beneficial plant parts. This practice is extensively used as primary modality, especially in rural areas. In a primarily agrarian society like ours, the farmers have to be provided with best-recommended practices for any specific crop to ensure that national crop yield remains high. As such, the necessary information must be provided to them about the various diseases and pests that can affect the crop. Further, knowing what a healthy plant looks like can help in early detection of disease. Culturally, plants and their parts play a significant role in many rituals and festivals. A systemic digital catalogue of the native species can have far-reaching consequences. Firstly, this catalogue is a part of digital heritage that can boost conservation efforts by helping identify various local species. Such a catalogue can help differentiate between similar species and allow for selective cultivation of more beneficial plants. It can be used to create Biodiversity parks to promote ecotourism. Having a digital platform can make plant-related education more accessible, allowing for generations of students to get interested in our bio-heritage.

Fig. 1. This figure shows images from level-0 and Level-1 of Indic-Leaf dataset. The top row shows images from Level-0 and the bottom row from Level-1. Each column shows images of different species.

1.2   Related Works

Early work on plant species classification used handcrafted features to describe plant parts. Gu *et al.* [7] extract leaf skeleton from scan-like images and use it to classify leaf images. There are studies which used the venation pattern of the leaves for the same [14]. Some use the texture of the leaf as a key feature [11]. The shape information is also used by the leaf-based methods [13]. Several studies used the combination of texture and shape [10] while other studies used the features from shape and veins [15]. Some used colour and polygon models to segment a leaf followed by extracting handcrafted shape features for leaf recognition [4]. Handcrafted features designed for leaf classification based on its morphological characteristics often assume an image with a simple background of uniform colour. They fail in the context of the natural environment as it is often hard to capture an image containing only a single leaf in a cluttered natural environment.

Neural networks automate the process of obtaining the features by learning a representation of training data. Sun *et al.* [19] and Barré *et al.* [3] propose custom architectures for plant identification. Existing VGG model is modified [8] and used in classifying PlantCLEF dataset [6]. Pl@ntnet, a plant identification system has also shifted from using classic handcrafted features [12] to a CNN based architecture for plant identification. We also take an approach of starting with pre-trained state-of-the-art convolutional neural networks and fine-tune them on a challenging leaf classification dataset.

Fig. 2. This figure shows images from level-2 and Level-3 of Indic-Leaf dataset. The top row shows images from Level-2 and the bottom row from Level-3. Each column shows images of different species.

1.3   Existing Datasets: Problems and a Solution

An image-based dataset should capture features that help human experts identify the object of interest. For plant recognition, experts analyze foliage from various distances to take note of the plant shape, arrangement of leaves, and characteristics of the leaf. They study a plant from different levels of distance to identify it. Publicly available datasets such as Herbarium [1], Flavia [20], Swedish Leaf [18], Leafsnap [13], PlantCLEF [6] have assisted in furthering the work in plant species classification. Other than PlantCLEF, all the others are composed of scan-like images in a lab constrained environment. PlantCLEF that captures plants in their natural environment doesn't organise the images of the species according to different distance levels mentioned above. Moreover, none of these datasets contain images specific to Indian sub-continent. Keeping this in view, we created the Indic-Leaf dataset.

Our proposed Indic-Leaf dataset is composed of 27,000 images belonging to 112 Indian plant species. It is divided into groups based on distance levels between the camera and the plant. This will allow for a broader set of tasks to be done using our dataset. As per our knowledge, this is the first dataset where the images are grouped according to different levels. More details about the dataset are provided in Sect. 2. Further sections describe the methods and our experimental setup. They detail the qualitative and quantitative analysis that has been done on the dataset to achieve a Precision@1 of 90.08.

2   Indic-Leaf Dataset

The Indic-Leaf dataset contains 27K images belonging to 112 plant species found in IIIT-H campus. For every image, there is an associated XML file containing annotations that include attributes of the leaf present in the image. Further, images from each species are divided into groups: Level-0, Level-1, Level-2, and Level-3. Level-0 contains scan-like images. The rest of the groups contain "in the wild" images of the leaves. These groups are designed to act as distinct datasets to assist with relevant research problems. The above-mentioned groups are explained in detail below.

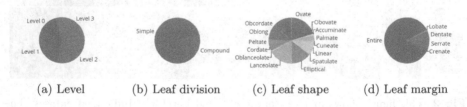

    (a) Level   (b) Leaf division   (c) Leaf shape   (d) Leaf margin

Fig. 3. Figure shows the distribution of different dataset attributes. Contribution of each (a) level, (b) leaf divison type, (c) leaf shape, and (d) margins.

Level 0: Scan-like images in our dataset are grouped into this *level*. Leaves collected from a plant are pressed for a short time to make them relatively flatter. Each leaf is placed on a sheet of white paper; its picture is taken from a camera at a fixed height with no flash.

Level 1: Leaves can be simple(a single leaf blade or lamina) or compound(with several leaflets). Level-1 contains images that capture a single leaf in its entirety so that the visibility of the blade area is maximized as shown in the bottom row of Fig. 1. The process of capturing is simpler in the case of simple leaved plants that have one leaflet. For plants with compound leaves, where a leaf is divided into many small leaflets, this process is rather challenging. In this case, the image is captured to contain the majority of these leaflets belonging to the leaf. Level-1 images capture the finer details of the leaf such as its shape, colour, texture, and veins.

Level 2: Images in this *level* capture details of a leaf cluster; the arrangement of the leaves along a stem/branch. The top row of Fig. 2 shows different types of leaf groups in different species. For example, the second image in this row shows leaves arranged in a rosette pattern.

Level 3: Images capturing partial/full view of the plants are grouped into this *level*. Images in this *level* give an overview of the shape of the plant/tree.

2.1 Annotation Schema

Each image in our dataset has an associated XML file that provides the annotations. These annotations describe the morphological characteristics of the leaf along with other information related to plant species captured in the image. These annotations are as follows:

- *Scientific Name:* This tag specifies the scientific name of the species captured in the image. It is a two-part name based in Latin.
- *Common Name:* Common name varies with the geography of the species. A species can have multiple common names.
- *Family:* Every plant species belongs to a family. The name of the family usually ends with "aceae" for plants. This tag gives the family of the species captured in the image.
- *Picture Type:* As mentioned in Sect. 2, each image is grouped into one of the levels. This tag records it.
- *Leaf Shape:* This tag describes the shape of the leaf in the image. Figure 3c shows different shapes of leaves available in Indic-Leaf dataset.
- *Leaf Margin:* Leaf margin refers to the outside perimeter of a leaf. Figure 3d shows different types of leaf margins found in Indic-Leaf dataset.
- *Leaf Divison:* Two basic forms of leaves can be described considering the way the blade (lamina) is divided. This tag describes whether the division of the plant species is simple or compound.
- *Picture season:* This tag captures the season in which the image was taken.
- *Disease:* This tag informs us of any common diseases that affect the leaves of the species captured in the image.
- *Description:* Detailed information about the plant species is provided in this tag. It contains a visual description of the species; detailing height of the plant/tree, colour and size of flowers and fruits, etc.
- *Utility:* Utility tag describes how the resources from a plant species are utilized.

3   Methods

Plant recognition "in the wild" is a challenging classification task. During classification, all the images of a particular species are considered into one class. Some species can be recognized from afar, while some need a closer inspection. This is emulated by using levels mentioned in Sect. 2 during classification task. A significant portion of plants have a variation of green hue as the leaf colour. The dataset was used in different colour spaces to identify any significant differences in class predictions. We wanted to understand whether the problem of plant classification is inherently a difficult one or it depends on the complexity of the model. We used VGG-16 and various architectures of ResNet to experiment on different dataset configurations.

3.1   VGG-16

VGG-16 [17] is a feed-forward convolutional neural network with 16 weight layers. This network is characterized by its simplicity for using convolutional filters with a receptive field of 3×3 in every layer. Convolutional layers in the network are followed by two fully connected layers and a softmax classifier. Due to its known efficacy in classification tasks, we use VGG-16 as our baseline model.

3.2   ResNet

Residual networks (ResNet) [9] are feed-forward neural networks that use skip connections in their architecture. ResNet based architectures out-rank their predecessors [2] in classification ability since they do not suffer from the vanishing gradient problem. We use ResNets of 18, 34, 50, 101, and 152 layers in our work. All of them have similar architectures with a single conv. layer that takes $224 \times 224 \times 3$ image as an input. This conv. layer is followed by 4 parent blocks. A block or a basic block represents stacked convolutional layers. Each parent block contains multiple basic blocks and their number varies with the position of the block and the depth of the ResNet. Each basic block in ResNet-18, 34 has two conv. layers while each block in ResNet-50, 101, 152 have three conv. layers. Table 1 explains the detailed architecture of different ResNets.

4   Experiments, Results, and Discussion

In this section, we present the experimental results of the networks used for classifying the test dataset. We then proceed to discuss the obtained results.

4.1   Experiments

Data Augmentation: This is a crucial strategy employed to improve the diversity of the data available for training the networks. It improves the performance

Table 1. This table shows different ResNet architectures with stacked building blocks. The first column displays the name of the parent blocks and the second column shows the size of the output of the block. Columns 3–8 specify the size, depth, number of the filters and blocks.

Layer	Output size	ResNet18	ResNet34	ResNet50	ResNet101	ResNet152
conv1	112×112	7×7, 64, stride 2				
		3×3 max pool, stride 2				
conv2_x	56×56	$\begin{bmatrix}3\times3,\ 64\\3\times3,\ 64\end{bmatrix}\times2$	$\begin{bmatrix}3\times3,\ 64\\3\times3,\ 64\end{bmatrix}\times3$	$\begin{bmatrix}1\times1,\ 64\\3\times3,\ 64\\1\times1,\ 256\end{bmatrix}\times3$	$\begin{bmatrix}1\times1,\ 64\\3\times3,\ 64\\1\times1,\ 256\end{bmatrix}\times3$	$\begin{bmatrix}1\times1,\ 64\\3\times3,\ 64\\1\times1,\ 256\end{bmatrix}\times3$
conv3_x	28×28	$\begin{bmatrix}3\times3,\ 128\\3\times3,\ 128\end{bmatrix}\times2$	$\begin{bmatrix}3\times3,\ 128\\3\times3,\ 128\end{bmatrix}\times4$	$\begin{bmatrix}1\times1,\ 128\\3\times3,\ 128\\1\times1,\ 512\end{bmatrix}\times4$	$\begin{bmatrix}1\times1,\ 128\\3\times3,\ 128\\1\times1,\ 512\end{bmatrix}\times4$	$\begin{bmatrix}1\times1,\ 128\\3\times3,\ 128\\1\times1,\ 512\end{bmatrix}\times8$
conv4_x	14×14	$\begin{bmatrix}3\times3,\ 256\\3\times3,\ 256\end{bmatrix}\times2$	$\begin{bmatrix}3\times3,\ 256\\3\times3,\ 256\end{bmatrix}\times6$	$\begin{bmatrix}1\times1,\ 256\\3\times3,\ 256\\1\times1,\ 1024\end{bmatrix}\times6$	$\begin{bmatrix}1\times1,\ 256\\3\times3,\ 256\\1\times1,\ 1024\end{bmatrix}\times23$	$\begin{bmatrix}1\times1,\ 256\\3\times3,\ 256\\1\times1,\ 1024\end{bmatrix}\times36$
conv5_x	7×7	$\begin{bmatrix}3\times3,\ 512\\3\times3,\ 512\end{bmatrix}\times2$	$\begin{bmatrix}3\times3,\ 512\\3\times3,\ 512\end{bmatrix}\times3$	$\begin{bmatrix}1\times1,\ 512\\3\times3,\ 512\\1\times1,\ 1024\end{bmatrix}\times3$	$\begin{bmatrix}1\times1,\ 512\\3\times3,\ 512\\1\times1,\ 2048\end{bmatrix}\times3$	$\begin{bmatrix}1\times1,\ 512\\3\times3,\ 512\\1\times1,\ 2048\end{bmatrix}\times3$
	1×1	average-pool, fc, softmax				

of the networks by making them robust to variance in new data. During training, we used random vertical-horizontal flipping, and rotation. The smaller side of the image is then resized to 672 pixels followed by cropping the central 560 × 560 patch. A 448 × 448 region from this patch is then randomly cropped. This region is resized to 224 × 224 pixels to be used as an input to the networks.

Experimental setup: All the deep networks used in our work are pre-trained on ImageNet dataset. Fine-tuning of each network parameters was done on Indic-Leaf dataset. The dataset is split into train, validation, and test sets in the order of 60:20:20. The batch size is set to 100 and cross-entropy is used as the loss function. Stochastic gradient descent (SGD) with the momentum of 0.9 is used for optimization. All the networks have been trained for 100 epochs with an initial learning rate of 0.01. It is decayed by a factor of 0.5 when there is no reduction in validation loss for 3 consecutive epochs.

We evaluate ResNet-18, 34, 50, 101, 152, and VGG16 models on our dataset. Each one of these models is trained and tested on two configurations of the dataset and three colour spaces. Each species in Indic-Leaf dataset is categorized into levels as mentioned in Sect. 2. The images in one *level* look visibly different from images in another. We use this information to create two different data configurations for experimentation. In the first configuration (*cfg1*), all the images belonging to a species are considered into one training class (*label = specie*). In the second configuration (*cfg2*), each *level* of a species is considered a training class(*label = specie_level*). If there are s species and each has maximum of l levels, then *cfg1* will have s classes where as *cfg2* will have maximum of $s \times l$ classes in the softmax layer.

Table 2. This table presents P@K values obtained by all the models on the test sets for K = 1, 3, 5. The first column shows the name of the model and the second column shows the configuration. Each of the rest of the columns have three sub-columns showing P@K value for different colour spaces. Each row displays the P@K values for the model used for different colour spaces. Each of these rows have two sub-rows, one for each dataset configuration. The first sub-row displays the results from *cfg1* and the second, *cfg2*.

Model	Cfg	P@1			P@3			P@5		
		YCbCr	RGB	HSV	YCbCr	RGB	HSV	YCbCr	RGB	HSV
VGG-16	*cfg1*	88.49	89.30	88.99	94.43	94.82	94.93	96.34	96.54	96.29
	cfg2	85.47	85.21	86.08	93.07	93.39	93.48	95.08	95.24	95.28
Res-18	*cfg1*	86.97	85.90	86.50	93.64	92.85	93.57	95.24	94.67	95.38
	cfg2	82.63	82.95	82.46	91.62	91.70	91.26	93.83	93.66	93.63
Res-34	*cfg1*	86.99	86.92	87.24	93.48	93.20	93.70	94.93	94.99	95.37
	cfg2	83.98	84.35	84.11	92.31	92.53	92.71	94.79	94.90	94.93
Res-50	*cfg1*	89.85	88.84	89.43	95.35	94.40	95.15	96.62	95.90	96.80
	cfg2	86.05	86.50	86.50	93.43	93.45	94.10	95.22	95.46	95.95
Res-101	*cfg1*	89.45	**90.08**	89.94	95.11	95.35	**95.51**	96.71	**96.90**	96.74
	cfg2	86.75	87.39	86.92	94.30	94.28	94.28	96.25	95.96	96.49
Res-152	*cfg1*	89.25	89.65	89.11	94.79	94.79	95.00	96.24	96.49	96.49
	cfg2	87.21	87.20	86.72	94.41	94.40	94.17	96.22	96.00	95.80

4.2 Results

Table 2 shows the exhaustive set of experiments performed on Indic-leaf dataset. As seen in Table 2, Res101 *cfg1* in RBG colour space outperforms other models with P@1 of 90.08. Our baseline, VGG-16 achieves P@1 of 89.30 outperforming ResNet-18, 34, and 50 architectures. It can be observed that models using images in RBG colour space outperform models using images in other colour spaces.

Table 3. Table shows the P@1 values of different models when training set is constrained to specific *levels*. The header of each column specifies the *levels* used for training the specified model in each row.

Model	Levels							
	0, 3	1, 3	1, 2	2, 3	0, 1, 2	0, 1, 3	0, 2, 3	1, 2, 3
VGG-16	44.73	61.89	54.65	56.39	61.06	68.80	68.10	68.60
Res-18	45.25	60.36	54.20	57.31	60.21	67.12	66.64	66.99
Res-101	48.07	64.09	56.75	60.41	63.24	69.54	69.70	69.90

Table 2 shows that in each colour space, models trained in *cfg1* outperform the models trained in *cfg2*. This is expected due to models in *cfg2* having more than thrice the number of classes compared to *cfg1* in their softmax layer and low inter-class difference due to the split of each species into multiple levels. To test this hypothesis, the best performing model in *cfg2* is made to predict species(*label*

= *specie*) from the test data. We noticed an increase in P@1 value from 87.39 to 89.47. This significant improvement in P@1 supports our hypothesis.

To ascertain the significance of different *levels* in the dataset, a series of experiments were conducted by constraining the training set to contain only specific levels. The best performing model from Table 2 along with the baseline VGG-16 are used to analyse the impact of different levels on the test set from Table 2. ResNet-18 architecture is used to understand the impact of depth in obtained predictions. Obtained results are presented in Table 3.

4.3 Discussion

In both the experimental configurations, the best performing models use data in RGB colour space. We find ResNet-101 achieving P@1 of 90.08 to be the best tradeoff between model capacity and optimization difficulty. The increase in P@1 for *cfg2* model (*label = specie_level*) when made to predict species (*label=specie*) implies an accurate prediction of species when compared with the species prediction along with their level by the model. Moreover, the models in *cfg2* have low P@K values than their *cfg1* counterparts suggesting a complex nature of *cfg2* variant of dataset. From Table 3, it is evident that the higher the number of *levels* in the training process, better the performance of the model. But, from second column we can deduce that the higher inter-level variance also provides for better performance of the models (Fig. 4).

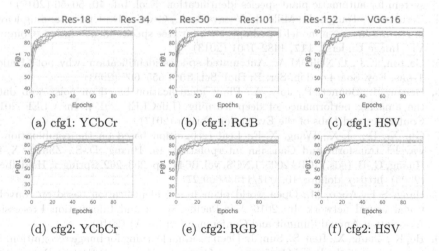

(a) cfg1: YCbCr	(b) cfg1: RGB	(c) cfg1: HSV
(d) cfg2: YCbCr	(e) cfg2: RGB	(f) cfg2: HSV

Fig. 4. This figure depicts P@1 of validation data plotted against epochs for different models in multiple colour spaces. Top row (a, b, c) shows P@1 from *cfg1* models and Bottom row (b, d, f) shows P@1 from *cfg2*. First column (a, c) shows P@1 for models trained on YCbCr colour space, second column (b, d) shows the same for RGB colour space and the third column (c, f) for HSV colour space.

5   Conclusion

We introduced and described a new dataset for recognizing Indian plant species in the natural environment. Images of the plant species are collected from various distances and emphasis was placed on categorizing them into different levels. We conducted quantitative analysis by using different convolutional neural network models on our dataset in different colour spaces. Our experiments into different dataset configurations show that the models perform better when all the images of a species are considered under a single class. We also observed that the complexity of the classification task increases when models are made to predict the *level* of the species (*label = specie_level*). The results obtained from experiments constraining the dataset to specific levels during training phase ascertain the importance of different levels of data for identifying "in the wild" test data. Apart from the name of the species, additional information like leaf shape, family of the species can be used in future work to improve the models.

References

1. Agarwal, G., et al.: First steps towardan electronic field guide for plants. Taxon **55**, 597–610 (2006)
2. Alom, M.Z., et al.: The history began from AlexNet: a comprehensive survey on deep learning approaches. arXiv preprint arXiv:1803.01164 (2018)
3. Barré, P., Stöver, B.C., Müller, K.F., Steinhage, V.: LeafNet: a computer vision system for automatic plant species identification. Ecol. Inf. **40**, 50–56 (2017)
4. Cerutti, G., Tougne, L., Mille, J., Vacavant, A., Coquin, D.: Understanding leaves in natural images-a model-based approach for tree species identification. Comput. Vis. Image Underst. **117**, 1482–1501 (2013)
5. Gaston, K.J., O'Neill, M.A.: Automated species identification: why not? Philos. Trans. Roy. Soc. London. Ser. B: Biol. Sci. **359**, 655–667 (2004)
6. Goeau, H., Bonnet, P., Joly, A.: Plant identification based on noisy web data: the amazing performance of deep learning (LifeCLEF 2017). In: CLEF 2017-Conference and Labs of the Evaluation Forum (2017)
7. Gu, X., Du, J.-X., Wang, X.-F.: Leaf recognition based on the combination of wavelet transform and Gaussian interpolation. In: Huang, D.-S., Zhang, X.-P., Huang, G.-B. (eds.) ICIC 2005. LNCS, vol. 3644, pp. 253–262. Springer, Heidelberg (2005). https://doi.org/10.1007/11538059_27
8. Hang, S.T., Aono, M.: Open world plant image identification based on convolutional neural network. In: 2016 Asia-Pacific Signal and Information Processing Association Annual Summit and Conference (APSIPA) (2016)
9. He, K., Zhang, X., Ren, S., Sun, J.: Deep residual learning for image recognition. In: Proceedings of the IEEE Conference on Computer Vision and Pattern Recognition (2016)
10. Husin, Z., et al.: Embedded portable device for herb leaves recognition using image processing techniques and neural network algorithm. Comput. Electron. Agric. **89**, 18–29 (2012)
11. Jamil, N., Hussin, N.A.C., Nordin, S., Awang, K.: Automatic plant identification: is shape the key feature? Proc. Comput. Sci. **6**, 436–442 (2015)
12. Joly, A., et al.: Interactive plant identification based on social image data (2014)

13. Kumar, N., et al.: Leafsnap: a computer vision system for automatic plant species identification. In: Fitzgibbon, A., Lazebnik, S., Perona, P., Sato, Y., Schmid, C. (eds.) ECCV 2012. LNCS, pp. 502–516. Springer, Heidelberg (2012). https://doi.org/10.1007/978-3-642-33709-3_36

14. Larese, M.G., Namías, R., Craviotto, R.M., Arango, M.R., Gallo, C., Granitto, P.M.: Automatic classification of legumes using leaf vein image features. Pattern Recogn. **47**, 158–168 (2014)

15. Lee, K.B., Hong, K.S.: An implementation of leaf recognition system using leaf vein and shape. Int. J. Bio-Sci. Bio-Technol. **5**, 57–66 (2013)

16. Pimm, S.L., et al.: The biodiversity of speciesand their rates of extinction, distribution, and protection. Science (2014)

17. Simonyan, K., Zisserman, A.: Very deep convolutional networks for large-scale image recognition. arXiv preprint arXiv:1409.1556 (2014)

18. Söderkvist, O.: Computer vision classification of leaves from Swedish trees. Master's thesis, Linköping University (2001)

19. Sun, Y., Liu, Y., Wang, G., Zhang, H.: Deep learning for plant identification in natural environment. Comput. Intell. Neurosci. (2017)

20. Wu, S.G., Bao, F.S., Xu, E.Y., Wang, Y.X., Chang, Y.F., Xiang, Q.L.: A leaf recognition algorithm for plant classification using probabilistic neural network. In: 2007 IEEE International Symposium on Signal Processing and Information Technology (2007)

Semantic Segmentation Datasets for Resource Constrained Training

Ashutosh Mishra[1]([✉]), Sudhir Kumar[1,2], Tarun Kalluri[1,3], Girish Varma[1],
Anbumani Subramaian[4], Manmohan Chandraker[3], and C. V. Jawahar[1]

[1] IIIT Hyderabad, Hyderabad, India
ashutosh.mishra@research.iiit.ac.in
[2] University at Buffalo, State University of New York, Buffalo, USA
[3] University of California, San Diego, USA
[4] Intel Bangalore, Bangalore, USA

Abstract. Several large scale datasets, coupled with advances in deep neural network architectures have been greatly successful in pushing the boundaries of performance in semantic segmentation in recent years. However, the scale and magnitude of such datasets prohibits ubiquitous use and widespread adoption of such models, especially in settings with serious hardware and software resource constraints. Through this work, we propose two simple variants of the recently proposed IDD dataset, namely *IDD-mini* and *IDD-lite*, for scene understanding in unstructured environments. Our main objective is to enable research and benchmarking in training segmentation models. We believe that this will enable quick prototyping useful in applications like optimum parameter and architecture search, and encourage deployment on low resource hardware such as Raspberry Pi. We show qualitatively and quantitatively that with only 1 h of training on 4 GB GPU memory, we can achieve satisfactory semantic segmentation performance on the proposed datasets.

Keywords: Semantic segmentation · Neural architecture search

1 Introduction and Related Work

Semantic segmentation is the task of assigning pixel level semantic labels to images, with potential applications in fields such as autonomous driving [5,16] and scene understanding. Many approaches have been proposed to tackle this task based on modern deep neural networks [4,12,14,18]. Majority of the proposed approaches use encoder-decoder networks that aggregate spatial information across various resolutions for pixel level labeling of images. For example, [12] proposes an end-to-end trainable network for semantic segmentation by replacing the fully connected layers of pretrained AlexNet [8] with fully convolutional layers. Segmentation architectures based on dilated convolutions [17] for real time performance have also been proposed in [14,18]. However most of these approaches come with huge overhead in training time and inference time since

---

A. Mishra, S. Kumar and T. Kalluri—Equal contribution.

© Springer Nature Singapore Pte Ltd. 2020
R. V. Babu et al. (Eds.): NCVPRIPG 2019, CCIS 1249, pp. 450–459, 2020.
https://doi.org/10.1007/978-981-15-8697-2_42

it requires multi-GPU training with very high GPU memory requirements. This poses multiple challenges for widespread use of semantic segmentation datasets and architectures, resulting in huge roadblocks for research and development of such real time systems, especially in developing regions of the world with resource constraints. We believe that there are multiple challenges posed by these current approaches. Firstly, compared to image classification tasks on datasets like MNIST [9] or CIFAR [8], semantic segmentation is limited in its scope for ubiquitous adoption which essentially rules out the introduction of any such project as part of a curriculum. Although large scale datasets for training the semantic segmentation models such as KITTI [6], CamVid [1] or recently introduced Cityscapes [5] and India Driving Dataset [16](IDD) which provide finely annotated images to train semantic segmentation models with a focus on autonomous navigation exist, the scale and the size of these datasets limit their widespread use, particularly in scenarios where computation resources are limited.

Fig. 1. Sample images with ground truth from IDD-lite, IDD-mini with second and third column representing 7 and 16 labels *(Best viewed when zoomed).*

Secondly, navigating through the hyperparameter space for coming up with the most optimum configuration and architecture for semantic segmentation is a demanding task due to huge training costs involved with deep neural networks. In the context of classification, previous works [11] perform architectural search on CIFAR dataset to show that the best performance also applies on larger scale datasets like ImageNet. Several works also use reinforcement learning [2,20], evolutionary algorithm [11] etc. for this purpose. However, there have been fewer works [3,10] to conduct architectural search on dense segmentation task due to resource intensiveness of the task. Hence smaller datasets that enables quick prototyping for hyper parameter search, and help in replicating the results on larger datasets is essential. This would bring down the cost of training, and would aid in improving the overall performance.

Finally, there is a need to drive the research in vision community towards achieving state of the art results for various tasks using only limited labeled data. Such a research direction would have huge impact, more so on semantic segmentation tasks that requires huge annotation of pixel level semantic labels.

Table 1. Comparison of state of the art datasets against proposed IDD-mini and IDD-lite.

Dataset	Average resolution	#Annotated pixels[10^6]	#Train images	#Val images	Disk space (in GB)	Label size
IDD [16]	968 × 1678	11811	6993	981	18	26
Cityscapes [5]	1024 × 2048	9430	2975	500	12	20
IDD-mini	512 × 720	535	1794	253	4	16
IDD-lite	227 × 320	39.75	673	110	<1.5	7

To address these challenges, we come up with two variants of the recently proposed India Driving Dataset (IDD) [16], namely *IDD-mini* and *IDD-lite*, as shown in Fig. 1, which are aimed at improving the state of semantic segmentation for autonomous driving in developing regions. We believe that having these datasets would help alleviate the challenges discussed above in resource constrained settings. Resource constraint can mean lack of availability of high end GPUs, limited time access to GPU resources or lack of infrastructure to store large scale datasets. The scenes and labels presented in our dataset are very different from those available in semantic segmentation datasets such as Cityscapes [5], KITTI [6] or CamVid [1]. Moreover, by developing such standardized small scale datasets, we wish to coalesce the efforts of the research community towards developing algorithms that need only few labels to match state of the art performance.

In summary, our contributions can be stated as follows.

- We provide IDD-mini and IDD-lite, which are subsampled version of IDD with very similar label statistics and smaller number of labels (See Sect. 2).
- We show that models trained only for an hour on a single 4 GB GPU still achieve reasonable prediction accuracies, making it possible to include them as part of short courses, workshops and labs in universities and other training centers (See Sect. 4).
- We establish that the accuracy of various models trained on our datasets correlates well with the accuracy on large scale datasets especially in cross-domain setting. This allows for fast prototyping and architectural search for semantic segmentation algorithms (See Sect. 4).
- We deploy models trained using our datasets on Raspberry Pi and report the accuracy and runtime, giving a standardized measurement of the performance characteristics on the device (See Sect. 4).

2   Dataset

We designed the two variants of the datasets with an aim to reduce the overall hardware footprint for storing and processing, keeping intact the diversity and variety from the original IDD dataset. In this section, we present the procedure used to come up with the train-val splits for IDD-mini and IDD-lite. We also provide statistical properties of the proposed datasets, and compare it with the original IDD dataset, along with another state of the art driving dataset, Cityscapes [5].

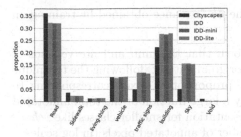

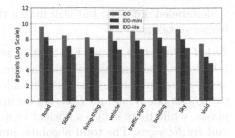

Fig. 2. Proportion of labels in total dataset for IDD, IDD-mini and IDD-lite *(Best viewed when zoomed).*

Fig. 3. Absolute value of annotated pixels (in powers of 10) for categories in IDD, IDD-mini and IDD-lite *(Best viewed when zoomed).*

Dataset Specifications

IDD-mini. The motivation behind designing IDD-mini is to have a small scale segmentation dataset that is useful for training image segmentation models on low resource hardware. The full IDD dataset[1] consists of 7974 high-resolution images in the train-val set with 26 labels at the L3 label hierarchy, taken from 182 different drive sequences. To create IDD-mini out of this dataset, we resize the images such that the largest dimension is downsampled to 720 while preserving the aspect ratio, and use the 16 labels from the L2 hierarchy of the original dataset. We subsample the number of images from the dataset by a factor of 4, uniformly across the drive sequences in such a way that the resultant split gives us the same proportion of labels as the full version of the dataset. The train set contains 1794 training images and 253 validation images.

IDD-lite. The major aim of having IDD-lite, in addition to IDD-mini, is to enable very quick prototyping of semantic segmentation models which, we believe, is very essential for demonstration or teaching purposes in settings with resource limitations. Following a similar technique as explained above, we subsample the dataset by a factor of 10, which gives us 673 training and 110 test images. We rescale the largest dimension to 320 while preserving the aspect ratio of the image while using the L1 hierarchy with 7 coarse labels. This also reduces the required disk space to store the dataset from 18 GB for IDD to <1.5 GB for IDD-lite, which helps in optimizing the storage footprint.

While we provide training and validation splits along with the IDD-mini and IDD-lite datasets, we do not propose a separate test set different from the IDD test set which consist of 2029 images at the original resolution. We believe that this provides the models trained on different datasets with a common platform for bench marking. We hope that this will encourage the research community to come up with innovative architectures or algorithms for structure learning or semi supervised learning to train models on such standard smaller

[1] https://idd.insaan.iiit.ac.in/.

scale labeled datasets, but still match the performance obtained by training on bigger datasets.

Label Statistics. From Fig. 2, it is shown that the mini and lite versions of IDD follow the same distribution as the original dataset, following the technique we used to subsample the dataset. The proportion of pixels corresponding to categories like *Road* and *Building* occupy a large fraction of the total annotated pixels, while there is also sufficient representation for smaller classes like *vehicle* and *traffic signs*. The total absolute number of annotated pixels (in log scale) is given in Fig. 3, to show that the number of pixels in IDD-mini, IDD-lite are an order less than that of the original dataset.

Comparison with Other Datasets. Comparison to another large scale and widely used dataset, Citycapes [5], is also presented in Fig. 2. Cityscapes consists of 2975 training images and 500 validation images at a uniform resolution of 1024×2048, with images taken from various cities and weather conditions. However, one major advantage that our datasets offer compared to cityscapes is that IDD-mini and IDD-lite contain scenes from more unstructured environments, with images captured from complex traffic and driving situations. Furthermore, the comparison from Fig. 2 shows that on most categories, the smaller datasets match Cityscapes on the proportion of the pixels.

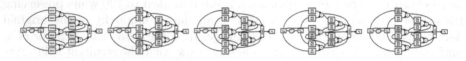

Fig. 4. To the left is Conv-module skeleton. From there to the right are the ERFNet modified models with Conv-module Cell structures named as A*, B*, C*, D* *(Best visualized when zoomed).*

3 Architecture Search

In this section, we demonstrate how IDD-lite and IDD-mini datasets can be useful for architecture search with limited resources. Neural Architecture Search [13] (NAS) on tasks like dense semantic segmentation need thousands of iterations GPU-days for convergence. Architecture search can be computationally very intensive as each evaluation typically requires training a neural network. Therefore, it is common to restrict the search space to reduce complexity and increase efficiency of architecture search. More recent papers on architecture search have shifted to searching the repeatable cell structure, while keeping the outer network level structure fixed by hand. This strategy needs less number of GPU hours and can conduct large experiments in constrained time. This would be a major advantage in resource constrained environments. Currently, this strategy is limited to tasks like image classification where small scale datasets are available but not for semantic segmentation due to lack of such small scale datasets.

We propose that IDD-mini, IDD-lite can be used to do architecture search in resource efficient way for semantic segmentation task.

We consider a scenario where we need to come up with best architecture with limited resource budget. We even explicitly consider a scenario where we can only afford fixed set of parameters for the architecture. Now, we need to find the best performing architecture among them. We conduct two experiments and show that architecture search results conducted on IDD-lite with custom ERFNet model actually translates to different domain like Cityscapes. Thus, we are also exploring generalizability of architectural search through such experiments.

Identifying Optimal Cell Structure. Our aim is to find best architecture in custom designed architectural space using IDD-lite. Also, we show that the results correlate to Cityscapes dataset. We use ERFNet [14] outer network level structure as the basis for our model. Within this structure we replace non-bottleneck layer proposed in original ERFNet with custom structure with architecture skeleton (Conv-module) as shown in Fig. 4.

Table 2. Modified version (left) and Compressed version (right) of ERFNet architecture that is used to run experiments on Cityscapes dataset and IDD-lite respectively.

Layer	Type	Layer	Type
1	Downsampler block	1	Downsampler block
2	Downsampler block	2	Downsampler block
3-5	3 x Conv-module	3	1 x Conv-module
5-7	2 x Conv-module	4	1 x Conv-module
8	Downsampler block	5	Downsampler block
9-16	8 x Conv-module(dilated)	6	Conv-module(dilated 2)
17	Deconvolution(upsampling)	7	Deconvolution(upsampling)
18-19	2 x Conv-module	8	1 x Conv-module
20	Deconvolution(upsamling)	9	Deconvolution(upsamling)
21-22	2 x Conv-module	10	1 x Conv-module
23	Deconvolution(upsampling)	11	Deconvolution(upsampling)

Each of the block in this Conv-module (skeleton) is filled from a set of 1 atrous 3×3 layer, 3 separable 5×5 layers, 2 atrous 5×5 layers, 4 seperable 3×3 layers, to ensure that we have same number of parameters overall. This forms the search space for architecture search. We use architectures given in Table 2 to conduct experiments on Cityscapes dataset and IDD-lite respectively.

4   Experiments and Results

Semantic Segmentation Performance Benchmarking. In this section, we benchmark the results of the proposed datasets on two state of the art architectures used for semantic segmentation, DRNet [18] and ERFNet [14]. More details regarding these networks are present in [16], which we do not present here again in the interest of space. For DRNet, we use a ResNet-18 backbone(*drn-d-22*).

Table 3. (a) Performance (in mIoU) of the proposed datasets on semantic segmentation architectures ERFNet and DRN-d-22. Note that *val. res.* corresponds to the validation resolution for each dataset, which is obtained by cropping and resizing the original images from Table 1, #L is the number of trainable classes in that dataset. (b) Depthwise Separable Convolution, Groups on ERFNet Architecture tested over IDD-lite dataset using Compressed ERFNet from Table 2.

Dataset	#L	Val. Res.	mIoU ERFNet [14]	mIoU DRN [18]
CS [14]	20	512×1024	71.50	68.00
IDD [16]	26	512×1024	55.40	52.24
IDD-mini	16	480×640	57.91	53.31
IDD-lite	7	128×256	66.14	55.03

(a)

Models	IoU (CS)	Params	IoU (IDD-lite)
ERFNet	70.45	2038448	53.975
D*	68.55	547120	52.01
DG2*	65.35	395568	50.71
DG4*	61.42	319792	48.88
DG8*	59.15	281904	46.40

(b)

Table 4. (a) Custom Cell architecture on compressed ERFNet tested over IDD-lite dataset correlate with the same tests on Cityscapes Dataset with modified ERFNet from Table 2. (b) Inference time (in sec.) of different semantic segmentation models on various versions of IDD on Raspberry Pi 3B.

Models	IoU(CS)	IoU(IDD-lite)
A*	64.54	58.15
B*	59.21	56.93
C*	55.96	55.46
D*	52.35	53.64

(a)

	IDD-lite	IDD-mini	IDD
ERFNet	1.12	5.99	10.60
DRNet-18	56.61	78.47	95.94

(b)

We take mIoU (mean intersection over union) as the performance metric for all our experiments.

The models ERFNet and DRNet-18 were trained using the resolution depicted in Table 1 and validated using the resolution shown in Table 3(a). The models achieve an mIoU of 57.91% and 53.31% on IDD-mini using ERFNet and DRNet-18 respectively. Similarly, IDD-lite gives mIoU values of 66.14% on ERFNet and 55.03% on DRNet respectively.

From Fig. 5, it is can be seen that IDD-lite dataset gives reasonably good mIoU results with just 15–20 min of training within 4 GB GPU memory *(Best visualized when zoomed)*. We also note that while models trained on such datasets cannot directly be employed in state of the art semantic segmentation applications, they will nevertheless be very useful in for teaching or workshop purposes in cases with limited technical support and overall resource availability.

Results on Architecture Search. Here, we present results on experiment to identify optimal cell structure and experimental correlation of IDD-lite and Cityscapes as mentioned in Sect. 3.

Implementation Details. The best cell structure identified using architecture search gave 64.54% IoU (Model A) on Cityscapes dataset. We also take 3 models (B, C, D) from the pool of possible Conv-modules and verify if the performance on smaller dataset match with that on Cityscapes. The results are presented in

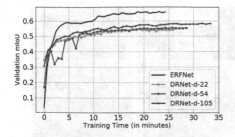
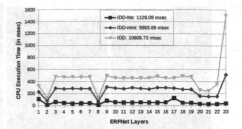

Fig. 5. Training time (x-axis) vs. Validation mIoU (y-axis) plot for IDD-lite. Note that with only 15 min of training on 1 GPU using only 4 GB, the model obtains >50% mIoU

Fig. 6. Runtime statistics per layer for ERFNet model on all three datasets (IDD, IDD-mini and IDD-lite). Total run time for each dataset is mentioned in the legend *(Best viewed when zoomed).*

Table 4(a). It is to be noted that though the architecture search was conducted on IDD-lite, we are able to get best performing architecture for a different domain like Cityscapes.

Correlation to Efficient Segmentation Models. There have been lots of interest in efficient CNN module designs that have lower compute needs, while still achieving good prediction accuracies [7,19]. [15] reports results with architecture variations of ERFNet named as D*, D2*, D4*, D8* on Cityscapes. These correspond to the usage of depthwise separable convolutions instead of the bottleneck modules of ERFNet along with grouping parameter on the 1×1 convolution. We conduct the same experiments on IDD-lite dataset with compressed ERFNet architecture (Table 2) and show that our results correlate with [15]. The results are presented in Table 3(b).

Models for Raspberry Pi. In order to make deep learning models scalable for real time application in resource constrained environments, factors such as real time performance, feasible cost of the hardware and low power consumption are essential. Hence, we provide the benchmarking values of segmentation on Raspberry Pi. This device is widely available as a single board compute platform which comes at an affordable cost, apart from being customizable and energy efficient.

More specifically, we chose Raspberry Pi 3B as the deployment hardware device for our semantic segmentation models. The device contains 1 GB RAM, and has a 1.2 GHz Quad-Core 4XARM Cortex-A53 CPU. We tested ERFNet and DRNet-18 networks on Raspberry Pi to calculate the inference time on the validation datasets at various resolutions. Table 4(b) shows the inference time of different semantic segmentation models at various resolutions on our validation datasets (Fig. 7).

Fig. 7. Qualitative examples of ERFNet model run on IDD-mini, IDD-lite dataset. From top to bottom - image, prediction and ground truth. First two columns correspond to results from IDD-mini and last two columns are for IDD-lite *(Best viewed when zoomed)*.

Figure 6 shows the run time information of each layer defined in the ERFNet architecture. Although the IDD and the IDD-lite datasets have equal trends, IDD-lite time is significantly lesser, in addition to being uniformly consistent across layers. This further reinforces our proposition that such a dataset can add more value to quick prototyping and help move towards real time deployment of segmentation models.

5   Conclusion

We propose two small scale datasets, IDD-mini and IDD-lite, to address some of the relevant issues in training semantic segmentation models on resource constrained environments. We show that these carefully designed datasets give decent qualitative and quantitative results enabling fast prototyping on low resource hardware and hugely reducing the training and deployment costs. We also demonstrate the usefulness of such small scale datasets in performing architecture search by showing that the parameters obtained using smaller network on these datasets actually translate to larger network with high resolution images.

References

1. Brostow, G.J., Fauqueur, J., Cipolla, R.: Semantic object classes in video: a high-definition ground truth database. Pattern Recogn. Lett. **30**(2), 88–97 (2009)
2. Cai, H., Chen, T., Zhang, W., Yu, Y., Wang, J.: Efficient architecture search by network transformation. In: Thirty-Second AAAI Conference on Artificial Intelligence (2018)
3. Chen, L.C., et al.: Searching for efficient multi-scale architectures for dense image prediction. In: Advances in Neural Information Processing Systems, pp. 8713–8724 (2018)

4. Chen, L.C., Papandreou, G., Kokkinos, I., Murphy, K., Yuille, A.L.: Deeplab: semantic image segmentation with deep convolutional nets, atrous convolution, and fully connected CRFs. IEEE Trans. Pattern Anal. Mach. Intell. **40**(4), 834–848 (2018)

5. Cordts, M., et al.: The cityscapes dataset for semantic urban scene understanding. In: Proceedings of the IEEE Conference on Computer Vision and Pattern Recognition, pp. 3213–3223 (2016)

6. Geiger, A., Lenz, P., Urtasun, R.: Are we ready for autonomous driving? the kitti vision benchmark suite. In: 2012 IEEE Conference on Computer Vision and Pattern Recognition, pp. 3354–3361. IEEE (2012)

7. Howard, A.G., et al.: Mobilenets: efficient convolutional neural networks for mobile vision applications. arXiv preprint arXiv:1704.04861 (2017)

8. Krizhevsky, A., Sutskever, I., Hinton, G.E.: Imagenet classification with deep convolutional neural networks. In: Advances in Neural Information Processing Systems, pp. 1097–1105 (2012)

9. LeCun, Y.: The MNIST database of handwritten digits (1998). http://yann.lecun.com/exdb/mnist/

10. Liu, C., et al.: Auto-deeplab: hierarchical neural architecture search for semantic image segmentation. arXiv preprint arXiv:1901.02985 (2019)

11. Liu, H., Simonyan, K., Vinyals, O., Fernando, C., Kavukcuoglu, K.: Hierarchical representations for efficient architecture search. arXiv preprint arXiv:1711.00436 (2017)

12. Long, J., Shelhamer, E., Darrell, T.: Fully convolutional networks for semantic segmentation. In: Proceedings of the IEEE Conference on Computer Vision and Pattern Recognition, pp. 3431–3440 (2015)

13. Pham, H., Guan, M.Y., Zoph, B., Le, Q.V., Dean, J.: Efficient neural architecture search via parameter sharing. arXiv preprint arXiv:1802.03268 (2018)

14. Romera, E., Alvarez, J.M., Bergasa, L.M., Arroyo, R.: ERFNet: efficient residual factorized convnet for real-time semantic segmentation. IEEE Trans. Intell. Transp. Syst. **19**(1), 263–272 (2018)

15. Vallurupalli, N., Annamaneni, S., Varma, G., Jawahar, C., Mathew, M., Nagori, S.: Efficient semantic segmentation using gradual grouping. In: Proceedings of the IEEE Conference on Computer Vision and Pattern Recognition Workshops, pp. 598–606 (2018)

16. Varma, G., Subramanian, A., Namboodiri, A., Chandraker, M., Jawahar, C.: IDD: a dataset for exploring problems of autonomous navigation in unconstrained environments. In: 2019 IEEE Winter Conference on Applications of Computer Vision (WACV). IEEE (2019)

17. Yu, F., Koltun, V.: Multi-scale context aggregation by dilated convolutions. arXiv preprint arXiv:1511.07122 (2015)

18. Yu, F., Koltun, V., Funkhouser, T.: Dilated residual networks. In: Proceedings of the IEEE Conference on Computer Vision and Pattern Recognition, pp. 472–480 (2017)

19. Zhang, X., Zhou, X., Lin, M., Sun, J.: Shufflenet: an extremely efficient convolutional neural network for mobile devices. In: Proceedings of the IEEE Conference on Computer Vision and Pattern Recognition, pp. 6848–6856 (2018)

20. Zhong, Z., Yan, J., Wu, W., Shao, J., Liu, C.L.: Practical block-wise neural network architecture generation. In: Proceedings of the IEEE Conference on Computer Vision and Pattern Recognition (2018)

Dear Commissioner, Please Fix These: A Scalable System for Inspecting Road Infrastructure

Raghava Modhugu[✉], Ranjith Reddy, and C. V. Jawahar

CVIT, IIIT-H, Hyderabad, India
durga.nagendra@students.iiit.ac.in, ranjithreddy1061995@gmail.com,
jawahar@iiit.ac.in

Abstract. Inspecting and assessing the quality of traffic infrastructure (such as the state of the signboards or road markings) is challenging for humans due to (i) the massive length of roads that countries will have and (ii) the regular frequency at which this needs to be done. In this paper, we demonstrate a scalable system that uses computer vision for automatic inspection of road infrastructure from a simple video captured from a moving vehicle. We validated our method on 1500 KMs of roads captured in and around the city of Hyderabad, India. Qualitative and quantitative results demonstrate the feasibility, scalability and effectiveness of our solution.

Keywords: Road infrastructure · Scalable audit · Indian roads

1 Introduction and Related Work

Ever increasing traffic activity makes the regular audit and maintenance of road infrastructure extremely critical for safety. However, the scale at which this has to be performed in India is massive with thousands of kilometres of highways and rural roads in every state. In general road infrastructure maintenance and diligence are determined by financial constraints, and associated social factors. Road infrastructure inspection is a relentless process. The existing methods primarily use manual verification, which is tedious, cost ineffective and not scalable. Gaining insights through analytics is also difficult because of the lack of a unified system that stores all the necessary information of road infrastructure. In order to overcome these limitations and establish a robust road infrastructure management plan, we believe that inspection system needs to be highly automated, cost effective and scalable. In this paper, we propose a system that uses computer vision to automatically detect the road infrastructure and geotag[1] them

---

[1] Geotagging is the process of adding geographical information to various media in the form of metadata.

R. Modhugu and R. Reddy—Equal contribution.

with relevant attributes that state the condition of the infrastructure. We also measure the information about the visibility range of infrastructure, which plays an important role in case of traffic signs (Fig. 1).

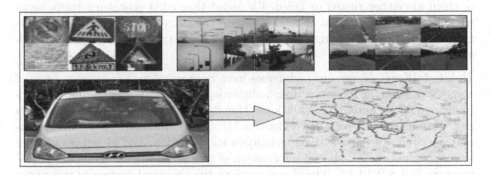

Fig. 1. In the proposed system, we aim to detect and classify the quality of the traffic signs, street lights and road lane markings to create database with geo-spatial information.

There is an increased interest in the field of computer vision for autonomous navigation in the recent years [6]. Computer vision based autonomous navigation systems try to exploit the visual instructions such as traffic signs and lane markings primarily meant for human navigational clarity. The advances in the areas of semantic segmentation and object detection paved way to numerous real world applications. In this paper, we propose a system that uses these aspects of computer vision to automatically detect the road infrastructure and geotag them with relevant attributes and their visibility. The proposed system helps in dealing with the challenges mentioned earlier. Our contributions in this paper are as follows:

1. We propose a scalable road infrastructure inspection system for detection based on state of art object detection approaches.
2. We propose a framework to geotag the detected infrastructure for precise location to save maintenance time.
3. We propose a framework to identify the condition of the road infrastructure and their visibility.
4. We release a dataset of road scenes for quality assessment of the infrastructure

A wide variety of road infrastructure requires maintenance, however in this work we choose to inspect traffic signs, street lights and lane markings. This choice is primarily based on the point that these infrastructure is present widely across the road. Therefore, these are a good choice for testing the scalability of the system. Secondly, we want to include not only just the object type infrastructure like traffic signs but also the infrastructure that is continuous and spread across regions, so that we can leave a very strong precedent on the road infrastructure inspection.

On testing our proposed system over 1500 KMs of road in Hyderabad to geotag the existing infrastructure with relevant attributes which will help in identifying in the state of traffic signs, roads without street lights and proper lane marking. Out of the total 8323 traffic signs geotagged, 3308 (nearly 40%) of them are either rusted or faded. We found that 8323 geotagged traffic signs with attribute information and also contains information about street light distribution and lane marking quality on over 30000 stretches of road, with each stretch being 50 m long.

Related Work. Numerous techniques have been developed in various parts of the world for road infrastructure audit independently. These techniques vary from manual to automated solutions. Manual techniques include field surveys and examination of recorded videos [5,11]. The automated solutions in general use computer vision based techniques for detection, and global positioning systems to obtain geo-spatial information of the automatically detected infrastructure [2,3,8,9,12,13]. The closest work to the proposed system in this paper is by Sudhir *et al.* [13] that focuses on auditing condition of roads, Whereas our audit system inspects a variety of infrastructure. Jones *et al.* [5] proposed a manual method where the personnel produces a detailed field survey and collect the GPS location of the infrastructure. A semi automated approach with the details of mobile mapping system (MMS) which requires data collection with a vehicle equipped with a global positioning system, distance measuring instrument and inertial navigational system is discussed by Khattak *et al.* [3]. It was experimentally concluded that the manually collected information is much more accurate than what was proposed by Khattak *et al.* [3]. A mobile data collection system presented by Maerz *et al.*[11] involves a post processing workstation to go through the recorded video to detect and classify the objects of interest. Jeyapalan *et al.* [8] used a method to determine the three-dimensional location of roadside features that appear in multiple images. This method maps the infrastructure without any classification or distinction between the features. A similar method as ours to recognise traffic signs and track them to avoid counting multiple times and map them using the GPS signal is proposed in Wang *et al.* [9]. In our system, we also track detected signs to avoid redundant counts. However, our system uses YOLOv3 as opposed to traditional image processing methods for detection, and tracking is used to determine the GPS position of the traffic sign. Unlike Wang *et al.* [9], our system is not just limited to traffic signs in road infrastructure. The traffic signs are detected and identified for inspection in Gonzalez *et al.* [2], but unlike our method it does not deal with the condition of the traffic signs. A compound architecture is proposed by Segvic *et al.* [12] for integrating independently developed vision components with the use of GPS to locate the traffic infrastructure. However, this system is restricted to object detection whereas our system inspects lane markings on the road also.

2 Framework and Model

In this section, we discuss the architecture of the proposed system. The key aspects of the system is detecting, geotagging and inspection (quality identification). An overview of the system pipeline can be seen in Fig. 2.

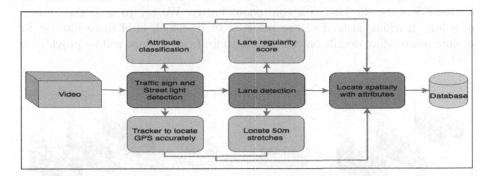

Fig. 2. The above figure illustrates the architecture of the proposed system for road infrastructure inspection. The traffic signs are detected using the YOLOv3. Once detected, these signs/lights are tracked to find the geographical location. In the next stage of the pipeline, SCNN is used to detect the lane markings. Using the detected lane markings by the SCNN, we generate a regularity score for every 50 m stretch. Then using the obtained information of attributes and location we map the infrastructure to create a database.

Detection. In this paper, the proposed system for road infrastructure inspections uses YOLOv3 [7] for detecting the traffic signs and street lights. Several object detection models can be trained to detect traffic signs and street lights, but YOLOv3 has many advantages such as object detection with global context, faster processing speed at test time. YOLOv3 can detect the objects at test time with 30 FPS on a Pascal Titan X and its single network evaluation makes it 1000× faster than R-CNN and 100× faster than fast R-CNN [7]. As the proposed system has to detect the traffic signs and street lights at real time speeds, YOLOv3 is a very natural choice for the proposed system.

As discussed in the introduction, we want to detect not only the traffic signs and street lights but also lane markings on the road. The proposed system detects lane markings using SCNN [15]. Unlike object detection, lane marking detection needs to tackle objects with strong structural prior but with less appearance clues. Lanes are continuous and might have been occluded by the vehicles in the traffic. It also requires precise prediction of the road curvature. In general, this can be done using probability maps on the image for lane markings [15]. SCNN [15] creates the probability maps for lane markings to identify them.

Geo Tagging. Geo-spatial information of the road infrastructure plays a very important role in decreasing the maintenance time by helping in easy identification. There are some methods proposed in the literature on locating the infrastructure with using GPS signal. The idea of mapping the infrastructure on a location where its bounding box area is maximum is proposed [14]. The other works that attempted to map the location of the infrastructure using photogrammetry are proposed in [1,4]. In our work, we track the detected traffic signs or street light and map them to the location of the last frame it was detected while driving along the road. In case of lane marking detection, this method may not be feasible since the lane is a continuous entity. We try to map the absence of a lane marking instead of the presence of it, which is of more interest for maintenance. More details on the criteria to find the absence will be provided in Sect. 3.

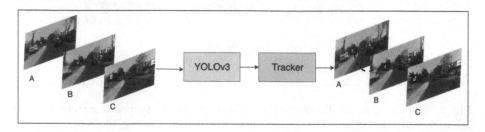

Fig. 3. The image illustrates the detection of infrastructure and tracking of it. We use tracker to identify the approximate GPS location and to find the visibility range of the traffic signs. Visibility range is calculated as the sum of distance between all the consecutive frames where the same traffic sign is detected using the GPS coordinates.

Inspection. The key aspects of road infrastructure inspection involves assessing quality of the infrastructure. As the characteristics of quality are subjective to the type of infrastructure involved in assessment, different measures for quality assessment are required.

The traffic signs that are detected by the YOLOv3 are classified using a trained convolution neural network classifier with VGG16 architecture to find whether the detected sign is rusted, faded or normal. The attribute information extracted from the traffic sign is stored along with the geo-spatial information. As shown in Fig. 3, We also find the visibility range of each traffic sign as distance along the path traced by the vehicle from its first to final detection by tracking it. In case of street lights, we detect the streetlights using YOLOv3 to tag them geographically and identify all the stretches that donot have any street lights along the road. The lane markings are generally expected to be present continuously all along the road. The stretches of interest in this case are the ones without lane markings. We defined a metric that can take into account the percentage of pixels that have been identified as lane marking along a stretch of 50 m of road to classify it accordingly (Fig. 4).

Experimental Setup. We have captured the data of 1500 km of real time data in and around the city of Hyderabad. Hyderabad region is deemed to be an

Fig. 4. Left: In anti clockwise direction: Intel's NUC, ZED camera, GPS unit and setup of all the components Right: Samples of images/frames from the collected data.

appropriate region to collect the data to build and test the system because of various reasons such as high traffic activity, unstructured environment. The data is captured using a ZED camera which is mounted on a car. This captures 15 frames per second at a resolution of 1920 × 1080 pixels along with the GPS coordinates. The GPS is captured at baud rate of 4800 to synchronise it with the video using the time of capture. The data is captured in various areas to include culture wise, maintenance wise, lighting wise and traffic conditions wise variety to suit the needs of the proposed inspection system.

3 Experiments and Results

Traffic Signs. We have used YOLOv3 for detection of traffic signs. A total of 2K frames are annotated manually which are used for training and validating the object detection model with a train-validation split of 80:20. The hyper parameters of the model are setup as suggested YOLOv3 [7] for custom object detection and trained for 6000 iterations and got an mAP of 0.58. We were able to achieve high recall of 0.91 on the unseen routes which is of key interest to the proposed system. The qualitative results in a wide variety of lighting and traffic conditions are illustrated in the Fig. 5.

Fig. 5. Qualitative results of traffic sign detection: The traffic signs are detected as objects using a trained YOLOv3. A variety of driving scenes where traffic signs are detected with variations in lighting and traffic conditions.

The proposed system characterizes the detected signs to be rusted, faded or normal to aide the inspection. For this purpose we used VGG16 network. The pretrained VGG16 network is fine-tuned with a learning rate of 0.0001, L2 regularisation with decay of $1e-6$ using Adam on cross entropy loss. The data required to train the classifier to characterise the traffic signs as rusted and faded are low in number. The collection of such data is very difficult and tedious. Therefore, we collected a few samples of rusted and faded traffic signs and used them for style transfer [10] on the traffic signs obtained from detected traffic signs using the trained YOLOv3 and also performed data augmentation techniques like data jittering, image transformation etc. to obtain around 7000 samples of rusted and faded traffic signs each. The accuracy obtained by the classifier is 91% on the validation data.

Fig. 6. Qualitative results of street lights detection: street lights along the road are detected using YOLOv3. The above figure shows a few scenes with street light detection.

Street Lights. Street lights are also detected using YOLOv3. Street lights are manually annotated from the frames of the collected data to train the model with a train-validation split of 80:20. YOLOv3 [7] is trained for 4000 iterations to detect the street lights and obtained an mAP of 0.53. The qualitative results of detection are illustrated in Fig. 6. The street lights are mapped with GPS obtained and located on a map. This gives the information to gather the stretches where street lights are not installed.

Road Lane Marking. As discussed earlier, the method used to detect lane markings is very different from object detection methods in traffic signs and street lights images. The lane markings on the road are assumed to be a continuous entity. We choose pretrained SCNN proposed in [15] for lane marking detection in the system presented in this paper, majorly because of the reason that the network is trained with the data in an unstructured and heavy traffic environment which suits the proposed system. SCNN can also extrapolate the lane markings occluded by the vehicular traffic on the road based on structural priors obtained from the unoccluded parts as shown in the Fig. 7.

We are more interested in the stretches where the lane markings are absent. In order to find that out, we define a metric that uses the regularity of the lane markings for every 50 m of distance as per the GPS data collected. Along with

Fig. 7. Qualitative results of road lane marking detection: The proposed system uses SCNN [15] to detect the lane marking along the road. The above figure illustrates lane marking detection in different conditions of traffic.

the distance, the system considers the time taken to cover that distance as well. There could be scenarios where video recording vehicle might have been stuck in traffic during the inspection, which we should be in a position to handle. Therefore we consider the metric as summation of percentage of pixels present across all the frames to cover 50 m. Lane regularity score (r) = $\dfrac{\sum_{i \in f} \dfrac{l_i}{n_i}}{d \cdot |f|}$.

l_i is number of pixels identified as lane marking in i^{th} frame, n_i is number of pixels in the ith frame, d is length of the stretch, f is set of frames recorded to cover the stretch of distance

The number of pixel that belongs to lane marking are far less than total number of the pixels in an image. Therefore by definition lane regularity is a very small value generally ranging in the order of magnitude of 10^{-3} to 10^{-6} depending on the scene. So we normalised the lane regularity scores to bring all the values in the range of [0, 1]. Normalized lane regularity score = $\dfrac{r - r_{min}}{r_{max} - r_{min}}$. The r_{max} and r_{min} are maximum and minimum regularity scores determined experimentally.

Quantitative Analysis. After testing the system on 1500 KMs of data, we made the observations that are illustrated in the Table 1. The median of average distance between two consecutive street lights in each route that was tested by the proposed system in Hyderabad is 24.84 m and it is also observed that 49.43% of the total stretch of the road needs immediate attention to fix the lane markings. We also provided an analysis on the regularity of the lane markings by classifying all the 50 m road stretches as fair, faded and unfair with the experimentally determined thresholds on normalised lane regularity score. The stretch with normalised lane regularity <0.2 is considered an unfair road, if it is ≥0.2 and ≤0.5 is considered to be faded, it is >0.5 then it is considered as a fair road with respect to the lane markings (Table 2).

Discussions. The quantitative and qualitative results illustrated in the previous Sect. 3 strongly support our assumption that there is a lot of scope for improvement in road infrastructure maintenance in Hyderabad. It also supports

Table 1. Quantitative results of road infrastructure in Hyderabad: The results shown above are obtained on 1500 KMs of test data that includes culturally, socially and financially diverse regions. With results shown in the above table we can conclude that the road maintenance is relatively better in the areas of industrially active areas than the other parts of the city, suburban areas and near by rural areas.

Regions in Hyderabad	Defective signs	Average distance between street lights	Lane marking thatneed attention
Industrially active region	712	10.46 M	143.1 KM
Old city region	1000	19.58 M	169.85 KM
Suburban region	895	38.612 M	206.5 KM
Near by rural region	701	324.59 M	221.7 KM

Table 2. Quantitative results: The results shown in the above table are obtained on a 10 KMs of test road stretch. We manually annotated the road for street lights and traffic signs to find the recall and precision separately.

	Frames with detections	True positives	False positives	False negatives	Recall	Precision
Traffic Signs	4999	80	43	6	0.93	0.65
Street lights	1408	112	4	47	0.70	0.96

our argument that the scalable and automated system is need of the hour and the proposed system is fit for that purpose. On observing the average consecutive street light separation of 24.84 m, it can be concluded that the street light distribution is very sparse[2]. The results on lane marking with normalised regularity score of 0.2723 clearly state that the existing state of maintenance of lane markings is subpar and has to improve massively to meet the present day traffic. 40% of the total traffic signs are either rusted or faded, which again needs an massive upgrade in infrastructure. The observations are in concord with the general perception on the road infrastructure maintenance that the urban areas are well maintained when compared to the suburban and rural areas. In this work, we are able to detect and identify the quality of infrastructure that is present along the road at FPS of 2.

---

[2] The length of the stretch that is illuminated by a street light is highly dependent on its wattage and intensity. Even with a very optimistic consideration of 10 m illumination by one street light, still the road is not optimal lit.

4 Conclusion

We have presented an approach to build a road infrastructure audit system which can create a database of the targeted infrastructure with the geo-spatial information along with relevant tags. Several future extensions to this work are possible such as recommending the missing infrastructure based on the scene and identifying the structures that creates occlusion on the road etc.

References

1. Gonzalez, A., Bergasa, L.M., Yebes, J.J.: Text detection and recognition on traffic panels from street-level imagery using visual appearance. In: IEEE Transactions on Intelligent Transportation Systems (2014)
2. Gonzalez, A., et al.: Automatic traffic signs and panels inspection system using computer vision. In: IEEE Transactions on Intelligent Transportation Systems (2011)
3. Khattak, A.J., Hummer, J.E., Karimi, H.A.: New and existing roadway inventory data acquisition methods. J. Transp. Statist. (2000)
4. Campbell, A., Both, A., Sun, Q.: Detecting and mapping traffic signs from google street view images using deep learning and GIS. Comput. Environ. Urban Syst. (2019)
5. Jones, F.E.: GPS-based sign inventory and inspection program. IMSA J. **42**, 30–35 (2004)
6. Janai, J., Güney, F., Behl, A., Geiger, A.: Computer vision for autonomous vehicles: problems, datasets and state-of-the-art. ArXiv (2017)
7. Redmon, J., Divvala, S., Girshick, R., Farhadi, A.: You only look once: unified, real-time object detection. In: IEEE Conference on Computer Vision and Pattern Recognition (2016)
8. Jeyapalan, K.: Mobile digital cameras for as-built surveys of roadside features. Photogrammetr. Eng. Remote Sens. **70**, 301–312 (2004)
9. Wang, K., Hou, Z., Gong, W.: Automated road sign inventory system based on stereo vision and tracking. Comput. Aided Civil Infrastruct. Eng. **25**, 468–477 (2010)
10. Bethge, M., Gatys, L.A., Ecker, A.S.: A neural algorithm of artistic style. Nat. Commun. (2015)
11. Maerz, N.H., McKenna, S.: Surveyor: mobile highway inventory and measurement system. Transp. Res. Rec. **1690**, 135–142 (1999)
12. Segvic, S., et al.: A computer vision assisted geoinformation inventory for traffic infrastructure. In: IEEE Conference on Intelligent Transportation Systems (2010)
13. Yarram, S., Varma, G., Jawahar, C.V.: City-scale road audit system using deep learning. In: International Conference on Intelligent Robots and Systems (2018)
14. Balali, V., Rad, A.A., Golparvar-Fard, M.: Detection, classification, and mapping of U.S. traffic signs using google street view images for roadway inventory management. Vis. Eng. **3**, 15 (2015). https://doi.org/10.1186/s40327-015-0027-1
15. Pan, X., Shi, J., Luo, P., Wang, X., Tang, X.: Spatial as deep: spatial CNN for traffic scene understanding. In: AAAI (2018)

Automatic Text Localization in Scene Images: A Transfer Learning Based Approach

Mridul Ghosh[1]($\boxtimes$), Sayan Saha Roy[2], Himadri Mukherjee[3],
Sk Md Obaidullah[4], K. C. Santosh[5], and Kaushik Roy[3]

[1] Department of Computer Science, Shyampur Siddheswari Mahavidyalaya,
Howrah, India
mridulxyz@gmail.com
[2] Department of Radio Physics and Electronics, Calcutta University, Kolkata, India
sayansaharoy97@gmail.com
[3] Department of Computer Science, West Bengal State University, Kolkata, India
himadrim027@gmail.com, kaushik.mrg@gmail.com
[4] Department of Computer Science, and Engineering, Aliah University,
Kolkata, India
sk.obaidullah@gmail.com
[5] Department of Computer Science, University of South Dakota, Vermillion, SD, USA
santosh.kc@usd.edu

Abstract. In this paper, a novel procedure of text localization has been discussed using deep neural network which is based on transfer learning. The set of images are fed to deep neural network framework using pre-trained model of EAST text detection and blobs are detected which are sent to the two convolution layers to measure the probability of text and non-text regions and coordinates of bounding boxes extraction respectively. By using non-maximum suppression the tight-fitting boundary box is obtained. Two publicly available datasets named, ICDAR 2003 and SVT have been employed to test the efficiency of our method and it has been observed that our method gives encouraging accuracy comparing with other existing work.

Keywords: Text localization · DNN · Non-maximum Suppression

1 Introduction

The automatic text localization in scene image is an interesting and active research topic for automatic script identification and recognition from the scene. Text in the scene images often carries vital information which helps in content-based image retrieval, traffic navigation, vehicle license plate number detection, landmarks detection for pedestrian, knowing unknown places, etc. Text localization in scene images is a challenge because it involves many factors like low resolution, noisy and blur effects, orientation, complex background, styles, fonts,

© Springer Nature Singapore Pte Ltd. 2020
R. V. Babu et al. (Eds.): NCVPRIPG 2019, CCIS 1249, pp. 470–479, 2020.
https://doi.org/10.1007/978-981-15-8697-2_44

etc. Two major tasks involved in scene text images i.e., text localization and text recognition. But without text localization, text recognition is not possible. Comparing with the scanned images, the text localization and text recognition in natural scene images are really difficult since along with the above-mentioned factors, often it has been found that the texts are written in a very artistic way. After the text localization and script identification, the documents can be recognized through appropriate OCR. But, to locate the text portion in the scene image, it has been observed that the texture of the background may go similarly with the text. For example, in some wall writing it is seen that the texture of the wall and the text written on the wall are in a similar style, automatic text localization makes more difficult in such cases and affects the performance of the OCR also. Researchers are working hard in this field since last decade and many methods [1–4] have been proposed. Also, competitions had already been organised in this topic at ICDAR 2003, 2005, 2011, 2013, 2015 and 2017 [5–10] to showcase the imperative need of better solution.

In [11] authors used stroke width transform to extract features to find out the 'estimate' (set of bounding boxes) to locate the text in the natural images. Neumann et al. in [12] discussed a novel procedure of text localization and recognition by introducing the hypotheses-verification framework, synthetic fonts and applying MSER method. In [13] a text detection procedure in scene images with an arbitrary orientation by component analysis has been discussed. In [14] the characters are enclosed by bounding boxes from the concept of extremal region detection. In the first phase, shape-based features have been extracted to have the probability of being extremal region (ER) and in the next phase, the ER's are retained which gives a maximal probability. In [15] authors discussed the pruning method on the output of MSER and single-link cluster algorithm is used to group the text regions by the proposed self-training distance metric algorithm. A connected component-based method which includes color clustering, bit dropping, image decomposition was discussed by Jain and Yu [16]. Zhong Yu et al. [17] proposed their two-phase method for text localization. In the first phase, connected components are made based on color uniformity, size, orientation, proximity, etc., and in the second phase, according to gray level variations, the text regions are identified and then combine the outcomes of these two phases to infer final result. Liao M. et al. [18] proposed a text detection and recognition method where 28-layered CNN and a layer of 6 text boxes architecture has been discussed and by word spotting the words are extracted for recognition.

The contribution in our work is we proposed text localization technique based on transfer learning using DNN for blob creation and using two convolution layers we created the network architecture. We also used non-maximum suppression to correct bounding box extraction and generated images with only text regions.

The rest of the paper is organized as follows: the proposed work is discussed in Sect. 2 followed by experiments in Sect. 3 and conclusion in Sect. 4. The flowchart of our proposed work is shown in Fig. 1.

2   Proposed Method

A deep neural network (DNN) [19] is a variant of Artificial Neural Network with multiple hidden layers between the input and output layers. The advantage of using DNN is that complex non-linear relationships can be modelled by it. DNN assigns random weights to the connecting neurons at the beginning and the weights and the inputs are multiplied to recognize the particular pattern by the output of 0 or 1 and if the recognition is unsuccessful then the weights are adjusted to minimize the difference between target and evaluated values in the training phase. A massive quantity of training data and high computation power is required to train a DNN. So, we use transfer learning [20] process where we take pre-trained model of EAST text detector [21] and use it in our DNN model, restricting ourselves from initiating the training procedure from the scratch.

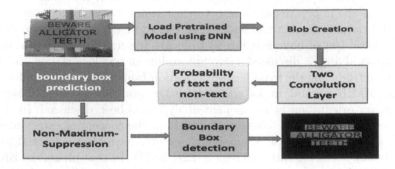

Fig. 1. The flowchart of our proposed text localization method.

Before feeding into DNN model, we normalize the images with predefined height and width of [300,300]. From DNN, the blobs are created. In blob detection, the large objects in an image which is a group of 4 or 8 connected pixels are detected. It signifies the detection of points or regions where there is a significant difference in colors, contrasts, brightness compared to the surrounding regions. Blobs are having similar pixel values surrounding some portion of an image. It is based on the parameters: scale factor for channel normalization, blob size, average pixel intensity value. The created blobs are forwarded to the two output layers which are basically convolution layers. The first output layer calculates the probability or score of the blobs. Lower the probability denotes the particular blob belongs to in the non-text region and higher value denotes text region. The blobs having lower probabilities are ignored.

The second output layer helps to derive prospective bounding box coordinates that encloses the text. The required boundary boxes may be oriented with respect to the horizontal line. The initial point of the bounding box is treated as the offset point. To access other coordinate value of the same bounding box, the following equations are followed.

$$offsetC = offsetA + W0 * cos\theta + H0 * sin\theta \qquad (1)$$

$$offsetD = offsetB - W0 * sin\theta + H0 * cos\theta \qquad (2)$$

where, $(offsetA, offsetB)$ denotes the initial point of the bounding box, and $(offsetC, offsetD)$ denotes the required coordinate point of the oriented bounding box having angle θ with the horizontal level. From Fig. 2, it is seen that the bounding box so obtained by this method. H0 and W0 represents the length of the two sides of the rectangle.

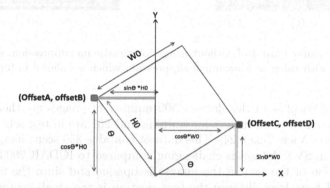

Fig. 2. Coordinate point calculation when the bounding box creates an angle with respect to the horizontle.

The pre-trained model reduces the size of the input image. The coordinate values obtained is actually $1/4^{th}$ times compared to the original input image. So, we have to multiply by a factor of 4 to have the coordinate values which is actually scaled according to the original image.

By using non-maximum suppression [22], tight-fitting window is selected for the genuine bounding box detection. In this process, out of many windows, the best scoring window is selected suppressing the remaining windows that were close to the best score by iteratively updating the best scoring window and suppressing the windows that were close to the best scored windows until there is no window left to be chosen. In Fig. 3 the results of without using non-maximum suppression and with using non-suppression are depicted. After selecting proper boundary boxes, we have created the same number of images as of in the datasets having zero intensity values and with same height and width with the original normalized images. Then copied the boundary boxes from to the created black images by extracting the coordinate values of each image's boundary boxes.

3 Experiments

3.1 Datasets

In this paper, two Different publicly available scene text image datasets have been considered.

(a) (b)

(c) (d)

Fig. 3. The sample output of without using non-maximum suppression, shown in (a) and (b) and with using non-maximum suppression which are shown in (c) and (d)

1. ICDAR 2003 [23]- In this dataset 509 number of images are there in which 258 numbers of scene images for training and 251 are in test set.
2. SVT(Street View Text) [24]- This dataset contains 350 scene images. Detecting text in SVT dataset is challenging compared to ICDAR 2003 dataset as the portion of the text in the images is opaque and since the images were captured from long distance the text portion is too small compared to the non-text region, and also there is a low-resolution issue in some images.

3.2 Evaluation Protocol

The bounding box extracted denoted by E after non-maximum suppression, are compared with the ground truth value G given by ICDAR 2003 and SVT using standard evaluation protocol [13]. The protocol uses the matching procedure of bounding rectangle γ over the set of rectangles χ. The matching formula can be described as follows:

$$match(\gamma; \chi) = maxB(\gamma; \delta | \delta \in \chi) \tag{3}$$

where, $B(\gamma; \delta)$ denotes the ratio of the area of intersection to the area of the bounding box enclosing both the rectangles. From this notion the precision and recall can be defined as

$$Pr = \frac{\sum_{ra \in A} match(ra; G)}{|A|} \tag{4}$$

$$Rc = \frac{\sum_{rg \in G} match(rg; A)}{|G|} \tag{5}$$

where, Pr and Rc denote the precision and recall measure respectively and A, G denotes the set of estimated rectangles and ground-truths respectively. Another standard measure for text localization, named f-measure which can be defined as follows.

$$f_m = \frac{2 * (Pr * Rc)}{Pr + Rc} \tag{6}$$

f_m represents f-measure parameter.

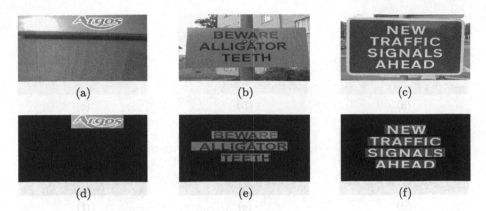

Fig. 4. Sample original images from ICDAR 2003 dataset (a–c) and corresponding localized text (d–f)is shown.

Table 1. The performance of our proposed method has been measured with respect to ground truth.

Dataset	Precision	Recall	f-measure	Time (Sec.)
ICDAR 2003 Train set	0.8765	0.823	0.8489	0.49
ICDAR 2003 Test set	0.786	0.698	0.7394	0.58
SVT	0.6972	0.601	0.6455	0.54

3.3   Results and Analysis

In Fig. 4 and Fig. 5 the sample images from ICDAR 2003 and SVT and corresponding localized outputs are shown. Along with good output, there are also instances of bad result which can be observed in Fig. 6. In Fig. 6 images (a)-(c) have been taken from ICDAR 2003 and SVT datasets and corresponding outputs of localized text are shown in (e-f). The possible reasons for bad output are reflection of light on images, low resolution, and brightness, capturing of images from long distance, similarity with the background texture, blur effect, etc. In Fig. 6 it can be realized that images (a) and (b) suffers from the reflection of the light issue and in image (c), similarity with background texture and low resolution, blur effect issues are involved.

From Table 1 it is observed that using ICDAR 2003 dataset average precision, recall and f-measure values are obtained 0.8313, 0.7605 and 0.7943 respectively having average time taken 0.535 sec and using SVT dataset 0.69, 0.60, 0.64 precision, recall and f-measure values are obtained respectively with time elapsed 0.54 sec. Comparing our method with other existing methods which are shown in Table 2 and Table 3 for ICDAR 2003 and SVT datasets, it is obvious that our proposed method gives good output.

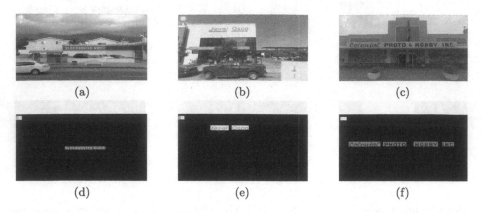

Fig. 5. Sample original images from SVT dataset (a–c) and corresponding localized text (d–f)is shown.

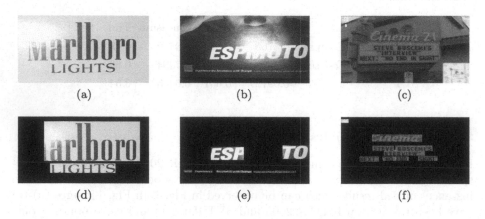

Fig. 6. Missing some text in localization.

Table 2. The performance comparison of our proposed method using ICDAR 2003 dataset.

Method	Precision	Recall	f-measure	Time
Our Result	0.8313	0.7605	0.7943	0.535
Huang et al. [25]	0.81	0.74	0.72	-
Epshtein et al. [11]	0.73	0.60	0.66	0.94
Hinnerk Becker [6]	0.62	0.67	0.62	-
Alex Chen [6]	0.60	0.60	0.58	-
Lukas Neumann [12]	0.59	0.55	0.57	-

Table 3. The performance comparison of our proposed method using SVT dataset.

Method	Precision	Recall	f-measure	Time
Our Result	0.6972	0.601	0.6455	0.54
Jaderberg [26]	0.56	-	-	-
FCRNall+filts [27]	0.53	-	-	-
TextBoxes [18]	0.64	-	-	-

4 Conclusion

In this work, an automatic text localization technique has been proposed using a transfer learning based approach where a pre-trained model has been taken into deep neural network to avoid training the network from scratch. Two datasets are used namely, ICDAR 2003 and SVT to test the performance of our work. This method gives good result compared with other existing methods. We will also consider other publicly available datasets to test our method. In this work, the text detection has been done with the assumption that the text are horizontally oriented. Whenever any orientations occur in the text, the whole rectangle surrounded by the text region is considered without considering the exact arch or exact orientation of the rectangle which is the drawback of our work. In future, we will implement text localization method considering arbitrary orientations of text in images.

References

1. Wu, V., Manmatha, R., Riseman, E.M.: Textfinder: an automatic system to detect and recognize text in images. IEEE Trans. Pattern Anal. Mach. Intell. **21**(11), 1224–1229 (1999)
2. Chen, X., Yang, J., Zhang, J., Waibel, A.: Automatic detection and recognition of signs from natural scenes. IEEE Trans. Image Process. **13**(1), 87–99 (2004)
3. Ezaki, N., Bulacu, M., Schomaker, L.: Text detection from natural scene images: towards a system for visually impaired persons. In Proceedings of the 17th International Conference on Pattern Recognition, 2004. ICPR 2004, vol. 2, pp. 683–686. IEEE (2004)
4. KEpshtein, B., Ofek, E., Wexler, Y.: Detecting text in natural scenes with stroke width transform. In: 2010 IEEE Computer Society Conference on Computer Vision and Pattern Recognition, pp. 2963–2970. IEEE (2010)
5. Lucas, S.M., Panaretos, A., Sosa, L., Tang, A., Wong, S., Young, R.: ICDAR 2003 robust reading competitions. In Seventh International Conference on Document Analysis and Recognition, 2003. Proceedings, pp. 682–687. IEEE (2003)
6. Lucas, S.M.: ICDAR 2005 text locating competition results. In: Eighth International Conference on Document Analysis and Recognition (ICDAR 2005), pp. 80–84. IEEE (2005)

7. Shahab, A., Shafait, F., Dengel, A.: ICDAR 2011 robust reading competition challenge 2: reading text in scene images. In: 2011 International Conference on Document Analysis and Recognition, pp. 1491–1496. IEEE (2011)

8. Karatzas, D., et al.: ICDAR 2013 robust reading competition. In: 2013 12th International Conference on Document Analysis and Recognition, pp. 1484–1493. IEEE (2013)

9. Karatzas, D., et al.: ICDAR 2015 competition on robust reading. In: 2015 13th International Conference on Document Analysis and Recognition (ICDAR), pp. 1156–1160. IEEE (2015)

10. Shi, B., et al.: ICDAR2017 competition on reading Chinese text in the wild (RCTW-17). In: 2017 14th IAPR International Conference on Document Analysis and Recognition (ICDAR), vol. 1, pp. 1429–1434. IEEE (2017)

11. Epshtein, B., Ofek, E., Wexler, Y.: Detecting text in natural scenes with stroke width transform. In: 2010 IEEE Computer Society Conference on Computer Vision and Pattern Recognition, pp. 2963–2970. IEEE (2010)

12. Neumann, L., Matas, J.: A method for text localization and recognition in real-world images. In: Kimmel, R., Klette, R., Sugimoto, A. (eds.) ACCV 2010. LNCS, vol. 6494, pp. 770–783. Springer, Heidelberg (2011). https://doi.org/10.1007/978-3-642-19318-7_60

13. Yao, C., Bai, X., Liu, W., Ma, Y., Tu, Z.: Detecting texts of arbitrary orientations in natural images. In: 2012 IEEE Conference on Computer Vision and Pattern Recognition, pp. 1083–1090. IEEE (2012)

14. Neumann, L., Matas, J.: Real-time scene text localization and recognition. In: 2012 IEEE Conference on Computer Vision and Pattern Recognition, pp. 3538–3545. IEEE (2012)

15. Yin, X.C., Yin, X., Huang, K., Hao, H.W.: Robust text detection in natural scene images. IEEE Trans. Pattern Anal. Mach. Intell. **36**(5), 970–983 (2013)

16. Jain, A.K., Yu, B.: Automatic text location in images and video frames. Pattern Recogn. **31**(12), 2055–2076 (1998)

17. Zhong, Y., Karu, K., Jain, A.K.: Locating text in complex color images. Pattern Recogn. **28**(10), 1523–1535 (1995)

18. Liao, M., Shi, B., Bai, X., Wang, X., Liu, W.: Textboxes: a fast text detector with a single deep neural network. In: Thirty-First AAAI Conference on Artificial Intelligence (2017)

19. Hinton, G., et al.: Deep neural networks for acoustic modelling in speech recognition. IEEE Sig. Process. Mag. **29**, 82–97 (2012)

20. Krizhevsky, A., Sutskever, I., Hinton, G.E.: ImageNet classification with deep convolutional neural networks. In: Advances in Neural Information Processing Systems, pp. 1097–1105 (2012)

21. Zhou, X., et al.: EAST: an efficient and accurate scene text detector. In: Proceedings of the IEEE conference on Computer Vision and Pattern Recognition, pp. 5551–5560 (2017)

22. He, W., Zhang, X.Y., Yin, F., Liu, C.L.: Deep direct regression for multi-oriented scene text detection. In: Proceedings of the IEEE International Conference on Computer Vision, pp. 745–753 (2017)

23. Lucas, S.M., et al.: ICDAR 2003 robust reading competitions: entries, results, and future directions. Int. J. Doc. Anal. Recogn. (IJDAR) **7**(2–3), 105–122 (2005)

24. Wang, K., Babenko, B., Belongie, S.: End-to-end scene text recognition. In: 2011 International Conference on Computer Vision, pp. 1457–1464. IEEE (2011)

25. Huang, W., Lin, Z., Yang, J., Wang, J.: Text localization in natural images using stroke feature transform and text covariance descriptors. In: Proceedings of the IEEE International Conference on Computer Vision, pp. 1241–1248 (2013)
26. Jaderberg, M., Simonyan, K., Vedaldi, A., Zisserman, A.: Reading text in the wild with convolutional neural networks. Int. J. Comput. Vis. **116**(1), 1–20 (2016)
27. Gupta, A., Vedaldi, A., Zisserman, A.: Synthetic data for text localisation in natural images. In: Proceedings of the IEEE Conference on Computer Vision and Pattern Recognition, pp. 2315–2324 (2016)

Automated Detection of Mine Water Bodies Using Landsat 8 OLI/TIRS in Jharia

Jit Mukherjee[1,4(✉)], Jayanta Mukherjee[2,4], and Debashish Chakravarty[3,4]

[1] Advance Technology Development Centre, Kharagpur, India
jit.mukherjee@iitkgp.ac.in
[2] Department of Computer Science and Engineering, Kharagpur, India
jay@cse.iitkgp.ac.in
[3] Department of Mining Engineering, Kharagpur, India
dc@mining.iitkgp.ernet.in
[4] Indian Institute of Technology, Kharagpur, Kharagpur, West Bengal, India

Abstract. Mine water bodies create enormous water pollution due to heavy use of water in different stages of mining. Detection and monitoring of such water bodies are necessary for environmental benefits. In the past, mine water bodies are classified along with non mine water bodies through manual intervention. The motivation of this work is to automate the process of detection of mine water bodies from Landsat 8 OLI/TIRS images. First, automated water extraction index ($AWEI$) is used to detect water bodies in adaptive manner. Most mine water bodies can be found near mining regions. Further, mine water bodies are detected through connected component and bounding box analysis using this cue. Coal Mine Index (CMI) can differentiate coal mine regions from other land classes. The proposed method uses the feature space of CMI to detect mine water bodies in an automated fashion with average precision, and recall of 87.46%, and 65.74% respectively.

Keywords: Mine water body · Coal mine index · AWEI · Short wave infra-red · K-means clustering

1 Introduction

Mining has various environmental impacts, specially on surface and ground water. It causes drastic changes in land cover. Mining techniques, specifically surface mining directly effect the environment, soil condition, air pollution, regional biodiversity, [4,10] etc. Along with air pollution, water pollution is one of the major adversities of different mining techniques. Water is used in various steps of mining such as mine cooling, mine drainage, etc. Fresh water is needed in different stages of mining. There are various impacts of mining in water quality such as, acid mine drainage, heavy metal contamination, leeching, etc. [19]. Water bodies polluted with such high concentration of chemicals become unsuitable for sustaining biodiversity and prone to cause soil erosion. Therefore, it

© Springer Nature Singapore Pte Ltd. 2020
R. V. Babu et al. (Eds.): NCVPRIPG 2019, CCIS 1249, pp. 480–489, 2020.
https://doi.org/10.1007/978-981-15-8697-2_45

is of paramount importance to monitor such contaminated water bodies even after abandoning the mining activity. Detection and monitoring of different land classes in mining regions through satellite images have been explored by various works [8,9,13–17]. Hence, detection and monitoring of mining water bodies have several challenges and impacts on eco-environment.

1.1 Related Works

Detection and monitoring of different land classes in mining regions are obtained mostly by various supervised and semi-supervised techniques. Various surface mining land classes are detected using support vector machine by [4,16]. In [8], two classification techniques, namely object based, and spectral based have been proposed to detect different land classes in surface mines. A coal mine region is classified using different spectral responses [17]. A spectral index of short wave infra-red one ($SWIR-I$), and short wave infra-red two ($SWIR-II$) bands is proposed to detect surface coal mines [13]. Most of these works in literature do not detect mine water bodies separately from non mine water bodies, while classifying different land covers in surface mining regions. There are various research challenges regarding water body detection such as, wetland estimation [18], flood area detection [3], shallow water body detection [5], etc. There are various indices to detect water bodies from remotely sensed images, such as Normalized Difference Water Index ($NDWI$) [7,11], Modified Normalized Difference Water Index ($MNDWI$) [20], Automated Water Extraction Index ($AWEI$) [6], etc. $NDWI$ is one of the most widely used techniques to detect water bodies. There are two variants of $NDWI$ to detect water bodies. In [7], $NDWI$ is proposed as a spectral index of near infra-red and short wave infra-red bands. Another variant proposes a spectral index of green and near infra-red bands as $NDWI$ [11]. Modified Normalized Difference Water Index ($MNDWI$) detects water bodies using a spectral index of green and short wave infra-red one bands [20]. In [6], two indices have been proposed named as $AWEI_{nsh}$ and $AWEI_{sh}$. $AWEI_{nsh}$ detects water bodies in automated fashion by removing non water elements along with dark build surfaces. $AWEI_{sh}$ further improves the accuracy of $AWEI_{nsh}$ by removing shadowy pixels.

1.2 Motivation and Application

Water bodies in mining areas show distinct characteristics from other water bodies because of their chemical contents and surrounding areas. This idea has been explored in few works. Clay mineral ratio can differentiate mine water bodies from non mine water bodies using empirical threshold [14]. In this work, water bodies are treated separately, and bounding boxes of every water body regions are analysed. The method has been extended using difference of clay mineral ratio and iron oxide index to separate them in automated fashion [12]. These techniques use $NDWI$, and bare soil index (BI) [2] to detect water bodies and removal of bare soil regions, respectively. This requires manual intervention for

empirically choosing parameters. Therefore, these techniques are not fully automated. The technique discussed in [12] has been found to be erroneous in presence of river bed. The motivation of this work is to detect mine water bodies in
adaptive fashion and to make the process robust in presence of river bed regions.
It has been observed that coal mine index (CMI) can significantly differentiate
coal mine areas from non mine areas [13]. Therefore, another motivation of this
work is to explore the feature space of CMI while detecting mine water bodies.
In this work, a novel pipeline of methods is proposed where mine water bodies are detected without manual intervention. First, automated water extraction
index ($AWEI$) is used to detect water bodies in adaptive manner [6]. Further,
these water body regions are treated separately to detect mine water bodies. As
mine water bodies have various effects on water pollution, this method can be
found useful in various aspects such as, de-watering scheme, area monitoring of
water bodies, safety measures, etc.

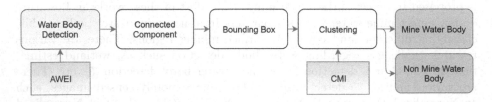

Fig. 1. Flow of adaptive detection of mine water bodies from landsat 8 OLI/TIRS

2   Methodology

The proposed method follows a pipeline of techniques to detect mine water
bodies in automated fashion as shown in Fig. 1. First, water bodies are detected
using $AWEI$. Further, water bodies are treated individually using connected
component analysis. CMI values of each bounding box over each connected
component are further analysed. Finally, Mine water bodies are obtained by
clustering mean values of CMI responses of each bounding box as shown in
Fig. 1. In this work, top of atmosphere reflectance values are computed from raw
pixel values of Landsat 8 $L1$ data as per [1].

2.1   Automated Water Extraction Index (AWEI)

There are various techniques to detect water bodies from satellite images. These
techniques primarily use manual observations to detect water bodies. In this
work, automated water extraction index ($AWEI$) has been used, which detects
water bodies eliminating different ambiguous land classes in automated fashion [6]. It proposes two indices, namely, $AWEI_{nsh}$, and $AWEI_{sh}$ as shown in
Eq. 1 [6].

$$AWEI_{nsh} = 4 \times (\lambda_{Green} - \lambda_{SWIR-I}) - (0.25 \times \lambda_{NIR} + 2.75 \times \lambda_{SWIR-II})$$
$$AWEI_{sh} = \lambda_{Blue} + 2.5 \times \lambda_{Green} - 1.5 \times (\lambda_{NIR} + \lambda_{SWIR-I}) - 0.25 \times \lambda_{SWIR-II} \quad (1)$$

Here, λ_{Blue}, λ_{Green}, λ_{NIR}, λ_{SWIR-I}, and $\lambda_{SWIR-II}$ denote top of atmosphere (*TOA*) reflectance values of *Blue*, *Green*, near infra-red (*NIR*), short wave infra-red one (*SWIR-I*), and short wave infra-red two (*SWIR-II*) bands, respectively. These parameters are chosen by analysing reflectance patterns of pure class reflectance values. Positive values of $AWEI_{nsh}$ are treated as water body regions [6]. $AWEI_{nsh}$ eliminates dark build surface in urban regions, which has been found falsely being classified as water body regions. $AWEI_{sh}$ enhances $AWEI_{nsh}$ by eliminating shadowy pixels [6]. In this work, $AWEI_{nsh}$ has been used in Jharia Coal Fields (*JCF*) to detect water bodies as we have not found any further improvement in performance by using $AWEI_{sh}$ instead of $AWEI_{nsh}$.

2.2 Connected Component Analysis

A satellite image can have vast number of water bodies with different categories. These water bodies are needed to be treated independently to detect mine water bodies. Connected component analysis is used here to treat each water bodies separately. In connected component analysis every unmarked pixels are categorised into similar groups based on pixel connectivity. The surrounding areas of mine water bodies are distinctive. Hence, surrounding areas of each connected component are analysed using bounding boxes. Few mine water bodies are small in size, which makes it difficult to infer their distinctive spectral characteristics. Hence, bounding boxes of each connected component are padded with 5 pixels on every sides. The method uses *CMI*, which is a spectral ratio of *TOA* reflectance values of *SWIR-I* and *SWIR-II* i.e. ($\frac{\lambda_{SWIR-I} - \lambda_{SWIR-II}}{\lambda_{SWIR-I} + \lambda_{SWIR-II}}$). Mean of *CMI* values of each such bounding boxes are further analysed. These mean values are clustered using K-means clustering. K is considered here as 2. As, coal mines are prone to have lower *CMI* values [13], the cluster centre associated with lowest value is considered to preserve mine water bodies. Whereas, non mine water bodies are considered to be present in the cluster with highest cluster centre. The connected component analysis of the proposed method have similar approach to [12,14] but the feature space of *CMI* has been explored here to improve accuracy. For automated mine water body detection *Blue*, *Green*, *NIR* bands are considered along with *SWIR-I*, and *SWIR-II* bands. Therefore, the proposed technique can be applied to any satellite modality, which have these bands.

3 Data and Study Area

In this work, Jharia Coal Field (*JCF*) has been used as study area. *JCF* is located in between latitudes 23°38′ N and 23°50′ N and longitudes 86°07′E and 86°30′E in Dhanbad district of the state of Jharkhand in India as shown in Fig. 2. The bounding box on the right most image in Fig. 2 shows the location of

JCF. It has vast geographical features of fresh water lake, river, dam, mine water bodies, croplands, prominent river beds, reserve forest, urban area, mining, dense vegetation, etc. For experimentation, Landsat 8 *L*1 images have been used. *L*1 data provides *TOA* reflectance values. Landsat 8 provides nine multi-spectral bands with two thermal bands. The spatial resolutions of Landsat 8 images are of 30 meter, except the panchromatic band. In this work, Landsat 8 images, which have <10% cloud cover, are considered. Satellite images from the path 140, and row 44 as per Landsat reference system in different months have been obtained for experimentation in *JCF*. Various mine and non mine water bodies are marked from High resolution Google Earth images. These water bodies are treated as ground truth for this work.

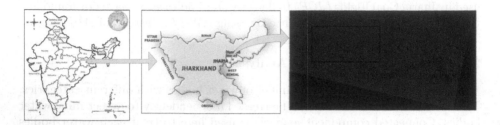

Fig. 2. Jharia Coal Field location in Jharkhand, India

4   Results

Landsat 8 images from path 140 and row 44 as per Landsat reference system of 2017 have been used for experimentation. As discussed in Sect. 2, water bodies are detected from these images using *AWEI* in automated fashion. Further, these water bodies are treated independently in the feature space of *CMI*. In [12,14], it is found that clay mineral ratio, iron oxide ratio, and difference of clay mineral and iron oxide ratio (*CLM-IO*) can distinguish mine water bodies from other water body regions. *CLM-IO* has been found more suitable than using these indices independently [12] for automated segregation of mine and other water bodies. In this paper, the performances of *CLM-IO* and *CMI* are discussed and compared using the proposed method. $AWEI_{nsh}$ is used to detect water body regions as shown in Fig. 3(A) from Landsat 8 images in December 2017. In [12,14], an additional step of bare soil removal after water body detection has been performed. It has been observed that very few bare soil regions are falsely classified as water bodies using $AWEI_{nsh}$. Hence, the additional step of bare soil removal is omitted in this work. Further, connected component analysis is used to treat each water body separately. A bounding box with 5 pixel padding on each side are computed over each connected component as shown in Fig. 3(B). Mean values of these bounding boxes are considered for clustering. Detected mine and other water body region using *CLM-IO* and *CMI* are shown in Fig. 3.

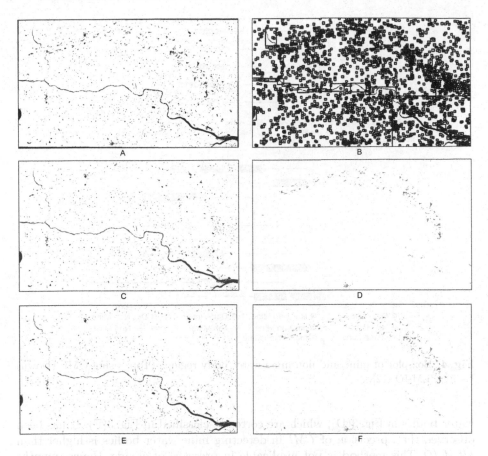

Fig. 3. Results in Jharia Coal fields in december. (A) Detected water bodies by $AWEI_{nsh}$, (B) Bounding boxes over each water body, (C) Non mine water bodies by CMI, (D) Mine water bodies by CMI, (E) Non Mine Water Bodies by CLM-IO, (F) Mine water bodies by CLM-IO

Mine and other water bodies using CMI are shown in Fig. 3(C), and (D), respectively. Mine and other water bodies using CLM-IO are shown in Fig. 3(E), and (F), respectively. It can be observed from Fig. 3 that few river regions are detected as mine water bodies using CLM-IO, which is a bottleneck of [12]. These regions got missclassified because of vast mineral proportion in river bed regions. It is observed that these regions are correctly classified as non mine water bodies using CMI. CLM-IO values of river bed regions are close to mining regions. Whereas, it has been found that CMI can significantly differentiate mine and river bed regions [13,15]. As observed in Fig. 3(E), CLM-IO also falsely classify various small non mine water bodies as mine water bodies. Figure 3(C) shows very less number of non mine water bodies detected as mine water bodies. However, some mine water bodies can be found as falsely classified as non mine

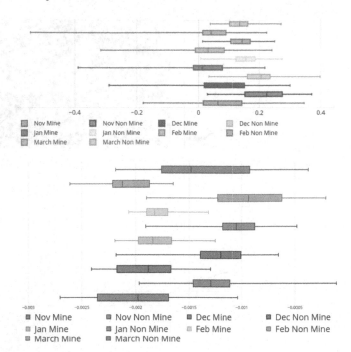

Fig. 4. Box plot of mine and non mine water body regions (Top) using CMI, (Down) Using CLM-IO [12].

water bodies in Fig. 3(D), which are correctly classified in Fig. 3(F). It has been observed that, precision of *CMI* in detecting mine water bodies is higher than *CLM-IO*. This method is not applicable in presence of clouds. Hence, months from June to October are not considered for analysis. Few ground truth mine and other water body regions are selected from High resolution Google Earth images. These ground truth water body regions are further used for validation.

4.1   Validation

Random samples over each bounding boxes of different ground truth mine and other water body regions are considered for validation. Box plot of *CMI* values of these regions over different months are shown in Fig. 4 (Top). Figure 4 (Bottom) shows box plot of *CLM-IO* over different months as discussed in [12]. *CLM-IO* and *CMI* both show less overlapping in mine and other water bodies over the seasons. Yet, the differences of mine and other water bodies in *CLM-IO* are less than *CMI*. Hence, the feature space of *CMI* can be found more useful than the feature space of *CLM-IO*. Further, a two tail t-test has been performed over the null hypothesis $\mu_{mineWater} = \mu_{nonMineWater}$, where $\mu_{mineWater}$, and $\mu_{nonMineWater}$ are denoted as mean of *CMI* values over bounding boxes of ground truth mine, and other water bodies, respectively. Here, $S_{mineWater} \neq S_{nonMineWater}$ is considered, where $S_{mineWater}$, and $S_{nonMineWater}$ are variances of mine, and other water bodies, respectively. t_0, degree of freedom and P value over the seasons are shown in Table 1. t_0, P values, and degree of freedom indicate the significant difference value between two populations, significance of the result, and the number of independent variables, respectively. Higher value of t_0 shows higher difference between two populations. Small P values show strong evidence against the null hypothesis. It can be observed from Table 1, that the null hypothesis $\mu_{mineWater} = \mu_{nonMineWater}$ can be rejected by alternative hypothesis $\mu_{mineWater} \neq \mu_{nonMineWater}$ over the seasons. Therefore, mine and non mine water bodies can be significantly differentiated using CMI. As discussed in [12], CLM-IO can also significantly separate mine and other water bodies over the seasons. Yet, t_0 values of CLM-IO [12] are less than t_0 values of CMI. Therefore, the separation of mine and other water bodies in CMI is more significant than CLM-IO. Further, it has been observed that the null hypothesis can be rejected by the alternative hypothesis of $\mu_{mineWater} < \mu_{nonMineWater}$ over the seasons.

Table 1. T-test Results over Null Hypothesis $\mu_{MineWater} = \mu_{NonMineWater}$ using CMI

	Nov	Dec	Jan	Feb	March
t_0	-10.61	-11.24	-12.05	-10.52	-8.59
df	191.68	162.02	170.41	172.13	133.85
P value	<0.00001	<0.00001	<0.00001	<0.00001	<0.00001

Table 2. Precision and Recall of the Proposed Method over CMI and CLM-IO

Features	Water Body	Nov		Dec		Jan		Feb		March	
		Precision	Recall	Precision	Recall	Precision	Recall	Precision	Recall	Precision	Recall
CMI	Mine	88	61.11	83.87	66.66	90	72.97	88	62.85	47.36	64.28
	Non Mine	74.07	93.02	76.36	89.36	80.39	93.18	75	92.85	66.66	50
CLM-IO	Mine	71.42	78.12	70.45	72.09	66.66	64.86	76.92	62.5	42.85	56.25
	Non Mine	83.72	78.26	75.51	74	71.11	72.72	74.46	85.36	58.82	45.45

For computation of accuracy, two-class precision and recall[1] is considered. In this work, $AWEI_{nsh}$ has been used. It detects water bodies in automated fashion and number of missclassifed land classes are less than $NDWI$. Yet, few land classes mostly, land covers in mining regions are falsely classified. Therefore, only true positive water body regions are considered. Seasonal precision and recall of the proposed method with the feature space of CLM-IO and CMI are shown in Table 2. The proposed method concentrates more on detecting mine water bodies precisely. As shown in Table 2, the proposed method has been found to be erroneous in the month of March. $AWEI$ could not detect some water bodies, mostly

---

[1] Precision, and Recall are defined as $t_p/(t_p + f_p)$, and $t_p/(t_p + f_n)$, where t_p, f_p, and f_n, are true positive, false positive, and false negative, respectively. F_1 Score is harmonic mean of Precision and Recall.

in mining regions from March to May. Hence, the performance of the proposed method declines in this period. Detection of mine water bodies in this season has been considered as a future direction of this work. The seasonal mean precision, recall, and F_1 score of mine, and non mine water bodies by CLM-IO are found as [71.36%, 69.39%, 70.36%], and [76.2%, 77.58%, 76.88%], respectively considering November to February. The seasonal mean precision, recall, and F_1 score of mine, and non mine water bodies by CMI are as [87.46%, 65.89%, 75.16%], and [76.45%, 92.10%, 83.54%], respectively, considering November to February. CMI has been found to be more effective than CLM-IO. In [12], precision, recall, and F_1 score of mine and other water body regions are detected as [75.55%, 74%, 74.76%], and [75.47%, 76.92%, 76.18%], respectively. Therefore, the proposed method automates the detection of mine water bodies with improved precision. The recall of mine water body is less than [12]. However, the F_1 scores have been improved for both mine and other water bodies. Additionally, the method classify ambiguous river regions with prominent river beds as non mine water body regions. The method has been analysed in Barakar region, West Bengal, India. It has been observed that the number of misclassified water bodies with prominent river bed has been decreased in CMI. Further experimentation with other regions is considered as a future direction of this work.

5   Conclusion

The paper proposes a novel method to detect mine water bodies adaptively using the features space of $AWEI$ and CMI. The method has been analysed over the seasons. Water bodies are detected by automated manner using $AWEI$. Further, mean values of CMI response have been analysed over each water bodies to detect mine water bodies. In the past, segregation of mine and non mine water body regions has been found erroneous in the presence of prominent river beds. The propose method is found to be effective in the presence of river bed regions. It shows average precision and recall for mine, and non mine water bodies as [87.46%, 65.74%], and [76.45%, 92.1%], respectively. The proposed method can be further used for classification and monitoring of surface mining regions. Application of this technique in other mining regions and with surface reflectance values are considered as future works.

References

1. Using the USGS landsat8 product. https://landsat.usgs.gov/using-usgs-landsat-8-product. Accessed 29 Mar 2017
2. Chen, W., Liu, L., Zhang, C., Wang, J., Wang, J., Pan, Y.: Monitoring the seasonal bare soil areas in beijing using multitemporal tm images. In: 2004 IEEE International Proceedings of the Geoscience and Remote Sensing Symposium, IGARSS 2004, vol. 5, pp. 3379–3382. IEEE (2004)
3. Chignell, S.M., Anderson, R.S., Evangelista, P.H., Laituri, M.J., Merritt, D.M.: Multi-temporal independent component analysis and landsat 8 for delineating maximum extent of the 2013 colorado front range flood. Remote Sens. 7(8), 9822–9843 (2015)

4. Demirel, N., Emil, M.K., Duzgun, H.S.: Surface coal mine area monitoring using multi-temporal high-resolution satellite imagery. Int. J. Coal Geol. **86**(1), 3–11 (2011)

5. Eugenio, F., Marcello, J., Martin, J.: High-resolution maps of bathymetry and benthic habitats in shallow-water environments using multispectral remote sensing imagery. IEEE Trans. Geosci. Remote Sens. **53**(7), 3539–3549 (2015)

6. Feyisa, G.L., Meilby, H., Fensholt, R., Proud, S.R.: Automated water extraction index: a new technique for surface water mapping using landsat imagery. Remote Sens. Environ. **140**, 23–35 (2014)

7. Gao, B.C.: NDWI'a normalized difference water index for remote sensing of vegetation liquid water from space. Remote Sens. Environ. **58**(3), 257–266 (1996)

8. Gao, Y., Kerle, N., Mas, J.F.: Object-based image analysis for coal fire-related land cover mapping in coal mining areas. Geocarto Int. **24**(1), 25–36 (2009)

9. Kuenzer, C., et al.: Uncontrolled coal fires and their environmental impacts: investigating two arid mining regions in north-central china. Appl. Geogr. **27**(1), 42–62 (2007)

10. Lima, A.T., Mitchell, K., O'Connell, D.W., Verhoeven, J., Van Cappellen, P.: The legacy of surface mining: remediation, restoration, reclamation and rehabilitation. Environ. Sci. Policy **66**, 227–233 (2016)

11. McFeeters, S.K.: The use of the normalized difference water index (NDWI) in the delineation of open water features. Int. J. Remote Sens. **17**(7), 1425–1432 (1996)

12. Mukherjee, J., Mukherjee, J., Chakravarty, D.: Automated seasonal separation of mine and non mine water bodies from landsat 8 OLI/TIRS using clay mineral and iron oxide ratio. IEEE J. Sel. Top. Appl. Earth Observ. Remote Sens. **12**(7), 2550–2556 (2019)

13. Mukherjee, J., Mukherjee, J., Chakravarty, D., Aikat, S.: A novel index to detect opencast coal mine areas from landsat 8 OLI/TIRS. IEEE J. Sel. Top. Appl. Earth Observ. Remote Sens. **12**(3), 891–897 (2019)

14. Mukherjee, J., Mukhopadhyay, J., Chakravarty, D.: Investigation of seasonal separation in mine and non mine water bodies using local feature analysis of landsat 8 OLI/TIRS images. In: IEEE IGARSS 2018, Valencia, Spain, 22–27 July 2018, pp. 8961–8964 (2018)

15. Mukherjee, J., Mukhopadhyay, J., Chakravarty, D., Aikat, S.: Automated seasonal detection of coal surface mine regions from landsat 8 oli images. In: IEEE IGARSS 2019, Yokohama, Japan, 27 July–3 August 2019 (2019)

16. Petropoulos, G.P., Partsinevelos, P., Mitraka, Z.: Change detection of surface mining activity and reclamation based on a machine learning approach of multi-temporal landsat tm imagery. Geocarto Int. **28**(4), 323–342 (2013)

17. Prakash, A., Gupta, R.: Land-use mapping and change detection in a coal mining area-a case study in the jharia coalfield, india. Int. J. Remote Sens. **19**(3), 391–410 (1998)

18. Rebelo, L.M., Finlayson, C.M., Nagabhatla, N.: Remote sensing and GIS for wetland inventory, mapping and change analysis. J. Environ. Manage. **90**(7), 2144–2153 (2009)

19. RoyChowdhury, A., Sarkar, D., Datta, R.: Remediation of acid mine drainage-impacted water. Curr. Pollut. Rep. **1**(3), 131–141 (2015)

20. Xu, H.: Modification of normalised difference water index (NDWI) to enhance open water features in remotely sensed imagery. Int. J. Remote Sens. **27**(14), 3025–3033 (2006)

Deep Learning-Based Bangla Isolated Character Recognition from Online and Offline Data

Himadri Mukherjee[1], Shibaprasad Sen[2], Ankita Dhar[1(✉)],
Sk. Md. Obaidullah[3], and Kaushik Roy[1]

[1] Department of Computer Science, West Bengal State University, Kolkata, India
himadrim027@gmail.com, ankita.ankie@gmail.com, kaushik.mrg@gmail.com
[2] Department of Computer Science & Engineering, Future Institute of Engineering
and Management, Kolkata, India
shibubiet@gmail.com
[3] Department of Computer Science & Engineering, Aliah University, Kolkata, India
sk.obaidullah@gmail.com

Abstract. In spite of the introduction of modern technologies, handwriting is still considered as one of the key means of communication and disseminating information in our daily life. Though commercial handwriting recognizers are available for several Western languages but same is not true for Bangla. The complexity of the script is one of the reasons. Recognizing both online and offline handwriting has pros and cons of their own. In this paper, a deep-learning based approach has been adopted to recognize isolated Bangla characters in both online and offline modes. The experiments have been performed on a database of 15000 handwritten Bangla character samples and highest accuracies of 99.91% and 99.92% have been obtained for offline and online modes respectively.

Keywords: Deep learning · Online handwriting · Offline handwriting.

1 Introduction

Handwriting recognition is the mechanism by which a computer system can recognize handwritten characters and other symbols collected from sources like scanned document images or directly taking input from touch sensitive screen and then convert it as machine readable format. Handwriting recognition has gained much of the researchers interest in recent years. Based on the source of input data, handwriting recognition can be broadly divided into online and offline recognition. In offline recognition, the information are collected as images by using a scanner. Whereas, in online recognition the information is captured from the movements of stylus on the writing surface. This information includes the position, velocity, acceleration and pen angles at coordinate level. The supplied information in online mode are stored in form of pixels as function of time.

Paper ID-62.

© Springer Nature Singapore Pte Ltd. 2020
R. V. Babu et al. (Eds.): NCVPRIPG 2019, CCIS 1249, pp. 490–497, 2020.
https://doi.org/10.1007/978-981-15-8697-2_46

Due to the presence of ordered pixel information, the stroke order information is also available in online mode which is not true for offline scheme. This is one of the advantages of online recognition over its counterpart. In general, inherent writing styles of different individuals, size of the component characters, different writing speed of different persons poses challenge in online recognition. Sometimes people overwrite characters that makes the recognition more challenging. Figure 1 highlights such an input signal that can be analyzed in both offline and online recognition mode.

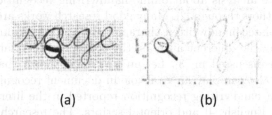

(a)   (b)

Fig. 1. (a) Example of an offline word sample where scanner converts the image into grey level pixels. (b) Online word sample where pen tip represents the function of time along x and y coordinates.

In this paper, we have analyzed the recognition performance of both online and offline approaches applied on same handwritten Bangla character database. A block diagram of the present work is shown in Fig. 2.

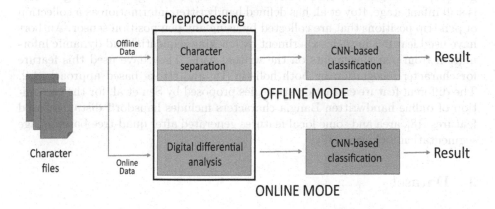

Fig. 2. Block diagram of the present work.

This paper is structured as follows: Sects. 2 and 3 presents the literature survey and dataset details respectively. Section 4 highlights the proposed methodology whereas Sect. 5 describes and analyze the obtained outcome. Lastly Sect. 6 summarizes the contributions along with mentioning few future directions of this work.

2   Literature Survey

During past decade a noticeable growth on offline handwriting recognition has been observed in terms of its application. The examples of few such applications include document processing, bank processing, mail sorting, postal addresses recognition/verification and writer identification. Again, as automatic processing of the supplied information is done in online recognition, researchers are trying to develop technology driven applications like sign verifiers, pen based computers, home safety using handwritten pattern recognition system [1].

An exhaustive analysis about offline handwriting recognition has been discussed by the authors through [2]. Many good research works are available in the literature for isolated handwritten character recognition. Among various techniques applied by the different authors, the concept of template matching procedure has been discussed in [3]. LeCun in [5] has shown that Convolutional Neural Network also can play an vital role in document recognition tasks. Most of the studies on handwriting recognition reported in the literature have been implemented on English [4] and oriental scripts. The research works in handwriting recognition domain under Indic scripts are very limited. Authors in [6] have extracted stroke-based features from handwritten Devanagari numerals and used a tree classifier for the classification purpose. Dutta et al. [16] have also experimented with Devanagari handwriting recognition on benchmark dataset. Authors in [7] have applied a neural net classifier for the recognition of handwritten alphanumeric characters. Rahman et al. have proposed a multistage scheme in [11] to recognize Bangla alphabetic characters.

For online handwriting recognition, researchers have done works on Devanagari [13] and English [12] to list a few. In contrary, the progress on Bangla script is still infant stage. Roy et al. has defined handwritten information as a collection of pen trip positions that are collected by using any pen position sensor. Authors have used features in their experiment by tracking sequential and dynamic information from pen movements on the writing pads. They have used this feature for character recognition by both holistic [15] and stroke based approach [14]. The different feature extraction strategies proposed by Sen et al. for the recognition of online handwritten Bangla characters includes hausdorff distance based features [18], area and some local features generated after quad-tree based image segmentation technique [17].

3   Dataset

Building dataset is pre-requisite and plays an important role in any research work and this dataset always need to uphold real world varieties to aid in the development of robust systems. In the present experiment, online handwritten

Bangla character database is considered. The Bangla character database contains 11 vowels and 39 consonants. The collected characters are presented in Table 1.

Table 1. Collected Bangla alphabets.

Data Type	Characters
Vowel	অ, আ, ই, ঈ, উ, ঊ, ঋ, এ, ঐ, ও, ঔ
Consonant	ক, খ, গ, ঘ, ঙ, চ, ছ, জ, ঝ, ঞ, ট, ঠ, ড, ঢ, ণ, ত, থ, দ, ধ, ন, প, ফ, ব, ভ, ম, য, র, ল, শ, ষ, স, হ, ড়, ঢ়, য়, ৎ, ং, ঃ, ঁ

The writers were given data collection forms as shown in Fig. 3. The forms were placed on a iball Take Note A414 to collect the character information in online mode as well as to provide a writing board to make the writers feel natural. Writers were aged in between 18–40 years and the number of sets varied from writer to writer. An ultimate dataset of 15000 characters were put together with the aid of the writers having 300 instances of each character.

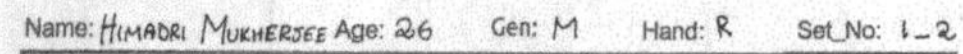

Fig. 3. A filled up data collection form.

4   Proposed Method

4.1   Preprocessing

During data collection it was observed that there were scribbles at times which were first removed. Then the characters were separated using a semi automatic approach for offline mode recognition. There were various noises like minute ink spills and stains which were not removed to ensure real world scenario.

As for the online recognition, the characters were generated by joining the sample points as obtained from the Take Note. We had used a digital differential analysis-based approach [10] for generating the strokes which were then joined to form the characters. The offline and online version of an alphabet is presented in Fig. 4.

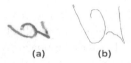

(a)   (b)

Fig. 4. The online and offline version of a single character.

4.2   Deep Learning-Based Classification

Deep learning [8] has recently gained much popularity in the field of machine learning. It has demonstrated merit in solving disparate pattern recognition problems. In this experiment, we have used deep learning-based classification with the aid of convolutional neural network [9]. The data are first fed to a 32 filter convolution layer which used a convolution size of 5 with a ReLU activation function as detailed in Eq. 1. The result of this layer is passed on to a pooling layer where maxpooling is performed on a window size of 3. Next the data are passed to a second convolution layer of 16 filters having the same activation function with a convolution size of 3. The output of this layer is again pooled which is then fed to a fully connected layer of 256 dimensions and finally to a 50 dimensional output layer having a softmax activation as pre-set as presented in Eq. 2. The network structure along with its parameters were set based on experimental trials. The used CNN architecture is illustrated in 5.

$$f(x) = max(0, x), \tag{1}$$

here, x is the input to a neuron.

$$\sigma(z)_j = \frac{e^{z_j}}{\sum_{k=1}^{K} e^{z_k}}, \tag{2}$$

where z is an input vector of length K.

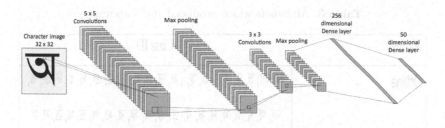

Fig. 5. Architecture of CNN used in the experiment.

5   Result and Discussion

The offline as well as the processed online versions of the dataset were fed to the CNN-based classifier. The network was tested with both 5 and 10-fold cross validation for different training iterations whose results are tabulated in Table 2.

Table 2. Obtained accuracies for online and offline data using different training epochs.

Online			
Training epochs	100	200	300
5 Fold cross validation	99.36	99.39	99.45
10 Fold cross validation	99.89	**99.92**	99.90
Offline			
5 Fold cross validation	99.56	99.52	99.42
10 Fold cross validation	99.89	99.80	99.91

It is observed from the Table that the best result for offline recognition (99.91%) was obtained with 300 training iterations and 10 fold cross validation. In case of online recognition, the best result (99.92%) was obtained for when 10 fold cross validation scheme was applied with 200 iteration. This is also the overall highest in our experiment. The alphabets which were classified with 100% accuracy is presented in Table 3.

The highest misclassifications both in the case of online and offline recognition occurred for শ. In the case of offline recognition, 6 instances of শ were misclassified out of which 4 were misclassified as প. The remaining 2 were classified as স and ষ respectively.

In the case of online recognition, only 4 instances of class 18 were misclassified as class প thereby demonstrating an improvement in performance over the offline scheme. This confusion is mainly due to the similarity of the type of strokes of these classes.

Table 3. Alphabets which produced 100% accuracy.

Method	Class ID
Offline	অ, আ, ঢ়, ব, ভ, ঃ, চ, ছ˝, দ, ড, ঢ, ধ, ড়, এ, ঞ, ঘ, হ, ঈ, জ, ঝ, ক, খ, ৎ, ল, ম, ণ, ষ, ন, ঐ, ঙ, প, ফ, র, খ, শ, ত, থ, ঠ, য়, য
Online	অ, আ, ঢ়, ৎ, ব, ভ, ঃ, ছ˝, ড, ঢ, ধ, ড়, এ, ঞ, ই, ঈ, জ, ঝ, ক, খ, ৎ, ল, ম, ষ, ন, ঙ, ঐ, ঙ, প, ফ, র, স, শ, ট, ত, থ, ঠ, ঙ, উ, য়, য

6   Conclusion

In this paper, we have classified handwritten Bangla isolated characters both in online as well as offline mode. The experiments had been performed on a single database and the best result was obtained for online mode. In future, we will experiment on a larger dataset comprising of compound characters as well. We will also experiment with a deeper network architecture. We also plan to test the performance of other approaches available in literature for the task of character identification. The system will also be extended towards recognition of words and sentences. Finally, we will test the performance of the system with extremely noisy data which is often the case in real world scenario.

Acknowledgement. The authors would like to thank SERB, DST for financial support in the form of project.

References

1. Lian, K.-Y., Hsiao, S.-J., Sung, W.-T.: Home Safety Handwritten Pattern Recognition System
2. Govindan, V.K., Shivaprasad, A.P.: Feature extraction methods for character recognition'a survey. Pattern Recogn. **29**(4), 641–662 (1996)
3. Uchida, S., Sakoe, H.: A survey of elastic matching techniques for handwritten character recognition. IEICE Trans. Inf. Syst. **E88–D(8)**, 1781–1790 (2005)
4. Camastra, F.: SVM-based cursive character recognizer. Pattern Recogn. **40**, 3721–3727 (2007)
5. LeCun, Y., Bottou, L., Bengio, Y., Haffner, P.: Gradient-based learning applied to document recognition. Proc. IEEE **86**(11), 2278–2324 (1998)
6. Sethi, I.K., Chatterjee, B.: Machine recognition of constrained handprinted Devanagari. Pattern Recogn. **9**(2), 69–75 (1977)
7. Dutta, A.K., Chaudhuri, S.: Bengali alpha-numeric character recognition using curvature features. Pattern Recogn. **26**, 1757–1770 (1993)

8. LeCun, Y., Bengio, Y., Hinton, G.: Deep learning. Nature **521**(7553), 436 (2015)
9. Krizhevsky, A., Sutskever, I., Hinton, G.E.: Imagenet classification with deep convolutional neural networks. In: Advances in Neural Information Processing Systems, pp. 1097–1105 (2012)
10. Harris, R.H., Owen, P.L.: U.S. Patent No. 3,564,223. Washington, DC: U.S. Patent and Trademark Office (1971)
11. Rahman, A.F.R., Rahman, R., Fairhurst, M.C.: Recognition of handwritten Bengali characters: a novel multistage approach. Pattern Recogn. **35**, 997–1006 (2002)
12. Agarwal, S., Kumar, V.: Online character recognition. In: Proceedings of the 3rd International Conference on Information Technology and Applications, pp. 698–703 (2005)
13. Connell, S.D., Sinha, R.M.K., Jain, A.K.: Recognition of unconstrained online Devanagari characters. In: 15th international conference on Pattern Recognition, pp. 368–371 (2000)
14. Roy, K.: Stroke-database design for online handwriting recognition in Bangla. Int. J. Modern Eng. Res. **2012**, 2534–2540 (2012)
15. Roy, K., Sharma, N., Pal, U.: Online Bangla handwriting recognition system. In: International Conference on Advances in Pattern Recognition, pp. 117–122 (2007)
16. Dutta, K., Krishnan, P., Mathew, M., Jawahar, C.V.: Offline handwriting recognition on Devanagari using a new benchmark dataset. In: 2018 13th IAPR International Workshop on Document Analysis Systems (DAS), pp. 25–30. IEEE (2018)
17. Sen, S., Mitra, M., Chowdhury, S., Sarkar, R., Roy, K.: Quad-tree based image segmentation and feature extraction to recognize online handwritten Bangla characters. In: 7th IAPR TC3 Workshop on Artificial Neural Networks in Pattern Recognition, Ulm, Germany, pp. 246–256 (2016)
18. Sen, S., Sarkar, R., Roy, K., Hori, N.: Recognize online handwritten Bangla characters using Hausdorff distance based feature. In: 5th International Conference on Frontiers in Intelligent Computing: Theory and Application, pp. 541–549 (2016)

Super Resolution Land Cover Mapping Using Deep Multi Scale Residual Dense Network

D. Synthiya Vinothini[(⊠)], B. Sathya Bama, Nirmal Selva, and Naveen Kumar

Thiagarajar College of Engineering, Madurai 625015, Tamilnadu, India
{synthiya,sbece}@tce.edu, {nirmal,naveenkumar}@student.tce.edu

Abstract. Super Resolution Mapping (SRM) is a land cover mapping method that generates land surface cover maps at fine spatial resolution from a coarse spatial resolution Remote Sensing (RS) image. Recently deep networks have shown impressive performance for image super resolution and image segmentation. Inspired by this performance a deep Multi-Scale Residual Dense Network (MSRDN) is proposed for SRM application of satellite data which extracts hierarchical features that can efficiently map sub-pixels to an accurate class. A MSRDN network is trained with coarse resolution images and its corresponding fine resolution class cover patches to learn a super resolution mapping of land cover. The accuracy of the Conventional SRM techniques is restricted by the performance of soft classification methods. Hence this work utilizes the full power of deep learning to generate a fine resolution land cover map directly from a coarse resolution image neglecting the intermediate soft classification result. The results of the experiments show that MSRDN can become a best alternative to the conventional SRM techniques, to generate a precise land cover information directly from a coarse data.

Keywords: Super Resolution Mapping · Class proportion image · Coarse resolution · Fine resolution · Land cover class

1 Introduction

Whenever Land and Land cover is being spoken of, there is often a propensity to disregard the fact that it is a natural resource too, that needs preservation and wise usage. It is a limited resource we cannot afford to take lightly. Since most of the land cover is frequently being lost to floods, erosion, deforestation, overgrazing and other such adversities, effective Land cover monitoring is a subject of eternal importance, for its sustainable usage which requires accurate land cover mapping.

Accurate land cover mapping has important significance in multiple remote sensing applications like wetland inundation [1], urban floods map [2], city planning, environmental assessment and monitoring, land surface change detection, etc. But land cover mapping of remotely sensed imagery always suffers from a bottle neck of mixed-pixel problem especially when obtained from a coarse resolution sensor. Hard classification usually neglects this and consider only one class per pixel thus losing significant class

© Springer Nature Singapore Pte Ltd. 2020
R. V. Babu et al. (Eds.): NCVPRIPG 2019, CCIS 1249, pp. 498–507, 2020.
https://doi.org/10.1007/978-981-15-8697-2_47

covers. Soft classification considers this mixed pixel problem and provides a convenient method to estimate the proportion of different classes within a mixed pixel. The core of Super Resolution Mapping (SRM) stems from the concept of dividing pixel into sub-pixels, thereby increasing the number of pixels per unit area providing a more useful High-Resolution Map for a coarse resolution image.

1.1 Related Works

Many SRM methods have been a proven method to address the mixed pixel problem. The most prevalent technique that addresses the mixed pixel problem is based on maximum spatial affinity model [3] in which a coarse mixed pixel is subdivided into subpixels. Each subpixel is assigned a class value such that it increases the spatial attractiveness within the pixel and its neighboring subpixels. This spatial affinity may be estimated at sub-pixel level [3], sub-pixel/pixel level [4, 5] or multiple levels [6, 7]. These spatially attractive models have been extensively used in SRM, but they are not appropriate for representing complex land cover structures like highly disjoint lands [8] also the model employed and the soft classifier used impacts the quality of the generated map strongly [9].

Many learning based SRM models have been developed to overcome the difficulty associated with explicit spatial dependency of land cover. These algorithms learn from an available fine resolution map. It works on the assumption that the coarse class proportion is related to the fine resolution map [8], thus the model learns this relationship from the available data to yield a SR map from a coarse class proportion image. These learning models can also be present as isolated ones or in fusion with another model. Learning models like back-propagation neural networks [10] and support vector regression [11] have been modelled to learn this relationship. Many hybrid learning models have also been developed to serve this purpose. Integration of Back Propagation Neural Network with Genetic Algorithm [1] for Super Resolution Mapping of Wetland Inundation wherein, a fusion of the GA and BPNN is present to ultimately perform SRM. The datasets used for this particular work were obtained from LANDSAT - TM/ETM Satellites, captured over two regions namely, Poyanghu in China and the Macquarie Marshes in Australia. This work was focused on Marshy Area mapping, and further works went on to explore the possibilities of Land Cover Mapping [12] as well as Urban Flood Mapping [2]. But practically its performance is limited in learning the complex non-linear relationships.

Currently in many computer vision and remote sensing applications Deep learning models have shown remarkable performance by learning the non-linear relationship between various parameters. One such work focused on Deep Learning for SRM is DeepSRM [13] that learns the non-linear relation between fraction classes and fine resolution map. But this class proportion is not readily available and not always reliable. Though SRM techniques yield enhanced class cover map with coarse class proportion image, its accuracy is always defined by the accuracy of the soft classification algorithm.

The implementation of Deep Learning in obtaining Super Resolution Maps (SRMap) is a domain which is still in the incubator, not many works have been reported in this regard, but a few, only in the recent past. Thus, a paradigm shift, leading to the development and application of various algorithms in SRM, became the primal subject of research. In this paper Deep Learning is implemented to learn a Multi-Scale Residual

Dense Network for SRM application to obtain High Resolution Maps directly from LR images as a single step process. Our work is devoted towards the induction of only Deep Learning in obtaining HRM, thereby excluding the possible use of class proportion data.

1.2 Contribution

Remarkable success in deep learning technology has led to the development of many computer vision task including Super resolution and image semantic segmentation to achieve greater heights. But very few networks have been reported for SRM application. Inspired by the performance of the Residual Dense Network (RDN) for image super resolution [14], this work adopts the RDN model to generate SRmap by exploiting the hierarchical features. Conventional SRM algorithms use class proportion data for mapping and its performance relies on the accuracy of the soft classification algorithm that gives the class proportion data. DeepSRM [13], the first paper on deep learning for SRM application also make use of this class proportion data. But the proposed work MSRDN, extracts multi scale features and does not rely on the accuracy of the output of soft classification but rather takes the full advantage of deep learning to yield an accurate land cover class map directly from a coarse image.

1.3 Organization

The rest of this paper is organized as follows. Section 2 introduces the proposed Multi-Scale Residual Dense Network for SRM. This section deals in detail about the network architecture and the process flow involved in training, testing and land cover generation. Section 3 presents the experimental results, quality measurements and its analysis. Finally, Sect. 4 concludes with a brief summary.

2   MSRDN: Multi-scale Residual Dense Network for SRM

Super Resolution Mapping generates a High-Resolution land cover information C_i, given a Low-Resolution image 'y', where C is a binary image representing the presence of ith land cover class. The proposed model is trained to accurately generate the land cover information. This involves three steps: Dataset pre-processing, Training the MSRDN net, SRmap generation. Figure 1 show an overview of our proposed method for network training and SR land cover map generation.

2.1 Data Pre-processing

Generally Remote Sensing (RS) image data are too large to be processed by a network model in a single pass. The minimum dimension of the image data tile from the dataset Vaihingen provided by ISPRS is 2336 × 1281, which is way too large for a network's input considering the GPU memory limitations. The other constraint is the limited availability of RS data along with its ground truth, whereas a deep network requires more data for training. Considering both the GPU memory limitation and more training data requirement the available large dataset tile and its corresponding ground truth information is divided into smaller overlapping patches with a simple sliding window. Now it is possible to process the entire large data linearly. The dataset consists of classified map for a remotely sensed image. The image is down-sampled to give a coarse image 'y'. The training pair $\{y^p, C_i^p\}_{p=1}^P$ is generated by dividing into 'P' patches, the coarse image and its corresponding HR classified map.

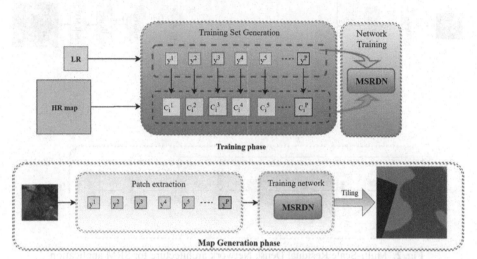

Fig. 1. Overview of Multi-Scale Residual Dense Network model for SRM application

2.2 MSRDN Network Training

The Fig. 2 shows the architecture of Multi Scale Residual Dense Network (MSRDN) comprising of Residual Dense Blocks (RDB) [14] at multiple scales as the name suggests, which extracts features at multiple level. The network is composed of three steps: **Shallow feature extraction** (F_{SF}) from two successive convolution blocks containing Convolution, Batch Normalization and Relu layers, **Dense feature extraction** (F_{Di}) at multiple scales by making use of the RDB Blocks and the Transition Upscaling (TU) Blocks. F_{SF} is fed as the input to both the stages and the presence of multiple stages can be justified by the order in which the TU Block and RDB blocks are brought to the vicinity of the shallow feature input. Either upscaling is followed by feeding of the corresponding output to the RDB Block or vice-versa. Finally, the **fusion of multi-scale dense features** (F_{MSD}) by concatenation followed by dropout layer.

Let y_m be the input image patch for the network.

$$F_{SF} = H_{SFE}(y_m) \tag{1}$$

where H_{SFE} represents shallow feature extraction. F_{SF}, is the input to both the stages of the MSRDN net. First stage comprises of the entry of F_{SF} into the RDB Block (H_{RDB}) after which upscaling is performed by TU Block (H_{TU}). The swapping of these events occurs at the second stage. The TU block consists of convolution layer with stride '2' to upsample the input feature by a factor of '2'.

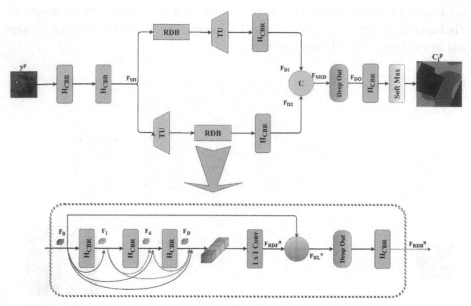

Fig. 2. Multi-Scale Residual Dense Network architecture for SRM application

RDB block comprises of residual connection of dense block, dense feature fusion (F_{RDF}) and residual learning. The input to RDB block is denoted as F_0 and the functionality of nth stage RDB is represented as follows

$$F_{RDB}^n = H_{RDB}(F_0) \tag{2}$$

The dense block constitutes of dense connection of d convolution blocks.

$$F_{RDF}^n = H_{RDF}([F_0, F_1, F_d, \ldots F_D]); (1 <= d <= D) \tag{3}$$

where [..] represents concatenation of the features, H_{RDF} represents the functionality of fusion of dense feature within RDB block. The features from d convolution blocks are concatenated and are subjected to a 1×1 convolution layer. F_d is the output of dth convolution block of RDB block. Each convolution block consists of a convolution layer followed by Batch normalization and RELU layer and its functionality is denoted by H_{CBR}.

$$F_d = H_{CBR}([F_0, F_1, .., F_{d-1}]) \tag{4}$$

The residual learning feature (F_{RL}) is the sum of the input feature F_0 and residual dense feature F_{RDF}. This is followed by dropout layer (H_{DO}) and a convolution block (H_{CBR}).

$$F_{RL}^n = F_{RDF}^n + F_0 \tag{5}$$

$$F_{RDB}^n = H_{CBR}\left(H_{DO}\left(F_{RL}^n\right)\right) \qquad (6)$$

The outputs of both the stages are marked as F_{D1} and F_{D2} respectively. F_{D1} is the upscaled residual dense feature, whereas F_{D2} is the residual dense feature of the upscaled shallow feature.

$$F_{D1} = H_{CBR}(H_{TU}(H_{RDB}(F_{SH}))) \qquad (7)$$

$$F_{D2} = H_{CBR}(H_{RDB}(H_{TU}(F_{SH}))) \qquad (8)$$

After which fusion of F_{D1} and F_{D2} by concatenation is performed and F_{MSD} is obtained. The dropout layer receives F_{MSD}, which aids in removal of the correlated features and prevents overfitting of the network. Finally

$$F_{MSD}=[F_{D1}, F_{D2}] \qquad (9)$$

$$C_m = H_{CBR}(H_{DO}(F_{MSD})) \qquad (10)$$

3 Experimental Results and Discussion

This section analyzes the performance of the proposed network. It includes dataset description, the experimental setup used for training the network and finally the evaluation of the network and discussion on the results.

3.1 Dataset Description

This work uses the standard dataset provided by ISPRS covered over Vaihingen, Germany. The data set is associated with 33 patches of different dimensions with an average dimension of 2064 × 2494 and each of them corresponds to True OrthoPhoto (TOP), extracted from the larger TOP mosaic. The TOP and its ground truth arc 9 cm which corresponds to both the ground sampling distance. TOP contains three bands *viz.*, Near infrared, red and green bands. Dataset have defined six categories *viz.*, Impervious surfaces, building, low vegetation, tree, car and clutter.

3.2 Experimental Setup

Stochastic gradient descent (SGD) algorithm is used to minimize the objective function. The SGD weight decay is set to 10^{-7}, momentum to 0.9 and mini-batch size to 16. The network training is done for 100 epochs and 544 iterations per epoch. The initial learning rate was set to 0.1 and decreased by a factor 10 at every 20 epochs and trained with NVIDIA GeForce GTX 1050 Ti GPU.

3.3 Network Evaluation

A total of 33 data patches is split into 60/40% for training and testing with 20 and 13 patches respectively. The training set is limited for training deep network hence the data patches are divided into overlapping patches with a stride of 70 and a uniform patch dimension of 128 × 128 resulting in 8754 and 5767 disjoint training and testing patches. The TOP data is further downsampled at fds = 2. The network parameters *viz.*, the number of convolution layers (D) in the RDB dense block and the growth rate (G) is set to D = 3 and G = 16.

The network evaluation is done by comparing it with Unet [15] and Segnet [16] based segmentation model. Since conventional SRM models use soft classified result as an input for mapping, this work finds it meaningful in using a modified semantic segmentation network for comparison. In this regard image segmentation models used for Remote sensing images are modified by including an extra decoding layer at the end to increase the resolution of segmentation result thus resulting in a SRmap. The comparative results of super resolution mapping networks are shown in Fig. 3. It is obvious from the observed result that proposed MSRDN has performed better than the Unet and Segnet.

3.4 Quality Metrics

The assessment is performed using the following quality metrics: Accuracy, IoU accuracy, and weighted IoU. Accuracy is the ratio of correctly classified pixels to the total number of pixels in that class, according to the ground truth.

$$Accuracy\ Score = \frac{TP}{TP + FN} \tag{11}$$

For the aggregate data set, Mean Accuracy is the average Accuracy of all classes in all images. Intersection over Union (IoU) accuracy is the ratio of correctly classified pixels to the number of ground truth and predicted pixels in that class *i.e.*,

$$IoU\ Score = \frac{TP}{TP + FP + FN} \tag{12}$$

where TP, FP and FN are the number of True Positives, False Positives and False Negatives. Weighted-IoU is the Average IoU of each class, weighted by the number of pixels in that class. This metric is useful when images have disproportionally sized classes, to reduce the impact of errors in the small classes on the aggregate quality score (Table 1).

3.5 Robustness to Ambiguities and Mislabeled Ground Truth

In the ISPRS dataset the provided ground truth suffers from few uncertainties resulting in erroneous labeled data. The ambiguities arise due to missing some objects while labelling, sharp transitions in labelled data for unsharp true data. This has led the trained network to overfit and misclassify compared with the ground truth but actually the network has performed better than the ground truth. This is obvious in Fig. 4. To explain

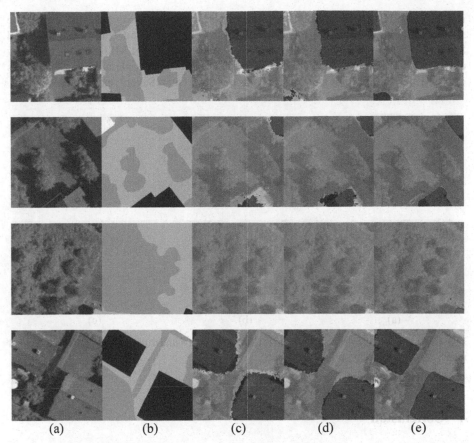

(a)   (b)   (c)   (d)   (e)

Fig. 3. Comparative results of super resolution mapping networks. Patches from (a) TOP, (b) HR ground truth, (c) Unet results overlayed, (d) Segnet results overlayed, and (e) MSRDN (proposed) results overlayed.

Table 1. Results on ISPRS Vaihingen dataset.

Methods	Global accuracy	Mean accuracy	Mean IoU	Weighted IoU	Training time (sec)
Unet	0.7389	0.6568	0.4021	0.4985	31149
Segnet	0.7564	0.6729	0.4356	0.5687	26517
MSRDN (proposed)	0.7732	0.7181	0.5281	0.6462	21093

better, there is visible presence of an impervious surface at the western corner of the true image (TOP) in Fig. 4(a). Ironically, the Ground Truth displays it as a part of low vegetation whereas the Unet and Segnet results map it as a building rather than labeling it as an impervious surface. In the second case of ambiguity, two small buildings at the southern end in the True Image have been missed out by Ground Truth while Unet and Segnet has mapped it along with the low vegetation cover but MSRDN has correctly classified as building. The labeling in such scenarios is perfect pertaining to the results of the MSRDN, dethroning the errors committed by Unet, Segnet and Ground Truth.

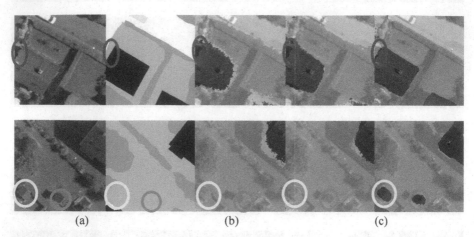

(a)   (b)   (c)

Fig. 4. Ambiguous results. Patches from (a) TOP, (b) HR ground truth, (c) Unet results (d) Segnet results, and (e) MSRDN (proposed) results

4   Conclusion

Super Resolution Mapping (SRM) is a land cover mapping method that generates land surface cover maps at fine spatial resolution from a coarse spatial resolution Remote Sensing (RS) image. The performance of conventional SRM techniques is limited by the accuracy of the soft classifier result, thus this work proposes a novel method fully utilizing the power of deep learning to learn a non-linear relationship that exist between the coarse resolution image and high-resolution map. In this regard, a deep Multi-Scale Residual Dense Network (MSRDN) is proposed for SRM application of satellite data which extracts hierarchical features that can efficiently map sub-pixels to an accurate class. This network is trained with coarse resolution image and a fine resolution map patches to learn a super resolution mapping of land cover. The results of the experiments show that the proposed network provides an alternate solution to conventional SRM techniques, in generating a precise land cover information directly from low resolution images.

References

1. Li, L., Chen, Y., Xu, T., Liu, R., Shi, K., Huang, C.: Super-resolution mapping of wetland inundation from remote sensing imagery based on integration of back-propagation neural network and genetic algorithm. Remote Sens. Environ. **164**, 142–154 (2015)

2. Li, L., et al.: Enhanced super-resolution mapping of urban floods based on the fusion of support vector machine and general regression neural network. IEEE Geosci. Remote Sens. Lett. (2019)

3. Thornton, M.W., Atkinson, P.M., Holland, D.A.: Sub-pixel mapping of rural land cover objects from fine spatial resolution satellite sensor imagery using super-resolution pixel-swapping. Int. J. Remote Sens. **27**(3), 473–491 (2006)

4. Ling, F., Du, Y., Li, X.D., Li, W.B., Xiao, F., Zhang, Y.H.: Interpolation-based super-resolution land cover mapping. Remote Sens. Lett. **4**(7), 629–638 (2013)

5. Mertens, K.C., De Baets, B., Verbeke, L.P.C., De Wulf, R.R.: A sub-pixel mapping algorithm based on sub-pixel/pixel spatial attraction models. Int. J. Remote Sens. **27**(15), 3293–3310 (2006)

6. Ling, F., Du, Y., Li, X.D., Zhang, Y.H., Xiao, F., Fang, S.M., Li, W.B.: Superresolution land cover mapping with multiscale information by fusing local smoothness prior and downscaled coarse fractions. IEEE Trans. Geosci. Remote Sens. **52**(9), 5677–5692 (2014)

7. Chen, Y.H., Ge, Y., Chen, Y., Jin, Y., An, R.: Subpixel land cover mapping using multiscale spatial dependence. IEEE Trans. Geosci. Remote Sens. **56**(9), 5097–5106 (2018)

8. Ling, F., et al.: Learning-based superresolution land cover mapping. IEEE Trans. Geosci. Remote Sens. **54**(7), 3794–3810 (2016)

9. Muad, A.M., Foody, G.M.: Impact of land cover patch size on the accuracy of patch area representation in hnn-based super resolution mapping. IEEE J. Sel. Top. Appl. Earth Observ. Remote Sens. **5**(5), 1418–1427 (2012)

10. Zhang, L.P., Wu, K., Zhong, Y.F., Li, P.X.: A new sub-pixel mapping algorithm based on A BP neural network with an observation model. Neurocomputing **71**(10–12), 2046–2054 (2008)

11. Zhang, Y.H., Du, Y., Ling, F., Fang, S.M., Li, X.D.: Example-based super-resolution land cover mapping using support vector regression. IEEE J. Sel. Top. Appl. Earth Observ. Remote Sens. **7**(4), 1271–1283 (2014)

12. Yang, X., Xie, Z., Ling, F., Li, X., Zhang, Y., Zhong, M.: Spatio-temporal super-resolution land cover mapping based on fuzzy C-means clustering. Remote Sens. **10**(8), 1212 (2018)

13. Ling, F., Foody, G.M.: Super-resolution land cover mapping by deep learning. Remote Sens. Lett. **10**(6), 598–606 (2019)

14. Zhang, Y., Tian, Y., Kong, Y., Zhong, B., Fu, Y.: Residual dense network for image super-resolution. In: Proceedings of the IEEE Conference on Computer Vision and Pattern Recognition, pp. 2472–2481 (2018)

15. Ronneberger, O., Fischer, P., Brox, T.: U-net: convolutional networks for biomedical image segmentation. In: Navab, N., Hornegger, J., Wells, W.M., Frangi, A.F. (eds.) MICCAI 2015. LNCS, vol. 9351, pp. 234–241. Springer, Cham (2015). https://doi.org/10.1007/978-3-319-24574-4_28

16. Audebert, N., Le Saux, B., Lefèvre, S.: Semantic segmentation of earth observation data using multimodal and multi-scale deep networks. In: Lai, S.-H., Lepetit, V., Nishino, K., Sato, Y. (eds.) ACCV 2016. LNCS, vol. 10111, pp. 180–196. Springer, Cham (2017). https://doi.org/10.1007/978-3-319-54181-5_12

Fundus Image Quality Assessment Through Analysis of Illumination, Naturalness, and Structure Level

J. Kanimozhi[1]([✉]), P. Vasuki[2], and S. Mohamed Mansoor Roomi[3]

[1] ECE Department, K. L. N. College of Information Technology,
Pottapalayam, Sivagangai District, Tamilnadu, India
kanimozhibalamurugan@gmail.com
[2] ECE Department, Sethu Institute of Technology,
Kariyapatti, Virudhunagar, Tamilnadu, India
vasakime@gmail.com
[3] ECE Department, Thiagarajar College of Engineering,
Madurai, Tamilnadu, India
smmroomi@tce.edu

Abstract. Optical diseases such as diabetic retinopathy, cataract and glaucoma generally have affected a more quantity of the populace international. Image-based medical diagnosis relies upon adequate image quality and clarity. Mostly the fundus image acquisition are more vulnerable to distortions due to changes from a fixed place camera to portable fundus camera. The fundus images are the main tool for many retinal disease analyses. Repeated image acquisition is required for diagnosis because most of the images captured are of low quality. So, the automatic system is needed to evaluate the quality of the fundus image in terms of illumination level, naturalness level, and structure level. During the capturing time the Non-mydriatic image quality is more vulnerable to distortions. This kind of image quality distortions is called as generic quality distortions. The proposed work is about classification of the fundus image using the Adaptive Migration Biogeography based Optimization (AMBBO) Algorithm based Radial Basis Function Network (RBFN) where the Fundus Image Quality is assessed through the Analysis of Illumination, Naturalness, and Structure level (FIQAINS) model. Changes have been proposed to the original BBO algorithm since it does not have the intrinsic property of clustering which is necessary in fundus image classification. Hence the modified algorithm is used to classify the fundus image based on the generic illumination feature, the critical naturalness feature and the necessary structure feature. The experimental results that make use of MATLAB tools to accomplish the generic overall quality classification such as sensitivity, specificity, accuracy and AUC and different threshold values from DRIMDB Dataset of fundus images and furthermore discover accept or reject class based on the AMBBO Algorithm.

Keywords: Fundus images · Quality distortions · Illumination · Structure level · Naturalness · AMBBO algorithm

© Springer Nature Singapore Pte Ltd. 2020
R. V. Babu et al. (Eds.): NCVPRIPG 2019, CCIS 1249, pp. 508–526, 2020.
https://doi.org/10.1007/978-981-15-8697-2_48

1 Introduction

The interior facing of the eye taken as image known as Fundus image. For many ocular disease diagnosis purpose, fundus image is a significant tool. To perform diagnosis, from local clinics the captured Fundus images are digitally transmitted to another location. The captured Fundus images suffer from different issues like inappropriate positioning, unacceptable illumination, out-of-focus, field mis-labeling etc. The quality of a fundus image degrades due to these problems making them unsuitable for diagnosis. It repeats acquisition of images that enlarges the burden to patients. Hence an automatic system is desirable during image acquisition to assess the quality of the images.

The Human Visual System (HVS) has many characteristics described that humans can recognize as various patterns such as colour, orientation, contour, motion and frequency variation. Applied to retinal image quality assessment, low-level characteristics of the HVS can extract generic features such as illumination and colour, while high-level characteristics can extract structural features such as vessel edges and macular texture. Apply low-level HVS characteristics to generic quality assessment and propose an integrated HVS-based generic quality assessment and generic quality involves three parameters they are illumination and colour, focus and contrast.

To assist ophthalmologists to detect eye diseases [3], such as age-related macular degeneration [4], glaucoma [5, 6], and diabetic retinopathy [7], an automated retinal image analysis-system is designed. The objective quality evaluation of fundus images plays a major role in automatically selecting diagnosis-accessible fundus images among the outputs of digital fundus images. It is a descendant of subjective quality evaluation. Subjective quality evaluation is done by experienced ophthalmologists who grade the quality of fundus images by comparing differences in the images to be graded with excellent quality images, based on their prior knowledge of excellent image quality. Such prior knowledge is acquired either from the human visual system (HVS), which is a complex biological system.

The rest of the paper is organized as follows Sect. 2 related works describes about retinal fundus images; Sect. 3 describes the proposed algorithm which consists of three parts of fundus image analysis; naturaless, illumination and structure level Sect. 4 presents the result of tests of the proposed work and Sect. 5 presents the discussion and conclusion, respectively.

2 Related Works

Luca Giancardo et al. [1] the retinopathy diagnosis as the characteristics of an image by a human needs the quality assessment for fundus images. The survey of this finds techniques that help to achieve this goal. Here, the datasets of four different types were used. By calculating comparatively easy features and matching them to a model of a good quality image the image quality assessment (QA) approached the problem. Few of the steps fail due to unpredictable results and time needed to position the various structures and the poor image qualities in reality are the main drawbacks.

Shaoze Wang et al. [3] and Kanimozhi J et al. [11] authors aimed to assess the generic quality of retinal images, especially for portable fundus camera applications in non-mydriatic ocular fundus images. An algorithm is proposed to assess image quality using a human vision system-based evaluation of three partial quality factors: illumination and color focus and contrast. In order to assist inexpert individuals in gathering significant and interpretable data with constancy an algorithm is proposed capable of selecting images of fair generic quality.

Coyner AS et al. [4] authors aimed, the image quality and clarity is an adequate than image based medical diagnosis. This important implication is for promising methods such as image analysis based on computer and telemedicine and clinical diagnosis. Here, to automatically assess the quality of fundus images in a representative disease, retinopathy of prematurity (ROP) a convolutional neural network (CNN) is trained. Images were assessed by clinical experts for quality regarding ability to diagnose ROP accurately and were labeled "acceptable" or "not acceptable". The test set accuracy was 89.1% with area under the receiver operating curve and area under precision-recall curves.

Aditya Raj et al. [2] this survey paper discusses about the real-time distortions in fundus image capturing and the fundus image quality affecting factors. The retinal IQA algorithms have been analyzed based on similarity, segmentation and machine learning. It provides the importance, present condition, restrictions and future scope of the retinal IQA research in detail as information.

Michael D. Abràmoff et al. [5] reviewed the retinal imaging and image analysis methods devoted to clinical implications. Here, 3-D OCT (optical coherence tomography) imaging and 2-D retinal imaging methods and procedures are reviewed. All through the paper, characteristics of image analysis, image acquisition, and clinical significance are considered together.

Gajendra Jung Katuwal et al. [8] developed an automatic approach based upon the intrinsic regularity of retinal blood vessels to assess quality of the captured fundus retinal image. A complete quality assessment of a set of fundus images of different fields of an eye and individual quality assessment of a single fundus image are the two ways approached to solve the problem of quality assessment. Using the position of optic disc this method identifies the field and side of the fundus image and the intensity information in two local windows.

Lamiaa Abdel-Hamid et al. [16] author presents a no-reference transform-based Retinal Image Quality Assessment (RIQA) algorithm to evade wrong diagnosis caused by meager quality retinal fundus images and assesses images based on roughness, illumination, homogeneity, field definition and details. For homogeneity assessment, a fundus image saturation channel is utilized beside with wavelet-based features and colour details is utilized to eliminate nonretinal images and roughness and illumination features are used to guarantee sufficient field definition. Thus, the combined features given as an input vector to a classifier to assess the on the whole quality.

F. Shao et al. [9] proposed a fundus image quality classifier via the analysis of illumination, naturalness, and structure level and achieved accuracy of 93.60%

To classify a satellite image BBO Algorithm was modified by V. K. Panchal et al. [21]., and Navdeep Kaur Johal et al. [22], to make the clusters of different classes present in the image. Geographic spreading of animals and birds are studied in Biogeography. An application of biogeography to optimization problems is Biogeography based Optimization (BBO). In BBO, islands are used to represent problem solutions and the emigration and immigration is used to represent allocation of features between solutions. The original population is modified by migration after each generation, rather it is not discarded is one of the characteristic of BBO. To measure the suitability of individual, a habitat is considered for each individual solution In BBO, with a habitat suitability index (HSI), which is same as the fitness of Evolutionary Algorithms. To characterize the habitability of an island, SIV (suitability index variable) is used [15].

Inspired by the classification framework in [9], we have proposed a modified BBO Algorithm as Adaptive Migration Biogeography-Based Optimization (AMBBO) algorithm for Fundus Image Classification where the fundus image quality is assessed through the analysis of illumination, naturalness, and structure level (FIQAINS Model).

3 Proposed Methodology

The Pipeline for Fundus Image Quality Assessment Using AMBBO Algorithm is illustrated in the below Fig. 1. The first process of image quality assessment is pre-processing. Next, the illumination, naturalness and structural level analysis for the preprocessed fundus images are performed. The features taken from these levels are used to determine the overall 'accept' or 'reject' class of a fundus images. The adaptive migration BBO is used for feature selection process.

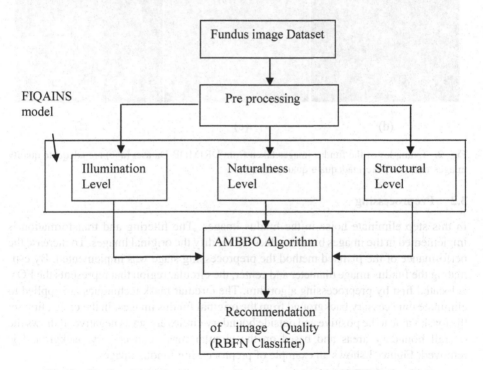

Fig. 1. Pipeline for fundus image quality assessment using AMBBO algorithm

3.1 Fundus Image Dataset

The fundus retinal images are utilized for the assessment of the proposed method which is taken from DRIMDB database for quality recommendation. It has 125 good images, 69 bad images and 22 outlier images with a resolution of 570×760 pixels. Only good and bad images are taken for our work. Good quality images from other publicly available datasets such as Messidor [13] with 1200 images, Drive [17] with 40 images, Stare [19] with 400 images and Chase_DB [18] with 28 images are utilized to evaluate the proposed model (Fig. 2).

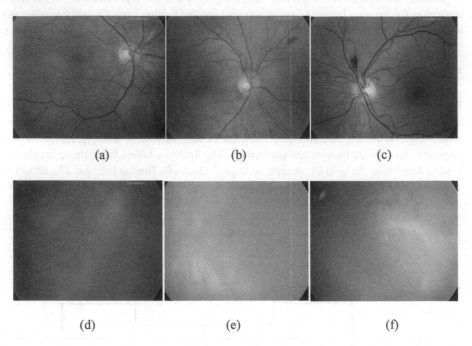

Fig. 2. Examples of the fundus images taken from DRIMDB Dataset (a–c) are adequate quality images and (d–f) are inadequate quality images.

3.2 Preprocessing

In this step eliminate noise in the fundus images. The filtering and transformation is implemented in the images but these does not modify the original images. To increase the performance of the planned method the preprocessing stage was implemented. By estimating the fundus image diameter and center, the circular region that represents the FOV is located first by preprocessing algorithm. The circular mask techniques are applied to eliminate unnecessary background from the original fundus images. In the circle, first set the mask value to be positive and outside boundary circles are set as negative. It draws the overall boundary areas and based on the circular mask unnecessary background is removed. Figure 3 shows an example of preprocessing fundus images.

3.3 Illumination Level

Red, green and blue are the three channels in an acquired fundus color image which concurrently contains the luminosity and color data that are interconnected with each other. The fundus color image is changed into the YUV color space to obtain the color invariant luminance gain matrix, where the luminosity channel (Y) is separated from the two chrominance components (UV) represented by transformation matrix as:

$$\begin{bmatrix} Y \\ U \\ V \end{bmatrix} = \begin{bmatrix} 0.299 & 0.587 & 0.114 \\ -0.147 & -0.289 & 0.436 \\ 0.615 & -0.515 & -0.100 \end{bmatrix} \begin{bmatrix} R \\ G \\ B \end{bmatrix} \tag{1}$$

To differentiate the dark and bright illumination, the defined thresholds denoted as T_{low} and T_{high} using the threshold operation;

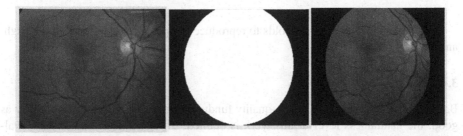

Fig. 3. Example of preprocessing fundus images (a) Original image (b) circle Mask (c) Image masked with Circle

$$M_1(x, y) = \begin{cases} 1, if\ Y(x, y) < T_{low} \\ 0, else \end{cases} \tag{2}$$

$$M_2(x, y) = \begin{cases} 1, if\ Y(x, y) < T_{high} \\ 0, else \end{cases} \tag{3}$$

The following μ_{OD} and μ_{OB} are utilized to measures the ratio of fundus images dark and bright regions and by applying the masks on the components.

$$\mu_{OD} = \frac{1}{W \times H} \sum_{y=1}^{H} \sum_{x=1}^{W} M_1(x, y) \tag{4}$$

$$\mu_{OB} = \frac{1}{W \times H} \sum_{y=1}^{H} \sum_{x=1}^{W} M_2(x, y) \tag{5}$$

Where,
W and H are the processed fundus image width and height.

Moreover, with a size of 9 × 9, the illumination component is separated into numerous un-overlapping patches and to measure the degree of uneven illumination, the average variance among the patches is calculated.

$$\sigma_{UI} = \frac{1}{n \times n} \sum_{i=1}^{n} \sum_{j=1}^{n} (\mu_{i,j} - \overline{\mu})^2 \tag{6}$$

Where,

$\overline{\mu}$ - global image average luminance $\mu_{i,j}$ - the patch average luminance.

Lastly, the illuminance index is determined as

$$S_1 = \begin{cases} 1, & \text{if } \mu_{OD} \leq T_1 \text{ and } \mu_{OB} \leq T_2 \text{ and } \sigma_{UI} \leq T_3 \\ 0, & \text{else} \end{cases} \tag{7}$$

Where,

T1, T2 and T3 are the thresholds to reproduce the power of over dark, over bright and uneven illuminations.

3.4 Naturalness Level

Based on the statement that a high-quality fundus image be supposed to look likely as good, the naturalness level in this work is defined. The good illuminations are evaluated in the naturalness. The Naturalness Image Quality Evaluator (NIQE) compares a default model computed from the images with the calculated no-references image quality score of fundus images. Better perceptual quality indicated from least score. The NIQE is used to remove the noisy and blurry images. The NIQE is transferring the input images into a specified grayscale or RGB images. The NIQE Model object is derived as custom model of image features and natural scene statistics (NSS). The nonnegative scalar output is returned. The distance between the NSS-based features calculated to the features obtained from a fundus image measured by the NIQE algorithm is used to train the model. From high-quality fundus image a perfect multivariate Gaussian (MVG) model is trained. The trained MVG Model is:

$$f(x) = \frac{1}{(2\pi)^{m/2}|\Sigma|^{1/2}} \exp\left(-\frac{1}{2}(x-\mu)^T \Sigma^{-1} (x-\mu)\right) \tag{8}$$

x - feature vector

μ and Σ – mean vector and covariance matrix of x

To train the MVG model, NSS features extracted from patches are evaluated here. To make a confined quality score of patch i, compute the distance between (μ_i, Σ_i) and the pristine MVG model (μ, Σ).

$$q_i = \sqrt{(u - u_i)^T \left(\frac{\Sigma + \Sigma_i}{2}\right)^{-1} (u - u_i)} \tag{9}$$

qNA=47.9991 S2=1   qNA = 67.6078   S2=0   qNA =72.6443 S2=0

Fig. 4. Illustrations with various naturalness quality scores of fundus images.

The image quality is good with a small distance. The on the whole quality score q_{NA} of a fundus retinal image is collected as the average of $\{q_i\}$. At last, the naturalness index is determined by

$$S_2 = \begin{cases} 1 & \text{if } q_{NA} \leq T_4 \\ 0 & \text{else} \end{cases} \tag{10}$$

qNA = 47.9991 S2 = 1 qNA = 67.6078 S2 = 0 qNA = 72.6443 S2 = 0

As exposed by the illustrations in Fig. 4, the trends in quality change reflected basically by the predictable naturalness quality scores.

3.5 Structure Level

The Optic Disc (OD) detection plays a significant role in the retinal fundus image classfication based on quality assessment. The visibility of OD is used to identify the good image quality. Retinal blood vessels converge at the Optic Disc which is a bright yellow disc in the retina. The OD can be located simply in a retinal fundus image from its distinctive features of high-intensity and circular in shape.

The mean value is filled in the backdrop area of the fundus image calculated from the retinal grayscale image. Here, the threshold is set to 10 assuming that the disc position does not emerge at the top and bottom of the retinal fundus image. Blood vessels are detected first from the image, since it is converged at the Optic Disc. For this red and green channels intensity images are computed.

The gobar filter is used for energy information extraction [10, 12, 14]. The computation of the response $S_{\theta,\omega}(x)$ of the gobar filter is

$$S_{\theta,\omega}(x) = g_{\theta,\omega}(x) \otimes I(x) \tag{11}$$

Where, $g_{\theta,\omega}(x)$ is the energy information extracted from gobar filter and $I(x)$ s the input.

Figure 5 shows the illustration of retinal vessels extraction Fig. 5(a) intensity map, Fig. 5(b) response map, Fig. 5(c) PC map, and Fig. 5(d) detected vessels. For the vessel distribution and overall directional characteristic description a simple thresholding operation is performed to obtain binary vessel map. The response map from the image that have problem in serious local quality degradation but extorted PC map is successful in local assessment. By moving a circular mask the intensity map position is obtained. Thus maximum point is chosen as location of OD.

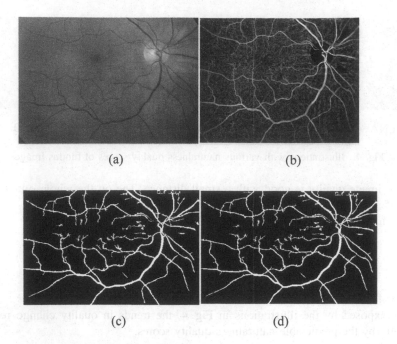

(a)   (b)

(c)   (d)

Fig. 5. Illustration of retinal vessels extraction

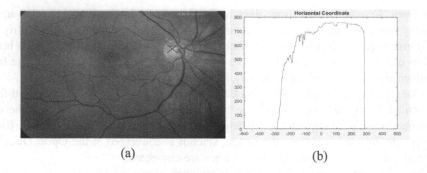

(a)   (b)

Fig. 6. Illustration of OD marked

The Fig. 6 shows the location of OD marked in the image from the maximum point of its horizontal coordinate. Figure 6(a) shows the Optic disk located in the fundus image and Fig. 6(b) shows its horizontal coordinate.

The structure level is used to divide an image into 64 parts of the same size and find out if the OD is situated in the left and right positions of the fundus image. At last the OD structure is determined as

$$S_3 = \begin{cases} 1, & \text{if } O_{OD \in \mathbb{R}} \\ 0, & \text{else} \end{cases} \tag{12}$$

where O_{OD} is the identified location of OD and $\mathbb{R}$ is a set of defining location.

3.6   Recommendation Image Quality

Image with even illumination represented as illumination index $S1 = 1$, Image with high contrast, clear contour, etc., represented as naturalness index $S2 = 1$ and Center of Optics disk located in the defined locations represented as structure (OD location) index $S3 = 1$ based on these illumination index $S1$, naturalness index $S2$ and structure (OD location) index $S3$, we can straightly determine on the whole 'accept' or 'reject' class by

$$S = \begin{cases} 1, & \text{if } S_1 = 1 \& S_2 = 1 \& S_3 = 1 \\ 0, & \text{else} \end{cases} \tag{13}$$

To derive four recommendation indices (0, 1, 2 and 3) based on the perspective of quality recommendation, the grade of recommendation is determined by

$$\gamma = \begin{cases} 0, & \text{if } S_1 = 0 \\ 1, & \text{if } S_1 = 1 \ \& \ S_2 = 0 \\ 2, & \text{if } S_1 = 1 \ \& \ S_2 = 1 \& S_3 = 0 \\ 3, & \text{if } S_1 = 1 \ \& \ S_2 = 1 \& S_3 = 1 \end{cases} \tag{14}$$

For the fundus images with good illumination, the recommendation index ($\gamma = 1$) is calculated, and for the images with good illumination and naturalness, the recommendation indices ($\gamma = 2$) and ($\gamma = 3$) are predicted.

3.7   Biogeography-Based Optimization Algorithm

Migration is a probabilistic operator that adjusts a habitat H. The probability that Hi is modified is proportional to its immigration rate λi, and the probability that the source of the modification comes from Hj is proportional to the emigration rate μj. Migration is defined by

$$Hi(SIV) \leftarrow Hj(SIV) \tag{15}$$

In biogeography, an SIV is a suitability index variable which characterizes the habitability of an island. In BBO, an SIV is a solution feature, equivalent to a "gene" in other population-based optimization algorithm (GAs, for example).

Migration process can be described as follows:

Select Hi with probability based on λi;

If Hi is selected

Select Hj with probability based on µj;

If Hj is selected

Randomly select an SIV s from Hj;

Replace a random SIV in Hi with s;

End

End

Mutation is a probabilistic operator that randomly modifies a habitat's SIV based on the habitat's a priori probability of existence. For classic BBO, the mutation rate m is inversely proportional to the solution probability, which is defined by

$$m = m_{\max}\left(1 - \frac{P}{P_{\max}}\right) \tag{16}$$

Where m max is a user-defined parameter. This mutation scheme tends to increase diversity among the population.

Mutation can be described as follows:

Use λi and µi to update the probability Pi;

Compute mutation probability mi;

Select an SIV s in Hi with probability based on mi;

If Hi(SIV) is selected

Replace Hi(SIV) with a randomly generated SIV s;

End

The basic structure of BBO algorithm is as follows:

Step 1. Initialize the BBO parameters, including the maximum migration rates E and I, the maximum mutation rate mmax, and the minimal emigration rate θ. Migration rate is similar to crossover rate in GAs. Mutation rate is the same as in GAs.

Step 2. Initialize a random set of habitats, each habitat corresponding to a potential solution to the given problem.

Step 3. For each habitat, map the fitness to the number of species k, the immigration rate λk, and the emigration rate µk based on migration models as discussed earlier.

Step 4. Probabilistically use immigration and emigration to modify each habitat based on (28) as discussed, then compute each habitat's fitness.

Step 5. For each habitat, update the probability of its species count using (2.19). Then mutate each habitat based on (2.30), and recompute each habitat's fitness.

Step 6. Go to step 3 for the next iteration. This loop can be terminated after a predefined number of generations, or after an acceptable problem solution has been found.

3.7.1   AMBBO (Adaptive Migration Biogeography-Based Optimization)

The BBO approach has method of sharing information between solutions. The original BBO algorithm does not have the intrinsic property of feature extraction to classify a fundus image for this purpose we proposed a modified form of Biogeography based algorithm to classify the fundus image known as adaptive migration biogeography-based optimization (AMBBO) Algorithm. Here each feature based on the recommendation indices represented as the independent variable is called suitability index variable (SIV) in AMBBO. Based on these modified features, the island suitability index (ISI) also modified, making ISI as the dependent variable. A classification problem with n-SIV (independent variables) and k-ISI (islands or individuals) can be expressed as:

$$ISI_i = f(SIV1, SIV2, \ldots, SIVn\,)i = 1, 2, \ldots, \tag{17}$$

In the AMBBO method, the immigration rate and emigration rate is probabilistically changed according to the difference between the values. The probability for migration is computed based on the difference. From the differences, mean value, minimum value and maximum value of differences are computed. Based on these values the probability of migration is computed. Using the probability value, the new probabilistic immigration rate and probabilistic emigration rate are computed

Algorithm AMBBO Based Fundus Image Classification

Step 1. Get the Fundus image

Step 2. Analyze the fundus image by FIQAINS model i.e., fundus image quality is assessed through the analysis of illumination, naturalness, and structure level

Step 3. Consider Extracted features from illumination, naturalness, and structure level as a species of universal habitat.

Step 4. Consider other habitats even illumination, naturalness quality scores and localization of optic disc as their members.

Step 5. Define HSI, Smax, immigration rate (λ) and emigration rate (μ) as in BBO.

Step 6. Calculate HSI of each feature habitat.

Step 7. (i) Select a species from the Universal Habitat and migrate it to one of the feature habitat.

(ii) the immigration rate and emigration rate is probabilistically changed according to the difference between the values.

Step 8. Using the probability value, the new probabilistic immigration rate and probabilistic emigration rate are computed

Step 9. Recalculate the HSI of feature habitat after the migration of the species to it.

Step 10. If there is any species left in the universal habitat

(i) Go to step 6

Else: Stop the process.

End

Flowchart of AMBBO Algorithm

In this process, after initialize BBO parameters, find the immigration rate, emigration rate and is probabilistically changed according to the difference between the values (Fig. 7).

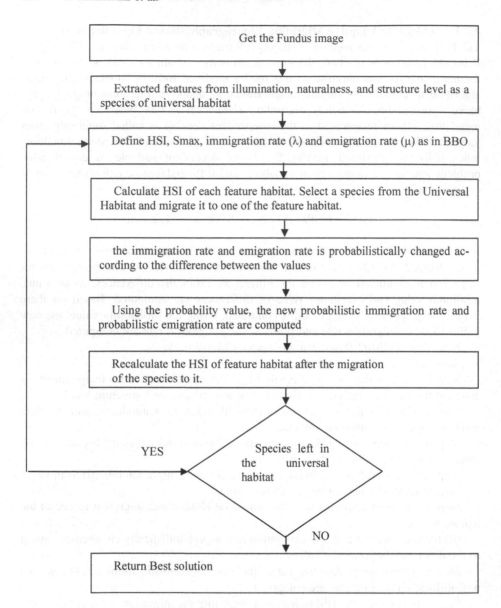

Fig. 7. Flowchart of AMBBO algorithm

3.7.2 Implementation of AMBBO Algorithm

The Adaptive Migration Biogeography based optimization algorithm (AMBBO) is a relationships between the different species located in different fundus regarding migration. The Habitat suitability index are relatively larger number of species. The feature extraction is a type of dimensionality reduction and efficiently representing an images as a compact feature vector. This approach is useful when image sizes are large and reduced feature representation such as image matching and retrieval.

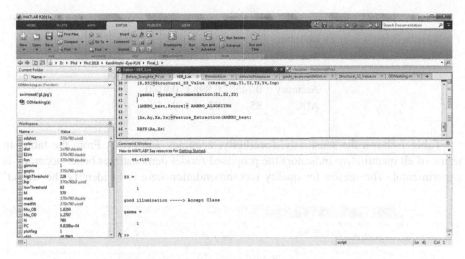

Fig. 8. Implementation Code of AMBBO algorithm

The Fig. 8 above shows the implementation of AMBBO algorithm and feature extraction function to find the good illumination and naturalness images.

4 Experimental Results

The experimental results for the proposed method obtained using MATLAB tools and the performance measures such as sensitivity, accuracy, specificity and roc curve (AUC) are evaluated. The sensitivity represents the correctly identified as 'accept' class and specificity represents the correctly identified as 'reject' class.

$$\text{Sensitivity} = \frac{\text{TP}}{\text{TP} + \text{FN}} \tag{18}$$

$$\text{Specificity} = \frac{\text{TN}}{\text{TN} + \text{FP}} \tag{19}$$

$$\text{Accuracy} = \frac{\text{TN} + \text{FP}}{\text{TN} + \text{TP} + \text{FN} + \text{FP}} \tag{20}$$

4.1 Threshold Determination

The dark and bright images are grouped and thresholds are computed from the average values of illumination for all pixels inside the circular masks of these images. To better illustrate the thresholds T_1, T_2, T_3 and T_4 and accuracy rates is tested to select the optimal threshold. The Fig. 9 shows the different threshold values and the accuracy rates.

Table 1. Performance of partial and overall quality recommendation

Indicator	IL	NA	ST
Sensitivity	0.9668	0.9996	0.9826
Specificity	0.6118	0.9008	0.8724
Accuracy	0.7458	0.8983	0.9140
AUC	85	92	93.5

Table 1 shows the sensitivity, specificity, accuracy and AUC. From the table, in terms of all quantitative indicators the proposed model demonstrates better accuracy is experimental. The reason for quality recommendation here is to identify the 'reject'

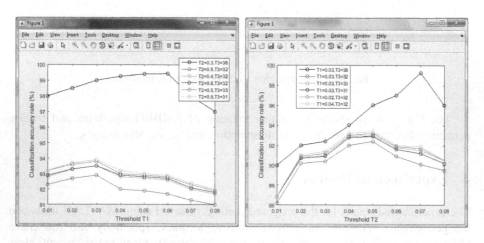

(a)Threshold T1 for Over Dark   (b) Threshold T2 for Over Bright

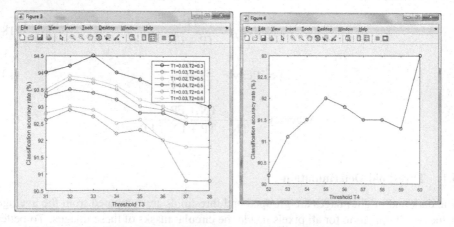

(c) Threshold T3 for Uneven Illumination   (d) Threshold T4 for

Naturalness

Fig. 9. The correlation between various threshold values and the accuracy rates on the database.

retinal images that experience from illumination, naturalness or structure degradations. The Fig. 10 shows the ROC curves of the illumination, the naturalness, the structure level, and the overall, respectively.

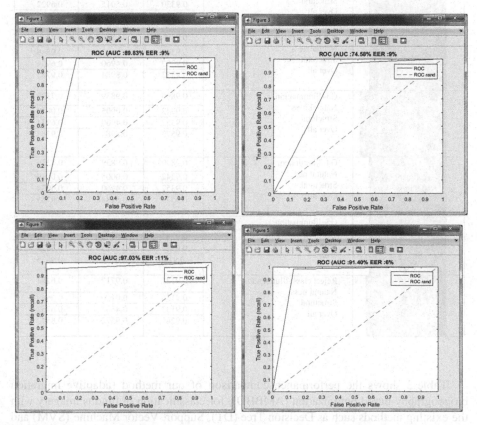

Fig. 10. ROC curves of (a) illumination classification result, (b) naturalness classification result, (c) structure classification result, and (d) overall quality classification result.

The Table 2 shows the accuracy, sensitivity and specificity values for the fundus database images.

Here, G stands for good images and R stands for Reject class images. The illumination, structure, naturalness and overall level are measured for all the images and found that most of the images have good quality.

Table 2. Accuracy, Sensitivity and Specificity of different fundus images in dataset

Image	Data	Accuracy	Sensitivity	Specificity
	G1 –Illumination	0.8958	0.9668	0.6118
	Natural ness	0.9283	0.0005	0.0794
	Structural	0.9330	0.5015	0.6922
	Over all	0.9116	0.8233	0.9675
	G2–Illumination	0.9890	0.9839	0.7336
	Natural ness	0.9342	0.0005	0.0849
	Structural	0.9352	0.4960	0.6934
	Over all	0.9573	0.8984	0.9753
	G3–Illumination	0.9890	0.9839	0.7336
	Natural ness	0.9342	0.0005	0.0849
	Structural	0.9352	0.4960	0.6934
	Over all	0.9573	0.8984	0.9753
	G4–Illumination	0.9890	0.9839	0.7336
	Natural ness	0.9342	0.0005	0.0849
	Structural	0.9352	0.4960	0.6934
	Over all	0.9573	0.8984	0.9753
	G5–Illumination	0.8958	0.9668	0.6118
	Natural ness	0.9283	0.0005	0.0794
	Structural	0.9330	0.5015	0.6922
	Over all	0.9116	0.8233	0.9675
	Reject class–Illumination	0.9121	0.9717	0.6284
	Natural ness	0.9136	0.0120	0.0649
	Structural	0.9133	0.4631	0.6732
	Over all	0.9247	0.9572	0.8540

Table 3 shows the performance comparison of our method (adaptive migration biogeography-based optimization (AMBBO)) for classification of fundus imagery with the existing methods such as Decision Tree (DT), Support Vector Machine (SVM) and Dictionary Learning (DL) on DRIMDB Database [20].

Table 3. Classification results on DRIMDB Database

Model	Sensitivity	Specificity	Accuracy	AUC
DT	97.10%	81.60%	87.11%	86.31%
SVM	94.14%	83.25%	89.58%	88.69%
DL	75.82%	63.30%	71.05%	71.06%
AMBBO	0.8233	0.9675	0.9816	97.03%

Table 4 shows the Predicted Percentage of 'Accept' images on MESSSIDOR, DRIVE, CHASE_DB and STARE Database using AMBBO algorithm.

Table 4. Predicted Percentage of 'Accept' images on MESSSIDOR,DRIVE,CHASE_DB and STARE Database

Database	IL	NA	ST
MESSSIDOR	92.83%	64.00%	95.58%
DRIVE	100.00%	95.00%	97.50%
CHASE_DB	89.29%	71.73%	3.57%
STARE	96.47%	25.44%	40.05%
DRIMBD	98%	96.68%	97.53%

5   Conclusion

In this chapter, we propose Fundus Image Classification using Adaptive Migration Biogeography based Optimization (AMBBO) Algorithm and RBFN neural network classification where the fundus image quality is assessed through the analysis of illumination, naturalness, and structure level termed as FIQAINS model and was tested and assessment results quantitatively confirmed that our proposed algorithm is consistent in terms of repeatability and also achieved high accuracy. Our results sturdily performed well and achieved sensitivity 94.95%, specificity 99.47%, accuracy 97.03% and AUC of 94% for the fundus image classification.

References

1. Giancardo, L., Meriaudeau, F., Karnowski, T., Chaum, E.: Quality assessment of retinal fundus im- ages using elliptical local vessel density. Biomed. Eng. 201–223 (2010)
2. Raj, A., Tiwari, A.K., Martini, M.G.: Fundus image quality assessment: survey, challenges, and future scope. IET Image Process. 13(8), 1211–1224 (2019)
3. Wang, S., Jin, K., Lu, H., Cheng, C., Ye, J., Qian, D.: Human visual system-based fundus image quality assessment of portable fundus camera photographs. IEEE trans. Med. Imaging 35(4), 1046–1055 (2016)
4. Coyner, A.S., et al.: Deep learning for image quality assessment of fundus images in retinopathy of prematurity. In: AMIA Annual Symposium Proceedings (2018)
5. Abràmoff, M.D., Garvin, M.K., Sonka, M.: Retinal imaging and image analysis. IEEE Rev. Biomed. Eng. 3, 169–208 (2011)
6. Liu, S., Faloutsos, C., Galdran, A.: EyeQual: accurate, explainable, retinal image quality assessment. In: 2017 16th IEEE International Conference on Machine Learning and Applications pp-323–340 (2017)
7. Fu, H., et al.: Evaluation of retinal image quality assessment networks in different color-spaces. In: Shen, D., et al. (eds.) MICCAI 2019. LNCS, vol. 11764, pp. 48–56. Springer, Cham (2019). https://doi.org/10.1007/978-3-030-32239-7_6
8. Katuwal, G.J., Kerekes, J., Ramchandran, R., Sisson, C., Rao, N.: Automatic fundus image field detection and quality assessment. IEEE Western New York Image Processing Workshop (WNYIPW) (2013)
9. Shao, F., Yang, Y., Jiang, Q., Jiang, G., Ho, Y.: Automated quality assessment of fundus images via analysis of illumination, naturalness and structure. IEEE Access 6, 806–817 (2018). https://doi.org/10.1109/ACCESS.2017.2776126

10. Kanimozhi, J., Vasuki, P.: Iterative Vessel segmentation with stopping criterion for fundus imagery. Int. J. Sci. Res. Netw. Secur. Commun. (IJSRNSC) 6(3), 6–12 (2018). ISSN 2321-3256

11. Kanimozhi, J., Vasuki, P.: Generic image quality assessment of portable fundus camera photographs. Adv. Nat. Appl. Sci. 11, 34–40 (2017). ISSN 1995-0772, EISSN 1998-1090

12. Kanimozhi, J., Vasuki, P.: Optic disc detection using vessel distributional and directional characteristics in retinal imagery. In: IEEE Sponsored International Conference on Innovations in information Embedded and Communication Systems (ICIIECS) on 17th and 18th March 2017 (2017)

13. Messidor (2008). https://www.messidor.crihan.fr/index en.php

14. Adalarasan, R., Malathi, R.: Automatic detection of blood vessels in digital retinal images using soft computing technique. Mater.: Today Proc. 5(1), 1950–1959 (2018)

15. Sarkar, D., Das, S.: Automated glaucoma detection of medical image using biogeography based optimization. In: Bhattacharya, I., Chakrabarti, S., Reehal, H.S., Lakshminarayanan, V. (eds.) Advances in Optical Science and Engineering. SPP, vol. 194, pp. 381–388. Springer, Singapore (2017). https://doi.org/10.1007/978-981-10-3908-9_46

16. Abdel-Hamid, L., El-Rafei, A., El-Ramly, S., Michelson, G., Hornegger, J.: Retinal image quality assessment based on image clarity and content. J. Biomed. Opt. 21(9), 096007 (2016)

17. Niemeijer M., et al.: DRIVE: digital retinal images for vessel extraction (2004).https://www.isi.uu.nl/Research/Databases/DRIVE

18. CHASE_DB1 Retinal Image Datbase. https://www.idiap.ch/software/bob/docs/bob/bob.db.chasedb1/master/index.html

19. Hoover, A., et al.: Locating blood vessels in retinal images by piece-wise threshold probing of a matched ilter response. IEEE Trans. Med. Imaging 19(3), 203–210 (2000)

20. DRIMDB (Diabetic Retinopathy Images Database) Database for Quality Testing of Retinal Images (2014). https://academictorrents.com/details/99811ba62918f8e73791d21be29dcc372d660305

21. Panchal, V.K., Singh, P., Kaur, N., Kundra, H.: Biogeography based satellite image classification arXiv preprint arXiv:0912.1009 (2009)

22. Johal, N.K., Singh, S., Kundra, H.: A hybrid FPAB/BBO algorithm for satellite image classification. Int. J. Comput. Appl. 6(5), 31–36 (2010)

CaReNet: CapsNet Based Regression Network

Abhinay Badam, Basanta Sharma, Darshan Gera, S. Balasubramanian$^{(\boxtimes)}$,
and Srikanth Khanna

Sri Sathya Sai Institute of Higher Learning, Anantapur, AP, India
abhinayb.sssihl@gmail.com, basantanickal@gmail.com,
{darshangera,sbalasubramanian,srikanthkhanna}@sssihl.edu.in
http://sssihl.edu.in

Abstract. We propose a capsule based regression network (CaReNet),
a framework that is based on capsule networks (CapsNet), rather than
on the conventional convolutional neural networks (CNNs) to determine
estimates of continuous variables. The core principles of CaReNet remain
that of routing-by-agreement and translation equivariance proposed in
the CapsNet architecture for classification problems. However, unlike the
CapsNet architecture, the final layer capsules in CaReNet architecture
capture the number of values to regress in their dimensionality. An output vector returned by each of these capsules contains all the regressed
values while the corresponding activity vector, determined by squashing
an output vector, captures the likelihood of the regressed values being
present in the corresponding capsule. We show that our novel CaReNet
architecture achieves state-of-the-art performance on regressing facial
keypoints from images, an important problem that plays a significant
role in face recognition systems. The performance of CaReNet has been
evaluated on the dataset from Kaggle Facial Keypoints Detection competition. Further, the flexibility in CaReNet architecture allows it to be
easily extendable to any other regression problem such as 3D reconstruction of facial models from 2D images.

Keywords: Capsule networks · Regression · Facial Keypoint Detection

1 Introduction

Given a continuous dependent variable Y and an independent variable X, regression computes the most probable value of Y for each value of X using a finite
set of instances of X and the corresponding instances of Y. Unlike classification
which involves the prediction of a class label, regression involves the prediction of
a continuous variable. Detecting facial keypoints is one such regression problem
that finds its use in tracking and recognizing faces, analyzing facial expressions
and in detecting dysmorphic facial signs for medical diagnosis [4]. CNN-based

Supported by SSSIHL.

R. V. Babu et al. (Eds.): NCVPRIPG 2019, CCIS 1249, pp. 527–536, 2020.
https://doi.org/10.1007/978-981-15-8697-2_49

regression have achieved more accurate and efficient results compared to the traditional methods in the recent past. For example, traditional methods that detect local features in an image for facial keypoint detection fall into local minima due to ambiguous patches in an image [6,13]. Cascading CNNs [10] avoid this problem by using multiple CNNs at various levels to predict and fine tune the values. Data augmentation is also used to obtain better results [5]. However, CNNs are limited by the availability of large number of ground truths. For instance, in facial keypoint detection, some of the ground truth keypoints are not disclosed due to difference of angles in view points. As CNNs are not robust to viewpoint variance, these images can lead to misclassification. Removing these images will also not do good as the training set will become smaller.

Capsule network (CapsNet) [9], is a state-of-the-art method in deep learning, based on the principles of viewpoint equivariance and inverse rendering. It has been proven to work well in the domain of classification such as vehicle type recognition [12], traffic sign recognition [2], fire hazard detection [11], etc. Development work of regression models based on CapsNet has just begun [1], [8]. We propose a general capsule based regression network (CaReNet) for facial keypoint detection. We also highlight the improved accuracy obtained by the proposed method on the Kaggle Facial Keypoints Detection dataset [4]. Section 2 discusses the existing work while Sect. 3 elaborates on the proposed CaReNet architecture. Performance of the proposed method is demonstrated in Sect. 4. Section 5 concludes our work and discusses possible future work.

2   Background

2.1   Limitations of CNN

CNNs have three main limitations: Firstly, they need a large dataset to correctly classify or regress from the given data. Secondly, CNNs achieve positional invariance through max pooling and accurately classify even unknown objects with minor changes in positions compared to the objects in the training set. However, positional invariance can lose a lot of important spatial information leading to misclassification. Thirdly, CNNs are not robust to variances in pose. To overcome these limitations, Hinton et al. [3,9] have come up with the concept of positional and view equivariance through the idea of CapsNet.

2.2   Capsule Networks

A CapsNet is essentially a network of many layers of capsules. Each capsule is a group of neurons. Unlike a neuron in a traditional CNN whose I/O is a scalar, a capsule operates on a vector and squashes it using a non-linear activation.

The magnitude of the squashed output vector quantifies the probability of the feature detected by the respective capsule while the vector's direction represents the state, orientation or any other instantiation parameters of the detected feature.

Sabour et al. [9] proposed a routing-by-agreement algorithm between the layers of capsules to dynamically determine the path taken by the passage of information from one capsule layer to another. For every capsule g_i^l in layer l and capsule g_j^{l+1} in layer $l+1$, a coupling coefficient c_{ij} is iteratively learnt from the agreement between the g_i^l's prediction of g_j^{l+1}'s output and the actual output of g_j^{l+1} (which is captured using cosine similarity).

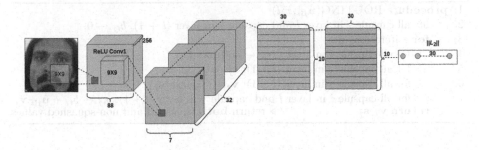

Fig. 1. Our proposed 2D CaReNet encoder architecture.

3   Design of 2DCaReNet for Regressing Facial Keypoints

The architecture of our 2D capsule-based regression network (2D CaReNet) for facial key point detection has an encoder structure (as shown in Fig. 1) with the following layers similar to that in [9]:

1. Convolutional layer: This layer has 256 convolution kernels of size 9×9 with a stride of 1 and ReLU activation unit.
2. PrimaryCapsule layer: This layer is made up of 32 capsules and each capsule has 8 convolutional units with each having a kernel of size 16×16 and stride of 12.
3. RoutingCapsule layer: This layer is made up of ten 30D capsules. Each of the capsules obtains the input from all the capsules in PrimaryCapsules. Further, each capsule outputs a vector that gives the corresponding activity vector of the capsule when squashed using the squash function given in equation. As the length of an activity vector determines the probability that an entity exists at the corresponding capsule, we use the squashed vectors or the activity vectors to determine the most probable capsule to be routed dynamically. The non-squashed values are not used for any other purpose in this layer.
4. DetectionCapsule layer: This layer is also made up of ten 30D capsules and the squashed vectors are used to dynamically determine the capsule to be routed to. Further, in this layer, the **non-squashed vector with the highest length** in the corresponding activity vector is considered as the regressed output vector that captures the expected keypoints in its dimensions. Note

that both the non-squashed values and the squashed values are used here. The squashed values give the probability of routing to a particular capsule (as proposed in CapsNet) while non-squashed values give the expected key points regressed by that capsule(proposed in this work).

Algorithm 1. Routing algorithm

1: **procedure** ROUTING($\hat{\mathbf{u}}_{j|i}, r, l$)
2:    for all capsule i in layer l and capsule j in layer $(l+1)$: $b_{ij} \leftarrow 0$.
3:    **for** r iterations **do**
4:        for all capsule i in layer l: $\mathbf{c}_i \leftarrow$ softmax($\mathbf{b}_i$)
5:        for all capsule j in layer $(l+1)$: $\mathbf{s}_j \leftarrow \sum_i c_{ij} \hat{\mathbf{u}}_{j|i}$
6:        for all capsule j in layer $(l+1)$: $\mathbf{v}_j \leftarrow$ squash($\mathbf{s}_j$)
7:        for all capsule i in layer l and capsule j in layer $(l+1)$: $b_{ij} \leftarrow b_{ij} + \hat{\mathbf{u}}_{j|i}.\mathbf{v}_j$
   return $\mathbf{v}_j, \mathbf{s}_j$ ▷ return **both** squashed and non-squashed values

---

We use routing-by-agreement between PrimaryCapsule layer and the RoutingCapsule layer, and between RoutingCapsule layer and the DetectionCapsule layer. However, unlike the routing algorithm in [9] which returns only the squashed values, our routing algorithm returns **both the squashed values and the non squashed values**. The non-squashed values are used in the final layer, namely, DetectionCapsule layer as the output vectors as explained before.

The loss used to compare the output and the ground truth is MSE instead of the margin loss defined for classification in [9].

The decoder structure is similar to the CapsNet classification architecture as in [9]. The dimensions of the three fully connected layers are 30×1024, 1024×4096 and 4096×9216 respectively. The reconstruction loss is calculated using sum of squared errors (SSE). The over all loss is calculated as in [9]:

$$loss = MSE_{encoder} + 0.00005 * SSE_{decoder} \tag{1}$$

Here, the decoder loss is scaled down by 0.00005 so that the it does not dominate the encoder loss during the training phase. In the absence of scaling, the few regressed points try to decode the whole of the original image leading to an under-fitted model and inaccurate results. On scaling down the decoder loss, the decoder only captures and reconstructs the most relevant features in the original image (just as in [9]).

4 Performance Evaluation

4.1 Dataset

In our implementation of CaReNet for facial keypoints detection, we used the Kaggle dataset [4], a dataset that consists of 7049 96×96 images out of which, only 2140 images have all the 15 key points labelled.

4.2 Training

With the given dataset, we performed three experiments:

1. In the first experiment, we created a test set named, $test_{split}$ containing 100 (i.e 1.5%) of the given 7049 training images with complete labels. This test set was essential for performing quantitative analysis in the evaluation phase as the test images provided by Kaggle do not have any labels. The rest of the training set named, $training_{split}$ was used in the training phase for both quantitative and qualitative analysis.
2. In the second experiment, we created a training set named $train_{allLabels}$ containing the 2140 images of the given training set with all the labels present. The test evaluation was done on the given 1783 test images provided in the Kaggle platform.
3. In the third experiment, we used all of the images provided for training and performed the quantitative model evaluation on the test set provided in the Kaggle platform.

The given test images were also used for qualitative analysis in all the experiments. The hyper-parameters of the architecture model were obtained using *random search* and were set to the various values as shown in the Table 1.

Table 1. Hyperparameters set (using random search where applicable) for CaReNet

Hyper-parameters	Values
Data split	80% - 20%
Optimizer	Adam
Learning rate	0.0001
Batch size	16
Weight initialization	Uniform distribution with mean 0 and variance 1
Total training epochs	300

4.3 Results

Training Error. In the training phase, the quantitative analysis between the output vector o and the ground truth vector g was performed using MSE (defined in Eq. 2) averaged over all the training images. Figure 2 shows the training evaluation of CaReNet with all the datasets used in the various experiments. Clearly, the model converges after 200 training epochs in all of the experiments. The average MSE converged to 0.0107, 0.008 and 0.1756 when our model was built on the $training_{split}$, $training_{allLabels}$ and the given complete training set respectively. However, this only shows that the model works well on training set. The next subsection evaluates the model on a test set.

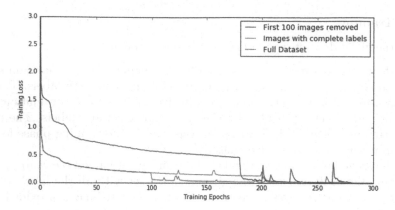

Fig. 2. Training evaluation of CaReNet with various experiments & their training sets. CaReNet converges after 200 epochs in all the experiments

$$MSE = \frac{1}{n}\sum_{i=1}^{n}(g_i - o_i)^2 \tag{2}$$

Test Error / Prediction Accuracy. In the test phase, we evaluate the prediction accuracy of the output o compared to the ground truth g using the root-mean-square error (RMSE) (defined in Eq. 3).

$$RMSE = \sqrt{\frac{1}{n}\sum_{i=1}^{n}(g_i - o_i)^2} \tag{3}$$

As there are two convolutional layers in our network, we used a **baseline model** that also contained two convolutional layers of 256, 128 channels with respective kernels of size 6×6, 4×4 and strides of size 4 and 2. Two fully connected layers of sizes 1152, 512 interspersed with a ReLU unit follow the last convolutional layer. Table 2 shows the results obtained with these models when run on the various training sets and the test sets.

In the first experiment, we obtained a total RMSE of 2.217 on the 100 images of $test_{split}$ and a RMSE of 3.100 on the Kaggle test set using the Kaggle platform. In the second and third experiments, we obtained a RMSE of 3.108 and 3.113 respectively on the Kaggle test set using Kaggle platform. In all the cases, the errors obtained are lesser than the corresponding baseline models. Further, such low test errors that have been obtained on our 4-layer network were previously attained by much deeper networks [7] that are convolutional. Another observation is that both the baseline and CaReNet models performed best when trained on $training_{split}$ dataset. However, the growth of error differs significantly between these models when the training set changes from $training_{split}$ to $training_{allLables}$. The ratio of test error growth in the baseline model and

Table 2. Evaluation of models (refer Sect. 4.3) using various training sets (refer Sect. 4.2)

Model	Training set		RMSE on	
	Name	Size	$test_{split}$	Kaggle test set
Baseline	$training_{split}$	6949 images	2.355	3.314
Baseline	$training_{allLabels}$	2143 images	–	3.349
Baseline	Kaggle training set	7049 images	–	3.350
CaReNet	$training_{split}$	6949 images	2.217	3.100
CaReNet	$training_{allLabels}$	2143 images	–	3.108
CaReNet	Kaggle training set	7049 images	–	3.113

CaReNet is 4 : 1. Further, the difference between the test errors of CaReNet in the two experiments is infinitesimal while the size of the dataset reduces by 77%. This emphasises that CaReNet not only performs better than CNN, but also achieves optimal performance even on small datasets. However, the time taken to train the current implementation of CaReNet is much higher than that of CNN, a set back we wish to overcome as part of our future work.

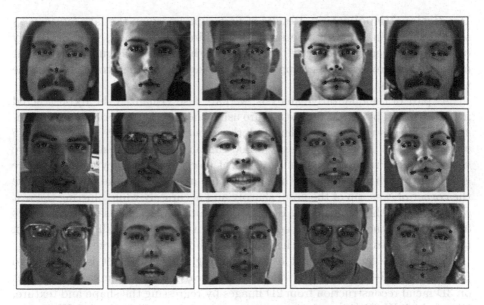

Fig. 3. Results with $test_{split}$ images. Model output is plotted using red dots (.) and ground truth is using green stars (*). (Color figure online)

Fig. 4. Results with test images. Model output is plotted using red dots (.) (Color figure online)

Prediction Visualization Results of first experiment on the labelled $test_{split}$ set are shown in Fig. 3. In the second and third experiments, we relied solely on the visual perception of the test images with no labels. Figure 4 shows that our model has regressed very appealing facial keypoints when trained on all the training images.

As part of the qualitative analysis, we have also visualized the reconstructed image returned by the decoder structure using the encoded keypoints. The reconstructed images were very similar in all the experiments and are shown in Fig. 5 when our model is trained on $test_{split}$ and run on the Kaggle test set. The figure shows that the reconstructed images, learnt solely from the keypoints with the given image as the ground truth, capture the areas around the keypoints (like the corner of eyes, tip of the nose) sharply and accurately while blurring the rest of the areas of the input image. Hence, the decoder structure uses the keypoints obtained from the encoder and acts like a filter that blurs out all the features in the input images which do not lie in the neighbourhood of the keypoints.

Though the facial keypoint detection using Kaggle dataset is sufficient to prove that CaReNet works for regression, we carried out a similar experiment on 3D facial reconstruction from 2D images by regressing the shape and texture. We used 300W-3D [14], a dataset that contains images from the 300-W dataset and the corresponding 3DMM parameters. Hyper-parameters such as the length of the capsules in detectionCapsule layer were changed and the results obtained are shown in Fig. 6. Clearly, this shows that the architecture is flexible and can be easily modified for other regression problems.

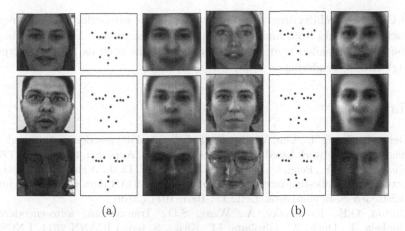

(a)   (b)

Fig. 5. Results of CaReNet - in both (a) and (b): Left: input image, Middle: encoded keypoints, Right: image decoded from the keypoints.

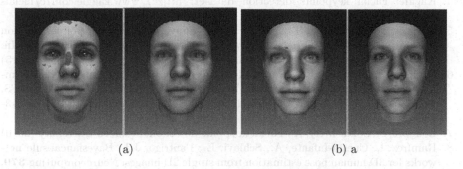

(a)   (b) a

Fig. 6. Results CaReNet on 3D reconstruction - in both (a) and (b): Left: ground truth, Right: output.

5   Conclusion and Future Work

We have proposed a framework for regression network called capsule based regression (CaReNet) which uses capsule networks (CapsNet) rather than the traditional convolutional neural networks (CNNs) to determine estimates of continuous variables. CaReNet is based on the principles of routing-by-agreement and translation equivariance proposed in the CapsNet architecture for classification problems. However, unlike the CapsNet architecture that captures the localized part of the target object in the dimensions of its final layer, CaReNet captures the number of values to regress in their dimensionality. Each of these capsules select an output vector that contains the regressed values based on the corresponding activity vector that captures the likelihood of the regressed values being present in that output vector. We achieved impressive performance on the dataset from Kaggle Facial Keypoints Detection competition that were achievable with much deeper convolution networks in the past. This shows that our novel CaReNet architecture can achieve state-of-the-art performance on regressing facial keypoints from images. Further, our architecture is very flexible and can be easily extended to other regression domains such as 3D reconstruction through inverse rendering.

References

1. Deng, C., Zhang, L., Cen, Y.: Retrieval of chemical oxygen demand through modified capsule network based on hyperspectral data. Appl. Sci. **9**(21), 4620 (2019)
2. Guan, H., Yu, Y., Peng, D., Zang, Y., Lu, J., Li, A., Li, J.: A convolutional capsule network for traffic-sign recognition using mobile LiDAR data with digital images. IEEE Geosci. Remote Sens. Lett. **17**, 1067–1071 (2019)
3. Hinton, G.E., Krizhevsky, A., Wang, S.D.: Transforming auto-encoders. In: Honkela, T., Duch, W., Girolami, M., Kaski, S. (eds.) ICANN 2011. LNCS, vol. 6791, pp. 44–51. Springer, Heidelberg (2011). https://doi.org/10.1007/978-3-642-21735-7_6
4. Kaggle: Facial keypoints detection dataset. https://www.kaggle.com/c/facial-keypoints-detection/data
5. Kimura, M., Yamashita, T., Yamauchi, Y., Fujiyoshi, H.: Facial point detection based on a convolutional neural network with optimal mini-batch procedure. In: IEEE International Conference on Image Processing (ICIP), pp. 2860–2864 (2015)
6. Liang, L., Xiao, R., Wen, F., Sun, J.: Face alignment via component-based discriminative search. In: Forsyth, D., Torr, P., Zisserman, A. (eds.) ECCV 2008. LNCS, vol. 5303, pp. 72–85. Springer, Heidelberg (2008). https://doi.org/10.1007/978-3-540-88688-4_6
7. Longpre, S., Sohmshetty, A.: Facial keypoint detection. Stanford University (2016)
8. Ramírez, I., Cuesta-Infante, A., Schiavi, E., Pantrigo, J.J.: Bayesiancapsule networks for 3D human pose estimation from single 2D images. Neurocomputing **379**, 64–73 (2019)
9. Sabour, S., Frosst, N., Hinton, G.E.: Dynamic routing between capsules. In: Advances in Neural Information Processing Systems, pp. 3859–3869 (2017)
10. Sun, Y., Wang, X., Tang, X.: Deep convolutional network cascade for facial point detection. In: IEEE Conference on Computer Vision and Pattern Recognition (CVPR), pp. 3476–3483 (2013)
11. Yaloveha, V., Hlavcheva, D., Podorozhniak, A., Kuchuk, H.: Fire hazard research of forest areas based on the use of convolutional and capsule neural networks. In: 2019 IEEE 2nd Ukraine Conference on Electrical and Computer Engineering (UKRCON), pp. 828–832. IEEE (2019)
12. Zhang, Z., Zhang, D., Wei, H.: Vehicle type recognition using capsule network. In: 2019 Chinese Control And Decision Conference (CCDC), pp. 2944–2948. IEEE (2019)
13. Zhu, X., Ramanan, D.: Face detection, pose estimation, and landmark localization in the wild. In: IEEE Conference on Computer Vision and Pattern Recognition (CVPR), pp. 2879–2886 (2012)
14. Zhu, X., Lei, Z., Liu, X., Shi, H., Li, S.Z.: Face alignment across large poses: a 3D solution. In: Proceedings of the IEEE Conference on Computer Vision and Pattern Recognition, pp. 146–155 (2016)

Analyzing Image Classification via EEG

Rahul Mishra[✉] and Arnav Bhavsar

Multimedia Analytics, Networks and Systems Lab,
School of Computing and Electrical Engineering, IIT Mandi, Mandi, India
d16043@students.iitmandi.ac.in, arnav@iitmandi.ac.in

Abstract. Electroencephalogram (EEG) has been a popular technique for brain-computer interface (BCI) and brain decoding studies. However, decoding perceptual information (e.g. images and sound) is only recently being considered. In this work, we make an attempt to experimentally analyze and address the task of classification of images that a person sees, based on the captured EEG during the visual task. For this work, we used a publicly available dataset and, as a part of our analysis, find some important concerns associated with that dataset, which also highlights challenges in EEG based image classification. After we process the data to address these concerns, we show that there may still be some discriminative traits in the EEG data for classifying a small number of classes.

Keywords: EEG · Image classification · LSTM networks · Filtering

1 Introduction

Typically, for a brain-computer interface (BCI) or a brain decoding task, a manifestation of physiological activity generated in the brain is recorded, and some machine approach [13] is further used to interpret it. Since its discovery in 1924 by Hans Berger [1], electroencephalography (EEG) was earlier used for medical applications like seizure detection [1], but recent research also includes its applications in neuroscience, and biomedical engineering (e.g. brain-computer interfaces) [7]. The main advantage of this technique is its non-invasiveness along with high temporal resolution and relatively low cost.

Having said that, it is quite challenging to understand what happens in the human brain from the EEG. Nevertheless, there have been successful work on BCI for decoding emotion, analyzing attention [2,3,5] etc. Inspired by such methods, we explore the possibility of decoding brain activity while performing visual tasks. More specifically, we experimentally analyze and address the task of classification of images that a person sees, based on the captured EEG during the visual task.

In humans, the interface between perception and cognition [14] is responsible for visual object classification. In the area of cognitive neuroscience, there have been investigations about which parts of the brain are responsible for these

© Springer Nature Singapore Pte Ltd. 2020
R. V. Babu et al. (Eds.): NCVPRIPG 2019, CCIS 1249, pp. 537–547, 2020.
https://doi.org/10.1007/978-981-15-8697-2_50

cognitive processes. However, there is still scope for better answers. In some sense, this reflects the complexity of understanding the visual image classification task.

The traditional approaches for the EEG classification task include a series of steps like artefact removal, feature extraction, classification using a machine learning method [10]. A large number of machine learning algorithms have already applied to EEG data. For example, we can use PCA (Principal Component Analysis) for dimensionality reduction [15] and ICA (Independent Component Analysis) for representing EEG signals [15], and algorithms such as adaptive classifiers or SVM (support vector machine) are used for classification [10]. In the past few years, deep learning methods have also been considered for classification of EEG [3]. Indeed, a recent attempt to classify EEG signals for the visual task, that we too envision, was reported in [14].

While the work in [14], appears to be interesting at first, in this work we demonstrate that a careful experimental analysis (which we term as 'reanalysis') of the data associated with [14], brings out some interesting findings and important concerns with the EEG based classification task, as depicted in [14].

However, in the next part of this work, with a belief that there may still be some discriminatory information between the EEG signals corresponding to different classes, after addressing some concerns referred to above, we again use the same dataset [14] for classification with a fewer number of classes and demonstrate some encouraging indications. Indeed, classification over fewer classes can also have some useful applications such those involving classifying numbers, symbols, limited number surrounding objects etc.

2   Related Work

While there is much literature on EEG analysis for various applications using traditional machine learning methods, we only discuss work employing contemporary deep learning approaches. The works on EEG classification based on deep learning focus on tasks such as seizure detection [1], event-related potential detection [11], emotion recognition [2], mental workload [4], motor imagery [7] and sleep scoring [6] etc. The authors in [3] discussed all the significant current practices and performance outcomes with deep learning for EEG classification. In [2,5], the authors propose deep learning algorithms (KNN, ANN and deep CNN network) to simultaneously learn the features and classify the emotions with EEG signals. The next attempt to classify emotions using EEG signals was done in [2], wherein the authors suggested a deep convolution neural network (CNN) based on temporal features, frequential features, and their combinations of EEG signals. They employ the DEAP dataset.

The work in [11] is a benchmark work in the field of EEG signals as the authors proposed an automatic image annotation system based on EEG signals. This study used the P300 ERP signature for the task of image annotation. This study is different from that of Spampinato et al. [14] as the later employed EEG features for multi-class image classification.

Indeed, parallel to our efforts, the authors in [9] also challenge the claims made by Spampinato et al. [14]. In [9], the authors with the help of their experiments suggest that the high accuracy mainly depends on the block level design of the data acquisition protocol. In the block-level design, all images of a single class (a block) are shown sequentially, followed by block corresponding to another class. This raises a hypothesis that the brain may get biased after the first few images for a single class. They demonstrate that the classification fails in a rapid event design where stimuli from different classes are randomly mixed. Also, in EEG pre-processing, filtering is an essential step. But, in this case, after filtering the classification performance is significantly reduced (an aspect that we reanalyse in this work). In our work, a) in addition to the reanalysis in [9], we highlight an issue with the dataset in terms of the temporal window considered for processing, and as indicated above, we provide some more insights on the issue of filtering. b) Moreover, with regards to the argument of the block-level design posed in [9], we consider a different question. We explore, whether in a block-level design, be that as it may, if there is still some discriminatory information after correctly factoring out the issues in a). i.e. even if the brain is biased to viewing one class of images after the first few images shown in a block (a possibility with the dataset of [14]), there can be some useful discriminatory information in EEG signals. We provide some indications about this for a small number of classes.

3   Methodology

In this section, we discuss our study in two parts a) Reanalysis, and b) Classification. For both the tasks, we use Long Short Term Memory (LSTM) networks [12]. For first task, we use stacked LSTM (128, 128) while for the next task, a straightforward single layer LSTM network with 256 units is implemented, which is followed by a softmax classifier.

3.1   Reanalysis

The reanalysis involves two sub-tasks, a) Temporal analysis, and b) Filtering.

Temporal Analysis: In this task, we try to analyze EEG data by considering fixed time windows of 200 ms, 5 ms and 1 ms in subsequent trials, instead of whole time series (EEG signals). This partition of signal helps in getting more insight about EEG data. We then analyze the classification performance for these time windows. During the temporal analysis, we also neglect initial 40 ms of samples as these initial samples may have interference from those related to the previous image [8].

Filtering: Typically, methods of analyzing EEG data involve steps like filtering, feature extraction etc. Here also, we follow the standard filtering paradigm by filtering out the dc components, and preserving alpha, beta and gamma bands, before classification.

3.2 Classification

As indicated earlier, after our reanalysis (which highlights some concerns, as demonstrated in the results), the second part of this study is to consider the possibility of classification using data of [14] for smaller number of classes, to indicate some discrimination between the visual classifier using EEG. Note that, we do not make any claim against the argument about the block level design highlighted in [9]. We wish to consider if some discrimination still exists between classes, even in the block level design. To address this, we use filtered data (alpha, beta and gamma band), for the classification task. Here, to analyze the effectiveness of classifier, the classes residing in the dataset are arranged in different combinations. These arrangements are defined as:

Serial Combination: Here, the classes selected for the classification are those which are sequentially shown to the subject during the EEG acqustion. In this case, there is a high possibility of biasing with respect to the previous class.

Random Combination: In order to avoid the possibility of biasing condition defined above, we consider another type of class arrangement, wherein the selected classes are not sequentially shown (and are otherwise randomly chosen).

4   Experiments

We start with the experimentation using the stacked LSTM model (128, 128) [14] and dataset released by the Spampinato et al. [14].

4.1   Dataset

Spampinato et al. [14] collected EEG data by using the following experimental protocol. They randomly selected 40 classes from ImageNet [14] along with 50 random images of each class. These images were presented on a computer screen in front of 6 human beings undergoing EEG. Each person is watching all images of a class and after that the next class starts. So, as mentioned in [9], this represents a block design in which one block contains one class. During EEG acquisition each image was presented once in whole process. This process is same for all human subjects (6 subjects), i.e., each subject has seen the same 2,000 images. The order in which the subjects are watching the images of a class is unknown to us. Each image from a class was presented for 0.5 s. There is a time gap of 10 s, between displaying of subsequent classes. The total time for EEG acquisition was 1400 s from 128 channels, at 1 KHz sampling frequency and 16 bit resolution.

For training the classifier, the k-fold cross validation is used. The value of k is 3. Figure 1 demonstrates an example of raw and filtered data.

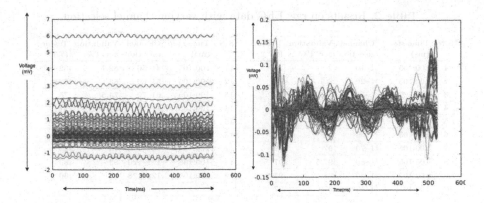

Fig. 1. Raw data (left), and filtered data (right)

4.2 Reanalysis

For our experimentation, we choose 33 random images from each class as training data and 9 images are selected for test data, from the remaining data. In each case, remaining 8 images are used as validation data. The results of the initial experimentation are quite surprising as, with raw EEG signals, the learning process converges in a very few epochs to yield results, which are higher than those reported in [14]. Motivated (and unsettled by) this observation, we perform some more experiments as described in next sub-sections.

Temporal Analysis: We first consider the time window of 40–240 ms from all channels. So the section of raw EEG data (40–240 ms with batch size = 128) is considered as input for LSTM network, and quote the classification performance in Table 1. For classification task, a softmax layer has been added at the end of the network. The number of epochs are 100 for this experiment.

Table 1. Results on raw EEG data

Channel	Time step	Validation accuracy	Test accuracy
1–128	40–240	97%	97%

• **Experimentation with varying channel selection:** In above experiment, both validation and test accuracies are much higher than the results reported in [14]. Considering this as a bit surprising, we consider a fix (and a small) time window and but with different EEG channel. We performed multiple experiments with multiple such selections and almost all are giving the similar type of results. Table 2 (S. No. 1–10) includes all the results with different channel selection and an example fixed time window of 100:105 ms.

Table 2. Results on raw EEG data with varying channel selection

S.No	Time-step (ms)	Channel selection	Validation acc. (%)	Test acc. (%)	S.No	Time-step (ms)	Channel selection	Validation acc. (%)	Testacc. (%)
1	100:105	1–10	2	2	11	100:105	41–50	82.7	82
2	100:105	1–20	3.5	3	12	100:105	51–60	83	83
3	100:105	1–30	3.5	3	13	100:105	61–70	74.5	75
4	100:105	1–40	79	77	14	100:105	71–80	87	87
5	100:105	1–50	92	93	15	100:105	81–90	83	83
6	100:105	1–60	96	96	16	100:105	91–100	76%	75
7	100:105	1–70	97	97	17	100:105	101–110	74	75
8	100:105	1–80	97.5	97	18	100:105	111–120	83	83
9	100:105	1–90	98	97.5	19	100:105	121–128	61	60
10	100:105	1–128	97	97					

- First, from the results of Table 2 (left side), one can say that the initial 30 channels are contributing almost nothing for the classification task. This finding is concerning as this indicates that the use of the initial 30 channels is worthless. Further, the results in the right-half demonstrate that only 10 channels (e.g. 71–80) are enough to produce very high classification accuracy. Finally, in general, it is also not convincing that only 5 s of EEG data is enough to get a high quality classification.

Table 3. Results on raw EEG data for single time-step

S. No	Time-step (ms)	Channel selection	Validation accuracy	Test accuracy
1	100:101	40–50	82.7%	82%
2	100:101	50–60	83%	83%
3	100:101	60–70	75%	74%
4	100:101	70–80	83%	83%
5	100:101	80–90	82%	83%
6	100:101	90–100	74%	73%
7	100:101	100–110	74%	75%

- Dissecting further, Table 3 gives provides a similar analysis while taking a single time window of 1 ms (100:101 ms). The results of this experiments are even more surprising and raise further doubts, as the results convey that only 1 time sample is enough to produce high classification accuracy. Hence, questioning these observations, we next consider the role of filtering.

Filtering: The filtering process involves removal of dc component and 50 Hz component, using notch filters Then, we filter the rest, except for preserving alpha (7–13 Hz), beta (14–30 Hz) and gamma (30–70 Hz) bands, as these bands contain most of the information, when EEG is captured in the alert and active state of a person. The classification performance on this filtered data yields very poor results (top part of Table 4).

- Considering that filtering is a common operation in EEG processing, this is again an unnatural observation. More so, when the raw EEG data yeilds very high performance even with a small number of samples and channels, as shown earlier.

Table 4. Some results on filtered EEG data

Results on filtered EEG data			
Channel	Time step (ms)	Validation accuracy	Test accuracy
1–128	40–400	16%	15%
1–128	40–240	5%	4%
Results on filtered raw EEG data (notch filter and 50 Hz & 0 Hz)			
Channel	Time step (ms)	Validation accuracy	Test accuracy
1–128	40–240	4.8%	4%
Results on dc values on EEG signals			
Channel	Data	Validation accuracy	Test accuracy
1–128	dc value	97%	96.5%

- Thus, we further experiment includes only the application of notch filter at 0 Hz and 50 Hz on raw data, without filtering anything else, and the results are shown in mid part of Table 4. These results are almost same with the ones given above. Thus, this indicates that strangely, the high results observed earlier could be because of the 0 Hz or 50 Hz component, and not with the actual information in the EEG signal.
- To verify this indication, we only preserve the dc values and perform the classification. The results of Table 4 (bottom part) indicates that the classification accuracy is case of dc value of the EEG signals is very high. To get more insights, we plot the t-SNE (shown in Fig. 2) of dc values of the EEG signals corresponding to different images. One can note that the dc values are reasonably well separated from each other, and hence it is not surprising that these are the ones responsible for high accuracy.

4.3 Classification on Filtered Data (Alpha, Beta and Gamma Bands)

The authors in [9] claimed that the high accuracy is due to the block level design. However, as shown above, the dc value is also contributing to high accuracy. Thus, we now question the role of actual information in the EEG signals

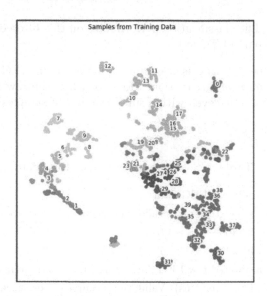

Fig. 2. t-SNE plot of DC values of EEG signals (40 classes).

(notwithstanding the block-level design), for discrimination between the classes. Clearly, we note that, on the filtered data, for large number of classes, the LSTM based classifier is not able to learn the discrimination effectively with classification performance of the order of 5% to 15%. Thus, to comment on whether there is any discrimination potential in the EEG, we consider only a few classes, and perform classification with different combination of such few number of classes (2-class, and 3-class cases). From here onwards, all the results reported below are with channels 40–128 and time step 40:400 ms.

4.4 Result on 2-Class Data

For the 2-class classification problem, we different 2-class combinations. As mentioned earlier, two different strategies have been used to prepare these class combinations: serial and random combinations. We use another strategy of selecting visually highly distinct class pairs, in a deliberate manner.

From the results in Table 5, we infer that there still exists some discriminibility in the EEG data. The results in case of (much) fewer classes are much better than those for all classes with filtered EEG signals. We also infer that the results in the random combination case are, on an average, better than those for the serial combination. This is reasonable, as it is quite possible that neural responses for temporally adjacent classes can involve a bias (similar to the argument for the block based design). For distinct classes (Table 6), the results are better than those for the serial case (which is expected), but are lower than those in the case of random combinations; an observation that needs to be further analyzed. Note

Table 5. Classification accuracy of 2-class filtered random and serial data

S.No	Random data pairs	Test accuracy	Serial data pairs	Test accuracy
1	data1 (Capuchin & Computer)	65.83%	data1 (Capuchin & Elephant)	51.66%
2	data2 (Elephant & Watch)	59.16%	data2 (Phone & Mug)	59.16%
3	data3 (Panda & Guitar)	70.00%	data3 (Computer & Watch)	58.33%
4	data4 (Broom & Guitar)	61.66%	data4 (Chair & Golf)	50.00%
5	data5 (Fish & Locomotive)	64.16%	data5 (Iron & Jack)	55.88%
6	data6 (Airliner & Espresso)	60.18%	data6 (Mail bag & Missile)	50.00%
7	data7 (Broom & Chair)	58.33%	data7 (Bike & Tent)	51.66%
	Average accuracy	62%	Average accuracy	53.81%

that in all cases in a particular strategy, the order of accuracies is similar, which indicates statistical reliability of results, irrespective of the classes considered.

Table 6. Classification accuracy of 2-class filtered distinct data

S.No	Distinct data pairs	Test accuracy
1	data1 (Fish & Missile)	60.83%
2	data2 (Elephant & Chair)	63.33%
3	data3 (Golf & Pyjama)	49.16%
4	data4 (Panda & Broom	47.50%
5	data5 (Dog & Computer)	63.00%
	Average accuracy	56.66%

4.5   Results on 3-Class Data

Here, we discuss the results for 3-class data classification. The results are summarized in Table 7. From these results too, we can observe that the classification

Table 7. Classification accuracy of 3-class filtered random and serial data

S.No	Random data pairs	Test acc.	Serial data pairs	Test acc.
1	data1 (Broom & Watch & Guitar)	50.55%	data1 (Dog & Cat & Butterfly)	42.22%
2	data2 (Phone & Guitar & Piano)	38.55%	data2 (Sorrel & Capuchin & Elephant)	37.22%
3	data3 (Cat & Broom & Chair)	55.66%	data3 (Panda & Fish & Airliner)	34.44%
4	data4 (Fish & Mug & Locomotive)	44.44%	data4 (Broom & Canoe & Phone)	46.11%
5	data5 (Cat & Panda & Guitar)	48.33%	data5 (Mug & Convertible & Computer)	38.88%
	Average accuracy	47.5%	Average accuracy	39.7%

accuracy for random data pairs are much higher than those in the serial data pairs. Thus, we can draw the same inference as that in the 2-class case.

5   Discussion and Conclusion

The reanalysis of the public dataset, released by Spampinato et al. [14], via various experiments, demonstrate that the results reported in [14] do not depend on the EEG signal, but only on the DC value, and these results are largely independent of the time-duration on the number of channels, thus suggesting the invalidity of the results. With standard filtering operation on EEG data, the results are poor for the overall classification problem considering images from all 40 classes, thus indicating that the problem of EEG based image classification is quite harder than what seems based on the results in [14]. In [9], the authors claimed that the achieved classification accuracy is due to the block level design of the experimental protocol, which seems not to be completely satisfactory. With the block level design too, the overall classification results is poor on filtered data.

Having said that, we then demonstrate an encouarging sign that the filtered (and hence properly processes) EEG data may still have some discriminatory information with respect to the classes. This is indicated by our experiments with 2-class and 3-class cases, which achieves an encouraging performance over the harder case of 40-classes. Moreover, the analysis with different class selecting strategies, show that classes whose images are shown temporally closer to each other, have a somewhat inferior performance.

Considering the above discussion, we suggest the following: a) We agree with [9] that block-level experiment can induce bias, and which can also affect EEG signatures related to classes which are temporally closer during acqusition. b) To further reduce such biases, perhaps a larger time between displayed images, can help. However, confirming this requires further experimentation. c) Finally, considering the encouraging signs of discriminblitly in case of fewer classes, we believe that approaches which can project EEG data into discriminative subspaces or computing embedding which improves discrimination, can further improve results, and this direction can be explored further.

References

1. Chen, G.: Automatic eeg seizure detection using dual-tree complex wavelet-fourier features. Expert Syst. Appl. **41**(5), 2391–2394 (2014)
2. Chen, J., Zhang, P., Mao, Z., Huang, Y., Jiang, D., Zhang, Y.: Accurate EEG-based emotion recognition on combined features using deep convolutional neural networks. IEEE Access **7**, 44317–44328 (2019)
3. Craik, A., He, Y., Contreras-Vidal, J.L.: Deep learning for electroencephalogram (EEG) classification tasks: a review. J. Neural Eng. **16**(3), 031001 (2019)
4. Di Flumeri, G., et al.: EEG-based mental workload neurometric to evaluate the impact of different traffic and road conditions in real driving settings. Front. Hum. Neurosci. **12**, 509 (2018)
5. Gao, Y., Lee, H.J., Mehmood, R.M.: Deep learninig of EEG signals for emotion recognition. In: 2015 IEEE International Conference on Multimedia & Expo Workshops (ICMEW), pp. 1–5. IEEE (2015)

6. Ghimatgar, H., Kazemi, K., Helfroush, M.S., Aarabi, A.: An automatic single-channel EEG-based sleep stage scoring method based on hidden Markov model. J. Neurosci. Methods 108320 (2019)

7. He, Y., Eguren, D., Azorín, J.M., Grossman, R.G., Luu, T.P., Contreras-Vidal, J.L.: Brain-machine interfaces for controlling lower-limb powered robotic systems. J. Neural Eng. **15**(2), 021004 (2018)

8. Heckenlively, J.R., Arden, G.B., Bach, M.: Principles and Practice of Clinical Electrophysiology of Vision. MIT Press, Cambridge (2006)

9. Li, R., et al.: Training on the test set? An analysis of Spampinato et al. [arxiv: 1609.00344]. arXiv preprint arXiv:1812.07697 (2018)

10. Lotte, F., et al.: A review of classification algorithms for EEG-based brain-computer interfaces: a 10 year update. J. Neural Eng. **15**(3), 031005 (2018)

11. Parekh, V., Subramanian, R., Roy, D., Jawahar, C.V.: An EEG-based image annotation system. In: Rameshan, R., Arora, C., Dutta Roy, S. (eds.) NCVPRIPG 2017. CCIS, vol. 841, pp. 303–313. Springer, Singapore (2018). https://doi.org/10.1007/978-981-13-0020-2_27

12. Sherstinsky, A.: Fundamentals of recurrent neural network (RNN) and long short-term memory (LSTM) network. CoRR abs/1808.03314 (2018). http://arxiv.org/abs/1808.03314

13. Shih, J.J., Krusienski, D.J., Wolpaw, J.R.: Brain-computer interfaces in medicine. Mayo Clin. Proc. **87**(3), 268–79 (2012)

14. Spampinato, C., Palazzo, S., Kavasidis, I., Giordano, D., Shah, M., Souly, N.: Deep learning human mind for automated visual classification. CoRR abs/1609.00344 (2016). http://arxiv.org/abs/1609.00344

15. Velu, P., de Sa, V.R.: Single-trial classification of gait and point movement preparation from human EEG. Front. Neurosci. **7**, 84 (2013)

Relocalization of Camera in a 3D Map on Memory Restricted Devices

Deepti Hegde[(✉)], Dikshit Hegde, Ramesh Ashok Tabib, and Uma Mudenagudi

KLE Technological University, Hubballi, India
deeptihegde@gmail.com
https://www.kletech.ac.in/

Abstract. Simultaneous Localization and Mapping (SLAM) is a core component in navigation systems of numerous vehicles such as UAVs and field robots. Relocalization in visual SLAM is the identification of camera position in a mapped area. The necessity for such a system arises in case of failed tracking or errors in loop closing. These processes are computationally intensive, and have real-time requirements and must run on processors with power and memory restrictions. We propose a system for relocalization which identifies 6 degrees of freedom camera pose and trajectory based on a single query image by using a vocabulary tree to create a visual word dictionary for quick and efficient image retrieval. This system eliminates the need to build and run computationally heavy complete SLAM systems and does not require storage of large video files/datasets on the device. We demonstrate the proposed system on a low memory embedded system, the ARM Cortex A53 board (Raspberry Pi 3 Model B). The proposed system enables faster, low memory relocalization with improved memory usage and time taken for inference in specialized, low cost systems such as smaller autonomous robots and drones.

Keywords: SLAM · Relocalization · K-means clustering

1 Introduction

Simultaneous localization and mapping (SLAM) [4] includes the estimation of position of a camera as well as the relative orientation and structure of its surroundings. SLAM can be broadly categorized into landmark-based approaches and raw data based approaches. Landmark-based solutions of SLAM use the extended Kalman Filter [21] to represent the model [9] and use range measuring devices such as LiDar [1,10], SONAR [22], or laser range finders [5]. Visual SLAM [7,17] is a raw-data approach and is odometry based. A camera or camera rig is used for sensors. Landmark-based approaches yield results under restrictive conditions of robots undergoing planar movements on simple, easy to map terrain [3]. Visual SLAM has no such constraint. The nature of the captured data enables the map to provide texture and visual information of the surroundings.

© Springer Nature Singapore Pte Ltd. 2020
R. V. Babu et al. (Eds.): NCVPRIPG 2019, CCIS 1249, pp. 548–557, 2020.
https://doi.org/10.1007/978-981-15-8697-2_51

With the increasing availability of economically viable, high quality cameras, this approach has become a low cost solution. Visual SLAM is used extensively in small scale vehicles such as rovers, drones, and other autonomous vehicles [7,14,19]. While the use of visual SLAM eliminates the need to use expensive range finding equipment, the problem of increased computational requirements arises with the use of image data. Real time processes must be kept as less computationally expensive as possible. Autonomous vehicles use SLAM to navigate unknown territory. The identification of camera pose in the mapped area, or relocalization, becomes necessary in cases of occlusion, errors in tracking, etc. [11]. Most works [7,11–13,17] in SLAM literature provide robust loop closing and relocalization capabilities in SLAM systems, but run on conventional computers and processors with high computational capability [15]. Small scale vehicles use processors with restricted memory and less computational power [1] and do not run these systems efficiently. For example, ORB SLAM [12] provides real-time relocalization capabilities, but requires a powerful processor (Intel CORE i7). To solve this problem, we propose a system for memory and computationally efficient relocalization of a camera in a SLAM generated 3D map, capable of being run on low memory edge devices. Using ORB SLAM2 for feature extraction and map generation, we demonstrate a stand-alone system for fast relocalization. Our main contribution is a lightweight system for camera pose estimation based on hierarchical cluster tree of ORB features. In Sect. 2, we discuss the related work on visual SLAM and relocalization. In Sect. 3, we provide details of the proposed methodology. In Sect. 4, we demonstrate the experimentation analysis. In Sect. 5, we provide the concluding remarks.

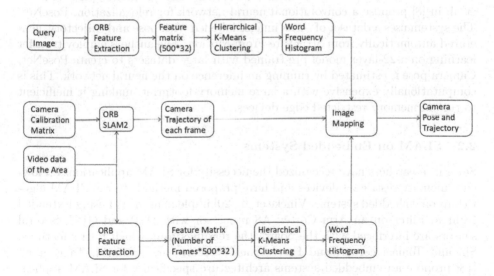

Fig. 1. Block diagram of camera pose estimation

2   Related Work

In this section, we discuss various approaches to relocalization based on image mapping in literature, as well as implementations of SLAM on memory restricted devices.

2.1   Relocalisation in Visual SLAM

Relocalization is the recovery of camera pose and trajectory in case of tracking failure by correlating map points to feature points in the current frame. SLAM systems such as ORB SLAM2 [12] by Mur-Artal et al. have relocalization modules which uses bundle adjustment and feature mapping to find camera pose. Several other approaches for relocalization have also been proposed. Galvez-Lopez et al. [6] propose a method for place recognition using bag of binary words. FAST keypoints and BRIEF descriptors are extracted to avoid bottleneck scenarios in real time applications. Their proposed loop closure algorithm includes image database query using bag of words vector, match grouping, temporal consistency, and geometric consistency. Moteki et al. propose a method for real time relocalization for keyframe based mapping using Parallel Tracking and Mapping [11]. The authors aim to rectify speed and accuracy drawbacks of the image-to-image mapping solution of Klein et al. [9]. and the image-to-map solutions of Straub et al. [15]. They do so by choosing adaptively between two algorithms based on the relative camera pose between current and target keyframes. The process flow begins as tracking fails. The steps include keyframe detection, feature matching, outlier detection, model selection, and image mapping. Kendall et al. in [8] propose a convolutional neural network for relocalization, PoseNet. The system uses a dataset of scene images labelled with pose and trajectory, generated automatically from Structure-From-Motion. The authors employ transfer learning on a 22-layer model pre-trained with large datasets to create PoseNet. Camera pose is estimated by running an inference on the neural network. This is computationally expensive with a large memory footprint, making it inefficient to run on memory restricted edge devices.

2.2   SLAM on Embedded Systems

Several researchers have recognized the necessity for SLAM applications on low-end, memory restricted devices and have proposed methods to run SLAM algorithms on embedded systems. Vincke et al. [20] implement SLAM using Extended Kalman Filter on an Arm Cortex A8 processor with DSP and GPU. Several sensors are interfaced with the board, the readings from which Harris features, Shi and Tomasi corner, and Fast corner detectors are obtained. Tang et al. [18] propose an embedded systems architecture specifically for SLAM applications. The proposed architecture consists of direct IO for DSP, feature buffers to reduce memory access latency, and a notification mechanism for synchronization between CPU threads. SLAM is implemented on a System On Chip with Arm v8A four core CPU with feature extraction, propagation, updating and mapping

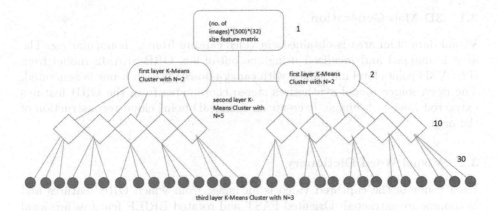

Fig. 2. Hierarchical K-means tree

on each thread. Neither of the proposed implementations allow relocalization of the vehicle on a well mapped area in case of tracking failure.

3 Proposed Methodology for Camera Pose Estimation

We propose a method of relocalization of camera in a well mapped area using hierarchical k-means clustering of ORB features. The proposed re-localization system is capable of being run on resource limited devices using a monocular camera rig. The process consists of 3 stages:

1. Generation of a 3D map
2. Creation of a visual word dictionary for captured video frames
3. Image mapping and retrieval to obtain camera pose and trajectory

The methodology in the form of a flow diagram may be seen in Fig. 1.

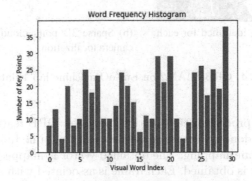

Fig. 3. Visual word frequency histogram

3.1 3D Map Generation

Visual data of an area is obtained via video capture from a monocular rig. The area is mapped and localized using the out-of-box ORB-SLAM2 model from [12], A 3D point cloud map along with camera poses for each frame is generated. The open source model synthesizes stereo coordinates from the ORB features extracted from each image. It creates a sparse 3D point cloud reconstruction of the area.

3.2 Visual Word Dictionary

Each frame of the captured video is an image from which ORB features and keypoints are extracted. Oriented FAST and rotated BRIEF features are ideal for this implementation. ORB [4] is a fast and efficient alternative to SIFT, and is a combination of FAST and BRIEF features which accommodate for rotation and scaling. A set of 500 key points, each with a 32 dimensional descriptor array is obtained from each frame. Feature are concatenated to a single large set of data points representing the entire image corpus. Hierarchical K-means clustering is used to create a vocabulary of visual words, with each cluster center comprising a word. A word frequency histogram characterizes each image. The dimensionality of the feature matrix is thus reduced from (number of frames) × (500) × (32) to a vector for each image with dimensions (number of frames) × (number of words). The tree structure can be seen in Fig. 2.

 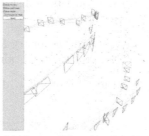

(a) Keypoints being identified for each frame

(b) Sparse 3D point cloud reconstruction and camera localization

Fig. 4. ORB SLAM2 on EuRoC machine lab 1 dataset

Similar to the process done to entire image set, ORB features are extracted and clustering is done to create a frequency histogram. Image search is conducted by histogram mapping. The obtained vector is mapped to the dictionary and frame number is obtained. Each frame is associated with a camera pose and trajectory in the form of Cartesian coordinates in a 3D space and a set of quaternions. The descriptor matrices for each image are reduced to one dimensional word frequency histograms as seen in Fig. 3.

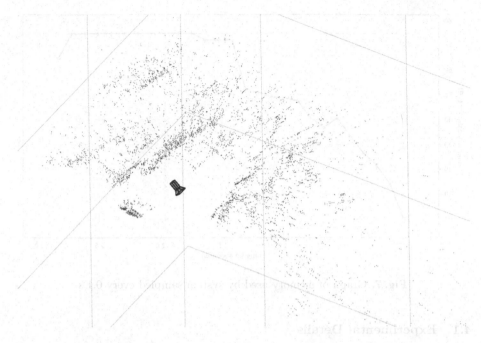

Fig. 5. Predicted camera pose plotted on sparse 3D map for EuRoC Machine Lab 1 dataset

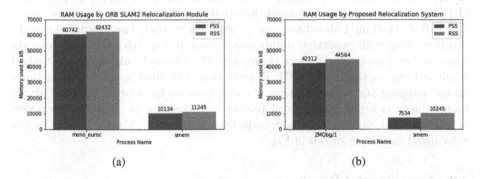

(a)   (b)

Fig. 6. Comparison of memory usage in terms of Resident Set Size (RSS) and Proportionate Set Size (PSS) of (a) ORB SLAM2 relocalization module and (b) proposed relocalization module run on EuRoC dataset.

4 Experimental Results and Evaluation

In this section we demonstrate the proposed system on a memory restricted device and compare the memory and time profiles against the state-of-the-art. Section 4.1 consists of the details of the experiments conducted, including hardware specifications and datasets used. Results obtained and the analysis of the same comprises Sect. 4.2.

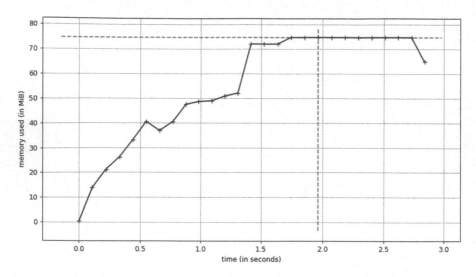

Fig. 7. Graph of memory used by system sampled every 0.1 s

4.1 Experimental Details

We demonstrate the system on three standard datasets, EuRoC Machine Lab 1 [2] and the TUM xyz videos [16] on an 8 GB RAM, Intel CORE i5 processor. ORB SLAM2 is run on each dataset. Key points detected in a given frame run on the EuRoC Machine Lab dataset can be seen in Fig. 4(a). The estimated camera position along with generated points can be seen in Fig. 4(b). ORB features are extracted and descriptor matrix is created. The hierarchical clustering method is carried out on the Intel CORE i5 processor. The final stage, which includes image mapping and re-localization, is carried out on the Cortex board. A single image query is input and a word frequency histogram is created. The image is mapped and camera pose and trajectory are found. A visualisation of the relocalized camera is shown in Fig. 5.

4.2 Experimental Results

We analyse the results of our relocalization system in terms of error in pose estimation, computational efficiency, and memory footprint.

Accuracy of Camera Pose Estimation. Table 1 shows the average distance and angle error of the proposed relocalization system for three standard monocular video datasets.

Results of Memory Profiling. We analyse the memory footprint of our relocalization system when run on an ARM Cortex A53 processor by sampling memory used every 0.1 s. As seen in Fig. 6, the maximum memory used is 75 MiB.

Table 1. Table of average error of proposed relocalization system over 50 test cases for three datasets.

Dataset	Average distance error (meters)	Average angle error (degrees)
EuRoC Machine Lab 1	0.67	1.0564
TUM fr1/xyz	0.42	1.3245
TUM fr2/xyz	0.65	1.892

RAM usage and time taken for real time re-localization is analysed. Memory usage of the proposed method versus the complete ORB SLAM2 model running on the board are compared using smem memory profiler. Both Resident Set Size (RSS) [24] and Proportional Set Size (PSS) [23] are plotted for each process to provide a more meaningful representation. In a simplistic system with no shared memory, resident set size is a measure of the number of pages the process has. In the case of sufficient memory, i.e. non-thrashing, the RSS value represents the actual amount of RAM it needs to work at its current pace. However, due to the large amount of shared memory used in modern Linux systems, the use of RSS as a measure may overestimate memory usage by a process. Thus, we also show proportional set size, which is a more accurate measure of memory usage, as it gives the number of pages used by each process. The PSS value of a process is the number of pages in memory, where each page is divided by the number of processes sharing it (Fig. 7).

The ORB SLAM2 model takes approximately 30% more temporary memory than the proposed method for image mapping and re-localization, as shown in Fig. 6. We measure execution time of each model and compare. Predictably, inference slows considerably when run on the Cortex board due to limited RAM. The delay in ORB SLAM2 is considerably larger, and takes approximately 3 times longer to run on the ARM Cortex A53 board than the Intel CORE i5 processor.

5   Conclusion

We presented a light-weight relocalization system for 6DoF camera pose estimation in a SLAM generated 3D map capable of being run on memory restricted edge devices. Building and running complete SLAM models are computationally too expensive for devices such as the ARM Cortex A53. A low cost, specific robot or drone requires minimal hardware and simplistic design. The proposed method re-localization delegates computationally heavy tasks to steps run on more advanced machines, while the low memory device performs only the final steps of image matching and camera pose estimation.

References

1. Alexandersson, J., Nordin, O.: Implementation of slam algorithms in a small-scale vehicle using model-based development. Master's thesis, Linkping University, Computer Engineering (2017)

2. Burri, M., et al.: The EuRoC microaerial vehicle datasets. Int. J. Robot. Res. **35**, 1157–1163 (2016)
3. Davison, A.J., Reid, I.D., Molton, N.D., Stasse, O.: MonoSLAM: real-time single camera SLAM. IEEE Trans. Pattern Anal. Mach. Intell. **29**(6), 1052–1067 (2007)
4. Durrant-Whyte, H., Bailey, T.: Simultaneous localization and mapping: part I. IEEE Robot. Autom. Mag. **13**(2), 99–110 (2006)
5. Fu, S., Liu, H., Gao, L., Gai., Y.: SLAM for mobile robots using laser range finder and monocular vision. In: 2007 14th International Conference on Mechatronics and Machine Vision in Practice, pp. 91–96, December 2007
6. Galvez-Lpez, D., Tardos, J.D.: Bags of binary words for fast place recognition in image sequences. IEEE Trans. Rob. **28**(5), 1188–1197 (2012)
7. Karlsson, N., di Bernardo, E., Ostrowski, J., Goncalves, L., Pirjanian, P., Munich, M.E.: The VSLAM algorithm for robust localization and mapping. In: Proceedings of the 2005 IEEE International Conference on Robotics and Automation, pp. 24–29, April 2005
8. Kendall, A., Grimes, M., Cipolla, R.: Convolutional networks for real-time 6-DOF camera relocalization. CoRR, abs/1505.07427 (2015)
9. Klein, G., Murray, D.: Improving the agility of keyframe-based SLAM. In: Forsyth, D., Torr, P., Zisserman, A. (eds.) ECCV 2008. LNCS, vol. 5303, pp. 802–815. Springer, Heidelberg (2008). https://doi.org/10.1007/978-3-540-88688-4_59
10. Montemerlo, M., Thrun, S., Koller, D., Wegbreit, B.: FastSLAM: a factored solution to the simultaneous localization and mapping problem. In: Proceedings of the AAAI National Conference on Artificial Intelligence, pp. 593–598. AAAI (2002)
11. Moteki, A., Yamaguchi, N., Karasudani, A., Yoshitake, T.: Fast and accurate relocalization for keyframe-based SLAM using geometric model selection, pp. 235–236, March 2016
12. Mur-Artal, R., Tardos, J.D.: ORB-SLAM2: an open-source SLAM system for monocular, stereo and RGB-D cameras. CoRR, abs/1610.06475 (2016)
13. Qin, T., Li, P., Shen, S.: Relocalization, global optimization and map merging for monocular visual-inertial SLAM. CoRR, abs/1803.01549 (2018)
14. Steder, B., Grisetti, G., Stachniss, C., Burgard, W.: Visual slam for flying vehicles. IEEE Trans. Rob. **24**(5), 1088–1093 (2008)
15. Straub, J., Hilsenbeck, S., Schroth, G., Huitl, R., Mller, A., Steinbach, E.: Fast relocalization for visual odometry using binary features. In: 2013 IEEE International Conference on Image Processing, pp. 2548–2552, September 2013
16. Sturm, J., Burgard, W., Cremers, D.: Evaluating egomotion and structure-from-motion approaches using the TUM RGB-D benchmark. In Proc. of the Workshop on ColorDepth Camera Fusion in Robotics at the IEEE/RJS International Conference on Intelligent Robot Systems (IROS), October 2012
17. Taketomi, T., Uchiyama, H., Ikeda, S.: Visual slam algorithms: a survey from 2010 to 2016. IPSJ Trans. Comput. Vis. Appl. **9**(1), 16 (2017)
18. Tang, J., Liu, S., Gaudiot, J.: Embedded systems architecture for SLAM applications. CoRR, abs/1702.01295 (2017)
19. Terashima,T., Hasegawa, O.: A visual-slam for first person vision and mobile robots. In: 2017 Fifteenth IAPR International Conference on Machine Vision Applications (MVA), pp. 73–76, May 2017
20. Vincke, B., Elouardi, A., Lambert, A.: Design and evaluation of an embedded system based slam applications. In 2010 IEEE/SICE International Symposium on System Integration, pages 224–229, December 2010
21. Welch, G., Bishop, G.: An introduction to the Kalman filter. Technical report, Chapel Hill, NC, USA (1995)

22. Williams, S.B., Dissanayake, G., Durrant-Whyte, H.F.: Towards terrain-aided navigation for underwater robotics. Adv. Robot. **15**, 533–549 (2001)
23. PSS accounting in smaps. http://lkml.iu.edu/hypermail/linux/kernel/0708.1/3930.html
24. Understanding Resident Set Size and the RSS problem on modern Unixes. https://utcc.utoronto.ca/~cks/space/blog/unix/UnderstandingRSS

Scene Understanding in Night-Time Using SSAN Dataset

R Anandha Murugan[1], B Sathyabama[2(✉)], Sam Joshuva Paul Jeevan Shapher[2(✉)], Suryakiran Sureshkumar[2(✉)], and Nighil Krishna Rajaguru[2(✉)]

[1] K. L. N. College of Engineering, Sivaganga, India
anandhamurugan87@yahoo.co.in
[2] Thaigarajar College of Engineering, Madurai, India
sbece@tce.edu, sampauljeevan@gmail.com,
surya.kiran2872@gmail.com, Nighilkrishna63@gmail.com

Abstract. Night vision greatly affects the efficiency of our vision which we come across daily. Research work on night vision is very essential to solve the social problems in the present scenario, but there is still a lack of database to do research on night vision using deep-learning technique. Due to poor light the object detection is a very tedious process. To overcome such hardships, we collected the night vision datasets under various conditions. This work is about scene understanding during night-time with IR-cameras. The feature extraction from night videos is mainly affected by wavelength or the intensity of IR, illumination and distance factor. We proposed a novel algorithm exclusively for object detection during night time and we compare our algorithm with various yolo versions and we found that our night vision yolo performs better in detecting various objects like Male, Female, Car, bike, Van, Cycle during night time.

Keywords: Night vision · Night vision yolo · Object detection · IR camera · SSAN datasets

1 Introduction

Computer vision is used for the construction of meaningful description of physical objects from the obtained scenes. It is of two types day-time vision and night-time vision. In day-time the objects and its features can be easily extracted, but as a consequence of very low-light intensity it becomes difficult for the system to detect the objects and its features. In this work we mainly focus on the night vision system to improve the safety and security of people. Nowadays CCTV is mainly used for security systems in various sectors like banking, traffic, tourist places and educational sectors. However, in the videos obtained from IR-cameras, which are of low light intensity, research is more oriented towards enhancement of image, whereas the real challenge lies in object detection. Due to lack of benchmark datasets at night-time, research pertaining to this field has been

The original version of this chapter was revised: the names of the authors were corrected. The correction to this chapter is available at https://doi.org/10.1007/978-981-15-8697-2_59

superficial. There are many popular public object datasets such as PASCAL VOC [4, 5], ImageNet [6, 7], Microsoft COCO [8] and Exclusively Dark (ExDARK), which played a vital role in the object detection and recognition in low light environment

SSAN dataset is a compilation of 10 distinct circumstances. In the Indian scenario, the CCTV images are affected by high noise, poor illuminations, bad weather, so the above four datasets are not suitable for the Indian conditions during night time. First, we developed our own datasets called SSAN with IR camera which suits the Indian conditions for night time with various objects. Second, we developed our own neural network for night vision which satisfies various conditions. We have provided an object detection analysis for night time videos using night vision algorithms in both hand-crafted and learned features for the understanding of night vision and its difference from vision with sufficient illumination. In Sect. 2 we are going to discuss the popular dataset and in Sect. 3 is the proposed methodology and in Sect. 4 is the results and discussion and in Sect. 5 is the conclusion and references.

2 Popular Object Datasets

2.1 Existing Datasets

There are some popular datasets such as PASCAL VOC, IMAGENET, MICROSOFT COCO, ExDark. These are the datasets which are as benchmark for the low-light images.

2.2 Methods Proposed on Existing Datasets

PASCAL VOC: The first dataset for objects (Everingham et al. 2010) rose from 2005 to 2012, with regular difficulties that motivated scientists to constantly improve their advancement in their algorithms. It started with just 4 classes of objects and 3787 pictures from current datasets. Initially containing easy pictures of objects, it has been enhanced continually with more challenges.

IMAGENET: In 2010 ImageNet (Russakovskyet others, 2015 a) was accessible to the media as the greatest data collection of objects and became particularly famous in 2012 when the community had made possible the optimization of CNNs and created a fresh benchmark for the objects identification tasks with its database of more than 1 million pictures and 1000 picture levels.

Microsoft COCO: In 2014, latest notable object data set was released. The number of images supplied is not the same as ImageNet, although the benefit of the image annotations are complete. In particular, 80 categories of objects are notified for tracking assignment from the binding panel to the pixel stage for segmentation, and each frame is described for the underlying assignment.

Exclusively Dark dataset: In 2018 Exclusively Dark (ExDark) Image Dataset was introduced. Exclusively Dark (ExDARK) is a set of 7,363 low-light pictures, which are annotated both on the pictures category levels and on local object bonding systems, from very low light circumstances until dusk (i.e. the 10 distinct times), with 12 item groups (comparable to PASCAL VOC).

2.3 Issues

In the present day there is only one available dataset for low light, in which the images are quantized to be a dark image. There are also datasets for night-time object detection taken in IR camera. The existing datasets consist of images which are nearer to the camera, but in CCTV IR the object may be located nearer or far away from the camera, it may also be affected by illumination and others, so it becomes very complex to recognize the objects. In real time IR images are only used for surveillance security of the civilians. The existing dataset fail in the context, so there is a need of object detection using IR image. Moreover, the existing works in this area are involved only in object detection and not human detection which is more vital for the security and for some automation. So, there is a need for night vision datasets exclusively on IR images with objects and persons.

2.4 Main Contribution of Our Paper

1. Development of a night vision datasets using CCTV IR images.
2. A methodology for screen understanding in night vision for object detection.
3. A novel modified YOLO network for night vision.

2.5 SSAN Datasets

Night vision system is an essential component of our everyday environment and has a significant impact on the efficacy of our sight. Night vision research has seen constant development, especially in image enhancement during dark time, but the database is still missing as a benchmark. Our dataset is for night vision objects, in which a dark night videos is classified as light if its illumination changes are either small or substantial. Night vision videos are taken with different condition with different illumination objects. The main challenge in night vision videos depend on the IR led light illuminations. In our CCTV system we are using the IR Led lights which can reach the max distance of 25 meters with the image sensor camera of 920pixel. We have considered various condition CCTV footage with various objects like Human, car, bike, bicycle, van & etc. For each object we have taken around 50 videos with frame rate of 25FPS. In Fig. 1: describes the night CCTV-IR images with various conditions like multiple objects, IR reflections, object shadows and IR illuminations. We have developed an exclusive benchmark dataset for night vision systems which will be useful for the night vision research scholars.

3 Proposed Methodology

There are 24 convolutional levels and two fully linked levels are present in the network architecture of this model. The convolutional strata extract the features while the fully linked strata estimate the location and probabilities of the boundary layers. At first, we divide the complete image into a panel grid of size n × n. Each grid cell associates with two bounding boxes and their respective category confidences, so we can identify a maximum of two items in a single grid cell. When an item occupies over one grid cell, we choose the middle cell to be the point of prediction for that item. A bounding box with no items has zero confidence value while a bounding box near an item has a confidence value congruous to the bounding box score (Figure 2).

Fig. 1. Night-time CCTV IR footages with unequal lighting of SSAN datasets

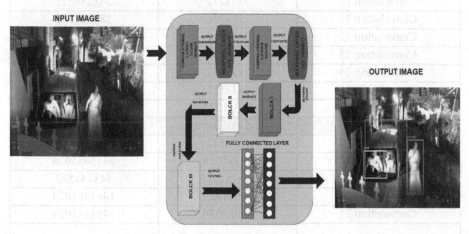

Fig. 2. Proposed Night Vision YOLO Architecture

3.1 Layer Description

Our model consists of 24 convolutional layers. Each layer is described in detail in the table below:

Name	Filters	Output Dimension
Convolution 1	7x7x64, stride=2	224x224x64
Maxpooling 1	2x2, stride=2	112x112x64
Convolution 2	3x3x192	112x112x192
Maxpooling 2	2x2, stride=2	56x56x192
Convolution 3	1x1x128	56x56x128
Convolution 4	3x3x256	56x56x256
Convolution 5	1x1x256	56x56x256
Convolution 6	1x1x512	56x56x512
Maxpooling 3	2x2, stride=2	28x28x512
Convolution 7	1x1x256	28x28x256
Convolution 8	3x3x512	28x28x512
Convolution 9	1x1x256	28x28x256
Convolution 10	3x3x512	28x28x512
Convolution 11	1x1x256	28x28x256
Convolution 12	3x3x512	28x28x512
Convolution 13	1x1x256	28x28x256
Convolution 14	3x3x512	28x28x512
Convolution 15	1x1x512	28x28x512
Convolution 16	3x3x1024	28x28x1024
Maxpooling 4	2x2, stride=2	14x14x1024
Convolution 17	1x1x512	14x14x512
Convolution 18	3x3x1024	14x14x1024
Convolution 19	1x1x512	14x14x512
Convolution 20	3x3x1024	14x14x1024
Convolution 21	3x3x1024	14x14x1024
Convolution 22	3x3x1024, stride=2	7x7x1024
Convolution 23	3x3x1024	7x7x1024
Convolution 24	3x3x1024	7x7x1024
Fully Connected I	-	4096
Fully Connected II	-	7x7x30(1470)

The first step towards YOLO explains how its output is encoded. The picture input is separated in the S × S cell grid. A grid cell is called "accountable" for anticipating each object present in the picture. This is the cell into which the object's core falls.

In each grid cell, bounding boxes B and C-probability are anticipated. The bounding box prediction has five components: (x, y, w, h, Confidence). The (x, y) coordinates are the center of the box, relative to the grid cell location (remember that if the center of the box does not fall inside the grid cell, this cell is not responsible for it). These coordinates are normalized between 0 and 1. The size of the (w, h) box is also normalized to [–0, 1] relative to the size of the image.

The class probabilities Pr (Class(i) Object should also be predicted. This probability is determined by the grid cell of an object (see if the conditional probability means you do not know this). In practice, this means that the loss function does not penalize it for an erroneous prediction in the class if no object is present on the grid cell, as we shall see later. The network only predicts one class probability per cell, irrespective of box number B. This gives total probabilities of class $S \times S \times C$

Note that the design has been designed to be applied to the Pascal VOC dataset and authors used $S = 7$, $B = 2$ and $C = 20$. The ultimate maps are therefore 7×7 and the input magnitude ($7 \times 7 \times (2* 5 + 20)$) are also explained. This network may involve a tuning of layer sizes, with distinct grid sizes or different class numbers.

The sequences of 1×1 reduction layers and 3×3 convolutional layers were inspired by the GoogLeNet (Inception) model

The final layer uses a linear activation function. All other layers use a leaky RELU ($\Phi(x) = x$, if $x > 0$; $0.1x$ otherwise)

Loss Function:

$$\lambda_{coord} \sum_{i=0}^{S^2} \sum_{i=0}^{B} 1_{ij}^{obj} \left(x_i - \hat{x}_i\right)^2 + \left(y_i - \hat{y}_i\right)^2 \tag{1}$$

where λ is a constant.

1 obj is defined as follows:

1, If an object is present in grid cell i^{th} and the jth bounding box predictor is "responsible" for that prediction

0, otherwise.

4 Results and Discussion

We run this project on environment using CUDA CUDNN and used a machine of the following specifications (intel i5 8th gen with 3.9 Ghz, 4 cores; NVIDIA GeForce GTX 1050 graphics card with 4 GB of memory, 8 GB RAM). We trained this model with dataset containing 2485 images and had a testing dataset of 4 videos.

In our dataset we have 10 videos for each class, from which we split the video in rate of 10 frames/sec. So hence, 3000 images are generated. From that we took 2485 images for training dataset and remaining we kept it for testing for trained model (Figure 3).

The following way we trained the model:

1. First, pretrain the first 24 convolutional layers using the ImageNet 1000-class competition dataset, using an input size of 1080×720
2. Then, decrease the input resolution to 448×448
3. Train the full network for about 20 epochs using a batch size of 64, size
4. Learning rate schedule: for the first epochs, the average loss rate was slowly down from 78 to 6.8. Train for about 15 epochs and then start decreasing it.

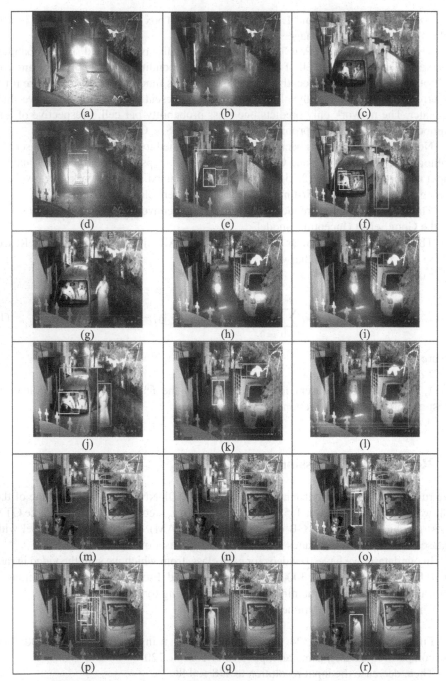

Fig. 3. {(a), (b), (c), (g), (h), (i)} – input images {(d), (e), (f), (j), (k), (l), (m), (n), (o), (p), (q), (r)} – output trained images

5. Use random scaling and translation of information increases and adjust visibility and saturation uniformly.
6. We train the model up to 20 epochs to get the better result and the average loss function is 2.3.

It is important to modify the features of failure for stronger outcomes. Two items are remarkable:

1. When multiple classes overlap, labelling should be done properly.

2. Predict the bounding box size and height square root for penalizing errors separately in tiny objects and big objects.

Training datasets are used to train the model, which can detect various objects like male, female, car, van, bike, cycle. And we tested the model for testing videos, our model can detect objects based upon the wavelength of IR camera. And the advantage of this model is that it can detect objects lively, with less loss. (Table 1 and Figure 4, 5 and 6).

Table 1. Comparison table with decreasing average loss with increasing epochs

Epochs	Average loss	Epochs
1	78.5	1
2	70.1	2
3	65.9	3
4	52.6	4
5	48.5	5
6	43.9	6
7	36.8	7
8	30.7	8
9	22.8	9
10	18.8	10
11	15.6	11
12	11.7	12
13	9.6	13
14	7.8	14
15	6.9	15
16	4.6	16
17	2.7	17
18	2.3	18
19	1.2	19
20	0.9	20

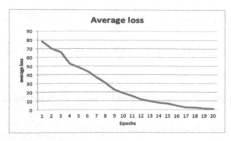

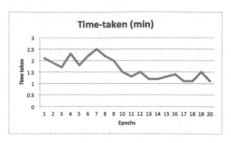

Fig. 4. Epochs vs Average loss   **Fig. 5.** Epochs vs Time taken

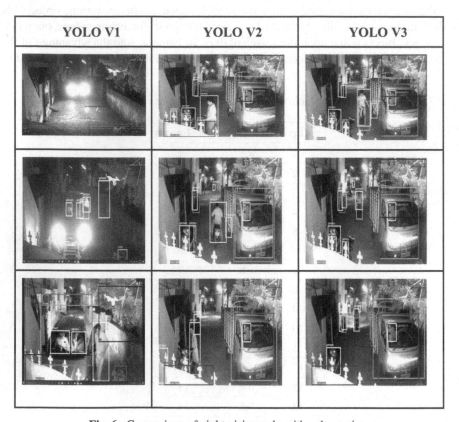

Fig. 6. Comparison of night vision yolo with yolo versions

5 Comparison of Various Yolo Versions with Our SSAN Datasets

In Table 2 we compare our proposed night vision yolo algorithm with present yolo versions. We found that our algorithm gives the better result when compared with others. It's given the efficiency of 92.25%.

Table 2. Comparison of our algorithm with various yolo versions

S. No.	Algorithm	No. of frames	Threshold	Efficiency (%)
1	yolo v1	606	0.7	72.5
2	yolo v2	606	0.68	80.5
3	yolo v3	606	0.75	86
4	**proposed night vision yolo algorithm**	**606**	**0.72**	**92.25**

6 Conclusion

This work introduces the SSAN data set in the hope of providing a complementary database for night time research work and encourages the community to address the challenges of long glossed night time environments, particularly in application-based research such as object detection.

Using this dataset, we analyzed in depth the computational behavior of the common, handmade and learned night time images in the context of the object detection and found some interesting information in them. The development of handcrafted characteristics was discovered to be primarily in bright circumstances, so that sound and absence of detailed information that often occur in nightlight pictures could not be properly addressed. Likewise, a modern denotational algorithm is not enough to manage the noise often occurring next to bright information.

Our research focuses on the assessment of features based on object detection and we think that in the night time domain more needs to be developed. Therefore, we hope that the SSAN database will be a useful database for future undertakings, both to further understand the vision behavior or to improve practical work performance at night. Our proposed algorithm gives the better result at 20 epochs with the average loss function is 2.3.

References

1. Loh, Y.P., Chan, C.S.: Getting to know low-light images with the exclusively dark dataset. Comput. Vis. Image Underst. **178**, 30–42 (2019)
2. Davis, J.W., Keck, M.A.: A two-stage template approach to person detection in thermal imagery. In: Seventh IEEE Workshops on Application of Computer Vision,WACV/MOTIONS'05. vol. 1. pp. 364–369. IEEE (2005)
3. Bilodeau, G.A., Torabi, A., St-Charles, P.L., Riahi, D.: Thermal–visible registration of human silhouettes: a similarity measure performance evaluation. Infrared Phys. Technol. **64**, 79–86 (2014)
4. Leo, M., Medioni, G., Trivedi, M., Kanade, T., Farinella, G.M.: Computer vision for assistive technologies. Comput. Vis. Image Underst. **154**, 1–15 (2017)
5. Everingham, M., Eslami, S.A., Van Gool, L., Williams, C.K., Winn, J., Zisserman, A.: The pascal visual object classes challenge: a retrospective. Int. J. Computer. Vis. **111**, 98–136 (2015)
6. Everingham, M., Van Gool, L., Williams, C.K.I., Winn, J., Zisserman, A.: The pascal visual object classes (voc) challenge. Int. J. Computer. Vis. **88**, 303–338 (2010)

7. Russakovsky, O., et al.: ImageNet large scale visual recognition challenge. Int. J. Comput. Vis. **115**(3), 211–252 (2015). https://doi.org/10.1007/s11263-015-0816-y
8. Russakovsky, O., et al.: Imagenet large scale visual recognition challenge. Int. J. Comput. Vis. **115**, 211–252 (2015)
9. Lin, T.Y., et al.: Microsoft COCO: common objects in context. In: Fleet, D., Pajdla, T., Schiele, B., Tuytelaars, T. (eds.) ECCV 2014. LNCS, vol. 8693, pp. 740–755. Springer, Cham (2014). https://doi.org/10.1007/978-3-319-10602-1_48
10. Dong, J., Ge, J., Luo, Y.: Nighttime pedestrian detection with near infrared using cascaded classifiers. In: 2007 IEEE International Conference on Image Processing (ICIP), IEEE, pp. VI–185 (2007)
11. Zeiler, M.D., Fergus, R.: Visualizing and understanding convolutional networks. In: Fleet, D., Pajdla, T., Schiele, B., Tuytelaars, T. (eds.) ECCV 2014. LNCS, vol. 8689, pp. 818–833. Springer, Cham (2014). https://doi.org/10.1007/978-3-319-10590-1_53
12. Wang, J., Yang, J., Yu, K., Lv, F., Huang, T., Gong, Y.: Locality-constrained linear coding for image classification. In: 2010 IEEE Conference on. IEEE Computer Vision and Pattern Recognition (CVPR), pp. 3360–3367 (2010)
13. Khosla, A., Bernstein, M., et al.: Imagenet large scale visual recognition challenge. Int. J. Computer. Vis. **115**, 211–252 (2015)
14. Russell, B.C., Torralba, A., Murphy, K.P., Freeman, W.T.: Labelme: a database and web-based tool for image annotation. Int. J. Computer. Vis. **77**, 157–173 (2008)
15. Donahue, J., et al.: Decaf: A deep convolutional activation feature for generic visual. convolutional neural networks. In: Advances in Neural Information Processing Systems. pp. 1097–1105 (2014)

Deep Learn Bananas: A Transfer Learning for Banana Variety Classification

Senthilarasi M[1(✉)], Md. Mansoor Roomi S[2], Maheesa M[2], and Sivaranajani R[3]

[1] Dr. Mahalingam College of Engg. and Tech, Pollachi, India
arasiece@gmail.com
[2] Thiagarajar College of Engineering, Madurai, India
smmroomi@tce.edu, maheesharoomi@gmail.com
[3] Sethu Institute of Technology, Kariapatti, India
bharathi_siva21@yahoo.com

Abstract. India produces nearly 29 million tons of Bananas (Musasp.) every year under diverse conditions and production systems. There are over 1000 different varieties of bananas growing around the world. Finding out the intra classification of a banana fruit is an essential task to cater them towards proper management of food product preparation, marketing and pricing. This paper proposes a technique for the identification of banana varieties using a deep convolution neural network model to classify eight varieties of bananas namely Karpuravalli(ABB), Rasthali(AAB), Poovan(AAB), Nendran(AAB), Hill/Malai(AAB), Nali Poovan(AB), Monthan(ABB) and Grand Naine(AAA). The proposed deep learnt banana variety classification has acquired better accuracy of 88.6% which is higher than banana variety classification using VGG16 network model.

Keywords: Deep learning · Banana · Variety identification · Vision

1 Introduction

Banana is the most cultivated and consumed fruit of the world. Global exports of banana plantain have attained nearly 18.1 million tons during 2017. The diverse banana varieties cultivated in India are Dwarf Cavendish, Robusta, Monthan, Poovan, Nendran, Red banana, Nyali, Safed Velchi, Basarai, Ardhapuri, Rasthali, Karpurvalli, Karthali and Grandnaine etc. Each of these varieties have their inherent nature of colour, taste, odour and shape. Their inherent characteristics of these diverse varieties are suitable for variety of dishes and products. Grand Naine banana fruits are highly suitable for preparing delicious milk shakes, baby food and ice creams. Monthan is used for bread, biscuit and cookies.

Poovan variety is very sweet, pulp is firm with good aroma and excellent edible qualities, which is suitable for juice processing and banana fig industries. Nendran is the ingredient for health drinks. Banana fruit bars are prepared from Karpuravalli variety. Rasthali is very tasty with apple flavor which is fit for jam preparation. Different varieties of bananas are shown in Fig. 1. Selection of these varieties, is therefore based on

© Springer Nature Singapore Pte Ltd. 2020
R. V. Babu et al. (Eds.): NCVPRIPG 2019, CCIS 1249, pp. 569–577, 2020.
https://doi.org/10.1007/978-981-15-8697-2_53

various kinds of needs and situations. Banana fruit processing industries are set world-wide to add value to the fresh banana fruits produce in a number of ways viz. canning, drying, freezing and new ingredient creation like chips, jam, pickles etc. Hence, the identification of banana variety is required to regulate the online transit of raw bananas to various processing chambers. Banana variety classification also finds its application in dietary guidance for the selection of fruits to suit health condition, supermarket and marketing industry for pricing of commodities and to develop an interactive tool for enhancing teaching and learning process for children. The major challenges of banana fruit industries are outdated equipment for processing operations, limited technical support services and inadequate quality control systems. The recent trends in electronics, vision and artificial intelligence can cater the banana fruit industries to automate the process of variety identification.

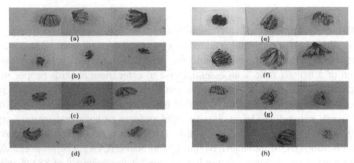

Fig. 1. Samples images of different banana varieties [a-Karpuravalli, b-Hill, c-Monthan, d-Grand Naine, e-NaliPoovan, f-Nendran, g-Poovan and h-Rasthali]

Many researches are being carried out in the horticulture for variety classification using machine learning and computer vision. Before 2012, the hand crafted features were prevalently extracted for object classification and recognition tasks. Chen et al. [1] have proposed an image processing method for corn variety identification by combining discriminant analysis and neural network. Here, 17 geometrical, 13 shape and 28 colour features are fed as the feature vector for classifier. Identification of plum varieties is performed based on shape, size, and fruit drupe color in [2]. The morpho-colorimetric endocarps features are applied through stepwise Linear Discriminant Analysis (LDA) to implement a statistical classifier to classify each variety. Kambo and Yerpude [3] have presented a technique to classify the basmati rice variety using principal component analysis. The accuracy achieved by their approach is around 80%. In [4], a classification method was proposed to discriminate pepper seed based on neural networks and computer vision. Image features representing color, shape, and texture were extracted and used to classify pepper seeds. Effective features were selected using sequential feature selection with different criterion functions. Sabzi et al. [5] presents a novel approach to automatically identify three common varieties of oranges. The 6 most effective features out of 263 parameters, including texture, color and shape features, were automatically selected using a hybrid approach with artificial neural network and particle swarm optimization algorithm (ANN-PSO). The accuracy of these techniques rely on the effectiveness of feature selection process. In machine learning, a model is constructed from the discriminative and robust features which are extracted from the raw data. This needs careful engineering and expertise to select suitable set of features. The hand crafted feature extraction process is overridden by the deep learning algorithm, where the features are learnt by a network model. Deep learning is feature learning where features from higher levels of the hierarchy are being formed by the composition of lower level features [6]. The significant advantages of using DL in image processing has reduced the need of feature engineering (FE). In [7], three plum varieties are classified in immature state using a deep convolutional neural network. This approach has attained the accuracy of about 91 to 97%. The objective of this paper is to identify banana variety from digital images for automating the fruit processing methods. The major contributions of the paper are

- Identification of suitable solution to solve banana variety classification.
- Database collection - Since deep learning requires enormous amount of data for training, a database is collected for eight varieties of bananas.
- Selection of suitable network architecture, implementation, proper selection of hyper parameters for deep learn banana variety classification.

2 Proposed Methodology

Many banana varieties are cultivated across the country to cater various purposes like jam, pickle, powder, candy, chips and etc. The intra-class variations among the banana varieties are less. Their variations are fruit end, fruit shape and the arrangement of banana fingers to the stalk. In order to retrieve these information, banana finger has to be segmented from hand to analyze the structure completely. But in real world applications, banana hands are usually handled. Shape of the banana hand varies with respect to the number of banana fingers, rotation and view point. Therefore, banana variety classification is difficult and error prone using shape feature based approach.

Selection of Suitable Technique for Banana Variety Classification. Descriptors of banana fruits are peel colour, fruit shape and fruit apex. Fruit shape is categorized into four types such as (1) Straight or Slightly curved (2) Straight at the distal end (3) Curved (4) Curved in 'S' shape as Fig. 2(A).

Various species of banana possesses different structure at their tip (referred as apex or distal end). The structure of apex can be pointed, lengthily pointed, blunt tipped, bottle necked and rounded as shown in Fig. 2(B). Variety of banana is characterized based on its fruit shape and fruit apex as shown in Fig. 2(C).

It could be inferred that Nendran banana (placed leftmost in Fig. 2(C)) is slightly curved and possess pointed apex, Monthan placed second has pointed apex with straight fruit shape and Morris placed at third position is curved and its apex is truncate. Likewise, each variety of banana has its own structure as tabulated in Table 1. Therefore, the structural information of fruit shape and fruit apex can be chosen as a key for banana fruit classification. All these eight varieties of banana changes from green to yellow during ripening process. Hence, colour feature is not suitable for discriminating the

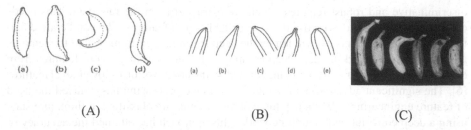

Fig. 2. (A) Fruit Shape (a) Straight (b) Straight at the distal part (c) Curved (d) Curved in S shape; (B) Fruit Apex (a) Pointed (b) Lengthily Pointed (c) Blunt tipped (d) Bottle necked (e) Rounded; (C) Differences in Fruit shape of bananas

Table 1. Banana variety and its shape characteristics.

Variety	Shape	Apex
Nendran	Straight at Apex	Pointed
Rasthali	Slightly Curved	Blunt tipped
Morris	Slightly Curved/S Curved	Truncate
Monthan	Straight	Pointed
Poovan	Straight	Bottle necked
NaliPoovan	Straight	Bottle necked
Karpuravalli	Slightly curved	Blunt tipped
Malai	Straight	Pointed

intra class of bananas. Usually, the structural variation of banana is learnt by the human brain, which makes a person to identify the banana variety easily by just looking at it.

Banana variety can be identified by partitioning a banana finger into top, middle and apex region. The structure of fruit apex and fruit shape can be retrieved by fitting medial axis transform as shown in Fig. 3. Before proceeding to shape analysis of banana fingers, it is important to isolate banana fingers from the hand. But the delineation of banana finger is impossible with RGB image, because the rinds of banana finger makes subtle edges and also their variation at these edges are not very significant. Therefore, the extraction of hand crafted shape features may not be an appropriate solution. Hence, deep learning has been chosen for banana variety classification.

In the last few years, multiple deep CNNs models have been designed. In this paper, two convolutional neural network model say Alexnet and VGG16 are selected for banana variety identification.

Alexnet. Alexnet [8] comprises of twenty-five layers, out of which there are 5 convolutional layers and three fully connected layers. Alexnet has 11×11, 5×5, 3×3, convolutions, max pooling, dropout, data augmentation, ReLU activations, SGD with momentum. Alexnet has the advantages of solving vanishing gradient problem by using ReLu (Rectified Linear Unit) and overfitting problem by using a Dropout layer. In the

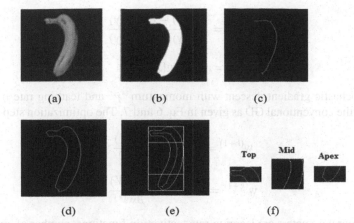

Fig. 3. Fruit Shape/Apex analysis (a) input image (b) Segmented object (c) Medial axis of fruit (d) Banana Contour (e) Partitioning of Banana (f) Partitioned segments

proposed work, the features of different variety of bananas are extracted by applying the Alexnet on the set of training images. The features are extracted from the fully connected layer fc7 of Alexnet model. The dimension of extracted features is 4096. The features acquired from the deep neural network are fed to the Support vector machine for banana variety classification. This is performed because Support vector machine classifier is preferred than softmax layer due to its superior regularization effects on loss function.

VGG16. VGG16 [9] Net consists of 16 convolutional layers and it is most widely used because of its uniform architecture. VGG16 is similar to Alexnet but with lots of filters. The proposed work is experimented using VGG 16 architecture and classified using SVM.

Selection of Activation functions/ Hyperparameters/Classifier. Activation function dictates how the weighted sum of inputs are transformed to activate the next node of the neural network model. The output of non-linear activations of weighted sum of inputs 'y' is $\hat{p}$ as given in Eq. 2.

$$y = w_0 + w_1x_1 + \ldots w_nx_n \tag{1}$$

$$\hat{p} = f_{NL}(y) \tag{2}$$

Non-linear activation functions that are preferred in neural network are sigmoid functions and hyperbolic tangent functions for learning complex data. Equation 3 and 4 gives the expression for sigmoid and hyperbolic function. The selection of these nonlinear function depends upon the values of activation as either 0 to 1 or −1 to +1. Gradient descent is a well-known optimization technique used to determine the optimal values for weights 'w' by minimizing loss function. Cross entropy is the loss function (J) used for training this network. The optimal weights are determined as in Eq. 5.

$$f_{NL}(y) = \frac{1}{1 + \exp(-y)} \tag{3}$$

$$f_{NL}(y) = \frac{\exp(y) - \exp(-y)}{\exp(y) + \exp(-y)} \tag{4}$$

$$W = \arg_w min\{J(W)\} \tag{5}$$

The stochastic gradient descent with momentum 'γ' and learning rate η is found better than the conventional GD as given in Eq. 6 and 7. The optimization step becomes

$$w^{(k+1)} = w^{(k)} - \eta \frac{\partial J(W)}{\partial w^{(k)}} \tag{6}$$

$$w^{(k+1)} = \gamma w^{(k)} - \eta \frac{\partial J(W)}{\partial w^{(k)}} \tag{7}$$

The hyper parameters are learning rate, activation functions, number of epochs and momentum. The performance of CNN high relies on the selection of these parameters If the learning rate is chosen high, collision is involved whereas its low value causes miss in learning of few patterns. Therefore, the appropriate selection of hyper parameters are important.

3   Results and Discussion

In any banana fruit processing industry and commercial places like departmental stores and market, bananas are mainly handled as a complete set (i.e. a bunch of bananas called as hand) rather than using it as single pieces (Fingers). Hence, in the proposed method the bunch of banana is used for training rather than single piece. Totally 1000 images of each banana variety are considered for experimentation and 70% of these images are used for training and remaining 30% for testing. Hence, 700 images per category are used to train the convolutional neural network. The resolution of these input images are 4608×3072. The training images are resized as 227×227 for further processing using Alexnet. Deep features from the training images are taken from the fully connected layer "fc7" of Alex net. The deep learnt features are fed to multiclass SVM (One versus all) for eight banana variety identification.

The proposed Deep banana variety identification is experimented in Intel core i7 8550U CPU@1.8 GHz processor, 8 GB RAM along with Nvidia GeForceMX130(4 GB RAM). The Alexnet and Vgg16 network libraries are used in Matlab 2017b environment. Database collection of eight varieties of bananas are carried under the controlled environment say a uniform white and non-reflective background with the light from four Philips trulite. NikonD3100 camera (3.5 MP) is used for data acquisition at different view angles and rotations. Different varieties of banana are cultivated across the world with AAB and ABB genome constitutions, where A and B represents Musa acuminata and Musa balbisiana. Eight varieties of banana considered for classification are Karpuravalli(ABB), Rasthali(AAB), Poovan(AAB), Nendran(AAB), Hill (AAB), Njali Poovan(AB), Monthan(ABB) and Grand Naine(AAA). These varieties of bananas are chosen due to their significant amount of sale in local market because of the amount of production, taste and ingredient for product preparation. Few sample images of these banana varieties are shown earlier in Fig. 1 are acquired at different view angles, rotation, translation and ripening levels. The banana samples used for the experimentation of the proposed work possess various challenges like

- Bananas are at various ripening levels.
- Bananas at different rotation and view angle which provides pose variation.
- Self-occlusion of banana fingers.
- The periphery of the banana hand varies with respect to number of fingers/hand within the intra-class.
- Inter class variation of banana is less. For example, Poovan and Nali Poovan appears to be almost similar. The same case for Karpuravalli and Rasthali, Poovan and Rathali and so on.
- The presence of senescent spots on banana like Malai/Hill.
- No differentiation of fruit colours across eight varieties.

The proposed banana variety identification is implemented using Alexnet and VGG16 architecture. The transfer learning of Alexnet for banana variety identification has resulted in the confusion matrix as shown in Fig. 4(a). In this confusion matrix, the class 1 to 8 corresponds Karpuravalli, Hill/Malai, Monthan, Grand Naine, NaliPoovan, Nendran, Poovan and Rasthali respectively. The overall accuracy attained is 88.86%. Poovan and Nali poovan has almost similar structural characteristics which has made the CNN to confuse as seen below. Also for comparison, the features are taken from "fc7" layer of VGG16 and classified using the support vector machine. The average accuracy attained by VGG16 is 13.68% which very less compared to the Alexnet. The classification results of Alexnet and VGG16 are shown in the below given Fig. 4(b). It is observed that the data similarity is high between different classes, where this has negatively affected the VGG neural networks learning ability. In deep neural network, not always the increase in number of layers would improve the performance of a network. Rather, there is a tradeoff between the model complexity and variance of the data. In the proposed work, the intraclass variation of banana is very less i.e. the data similarity is high among the different banana classes, which negatively affects the VGG neural networks learning ability. Usage of small size filters in VGG16 results in learning the local information than the generic details where it is required for the given data.

The features from three fully connected layers of Alexnet are taken for performance analysis. Feature from seventh fully connected layer with 4096 features are fed to the SVM classifier. This leads to the accuracy of about 88.61%. When the features are taken from fc6 layer the accuracy has reduced to 85.42%. The effects of hyper parameter used in the proposed Alexnet based transfer learning approaches are analyzed and presented in Fig. 5. The hyper parameters of CNN are learning rate and momentum. From the literature, it is seen that the learning rate and momentum can be varied between 0.1 to 0.0001 and 0.5 to 0.9 respectively. The effect of these hyper parameters are observed by varying the combinations of learning rates and momentum. It is noted that Alexnet with learning rate of 0.0001, momentum as 0.5 and number of epochs is chosen as 10 has provided better accuracy.

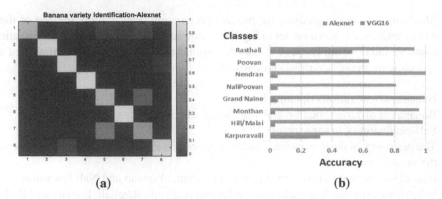

(a)   (b)

Fig. 4. (a) Confusion Matrix of proposed banana variety identification using Alexnet; (b) Comparative results of Alexnet and VGG16 in Deep learning banana for variety identification

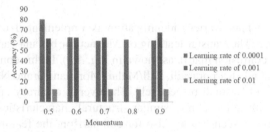

Fig. 5. Effect of learning rate and momentum

Table 2. Performance analysis of banana variety classification.

Techniques	Classification rate %)
HOG + Linear Discriminant	61.6
HOG + Linear SVM	65.6
HOG + Quadratic SVM	75.6
HOG + Cubic SVM	77.9
HOG + KNN	33.3
HOG + Ensemble Boosted Tree	42.4
Proposed Technique using Alexnet	**88.6**

To the best of knowledge, there are no papers on banana variety classification using image processing approach. But there are few literatures on variety classification of dates and corn, where their techniques are not suitable for bananas. Therefore, the implementation of deep learning for banana variety classification is evaluated and compared with the performance of various classifiers on HOG features. The application of Cubic SVM classifier has resulted 77.9% of accuracy whereas the deep learning technique has attained

88.62%. Alexnet provides higher accuracy than VGG16 and HOG features because more optimal filters for less variant data are obtained (Table 2).

4   Conclusion

In fruit processing industries, identification of fruit's intra class is one of the important task to regulate the process flow which is being performed manually. Advancement in deep learning can mimic the human decision making in this regard by deep learning the features from texture, fruit shape and structural variations. Each banana varieties have their inherent characteristics in both external and internal factors. A deep neural network model (Alexnet) is incorporated in the proposed banana variety classification technique. The banana features are deep learnt using Alexnet and the features from fully connected layer(fc7) are fed as the feature vector to support vector machine for banana variety identification. The performance of the Alexnet is much higher than VGG16.

References

1. Chen, X., Xun, Y., Li, W., Zhang, J.: Combining discriminant analysis and neural networks for corn variety identification. Comput. Electron. Agr. **71**(1), 48–53 (2010)
2. Sarigu, M., et al.: Phenotypic identification of plum varieties (Prunus domestica L.) by endocarps morpho-colorimetric and textural descriptors. Comput. Electron. Agr. **136**, 25–30 (2017)
3. Kambo, R., Yerpude, A.: Classification of basmati rice grain variety using image processing and principal component analysis. Int. J. Comput. Trends Technol. (IJCTT) **11**(2), 80–84 (2014)
4. Kurtulmuş, F., Alibas, İ., Kavdır, I.: Classification of pepper seeds using machine vision based on neural network. Int. J. Agr. Biol. Eng. **9**(1), 51–62 (2016)
5. Sabzi, S., Abbaspour-Gilandeh, Y., García-Mateos, G.: A new approach for visual identification of orange varieties using neural networks and metaheuristic algorithms. Inf. Process. Agr. **5**(1), 162–172 (2018)
6. LeCun, Y., Bengio, Y., Hinton, G.: Deep learning. Nature **521**(7553), 436–444 (2015)
7. Rodríguez, F.J., García, A., Pardo, P.J., Chávez, F., Luque-Baena, R.M.: Study and classification of plum varieties using image analysis and deep learning techniques. Progress Artif. Intell. **7**(2), 119–127 (2017). https://doi.org/10.1007/s13748-017-0137-1
8. Krizhevsky, A., Sutskever, I., Hinton, G.E.: ImageNet classification with deep convolutional neural networks. In: Proceedings of the 25th International Conference on Neural Information Processing Systems, vol. 1, pp. 1097—1105 (2012)
9. Karen, S., Andrew, Z.: Very deep convolutional networks for large-scale image recognition. In: ICLR (2015)

A Framework for Lane Prediction Based on Vehicle Detection and Tracking

Any Gupta(ID) and Ayesha Choudhary(✉)(ID)

School of Computer and Systems Sciences, Jawaharlal Nehru University,
New Delhi, India
any2027@gmail.com, ayeshac@mail.jnu.ac.in

Abstract. In this paper, we propose a novel, real-time, coupled framework for vehicle detection, unsupervised learning based vehicle tracking and lane prediction by an outside looking camera mounted on the dashboard of a vehicle. We detect the vehicle using YOLOv3 (You only look once) object detection method [1] and achieve 98.7% detection accuracy on an average. Then, we apply incremental clustering across frames for tracking the vehicles on-the-fly. Moreover, we detect and track lanes using unsupervised learning based algorithm [2], wherever the lanes are visible. Many-a-time, the lane markings are not visible due to wearing-off of the markings or occlusion caused by the vehicles on the road. In our proposed framework, we use the information of vehicle tracks and detected lane markings for predicting lanes where the lanes are not present or not visible on the road. Our framework detects and tracks the vehicles accurately in each frame and successfully predicts the lanes even in challenging scenarios such as, in the presence of occlusion, illumination variation, etc.

Keywords: Vehicle detection · Vehicle tracking · Lane estimation · Deep learning · Intelligent vehicles · Lane prediction.

1 Introduction

In this paper, we propose a novel and real-time coupled framework for vehicle detection, tracking and lane markings detection, tracking and prediction where the lane markings are not present or visible. We apply YOLOv3 (You only look once) [1] object detection technique for vehicle detection and use unsupervised learning based algorithm [2] for detecting and tracking lanes. We propose an incremental clustering algorithm to track the detected vehicles across frames in space and time. Furthermore, in case the lane markings are not present or visible, we use the vehicle tracks and the last detected lane markings to accurately predict the lane markings, so that the driver can be given a lane departure warning, even when the lanes are not actually visible or present.

Vehicle detection is to localize the vehicles in the current frame, while vehicle tracking is to keep localizing the same vehicle across frames as the vehicle moves. Vehicle detection and tracking system is part of an Advanced Driver Assistance Systems (ADAS) and plays an important role in collision avoidance. It guides

© Springer Nature Singapore Pte Ltd. 2020
R. V. Babu et al. (Eds.): NCVPRIPG 2019, CCIS 1249, pp. 578–588, 2020.
https://doi.org/10.1007/978-981-15-8697-2_54

the driver about surrounding vehicles and alerts him from possible collisions between the ego-vehicle and the leading vehicles. Lane detection and tracking is to find the lane markings within and across frames and is also part of ADAS and is needed for Lane Departure Warning to avoid accidents.

It is reported that millions of people are severely injured and many lose their life each year around the world due to collision of vehicles on the road. Therefore, there is need to develop a lane departure warning and collision avoidance system based on lane and vehicle detection and tracking.

There are various challenges and issues in robust and accurate lane and vehicle detection and tracking from a camera. Lane markings can be of different types, such as short or long lines, different colors such as white and yellow. In general, since there is no *a priori* information of the lanes and vehicles on the road, the system has to accurately track both the lanes and vehicles on-the-fly. Challenges because of shadows, illumination variation, environmental changes such as rain, fog, snow, etc. make both vehicle and lane detection and tracking difficult. The vehicle can be occluded by surrounding vehicles which makes it difficult for detection. Therefore, there is a need to make a robust lane and vehicle detection and tracking system which can deal with all of these challenges. Moreover, many a time, the lanes are not visible due to wearing off of the lane markings, heavy traffic, etc. In such cases, if the lanes can be predicted, the lane departure warning system can continue to play its role and keep the vehicle safe.

In this paper, we test our framework on the publicly available datasets, namely, Caltech dataset [3] and LISA dataset [4] and an internet video Dataset [5]. It can be seen that our framework is robust and accurate as described in Sect. 4. We organize the paper in the following manner: Sect. 2 describes the state-of-the-art. In Sect. 3, we discuss our proposed framework in detail. In Sect. 4, we describe and discuss the experimental results and conclude our work in Sect. 5.

2 Related Work

In this section, we discuss methods which are applied for vehicle detection and tracking, lane detection and tracking and lane prediction. Jihun et al. [6] used YOLO object detection method for vehicle detection and Kalman filter for vehicle tracking. After that, they used the tracker information for further path prediction. They achieved 95% accuracy in path estimation. John et al. [7] used road scene features for lane estimation using trees based and regression framework. They extracted color and depth features of road scene using a neural network. Their system works in the presence of occlusion also. Alexandru et al. [8] estimated the lanes using deep neural network. They calculated the distance of the straight lane from the vehicle and also computed lane orientation for lane estimation. Further, they also generate artificial lanes with random background to train the network. The hardware requirement is high for execution of this system. Joel et al. [9] first used steerable filters for lane detection and tracking then applied this lane markings and lane texture information and vehicle positioning data for estimating the lane curvature.

Akshay et al. [10] used Markov decision process for vehicle tracking. They used reinforcement learning for training the model using the features as

Euclidean distance, height. Yao et al. [11] develop a model for lane change analysis by vehicle based on analysis of extraction of lane change segments from a continuous driving scenario. Piyush et al. [12] used some parameters such as area, maximum length, horizontal length for extracting the vehicles from the input image and applied background subtraction for vehicle detection. Finally, they train a multi-layer feed-forward artificial neural network classifier with the features of vehicles for classifying them.

Satzoda et al. [13] trained Adaboost detector using Haar-like features on grey-level images for vehicle detection. They have also used color and geometrical information of vehicles for detection. Their system is trained on full vehicle images, therefore, it is sensitive if a partial vehicle is seen in front of the ego-vehicle in night vision. Wang et al. [14] develop an algorithm for vehicle detection using the geometric parameters of the vehicle taken from each viewpoint. Viewpoint maps are generated using the information of road structure and driving ways. Satzoda et al. [15] develop a vehicle detection algorithm using Haar-like features and Adaboost classifiers. Kristoffersen et al. [16] applied Deformable Parts Model (DPM) detector for vehicle detection and used the combination of Markov decision processes (MDP) and Tracking-Learning-Detection (TLD) tracker for vehicle tracking. Satzoda et al. [17] used lane and vehicle positions, type of lane markings, speed and orientation of vehicle for further lane and vehicle estimation. Eshed et al. [18] also used color and geometrical information for making the clusters of vehicle and then they trained Adaboost detector using decision tree on pixels level information but their system is sensitive to occlusion scenario. Chen et al. [19] used the combination of features from Accelerated Segment Test (FAST), HoG method and Hue, Saturation and Value (HSV) color space for vehicle detection. For vehicle tracking, A Forward and Backward Tracking (FBT) method is applied. Kosaka et al. [20] proposed a framework which detects the vehicle at night time using Laplacian of Gaussian operator. The classification takes place by applying Support Vector Machines (SVM). Tian et al. [21] used vehicle features such as color, texture, and region for detection and Kalman filter for vehicle tracking.

We compare our work with Jun et al. [22] and show it in experimental section. They first applied Inverse Perspective Mapping (IPM) for processing the images and used position and orientation of the detected lanes for further estimation of lane boundaries. They have used multitask deep convolutional network and recurrent neural network for lane structure prediction. In our framework, we use YOLOv3 object detection technique for vehicle detection and spatio-temporal clustering of the vehicles using parameters, such as color, vehicle position, orientation etc., across frames for tracking. We work in the 2D domain and propose a simple geometric algorithm for lane prediction that works efficiently in real-time.

3   Proposed Work

In this section, we discuss our novel, coupled framework for lane and vehicle detection and tracking and lane prediction. Our framework processes each incoming frame of the video captured by camera one by one in real-time. We divide our proposed work in four sections: 1) vehicle detection, 2) lane detection and tracking 3) vehicle tracking and 4) lane prediction and perform these steps for each appearing frame of the video as the vehicle moves on the road.

3.1   Vehicle Detection

We apply YOLOv3 object detection method [1] for vehicle detection in each frame. YOLO is a popular technique for object detection as it is efficient and accurate. It applies the CNN model to the full frame at once rather than applying it on multiple locations. Therefore, it is called one-stage object detector. Furthermore, it divides the frame into regions and predicts bounding boxes and confidence for each region using logistic regression.

We apply YOLOv3 in our framework which uses a custom deep learning architecture Darknet-53. Darknet-53 feature extractor is trained on Imagenet [23] database and has 53 layers of network in it. In YOLOv3, we get 106 fully convolutional layers as 53 more layers are added onto Darknet-53 framework for object detection. It gives mean average precision (MAP) for Intersection Over Union (IOU) of 0.5.

Training the Model. We use transfer learning for training the YOLOv3 model using pre-trained darknet53.conv.74 weight file. We use BBox-labeling tool for the annotations of our data. As we have only one class in our framework, i.e. vehicle, we train our dataset with batch, subdivisions, filters as 24, 8, 18 respectively. We train YOLOv3 for 500 epochs with the learning rate of 0.001 and save the weights after every 1000 iterations. We achieve precision, recall and f1-score as 0.98, 0.99 and 0.98 respectively at threshold value 0.85.

Testing Phase. We perform vehicle detection in real input images of our dataset. As the input frame appears, the vehicles are detected with bounding box. With the help of bounding box, we are able to locate the vehicle and determine the needed parameters for the tracking. The detected vehicle is then tracked across frames by incremental clustering as discussed in the Sect. 3.3.

3.2   Lane Detection and Tracking

Simultaneously, we detect lanes wherever possible. We apply unsupervised learning based algorithm for lane detection and tracking [2]. We detect the connected components using area and orientation to discover the actual lane markings. We then cluster these connected components in space and time across frames to detect and track the lane markings using orientation, size and distance parameters. The distance is measured by fitting a curve between two connected components and calculating the sum of squared error (SSE) of the curve using *least square fitting technique*. The connected components should satisfy the SSE and orientation threshold for being a part of the particular lane cluster. Each cluster represents a lane within and across the frame as shown in Fig. 1(a).

We use this algorithm [2] because it is fast and does not require any training data, which makes the system able to work in real-time in various scenarios. Also, it gives accurate results as well as works on straight as well as curved lanes. Moreover, it detects various types of lanes such as continuous, discontinuous, single and double lanes in each frame on-the-fly.

3.3 Vehicle Tracking

We track the vehicle in the frame using parameters such as, color, area, orientation, vehicle centroid and vehicle position in the lane. We determine the vehicle position with respect to the lane markings present on both sides of the vehicle by comparing the distance between the vehicle and detected lane markings as shown in Fig. 1(b). Vehicle position indicates the lane markings on which the vehicle is present and it is important because when the vehicle changes the lane then also it should be tracked as the same vehicle which was on the other side of the previous lane.

We represent each property of the vehicle as $V_j^i = \{O_j^i, C_j^i, P_j^i, R_j^i\}$, where V_j^i is the jth vehicle in the ith frame, O_j^i is the orientation, C_j^i is the centroid, P_j^i is the position and R_j^i is the color of the jth vehicle in the ith frame. Therefore, in frame f_i, let $V^i = \{V_1^i, V_2^i, \ldots, V_n^i\}$ be the collection of detected vehicle and it represents the initial set of clusters for further clustering. We perform incremental spatio-temporal clustering for each vehicle across frames based on the vehicle properties listed above in the following manner.

Let $V^{i+1} = \{V_1^{i+1}, V_2^{i+1}, \ldots, V_m^{i+1}\}$ be the vehicles present in frame f_{i+1} and $V_j^{i+1} = \{O_j^{i+1}, C_j^{i+1}, P_j^{i+1}, R_j^{i+1}\}$ is the jth vehicle in the $(i + 1)^{th}$ frame. We perform clustering in the hierarchical manner such as if the color and position of V_j^i and V_j^{i+1} matches, then we calculate the similarity between their orientations and the distance between their centroids using Euclidean distance given by Eq. 1.

$$d\left(C_j^i, C_j^{i+1}\right) = \sqrt{\left(q_1 - p_1\right)^2 + \left(q_2 - p_2\right)^2} \tag{1}$$

where, $C_j^i = (p_1, p_2)$, $C_j^{i+1} = (q_1, q_2)$. If the orientation and centroid distance satisfies the respective thresholds, then V_j^{i+1} becomes an element of the cluster V_j^i, otherwise we check the similarities with properties of the other clusters present in frame f_i. V_j^{i+1} becomes an element of the cluster with which it satisfies the threshold on all the parameters, otherwise a new cluster V_{n+1}^{i+1} is created with V_j^{i+1} as its first element. In the same manner, we cluster each vehicle in V^{i+1} and furthermore, this method is followed for clustering the vehicle within and across the frames for tracking. The cluster orientation is computed as an average of the orientations of the vehicles across time in the cluster, whereas, the centroid of the cluster is the centroid of the current vehicle present in the frame. Each cluster represents the same vehicle across frames and the centroid gives the track as shown in Fig. 1(a).

If the vehicle changes the lane, then we get this information by comparing the coordinates difference between centroids of the vehicle and lane markings

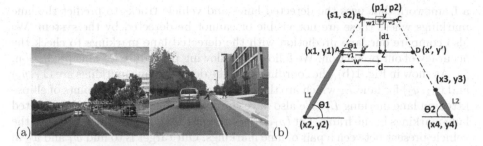

Fig. 1. (a) Lane and vehicle detection and tracking on LISA dataset [4] (b) Representation of the lane prediction based on the detected vehicle and lane markings.

as well as our clustering method is helpful for confirming that this is the same vehicle which has changed the lane or not. Therefore, our proposed method is also helpful for lane changing scenario and in that case, a lane departure warning can be given to the driver, if required.

Fig. 2. (First row) Lane detection and prediction on LISA dataset [4], (a) and (b) shows multiple lane predictions. (Second row) Lane prediction on dataset [5], where no markings are there in (b). We do lane detection and prediction in (a) and based on that we further predict the lanes in (b) after 30 frames.

3.4 Lane Prediction

Many a time, the lane markings are not visible in the image because of the reasons such as, non-presence, wearing-off of the paint, occlusion due to traffic, etc. This leads to bottlenecks for a lane departure warning systems. We propose a framework that uses the detected lanes and vehicle tracks to predict the lane markings where these are not visible or cannot be detected by the system. We also compare our lane prediction with the detected lane markings to check the accuracy of our prediction. We follow the following procedure for lane prediction.

As show in Fig. 1(b), the coordinates of the detected lane markings are (x_1, y_1) and (x_2, y_2) for lane L_1 which are the endpoints of the major axis points of ellipse fitted on lane marking L_1. We also have the orientation θ_1 and θ_2 of the detected lane markings in the frame. Let (p_1, p_2) represent the centroid of the cluster of the vehicle present between a pair of lane markings. Our target is to find w_1 and w_2 in Fig. 1(b), for the initial step towards lane prediction. It is not necessary that the detected lanes be of the same length, therefore first, we need to calculate the point (x', y') and then, the distance d as shown in Fig. 1(b).

Geometrically, $y' = y_1$ and $x' = \frac{y_4 - y'}{tan\theta_2}$. Therefore, distance $d = x' - x_1$.

Now, further calculation will be done for calculating w_1 and w_2. Now, z is the point of intersection of the perpendicular on the line joining (x_1, y_1) and (x', y') from the centroid of the vehicle. Then, coordinates of z are (p_1, y_1) or (p_1, y'). Furthermore, the length of the perpendicular is $d_1 = y_1 - p_2$.

We consider the region ABVZ and calculate the distance $v_1 = \frac{d_1}{tan\theta_1}$. From the Fig. 1(b), $w' = p_1 - x_1$ and distance $BV = w_1 = w' - v_1 = w' - \frac{d_1}{tan\theta_1}$. We calculate w_2 in the similar manner.

Further, we predict the lanes with θ_1 as angle and B as the starting point having the coordinates as (s_1, s_2), where, $s_1 = p_1 - w_1$ and $s_2 = p_2$. We extend the lane towards the base of the frame and consider the y-coordinate of the end point of the lane as the point lying on the base of the frame. The results of the lane prediction is shown in Fig. 2. We predict the lane markings based on the vehicle present in between the lane markings. For one lane marking, we may get more than one predicted lane marking, as shown in Fig. 2 (first row).

4   Experimental Results and Discussions

We perform our experiments on Intel Core i7-7500U CPU at 3 GHz with 16 GB RAM and NVIDIA GeForce GTX 1060 GPU. We detect the vehicles using YOLOv3 [1] and apply spatio-temporal incremental clustering for vehicle tracking in both space and time. We use unsupervised learning based algorithm [2] to simultaneously detect and track the lane markings wherever the lane markings are visible. However, when the lane markings are not detected, we predict the lane markings by using the previously detected lane markings and the tracks of the detected vehicles. We implement the experiments on two publicly available datasets, 1) Caltech dataset [3], 2) LISA dataset [4] and one internet video dataset [5]. The description of the datasets including the performance of our framework is given below.

Caltech dataset [3] has total of 526 images of cars having resolution of 320 × 240 pixels and are taken on the roads of Southern California. We train YOLOv3 model with 350 images after annotating them and rest of the images are used for testing phase. The dataset is captured from the random locations in the presence

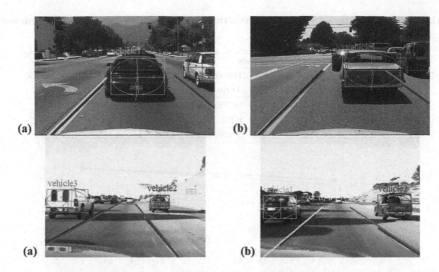

Fig. 3. (First row) Vehicle detection, tracking and lane prediction on Caltech dataset [3], (a) dark maroon and dark blue color shows lane detection and yellow and orange color shows lane prediction, (b) dark maroon, yellow and dark blue color shows lane detection and sky blue and orange color shows lane prediction. (Second row) Vehicle detection, tracking and lane prediction on LISA dataset [4], where, in (a) dark maroon and dark blue color shows lane detection and red and violet color shows lane prediction. (b) dark maroon and dark blue color shows lane detection and yellow and dark green shows lane prediction. (Color figure online)

of sunlight, and shadows. YOLOv3 method detects the vehicles in each frame and gives the bounding box coordinates of each detected vehicle. We localize the vehicle using the coordinates for further processing. We achieve 98.6% detection accuracy on this dataset. We do vehicle tracking and lane prediction on the detected vehicles and the complete dataset is processed within 15 s. This dataset results a lot of clusters since there are no consecutive frames of vehicles and after a few frames, the location is changed and a new vehicle is seen. We keep the history of few frames for tracking.

Figure 3 shows the result of our coupled framework in which we can clearly see that the lane prediction output is as accurate as lane detection [2]. Table 1 shows the vehicle detection and lane prediction performance by computing true positive, false positive and false negative. Figure 4 shows the comparison between our framework and Jun et al. [22] on the basis of Receiver Operating Characteristics (ROC) curve. They have used combination of two neural networks for predicting the lanes. They have achieved Area Under the Curve (AUC) as 0.96 on an average for Caltech dataset of lanes using recurrent neural network, whereas, we have achieved 0.98 AUC on Caltech dataset [3]. We calculate True Positive rate and False Positive rate for drawing the ROC curve.

LISA-Q Front FOV video dataset [4] consists three videos, namely dense, sunny and urban which consists 1600, 300 and 300 frames respectively. We resize

Table 1. Vehicle detection and lane prediction performance of our proposed framework on all datasets.

Methods	vehicle detection performance						Lane prediction performance		
	Caltech [3]		LISA [4]		Dataset [5]		Caltech [3]	LISA [4]	Dataset [5]
	Train	Test	Train	Test	Train	Test			
TP	99.6%	98.6%	98.5%	99.2%	98.7%	98.2%	98.9%	98.5%	98.8%
FN	0.12%	1.2%	1.3%	0.7%	0.5%	1.3%	-	-	-
FP	2.2%	1.9%	2.8%	1.6%	2.4%	2.1%	4.9%	5.5%	1.9%

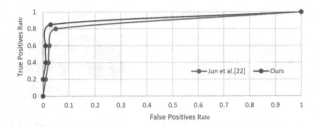

Fig. 4. Comparison of Jun et al. [22] and our work on the basis of ROC curve.

all the images with the resolution of 320 × 240. We take 1600 images for the training of YOLOv3 model and keep 600 images for testing. We achieve 99.2% detection accuracy. The vehicle tracking and lane prediction is completed within 20 s. All the three videos are captured in consecutive location, hence, makes the vehicle tracking more efficient as the number of clusters are less throughout the video. Figure 3 shows the result of vehicle detection, tracking and lane prediction. We show the performance of our framework in Table 1.

Dataset [5] is an internet video having 2000 frames, where we train 1200 images for training of YOLOv3 object detection model and use rest of the 800 images for testing. We are able to detect the vehicles accurately and achieve 98.3% detection accuracy. The lane prediction is also good in spite of having very light lane markings on the road as can be seen in Fig. 2 (second row).

5　Conclusions

In this paper, we propose a coupled framework for lane and vehicle detection, tracking and lane prediction. Many-a-time, the lane markings are not present, specially in unstructured environments, or are not visible because they are very light or worn-off. We apply YOLOv3 [1] object detection technique for vehicle detection and propose spatio-temporal incremental clustering based vehicle tracking method. We apply unsupervised learning based algorithm for lane detection and tracking [2]. Finally, we predict the lanes using the detected lane markings and the tracks of the vehicle. We achieve an average accuracy of 98.7% in detection phase, whereas, the lane prediction accuracy is 98.9%. The experimental results clearly show the performance of our framework.

References

1. https://pjreddie.com/darknet/yolo/
2. Gupta, A., Choudhary, A.: Real time lane detection using spatio-temporal incremental clusterin. In: Proceedings of IEEE Conference on Intelligent Transportation Systems, pp. 1–6 (2017)
3. Caltech computational vision Caltech (2001). http://www.vision.caltech.edu/html-files/archive.html
4. Sivaraman, S., Trivedi, M.M.: A general active-learning framework for on-road vehicle recognition and tracking. IEEE Trans. Intell. Transp. Syst. 11(2), 267–276 (2010)
5. https://www.youtube.com/watch?v=NS7ymLOPT-I
6. Kim, J., Han, D. S.: Vehicle path prediction based on radar and vision sensor fusion for safe lane changing. In: Proceedings of IEEE International Conference on Artificial Intelligence in Information and Communication, pp: 267–271 (2019)
7. John, V., Liu, Z., Mita, S., Guo, C., Kidono, K.: Real-time road surface and semantic lane estimation using deep features. Signal, Image Video Process. 12(6), 1133–1140 (2018). https://doi.org/10.1007/s11760-018-1264-2
8. Gurghian, A., Murali, V.N.: DeepLanes: end-to-end lane position estimation using deep neural networks. In: Proceedings of IEEE Conference on Computer Vision and Pattern Recognition, pp. 38–45 (2016)
9. McCall, J.C., Trivedi, M.M.: Video-based lane estimation and tracking for driver assistance: survey, system, and evaluation. IEEE Trans. on Intell. Transp. Syst. 7(1), 20–37 (2006)
10. Rangesh, A., Trivedi, M. M.: No Blind Spots: Full-Surround Multi-Object Tracking for Autonomous Vehicles using Cameras & LiDARs, arXiv preprint asXiv: 1802.08755 (2018)
11. Yao, W., Zeng, Q., Aioun, F.: On-road vehicle trajectory collection and scene-based lane change analysis: part ii. IEEE Trans. Intell. Transp. Syst. 18(1), 206–220 (2017)
12. Piyush, P., Rajan, R., Mary, L., Koshy, B.I.: Vehicle detection and classification using audio-visual cues. In: The Proceedings of International Conference on Signal Processing and Integrated Networks (SPIN), pp. 726–730 (2016)
13. Satzoda, R. K., Trivedi, M. M.: Looking at vehicles in the night: detection & dynamics of rear lights. IEEE Trans. Intell. Trans. Syst. 1–11 (2016)
14. Wang, C., Fang, Y., Zha, H.: Probabilistic inference for occluded and multiview on-road vehicle detection. IEEE Trans. Intell. Transp. Syst. 17(1), 215–229 (2016)
15. Satzoda, R.K., Trivedi, M.M.: Multipart vehicle detection using symmetry-derived analysis and active learning. IEEE Trans. Intell. Transp. Syst. 17(4), 926–937 (2015)
16. Kristoffersen, M.S., Satzoda, R.K., Trivedi, M.M., Moeslund, T.B.: Towards semantic understanding of surrounding vehicular maneuvers: a panoramic vision-based framework for real-world highway studies. In: The Proceedings of IEEE Conference on Computer Vision and Pattern Recognition Workshops (CVPRW), pp. 1584–1591 (2016)
17. Satzoda, R.K., Trivedi, M.M.: Drive analysis using vehicle dynamics and vision-based lane semantics. IEEE Trans. Intell. Transp. Syst. 16(1), 9–18 (2015)
18. Bar, E., Trivedi, M.M.: Learning to detect vehicles by clustering appearance patterns. IEEE Trans. Intell. Transp. Syst. 16(5), 2511–2521 (2015)

19. Chen, X., Meng, Q.: Robust vehicle tracking and detection from UAVs. In: The Proceedings of International Conference of Soft Computing and Pattern Recognition (SoCPaR), pp. 241–246 (2015)
20. Kosaka, N., Ohashi, G.: Vision-based nighttime vehicle detection using CenSurE and SVM. IEEE Trans. Intell. Transp. Syst. **16**(5), 2599–2608 (2015)
21. Ding, W., Ye, L., Tian, B.: Rear-view vehicle detection and tracking by combining multiple parts for complex urban surveillance. IEEE Trans. Intell. Transp. Syst. **15**(2), 597–606 (2014)
22. Li, J., Mei, X., Prokhorov, D., Tao, D.: Deep neural network for structural prediction and lane detection in traffic scene. IEEE Trans. Neural Networks Learn. Syst. **28**(3), 690–703 (2016)
23. http://www.image-net.org/

Detector-SegMentor Network for Skin Lesion Localization and Segmentation

S. Saini[✉], D. Gupta, and A. K. Tiwari

Department of Electrical Engineering, Indian Institute of Technology Jodhpur,
Jodhpur, India
saini.2@iitj.ac.in

Abstract. Melanoma is a life-threatening form of skin cancer when
left undiagnosed at the early stages. Although there are more cases of
non-melanoma cancer than melanoma cancer, melanoma cancer is more
deadly. Early detection of melanoma is crucial for the timely diagnosis of
melanoma cancer and prohibit its spread to distant body parts. Segmentation of skin lesion is a crucial step in the classification of melanoma
cancer from the cancerous lesions in dermoscopic images. Manual segmentation of dermoscopic skin images is very time consuming and error-
prone resulting in an urgent need for an intelligent and accurate algorithm. In this study, we propose a simple yet novel network-in-network
convolution neural network (CNN) based approach for segmentation of
the skin lesion. A Faster Region-based CNN (Faster RCNN) is used for
preprocessing to predict bounding boxes of the lesions in the whole image
which are subsequently cropped and fed into the segmentation network
to obtain the lesion mask. The segmentation network is a combination of
the UNet and Hourglass networks. We trained and evaluated our models
on ISIC 2018 dataset and also cross-validated on PH^2 and ISBI 2017
datasets. Our proposed method surpassed the state-of-the-art with Dice
Similarity Coefficient of 0.915 and Accuracy 0.959 on ISIC 2018 dataset
and Dice Similarity Coefficient of 0.947 and Accuracy 0.971 on ISBI 2017
dataset.

Keywords: CNN · Faster RCNN · Segmentation · Dermoscopic ·
Melanoma · Dice Similarity Coefficient

1 Introduction

It is estimated by the Indian Cancer Society that 55,100 new cases of melanoma
are being diagnosed each year in India [5]. Worldwide, it caused more than 60,000

S. Saini—Equal contribution.

Electronic supplementary material The online version of this chapter (https://
doi.org/10.1007/978-981-15-8697-2_55) contains supplementary material, which is
available to authorized users.

deaths out of the 350,000 cases reported in 2015 and causes one death in every 54 min in US [14]. Even after being accounted for as less as 1% of the total skin-related diseases, melanoma cancer has become the major cause of death in these diseases. The annual cost of healthcare for melanoma cancer exceeds $8 billion [8]. With early detection of melanoma, the 5-year survival rate can be increased up to 99%; whereas delaying the diagnosis can drastically reduce the survival rate to 23% [1] once it spreads to other parts of the body. Hence, it is of fundamental importance to identify the cancerous skin lesion at the earliest to increase the survival rate.

A huge amount of time and effort has been dedicated to increasing the accuracy and scale of diagnostic methods by researchers worldwide. The International Skin Imaging Collaboration (ISIC) provides a publicly available dataset of more than 25,000 dermoscopy images. They have been hosting the benchmark competition on skin lesion analysis every year since 2016. The previous year challenge comprised of 3 tasks on lesion analysis: Lesion Boundary Segmentation, Lesion Attribute Detection, and Lesion Diagnosis. The extraction of crucial information for accurate diagnosis and other clinical features depends heavily on the lesion segmented from the given dermoscopic image and therefore, segmentation of the lesion has been designated as a decisive prerequisite step in the diagnosis [2,12].

Our work majorly focuses on the segmentation of the skin lesions which in itself is a challenging task. Skin lesions are accompanied by a huge variance in shape, size, and texture. While melanomas have very fuzzy lesion boundaries, there are further artifacts introduced due to hair, contrast, light reflection, and medical gauze which makes it more difficult for the CNN-based approach to segment the lesions.

1.1 Related

In recent years, many pixel-level techniques for skin lesion segmentation have been developed. Initial work explored the visual properties of skin lesion like color and texture and applied classical techniques. Li et al. [26] proposed the use of above-mentioned features with classical edge detection for a contour-based methodology. Garnavi et al. [7] combined use of histogram thresholding and CIE-XYZ color space to segement the lesion. While classical approaches do not generalize well on unseen lesion images, deep convolutional neural network (DCNN) based approaches have proven to be a great success in generalization over such tasks with improved accuracy and precision [6,20]. Mishra et al. [16] presented an efficient implementation of UNet [20] and compared the improvement in performance with other classical methods. Many authors have used the same CNN-based method for segmentation as well as classification. In [29], two fully convolutional residual networks (FCRN) were used, to segment as well as classify skin lesions at the same time.

Instead of processing only the local features, much work has been focused on processing the global information with CNNs as well. In [21], the authors made use of pyramid pooling to incorporate global context along with spatial information to produce location precise masks. Some work has also introduced the concept of processing the features selectively. In [13], the authors made use of Squeeze-and-Excitation [11] network to incorporate attention for focusing only on the important parts of the feature maps. [27] and [23] made use of modified GANs (General Adversarial Network) which involves training a Generator and Discriminator network in an adversarial fashion to generate accurate segmentation maps. Recently, two-stage CNN pipelines have also been researched upon. In [24], they used YOLO [18], an object detection network for localising the skin lesion and then employed classical image segmentation algorithm for segmenting the lesion. Similarly, [25] first employed Faster RCNN [19] for detecting the lesion in the images and then employed a dilation-based autoencoder for segmenting the lesion.

2   Methods

We took inspiration from [24] and [25] and to apply the pre-processing step of extracting the region of interest (ROI). We implemented the faster region-based convolutional neural network (Faster RCNN) [19] on the lines of [25] as Stage 1 of our pipeline. The ROIs extracted through our detection network were give as input to our segmentation network to obtain the lesion mask which served as the Stage 2 of our pipeline. We named the Stage 1 as the Detector and the Stage 2 as the SegMentor. Our segmentation network is inspired from the UNet [20] and the Hourglass [17] network. As previously experimented in [24] and [25], the localized and cropped image of the lesion area by the detector in the given dermoscopic images, were used to train the network along with the cropped segmentation masks. Doing so, increased the over all performance of their segmentation algorithms. The reason behind this being that a prior removal of irrelevant features and other nearby pixels from the input images and present only relevant features at segmentation stage. This helps the segmentation network to achieve good and fast results. We used Dice Similarity Coefficient (DSC) as the evaluation metric which is similar to the Jaccard Index [28], to tackle the issue of imbalanced lesion to background ratio. We discuss the architectural uniqueness and the non-conventional training strategy followed for our model, where components of the model were trained sequentially to attain the optimal value of parameters. We have also shown a comparison between model performances with and without employing Stage 1 i.e. melanoma localization in Table 1. The overall pipeline is summarized in Fig. 1. We named the combined pipeline of localization and segmentation networks as Detector-SegMentor.

2.1   Dataset

The ISIC challenge 2018 [3, 22] dataset was used for training. The ISIC 2018 challenge provided datasets for skin lesion segmentation task along with attribute detection and lesion diagnosis tasks. The data was collected from various institutions and clinics around the word. ISIC archive is the largest dermoscopic image library available publicly. The challenge provided a total of 2594 images with their corresponding ground truth masks. Image dimensions varied from 1022×767 to 6688×4439. Out of the available dataset, we utilised 2000 images solely for training purpose. To extend our training data, we performed conventional augmentations such as horizontal and vertical flips, rotation, shear and stretc.h, central cropping, and contrast shift. The final training dataset consisted of 30,000 images with their corresponding ground truth masks. Moreover to showcase the generalisability of our model, we also used ISBI 2017 [4] and PH^2 [15] datasets for validation.

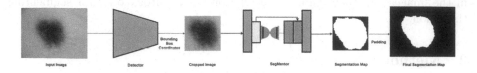

Fig. 1. An overview of the proposed pipeline.

2.2 Proposed Detector-SegMentor

Faster-RCNN network in Stage 1 task gave us the localised lesion. The Detector returns a set of coordinates corresponding to the input image which confines a lesion in it with a certain probability. The lesion area is cropped from the original image with the help of the obtained coordinates from the detector. The cropped image is then either resized (if aspect ratio larger than 512×512) or padded with zeros (if aspect ratio smaller than 512×512) to obtain the image size of $512 \times 512 \times 3$ to be fed into the SegMentor (Segmentation Network) to generate segmentation maps.

Stage - 1 : Detector. In Stage 1 of the proposed method, the skin lesion is localized in the input image and then passed on as input to the Stage 2. The Detector can be divided into three major components namely the base network, region proposal network (RPN), and the RCNN. The base network generates a feature map of the input image to be used by the RPN. We used the ResNet50 network [10] and its pre-trained weights on ImageNet. The RPN then acts on the feature map from the base network and outputs the region proposals in the form of set anchor boxes. These boxes have a high chance of containing the lesion from the input feature map. Thereafter, each proposed region is classified into lesion/non-lesion and the bounding box coordinates of the proposal are trimmed to fit the lesion entirely by the RCNN. As given in [25], time-distributed convolution layers were used for the RCNN to aid in avoiding repeated classification and also in accommodating the differing number of regions proposed by the RPN per image. Finally, Non-Maximum suppression was done with a threshold of 0.5 to remove the redundant boxes. Coordinates were scaled for the lesion in the original image. The network is depicted in Fig. 1 in supplementary material.

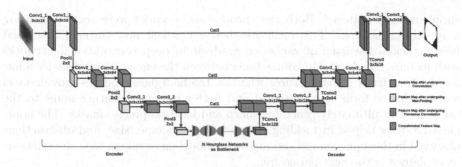

Fig. 2. SegMentor: Encoder, Hourglass bottleneck and Decoder of the Segmentation network.

Stage - 2 : SegMentor. After detecting the lesion at Stage 1, the detected section is cropped from the original image or padded appropriately to be given as input to the SegMentor. The segmentation network was designed in a network-in-network fashion. The base network has been derived from the well-known UNet [20] which was a major breakthrough in biomedical image segmentation.

We proposed the use of a sequence of hourglass modules which are smaller but effectively dense networks at the bottleneck of the autoencoder. The module enabled us to further compress and better represent the bottleneck features for them to be easily decoded by the decoder.

The encoder and decoder of the hourglass module are connected with processed skip connections instead of simple skip connections as in UNet [20]. We have demonstrated the effects of using multiple hourglass modules at the bottleneck in Table 1. The results showed that the segmentation accuracy reached a maximum for the optimum number of modules. Increasing the modules beyond the optimum number resulted in overfitting of the network. The following paragraphs give an insight into the encoder, decoder, hourglass modules, and training strategy followed for the SegMentor network. The SegMentor is depicted in Fig. 2.

Encoder - Decoder: The combination of an encoder and a decoder, termed autoencoder has been widely used across the literature for image-to-image translation tasks. Here, we exploited the same to obtain the mask for skin lesion. Our encoder comprises of convolution blocks where each block consist of 2 convolutional layers of filter size 3×3, each followed by batch normalization. We used max-pooling with steps 2×2 to downsample the features. Table 1 in supplementary material and Fig. 2 describe the detailed filter sizes and parameters for encoder. At the bottleneck of the encoder, feature map of size $64 \times 64 \times 128$ was fed into the hourglass modules to obtain the compressed feature map of size $64 \times 64 \times 256$ which was then fed into the decoder of the model. The decoder again comprises of convolutional blocks each having 2 convolutional layer of filter size 3×3 and number of filter for different blocks are 16, 64 and 128 same as that of the encoder, detailed filter sizes and parameters are given in Table 4 in supplementary material. Both the encoder and decoder were connected using long skip connections. This facilitates better gradient flow through them and hence, tackles the issue of vanishing gradient in deep convolutional networks such as ours. The long skip connections between the encoder and decoder allow for the transfer of global features whereas, the hourglass modules provide local features in the form of compressed and better extracted feature maps to the decoder. This ultimately generates sharp and location-precise masks. The hourglass modules helped in tackling the variation in shape, size, and obstructions observed in the input images and made the model more robust to such variations as explained in the next paragraph.

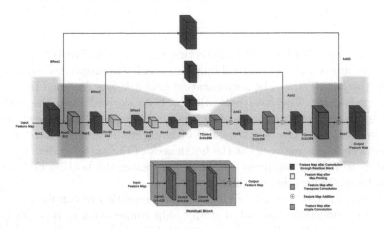

Fig. 3. Hourglass module and residual block.

Hourglass Module: Hourglass modules are dense autoencoders placed at the bottleneck of the main encoder-decoder model. Hourglass modules have long as well as short skip connections, allowing for the better flow of information across the network. This leads to better extraction of the required feature map at output. The short skip connection is incorporated to make the network residual and hence, avoid gradient vanishing while also transfer the information at every step. Each residual block has 3 convolutional layers with batch normalization and a skip connection from input layer to output layer of each block as given in Table 2 in supplementary material. Long skip connections between the hourglass-encoder and hourglass-decoder consist of intermediate residual blocks to process the skipped information before concatenating into the hourglass-decoder. This makes the network heavily dense allowing for better feature extraction and representation of bottleneck features. Table 3 in supplementary material and Fig. 3 shows the complete architecture of the hourglass module.

2.3   Training Strategy

The Detector was trained in step-wise manner where first, the RPN was trained followed by the regressor as described in [19] and [25]. Cross-entropy and categorical cross-entropy loss were used as classification loss in the RPN and RCNN respectively while the mean squared error (MSE) was used for both as regression loss. The masks obtained from the ISIC 2018 challenge were used to create synthetic ground truths for bounding box regression. Training strategy mentioned in [25] was followed for Faster-RCNN which is an standard approach in general.

We used a step-wise training strategy for SegMentor where first, the autoencoder was trained for few epochs to learn representation of the data. Afterwards, a single hourglass module was introduced at the bottleneck of the encoder-decoder pair for training while keeping the weights of the encoder-decoder pair frozen. Second hourglass module was introduced following the first one for training where the weights of all other components were kept frozen for few epochs and finally, the entire model was trained freely. Multiple modules can be introduced with similar strategy. Table 1 shows that as we increased the number of hourglass modules at the bottleneck of main network, the performance of framework increased till a certain point after which it started declining rapidly due to the overfitting on training dataset. Hence, we stopped at only 2 hourglass modules.

We used the dice coefficient loss for our segmentation model which is insensitive to class imbalance (poor foreground to background ratio) (Fig. 4).

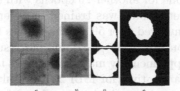

Fig. 4. Outputs at various stages of the pipeline. a) Lesion localized by the Detector, b) cropped image of the lesion, c) segmentation map from the SegMentor, d) final padded segmentation map.

3   Experimental Setup and Results

We evaluated our framework on Dice Similarity Coefficient, Jaccard Index, Accuracy, Sensitivity and Specificity. We used the Adam optimizer with a learning rate of 0.00001 and 0.0002 for the Detector and SegMentor respectively. It roughly took 6 h to train the Faster RCNN and 13 h to train the SegMentor alone for 90 epochs for final end-to-end training with single hourglass module, both on NVIDIA's GTX 1080 Ti with 12 GB memory.

Table 1. Results on ISIC 2018 validation set. In the table, UNet+nHG describes the network architecture used where 'n' represents the number of hourglass modules. Methods used to compare are taken from report [3] of the organisers of the ISIC 2018.

Method	Cropping Status	Accuracy	Dice	Jaccard	Sensitivity	Specificity
C. Qian (MaskRCNN)	-	0.942	0.898	0.802	0.906	0.963
Y. Seok (Ensemble + C.R.F.)	-	0.945	0.904	0.801	0.934	0.952
Y. Ji (Feature Aggregation CNN)	-	0.943	0.900	0.799	0.964	0.918
Y. Xue (SegAN)	-	0.945	0.903	0.798	0.940	0.942
UNet	W/o FRCNN	0.906	0.819	0.712	0.754	0.842
	With FRCNN	0.917	0.85	0.746	0.842	0.891
UNet + HG	W/o FRCNN	0.928	0.841	0.746	0.821	0.924
	With FRCNN	0.943	0.874	0.761	0.906	0.946
UNet + 2HG	W/o FRCNN	0.937	0.887	0.773	0.912	0.944
	With FRCNN	**0.959**	**0.915**	**0.809**	**0.968**	**0.973**
UNet + 3HG	W/o FRCNN	0.921	0.866	0.756	0.893	0.931
	With FRCNN	0.939	0.878	0.779	0.923	0.958

For evaluation, we randomly separated 594 images from ISIC 2018 challenge (training) dataset [3, 22] for pure testing purpose.

Apart from ISIC 2018 [3, 22], we evaluated our framework on PH^2 [15] and ISBI 2017 [4] datasets. The SegMentor was trained in multiple steps where initially only the encoder-decoder pair was trained for 20 epochs with a slightly smaller learning rate. Next, a single hourglass module introduced at the bottleneck and was trained alone for another 20 epochs with a slightly higher learning rate. Finally, the complete model was trained in an end-to-end manner for 90 epochs where the loss converged after 50 epochs. Tables 1 and 2 show the comparison among the results on ISIC 2018 [3, 22] and our results on ISBI 2017 [4] and PH^2 [15] as well. The supplementary material includes the qualitative (both success and failure) and quantitative (for ISBI 2017) results. Also, to further check the robustness of our proposed method, we performed 5-fold cross-validation on the ISIC 2018 dataset. The values obtained were 0.94 (Accuracy), 0.903 (Dice), and 0.783 (Jaccard). From Table 1, it can be seen that our method outperformed the famous MaskRCNN [9]. Though MaskRCNN also contains a detector and segmentor network, unlike ours, the training is done in an end-to-end fashion. In our method, the detector and segmentor are trained separately but resonate at the end. Also, MaskRCNN uses only simple 3×3 convolution layers to segment the lesion from the ROI but we have used a novel segmentation network altogether for the specified task.

Table 2. Results on ISBI 2017 validation and PH^2 dataset with UNet+2HG.

Dataset	Accuracy	Dice	Jaccard	Sensitivity	Specificity
PH^2	0.979	0.952	0.891	0.975	0.988
ISBI 2017	0.971	0.947	0.849	0.972	0.981
ISIC 2018	0.959	0.915	0.809	0.968	0.973

4 Conclusions

The proposed methodology with multiple networks achieved the state-of-the-art on publicly available datasets namely ISIC 2018. The results show, confident lesion mask boundary obtained from our network. However, the results were less than the present state-of-the art in terms of specificity. This was mainly in cases where the contrast of the lesion matched with the contrast of the normal nearby skin and so some background was segmented as foreground. In future, we will try to improve the performance in terms of specificity while simultaneously also aim for one single end-to-end network architecture to perform the detection and segmentation task together. Also, it is planned to extend the generalization of the network to enable segmentation of skin lesion from images taken from normal mobile cameras.

References

1. Cancer facts and figures 2018. American cancer society. https://www.cancer.org/content/dam/cancer-org/research/cancer-facts-and-statistics/annual-cancer-facts-and-figures/2018/cancer-facts-and-figures-2018.pdf. Accessed 3 May 2019
2. Celebi, M.E., Wen, Q., Iyatomi, H., Shimizu, K., Zhou, H., Schaefer, G.: A state-of-the-art survey on lesion border detection in dermoscopy images. Dermoscopy Image Anal. **10**, 97–129 (2015). https://doi.org/10.1201/b19107-5
3. Codella, N., et al.: Skin lesion analysis toward melanoma detection 2018: a challenge hosted by the international skin imaging collaboration (ISIC). arXiv preprint arXiv:1902.03368 (2019)
4. Codella, N.C., et al.: Skin lesion analysis toward melanoma detection: a challenge at the 2017 international symposium on biomedical imaging (ISBI), hosted by the international skin imaging collaboration (ISIC). In: 2018 IEEE 15th International Symposium on Biomedical Imaging (ISBI 2018), pp. 168–172. IEEE (2018)
5. Diwan, M.A., Meshram, S.K.: The study of skin cancer and its causes due to current scenarios in India (2017)
6. Milletari, F., Navab, N., Ahmadi, S.A.: V-net: fully convolutional neural networks for volumetric medical image segmentation. In: 3D Vision (3DV), pp. 565–571 (2016)
7. Garnavi, R., Aldeen, M., Celebi, M.E., Bhuiyan, A., Dolianitis, C., Varigos, G.: Skin lesion segmentation using color channel optimization and clustering-based histogram thresholding. In: International Conference on Machine Vision, Image Processing, and Pattern Analysis (MVIPPA09), World Academy of Science, Engineering and Technology, Bangkok, Thailand, vol. 60, pp. 549–557 (2009)

8. Guy, G.P., Machlin, S.R., Ekwueme, D.U., Yabroff, K.R.: Prevalence and costs of skin cancer treatment in the US, 2002–2006 and 2007–2011. Am. J. Prev. Med. **48**(2), 183–187 (2015)

9. He, K., Gkioxari, G., Dollár, P., Girshick, R.: Mask R-CNN. In: Proceedings of the IEEE International Conference on Computer Vision, pp. 2961–2969 (2017)

10. He, K., Zhang, X., Ren, S., Sun, J.: Deep residual learning for image recognition. In: Proceedings of the IEEE Conference on Computer Vision and Pattern Recognition, pp. 770–778 (2016)

11. Hu, J., Shen, L., Sun, G.: Squeeze-and-excitation networks. In: Proceedings of the IEEE Conference on Computer Vision and Pattern Recognition, pp. 7132–7141 (2018)

12. Burdick, J., Marques, O., Weinthal, J., Furht, B.: Rethinking skin lesion segmentation in a convolutional classifier. J. Digit. Imaging **31**(4), 435–440 (2018)

13. Kaul, C., Manandhar, S., Pears, N.: Focusnet: an attention-based fully convolutional network for medical image segmentation. In: International Symposium on Biomedical Imaging (ISBI) (2019)

14. Matthews, N.H., Li, W.Q., Qureshi, A.A., Weinstock, M.A., Cho, E.: Epidemiology of melanoma. In: Cutaneous Melanoma: Etiology and Therapy [Internet]. Codon Publications (2017)

15. Mendonça, T., Ferreira, P.M., Marques, J.S., Marcal, A.R., Rozeira, J.: Ph 2-a dermoscopic image database for research and benchmarking. In: 2013 35th Annual International Conference of the IEEE Engineering in Medicine and Biology Society (EMBC), pp. 5437–5440. IEEE (2013)

16. Mishra, R., Daescu, O.: Deep learning for skin lesion segmentation. In: 2017 IEEE International Conference on Bioinformatics and Biomedicine (BIBM), pp. 1189–1194. IEEE (2017)

17. Newell, A., Yang, K., Deng, J.: Stacked hourglass networks for human pose estimation. In: Leibe, B., Matas, J., Sebe, N., Welling, M. (eds.) ECCV 2016. LNCS, vol. 9912, pp. 483–499. Springer, Cham (2016). https://doi.org/10.1007/978-3-319-46484-8_29

18. Redmon, J., Divvala, S., Girshick, R., Farhadi, A.: You only look once: unified, real-time object detection. In: Proceedings of the IEEE Conference on Computer Vision and Pattern Recognition, pp. 779–788 (2016)

19. Ren, S., He, K., Girshick, R., Sun, J.: Faster R-CNN: towards real-time object detection with region proposal networks. In: Advances in Neural Information Processing Systems, pp. 91–99 (2015)

20. Ronneberger, O., Fischer, P., Brox, T.: U-Net: convolutional networks for biomedical image segmentation. In: Navab, N., Hornegger, J., Wells, W.M., Frangi, A.F. (eds.) MICCAI 2015. LNCS, vol. 9351, pp. 234–241. Springer, Cham (2015). https://doi.org/10.1007/978-3-319-24574-4_28

21. Shahin, A.H., Amer, K., Elattar, M.A.: Deep convolutional encoder-decoders with aggregated multi-resolution skip connections for skin lesion segmentation. In: 2019 IEEE 16th International Symposium on Biomedical Imaging (ISBI 2019), pp. 451–454, April 2019. https://doi.org/10.1109/ISBI.2019.8759172

22. Tschandl, P., Rosendahl, C., Kittler, H.: The HAM10000 dataset, a large collection of multi-source dermatoscopic images of common pigmented skin lesions. Sci. Data **5**, 180161 (2018)

23. Tu, W., Liu, X., Hu, W., Pan, Z.: Dense-residual network with adversarial learning for skin lesion segmentation. IEEE Access **7**, 77037–77051 (2019)

24. Ünver, H.M., Ayan, E.: Skin lesion segmentation in dermoscopic images with combination of yolo and grabcut algorithm. Diagnostics **9**(3), 72 (2019)

25. Vesal, S., Malakarjun Patil, S., Ravikumar, N., Maier, A.K.: A multi-task framework for skin lesion detection and segmentation. In: Stoyanov, D., et al. (eds.) CARE/CLIP/OR 2.0/ISIC -2018. LNCS, vol. 11041, pp. 285–293. Springer, Cham (2018). https://doi.org/10.1007/978-3-030-01201-4_31

26. Li, X., Aldridge, B., Ballerini, L., Fisher, R., Rees, J.: Depth data improves skin lesion segmentation. In: Yang, G.-Z., Hawkes, D., Rueckert, D., Noble, A., Taylor, C. (eds.) MICCAI 2009. LNCS, vol. 5762, pp. 1100–1107. Springer, Heidelberg (2009). https://doi.org/10.1007/978-3-642-04271-3_133

27. Xue, Y., Xu, T., Huang, X.: Adversarial learning with multi-scale loss for skin lesion segmentation. In: 2018 IEEE 15th International Symposium on Biomedical Imaging (ISBI 2018), pp. 859–863. IEEE (2018)

28. Yuan, Y., Chao, M., Lo, Y.C.: Automatic skin lesion segmentation using deep fully convolutional networks with Jaccard distance. IEEE Trans. Med. Imaging **36**(9), 1876–1886 (2017)

29. Li, Y., Shen, L.: Skin lesion analysis towards melanoma detection using deep learning network. Sensors **18**(2), 556 (2018)

Choroid Disease Classification Using Convolutional Neural Network

Neetha George[✉] and Jiji C. V

College of Engineering Trivandrum, Kerala, India
{neethageorge,jijicv}@cet.ac.in

Abstract. Enhanced depth imaging optical coherence tomography (EDI OCT) helps in better understanding of deeper layers of retina, the choroid, both qualitatively and quantitatively. Morphological variation in these images can lead to the identification of a spectrum of choroid related diseases. Early detection of these diseases make the treatment easier besides saving money and time. In this paper, we propose a deep learning based model using convolutional neural network (CNN) for automated classification of choroid diseases namely central serous chorioretinopathy (CSC), choroidal neovascularisation (CNV) and polypoid choroidal vasculopathy (PCV). Here, a 16 layer CNN network similar to VGG 16 is trained end-to-end using the choroid images to distinguish the spectrum of diseases. Experimental results show that prediction using our system is reliable and consistent. The method gives an accuracy of 93% and can be used as a powerful tool for automated diagnosis of choroid related diseases.

Keywords: Choroid diseases · Convolutional Neural Network · Classification.

1 Introduction

Optical coherence tomography (OCT) is a non invasive technique for obtaining high resolution images of living tissues. Presently, OCT finds wide application in ophthalmology for diagnosis and treatment of retinal diseases. Enhanced Depth Imaging Optical Coherence Tomography (EDI OCT) introduced by Spaide et al. [5] enabled more accurate and better analysis of the choroid. Development in the field of EDI OCT has recently provided new insights into variety of chorioretinal disorders. Choroid is the layer of tissue lying between retina and sclera. It consists of five layers - the upper Bruch's membrane, the choriocapillaris consisting of capillaries with fine fenestrations, Sattler's layer composed of medium sized capillaries, Haller's layer consisting of large capillaries or vascular patterns of the choroid and Choroid Sclera Interface (CSI) [8]. The architecture of the choroid is shown in Fig. 1. All these layers can be distinguished in the EDI OCT image of a normal eye. However, there can be variations when pathologies are present.

Pachychoroid is defined as thick choroid or abnormal choroid due to increase in the thickness of choroid layer which is mainly caused by dilation of choroid

R. V. Babu et al. (Eds.): NCVPRIPG 2019, CCIS 1249, pp. 600–608, 2020.
https://doi.org/10.1007/978-981-15-8697-2_56

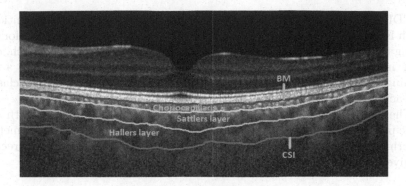

Fig. 1. Choroid layers

vessels in the Hallers layer. The increased thickness compresses the upper chori-ocapillaris and Sattler's layer [8]. Pachychoroid disease mainly emanate from three disorders viz. 1. Central serous chorioretinopathy (CSC) 2. Choroidal neo-vascularisation (CNV) and 3. Polypoid choroidal vasculopathy (PCV). All these are represented as pachy choroid and the individual stages can be identified using morphological changes. Pachy choroid spectrum is characterised by the thinning of choriocapillaris and Sattler's layer, thickening of Hallers layer and an increase in thickness of the choroid. With the progression of pathology, a gradual transition to a further stage of the disorder can take place.

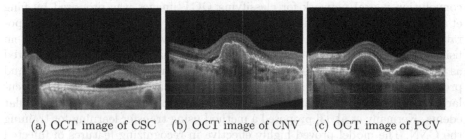

(a) OCT image of CSC   (b) OCT image of CNV   (c) OCT image of PCV

Fig. 2. OCT images with pathologies

CSC is an idiopathic disorder of the macula, which is characterised by serous detachment with or without ablation of the RPE. This is the first stage of pachy choroid disorder. CNV, considered as the second stage, is the development of a choroidal neovascular membrane which increases the thickness of the choroid. PCV is described as a rapid increase in thickness of the choroidal capillaries. This happens under the RPE and develops polyps. This is the last and most advanced stage of pachy choroid disease spectrum. Sample OCT images of choroid with CSC, CNV and PCV are shown in Fig. 2.

EDI OCT enables identification of pachy choroid disorders recognition of which is important for diagnosis and treatment. An automatic method for classifying these disorders would help in improving the diagnosis and research, especially in situations where experts are less. In this paper, we propose a deep learning based method using Convolutional Neural Network (CNN) for classifying pachy choroid OCT images.

The organization of the paper is as follows. Section 2 familiarises with some of the popular works using deep learning. Section 3 details the proposed method. Experimental results are presented in Sect. 4. Conclusions with future directions are given in Sect. 5.

2 Recent Works

Deep learning techniques have been applied to a variety of medical field applications to help understanding and classification of various problems. Oscar et al. [6] presented a CNN based model, OCTNET for automatic classification of diabetic macular edema images. The model was trained end to end using raw images and attained high accuracy when tested on OCT volumes. Results reported that the method effectively classifies OCT volumes as normal or pathogenic. Another model for detecting edema was proposed by Muhammad Awais et al. [1]. The method used pre trained CNN network for classifying normal and abnormal images. Features were extracted from different stages of the network and classification was performed based on these features using different classifiers. Results show good classification between normal and diseased images. A lesion-aware convolution neural network for classifying OCT images was proposed by fang et al. [2]. To improve classification, information from lesion regions were incorporated and good results were reported. Lu et al. [4] developed an intelligent system using 101-layer ResNet for multiclass OCT image classification. It was reported as the first one in multiclass detection. The method reported good efficiency and proved helpful for automatic diagnosis and classification of images with macular hole, epiretinal membrane, serous macular detachment and cystoid macular edema. Kermany et al. [3] proposed a method using transfer learning for training the CNN. The model proved highly effective in recognizing features of infected as well as normal images. Results demonstrated that this method could detect images with choroidal neovascularization, macular edema and drusen excellently with high accuracy.

Most of the methods discussed above focused mainly on binary classification between normal as well as abnormal images. But in real clinical setting, specific abnormalities need to be classified. A good detection system would help the ophthamologist for early detection and diagnosis of diseases. Here we propose a simple and efficient method for automatic detection of pachy choroid diseases using truncated VGG-16 network.

3   Proposed Method

VGG-16 is characterised by its simplicity, using small, 3×3 convolutional filters for implementing deep networks [7]. We propose a model using CNN similar to VGG-16 for the detection and classification of normal as well as abnormal choroid OCT images. Initially, a binary classifier model was trained to classify between normal and pachy choroid images. For this, the network was trained end-to-end randomly selecting weights for retraining during back propagation. Further, using the same CNN, pachy choroid diseases are also classified. The architecture was changed with four classifiers at the output.

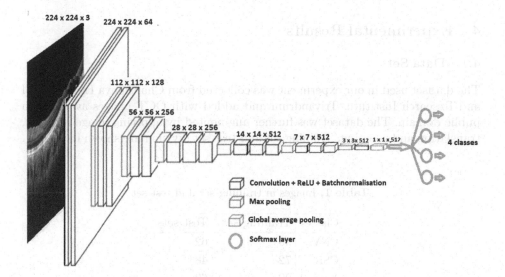

Fig. 3. CNN architecture

3.1   Deep Learning Model

The network model used in our work is a 16 layer CNN similar to VGG-16. OCT images of size $224 \times 224 \times 3$ are given as inputs. The architecture of the network is shown in Fig. 3. In each convolution layer, learnable filters are convolved with the input to generate activation map. A stack of 16 convolution layers followed by element wise ReLu and batch normalization is used for feature extraction. Different convolution layers learn features from the given image during training and updates weights continuously. The output from the convolution layers is passed through an activation function, ReLu, which decides the presence of a feature at a given point in the image. This is followed by max pooling which reduces dimensionality of the feature map by selecting maximum value in the max pool window. Drop out layers are added next to the max pool stage for random selection of input units for weight updation. The final convolution layer is followed by global average pooling layer which reduces overfitting and spatial dimensions. During training phase, the loss generated between the predicted class and the actual classes for each image is back propagated to update the selected weights. When a new image is fed to the network during testing, based on the probability generated, it is assigned to particular class.

The modified architecture for pachy choroid classification is shown in Fig. 3. In the convolution stage we have filter size 3×3 with depth 64, 64, 128, 128, 256, 256, 256, 256, 256, 512, 512, 512, 512, 512, 512, 512 followed by batch normalisation and ReLu and 6 max pooling layers in between. The final convolution layer is followed by a global average pooling layer and the final softmax layer which produces output class labels.

4 Experimental Results

4.1 Data Set

The dataset used in our experiment was collected from Chaithanya Eye Hospital and Research Institute, Trivandrum and added with OCT images available in public domain. The dataset was further augmented by applying image rotation, translation and zooming. Training set and test set division are shown in Table 1.

Table 1. Images in training set and test set

Classes	Training set	Test set
CNV	90	62
CSR	72	48
Normal	90	60
PCV	66	44

Dataset contains more than 100 OCT images of normal eyes as well abnormal images corresponding to each choroid abnormality. Example images from the data set are shown in Fig. 4

4.2 Training

For binary classification between normal and pachy choroid images, the CNN network is trained end to end with drop out layers. Using checkpoint, the snap shots of the weights were saved at regular intervals. This helps in reloading the weights from the previous saved state during training. To reduce over fitting and over training, the training process is automatically terminated by checking the loss by early stopping. Further, for multi class classification, the whole network is trained from the scratch using images from our data set.

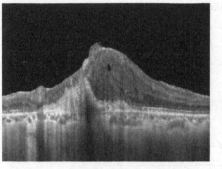 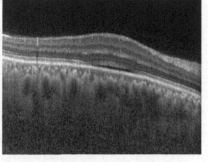

(a) EDI OCT image1   (b) EDI OCT image2

Fig. 4. Example images in the data set

4.3   Evaluation

The results of our network was analysed for binary and multi class classification. The system was given normal OCT images as one class and all pachy choroid images together as second class for binary classification. In the architecture shown in Fig. 3, the final number of outputs are set to two. The network was trained using images from our data set. Performance of the system is evaluated in terms of precision, recall and f1score. The metrices are defined as

$$recall = \frac{\sum(TP)}{\sum(TP) + \sum(FN)}, \tag{1}$$

$$precision = \frac{\sum(TP)}{\sum(TP) + \sum(FP)}, \tag{2}$$

$$f1\ score = \frac{2 \times recall \times precision}{recall\ +\ precision}, \tag{3}$$

TP represents true positive, FP is false positive and FN indicates false negative.

Accuracy obtained for binary classification is 100%. Our system was perfect in classifying normal versus abnormal images with precision, recall and f1 score 1.

For classifying pachy choroid images, the network used is the same shown in Fig. 3. Network was trained end-to-end using four different image sets. The system was evaluated for diagnosing central serous chorioretinopathy, Choroidal neovascularisation, polypoid choroidal vasculopathy and normal OCT images. An accuracy of 0.93 was obtained in the multiclass classification. The results obtained are tabulated in Table 2

We analysed VGG-16 network pretrained with ImageNet data for comparing our classification task. A comparison of average precision, recall and f1 score for the two architectures are shown in Table 3.

Confusion matrix shows assignment of test images to predictions. Matrix is generated with true labels represented along rows and predicted labels represented in columns. Diagonal elements of the matrix gives the number of images

Table 2. Summary of classification report for our model

	Precision	Recall	f1-score
CNV	1	0.68	0.81
CSR	0.94	1	0.97
Normal	1	1	1
PCV	0.78	1	0.88

Table 3. Comparison of classification result

	Precision	Recall	f1-score
VGG-16	0.8	0.8	0.8
Our network	0.93	0.91	0.91

classified correctly for a particular class and other elements show the number of misclassified images. Confusion matrix generated for VGG 16 and our network are shown in Fig. 5 for comparison.

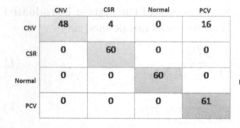

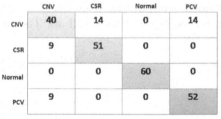

(a) Confusion Matrix for our model   (b) Confusion Matrix for VGG 16

Fig. 5. Comparison of Confusion matrix

Figure 6 shows the confusion matrix plot for the two models. For our network, out of 68 test images for CNV, 20 were misclassified. For all other classes, the predicted labels were same as the true labels. But for VGG 16, as shown in figure, there was misclassification for all pachy choroid classes. This shows that our system outperforms VGG 16 in pachy choroid classification.

Receiver Operating Characteristics (ROC), is a probability plot with false positive rate on x axis and true positive values on the y axis. ROC curve obtained for our model is shown in Fig. 7. This curve shows the capability of the classifier in differentiating different classes. Area under the curve in ROC plot gives a separability measure. Area near to one represents good separability. ROC curve obtained for our model is is shown in figure. Area value indicates that our classifier is good in distinguishing pachy choroid images.

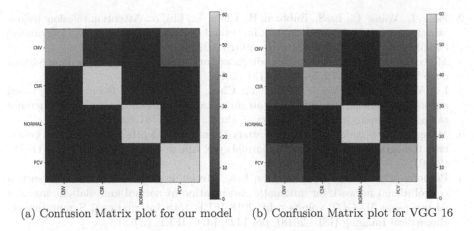

(a) Confusion Matrix plot for our model   (b) Confusion Matrix plot for VGG 16

Fig. 6. Confusion Matrix plot

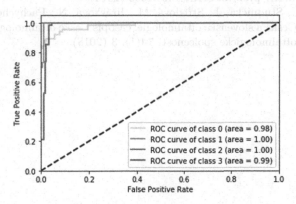

Fig. 7. Receiver Operating Characteristics

5   Discussion and Conclusion

We proposed a deep learning based system using CNN to classify pachy choroid diseases from OCT images. Our method has an accuracy of 93% and is highly consistent. A comparison of the experimental result with clinical finding proved high correlation between them. The method can be used as a powerful tool for the diagnosis and earlier detection of pachy choroid stage. This system can be applied in situations were expert opinion is not readily available.

References

1. Awais, M., Müller, H., Tang, T.B., Meriaudeau, F.: Classification of SD-OCT images using a deep learning approach. In: 2017 IEEE International Conference on Signal and Image Processing Applications (ICSIPA), pp. 489–492. IEEE (2017)

2. Fang, L., Wang, C., Li, S., Rabbani, H., Chen, X., Liu, Z.: Attention tolesion: lesion-aware convolutional neural network for retinal optical coherence tomography image classification. IEEE Trans. Med. Imaging (2019)
3. McKeown, A.: Identifying medical diagnoses and treatable diseases by image-based deep learning. Cell **172**(5), 1122–1131 (2018)
4. Lu, W., Tong, Y., Yu, Y., Xing, Y., Chen, C., Shen, Y.: Deep learning-based automated classification of multi-categorical abnormalities from optical coherence tomography images. Transl. Vis. Sci. Technol. **7**(6), 41–41 (2018)
5. Margolis, R., Spaide, R.F.: A pilot study of enhanced depth imaging optical coherence tomography of the choroid in normal eyes. Am. J. Ophthalmol. **147**(5), 811–815 (2009)
6. Perdomo, O., Otálora, S., González, F.A., Meriaudeau, F., Müller, H.: Oct-net: a convolutional network for automatic classification of normal and diabetic macular edema using SD-OCT volumes. In: 2018 IEEE 15th International Symposium on Biomedical Imaging (ISBI 2018), pp. 1423–1426. IEEE (2018)
7. Simonyan, K., Zisserman, A.: Very deep convolutional networks for large-scale image recognition. arXiv preprint arXiv:1409.1556 (2014)
8. Stepanov, A., Studnička, J., Středová, M., Jirásková, N.: Pachychoroid disease of the macula. Ceska a slovenska oftalmologie: casopis Ceske oftalmologicke spolecnosti a Slovenske oftalmologicke spolecnosti **74**(1), 3 (2018)

Hyper Vision Net: Kidney Tumor Segmentation Using Coordinate Convolutional Layer and Attention Unit

D. Sabarinathan[1], M. Parisa Beham[2]($\boxtimes$), and S. M. Md. Mansoor Roomi[3]

[1] Couger Inc, Tokyo, Japan
[2] Sethu Institute of Technology, Virudhunagar, Tamilnadu, India
parisaphd2011@gmail.com
[3] Thiagarajar College of Engineering, Madurai, Tamil Nadu, India

Abstract. Challenges in accurate tumor detection paves the way to haste the improvement of solid kidney tumor semantic segmentation methodologies. Accurate segmentation of kidney tumor in computer tomography (CT) images is a challenging task due to the non-uniform motion, similar appearance and various shape. Inspired by this fact, in this manuscript, we present a novel kidney tumor segmentation method using deep learning network termed as hyper vision Net model. All the existing U-net models are using a modified version of U-net to segment the kidney tumor region. In the proposed architecture, we introduced supervision layers in the decoder part, and it refines even minimal regions in the output. A dataset consists of real arterial phase abdominal CT scans of 300 patients, including 45964 images has been provided from KiTs19 for training and validation of the proposed model. Compared with the state-of-the-art segmentation methods, the results demonstrate the superiority of our approach on training dice value score of 0.9552 and 0.9633 in tumor region and kidney region, respectively.

Keywords: Kidney tumor segmentation · Coordinate convolution · U-net · Hyper vision net · Attention unit

1 Introduction

As per the study of American Cancer Society, Kidney cancer is among the 10 most common cancers in both men and women. Overall, the lifetime risk for evolving kidney cancer in men is about 1 in 48 and for women is 1 in 83. Many kidney cancers are found at an early stage but others are found at a more advanced stage. One of the main reasons for this is, the kidneys are deep inside the body so that small tumors cannot be seen during a physical exam [1]. Wide range of imaging techniques have been enabled to detect the kidney tumors at the early stage. In recent years, this approach has become more popular because it offers a chance to remove only the tumor lesion while preserving the much healthy kidney parenchyma. This method can also be useful for small renal masses treatment. After accurate segmentation of kidney tumor, some valuable information like renal volume, anatomy of kidney, etc., can be obtained. According to the clinical study

© Springer Nature Singapore Pte Ltd. 2020
R. V. Babu et al. (Eds.): NCVPRIPG 2019, CCIS 1249, pp. 609–618, 2020.
https://doi.org/10.1007/978-981-15-8697-2_57

[2], it is very difficult to predict the locations of various renal tumors in CT or MRI medical images. Moreover, these renal tumors are having dissimilar shapes and sizes, and most of the tumors have a similar appearance with their parenchyma and other nearby tissues. Thus the segmentation of kidney tumor region become a very challenging task in the CT images.

In the literature several algorithms and networks have been introduced to segment renal tumor from CT images. M G Lingararu et al. [3] proposed a computer-aided clinical tool based on adaptive level sets which was used to analyze 125 renal lesions from contrast-enhanced abdominal CT scans of 43 patients. In this method tumors are robustly segmented with 0.80 overlap between manual and semi-automated quantifications. The method also identified morphological discrepancies among various kinds of lesions. Lee et al. [4] presented an automated method for detecting and segmenting small renal mass (SRM) in contrast-enhanced CT images using texture and context feature classification. Their experimental results produced specificity of 99.63% in the SRM detection.

B Shah et al. [5] presented a computer aided segmentation technique using machine learning algorithms. Guanyu Yang et al. [6] presented an automated kidney segmentation in CT images based on multi atlas image registration. First they registered the down-sampled patient image with a set of low-resolution atlas images and thus the left and right kidneys are segmented. In the next step, the kidneys are cropped and aligned with the set of high-resolution atlas images to obtain final segmented results.

Recently more papers have been published on renal tumor segmentation using deep convolutional networks. In [7], a patch-wise approach is used to train the ConvNet to predict the class membership of the central voxel in 2D patches. Then densely processing the ConvNet over each slice of a CT scan produced a segmented kidney tumors. Skalski et al. [8] presented a novel hybrid level set method with elliptical shape constraints for kidney segmentation. Here RUSBoost and the decision trees technique were used to identify the kidney and tumor. This approach resolved the main problems like class imbalance and the number of voxels required to classify. Their proposed model produced an overall accuracy amounts to 92.1%. In [9] automated segmentation of kidneys using fully convolutional neural networks is presented, which is trained end-to-end, on slice wise axial-CT sections. Similarly Wang et al. [10] proposed an interactive segmentation by incorporating CNNs into a bounding box. They have also made the CNN model more adaptive by image specific fine tuning process.

Even though CNNs have achieved benchmark performance for automatic medical image segmentation, accuracy and robustness is still a challenging issue. To address these problems, U-Net is proposed [11] for automatic medical image segmentation where the U network synthesize the significant information by minimizing a cost function in the first half of the network and construct an image at the second half. Inspired by the U-Net model, we approached the present task of kidney tumor segmentation by proposing a novel Hyper vision Net model, in which we introduced Hyper vision layers in the decoder part of the U-net architecture and thus it refines even very small regions in the output tumor image. Our proposed framework segment the tumor regions of the kidney accurately and the results are proved quantitatively as well as qualitatively.

2 Dataset

A collection of multi-phase CT images, segmenting masks and their respective clinical reports of 300 patients have been provided in the challenging KiTs19 dataset [12]. For training, 210 (70%) of these patients CT images were selected randomly and released publicly for the 2019 MICCAI Kidney Tumor Segmentation (KiTS) Challenge. The objective of this dataset is to create a reliable learning-based kidney and kidney tumor semantic segmentation methods. Among the 210 patient's CT images, 32175 and 13790 images are used for the purpose of training and validation respectively. Figure 1 shows an example of CT images of 5 patients.

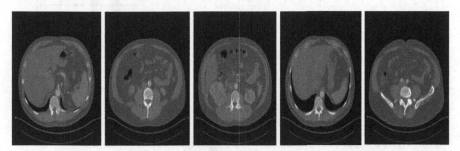

Fig. 1. An example of CT scan images from KiTs19 challenge dataset

3 Proposed Method

In this section, the detailed structure of the proposed Hyper vision net model and the modified loss function is described. Compared to othe architectures, In the proposed method, as the receptive field increases across successive layers of hyper vision net, predictions computed at different layers embed spatial information at different scales. Especially for imbalanced multi-class segmentation, different scales can contain complementary information. Also as the gradient is propagated in intermediate layers, the proposed network is able to update the weights more efficiently.

3.1 Image Preprocessing

In this work, before training the model, all the CT images are resized into 256 × 256 and divided by the value 255 to normalize the pixel value between 0 to 1.

3.2 Hyper Vision Net Model

Figure 2 shows the detailed architecture of the proposed Hyper vision Net model. The network has the properties of encoder and decoder structure of vanilla U-Net [13]. As proposed by [14], firstly the input image is passed into the coordinate convolution layer and then it is passed into the encoder part of the Hyper vision Net model. Here, to improvise the generalization capacity of the model, the coordinate convolutional layer is used which helps the network to select the features related to translation invariance. Also, with the support of this layer, spatial coordinates are mapped with the Cartesian coordinate's space through the use of extra coordinate channels. This kind of mapping provides power to the model to use either complete or varying degree of translation features. As suggested in the original paper [14], we have also used two extra coordinate channels (i, j) in the proposed work.

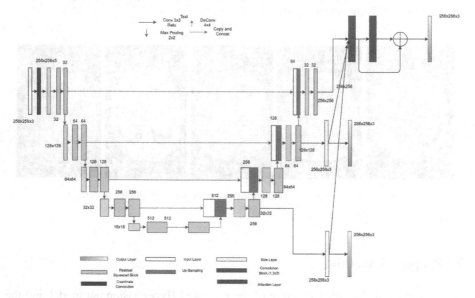

Fig. 2. An overview of detailed architecture of hyper vision net

During down-sampling in the encoder phase, there are four blocks have been used. In each block, the first layer is a 3 × 3 convolutional layer, followed by two residual blocks, and at the end, a 2 × 2 max-pooling layer is added. Our network also contains a deep residual block where the details of the block is shown in Fig. 3. We increased the depth of the residual block [17] to acquire multiple features, and in turn it enhances the performance of tumor segmentation. Similar to encoder phase, the decoder phase is also utilized the same blocks except the max-pooling layers replaced with the up-sampling layers. To get more robust feature maps after down-sampling, we added one 3 × 3 convolutional layer and residual block before passing the features into the encoder phase. Batch normalization and dropout layers are incorporated in both encoder and decoder phase. The network is trained with the exponential linear activation function.

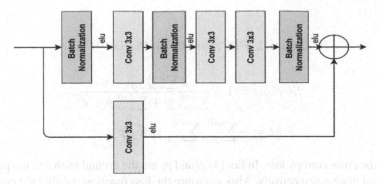

Fig. 3. Residual block used in the hyper vision net

Inspired by Skeleton network [15], two hyper vision layers are introduced in the decoder part which is used to refine even very small regions in the output. The output of two decoder layers is then fused with final decoder output. This fused output was given to the attention layer [16]. The attention layer is used to create a spatial attention on the channel attention of encoder output and the decoder output. Equation (1) and Eq. (2) shows the details of mathematical operations.

$$C_A = f_a \left[w_1 \left(w_0 \left(\frac{\sum_{i=1}^{n} x_i}{n} \right) \right) + w_1 (w_0(\max(x_i))) \right] \tag{1}$$

Where $w_0 \in R^{C/r \times C}$ and $w_1 \in R^{C \times C/r}$, f_a is denotes the Sigmoid activation

$$S_A = f_{con} \left(\left[\frac{\sum_{i=1}^{n} C_{Ai}}{n} \| \max(C_{Ai}) \right] \right) \tag{2}$$

where, f_{con} denotes the Sigmoid activation.

For the given intermediate feature map, the proposed model successively infers attention maps along channel and spatial, a two separate dimensions, then the attention maps are multiplied with the input feature map for adaptive feature refinement. The output of the attention layer is added with fused output. Further, the output of hyper vision layer and the final layer are passed through a soft max layer individually under the supervision of ground truth. The final output layer has three channels such as, tumor region, kidney region and the background.

3.3 Loss Function

In this work, Adam [18] optimizer is applied which perfectly update network weights in an iterative manner in training data. Adam makes average in first moment but also in second moments of gradients to adapt the learning rate parameter. Our Loss function is the sum of categorical cross entropy Dice loss channel one (C_0) and Dice Loss channel two (C_1) as defined in Eq. (3).

$$Loss = L + DiceLoss(C_0) + DiceLoss(C_1) \tag{3}$$

$$DiceLoss = 1 - \frac{2\sum_{n=k}^{i=0} y_i p_i + \in}{\sum_{n=k}^{i=0} y_i + \sum_{n=k}^{i=0} p_i + \in} \tag{4}$$

$$L = -\sum_{j=0}^{M} \sum_{i=0}^{N} y_{ij} \log(p_{ij}) \tag{5}$$

L is the cross entropy loss. In Eq. (4) y_i and p_i are the ground truth and the predicted segmented images respectively. Also, to ensure the loss function stability the coefficient $\in$ is used.

4   Experiment and Results

4.1   Training

The proposed network is trained with three outputs, which include the two hyper vision layers and one fused output layer. The weight updates performed with Adam optimizer using a learning rate of 0.001 and reduced after ten epochs to 10% if there is no improvement in the validation loss. The batch size is chosen to four, and the total epochs are set to 500. The model is trained using Nvidia 1080 GTX GPU.

4.2   Result and Discussion

To evaluate the performance of the proposed Hyper vision Net model, the standard Dice score is considered as an evaluation metric. For our experimentation, we were provided with 32175 and 13790 images as a training and validation images respectively. Table 1 shows the segmentation results of the proposed Hyper vision Net model for training and validation images with and without considering the attention layer. From the table it is observed that, during training, the proposed method achieves the Dice score of 0.8967 and 0.9535 for the tumor region and kidney region by involving attention layer in the proposed network respectively. Similarly, our network with attention layer achieves Dice score of 0.8967 and 0.9535 for tumor and kidney region respectively. It is also inferred that, without incorporating attention layer in the Hyper vision Net, Dice score of training and validation experimentation is reduced to 0.8186 and 0.84 respectively for tumor region, whereas for kidney region it is only 0.9375 and 0.93. From the experimental results we understand the power of attention layer in the proposed network. Attention layer helps the network to focus more in the segmentation region and utilize the fused features well.

Table 1. Results of the proposed hyper vision net model on KiTs19 dataset with and without attention layer

Model type	Image type	Number of images	Dice score of tumor region	Dice score of kidney region
Without attention layer	Training	32175	0.8186	0.9375
	Validation	13790	0.84	0.93
With attention layer	Training	32175	**0.9552**	**0.9633**
	Validation	13790	**0.8967**	**0.9535**

Table 2 shows the comparative analysis of various kidney segmentation methods with our proposed hyper vision net model. From the table it is observed that even for the minimal number of cases the dice coefficient (%) obtained is maximum of 96 by Cuignet et al. [21]. Comparatively our proposed method achieved 96.33% of Dice score for 300 cases which consist of 32175 training images.

Table 2. Comparison of segmentation methods for the right and left kidneys in CT scans according to the Dice score

Method	# Cases	Dice score of kidney region
Hierarchical atlases [19]	100	94
Atlas + graph cut [20]	100	90
Random forests + atlas [21]	233	96
ConvNet [7]	79	95
Deep learning [9]	165	86
KiTs19 Challenge [22]	300	97.37
Our method	300	92.55

The qualitative results of KiTs19 dataset on our proposed Hyper vision net model is shown in Fig. 4. Figure 4 (a) and Fig. 4 (b) shows the input images and their respective ground truth images used for experimentation. The segmented output images are depicted in Fig. 4 (c). In the output image the blue colored spot is a tumor region, whereas the red color spot is the kidney region. Total background other than the tumor and kidney regions are neglected for easy interpretation. From the qualitative results it is observed that the final segmented output is merely similar to the ground truth images which shows the efficacy of our proposed Hyper vision Network.

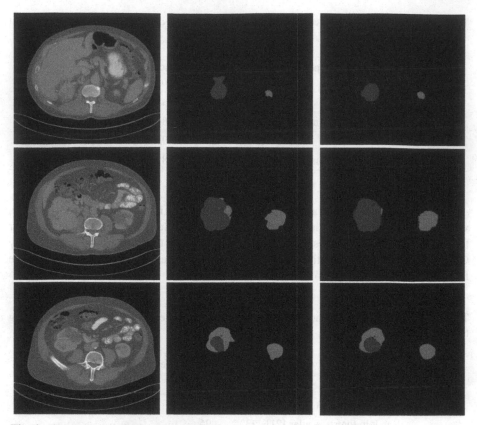

Fig. 4. Illustration of original input CT images and their respective kidney and tumor segmented output images (Color figure online)

5   Conclusion

Wide range of accurate image segmentation techniques are required to detect the kidney tumors at the early stage. Motivated by the superior performance of Convolutional Neural Networks, in this paper, a Hyper vision Net architecture is presented to segment the kidney and tumor region which is automatic and accurate. This challenge is carried out using KiTs19 dataset. The performance of our method is reported quantitatively and qualitatively for the given type of training and validation images. Our method achieved a maximum Dice score of 0.9633 for the training set and 0.9535 for the validation set. Comparatively the proposed Hyper vision Net reported best segmentation results in terms of Dice score.

References

1. https://www.cancer.org/cancer/kidneycancer/detection-diagnosis-staging/etection.html
2. Hesamian, M.H., Jia, W., He, X., Kennedy, P.: Deep learning techniques for medical image segmentation: achievements and challenges. J. Digit. Imaging **32**(4), 582–596 (2019). https://doi.org/10.1007/s10278-019-00227-x
3. Linguraru, M.G., et al.: Automated noninvasive classification of renal cancer on multiphase CT. Med. Phys. **38**(10), 5738–5746 (2011). https://doi.org/10.1118/1.3633898
4. Lee, H.S., Hong, H., Kim, J.: Detection and segmentation of small renal masses in contrast-enhanced CT images using texture and context feature classification. In: 2017 IEEE 14th International Symposium on Biomedical Imaging (ISBI 2017), Melbourne, VIC, pp. 583–586 (2017). https://doi.org/10.1109/isbi.2017.7950588
5. Shah, B., Sawla, C., Bhanushali, S., Bhogale, P.: Kidney tumor segmentation and classification on abdominal CT scans. Int. J. Comput. Appl. **164**(9), 1–5 (2017)
6. Yang, G., et al.: Automatic kidney segmentation in CT images based on multi-atlas image registration. In: 2014 36th Annual International Conference of the IEEE Engineering in Medicine and Biology Society, Chicago, IL, pp. 5538–5541 (2014). https://doi.org/10.1109/EMBC.2014.6944881
7. Thong, W., Kadoury, S., Piché, N., Pal, C.J.: Convolutional networks for kidney segmentation in contrast-enhanced CT scans. Comput. Methods Biomech. Biomed. Eng.: Imaging Vis. (2016). https://doi.org/10.1080/21681163.2016.1148636
8. Skalski, A., Jakubowski, J., Drewniak, T.: Kidney tumor segmentation and detection on computed tomography data. In: 2016 IEEE International Conference on Imaging Systems and Techniques (IST), Chania, pp. 238–242 (2016). https://doi.org/10.1109/ist.2016.7738230
9. Sharma, K.:Machine learning methods for segmentation in autosomal dominant polycystic kidney disease. Sharma2017MachineLM (2017)
10. Wang, G., et al.: Interactive medical image segmentation using deep learning with image-specific fine tuning. IEEE Trans. Med. Imaging **37**(7), 1562–1573 (2018). https://doi.org/10.1109/TMI.2018.2791721
11. Ronneberger, O., Fischer, P., Brox, T.: U-Net: convolutional networks for biomedical image segmentation. In: Navab, N., Hornegger, J., Wells, W.M., Frangi, A.F. (eds.) MICCAI 2015. LNCS, vol. 9351, pp. 234–241. Springer, Cham (2015). https://doi.org/10.1007/978-3-319-24574-4_28
12. Heller, N., et al.: The KiTS19 Challenge Data: 300 Kidney Tumor Cases with Clinical Context, CT Semantic Segmentations, and Surgical Outcomes, arXiv:1904.00445 (2019)
13. Shen, W., Wang, X., Wang, Y., Bai, X., Zhang, Z.: Deepcontour: a deep convolutional feature learned by positive-sharing loss for contour detection. In: Proceedings of the IEEE Conference on Computer Vision and Pattern Recognition, pp. 3982–3991 (2015)
14. Liu, R., et al.: An Intriguing Failing of Convolutional Neural Networks and the CoordConv Solution arXiv:1807.03247 (2018)
15. Nathan, S., Kansal, P.: SkeletonNet: Shape Pixel to Skeleton Pixel. CVPRw (2019). arXiv:1907.01683
16. https://arxiv.org/ftp/arxiv/papers/1910/1910.03274.pdf
17. He, K., Zhang, X., Ren, S., Sun, J.: Deep residual learning for image recognition. In: Proceedings of the IEEE Conference on Computer Vision and Pattern Recognition, pp. 770–778 (2016)
18. Kingma, D.P., Ba, J.: Adam: a method for stochastic optimization, arXiv:1412.6980 (2014)
19. Wolz, R., Chu, C., Misawa, K., Mori, K., Rueckert, D.: Multi-organ abdominal CT segmentation using hierarchically weighted subject-specific atlases. In: Ayache, N., Delingette, H., Golland, P., Mori, K. (eds.) MICCAI 2012. LNCS, vol. 7510, pp. 10–17. Springer, Heidelberg (2012). https://doi.org/10.1007/978-3-642-33415-3_2

20. Chu, C., et al.: Multi-organ segmentation based on spatially-divided probabilistic atlas from 3D abdominal CT images. In: Mori, K., Sakuma, I., Sato, Y., Barillot, C., Navab, N. (eds.) MICCAI 2013. LNCS, vol. 8150, pp. 165–172. Springer, Heidelberg (2013). https://doi.org/10.1007/978-3-642-40763-5_21

21. Cuingnet, R., Prevost, R., Lesage, D., Cohen, L.D., Mory, B., Ardon, R.: Automatic detection and segmentation of kidneys in 3D CT images using random forests. In: Ayache, N., Delingette, H., Golland, P., Mori, K. (eds.) MICCAI 2012. LNCS, vol. 7512, pp. 66–74. Springer, Heidelberg (2012). https://doi.org/10.1007/978-3-642-33454-2_9

22. https://kits19.grand-challenge.org/evaluation/results/6d366c1e-a5a6-4332-bb75-3c120c 0d2634

Texture Classification by Local Rajan Transform Based Descriptor

K. Priya$^{(\boxtimes)}$, S. Mohamed Mansoor Roomi, B. Sathyabama, and R. Neelavathy

ECE, Thiagarajar College of Engineering, Madurai, India
priyak@student.tce.edu, {smmroomi,sbece}@tce.edu,
rneelatce@gmail.com

Abstract. The texture is a significant factor used for the applications of recognizing objects and classifying the surface texture. This work presents a new texture feature descriptor based on Local Forward Rajan Transform (LFRT) for texture classification. The proposed method provides the features from the last stage key matrix of the LFRT. Based on the features the given texture images classified using K Nearest Neighboring (KNN) classifier. Experimental results are presented on a KTH-TIPS texture database, using KNN classifier algorithm. It shows good performance with 95.6% accuracy.

Keywords: Forward Rajan transform · Texture classification · Histogram · KNN

1 Introduction

The texture is defined as the display of a structure and frequent pattern at regular intervals. It refers to the appearance of objects and surface characteristics. The intensity variations compared with nearby pixels was measured from the surface texture descriptor. The texture feature extraction is the collection of features from feature analysis. Texture feature is an important function in applications like medical imaging, remote sensing and image retrieval [1].

The descriptor namely Schroedinger transform [2] was proposed to provide texture pattern in gray level texture images. This work dealt with random noise presented over the images also, which yields the best performance. The algebraic properties of Rajan transform [3] such as cyclic shift-invariance, Graphical inverse invariance property, Dyadic shift-invariance property, Dual-class invariance, Scalar property, Linearity property, Linear pair forming property was explained in this paper. Some sample algorithms pattern recognition using Rajan transform for image processing also dealt with this work

Sparsification property of the discrete Rajan transforms is used in compression techniques in audio data as well as video. This is used in speaker recognition applications and compression of images. The compressed data could be decompressed from inverse Rajan transform at the destination. This work obtained speaker recognition with 93.5% accuracy [4]. D.S Guru et al. proposed texture feature for flower classification using

© Springer Nature Singapore Pte Ltd. 2020
R. V. Babu et al. (Eds.): NCVPRIPG 2019, CCIS 1249, pp. 619–628, 2020.
https://doi.org/10.1007/978-981-15-8697-2_58

K Nearest Neighbor classifier (KNN). The texture features (Grey Level Co occurrence Matrix, Gabor) measured from distance formulas such as Euclidian, Cosine, City block for 25 classes [5]. Recently convolutional neural network (T CNN) has also been used [6] specifically to classify textures.

In the texture classification rotation variant is a challenge task. Most of the existing methods are sensitive to changes in rotation of texture images. In this work, a new texture descriptor based on Local Forward Rajan Transform Descriptor (LFRT) has been developed and the results justify that this descriptor is also rotation invariant.

2   Database Collection

There are many numbers of databases available on the internet. Brodatz database is a popular texture database available for research purposes. It is the collection of images with 640*640 pixel size. This database contains 112 images in gif format. The extension of Columbia-Utrecht Reflectance and Texture (CUReT) database is the KTH-TIPS (Textures under varying Illumination, Pose and Scale) image database which provides scale variation, pose variations and illumination changes in texture. This database contains images of 10 different materials such as Aluminium_foil, Brown_bread, Corduroy, Cotton, Cracker, Linen, Orange peel, Sandpaper, Sponge, Styrofoam with 200*200 image size (Fig. 1).

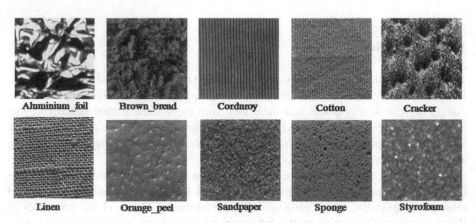

Fig. 1. Some sample images from KTH_TIPS texture database

The other database, UMD dataset consists of 1000 images of size 1280*960 pixels have 25 classes, 40 samples per class. Each class has scale variations and view point changes. This dataset contains images of diverse classes such as fruits, different types of plants, floors etc. Amsterdam library of Textures (ALOT) is the texture database containing 250 rough texture classes, each class having 100 images of size, 384*256 pixels. This collection is similar to CURET texture database (Figs. 2 and 3).

Fig. 2. Some sample images from UMD texture database

Fig. 3. Some sample images from ALOT texture database

3 Proposed Method

3.1 Local Forward Rajan Transform Texture Descriptor (LFRT)

A new texture descriptor called LFRT has been introduced to classify the textural images. The proposed texture feature descriptor based on the LFRT is shown in the Fig. 4. Let $I = \{i(x, y), x = 1, 2, 3..m, y = 1, 2, 3..n\}$ where m and n are the image size and i (x, y) is the intensity of the pixel at location (x, y). The input image is scanned by 3*3 mask and forward Rajan transform is applied on the boundary pixel value. The decimal equivalent of the third stage key value is taken as a texture feature

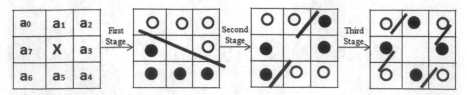

Fig. 4. Logical diagram - stages of LFRT

Consider the sequence a(n) of N where length N, is the power of 2. The first step of the forward Rajan transform divides the given sequence into half. Suppose N is 8, after division, each sequence has a length of 4 (N/2). The following equations represent the new sequences from performing summation and difference operation.

$$M(j) = a(i) + a\left(i + \left(\frac{N}{2}\right)\right); 0 \leq j \leq \frac{N}{2}; 0 \leq i \leq \frac{N}{2} \tag{1}$$

$$N(j) = a(i) - a(i + (N/2)); 0 \leq j \leq N/2; N/2 \leq i \leq N \tag{2}$$

Now both the sequences are further divided by half, then the length of the sequences are N/4. The following equations represent the sequences of length N/4.

$$M_1(k) = a(j) + a(j + (N/4)); 0 \leq k \leq \frac{N}{4}; 0 \leq j \leq \frac{N}{4} \tag{3}$$

$$M_2(k) = a(j) - a(j + (N/4)); 0 \leq k \leq N/4; N/4 \leq j \leq N/2 \tag{4}$$

$$N_1(k) = a(j) + a(j + (N/4)); 0 \leq k \leq N/4; 0 \leq j \leq N/4 \tag{5}$$

$$N_2(k) = a(j) - a(j + (N/4)); 0 \leq k \leq N/4; N/4 \leq j \leq N/2 \tag{6}$$

This process is continued up to no more division is possible. The number of stages in this transform is $\log_2 N$.

$$e_k = (-1)^k \tag{7}$$

$$K = \begin{cases} 1 \, for \, a\left(i + \frac{N}{2}\right) < a(i); 0 < i < \frac{N}{2} \\ 0 \, Otherwise \end{cases} \tag{8}$$

The operators ~ and+ **in the** Fig. 5 represent difference and sum of the operands. For example if the input sequence a(n) is 17, 70, 5, 19, 54, 7, 32, 25 which has length 8, forward Rajan transform is applied on input sequence a(n), denoted as A(K). The signal flow graph of the Rajan transform with key values (either 0 or 1) inside flow diagram is shown in the figure. In every stage Rajan transform produced key values which are denoted as E(r). The first stage key value is $E_1(r) = 0, 0, 0, 0, 0, 1, 0, 0$. The second stage key is $E_2(r) = 0, 0, 1, 1, 0, 1, 0, 1$. The third stage is $E_3(r) = 0, 0, 0, 1, 0, 0, 0, 0$. Now $E(r) = E_1(r) E_2(r) E_3(r)$. Then the sequence $A(K)E(r) = 229, 13, 67, 1, 133, 5, 67, 47, 0, 0, 0, 0, 0, 1, 0, 0, 0, 0, 1, 1, 0, 1, 0, 1, 0, 0, 0, 1, 0, 0, 0, 0$ is the forward Rajan transform of the input sequence. e_k is the function of key with key value K which is defined as in Eq. 7 and 8.

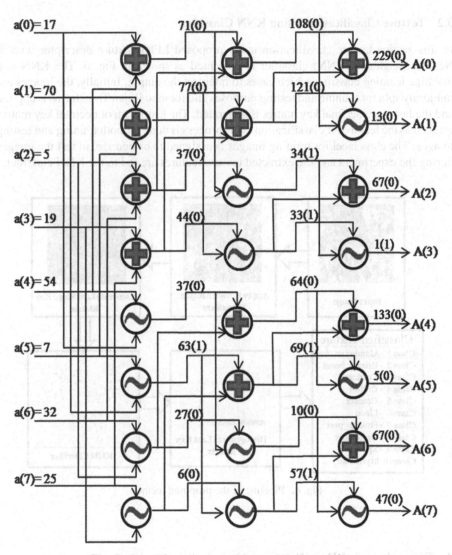

Fig. 5. Signal flow diagram of forward Rajan transforms

The last stage binary key value is 0, 0, 0, 1, 0, 0, 0, 0. The decimal equivalent of this binary key value is 16 and is taken as a feature for texture analysis. Likewise, the 3X3 mask is slid over the entire image to provide a host of integer values. A binned histogram is built using these integer values representing the whole image. This histogram feature is rotation invariant because it is the same for both the original and rotated images.

3.2 Texture Classification Using KNN Classifier

In this section texture classification using proposed LFRT texture descriptor with K Nearest Neighbors (KNN) classifier is presented as shown in Fig. 6. The KNN is a machine learning classifier which eases to interpret the output. Initially, the images are randomly split for training and testing purposes and forward Rajan Transforms is applied and the last stage decimal key matrix is generated. The histogram of decimal key matrix is taken as the feature for classification. This process is done for both training and testing images. The class label for training images is assigned to categorize, to test the images during the experiment and the extracted texture features are fed to the KNN classifier.

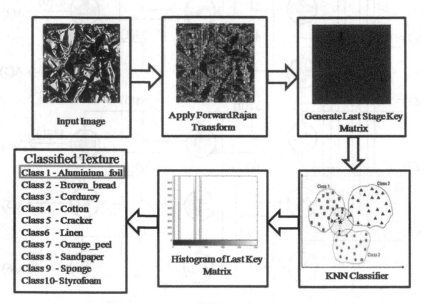

Fig. 6. Pipeline of the proposed method

4 Experimental Results

In this section, the experimental results of the proposed method for texture classification are explained.

4.1   Local Rajan Transform - Rotation Invariant Property Results

The histogram of the last stage key matrix for the sample image from CORDUROY class in KTH-TIPS database is shown in Fig. 7. This sample image is 90° rotated and the extracted histogram of last stage key matrix is shown in Fig. 8. Both the images have the same histogram which explains the rotation invariant characteristics of LFRT texture descriptor (Fig. 9).

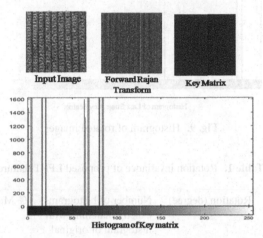

Fig. 7. Extraction of LRT texture descriptor (KTH_TIPS database)

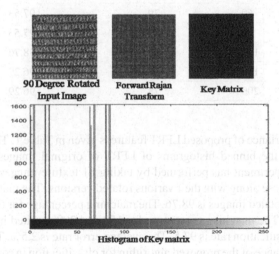

Fig. 8. Extraction of LFRT texture descriptor (90° rotation of I/P)

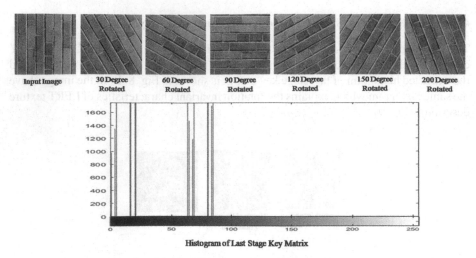

Fig. 9. Histogram of rotated images

Table 1. Rotation invariance of proposed LFRT feature

Number of images	Rotation (degree)	Number of histograms exactly matching with histogram of original images	% Matching	% Error
81	30	80	98.76	1.24
81	60	79	97.53	2.47
81	90	79	97.53	2.47
81	120	80	98.76	1.24
81	150	78	96.29	3.71
81	200	78	96.29	3.71

Rotation invariance of proposed LFRT feature is given in Table 1. This table provides how similar are the binned histograms of LFRT of original images with its rotated versions. The experiment has performed by taking 81 texture images from the class 1 KTH-TIPS database along with their various rotated versions. The matching percentage for 30 and 120° rotated images is 98.76. The matching percentage for 60 and 90° rotated images is 97.53. The matching percentage for 150 and 200° rotated images is 96.29%. The average classification rate is 97.5. The average error rate is 2.5%. The results justify the good performance of the proposed algorithm for classification in rotated images also.

4.2 Results of Texture Classification

The images from KTH-TIPS, UMD, A LOT texture database are used for texture classification. This database contains images in 10 material classes. The texture features based on LFRT are extracted for each class and classified using KNN classifier. The classification accuracy can be done by using the formula in Eq. 9 (Fig. 10 and Table 2).

$$Accuracy = \frac{Correctly \ classiifed \ image \ in \ class}{Total \ number \ of \ images \ in \ that \ class} \qquad (9)$$

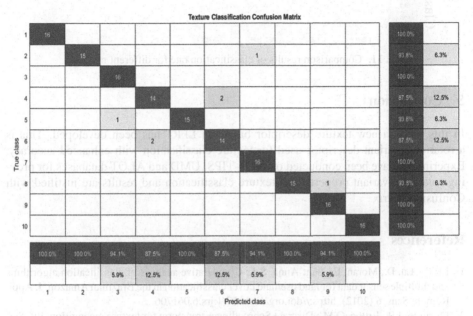

Fig. 10. Confusion matrix for texture classification (KTH-TIPS Database)

Table 2. Texture classification accuracy for various databases

Database name	No of classes	Sample size	Sample per class	Training sample per class	Testing sample per class	Accuracy (%)
KTH-TIPS	10	200*200	81	65	16	95.6
UMD	25	1280*960	40	32	8	92.3
ALOT	250	384*235	100	80	20	89.4

The accuracy of the proposed algorithm on KTH-TIPS database is 95.6% which is definitely higher than the existing T-CNN algorithm's accuracy of 48.7% for scratch network and 73.2% for Imagenet. The Imagenet increases the complexity as it is a database with 1000 classes where as the database used in the present work, is less complex with 10 classes (Fig. 11).

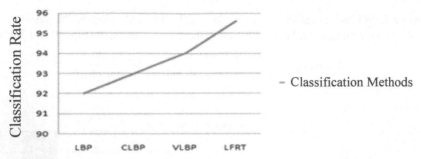

Fig. 11. Comparison results of classification rate for different methods

5 Conclusion

In this work, a new texture descriptor based on LFRT has been developed. This is a rotation invariant descriptor used for texture classification with enhanced accuracy. Experiments have been conducted on KTH-TIPS, UMD and ALOT databases for proving rotation invariant property and texture classification and results are justified with Confusion matrix.

References

1. Li, G., Lu, D., Moran, E., Sant'Anna, S.J.: Comparative analysis of classification algorithms and multiple sensor data for land use/land cover classification in the Brazilian Amazon. J. Appl. Remote Sens. **6** (2012). https://doi.org/10.1117/1.jrs.6.061706
2. Florindo, J.B., Bruno, O.M.: Discrete Schroedinger transform for texture recognition. Inf. Sci. **415**, 142–155 (2017)
3. Mandalapu, E.N., Rajan, E.G.: Rajan transform and its uses in pattern recognition. Informatica **33**, 213–220 (2009)
4. Prashanthi, G., Singh, S., Rajan, E.G., Krishnan, P.: Sparsification of voice data using discrete Rajan transform and its applications in speaker recognition, 978-1-4799-3840-7/14/$31.00 ©2014 IEEE (2014)
5. Guru, D.S., Sharath, Y.H., Manjunath, S.: Texture features and KNN in classification of flower images. IJCA Special Issue on "Recent Trends in Image Processing and Pattern Recognition" RTIPPR (2010)
6. Andrearczyk, V., Whelan, P.F.: Using filter banks in convolutional neural networks for texture classification. Pattern Recognit. Lett. (2016). https://doi.org/10.1016/j.patrec.2016.08.016

Correction to: Scene Understanding in Night-Time Using SSAN Dataset

R Anandha Murugan, B Sathyabama,
Sam Joshuva Paul Jeevan Shapher, Suryakiran Sureshkumar,
and Nighil Krishna Rajaguru

Correction to:
Chapter "Scene Understanding in Night-Time Using SSAN Dataset" in: R. V. Babu et al. (Eds.): *Computer Vision, Pattern Recognition, Image Processing, and Graphics,* CCIS 1249, https://doi.org/10.1007/978-981-15-8697-2_52

The original version of this chapter was revised. The names of the authors "Sam Joshuva Paul Jeevan Shapher, Suryakiran Sureshkumar and Nighil Krishna Rajaguru' were corrected.

The updated version of this chapter can be found at
https://doi.org/10.1007/978-981-15-8697-2_52

© Springer Nature Singapore Pte Ltd. 2020
R. V. Babu et al. (Eds.): NCVPRIPG 2019, CCIS 1249, p. C1, 2020.
https://doi.org/10.1007/978-981-15-8697-2_59

Author Index

Printed in the United States
By Bookmasters